ECONOMICS

DEALING WITH SCARCITY

THIRD EDITION

Also available from Glengarry Publishing for use with *Economics: Dealing With Scarcity*, Third Edition:

Study Guide

by Dale M. Sievert

ISBN 0-9621796-6-3

For a description of the study guide, see page viii in the Preface.

If your bookstore does not have the study guide in stock, please ask the manager to order copies for you and your fellow students.

ECONOMICS

DEALING WITH SCARCITY

THIRD EDITION

DALE M. SIEVERT
Milwaukee Area Technical College

GLENGARRY PUBLISHING

Front and Rear Cover Photos: Amazon Basin in Brazil
Cover Design: Peter Finn
Typesetting: Type Factory
Printer: TAN Books and Publishers, Inc.
Copy Editor: Barbara Salsini
Typist: Patricia Horschak

Printed in the United States of America.

1 2 3 4 5 6 7 8 9 10 - 96 95 94 93

ISBN 0-9621796-5-5

Glengarry Publishing
S 5977 Molla Drive
Waukesha, Wisconsin 53186
Telephone: 414-789-1164
Fax: 414-782-5579

This book is dedicated to the two most influential economists in my life, Leon Walrus (1834-1910) and Milton Friedman (1912-). To me, their most important impact has been the presentation of economic principles in a coherent body of interrelationships, showing clearly how the market system allows a society to maximize its economic welfare. Yet, they also show how easy it is for us, whether as individuals or groups, including government bodies, to reduce economic welfare and human happiness when we tinker with this beautiful system.

I was strongly motivated to shift my career to economics after two encounters with Professor Friedman in the 1960s. His work continues to inspire me.

I was in awe of Leon Walrus and his vision of the competitive world when I studied his work. I only wish he was still alive, so more people today would be influenced by his insights.

PREFACE

This book is intended for use in a one-term introduction to economics course. Such a course is usually taken by students who are not majoring in economics or business. However, some students may be taking the course as a foundation for further study, either at the undergraduate level or as preparation for an MBA where the student's undergraduate background was not in economics.

The Theme of This Book

Whoever reads this book, no matter what country in which they live, is part of a society that faces scarcity. They may live where there is a capitalist economic system, a socialist economic system, or a system that is a mix of these. But no society can produce everything its citizens want—resources are simply too scarce.

Thus, the subtitle of this book, *Dealing With Scarcity,* indicates what economics is about. Reference is continually made in the book to the fact that economic behavior is rooted in our desire for more goods and services than we have the resources with which to produce.

How the Book Is Organized

The first three chapters introduce the methods that have been developed over time to raise living standards from subsistence levels to the heights of today's standards. In essence, they show how we climbed so high. But of equal importance, the chapters show that our climb in living standards is far from over—in spite of what many doomsayers tell us about the future.

Chapter 4 focuses on economic systems, which are used by societies to direct the use of their resources.

Chapters 5 through 9, as well as Chapter 16, cover what is referred to by economists as microeconomics. It is the study of how individual elements of an economy operate, including consumers, laborers and others who sell resources, and business firms.

Chapters 10 through 15 cover macroeconomic concepts and principles. These refer to large elements of our economy and variables related to them. So, in macroeconomics students learn why whole sectors of the economy turn down in recessions, why prices in general rise (that is, why there is inflation), why interest rates fluctuate, and why the national debt rises. Much of the economics you hear or read about in the news is about macroeconomics.

Changes in the Third Edition

The main changes for the third edition include:

- In Chapter 1, the movement of introduction of production possibilities curves from the appendix to the chapter proper, plus an expansion of marginal analysis.
- In Chapter 3, a section was added on the post-industrial economy.
- In Chapter 4, the brief histories of the former Soviet Union and China are enlarged and placed in a new section.
- In Chapter 5, the relationships between specialization, exchange, rates of exchange, shortages, surpluses, and prices were made much clearer. In short, supply and demand are more understandable.
- In Chapter 11, GDP has replaced GNP in all contexts.
- In Chapter 13, the section on the multiplier was dropped, but there is still an appendix on the concept.
- In Chapters 13-15, the aggregate demand and supply functions were deleted from the appendices. However, they are available in the Instructor's Manual.
- The charts and graphs have all been reworked for greater clarity and a better appearance.
- Over three-fourths of the sentences have been changed at least by one word. Although the writing has been praised as very clear, after many rewrites I was able to find many ways to improve the writing. Of course, Barbara Salsini, my copyeditor, and my reviewers also were instrumental in this endeavor.

How to Study This Book

Each chapter begins with 10 Learning Objectives, which are directed at the main concepts of the chapter. The stars that appear in the left columns of the text indicate where a particular learning objective is first addressed. The number following the star tells which objective is being covered. In the back of each chapter, the Responses to the Learning Objectives contain the "answers" or appropriate responses.

Following the Learning Objectives is a list of Terms introduced in that chapter. Each appears in bold print the first time it is used. It is defined or explained immediately. The Glossary is at the back of the book, where each term (printed in bold letters) is defined and referenced to the page where it first appears. Accompanying the terms in the Glossary are many other words (printed in italics) and definitions, which are part of the jargon of economists.

Each chapter is divided into several main sections. The title of each section appears in large capital letters, extending from the left side of the page, and is underlined twice. In turn, these main sections are divided into several sub-sections. Each of these is titled in upper and lower case letters that begin at the left margin and is underlined once.

The summary at the end of each chapter provides a general description of the chapter rather than a listing of topics. Some students like to get a preview of the chapter by reading the summary first.

Each chapter ends with a list of five questions and/or projects especially designed to aid your understanding of some main points in the chapter.

Ancillaries

The Study Guide that accompanies this book begins with some Study Tips to clarify the more difficult concepts. A fill-in-the-blanks section tests your recall of the material. Exercises that focus on the main concepts are a key part of the guide. As students think about the concepts to complete the exercises, their understanding of them grows. The Study Guide includes a list of the terms on the left side of a page, with the definitions given on the right side. There is a similar list of the learning objectives and the responses. Finally, each chapter has 15 multiple-choice questions.

A set of two audio tapes contains the Learning Objectives/Responses and a third tape contains the Glossary. These tapes are sent to teachers and are able to be copied. They are useful for students who want to make good use of commuting time or for those who learn better by hearing than by reading.

An Instructor's Manual, in the form of a convenient three-ring binder, contains the following:

- A very detailed outline of each chapter
- A test bank containing nearly 2,000 multiple-choice and true-false questions

The questions are provided in printed form in the manual, and they are also available on computer disk

- Exercises, identical in form to those in the Study Guide, but with different examples and data
- Case applications, issues, and viewpoints, of which there are three per chapter
- More rigorous presentation of several concepts, including aggregate demand and supply functions
- Transparency masters for every graph and chart in the text
- Data updates for tables and charts, to be provided once a year

Acknowledgments

The third edition was most extensively reviewed by Robert Drago of the University of Wisconsin-Milwaukee and Dan Reavis of Guilford Technical/Community College. Others who deserve credit for their help include David Borst of Stratton College, Bret McMurran of Chaffey College, P.O. James of Fayetteville State University, Tobias Schwartz of Suffolk Community College, and Ghalib Baqir of Alabama State University.

I would appreciate any of your comments, both positive and negative.

Dale M. Sievert

CONTENTS IN BRIEF

TABLE OF CONTENTS

PROLOGUE

It takes a lot of time and considerable mental effort to study economics — so why should anyone bother? You already possess a great deal of information about economics, so who needs more? The trouble is, too often that information is a tangled mess of disorganized facts. In addition, many people also possess much *misinformation* about economics. A formal study of the subject will allow you to arrange your knowledge so you can better understand certain human behavior as well as economic concepts unrelated to human behavior. It will also allow you to function better in the economy — as a consumer; as a seller of resources, goods, and services; and as a taxpayer.

As this book often points out, economics is the study of how people deal with the fact that they have more materialistic goals than their scarce resources can produce.

Economics is a broad-based subject whose principles allow a wider understanding of your entire life. You might find little in this book which will directly improve your life dramatically — at least not immediately. Yet, sooner or later, your understanding of concepts within its covers will allow you to see clearly through the fog you might not now even realize exists. It can be likened to a person realizing how clearly they can see once they started wearing glasses after they were told they needed them.

Finally, do not take the mistaken view that economics only deals with money. Though materialism is at its core, economic principles are easily extended to many non-materialistic matters. In fact, economists realize the overall goal of any individual or group is the maximization of satisfaction from *all* goals — materialistic as well as non-materialistic ones.

> *The ideas of economists and political philosophers, both when they are right and when they are wrong, are more powerful than is commonly understood. Indeed, the world is ruled by little else. Practical men, who believe themselves to be quite exempt from any intellectual influences, are usually slaves of some defunct economist.* – John Maynard Keynes

CHAPTER 1

INTRODUCTION TO SCARCITY, RESOURCE USE, & ECONOMICS

★★★★★ LEARNING OBJECTIVES ★★★★★

1. List and give examples of the four classes of resources.
2. Explain how the economic problem arises.
3. Explain the reason for studying economics.
4. Explain the relationship between the efficiency of resource use and the economic problem.
5. Explain how to use scarce resources to maximize economic welfare.
6. Describe a production possibilities curve and what it shows.
7. Explain how to make decisions by using marginal analysis.
8. Indicate how errors are made in decision making and resource allocation and give examples of each of the four classes of such errors.
9. Explain the purpose of asking each of the Basic Economic Questions.
10. Describe the major concepts or beliefs of economists from ancient times to the present.

TERMS

social science
rational
economic model
materialistic goal
good
service
consumption process
non-materialistic goal
resource
production process
labor
capital
natural resource
entrepreneurship
scarce
the economic problem
economics
resource allocation
efficiency
cost-benefit analysis
benefit
opportunity cost
production possibilities curve
Basic Economic Questions
microeconomics
macroeconomics
mercantilism
Physiocrats
French Utopians
institutionalists

If you wish to understand why you act the way you do, it is useful to study the social sciences. Economics is one of the social sciences, as are psychology, sociology, political science, history, geography, and anthropology. A **social science** is any study of human behavior—how people think, act, and relate to each other.

SATISFACTION AND HUMAN BEHAVIOR

Economics assumes that the behavior of people is **rational**. This means that when people take action, they do so because they expect to be better off or more satisfied after taking that action. Conversely, to knowingly do something that reduces well-being or satisfaction is irrational.

To assume that people behave rationally might seem ridiculous, in light of the way some people behave, but let's assume it anyway. Without this assumption, understanding human behavior would be hopelessly complex. Too many factors would cloud the main forces driving human activity. Thus, in order to simplify complex situations and relationships that contain many variables, economists make assumptions. With these assumptions and relationships, they build **economic models** that give a clearer view of the primary relationships in the economy. These models leave out many details of reality, but this allows a better understanding of the fundamentals of situations and relationships.

One economic model, shown in Figure 1-1, shows how human goals and objectives relate to satisfaction derived from them. When people achieve a goal or objective, they feel satisfaction. The word "welfare" could be used as a substitute for satisfaction. It refers to the well-being of a person. This meaning of welfare is unrelated to public welfare programs.

Goals are arbitrarily split into two categories: materialistic goals and non-materialistic goals. A **materialistic goal** must be produced through the use of resources. Materialistic goals include both **goods**, which have physical substance, and **services**, which are intangible or have no physical substance. Examples of goods include pencils, cakes, radios, nuclear missiles, farm tractors, suits, highways, and compressed gas. Examples of services include auto repair, food preparation in restaurants, funeral services, police protection, education, and house painting.

To be precise, a materialistic goal is the *satisfaction one expects to receive* when making use of a good or service, not the good or service itself. Commonly, however, we think of having or using the good or service as the goal. Whereas welfare is the satisfaction enjoyed from all activities combined, *economic* welfare refers to the satisfaction derived from achieving materialistic goals. People get this satisfaction in what is called the **consumption process**. An example of this process is wearing a coat to keep warm.

Non-materialistic goals include the love of others, a walk in the woods, good grades, prestige, a place in the *Guinness Book of World Records*, friendship, and spiritual well-being. These are the concepts people have in mind when they say, "The best things in life are free." They're not. Although they require few if any resources of the type covered in the following section, they do require time and effort. Economics deals almost exclusively with materialistic goals, although

Figure 1-1 The Relationships Between Resources, Goals, and Welfare

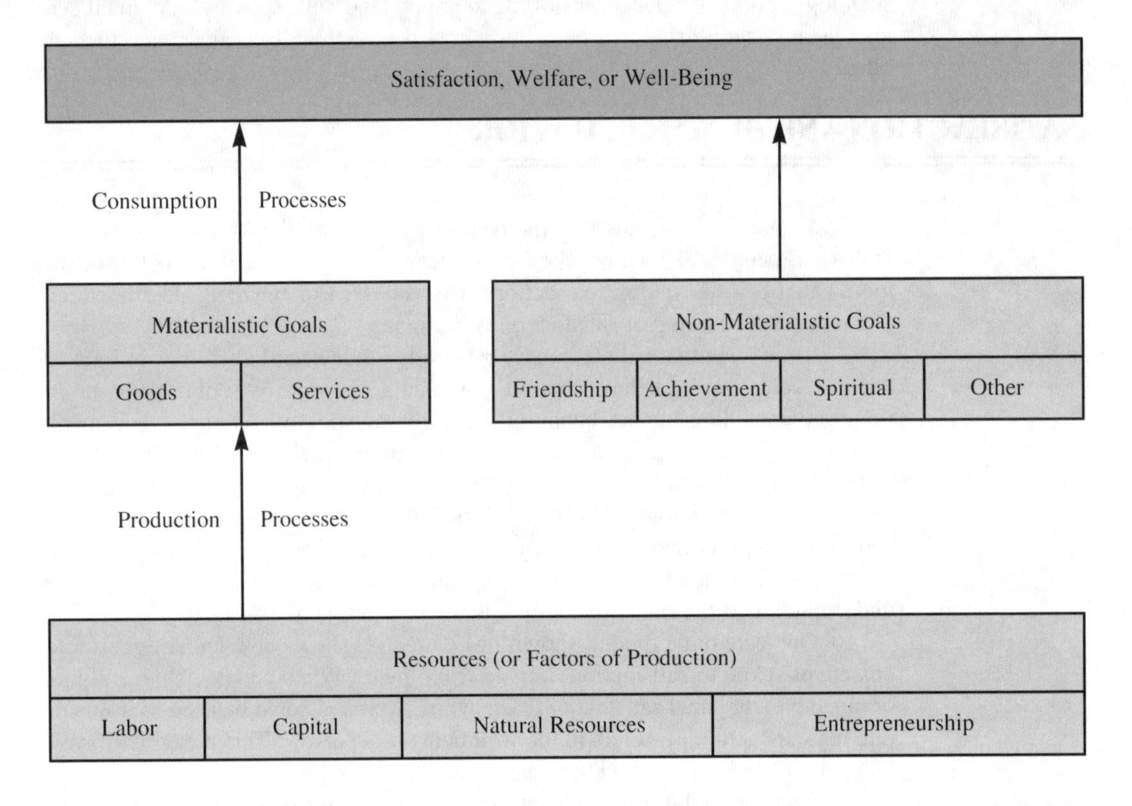

some economists (such as Gary Becker, the 1992 Nobel prize winner in economics) use economic concepts to explain behavior such as religious acts and beliefs and other "non-materialistic activity." Occasionally the production or consumption of goods and services prevents people from attaining some non-materialistic goal. In those cases, economics deals with more than materialism.

RESOURCES AND THE PRODUCTION PROCESS

A **resource** is anything necessary to produce a good or service, and this occurs in a **production process**. A common synonym for resource is factor of production. There are thousands of different resources that generally fit in one of four classes: labor, capital, natural resources, and entrepreneurship. ★1

■ **Labor** is any human effort to produce a good or service. Laborers not only include factory workers, but also teachers, accountants, and computer programmers. Usually each laborer is concerned with only a part of the production process. Laborers do not organize the entire production process, leaving that to others.

■ **Capital** is any good used to produce another good or service in a business or government enterprise. Examples of capital include lathes, drill presses, robots, buses, office buildings, roads, computers, copying machines, schools, and carpenters' saws. However, money is *not* capital because money doesn't directly produce anything. Money is considered "financial capital," and capital goods are "physical capital." Thus, money can be used to obtain capital. Another form of capital, "human capital," involves the education and training of workers. The concepts of physical and human capital will be covered in greater depth in Chapter 7.

■ The third class of resources, **natural resources**, appears in nature without human help. A synonym for natural resources is land. But land means more than just land used for farming or factory sites. Natural resources or land is a broad category that includes land and everything on it or in it that we can use, including iron ore, petroleum, limestone, and the like. Other natural resources include rivers, trees, and air.

■ **Entrepreneurship** refers to the enterprising nature of people. An entrepreneur oversees the entire production process, as distinct from the partial view of the laborer. Thus, an entrepreneur provides organizational or managerial talent. Besides that, an entrepreneur takes financial risks when entering a business that could fail. Although many people consider all business owners as entrepreneurs, this is not entirely true because entrepreneurs also possess a third characteristic: they introduce a new or improved good or service. Or they might significantly improve the production processes of existing goods and services. However defined, entrepreneurs go into business to profit from their ideas.

Although time and technology often are called resources, they are not separate classes of resources. Time already is included in the labor and entrepreneurship resources, which both require time when used. Technology is usually embodied in capital resources and refers to the level of sophistication, complexity, and scientific knowledge used or achieved in capital goods. An example of a technological change is the replacement of copper telephone cables with fiber optic cables. Thus, scientific discoveries in glass and laser technology lead to changes in the type of capital used in telephone communication.

SCARCITY AND ECONOMICS

Two facts of society lead us to study economics: 1) people have unlimited materialistic goals; and 2) resources are limited.

■ The first condition, people wanting unlimited amounts of materialistic goals, means there will never be a day when all people have everything they want. Most people will always be able to find use for another room in the house, another shirt, another vacation, another beer, another concert, and so on. This should not be confused with greed, where someone will do whatever is necessary to get something, often at the expense of others, even perhaps through stealing.

■ The second condition means that such resources as iron ore, metal-grinding machines, tool-and-die makers, and electricians are not in inexhaustible supply. Therefore, we can only produce limited amounts of goods and services. Although people also say resources are scarce, limited and scarce are not the same. Limited means a given or measurable amount of something. Something that is **scarce** is always limited, but it is also something that will increase economic welfare if more of it becomes available. Some things are limited but *not* scarce—litter on a playground and water in the Gulf of Mexico. More of them will do society no good. Scarce resources include engineers, milling machines, and freeways in Miami. If there are more of these, members of society will receive more satisfaction. You could also consider an item to be scarce if the amount available is less than the amount people would want if it were free.

★2 When considered simultaneously, these two conditions create **the economic problem**. The "problem" is that because resources are scarce, people can get only a fraction of the goods and services they want. This problem limits economic welfare, which causes frustration.

Faced with the economic problem, people have two alternatives: 1) do nothing; or 2) make the best of a bad situation. Economics is the practice of making the best of a bad situation—that is, finding ways to get more satisfaction by using (or allocating) resources more wisely (or efficiently). This narrows the gap that separates wants or needs from the filling of those needs.

★3 Because there are more things we want than we can make with our scarce resources, we must choose which things get produced—and do without the rest. Rational people make such choices to maximize their economic welfare. **Economics** studies how members of society choose to use scarce resources in order to maximize economic welfare.

You have similar problems in your own life. You probably want far more things than your money will buy. And you have more things to do than your time allows. Everyone faces this problem of scarce time and money (personal "resources"). Economic principles can help you use your time and money to increase your economic welfare. If you fritter away your funds and your time foolishly, the consequence will be less satisfaction or happiness from them.

THE ALLOCATION OF RESOURCES THROUGH COST-BENEFIT ANALYSIS

If different ways to use resources result in different levels of welfare, we need a framework to decide how to use them. This section considers decision making in resource use. **Resource allocation** refers to the directing of scarce resources to specific uses. Specifically, it refers to the decision to direct resources to the production processes of goods and services that are actually made. If decision makers are rational, resources should be allocated so they will maximize economic welfare. On the other hand, resource misallocation occurs if resources are used unwisely, leading to less than our potential economic welfare.

★4

Doing a good job of allocating resources means decision makers are efficient. Thus, **efficiency** means using resources in a way that maximizes economic welfare. More explicitly, efficiency means a given amount of resources produces a large amount of output. For example, an efficient secretary (the labor resource or input) can type 80 or 90 words (the output) per minute, whereas the average person can type about 50. Alternatively, efficiency means that just a few resources are needed to produce a given level of output. For example, an efficient carpet installer might be able to lay a 12-foot-square room in one hour. The average installer might take two hours. (One unit of input, an hour of labor, gives 144 square feet in the first case and 72 square feet in the second case.) In these examples, efficiency refers to the ratio of inputs to outputs of a specific production process. However, the concept can be extended to mean the input-to-output ratio of a particular firm, a whole industry, or even an entire economy.

How can it be assured that decisions will be made so that efficiency is achieved? Businesses, government agencies, and consumers all make such decisions, but consumers will be used as a model in an example below.

★5

Rational consumers make decisions about the use of their scarce resources of time and money by using **cost-benefit analysis**. This means they compare the benefits of spending time or money with the cost. The **benefit** is the amount of satisfaction derived from using resources. Let's assume you can measure the benefit you get from, say, a bag of popcorn or watching a play. After all, you probably often tell people that you like one product more than another. *How much* more is impossible to say or measure, but let's assume benefits can be "packaged" into so-called "satisfaction units." Each "unit" reflects a given amount of satisfaction received when consuming a good or service. Because each good or service provides different amounts of benefits, each yields different amounts of "satisfaction units" to the consumer.

For example, suppose Laura is thinking of buying a dress for $60, which she values at 640 "satisfaction units" (or "units" for short). Should Laura buy the dress? There's no doubt she likes it—640 "units" worth. Yet efficient use of Laura's resources requires that the dress "pass" cost-benefit analysis. Specifically, the dress must provide more benefits than costs. The benefit of the dress is 640 "units." And the cost is $60, right? Not really. That's the *price,* the amount of money needed to buy one unit of something. People often mistakenly equate cost and price. Cost is what you give up when doing something. (Let's repeat that because you will need to know that concept again and again: *cost is what you give up when doing something.*) You might think that because Laura gives up $60 if she buys the dress, $60 is the cost. That's not true. More correctly, cost is *the benefit or satisfaction* given up when doing something—not the money. In itself, the $60 is of no benefit or value. Laura doesn't even *want* the $60. Otherwise she would keep it. Nonetheless, if she parts with the $60 for the dress, she gives up *something*. She gives up the satisfaction she *could* have had from something else selling for $60.

But *what* else? Suppose Laura can think of three other ways to use the $60. She could use the money to buy a painting (which would provide 475 "units"), a subscription to Newsweek (360 "units"), or running shoes (810 "units"). If the cost of the dress is the benefit given up, is it 475, 360, or 810 "units"? Introducing a new term will help to answer the question. The **opportunity cost** of doing something, such as using resources, is the satisfaction given up from the *best* of the remaining alternative ways to use the resources. Laura's alternatives to the dress are the painting, the Newsweek subscription, and the running shoes. The pair of shoes, at 810 "units," is the most beneficial. If Laura buys the dress, she'll give up the satisfaction from the shoes. She'll get 640 "units"—but give up 810. It might be satisfying to buy the dress, but it would be a foolish buy because the shoes would be even more satisfying. And because Laura wants to *maximize* her welfare, she will not buy the dress.

But what if she had first considered buying the shoes, rather than the dress? Should she get them, given the same four options? Yes, for the benefit, 810 "units," is larger than the opportunity cost of 640 "units" (note that now the dress is the best remaining alternative).

This decision-making procedure is the same for any person, business, or government agency using something that is scarce. Always make certain that what is received (the benefit) exceeds what is given up (the opportunity cost). Then resources will be used only to produce things from which people get the most satisfaction.

PRODUCTION POSSIBILITIES CURVES

Saying that resources are scarce means we don't have enough of them to make everything we want. The other side of that coin says we can make only so many things with our available resources. That is the economic problem.

Perhaps a graph can help you understand the economic problem and the necessity of careful choice of resource use. Figure 1-2 shows a curve economists call a **production possibilities curve**. It shows all the possible combinations of two goods it is possible to produce with a given amount of resources.

★6

Imagine a simple economy that could produce only two goods, Good X and Good Y. Even if all this economy's resources produced only Good X, it could not produce an infinite amount of it. Rather, it could produce an amount represented by the distance between O and point A. Alternatively, if all the economy's resources were used to make Good Y, an amount represented by the distance between O and point D would be produced. Points A and D show two of the possibilities of production of Goods X and Y. There are more possibilities, such as B and C—an infinite number, in fact. And each of these combinations would be represented by a point. This infinite number of points traces out a line, and this line is the production possibilities curve.

Any point "outside" the curve (such as E and F) represents combinations of Good X and Good Y that cannot be obtained because there are not enough resources to produce them. This area is known as the zone of impossibility. Points "inside" the curve (such as G and H) represent levels of output that are less than what the economy was capable of producing. This could be the result of resources that were poorly (inefficiently) used. Thus, the area inside the curve is called the zone of inefficiency. Finally, notice that the curve is bowed out. This is because all resources are not equally suited to produce Good X and Good Y. It is one of the reasons why a nation that wishes to maximize its economic welfare will specialize in the use of its resources. The section on specialization in Chapter 2 will make this clearer. For a further presentation of production possibilities curves using a numerical example, see Appendix B at the end of this chapter.

MARGINAL ANALYSIS

Decision making is complicated somewhat because of a concept used in economics called marginal analysis. You will find several applications of this concept in this text.

Figure 1-2 Production Possibilities Curve

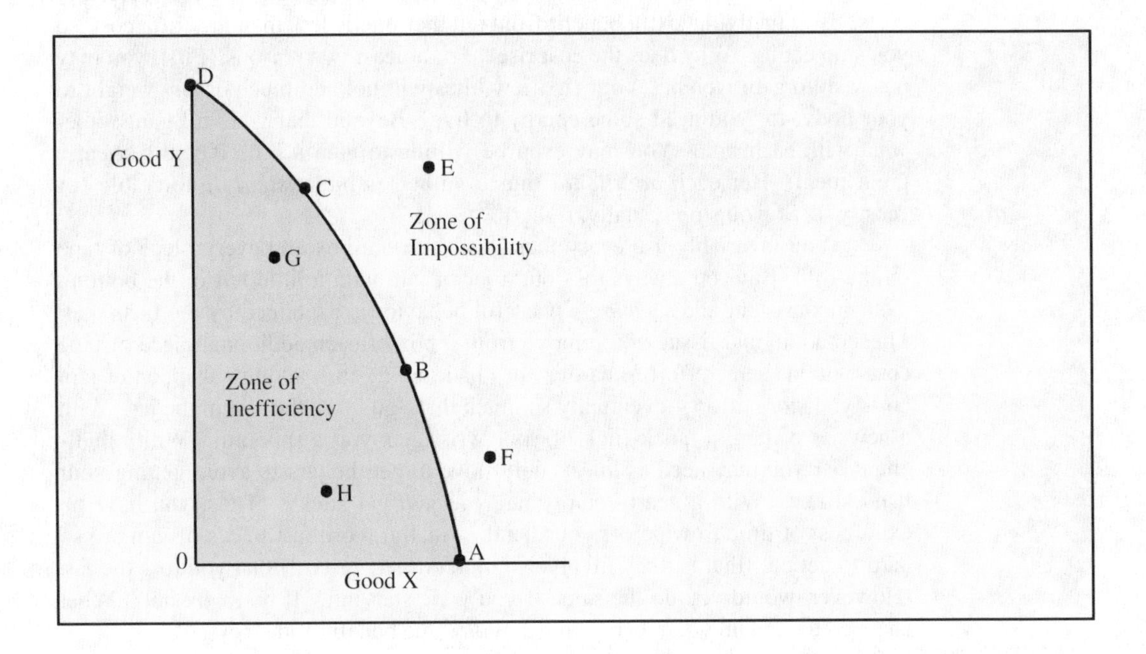

"Marginal" here means extra, additional, or the last of some action. The context usually helps explain what is meant by "marginal." For example, the marginal potato chip you *eat* is the last one before you put the bag away, but the marginal potato chip *purchased* is the last bag bought.

★7

The purpose of marginal analysis is to help us decide how to limit the amount of any activity—that is, how to know when to stop it. Since scarcity means we cannot have everything we wish, we need some way to allocate our time, money, and efforts. Marginal analysis performs this function. For example, if you have eaten 19 potato chips, the extra (or marginal) cost and the marginal benefit of eating the 20th potato chip can determine whether you eat it then and there. The marginal cost is the value of saving the potato chip for tomorrow, while the marginal benefit is the extra enjoyment from eating it now. On a larger scale, an automobile producer currently making 2,000 cars will weigh the marginal costs and marginal benefits from producing the 2,001st car. If the benefits are higher than the costs, the producer can make more profit by producing the extra car. But if marginal costs are higher than the marginal benefits, profit would be lost by making the car. Because the marginal benefits and costs change as we consume or produce more, eventually we stop eating more potato chips or producing more cars when the marginal costs exceed the marginal benefits.

Following are some situations in which you may find yourself. In some, your actions may not be completely understandable unless you use marginal analysis.

You enjoy a very good meal—but you leave some of it on the table. The rest (even an extra helping) would still taste good, and perhaps you are not even full. However, those extra mouthfuls involve increasingly large opportunity costs. Eventually the extra benefit from another bite is less than the extra cost, so you stop eating. Why does the cost rise? For at least two reasons. First, you may not wish to gain weight. Your first few bites will not add much or any weight to your body, for you need some energy to live. Beyond that you will gain somewhat with each bite. You may even be willing to gain a little if you can eat a great meal. But each *additional* ounce gained is *increasingly* intolerable (or "costly"). So you stop (usually, right?).

You invariably use every facial tissue in the box and every piece of tape on the roll. But you always toss out a jar of jam with a little left in the bottom. Your inconsistent and *seemingly* wasteful behavior is explained by the facts that: 1) each additional tissue you remove from a box or each additional piece of tape costs you the same effort as earlier ones had; but 2) each additional spoon of jam costs you *more* effort—eventually so much that you leave the rest in the jar. With a new jar of jam, a quick flick of your wrist gets you a spoonful. With a half-empty jar you may need a *slower,* deft move to get the jam to avoid getting your hand sticky. With a nearly empty jar, you *will* get sticky. Thus, you have an extra cost of time to wipe off your hand. Finally, those last traces of jam are so hard to get out (that is, they involve so much time—or cost) that you toss the jar. (However, would you do the same if you were starving? If not, why not? What changed to explain your change in behavior—the benefit or the cost?)

Do you always finish what you start, such as projects around the house, hobby projects, or even college courses? If you don't, someone might criticize you for throwing away the time or money you already invested in the activity. But a good marginal analyst knows that *the past is not important* when deciding whether to go forward. The past is "water over the dam" and must be ignored. The only things that count are the *extra* benefits and *extra* costs of continuing. And if those extra costs exceed the extra benefits—stop what you've been doing. Or as the saying goes, "Don't throw good money after bad." A good example is the supercollider, an $11 billion, 54-mile circular accelerator of sub-atomic particles being built in Texas. It is intended, among other things, to unlock the secrets of the formation of the universe. In October 1993, after already spending $2 billion on its construction, Congress cut off further spending for the project, believing that it wasn't worth the expense. (However, it is possible that Congress can reverse itself in the future.)

ERRORS IN DECISION MAKING

Making wise (efficient) decisions is easier said than done. Often decision makers derive less benefit than they give up, so they fail to maximize economic welfare. There are four common reasons why decision makers make bad decisions: 1) inaccurately measuring benefits and/or costs; 2) ignoring long-run costs; 3) ignoring external costs; and 4) paying only part of the costs of a decision. (Occasionally it is difficult to place an error in decision making into only one of these categories.)

★8

Figure 1-3 When Benefits or Costs Are Inaccurately Measured

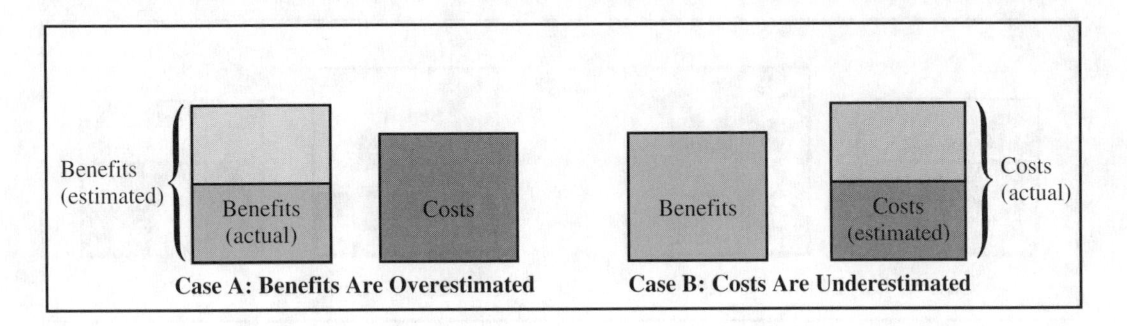

■ The first error in decision making is a failure to accurately measure benefits and/or costs. These errors occur even if there are rational decision makers, people who *try* to make decisions in their best interests. Such errors fall into two sub-classes. The first, Case A, involves an overestimation of benefits. Here, a decision maker believes the resources will yield more benefits than the opportunity cost. But fewer benefits than expected may result, even fewer than from an alternative use of the resources (that is, fewer than the opportunity cost). The diagrams on the left side of Figure 1-3 show this.

Examples of this include: watching a disappointing movie; buying clothes you seldom wear; spending a week on the Bahama beaches—in the rain. How can decision makers avoid such errors? They can't completely, but consumers can minimize errors by test-driving cars, selecting clothes carefully, reading movie reviews, and consulting owners of a product under consideration. Essentially, they're doing research. Businesses often do market research and even test-market products in selected areas to try to measure the chances of success.

The other problem of miscalculation, Case B, involves the underestimation of costs. What was thought to have less costs than benefits actually has *more.* The diagrams on the right side of Figure 1-3 show this case. Examples include: a car with more repairs than normal; a new missile system with massive cost overruns; and a drug maker with numerous lawsuits after its new drug caused birth defects.

Less evident examples involve what people *didn't get*, but wish they had: the person in the TV commercial who drinks some juice and has the revelation, "Wow, I could have had a V-8!"; somebody who finds in midlife that another career would have been more rewarding; and you regretting that you passed up the great restaurant meal your friend ordered.

With many decisions, there is a confusingly large number of options, each with different benefits. It's so hard to find the *best* option that people rarely do. There is almost always a *somewhat* better auto, career, suit—and, for a non-economic case, *several* better spouses than the one chosen (the best might be waiting in Sydney, Australia). Faced with such gloomy prospects for making good decisions, all people can hope to do is select *one of the best* alternative choices, thereby minimizing the losses. Bear in mind, too, that spending a lot of time making decisions can be costly in itself, as time also is scarce.

Figure 1-4 When Long-Run Costs or Benefits Are Ignored

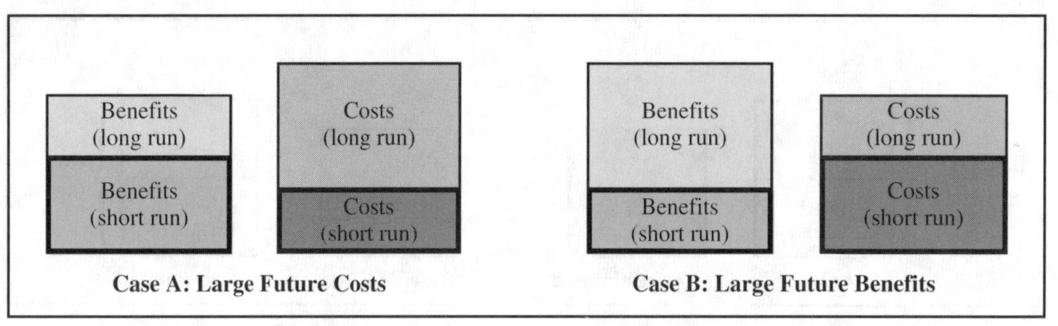

■ The second common error in making decisions involves ignoring or excessively downplaying long-run costs and benefits. It is a common mistake of irrational thought, stemming from the adage, "Eat, drink, and be merry, for tomorrow you may die!" That's great advice if you like parties—and if you will die soon. Figure 1-4 shows what happens when you mistakenly *don't* assume you'll live until 80 or so.

In the first set of such mistakes, or Case A, the decision maker sees only the cost or benefit in the heavily outlined boxes, labelled "short run." The short run is an arbitrarily chosen period—a few minutes, a day, or even years if a decision affects career planning. In the case shown, this irrational person would carry out this act, for the benefits exceed the costs—in the all-important short run. But this person would experience some substantial costs much later. There also could be some long-run benefits. Yet, when totaled over a *lifetime,* the benefits fall short of the costs. The person, older and wiser, will regret the error. Sometimes the person is only a day older, as is someone who wakes up with a hangover. Other examples include drug use that becomes addictive (thus, very costly and destructive) and overbuying on credit. Many people also would include smoking as an example, which it may be—but also may not be. It depends upon how the smoker, just before death, looks back on a lifetime of smoking. If the smoker never tried to quit nor wanted to, the decision to smoke was a good one for that person—no matter what financial costs or loss of health the smoker suffered. Apparently the benefits enjoyed from smoking exceeded these costs. (Incidentally, those who tell others not to smoke because it is self-destructive presume that their values are better than those of the smokers.)

With the second set of mistakes, in Case B, a person does *not* carry out some act that *should have* been done. That's because the only costs relevant to the irrational decision maker—the short-run ones—exceed the benefits of the present. But often the benefits of acts come much later. Attending high school is a good example because most of the benefits come after a graduate begins college or a career. Why should a 16-year-old finish the junior year, when the benefits from school *in the 16th year of life* are small—while the costs are high (time lost that could have been spent earning money or just messing around)? There is little reason, if the 16th year of life is the last one. Dropouts usually refuse to consider the future, but they suffer later when they face economic hardships and often make other people suffer as well.

Figure 1-5 When External Costs Are Ignored

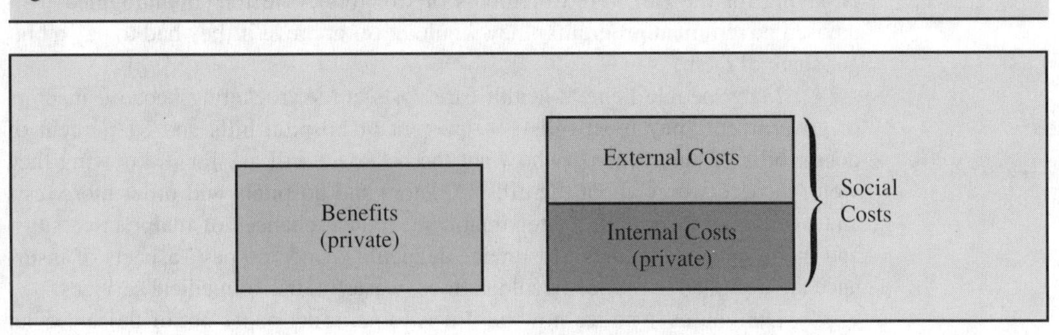

■ The third class of decision-making errors involves bystanders to the decision. Figure 1-5 shows one class of such errors. (Chapter 9 examines this and similar errors in greater detail.) The diagrams show a person receiving *individual* benefits (labelled "Private Benefits") in excess of *individual* costs ("Private Costs"). But, in many decisions, other people also have things to give up, called "external costs." Added up, these two costs equal "social costs," or what all of us as a whole give up when resources are used. In the diagram the social costs exceed the benefits. Thus, this decision, though a good one for the individual, is a poor one for society.

Examples of such external costs include: ruined fishing after a paper mill dumps chemicals into a river; spoiled tranquility when noisy motorcycles pass by; and lost aesthetic pleasure when you pass a house painted an atrocious color.

Figure 1-6 When Decision Makers Don't Pay All of the Costs of Their Decisions

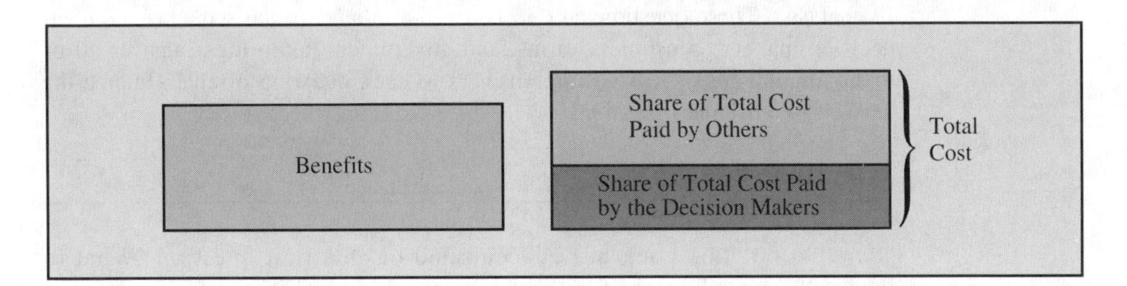

■ The last class of errors involving resource use occurs when the decision maker pays only some or none of the costs. Figure 1-6 shows the total cost of the decision exceeding the benefits. Although it is a bad use of resources, the person uses them anyway because the benefits exceed *that person's* cost, which is only a fraction of the total cost.

Some examples of this class of errors explain why life is the way it is. People attending parties often drink and eat more than they would if *they* had to pay for the food and drink consumed. Kids probably wouldn't take 10-minute showers if *they* paid the heat and water bills. A friend who receives a long-distance phone call is less likely to wish to end the conversation than the caller, who is paying for the call. And members of Congress vote for "boondoggles" (ill-advised government programs) they would never approve if they had to pay a bigger share of them.

Many people believe health care costs are skyrocketing because insurers or governments pay most bills—90 percent of hospital bills and 81 percent of doctor bills. Thus, patients who want the best care will ask for it, knowing they won't have to worry about the bills. Doctors and hospitals will order more tests and operations to provide better treatment, reduce chances of malpractice suits, and increase their incomes. Insurance deductibles and "co-pay" aspects of insurance are designed to reduce frivolous (thus, wasteful) use of medical services.

Did you ever notice how hard it is to get toilet paper out of those special dispensers in public restrooms? The maintenance department is not trying to frustrate you. Rather, the dispensers are designed to cut down on the waste of paper.

And what about your shameful behavior in motels? Don't you use more towels and water there than at home? Or have more lights on? Or mess up the bedding? Why? Because it's *their* problem—that of the owners and the staff, that is.

So now, if you find yourself among poor decision makers or feel penalized by the poor decisions of others, perhaps you see the wisdom of studying economics.

BASIC ECONOMIC QUESTIONS

★9

Virtually all decisions about resource use fit into three sets of questions, called **Basic Economic Questions**. If people are to maximize their economic welfare, they need to answer these correctly. They do so by practicing cost-benefit analysis. These questions are not answered in any special sequence. Rather, decision makers (consumers, firms, and government authorities) answer all of them simultaneously. Also, the answers to each question often influence the answers to other such questions.

What to Produce?

So far, this book has concentrated on this first question (What to Produce?). Literally tens of millions of things could be beneficial. Yet, because there are not enough resources to make them all, only relatively few are made. You might think most things that could be made *are* made. That isn't true because it's hard to visualize what *isn't* there—but could be. For example, carpets made of mink pelts, passenger trips to the moon, and wooden car bodies could be produced. But society has answered the question of whether to produce mink carpets, for example, with a "no." Alternatively, it says "yes" to the question of whether to produce nylon carpets.

How do we know whether to say "no" or "yes" in each case? We simply ask if the resources needed to make each item give the most satisfaction as compared with their use in making any other item. If it does, we make it. If not, we don't. Of course, remember that such decision making is difficult because it is hard to accurately measure the cost and benefit of each alternative use of our resources.

What to Produce questions often mean we must choose what to consume or buy. For example, decisions to order the steak or the pork on the menu ultimately lead farmers to raise more steers or, alternatively, more hogs. So, What to Produce questions might be thought of as What to Consume questions instead. We might also consider them as How Much to Consume (or Produce)? because we often choose between larger and smaller quantities of items, such as steaks.

How to Produce?

After a decision is taken to make something, selection must be made from among several possible production processes. Consider paper production. Paper comes from wood that is broken into tiny particles. That process could start either with: 1) people who cut off chunks of wood with knives; or 2) machines that lop off chunks. Next, the chunks are made into smaller bits until they look like oatmeal. Various machines or chemicals could do this job. Next, most of the water is extracted so the particles bind together to make sheets of damp paper. It is possible to hand-squeeze single sheets and air-dry them, as was done many years ago. But it is also possible to roll the sheets through a machine. Finally, cutting the paper into small sheets could be done with choppers, sharp rollers, or even lasers. Thus, there are many possible ways of making even simple things.

How to Produce questions are correctly answered by selecting production methods that use the least amount of all resources combined (labor, capital, entrepreneurship, and natural resources). In the case of paper, this ensures there will be as many resources as possible left over for making other things. In turn, that maximizes the output of goods and services and, therefore, economic welfare. Of course, minimizing resource use in production also ensures the lowest possible production cost.

For Whom to Produce?

Once goods and services are made, who will get them? Should everyone share equally in everything produced? Or should certain goods and services be distributed to selected groups? For example, should only people older than 60 be permitted to see Madonna perform? Should everyone who loves sailing get sailboats—or should people who get seasick get them? Should people who have hard, dangerous, or skilled jobs get more of everything—or less?

In the United States, the distribution of goods and services is determined largely by income levels. Those with more income get more goods and services. An individual's income depends mainly upon what price can be "commanded" in the marketplace for the resources that individual sells. Chapters 4 and 10 will consider alternative methods of income distribution.

Many Americans believe this system gives the closest approximation to the "right" distribution of goods and services, the one maximizing society's economic welfare. Yet, alternatives are sought when government leaders make changes in tax laws, welfare programs, minimum wage levels, and immigration practices. Such changes result in some people becoming worse off, while others become better off.

MICROECONOMICS AND MACROECONOMICS

Economic subjects and concepts can usually be split into two categories, microeconomics and macroeconomics.

Microeconomics deals with the economic behavior of individual (thus, micro) units in the economy. Examples of microeconomic units include a consumer, a firm, an industry, a laborer, a saver, and an investor. Microeconomic concepts cover such topics as: what affects the price of an individual good or service; what determines the output level of a firm; how tax rates affect the typical investor in stocks; and how increased competition affects prices in the airline industry.

Macroeconomics deals with the behavior of larger or aggregated sectors of the economy. These include all consumers combined, all manufacturing firms combined, the labor force, and the like. Macroeconomic concepts cover such topics as: the price level and how much it changes (the inflation rate), total output of the nation (measured by the gross domestic product), the unemployment rate, and the effect of changes in the tax rate on savings or interest rates.

A BRIEF SURVEY OF ECONOMIC THOUGHT

This final section of the chapter gives a brief introduction to major economic ideas and beliefs from ancient times to the present. This survey of economic thinkers is essentially Western in nature. Other societies would have a quite different list.

Economic Thought from Ancient to Medieval Times

★10

In 400 B.C., the ancient Greeks produced the first significant writings on economics. In fact, the word economics has its base in a Greek word, "oikonomos." Essentially, it means household management, referring to the management of resources of a community as well as a "house." Plato wrote in *The Republic* that there should be public or common ownership of property. He also saw the wisdom of specialization and the division of labor. His follower, Aristotle, defined wealth as the necessities of life that people possessed. He objected to the use of currency, lending for interest (usury), and commerce for personal gain. Like the Greeks, the Romans did not place a high regard on the accumulation of power and wealth through commerce.

After the Roman Empire fell in the fifth century, the lack of political order led to the development of feudalism in Europe. The Middle Ages feudal estate, led by the lord, directed production and determined consumption patterns of the serfs. Each estate was largely self-sufficient and self-governed in a nearly complete economy. There was very little trading or market activity as we know it. St. Thomas Aquinas, a prominent philosopher of the Middle Ages, proposed a system of "distributive and compensatory justice." Distributive justice focused on who should receive how many goods and services. Compensatory justice aimed at finding a fair or "just price" for whatever exchanges occurred. To this day people use the term "fair price" for an item, such as a used car. Many beliefs about economics in the Middle Ages stemmed from church doctrine. For example, the church condemned lending for interest and noted that the Bible says, "Love of money is the root of all evil."

Mercantilism and the Enlightenment

Feudalism declined significantly by the thirteenth and fourteenth centuries, accompanied by the formation of stronger nations. Throughout this period and later, people gradually gained the freedom to enter into market contracts, giving them the opportunity to accumulate material wealth. In the economic sense, a contract is an agreement between a buyer and a seller to exchange a given amount of some item for a specified amount of money or other thing of value (usually called the price). By about 1500, a philosophy had developed that a nation also could improve its lot by accumulating wealth in the form of gold and silver. Called **mercantilism**, it promoted exports, paid for in gold and silver. It also discouraged imports because they would drain gold and silver from the country. The plundering of New World gold and silver by the Spanish in the 1500s was partly a result of this philosophy. Mercantilist policy also included the granting of monopolies, regulation of wages and prices, and the exploitation of colonies—all designed to boost output to be sold abroad for gold and silver.

The eighteenth century, the century of the Enlightenment, was a period of discovery in all areas, starting with many scientific discoveries, such as Newton's laws. Then, because the church and the ancients were generally judged to be wrong in scientific areas, people began to question the church's views on materialistic matters. Newly aware that natural subjects such as rock and air obeyed natural laws, philosophers proposed that there were similar "natural laws" for humanity to obey in economic life. It was believed that human misery occurred because such laws were violated.

Much of the impetus of the American Revolution stemmed from such ideas. In 1625, Hugo Grotius (1583-1645) spoke of the "inalienable and indestructible rights of the individual" in such a "state of nature." John Locke (1632-1704) emphasized the "natural rights" of life, liberty, and property and said that all people had a right to the fruits of their individual labor. In 1762, Jean Jacques Rousseau (1712-1788) wrote the key phrase used in the Declaration of Independence 12 years later—the "inalienable rights of life, liberty, and the pursuit of happiness."

The first group of true economists, called the **Physiocrats**, appeared during this period. The term comes from the Greek word "physiocracy," which means "the rule of nature." They believed in natural law and that all wealth comes from the land. Thus, the "husbandmen" (farmers, fishermen, and miners) were the only true producers. The Physiocrats regarded industrialists, craftsmen, and tradesmen as "sterile" or unproductive. They wanted little government involvement in economic affairs, believing in *laissez faire et laissez passer*—that is, "don't interfere, for the world will take care of itself." Because "true" nature did not require government interference, the Physiocrats believed the economy didn't either.

Thomas Jefferson and many of the other Founding Fathers were strongly influenced by the concept of natural rights and the Physiocrats. Many were farmers (or "planters") and felt strongly that the success of democracy depended upon the ownership of land and farming of it by citizens. The Northwest Ordinance of 1787 and various land acts extending to the Morrill Act of 1862 aided the establishment of "smallholder agriculture" (small farms). These acts led to the establishment of "the family farm," which we still seek to maintain, and something like a purely competitive market structure (covered in more detail in Chapters 6 and 7).

The Classical Economists

The Physiocrats set the stage for the most influential writer in economics, Adam Smith (1723-1790). In 1776, he wrote *The Wealth of Nations,* in which he supported a new economic system based upon free markets with no government intervention. The book serves as the basis for capitalism, a system most Western nations generally use today. Smith fought for an end to government promotion of mercantilist policies, the granting of monopolies, and subsidies (money grants to businesses).

In 1798, another Classical economist, Thomas Malthus (1766-1834), predicted perpetual misery in his *Essay on the Principles of Population.* He believed population would increase at a geometric rate while food output would increase at only an arithmetic rate, leading to mass starvation. The essayist Thomas Carlyle branded economics "the dismal science" largely because of this pessimistic outlook, and economics never lost the name.

David Ricardo (1772-1823) extended and clarified Smith's work by explaining that rent on farmland was high as a consequence of high grain prices. This idea was revolutionary because people previously believed grain prices were high because land rents were high. Ricardo also explained how trade or exchange occurs by introducing the concept of the "law of comparative advantage" (covered in Chapter 2). Finally, he refined Malthus' "iron law of wages," which held that workers' wages would gravitate toward subsistence levels in a period of no economic growth.

Leon Walras (1834-1910) founded the Lausanne School of economic thought. He believed that economics could become more precise and useful if it used mathematics. In this he actually followed the father of mathematical economics, Antoine Augustin Cournot (1801-1877). Cournot introduced supply and demand curves into economics. Walras is best known for developing general equilibrium analysis, in which he showed how each individual market is connected to all other markets. He also explained how prices can be determined in competitive markets through *tatonement* (or adjustment). Walras wrote *Elements* (Volume I and II) in 1874 and 1877. Alfredo Pareto (1848-1923) elaborated on

Walras' work. He made general equilibrium analysis easier to understand and established the conditions necessary for maximizing welfare in society.

Alfred Marshall (1842-1924) wrote *Principles of Economics* (1890). Extremely respected, he is especially known for his theory of consumer behavior, for his connection of supply and demand, and for his insistence on precise analysis, especially in his use of mathematics.

Socialist Writers and Thought

Although many people believe that Karl Marx (1818-1883) was the father of socialism, some basic premises of this theory occurred in the Bible and other theological works. Marx was only one of many socialists. The **French Utopians** were the first modern proponents of socialism. A prominent Utopian was Francois Emile Babeuf (1760-1797), guillotined during the French Revolution for promoting a French socialist state. Other early framers of socialist thought include Louis Blanc (1811-1882), who coined "from each according to his ability, to each according to his needs." Another was Jeremy Bentham (1748-1832), who sought an economy that would provide the "greatest good to the greatest number." The more famous socialists Karl Marx and Frederich Engels (1820-1895) had their influence 50 to 100 years after these early socialist thinkers. It was their writings, including *The Communist Manifesto* and *Das Kapital*, (Vol. I, 1867; Vol. II, 1885; Vol. III, 1895) that aided the development of communist movements.

Although not classified as a socialist, John Stuart Mill (1806-1873) influenced socialist thought profoundly when he criticized the distribution of income and wealth in capitalist systems. His criticism also opened the door to government intervention in the economy, especially with respect to income distribution (the What to Produce question). He wrote *Principles of Political Economy* in 1848.

The Austrian School of Economics

The Austrian School consisted of several prominent economists, including the founder, Carl Menger (1840-1921). He was one of three economists who introduced the marginal utility theory (see Chapter 16), along with Walras and William Stanley Jevons (1835-1882). Menger and his students, including Eugen Bohm-Bawerk (1851-1914), developed models of capitalist economies. Bohm-Bawerk's student, Joseph Schumpeter (1883-1950), wrote *The Theory of Economic Development* (1912). He showed how entrepreneurs promote change through "creative destruction" of the existing economic order.

Ludwig Von Mises (1881-1973) founded the Modern School of Austrian Economics. Two of his books, *Socialism* (1922) and *Human Action* (1949), established his stature as a champion of freedom of the individual and the capitalist model. His student and like-minded follower, Friederich Hayek (1899-1992), gained fame with his own book, *The Road to Serfdom* (1944), in which he attacked government intervention in the economy.

20th Century Economic Thought

Several economists in the early 1900s rocked the boat of "laissez faire capitalism" (an economy free of government intervention). They are called **institutionalists** because they often attacked various economic and social institutions as roadblocks to higher economic welfare. They believed that institutions, customs, and social mores and values were as important in explaining economic behavior as the traditional economic concepts such as supply and demand. Some prominent institutionalists include: Thorstein Veblen (1857-1929), author of *The Theory of the Leisure Class* (1899); John R. Commons (1862-1945), who provided the political Progressives with ideas on tax reform, public utility regulation, and labor legislation; and Wesley C. Mitchell (1874-1948), who co-founded the National Bureau of Economic Research.

Irving Fisher (1867-1947) was the most famous American monetary economist of the early 20th century. He established the connection between the nominal rate of interest and the real rate of interest and did work on the equation of exchange (see pages 334 and 346).

Usually considered the most influential economist of the century, John Maynard Keynes (1883-1946) attacked the Classical belief that government should not interfere with an economy in the midst of a recession. Keynes' theories led to an active role for government in regulating national output, employment, price levels, and interest rates. To this day economists argue about the wisdom of such intervention.

Joan Robinson (1903-1983) and Edward Chamberlin (1899-1967) both did work on monopolistic competition (see Chapter 9), which made it easier to understand how firms that are not purely competitive determine their prices and output levels.

Perhaps today's well-known economists involved in such debates will become as prominent as those covered here. Recent or current leaders in contemporary economics include Kenneth Arrow, Robert Barro, Gary Becker, Alan Blinder, Milton Friedman, John Kenneth Galbraith, Robert Lucas, Robert Reich, Paul Craig Roberts, Paul Samuelson, Robert Solow, and Lester Thurow.

Chapter 1 SUMMARY

Economics is one of the social sciences, which are studies of how people think, as well as how they act, especially in their relations with others. This book assumes people are rational in their behavior, which means they seek to maximize satisfaction by attaining goals and objectives.

Economics deals for the most part with the materialistic goals of goods and services. They are produced with the resources of labor, capital, natural resources, and entrepreneurship. Desires for goods and services are unlimited, while resources are limited. Thus, resources are scarce, and the intent of studying economics is to help society deal with this scarcity.

People maximize their economic well-being by allocating or using resources efficiently. This is accomplished by using cost-benefit analysis, ensuring that resource users have more to gain (benefit) than they have to lose or give up (opportunity cost).

A production possibilities curve exhibits the economic problem graphically. It shows how the output of two goods is limited by the amount of resources available. It also shows that resources are not equally well-suited to producing all goods.

Marginal analysis shows that good decision making involves looking at just the extra benefits and costs one incurs. This means the benefits and costs of any past actions are irrelevant for future decisions.

Errors in decision making occur because of: 1) improper measure of costs and benefits; 2) failure to consider long-run effects; 3) refusal to consider the effects on others; and 4) someone else bearing much of the costs of a decision.

Cost-benefit analysis is properly carried out in a society when the three Basic Economic Questions are properly answered. What to Produce? is asked so that the most beneficial goods and services are made. How to Produce? is asked so that the most efficient production processes are used. For Whom to Produce? is asked to ensure that the goods and services provide the maximum economic well-being for all members of society combined.

Economics is split into microeconomics, the study of small elements of the economy, and macroeconomics, the study of large sections of the economy.

The best-known economist of the capitalist philosophy and founder of the Classical School was Adam Smith, who wrote *The Wealth of Nations* in 1776. Other major Classical economists include Thomas Malthus and David Ricardo. The major alternative body of thought has been that of the socialists, of which Karl Marx is the most prominent. The Austrian School, founded by Carl Menger, brought much of Classical thought into the modern era. Prominent economists of the Austrian School of the 20th century include Frederick Hayek and Ludwig Van Mises. The most revolutionary work in economics in the 20th century was done by John Maynard Keynes in the field of macroeconomics.

Chapter 1 RESPONSES TO THE LEARNING OBJECTIVES

1. The four classes of resources and examples include:
   a) labor—custodian, pilot, mason, machinist, accountant, bank teller
   b) entrepreneur(ship)—Ray Kroc, Walter Chrysler, Thomas Edison
   c) capital—dump truck, cement mixer, calculator, paper cutter, silo, factory
   d) natural resource—limestone, river, forest, farmland, salt mine
2. The economic problem is the consequence of:
   a) people wanting an unlimited amount of goods and services
   b) a limited amount of resources with which to produce goods and services
3. The purpose of studying economics is to ensure the maximum possible economic welfare from society's scarce resources through proper resource allocation.
4. Making the most efficient use of resources minimizes the problems caused by a scarcity of resources.
5. Resources should be used in an activity only if the benefit the activity provides exceeds the opportunity cost.
6. A production possibilities curve "bows out" from the origin or is concave outward. It shows all combinations of output of two goods or services it is pos-

sible to produce with a given set of resources.

7. Marginal analysis is used when a decision maker compares the extra benefit of using additional resources with the extra costs. The resources are used only if the extra benefits exceed the extra costs.
8. Errors are made in decisions regarding resources when:
   a) benefits are overestimated and/or costs are underestimated
   b) the long-run costs and/or benefits are ignored
   c) there are external costs
   d) decision makers pay little or none of the costs of a decision
9. The purpose of asking:
   a) What to Produce? is to ensure that goods and services that provide the most benefit from a given amount of resources are produced
   b) How to Produce? is to ensure that goods and services are produced with the least amount of resources
   c) For Whom to Produce? is to ensure that goods and services are received by those who derive much benefit from them
10. Until 300 years ago, most economic writing dealt with scattered matters. The mercantilists believed that a nation's wealth depended upon its gold and silver supplies, so they favored exports and discouraged imports. The Physiocrats said that all wealth came from the land, believed in natural law, and wanted little government in the economy. The Classical economists developed modern capitalist theory, which is based upon individuals seeking their own self-interest with a minimum of government interference. The socialists believe that government involvement in the economy and cooperation between individuals provides greater economic welfare. The Austrian School economists made economics more of a science and favored the market system of individuals seeking their own self-interest. The institutionalists rejected conventional explanations of human economic behavior, opposed unrestricted capitalism, and favored government intervention. Keynes brought about government involvement in such matters as employment and inflation rates.

Chapter 1 LEARNING ACTIVITIES AND DISCUSSION QUESTIONS

1. Which of the four classes of resources seems most important in producing all goods and services combined? Why?
2. If resources would cease being scarce, how would the economy change?
3. Explain how you used marginal analysis most recently?
4. Think of at least one error you made in decision making in each of the four "error categories."
5. Give an example of each of the Basic Economic Questions you saw being answered recently.

APPENDIX A SOME MATHEMATICS NEEDED IN ECONOMICS

Mathematics is useful and necessary in many subjects, including economics. This appendix covers concepts frequently used in this book, including percentages, factor changes, rates, and graphs.

MEASURES OF VARIABLES

A variable is any unit of measure that can range from a smaller amount to a larger amount. Land area, a person's weight, and income are all variables. The purposes of this section are: 1) to show how to calculate changes in variables; and 2) to show how to compare the magnitudes of two variables.

Percentage

The most elementary use of percentages is simple percentage, where, essentially, one seeks the ratio of one variable to another. It is found by:

Percentage = (Amount of A)/(Amount of B) x 100

For example, if B is a 32-gallon barrel of crude oil and A is the amount of gasoline that can be refined from the oil—say 20 gallons—then 62.5% of a barrel of crude oil is gasoline, or:

20/32 x 100 = 62.5%

Percentage changes are a bit more complex. They are usually expressed in one of two ways. Most common is a percentage increase or decrease in a variable, found by:

Percent Change in A = (Change in A)/(A in Time 1) x 100

= (A in Time 2 - A in Time 1)/(A in Time 1) x 100

For example, if a child's weight increases from 80 to 87 pounds between two birthdays, the child's weight increased by 8.75%, as:

(87 - 80)/80 x 100 = 7/80 x 100 = 0.0875 x 100 = 8.75%

Occasionally a variable is expressed as a "percent of" what it used to be. This is found by:

A in Time 2 as a Percent of A in Time 1 = (A in Time 2)/(A in Time 1) x 100

For example, if your income rose from $10,000 last year to $12,000 this year, your income this year is 120 percent of last year's income, or:

$12,000/$10,000 x 100 = 1.2 x 100 = 120%

Of course, variables can go down as well as up, so variables can have either percentage drops or increases.

Factor Changes

Another way to measure the changes in variables is through factor changes, given by the formula:

Factor Change in X = (Level of X in Time 2)/(Level of X in Time 1)

For example, if the value of a firm's capital rises from $4 million to $12.8 million, it experienced a factor increase of 3.2 times or a "3.2 fold" increase in its capital stock, as:

$12.8/4 = 3.2x factor increase

Factor changes and percentage changes in variables often are given simultaneously, and it is useful to know how to convert one into the other. The formula connecting the two is:

Percentage Change in X = 100(Factor Change in X - 1)

For example, a threefold increase or a tripling of a firm's debt is equivalent to saying its debt rose by 200 percent, for:

200 = 100(3 - 1)

The following columns for factor changes and percentage changes show equivalent changes on any given line.

Factor Change in x	Percentage Change in x
1.2x	20%
1.5x	50%
2.0x	100%
2.5x	150%
3.0x	200%
4.0x	300%

Rates

"Rate" is used to indicate several different measures of variables. First, it could mean a percentage change in a variable over time. For example, "wages were rising at a five percent yearly rate in the 1980s" means that wages were five percent higher each year than the previous year. Second, rate could mean the "flow" of one variable as compared with another. For example, the "wage rate" is the amount of money paid (variable one) or "flowing to" a worker for each hour of time worked (the amount of time is variable two). A secretary's typing rate might be 90 words (variable one) per minute (time being variable two). And the unemployment rate is the number of unemployed laborers (variable one) as a share or percent of the labor force (variable two). As a final example, the interest rate refers to the amount of interest paid (variable one) as a percent of the money borrowed (variable two).

GRAPHING

A picture is worth a thousand words—especially in economics. Generally a graph shows the relationship between two variables. Table A1-1 shows a relationship between two variables, x and y. This is a "direct relationship," which means both variables change in the same direction. Note that as x increases, so does y. Conversely, in an "inverse relationship," as one variable increases, the other decreases.

Two types of graphs are commonly used to display such relationships. The first is the bar graph or histogram, where variable x is measured along the horizontal line, called the x-axis. The vertical axis, called the y-axis, is used to measure the magnitude or the size of y. The height of each of the bar graphs can be measured on the y-axis by extending a horizontal line from the top of a bar graph over to the y-axis. Often bar graphs also have this magnitude stated within or next to the graph, as does the one in Figure A1-1. The same data in Table A1-1 is shown in Figure A1-1. The variable that does the causation, called the independent variable, is usually placed on the x-axis. The dependent variable, the one that is influenced by the independent variable, is placed on the y-axis.

The other type of graph, the line graph, is similar in concept. Again, there are two axes, called x and y, except now a point is located where the top of the bar graph would be in that form of graph, as is shown in Figure A1-2. The pair of numbers beside each point indicates the magnitudes of variable x and variable y, respectively. Finally, Figure A1-3 shows these points connected with a line—a graph. A line is really composed of an infinite number of points, just like the five that are shown. Any such point on a line graph always gives two "pieces" of information, found by dropping straight down to the x-axis to measure the amount of x and then by moving horizontally to the y-axis to find the magnitude of y.

Table A1-1 A Direct Relationship

Variable x	Variable y
1	16
2	20
3	24
4	28
5	32

Figure A1-1 A Bar Graph or Histogram

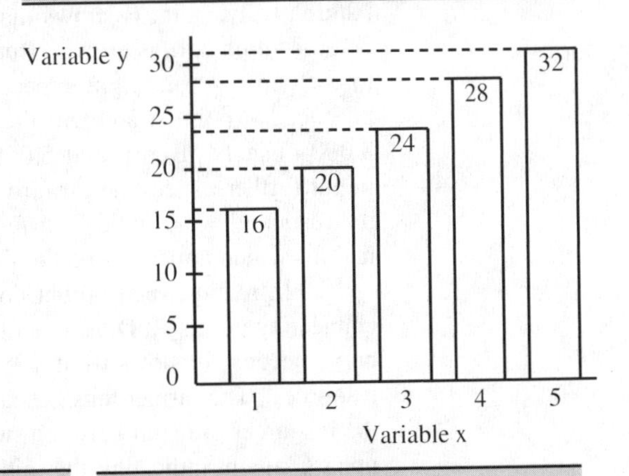

Figure A1-2 A Two-Variable System of Coordinates

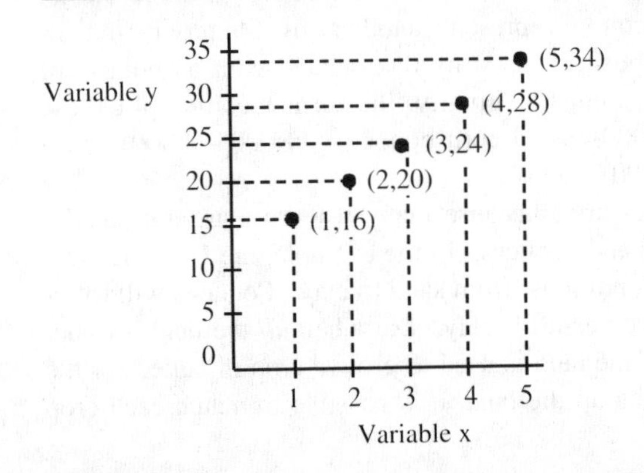

Figure A1-3 A Line Graph

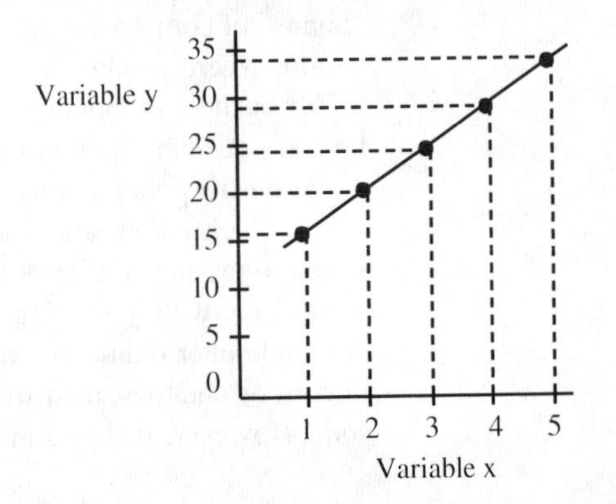

APPENDIX B PRODUCTION POSSIBILITIES CURVES

Suppose a farmer would like to grow as much corn and potatoes as possible. However, there is only a limited amount of resources with which to produce them—100 acres of land, 90 hours of labor, 70 hours of tractor time, and so on. The question then is: how much corn and potatoes *can* be produced with these scarce resources? The answer partly depends upon how the resources are distributed between the corn and potato enterprises.

The points along the bowed curve in Figure A1-4 show the *maximum possible* outputs of corn and potatoes. If the farmer makes any mistake in using the resources, such as driving over a row of corn while cultivating, the actual yield will be less than the curve indicates. Such situations are represented by points within the curve. Remember, this area is called the zone of inefficiency. In reality, since few producers answer the How to Produce question perfectly all the time, such interior points invariably describe real-life production processes.

The use of a production possibilities curve is based on the assumption of a given level of technology. That is, no innovations will change the way products can be made.

Point A in Figure A1-4 shows that if the farmer uses all the resources to grow corn, 16,000 bushels of corn will be produced, but no potatoes. Alternatively, point B shows that the resources could produce 10,000 bushels of potatoes if no corn is grown. But suppose the farmer devotes half of the resources to each crop. You might expect the farmer to get half the yield of corn that was produced at point A and half the potatoes that were produced at point B—that is, 8,000 bushels of corn and 5,000 bushels of potatoes, shown as point C. You might further expect the farm to yield other combinations of corn and potatoes if the resources were divided differently, but you might also expect that all combinations would appear along the line connecting points A, C, and B.

In reality, such output combinations would appear along the curved line connecting points A, D, E, F, and B. The curve is called a production possibilities curve because it shows what it is possible to produce of both crops, given a set of resources. The farmer thus gets a "bonus" (that is, a bigger yield than expected) if the resources are split between two crops, as the graph shows. For instance, note point C again, indicating the initial *expected* output of 8,000 bushels of corn and 5,000 bushels of potatoes. In reality, the farmer can produce 13,000 bushels of corn if 5,000 bushels of potatoes are grown, shown at point D—a 5,000 bushel "bonus" of corn. Alternatively, point F represents another possible production situation, where producing 8,000 bushels of corn is associated with a "bonus" of 3,700 bushels of potatoes over point C. Finally, the farmer could split these bonuses at point E, getting a 3,000-bushel corn bonus (= 11,000 - 8,000) and a 1,800-bushel potato bonus (= 6,800 - 5,000).

Such unexpected increases arise because many resources are not equally suited to produce different goods and services. In the example, the 100-acre field might have widely varying soil conditions, from sand to clay. Potatoes will tolerate sand better than corn, and vice versa for clay. But when *all* the land is either in corn or potatoes, then *some* of the land is used to grow a crop ill-suited for the soil. However, if the farmer splits up the land, it is possible to match each crop with its "favorite" soil, thereby boosting yields, the source of the "bonuses."

Such relationships between resources and the outputs of two goods and services are almost universal. It is a primary reason for the law of increasing cost, which states that higher levels of output of a particular good or service are increasingly costly. This is because increasingly ill-suited resources are used to make the extra output. Consequently, it takes more resources (thus, more costs) to make each additional unit of output. It's a bit like choosing players for a pick-up basketball game. The best player is chosen first, then the next best, and so on until the "scrubs" get picked. It might take the last three players picked to score as many points as the first player.

Production possibilities curves also can be used to show opportunity costs. Suppose the farmer was at point F and wanted to shift to point D by growing more corn—5,000 bushels more. It cost the opportunity of having 3,700 bushels of potatoes because potato output fell from 8,700 to 5,000 bushels. Conversely, moving from point D to point F means the opportunity cost of growing an extra 3,700 bushels of potatoes is 5,000 bushels of corn. Finally, if the move was from point D to point E, the cost of growing an extra 1,800 bushels of potatoes is 2,000 bushels of corn.

Figure A1-4 Production Possibilities of Corn and Potatoes

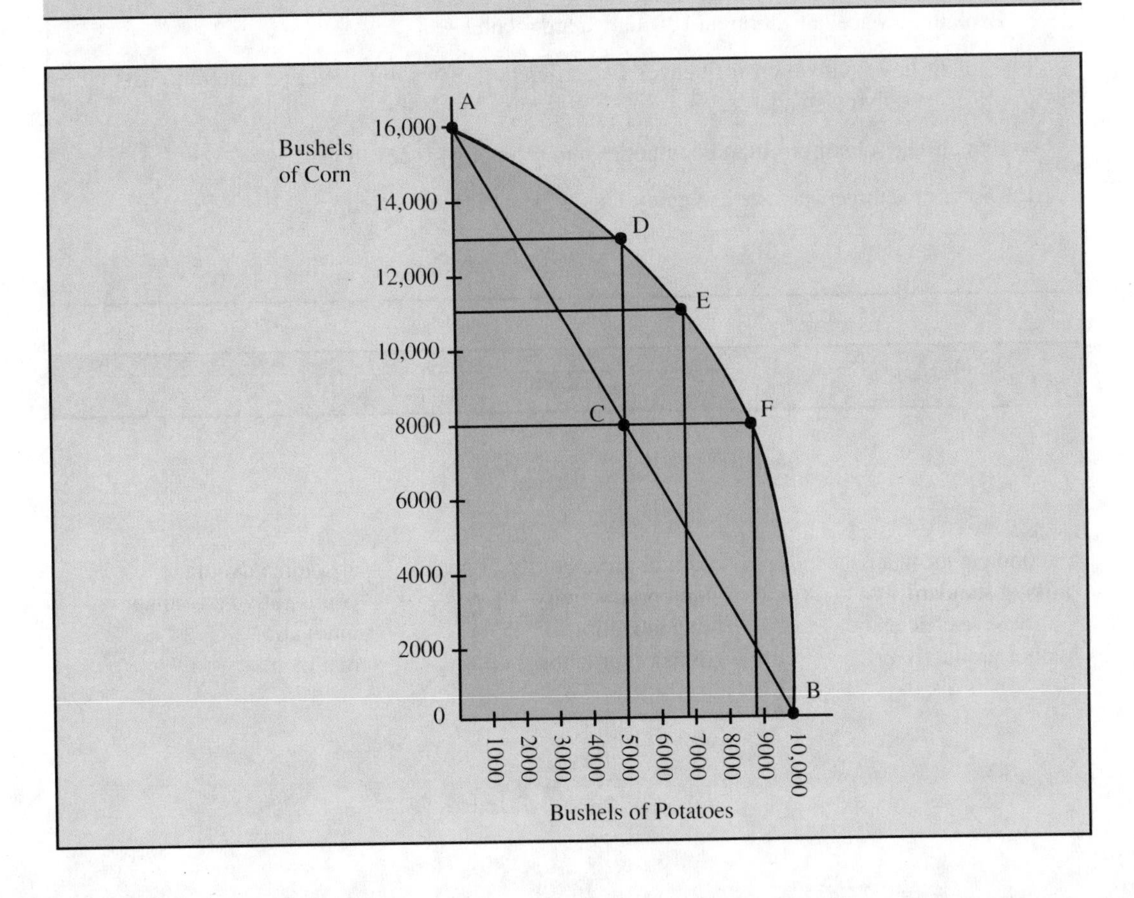

CHAPTER 2

RAISING ECONOMIC WELFARE THROUGH ECONOMIC GROWTH

★★★★★ LEARNING OBJECTIVES ★★★★★

1. Explain the concept of economic welfare.
2. Discuss the drawbacks in using living standards to reflect economic welfare.
3. List the primary ways to increase living standards.
4. Explain how to calculate the level of labor productivity for a resource in a production process.
5. Explain how specialization increases the efficiency of resource use.
6. Explain how to determine the comparative advantage of a particular resource.
7. Explain how specialization and exchange are related.
8. Explain how innovation influences the efficiency of resource use, production costs, prices, and living standards.
9. Explain the role of profit and competition in promoting innovation.
10. Discuss the three ways we can enjoy increases in economic welfare.

TERMS

economic growth
living standard
allocative efficiency
labor productivity
capital productivity
land productivity
specialization
division of labor
absolute advantage
comparative advantage
innovation
real income

Chapter 1 introduced "the economic problem," which occurs when unlimited wants combined with scarce resources force us to choose how to use our resources. Choosing wisely ensures that people will maximize satisfaction or economic welfare from their resources.

Although the system is not perfect, our economy has done rather well over its history. Still, people continue to seek an ever-increasing amount of satisfaction (or economic welfare). This chapter introduces the major ways of doing this—that is, of achieving **economic growth**, which is an increase in the output of goods and services. That, in turn, can increase economic welfare. More than anything else, this chapter shows how we got to our phenomenal level of materialistic richness in just a few centuries. It also will show why our descendants in the year 2100 will feel sorry we had to live in such "poverty"—that is, compared with their much higher incomes.

INTRODUCTION TO ECONOMIC WELFARE

Before exploring how economic welfare is raised, it is useful to discuss a way to measure it. This section introduces a measure of economic welfare and takes a broad look at how to raise it.

Measuring Economic Welfare

★1

Economic welfare refers to satisfaction achieved when consuming goods and services. Measuring satisfaction is difficult, at least objectively. Instead, your best available measure of economic welfare might be subjective. You could observe how often someone smiles, laughs, or makes cheerful remarks. But this wouldn't work perfectly because happiness has many sources besides materialistic ones.

However, economic welfare can be measured indirectly by measuring the output of goods and services. Table 2-1 shows some selected goods available to several nations, which could serve as a rough basis of economic welfare. It shows the number of automobiles, telephones, and televisions available in 1989 for every 1,000 persons. Not only do Americans surpass most foreigners in personal possessions, but today's Americans easily surpass earlier Americans in their pos-

Table 2-1 Possession of Selected Items per 1,000 People in 1989

	Country				
Item	United States	West Germany	Japan	Mexico	Soviet Union
Automobiles	572	446	235	65	42
Telephones	650	641	535	90	115
Televisions	621	377	250	108	300

Source: *International Marketing Fund*

sessions. For instance, only 25 percent of households in 1925 had radios, 94 percent did by 1953, and today virtually all do (and most have several). In 1910, *no* family had a vacuum cleaner, washing machine, refrigerator, dishwasher, toaster, coffee maker, or television—all items many people today call "necessities."

In a broader and more accurate sense, we measure *total* output for our nation in an entire year. This is a measure of the *collective* economic welfare of all the 260 million Americans combined. Similarly, the 27 million Canadians can add up their output. Nations measure their total output with the gross domestic product (GDP), or the total value of output in a year. This concept is presented in detail in Chapter 11.

But those figures don't indicate whether the *average* American has more goods and services than the *average* Canadian. To find that amount—the amount of *individual* economic welfare—you must divide total output by the population. This amount is called the **living standard** or standard of living. It refers to the amount of goods and services produced in a year for each person, on average (also known as per capita output). Its formula is:

$$\text{Living Standard} = \frac{\text{Total Output of Goods and Services}}{\text{Population}}$$

Of course, few people actually receive that exact amount of goods and services. They get either more or less than that. Yet the formula gives at least some idea of how prosperous we all are as compared with earlier generations as well as other nations today. Historically, each generation has seen a significant increase in living standards, though they have not risen every year.

★2

There are two major objections to the use of the living standard to measure economic welfare: 1) the problem of varying income distributions is not addressed; and 2) other goals and values are not addressed.

■ First, the living standard ignores the effect that varying income distributions have on the "collective satisfaction" of the whole society. In one possible income distribution, everyone would have an equal income. In another, 90 percent of the income would go to five percent of the population, with the remainder of the country barely surviving on the remaining 10 percent of the income. Although "collective satisfaction" cannot be measured in either case, perhaps the equal distribution would yield a happier society.

A greater "collective" economic welfare is the goal of legislatures, courts, and other government agencies when they make changes in taxes, earning power, and the public welfare system.

■ The second objection to using the standard of living to measure economic welfare is based on the fashionable criticism of our "quality of life." We have an economically rich society, but at what cost? Our air, rivers, and lakes reek; the stress of the "rat race" leads to phenomenal use of tranquilizers, cocaine, alcohol, and psychotherapy; the crime rate soars; and institutions—the family, schools, churches—collapse like dominoes. Because these situations often involve value judgments, it is difficult, perhaps impossible, to resolve this criticism.

Some First Steps in Raising Living Standards

Returning to our simpler measure, some clues to raising the living standard are found in the formula stated above. A nation can raise its living standard either by: 1) increasing the numerator (the output of goods and services); or 2) by decreasing the denominator (the population).

★3

■ Reducing the population obviously is not the answer. Yet controlling population *growth* does deserve attention. America's population grows around one percent per year, whereas those of many less-developed nations climb between two and three percent per year. A higher growth rate ensures that a higher percentage of the population is young—and not yet producing goods and services. Because these young people need food, clothing, and the like, the available output spreads more thinly in such nations. China's one-child-per-couple policy addresses that problem. Chinese couples who have more than one child suffer great financial and various social "negative rewards."

■ Thus, the primary way to increase the living standard is to produce more goods and services for a given population. Nations do this in two ways: 1) by finding or developing more resources; and 2) by becoming more efficient in using existing resources.

Before examining how this is done in our economy, let's consider how it might have worked in a self-sufficient, pioneer farm family. A family that lived at a subsistence level may have wished to increase its welfare (well-being). First, it could have done so by increasing the resources it already had. Labor resources could have been increased by working longer hours and by having larger families. More farmland could have been produced by clearing woodlands, draining swamps, and plowing prairie land. More capital would have been available after new tools were made, buildings constructed, and dams built as power sources and water reservoirs.

Second, the family could have been more efficient in using its resources. Trial and error in new production techniques would have improved crop yields and other outputs over time. Specialization would have raised productivity significantly. Men would have learned what tasks they were best at—probably those requiring strength and endurance, such as field work. So would have women—probably the lighter farm work, such as milking and tending chickens, as well as the household work of cooking, clothes-making, candle-making, and so on.

In a modern economy, such increases in the living standard come in the same two ways. Yet, the process is less obvious because it is harder to observe an entire economy than a single farm family. Nevertheless, let's consider how there can be an increase in the available resources in an entire economy. Rarely is this an overnight process, as you can see in the following examples.

Consider natural resources. Although the amount of natural resources can't be increased, the amount of *practically available* natural resources is increased when people: find and develop a new oil field; develop a mining process to extract a previously useless low-grade metal ore (like the fairly recent taconite iron ore process); drain wetlands for farm use or reclaim land from the seas as the Dutch did; and build roads into remote forests.

The labor resource can increase in several ways. Population can increase through normal excesses of births over deaths or by immigration. Often nations try to encourage the "right" people to immigrate and enter the labor force. U.S. immigration laws in the past limited immigration from various "undesirable nations," usually where people had few skills. Australia used to pay travel expenses for those who settled there—but only the "right people." The former Soviet Union kept people from *leaving* on the ground that the state educated people to become skilled laborers, and those people had an obligation to produce goods and services in the Soviet Union.

Labor availability could also be increased by: increasing the workweek from 40 to 50 or 60 hours, extending the retirement age and encouraging retired people to go back to work, setting up more workshops for the one million Americans in prisons, encouraging more homemakers to get jobs outside the home, and relaxing child labor laws. (Although these are *possible,* they generally are not *acceptable*—at least not in this country.)

Last, labor resources increase when otherwise "useless" raw human talent becomes educated. School "socializes" people (well, *usually*) so that they can work cooperatively with others and handle work discipline. It also provides them with complex mental and physical skills to be highly productive. Educated people are "human capital," for labor resources are created in schools, much as any machine (physical capital) is created in a factory.

The amount of capital resources (or capital stock) of the economy increases when, for example: Caterpillar builds a bulldozer, Apple makes a computer for an office at General Motors, and Stanley produces another hammer for a carpenter; the Army Corps of Engineers builds a dam to improve navigation, control floods, and supply irrigation water; a developer erects an office building in Los Angeles; and government expands the interstate highway system.

Finally, where do entrepreneurs come from? Some ways that government and private enterprise can encourage people to become entrepreneurs are: change tax laws to allow rich people to keep more of their income; develop sources of financial backing; stimulate original thinking and independence in schools; and expand Junior Achievement and similar programs.

RAISING THE EFFICIENCY OF RESOURCE USE

Recall that efficiency refers to how well resources are used. That is, it refers to how much output of a good or service is produced from a given amount of resources. Alternatively, it refers to how many resources it takes to make one unit of some good or service. Often people combine these two viewpoints and say that being efficient means getting the most output from the least amount of resources. This concept of efficiency has to do with producing things. Somewhat apart from that, economists often refer to **allocative efficiency**, which means firms produce the goods and services most preferred by consumers. Thus, the What to Produce question is answered so that any other way of answering it (that is, changing what is made) will reduce economic welfare. Another aspect of efficiency refers to how well the nation's total output is distributed. This is called distributive efficiency.

You often hear of another concept, called productivity, that seems identical to efficiency. Economists generally use the term efficiency when speaking of many resources being used in conjunction with each other. But productivity refers to the productiveness of a specific resource. Most commonly, people refer to **labor productivity**, or output per hour. It includes the hours worked by all laborers: assemblers, shipping clerks, secretaries, janitors, and so on. It is calculated for a particular production process in some given period with the formula:

★4

$$\text{Labor Productivity} = \frac{\text{Total Output}}{\text{Total Hours Worked}}$$

For example, say a window manufacturer makes 90,000 windows in a year with 30 employees working a 40-hour-week shift, 50 weeks per year. Total hours worked is then 60,000 hours (= 30 x 40 x 50), and labor productivity is 1.5 windows per hour (= 90,000 windows ÷ 60,000 hours). Thus, for each hour of every laborer's time, on average, the firm makes 1.5 windows.

A serious problem with this measure is that it cannot really tell us much about services, where output is much harder to measure than for windows or other goods. For example, practice may make a musician more productive if the quality of the play improves, but we have no way to measure this improvement. Government statisticians usually resort to measuring service output by the price consumers pay for services. Since most musicians do not receive higher pay every time they improve, most economists think service productivity is usually understated.

In addition, occasionally you hear of **capital productivity** (the amount of product produced by one hour of machine time) and **land productivity** (the yield of a crop per acre of land).

This section introduces the three primary ways of increasing efficiency: 1) eliminating waste in existing production processes; 2) increasing the specialization of resource use; and 3) innovation.

Achieving the Potential of Existing Production Processes

Everyone has a maximum output potential, whatever the job. A backhoe operator can dig just so many holes in an hour, and a dentist can fill just so many holes in an hour. Machines have similar capacities or potentials, as does farmland and other resources.

But few resources achieve their potential, even when producers use them in the best available production process. Here are a few of the millions of ways to cut the waste of resource use *without* changing the production process itself. Office workers could produce more by: stopping idle chatter, eliminating personal phone calls, reducing "paper shuffling" by better planning, and not calling in "sick" when they are not. Assembly line workers can boost their productivity by: speeding up the line, smoothing out the steps for a better job "flow," keeping parts handy, and reducing breakage by being more careful. Managers can be more effective by avoiding alcohol at lunch, being more skillful in dealing with subordinates, and restricting themselves to managing (rather than meddling in someone else's job).

Besides the waste of labor, often firms don't use their capital equipment to potential. Better maintenance would reduce breakdowns. Improved scheduling of supplies and production would reduce idle machine operation time. Adding second and third shifts is another way to increase capital productivity.

Natural resources also are often squandered. The loss of U.S. soil through wind and water erosion in the last hundred years or so is a national scandal. Wiser selection of crops and tillage practices would sharply reduce erosion. Our forest resources also suffered from mismanagement, especially in the upper Midwest in the late 1800s and early 1900s.

These examples of wasted resources are only a tiny share of the total. They point out how commonly we make errors in decisions about using the four types of resources you studied in Chapter 1.

Increasing the Specialization of Resource Use

The second way to raise the efficiency of resource use is by increasing the degree of **specialization**. When a resource's use is specialized, it produces only a few (or even one) goods or services. This is often called the division of labor by product. Bakers, auto workers, bus drivers, and telephone operators all produce one thing, or, at the most, several closely related items. In the case of capital, few machines make products other than those the designer intended. For example, cement mixers make concrete, not cake mixes or anything else.

Specialization can go a step further when a resource doesn't make the whole good or service. Because the resource participates in only one part of the production process, economists call this the division of labor by process. It's what usually is meant by the **division of labor**. In auto manufacture, for example, someone might work only on the engine, and just on the camshaft. This also occurs in medical services. The American Medical Association lists 25 specialties and 56 sub-specialties.

The value of specializing the use of land and natural resources is fairly obvious if we suppose that the only crops we can produce are wheat and rice. Since rice requires a lot of water and wheat only moderate amounts, land in Arkansas is ideal for growing rice. On the other hand, Kansas receives little rain and is a poor region for growing rice, but it has adequate rainfall for wheat.

The case for specializing capital is a little less obvious because some forms of capital, like trucks and buildings, can serve many functions. Even here, however, specialization can improve efficiency. For example, a general purpose truck could not carry much oil compared with a tanker truck designed for that purpose. Or if we wanted to deliver pizzas, the general purpose truck would not be as efficient in terms of energy use and maneuverability as a small car.

★5 Specialization in the use of labor, or the division of labor, increases labor efficiency for three main reasons: 1) many jobs take a long time to master; 2) people differ in their capabilities at different tasks; and 3) time between steps of a production process is saved.

■ First, because many jobs take a long time to master, if a worker does only one task, this minimizes the time the worker produces less than is possible.

Alternatively, a worker who does many tasks must spend a longer time learning all the tasks and, consequently, produces less than top output. Suppose a worker in a furniture factory does 10 jobs and that each job takes four years to learn perfectly. Then the worker needs to work 40 years—about as long as it takes to reach retirement age—to reach peak productivity in all 10 jobs.

■ Second, the division of labor increases efficiency because people differ in their capabilities at different tasks. It's foolish for every worker at a firm to share all the jobs because output wouldn't be as high as with specialization. (Incidentally, it's just as foolish for members of a household to share all the jobs around the house, unless the members feel that the extra time taken is more than offset by the "fairness" gained by sharing the work.) Similarly, farmers use the land in different parts of the country for different crops—corn and soybeans in the Midwest, pecans and peanuts in Georgia, and wheat in the Great Plains.

■ Third, the division of labor increases efficiency because it eliminates time that would otherwise be spent between the steps of a production process. For example, suppose six people are to make 500 pizzas for a club project. Each could make a complete pizza by following these steps: 1) put down the cardboard; 2) get a crust and set it on the cardboard; 3) get a ladle and spread some sauce on the crust; 4) get some cheese and put it on; 5) get some sausage and put it on; 6) package the pizza. Because so much time would be lost *between* steps, it would save time if each of the six people would do only one job. The same situation exists on assembly lines, in restaurants, and in offices.

Once it is decided to specialize the use of a resource, how is it decided what the resource should do? That seems easy. Shouldn't, for example, Michael, a laborer, do what he does well? Not always, for it's not that simple. When a resource (such as Michael) is the most productive of all such resources in making something, economists say that resource has an **absolute advantage** in that production process. But having an absolute advantage doesn't dictate how a resource should be used. A real example might help.

Once there was a good baseball pitcher, possibly the best in the league. But after he was traded, his new manager refused to let him pitch. He was sent to the outfield so he could play every day. The player's name was Babe Ruth. Did the manager make the right move? Obviously yes, most would say. But we'll never know. Although Ruth was a phenomenal home run hitter, maybe he would have done *even better* as a pitcher. Consequently, perhaps our best pitcher award would be the Babe Ruth Award—not the Cy Young Award.

★6

Many business managers face similar situations. If a particular employee is the best of all employees at two or more jobs, which job should be assigned to that employee? When laborers or other resources are very good at two or more things, hard choices must be made. It's equally hard when a resource isn't very good at producing *anything*. In either case, deciding how a resource should be used requires finding its **comparative advantage**. A resource has a comparative advantage when it can produce something with a lower opportunity cost than any similar resource. Recall that opportunity cost refers to what is given up. When Ruth pitched, he gave up the opportunity to hit more home runs (because pitchers play only about one-fourth of all games). It "cost" more home runs for him to pitch than for other pitchers who *couldn't* hit well. Because his manager believed that Ruth did not have a comparative advantage in pitching, he didn't pitch.

Table 2-2 gives three examples of finding comparative advantage, one each for labor, natural resources, and capital. In the first case, John and Bob are to split the production of bread and coats. Notice from the production figures that Bob can't brag about any of his talents. But John can, for he has an absolute advantage in both products. When asked what Bob should do, some people would say, "Just stay out of the way!" But remember that resources are scarce. So long as Bob can make *something,* that's better than producing nothing.

Table 2-2 Finding Comparative Advantages of Three Types of Resources

Person (Laborer)	**Production per Week of:** Bread	Coats	**Opportunity Cost of Producing:** 1 Loaf of Bread	1 Coat
John	1000 Loaves	100 Coats	0.100 Coat = 100 Coats / 1000 Loaves	10.0 Loaves = 1000 Loaves / 100 Coats
Bob	800 Loaves	60 Coats	0.075 Coat = 60 Coats / 800 Loaves	13.3 Loaves = 800 Loaves / 60 Coats

Field (Land)	**Yield per Acre of:** Beans	Hay	**Opportunity Cost of Producing:** 1 Bushel of Beans	1 Ton of Hay
Field A	40 Bushels	4 Tons	0.100 Ton Hay = 4 Tons / 40 Bushels	10 Bushels Beans = 40 Bushels / 4 Tons
Field B	60 Bushels	5 Tons	0.083 Ton Hay = 5 Tons / 60 Bushels	12 Bushels Beans = 60 Bushels / 5 Tons

Truck (Capital)	**Amount Hauled per Day of:** Steel	Boxes	**Opportunity Cost of Hauling:** 1 Ton of Steel	1 Box
Dump Truck	100 Tons	1000 Boxes	______ Boxes = ______	____ Tons Steel = ______
Van	20 Tons	600 Boxes	______ Boxes = ______	____ Tons Steel = ______

In Chapter 1 you learned that the purpose of economics is to find ways to get the most from our scarce resources. That is, we wish to maximize the output of all goods and services combined. Similarly here, the goal is to maximize the production of coats plus bread. Think of Bob and John as a team, each making one item, putting their products on a common pile of bread mixed with coats (figuratively speaking, of course). This pile will be higher if the person who makes each coat sacrifices the smallest number of loaves of bread. Remember, every

> *Ruth made a big mistake when he gave up pitching*
>
> – Tris Speaker, Baseball Hall of Fame Member

coat added to that pile means the maker *cannot* add bread to it. So, when John (or Bob) makes the pile grow by adding a coat, he *keeps it* from growing by *not* adding bread. Simply put, the benefit (the coat) is offset by the opportunity cost (the bread). Because the coat is the same whether Bob or John makes it, the only decision is to find how to minimize the opportunity cost—the bread given up. The table shows that John gives up 10.0 loaves when he makes a coat, and Bob gives up 13.3 loaves. Because John gives up less, he has the lowest opportunity cost and a comparative advantage in making coats.

Alternatively, Bob has a comparative advantage in bread making. He only gives up the opportunity to make 0.075 coats when he makes a loaf of bread. But John, making an identical loaf, gives up more of a coat—0.100 of one. So Bob, though lacking an *absolute* advantage, has a *comparative* advantage and should make bread. He won't make bread because he is *good* at it, but because he is better at bread making *as compared with* coat making.

Consider this in another way. Bob can make bread at 80 percent of John's rate (800 ÷ 1,000), but coats at only 60 percent of John's rate (60 ÷ 100). Thus, Bob is *closest to* John in bread making. So Bob should make bread. Similarly, comparative advantage explains why parents assign young children to relatively simple chores, such as trash removal, vacuuming, and garden watering. Children are almost as fast as parents at these tasks, but nowhere close when it comes to mending clothes or painting.

In the second example, Field B has an absolute advantage in growing both beans and hay. But notice that it is 50 percent more productive than Field A in beans (60 bushels to 40) and only 25 percent more productive in hay (five tons to four). Thus, Field B should produce beans. Also note that Field B has a lower opportunity cost than Field A in bean production (0.083 tons of hay compared with 0.100 tons). Thus, Field B has a comparative advantage in bean production. Alternatively, Field A has a comparative advantage in hay production. For each ton of hay grown, it gives up only 10 bushels of beans, while Field B could grow 12 bushels of beans on the same area that it needs to grow a ton of hay.

In the last example, one involving capital, you are to finish the calculations and find the comparative advantage for both the dump truck and the van.

In conclusion, just because a resource *can do* something doesn't mean it *should* do it. You must consider what else it could do as well. This concept, seemingly so simple, is often misunderstood. This will become more evident in Chapter 8 on international trade.

★7 This brings up the next point—trade, or exchange. Whenever you specialize in producing a certain good, you produce far more output of that good than you need personally. You have a "surplus." But you will not have any of the other goods and services needed for survival. You have personal "shortages." Because all specialists face this predicament, they must exchange their respective surpluses for the surpluses of other specialists. (Incidentally, this use of the words

> *Honest people like you and me who are free want only the opportunity to trade with our fellow men – either our labor or the fruits thereof. This has made America great.*
> – Harold Warp

Figure 2-1 How Specialization, Living Standards, and Exchange Are Related

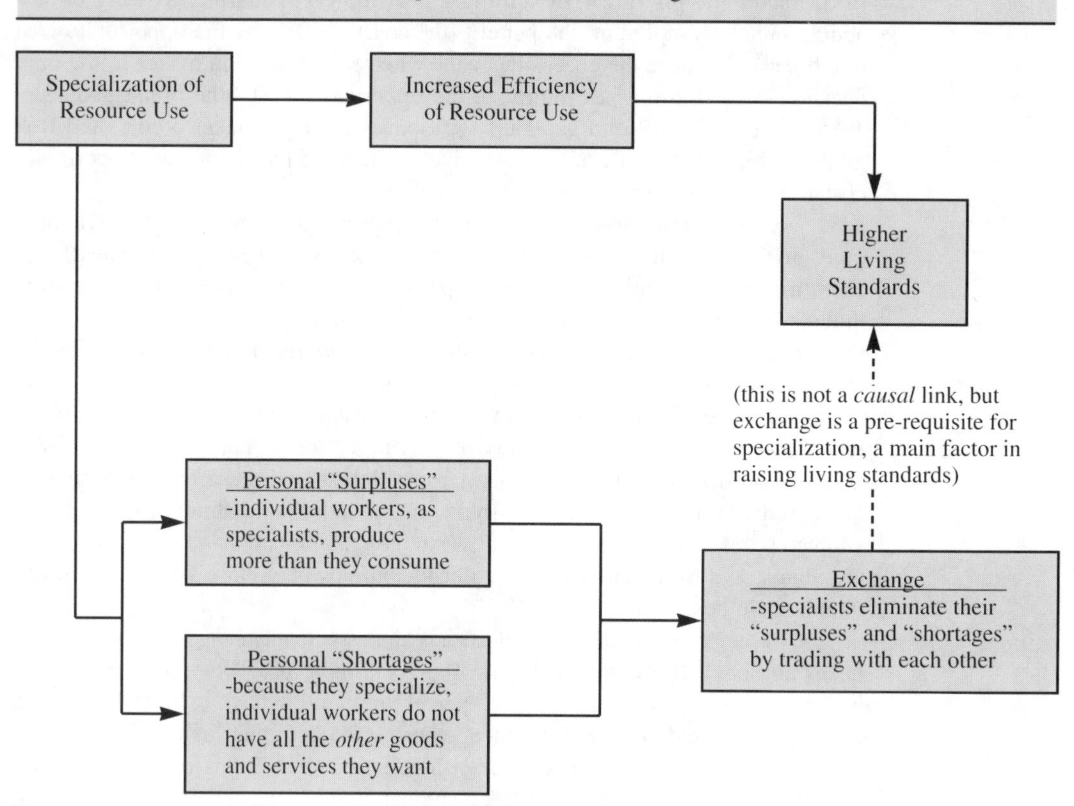

surplus and shortage differs from the normal use in economics, encountered in Chapter 5.) Figure 2-1 illustrates all these relationships about specialization.

Although specialization clearly has benefits, it has some negative side effects or problems: 1) boredom; 2) worker alienation; 3) changes in family structure; and 4) poverty.

■ The first problem of specialization is boredom, and this can bring on a *loss* in productivity. Many firms try to minimize this problem with frequent switches in jobs. Of course, this is practical only with jobs that are fairly easy to master.

■ The second problem is worker "alienation," which occurs when workers cannot always see the product they helped make. Years ago a worker could say, "I made this broom," or "I made that barrel." When workers can't say that, work itself becomes less fulfilling, and lower productivity may result. This is especially true in assembly line work. To prevent this problem, some firms assemble products with a team or "module" approach, where a group of workers builds one section of a product. That way, the whole team gains credit (and pride) for doing a good job. For example, a small group could assemble a hydraulic pump for a farm tractor. In addition, jobs can be frequently switched among the members of the group.

■ The next problem is not always recognized and is debatable. It involves the change in family structure when the agrarian (farm-based) subsistence economy gave way to the industrialized economy. Until the late 1800s, most families produced most of their needs by themselves. Thus, the home, the family, and work was a "way of life." Today most people commute to their jobs, and co-workers usually don't know each other's families. Consequently, the important bonds linking family members through work have been eroded by economic changes.

■ The last problem of specialization is poverty. In order to trade with other specialists, you need something of value, and most people trade some labor skill. But some people have few of the skills needed in a modern economy. Studies show one worker in five cannot read at an eighth-grade level. Yet the majority of written directions on most jobs require a high-school reading level. In centuries past, low-skilled and relatively unproductive people could find a place in a family-oriented, agrarian economy. Maybe they didn't always "pull their own weight," but at least they were cared for. Not today. In a capitalist society, those without skills to trade don't work. And those who don't work, don't eat.

Innovation

The last way to increase efficiency is through **innovation**, which is a change in the way resources are used. In a broad sense, innovation includes the elimination of waste in production processes, along with increased specialization, which was just covered. But in this section you will learn that innovation generally occurs when there is a change in the answers to What to Produce? and How to Produce? so that there is an increase in the efficiency of resource use. And if How to Produce? is answered differently, it means the production process itself has been changed.

★8 Most innovations fit into one of four classes: 1) mechanization of the production process; 2) reorganization of the production process; 3) alteration in energy sources; and 4) product innovations involving new consumer goods and services. The first three innovations increase the efficiency of production itself and reduce production costs. The last innovation leads to more consumer satisfaction and welfare from the same resources when a new and better product is made.

■ The first class of innovations involves mechanization. Essentially, mechanization means replacing some labor resource with some capital resource or, more plainly, replacing people with machines. Thus, What to Produce? is answered differently when a new machine is made. In turn, this leads to How to Produce? being answered differently. (Incidentally, people often mistakenly assume that mechanization and automation are the same. Automation involves the automatic control of one machine by another machine. An example is a computer that directs a milling machine to turn a piece of sheet metal into a finished part for a dishwasher.)

■ The second class of innovations involves a change in the organization of the production process or a fundamental change in production methods without any significant increase in mechanization. One example is tilting a product so that workers don't have to bend over to assemble it. The Nissan plant in Japan and the John Deere garden tractor plant in the United States use such techniques. Often such innovations are small and seemingly trivial. Yet, because there are so many of them, they add up to major productivity improvements in the long run. The Japanese even have a word for these innovations—*kaizen* (continuous improvement).

■ The third class of innovations involves changing the energy sources needed to accomplish work. Early humans used raw muscle power to produce everything, but eventually animals provided much of the power (at least for the heavier tasks, such as plowing land). Natural resources eventually replaced animal and human power. Early dependence upon water and wind power switched to fossil fuel (coal, gas, and oil) power in the 1800s. Finally, nuclear and solar energy emerged in the 1900s and may become the dominant energy sources in the 21st century.

■ The last class of innovations involves new products for consumers that are enjoyed more than older ones and require similar amounts of resources. Compact discs that replaced records, video cameras with sound that replaced silent film cameras, light beer that supplanted regular beer, and airplanes that replaced trains, buses, and ships are all examples.

New products of the 1990s also may increase our well-being. There's a new light bulb that uses a tiny radio transmitter to excite (stimulate) mercury gas. It wastes very little electricity in the form of heat, unlike incandescent bulbs. A new product that can be a lifesaver is the cardiopump that is used to restart the hearts of cardiac-arrest victims. It originated with the belief of a mother and son who thought a toilet plunger would work to revive the near-dead. The International Maize and Wheat Improvement Center in Mexico has released a strain of wheat that is resistant to the leaf rust blight caused by a fungus in humid areas. As a result, many areas of the world will be able to grow wheat for the first time. Finally, 10-year old Clint Lenz could shake up the world with his invention, a glow-in-the-dark toilet seat for nighttime guidance. Whatever it takes to raise our welfare...

★9

In a capitalist economy, most innovations occur in existing businesses or come from people who begin businesses to take advantage of their ideas. The incentive, of course, is profit. Also, if the competition between firms is strong enough, a firm must innovate just to stay in business. Such competition puts a business firm in a very precarious position. No one has explained this situation better than Joseph Schumpeter in his 1912 book, *The Theory of Economic Development.* According to Schumpeter's concept of "creative destruction," an innovator "creates" wealth by increasing the efficiency of resource use, which leads to more output (wealth). But firms that do not follow the lead of innovators or whose products become obsolete suffer "destruction" (are forced out of business).

Everything that can be invented has been invented.
– Charles H. Duell, Director of U.S. Patent Office, 1899

Cutting wheat with sickles in present-day Peru, as Americans did 150 years ago

Collection of sickles used for grain harvest, capable of cutting 3/4th acre per day

Reaper harvest of grain in the 1880s, the invention of Cyrus McCormick in 1834

Modern combine (which combines cutting and threshing) (Courtesy of J.I. Case Co.)

Threshing of grain (separating seeds from stalks) by walking cattle on stalks in present-day Peru

Figure 2-2 shows the sequence of events that follows an innovation in the manufacture of a good, called Good A. (This illustrates an innovation in the *production process* of a good and is distinct from a *product* innovation, such as the introduction of electric cars.) It initially takes X amount of resources to make one unit of Good A. The upper set of boxes represents the situation before the innovation, and the lower set represents the situation after the innovation. The blue box on the right represents the *physical* amount of resources needed to make just one unit of Good A. For example, if Good A is a house, the box would represent all the laborers, the wood, the tools, and whatever else it takes to build a house. The middle blue box represents the *dollar* amount of those resources, or the average cost of producing Good A (the house). The blue box on the left represents the price of Good A (the house), for price equals average cost plus the profit margin (or profit per unit).

Innovations of the first three types covered reduce the resources needed to make something. To see this, look at the lower set of blue boxes in Figure 2-2. The area on the right box labelled "Saved Resources" represents the resources saved in making one unit of Good A. In the house example, it might represent laid-off workers, leftover wood, and other resources after the innovation—for example, a switch to a pre-cut home (where much of the lumber is cut in a factory). Those resources are now "freed up" or available to produce something the economy previously never had the resources to make. Thus, the living standard increases when the resources are used elsewhere. (With the last category of innovations, product innovations, more satisfaction is obtained from the same resources. Thus, the living standard increases as well, but from a different source.)

Because average cost reflects the resources used in production, average cost drops with innovation, as indicated by the area labelled "Reduction in Average Cost of Good A" in the middle box. Finally, when there is competition from other firms, this innovative firm will reduce the price of Good A. Even without much competition, a firm might drop prices if it can sell many more products at a lower price. Finally, when the price of Good A falls, the effect on consumers is the same as if their incomes increased. They can buy more goods and services with the same amount of income—one unit of Good B in this case. Although their *money* income does not change, their **real income** (what their money income can buy) increases. Taking the house example, what other things would people buy if house prices fell? Anything, but one thing could be a product requiring wood, carpenters, and so on, such as a cabinet for the stereo equipment that earlier generations could never afford. Thus, the laid-off ("freed up") resources find new uses. Many people who actually experience such firing and hiring never make the connection between the two events and fail to see how our economy changes over time.

Some examples of the millions of innovations in the last few centuries will help you see their effects. Eli Whitney's cotton gin of 1793, which picked the seeds out of the cotton boll (the seed pod of the plant, which is made up mainly of fibrous white material), increased the output of laborers from three pounds of cotton per day to 17 pounds per day. It led to a sharp reduction in the price of cotton, transforming it from a luxury cloth to a cheap fabric. The Erie Canal, completed in 1825, allowed two mules to move 1,000 bushels of grain, instead of the six

Figure 2-2 The Effects of Innovation on Production Costs, Prices, and Real Income

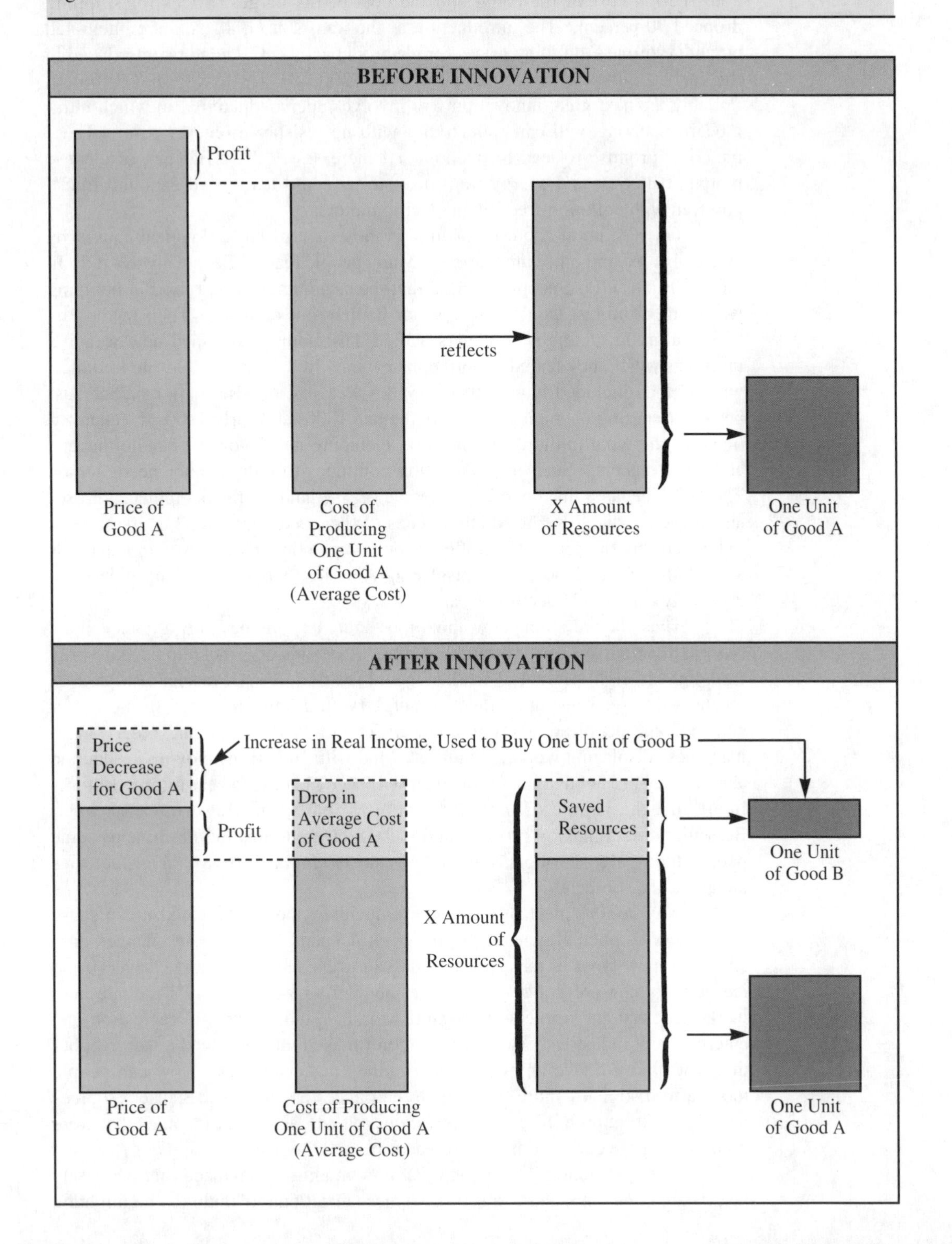

bushels they could carry on their backs. Consequently, even after covering the construction cost of the canal and the cost of the barges, prices for shipping dropped 90 percent. The introduction of the transistor (1948) and the integrated circuit (1969) led to falling prices for electronic goods. Calculators, introduced in the early 1970s and which sold for over $200, sell for less than $10 today. Possibly the next great innovation will involve superconductivity, in which ultra-modern materials will carry electricity with no resistance (energy loss). These materials promise to lead to phenomenal increases in the efficiency of electric motors, batteries, and energy transmission. It could lead to all cars and trucks powered with pollution-free, silent electric motors.

One last point about innovation is the extent of unemployment caused by mechanization and other innovations. Many people fear it. People always did. In the 1600s and 1700s, people worried that the steam engine, first used in pumping water out of mines, would throw water haulers out of work. Then in the late 1700s, a group of English weavers, called the Luddites, smashed new weaving machines which they feared would replace them. In the early 1800s, the Luddites, who by then included many others besides weavers, opposed *any* machine suspected of causing unemployment. By the late 1800s and early 1900s, mechanization was throwing millions out of work, including glass blowers, candle makers, and cigar makers. Such mechanization continues to reduce labor needs today. The 1920s began a mass exodus of people off the land as tractors replaced horses and also dramatically reduced labor needs. Whereas it required 32 hours of labor to tend an acre of corn in 1850, it takes only three hours today. And in the 1980s and 1990s, foreign laborers are displacing American laborers in many industries, especially auto, steel, electronics, and textiles.

Thus, the only thing new about jobs being lost are the *kinds* of jobs and the *reasons* for their losses. Throughout most of our history, including today, only from three to eight percent of workers could not find jobs. If mechanization does create widespread unemployment, it surely would have appeared by now. Of course, some people will say today is different. With robots and other "smart machines" displacing workers wholesale, and with U.S. firms moving production abroad, they predict that unemployment will skyrocket in the near future. But it is likely that the people of the 1800s were as fearful of McCormick's reaper, Bessemer's steel-making process, and Duke's cigarette-making machine as some people today are of robots, computers, and *maquiladoras* (Mexican factories along the U.S. border).

Why *doesn't* mechanization cause unemployment? Actually, it can cause some *types* of unemployment, but the *overall* unemployment rate changes only slightly as new types of jobs appear. Glass blowers, teamsters (horse drivers), and ice deliverymen are gone. New large labor groups of the 1900s include auto workers, restaurant workers, electronics workers, and workers in recreation and entertainment industries. Most of them don't make things we need to survive, but things we like to have anyway. That is, they make luxuries. How can people today afford so many more things than their ancestors could? Because resources were saved through millions of innovations, which raised real incomes that were used to purchase compact discs, airplane trips, and the like.

Now, be cautious. Although *you* now might be convinced that wholesale layoffs are *good*—not bad—don't praise mechanization too loudly. You might be able to convince some people that you are right. But if you make the attempt, some unemployed laborer might put a fist in your face. There are still Luddites today.

Also, bear in mind that it's painful to be forced to make career changes. Some people never make the transition to new positions. Stress and its accompanying problems often stem from "progress." No one said life would be easy. But, in a capitalist world, you are well-advised to keep your eyes open to innovations that could affect your job.

THE REWARDS OF INCREASES IN ECONOMIC WELFARE

Thus far you learned that either making more resources available or increasing the efficiency of their use allows the living standard to increase. This section takes a closer look at how increases in economic welfare change our lifestyles over long periods.

Ways to Enjoy Increases in Economic Welfare

★10

In Figure 2-2 you saw how innovation in a production process increases real income (in the form of more goods and services available from a given amount of resources). Increases in real income can also result from other ways of increasing the efficiency of resource use. These include innovations of new products, elimination of waste in production processes, and increased specialization of resource use. Finally, real income can increase if more resources are available for a given population.

Another way to gain more economic welfare (besides having more goods and services) is to spend more time at leisure and less at work. Suppose we doubled our capacity to produce goods and services. If the population remained constant, the living standard would double. Alternatively, with our new way to gain economic welfare, we could choose to cut by half the number of hours we all work. Of course, then the living standard would *not* increase because total output would remain constant (although productivity doubled, only half as many labor resources would be used). But people would still have more economic welfare because they would have the same living standard with half the effort.

Many of the examples given earlier on how labor waste can be reduced (less office chatter, for example) highlight an important difference between labor productivity and allocative efficiency. A machine receives no pleasure from idle chatter or calling in sick to take a holiday, but people do. Leisure itself is an economic good because time and our personal energies are scarce resources. Indeed, many economists view the dramatic reductions in working time achieved during the last century as an indicator of increased economic welfare. Therefore, it is not always true that higher labor productivity equals greater allocative efficiency. There even are cases where *lower* labor productivity, if it gives workers and managers more leisure, could *increase* allocative efficiency and economic welfare.

Figure 2-3 A Summary of How Economic Welfare Is Raised

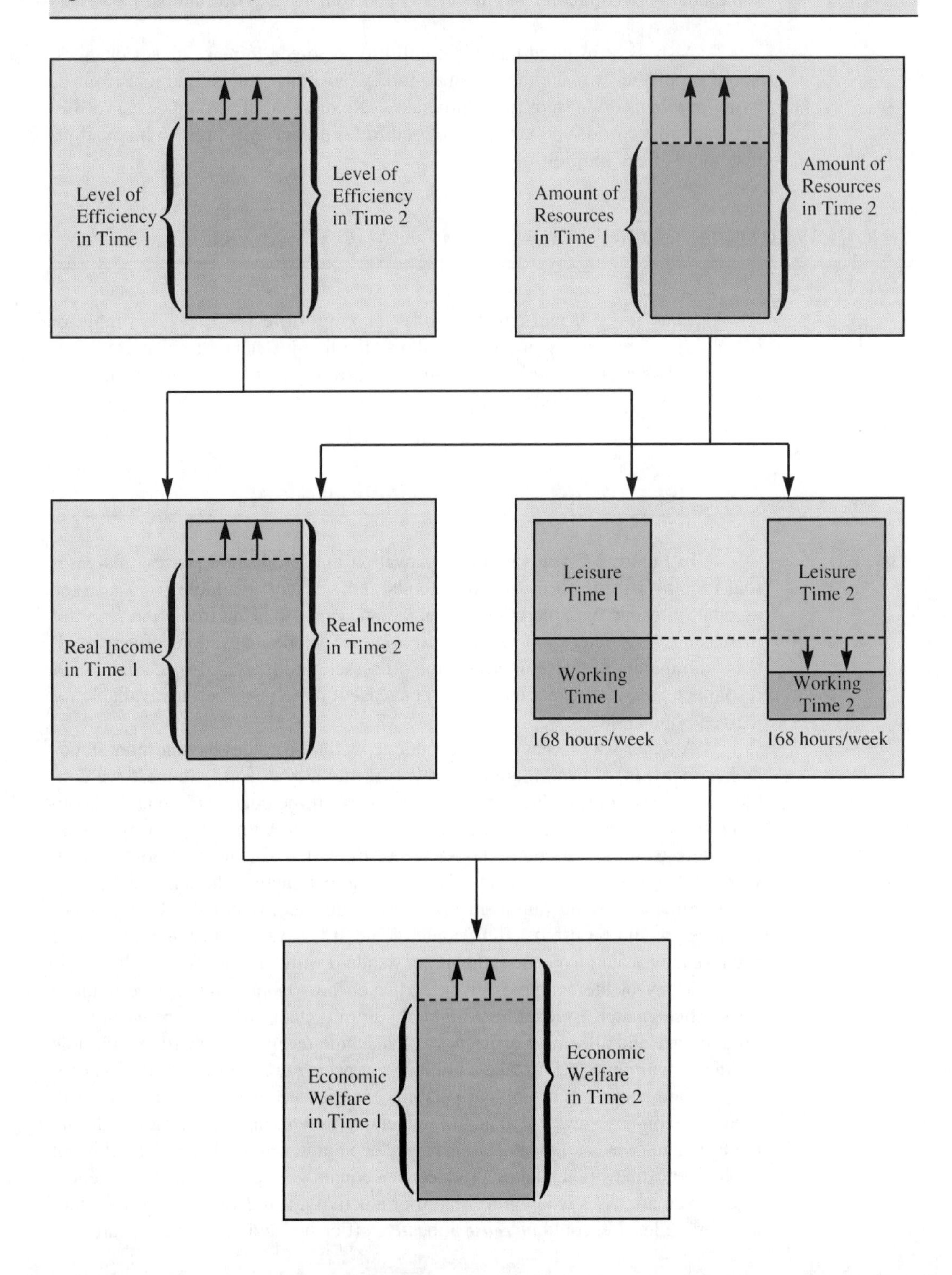

Figure 2-3 summarizes these two options of enjoying increased economic welfare as well as the two ways to raise economic welfare (higher efficiency and more resources available). The chart shows "before" (Time 1) and "after" (Time 2) situations for each variable involved. In the top row, notice that either the efficiency of resource use or resource availability can increase. Also notice that either of these increases can lead to: 1) an increase in real income; or 2) a reduction in working time (and an increase in leisure time) in each 168-hour week. The middle set of boxes shows this. The bottom box shows that economic welfare increases along with either of the two increases in the middle row.

In reality, Americans have taken their welfare increases over the centuries in both ways. Today we have vastly more goods and services than our ancestors had. Also, whereas a century ago people worked 60-80 hours per week, we now work about half as long (the average work week for men was 42.0 hours in 1991). In addition, we are retiring earlier. In 1950, 87 percent of men between 55 and 64 worked, whereas only 67 percent did in 1991. (Statistics for women are not as useful because of the recent dramatic shifts of women into the labor force.)

Ways to Enjoy Increases in Real Income

Besides having more goods and services, there is an alternative way to enjoy an increase in real income. With an increased capacity to produce, the same *quantity* of output could be produced, but it could be of a higher *quality*. Depending upon the product, it could have more: strength (car bodies), durability and longevity (refrigerators), efficiency of use (gasoline in car engines), taste and nutrition (foods), fidelity (stereo systems), or appearance (furniture). Quality of services also could be improved, such as better movies, faster restaurant service, and more reliable auto repairs.

Modern conveniences, such as paved roads and countless other items, were rare early in the 20th century. Car ownership was not common until around 1920.

In our history, there have been increases in both the quantity and the quality of goods and services. Although many people would argue that product quality has declined over time, overall it hasn't. Certain products are indeed of poorer quality today, but they are still the exception.

Figure 2-4 shows how increases in either the quantity of goods or services or in their quality can lead to increases in real income.

Figure 2-4 Alternative Ways of Exercising Increases in Real Income

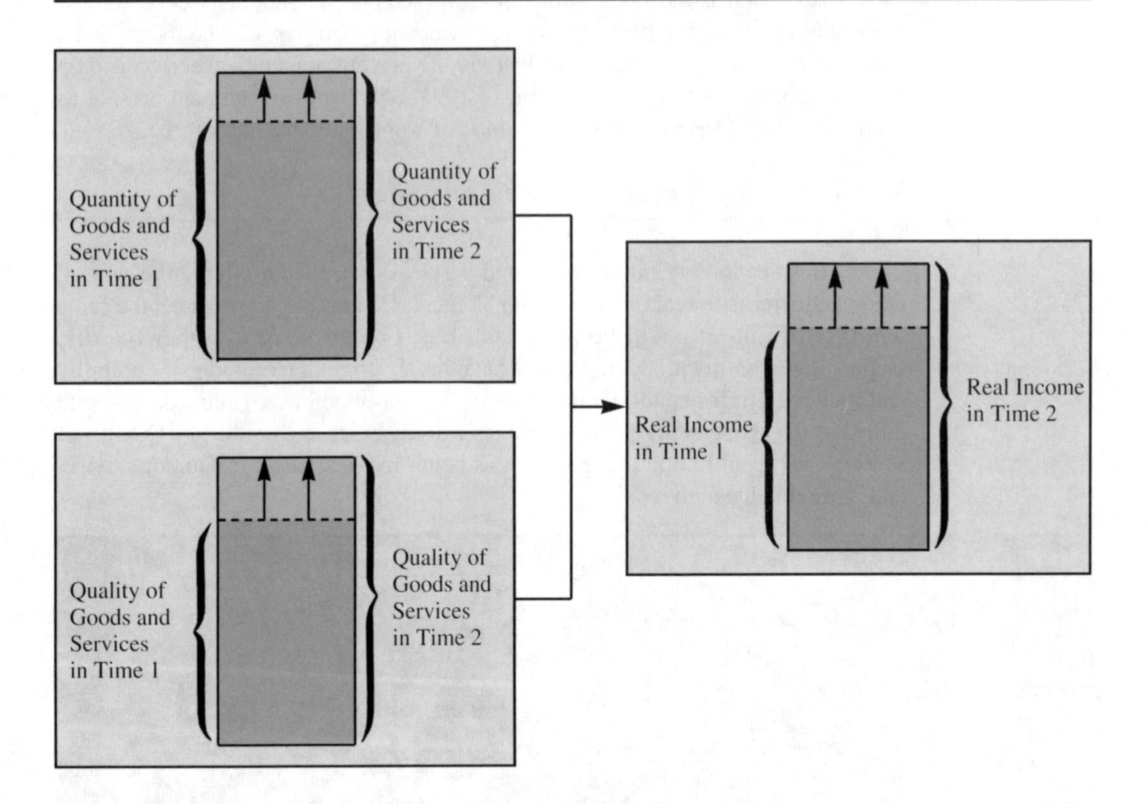

The Effect on Leisure Time of Purchasing More Services

Finally, how leisure time is spent explains changes in our lifestyles. "Leisure time" defies definition, but let's assume it is all time not spent on a paying job. Suppose all your time in a period is broken into three categories: 1) time spent on a job outside the home; 2) time spent in necessary activities that may or may not provide satisfaction; and 3) time spent on leisure activities that give you satisfaction.

The left box or column in Figure 2-5 shows an initial (Period 1) distribution of someone's time in, say, a week or year. A goal of that person would be to increase the share of time spent at pleasurable leisure. That increase could come from a decrease in the time spent on necessary activities. These activities would include cleaning the house, washing or repairing the car, mowing or fertilizing the lawn, washing and ironing clothes, painting the house, washing one's hair, and preparing meals.

Figure 2-5 The Effect on Leisure-Time Activities from Purchasing Certain Services

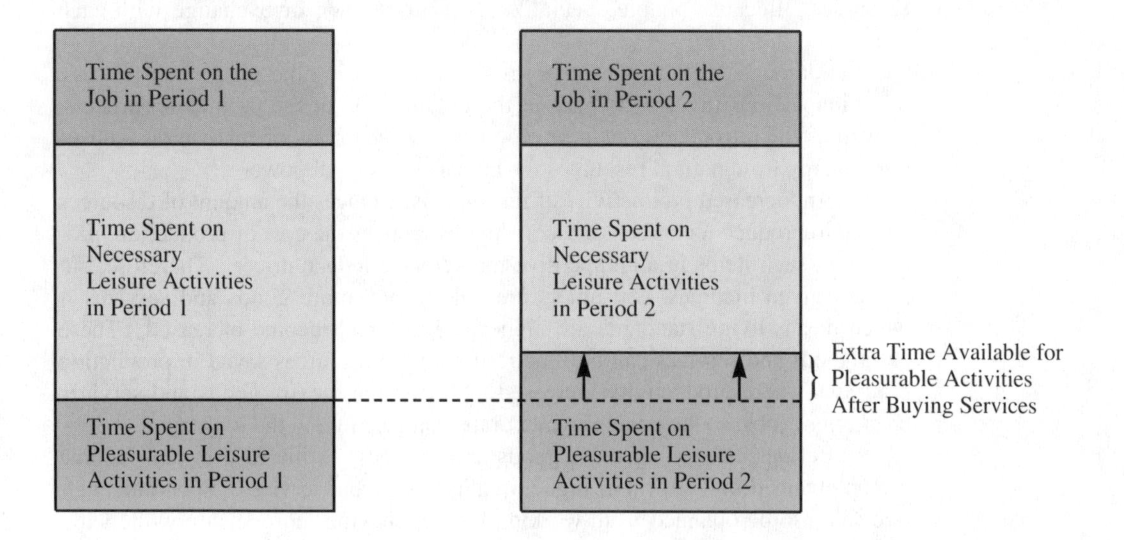

One way our lives differ from our ancestors is that today many of these tasks are done for us by service firms. These firms clean our homes, wash or repair our cars, maintain our lawns, do our laundry, care for our hair, prepare our meals (either for take-out or in restaurants), and paint our houses. This provides us with more "quality time" to engage in pleasurable leisure activities—playing games, traveling, reading, biking, watching TV or films, and attending cultural events.

Why didn't our ancestors buy such services (or buy them in the amounts that we do)? It's not that such services weren't available (there always were a *few* restaurants, beauty shops, house painters, etc.). It was because they couldn't afford to buy them. Remember, they used resources much less efficiently than we do. Consequently, their real incomes were too low to afford time-saving services.

For the same reason, will the 2090s be as different from the 1990s as the 1990s are from the 1890s? Why not? We still have not found all the best production processes, and we have not eliminated all the waste in using our resources.

Chapter 2 SUMMARY

Economic well-being, or economic welfare, has been increased primarily by increasing the amount of goods and services produced, known as economic growth. Economic welfare is measured by the standard of living.

Economic growth results from: 1) having more resources available with which to produce; and 2) increasing the efficiency of the existing resources, also known as increasing productivity. Productivity is raised by: 1) eliminating waste in the current production processes; 2) increasing the specialization of resource use; and 3) innovation.

A resource's use should be specialized in an area where it has a comparative advantage, meaning this resource will have the lowest opportunity cost of all resources. Because people specialize, they must trade or exchange with each other.

Although many innovations involve mechanizing the production process, other innovations involve changes in the organization of the production process, as well as the introduction of new products. A final class of innovations substitutes energy from natural resources for human and animal power.

An increased productivity of resource use reduces the amount of resources needed to produce a good or service. As this reduces the cost of production, producers of such items in a competitive marketplace reduce prices. Therefore, out of their given incomes, consumers are able to buy more goods and services—which means living standards are higher and that real income increased. These extra goods and services can be produced with the resources saved in production processes where productivity increased. Making these extra goods and services creates new jobs, so the unemployment rate changes little in the long run.

Besides consuming more goods and services, an increase in real income can be obtained in the form of higher quality goods and services. Economic welfare can also be obtained from working less and having more leisure while leaving the amount of goods and services unchanged. Over the years, people have purchased services that allow them to increase the amount of pleasurable leisure time they have.

Chapter 2 RESPONSES TO THE LEARNING OBJECTIVES

1. Economic welfare pertains to the well-being that people derive from consuming their materialistic goals.

2. The living standard is only a monetary reflection of economic welfare, so it might not perfectly represent well-being. It is not possible to objectively measure something perfectly that is as abstract as the concept of well-being. Also, the living standard does not consider income distribution, which could be very uneven. Finally, it does not consider non-materialistic goals, which might be undermined by a high living standard.

3. Living standards can be raised by controlling population growth and by raising the output of goods and services. In turn, output is raised by increasing either the amount of resources or the efficiency (productivity) of resources.
4. Labor productivity in some production process is found by dividing the total output of some enterprise in some period by the total number of hours worked by all employees combined in that period.
5. Specialization increases the efficiency of resource use because of:
   a) specialists spending a smaller share of their time learning how to do their jobs
   b) people and other resources finding the production processes to which they are best suited
   c) time saved by not moving from task to task in a production process
6. A resource has a comparative advantage in producing something if it has the lowest opportunity cost of all the resources in that class.
7. Exchange is the consequence of specialization, for specialists must trade their respective surpluses in order to obtain their wants and needs that they cannot or do not wish to provide for themselves.
8. Innovation raises the efficiency of resource use, which leads to a reduction in production costs. In turn, firms that face competition lower their prices, leading to higher living standards because people can buy more goods and services with their incomes.
9. Firms are induced to innovate by:
   a) profit, for their cost savings allow their profits to grow
   b) competition, for if one firm in an industry innovates and reduces its price, all competing firms must do so or lose business to the innovator
10. Increases in economic welfare can be enjoyed as:
    a) a larger quantity of goods and services
    b) a higher quality of goods and services
    c) less work and more leisure

Chapter 2 LEARNING ACTIVITIES AND DISCUSSION QUESTIONS

1. Try to estimate the economic welfare as well as the happiness of some people you know. Do you find any connection between their welfare and happiness?
2. If living standards were to be raised by having certain segments of the population "disappear," which segments should go?
3. If you have a job, calculate your efficiency as well as the efficiency of those in the same job.
4. Find a task or a job in which you believe you have a comparative advantage. What makes you believe you have that advantage?
5. Make a list of ten jobs that make convenient-but-not-necessary items (i.e., luxuries) that were not made in 1900. Which of the jobs do you think will still exist in the year 2050?

APPENDIX PRODUCTION POSSIBILITIES CURVES AND ECONOMIC GROWTH

The appendix to Chapter 1 presented a production possibilities curve for corn and potatoes. The concept is generalized in Figure A2-1, where the two axes measure any two goods, denoted by X and Y. The curve labelled PPC_1 gives all the possible combinations of Good X and Good Y that some set of resources can produce. As you learned in Chapter 2, many factors can increase the efficiency of resource use, resulting in an increase in output from a given amount of resources. This is indicated by a shift in the production possibilities curve to the curve labelled PPC_2. Consider point A_1 on PPC_1, which indicates that a given set of resources can initially produce X_1 amount of Good X and Y_1 amount of Good Y. But suppose an innovation makes possible more output of both Good X and Good Y from the same amount of resources. Point A_2 shows that situation, for X_2 exceeds X_1 and Y_2 exceeds Y_1. Figure A2-1 shows the effect of economic growth on just two goods. But, in general, economic growth has similar effects on virtually all production possibilities curves between any set of goods or services.

Figure A2-2 shows a special production possibilities curve. It is not one between two goods, but one between all consumer goods combined and all capital goods combined. Point D describes an economy that produces only consumer goods—no machines, factories, or the like. Point C shows an economy that makes only capital goods—no food, clothes, cars, and so on. Of course, neither of these extreme situations could go on for long, so economies always operate between these points, such as points A or B. An economy at point A leans more toward producing capital goods than does one at point B, as Y_A exceeds Y_B. Conversely, an economy at point B leans more toward producing consumer goods, as X_B exceeds X_A.

Generally, an economy at point A will grow faster than one at point B. That's because it will have more capital goods for producing goods and services in the future. Essentially, members of such a society sacrifice some consumer goods today so that they will have more of them tomorrow. A good analogy can be made with a person who spends much time and money today on education in order to have a great future. Good times today are sacrificed to get better times tomorrow.

Figure A2-3 shows the effects over time on production possibilities curves from being at points A and B in Figure A2-2. PPC_1 is the same curve as in Figure A2-1. Over time this economy experiences economic growth, but more if it operates at point A as compared with point B. Therefore, there are two curves representing the future, $PPC_{2\text{-}A}$ and $PPC_{2\text{-}B}$. Which one is better? Although the economy at point A has more economic welfare in the future, it is not necessarily better off *overall* (that is, over the entire time *between* Period 1 and Period 2). After all, its citizens had to live in the past, just as they will have to do in the future. Only they can determine when they should have their "good times." Incidentally, this issue—how fast an economy should grow by deciding on present or future consumption—is often considered a fourth Basic Economic Question in addition to What, How, and For Whom to Produce?

Figure A2-1 Economic Growth and Production Possibilities Curves

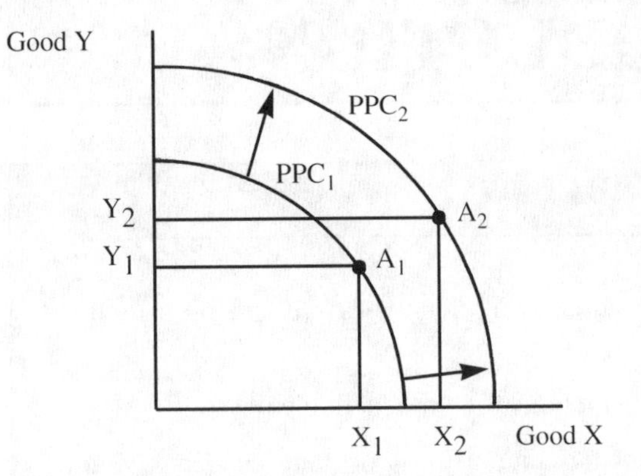

Figure A2-2 Production Possibilities of Capital and Consumer Goods

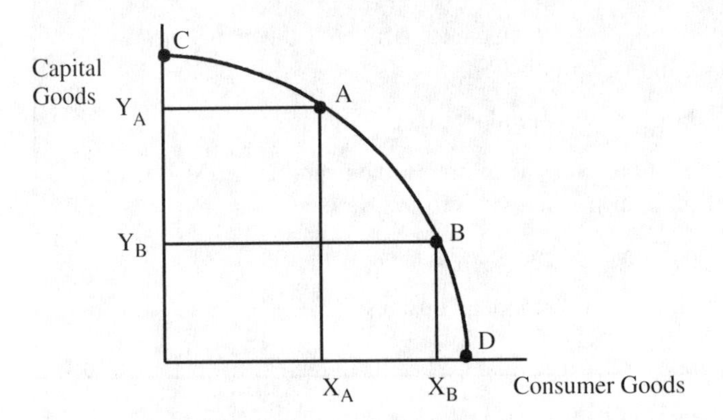

Figure A2-3 Differential Growth Rates

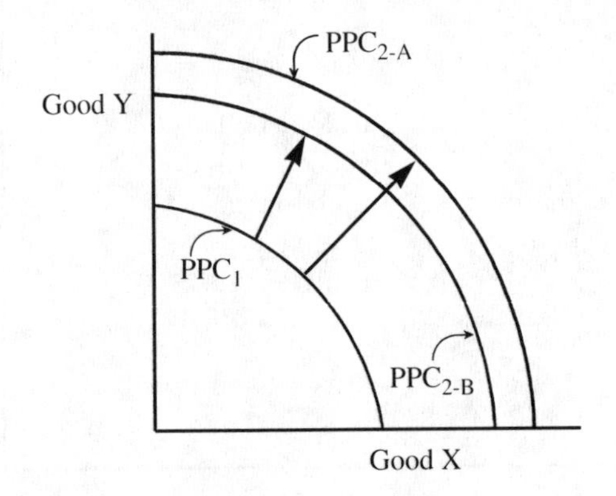

CHAPTER 3

THE ECONOMICS OF MASS PRODUCTION

★★★★★ LEARNING OBJECTIVES ★★★★★

1. Explain the three ways of increasing the output of a good or service in a production process.
2. Determine the point of diminishing marginal returns for a production process.
3. Determine whether a production process has increasing, constant, or decreasing returns to scale.
4. Explain the relationship between returns to scale and production costs.
5. List the five primary characteristics of a mass-production economy.
6. Explain the roles that standardization, interchangeable parts, and the transportation and communication systems have in mass production.
7. List the five consequences of a shift to a mass-production economy.
8. Explain the influence mechanization has on relative prices, the average firm size in an industry, the number of firms in an industry, and the shift to a service economy.
9. Explain how innovations that lead to mass production create new jobs.
10. Compare and contrast the four major eras of American business.

TERMS

marginal product
law of diminishing marginal returns
increasing returns to scale
constant returns to scale
decreasing returns to scale
standardization
interchangeable parts
continuous production process
mass markets
labor-intensive
capital-intensive
absolute price
relative price

Chapter 1 introduced the economic problem, caused by an unlimited desire for goods and services and a scarcity of resources. Chapter 2 showed how increasing the amount and the efficiency of resource use moderates that problem. This chapter examines production processes more fully to show how firms increase the efficiency of resource use by growing in size. In particular, this chapter concentrates on a particular type of production process—mass production. It ends with a brief view of the production processes in American business from colonial days to the present.

INCREASING THE OUTPUT OF A PRODUCTION PROCESS

Few of today's large firms started as giants. New firms usually operate on a small scale. After their startup, many firms grow in various ways until they achieve large-scale status, where they "mass produce." This section describes three ways a firm can increase its size of operations and the effect each has upon production efficiency. They are: 1) increasing a single resource; 2) increasing all resources at the same rate; and 3) increasing several resources at different rates.

★1

Increasing a Single Resource

Every good or service needs at least several different resources for production, including various types of laborers, capital equipment, and raw materials. A firm can boost its output by increasing just one of its resources (or inputs). The extra output from adding just one unit of a resource to a production process is the **marginal product**.

Consider a farmer's corn field as an example of increasing a single resource. Suppose the farmer wants to find what happens to corn yield (production) as extra tons of fertilizer are added to each acre of a field. Like many of the resources used to grow corn, including seeds and labor, fertilizer is a "variable resource." When variable resources change in quantity, the output also will change. Other resources are considered to be fixed or given in quantity, at least in the short run. For our corn farmer, examples would include the amount of land and machines that are available.

Examples of increasing a single resource in other production processes include: a tavern owner hiring extra bartenders, an electric power plant burning more coal, and a store hiring additional salesclerks.

For the corn example, Table 3-1 shows the input and output data up to the seventh ton of fertilizer. The marginal product is the difference in yield between successive tons of fertilizer used. The data show a common pattern in the production processes of most goods and services when firms increase a single resource. The marginal product increases initially, but it eventually declines. That is, the marginal product diminishes beyond a certain point—in this case with the third ton of fertilizer. Because this occurs so commonly, economists say there is a **law of diminishing marginal returns** that seems to hold in production processes. Notice further that marginal product becomes negative after the sixth ton of fertilizer.

★2

Table 3-1 Marginal Products of Fertilizer Used in Corn Production

In this example of adding a single resource to a production process, a one-acre plot of land is used to grow corn. With no fertilizer applied to the land, the yield (or total product) is 100 bushels. The following *increases* in yield (or marginal product) will result from applying the stated tons of fertilizer. The point of diminishing returns occurs with the 3rd ton.

	Tons of Fertilizer Used							
	0	1	2	3	4	5	6	7
Yield (Total Product)	100	120	150	175	195	210	210	190
Marginal Product	0	20	30	25	20	15	0	-20

In the other examples given above, diminishing marginal product exhibits itself as: additional bartenders selling fewer drinks than bartenders hired earlier, extra tons of coal producing fewer kilowatts of power than the first few tons, and the last-hired salesclerks selling less than those hired first. Observing such production data, you might think something is wrong with the *extra* or the last resources used. Perhaps the fertilizer or coal are of poor quality. Maybe the last bartenders and salesclerks are lazy or poorly trained. But marginal product falls even if all units of resources in each of these cases are identical. It falls primarily because the other resources in the production processes remain unchanged in quantity. This creates an imbalance of resources, in which the resources in constant supply become increasingly scarce compared with the resource being increased.

To elaborate, in corn production the extra fertilizer increases the nutrients available to the corn plants—but does nothing about the water needed. Because the same amount of ground water must support more vegetative matter, corn plants become increasingly "thirsty" as fertilizer is added. Consequently, water becomes a critically limiting factor, which holds down the gains expected from more fertilizer. Eventually, additional fertilizer *reduces* output because fertilizer is a salt that can "burn" plants if it is too abundant.

Similarly, in a tavern, the floor space and the beer taps and liquor bottles become increasingly scarce resources as more bartenders use them. While a single bartender can always find an available beer tap, with 10 bartenders there is likely to be a line at the tap. In the power plant example, the extra coal might produce less additional power because of the limited size of the steam lines. In the store example, extra clerks might sell less than those first hired because of the "bottleneck" at the cash register.

Why does the marginal product first *increase* before it eventually decreases? The initial increase in the marginal product generally stems from the gains in efficiency due to specialization. In the case of labor resources, workers divide the tasks of the production process. The marginal product figures suggest that each additional worker is more productive than those already working, until the point of diminishing returns is reached. That is misleading because *everyone* becomes more productive when specialization increases. But everyone's *increased* output is reflected in the output of the last worker hired. These gains from specialization end when there are no more ways to specialize. Then resources become so imbalanced that the marginal product falls.

The manager of a store like this must decide how many variable resources, such as laborers, to have in order to maximize profits. Such decisions require a thorough understanding of the principle of diminishing marginal utility.

The owner of this rice paddy in Korea has at last two decisions regarding variable resources: how many plants to set out in the paddy and how many workers to hire for planting.

Figure 3-1 gives a clearer view of the corn production example. Each box corresponds to the amount of extra corn from each additional ton of fertilizer. Because the second ton gives the highest marginal product, the third ton of fertilizer added is the so-called point of diminishing returns. Such data shown here are the basis for calculation of production costs, encountered in Chapter 6.

Figure 3-2 shows the yield per acre, a reflection of *all* the resources used, including *all* the fertilizer. Using no fertilizer, the farmer produces 100 bushels. The diagrams show the sources of extra corn yield from extra tons of fertilizer—as well as the total yield. Notice that total yield falls beyond the sixth ton of fertilizer. Do not confuse this point of declining *total* returns with the point of diminishing *marginal* returns, which occurs at the third ton of fertilizer.

In actual businesses, such data on the marginal product often are extremely difficult to attain. Also, in many cases, such as retail stores, finding "identical" workers is impossible.

Increasing All Resources Equally

The second way a firm can increase its output is to increase all resources at an equal rate. For instance, the corn farmer could increase all resources by 30 percent—the land area, the amount of seed planted, tillage implements, and cultivation labor. Likewise, the tavern owner could hire 40 percent more bartenders, lengthen the bar by 40 percent, and increase the seating area by 40 percent. Economists call such expansion an "increase in scale," as all resources expand proportionately. (Firms rarely if ever expand in this manner. But if we assume that they do in a simplified model, it will be easier to understand the effects of expansion on production costs. We become more realistic by relaxing this assumption in the next section.)

★3 Production processes fit into three categories, depending upon how much production increases in relation to proportionate increases in resources. If production increases at a faster rate than resources, the production process experiences **increasing returns to scale**, also called economies of scale. If production and resources expand at the same rate, there are **constant returns to scale**. **Decreasing returns to scale**, also called diseconomies of scale, occur when production climbs more slowly than resources.

This complex of factories of General Electric Medical Systems allows for efficient manufacture of sophistocated medical equipment, such as CAT scanners.
(Courtesy of GE Medical Systems)

Figure 3-1 Marginal Products of Fertilizer Used in Corn Production

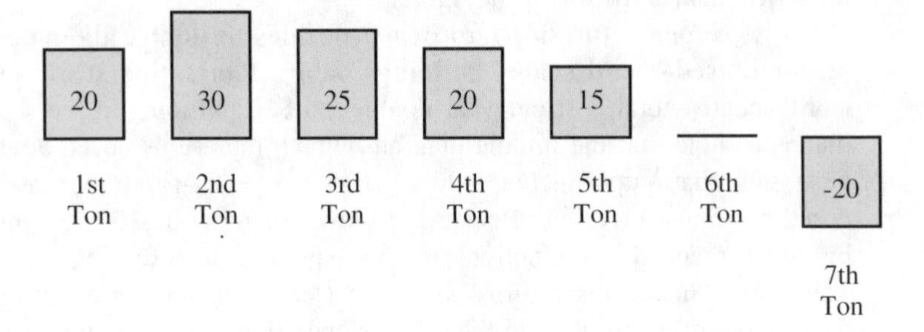

Figure 3-2 Yield (Total Product) of Corn at Different Fertilizer Levels Used

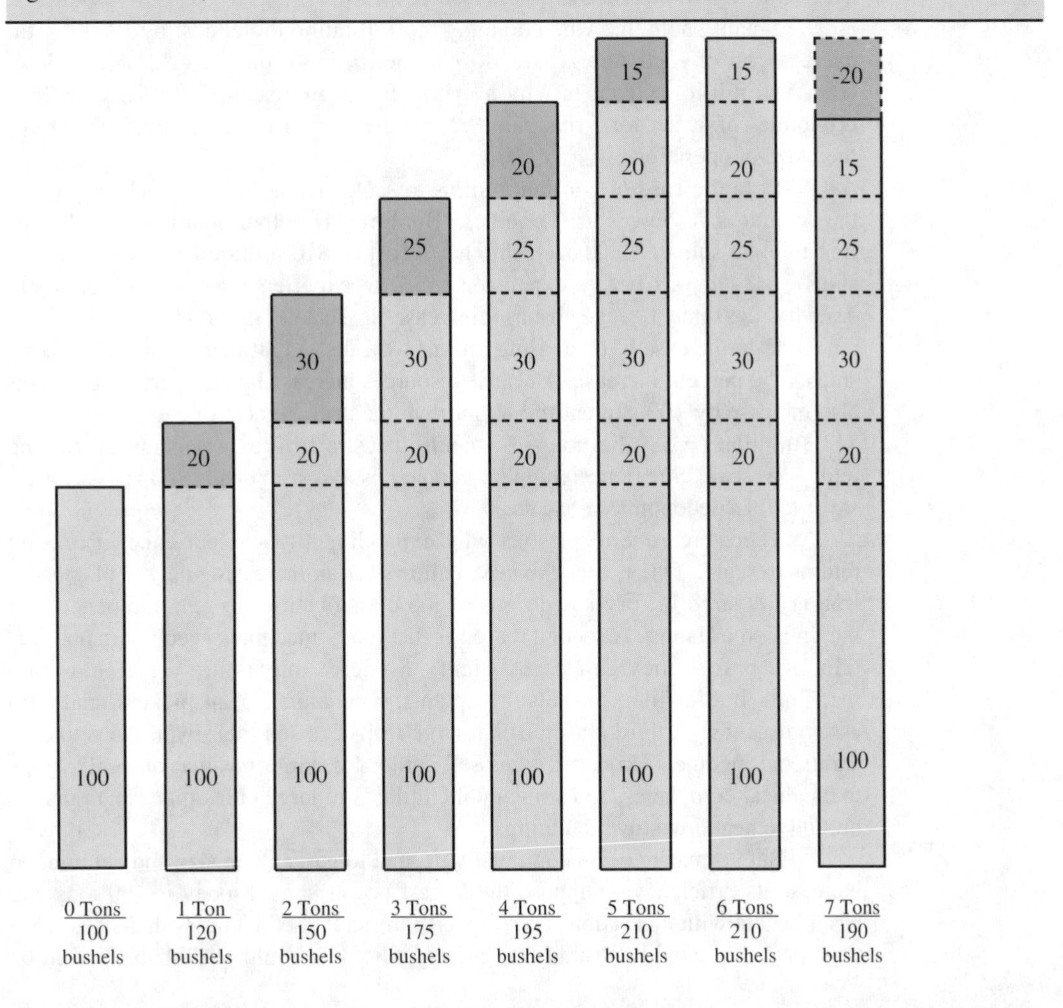

The example of a shipyard in Figure 3-3 illustrates each of these cases. Suppose the shipyard owner wants to expand from the present four-ships-per-year capacity. The yard now needs $40 million in resources to produce four ships, giving an average cost per ship of $10 million. The diagrams help to clarify this numerical data at the top of the figure.

■ Suppose the shipyard owner decides to double the amount of each resource used—yard space, buildings, labor, fabricating steel, and derricks. Consequently, total cost per year doubles to $80 million. In the second row of diagrams, note that the middle diagram, which represents costs, doubles in size. Next, note that output increases to 12 ships per year—triple the original amount, or a 200 percent increase. Because resources increase by 100 percent and output by 200 percent, the production process experiences increasing returns to scale. The words "increasing returns" imply that each resource now "returns" or produces more of a ship than in the smaller operation. For example, if two derricks are used in producing four ships in the smaller operation, then each derrick (helps to) produces two ships. But after expansion, each derrick produces *three* ships (= 12 ÷ 4). Thus, the "returns" to derricks climb from two to three, a 50 percent rise. The same thing holds for the other resources.

★4 Finally, note that when dividing the $80 million total cost by 12 ships, the average cost of each ship is now $6.7 million (= $80 million ÷ 12 ships), down from $10 million. That is why a synonym for increasing returns to scale is economies of scale, for firms gain "economies" or cost savings by "scaling up" their size of operations.

■ In the case of constant returns to scale, again the cost doubles because the amount of resources used doubles. But now the output doubles as well, from four to eight ships. Thus, each ship has a cost of $10 million (= $80 million ÷ 8 ships), the same as before expansion. A firm experiencing constant returns to scale has the same average cost as it increases its scale of operation.

■ In the case of decreasing returns to scale, output merely increases to six ships, a 50 percent increase. Because resources increase by 100 percent and costs also increase by 100 percent to $80 million, the average cost of each ship *rises* to $13.3 million (= $80 million ÷ 6 ships). Thus, a firm experiencing decreasing returns to scale experiences higher average costs as it expands. That is why we say it faces *dis*economies of scale.

There are several reasons why expanding firms experience increasing returns to scale. One is that expansion allows for an increasing degree of specialization. A large factory has dozens of job classifications to reap the benefits of the division of labor. A second reason is that many machines need to attain a certain size before they can be efficient. Some examples are metal stamping machines, bottle fillers in beverage plants, mechanical bean pickers, and auto assembly lines. A third reason is that large firms can sell their byproducts to earn additional income. Grocery chains sell cardboard, large meatpackers sell scraps to chemical companies, and some public utilities in large cities pipe steam underground to heat downtown buildings.

But no machine can continually expand to gargantuan size and continue to increase its efficiency. Suppose the largest power shovel today is 100 tons and has a bucket with a 60-cubic-yard capacity. A shovel of 10 times that size, 1,000 tons, probably would not hold 600 cubic yards. If it could, it probably would be

Figure 3-3 Increasing, Constant, and Decreasing Returns to Scale

A shipyard decides to double its scale of operation, thereby doubling its total cost. The top case shows the output of ships, the total cost of operation, and the average cost of each ship before the expansion. The three possibilities regarding returns to scale appear next, showing the results on output and cost following expansion.

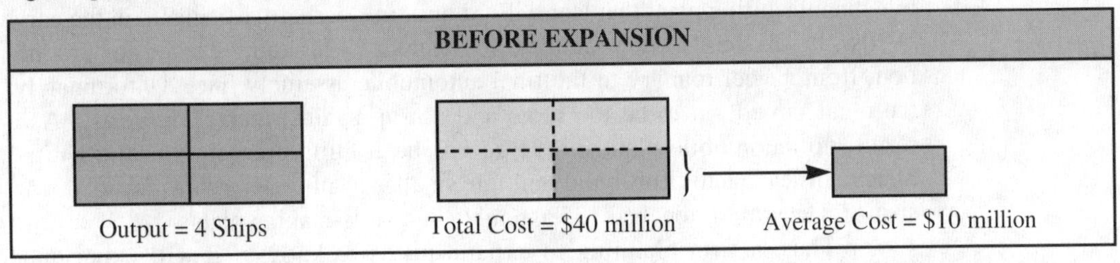

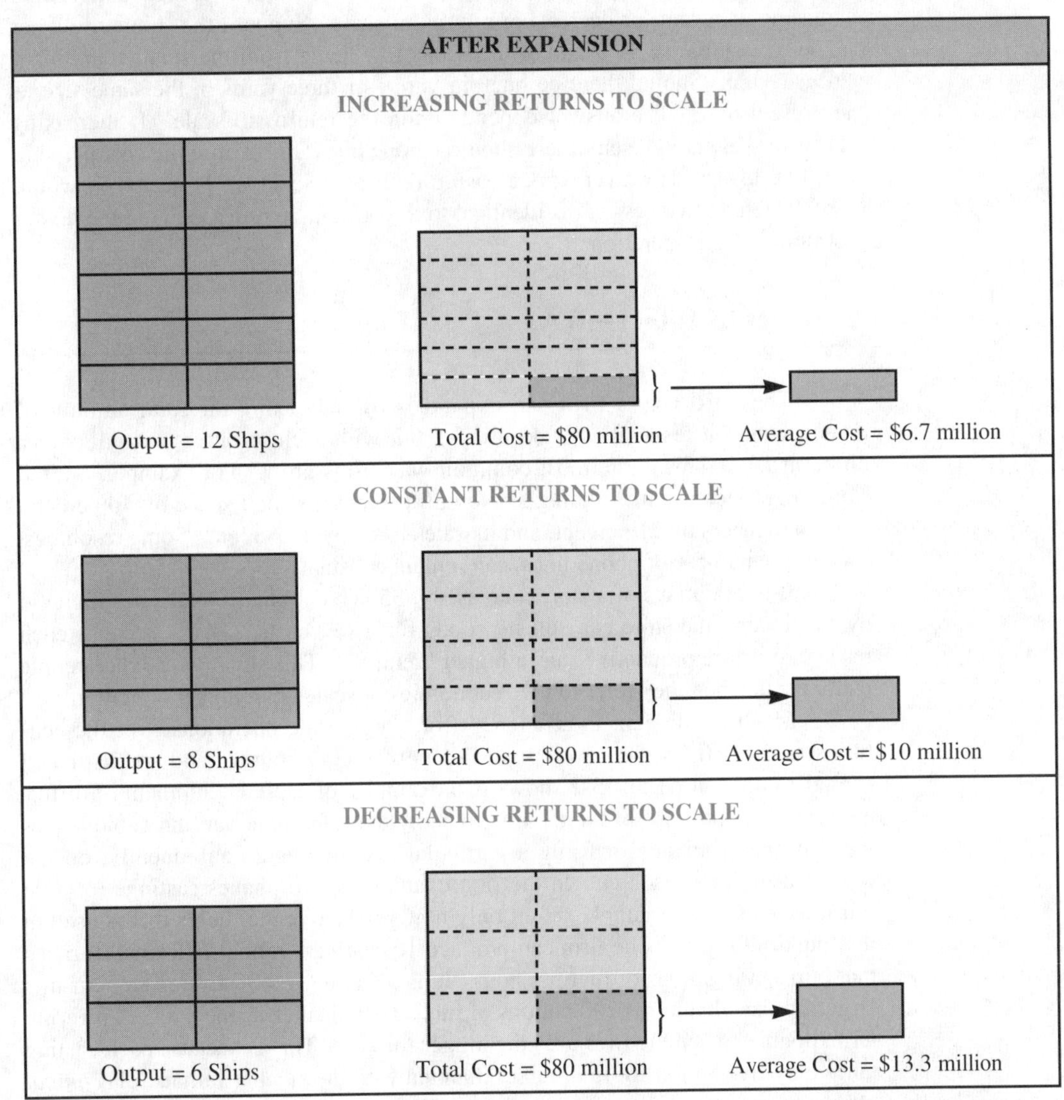

built. Thus, sooner or later firms experience decreasing returns to scale—partly because of the limits on capital size. Often a more important reason is that managers find extremely large businesses difficult to manage. This is the primary cause of diseconomies of scale.

An example of diseconomies of scale is the gigantic River Rouge automobile manufacturing plant that Henry Ford built in Dearborn, Michigan, in the early 1920s. It was nearly one mile long and included everything needed for production, from a steel foundry to the final automobile assembly line. Unfortunately, the plant turned out to be too large and ran up against increasing costs. As a result, no automobile plant this large has been built since then in the United States. Instead, auto firms build multiple smaller plants. Before its recent "downsizing," General Motors had 125 assembly and parts-making plants.

Thus, a firm planning to expand needs to know if it will experience increasing, constant, or decreasing returns to scale. Suppose the shipyard owner can sell 12 ships per year and, thus, wants to expand from the small four-ships-per-year yard. Should there be one big yard—or three yards of the same size as the present one? The answer depends upon the returns to scale. If increasing returns to scale are present, there should be one big yard because the cost per ship would be lower. However, if decreasing returns to scale are projected, it would be better to add two new yards identical to the original in order to avoid the higher cost of the larger operation.

Increases in Total Outlays

The third way a firm can expand is by increasing the total amount of money spent on resources (total outlays), but with each resource expanding at a different rate. This is the most common way firms grow. For example, a retail store might increase its building size by 30 percent, its shelf space by 40 percent, its cash registers by 21 percent, and its sales force by 26 percent. Some resources, such as the number of phone lines, can remain constant.

If total outlays of a store increase by 35 percent, and if total sales increase by 47 percent, the store can sell its goods for lower costs. That's because each resource is more productive (has a higher "return"). This situation is what people really mean when they refer to the "economies of scale" of a bigger operation.

Much of the gain in efficiency from large-scale operations over the centuries resulted from the development of new energy sources and sophisticated capital equipment. Table 3-2 shows two examples of capital equipment of different size. The purpose of the table is to show the effect that varying capital sizes have on the efficiency of using a particular resource and, consequently, on the cost of using that resource. In the first example, a firm makes castings for auto transmissions. The example shows only how productive the fuel is that is used in the foundry furnace. The firm can produce 10 castings an hour in a small furnace that burns 100 gallons of fuel per hour. It also can make 40 castings an hour in a larger furnace that burns 200 gallons of fuel. Technical efficiency, an engineering term, doubles when the firm uses the bigger furnace. This is because each casting takes only five gallons of fuel, rather than ten with the smaller furnace. *Technical* efficiency refers to a comparison of the *physical* amounts of resources used to the

Table 3-2 Effects of Capital Size on Efficiency of Resource Use and Production Costs

Example 1: A foundry makes transmission castings, and the effects of capital (furnace) size on fuel cost is considered. (The effects on other costs are ignored.) Assume that the price of fuel is $2 per gallon.

Furnace Size	Resources Used (fuel)	Output Level (Castings/hr)	Resources per Unit of Output (Gallons of Fuel/Casting)	Resource Cost (Fuel Cost/Casting)
Small	100 Gallons/hr	10 Castings/hr	10 Gallons/Casting	$20/Casting
Large	200 Gallons/hr	40 Castings/hr	5 Gallons/Casting	$10/Casting

Example 2: A farmer grows potatoes, and the effect of using different size tractors on harvesting cost is considered. Only capital (tractor) costs are considered. Capital is measured by tractor horsepower. Assume that each horsepower of tractor size costs $2 for each hour the tractor is used.

Tractor Size	Resources Used (HP)	Output Level (Tons/hr)	Resources per Unit of Output (HP Used in 1 Hour/Ton)	Resource Cost (Tractor Cost/Ton)
Small	40 HP	2 Tons/hr	20 HP/Ton	$40/Ton
Large	160 HP	16 Tons/hr	10 HP/Ton	$20/Ton

outputs produced. *Economic* efficiency refers to the *cost* of the resources needed to make a good or service. In the example, if fuel cost $2 a gallon, the fuel cost for each casting is only $10 with the larger furnace—half the cost of the smaller one.

Similarly, in the second example, a farmer cuts the tractor cost in half when harvesting potatoes with a larger tractor. In this case a fourfold increase in tractor engine size yields an eightfold increase in output.

Economies of scale are common in production processes. However, although the data for these two examples look favorable for larger size equipment, you must take care. Remember, the last column shows the effect on just one of the resources used. Perhaps the cost per unit of output of other resources used would increase. Managers can make a good (profit-maximizing) decision about the best size (or capacity) of capital and operation only after a detailed analysis.

Equally important to a firm is the market size—that is, how much it can sell. Suppose you are a soft drink bottler in sparsely populated Wyoming. You might be able to *bottle* drinks more cheaply in a vast plant. But you would be sorry (and broke!) if you could sell only one-tenth of your output. Thus, the cost per unit of what little you actually can sell would be very high.

In a somewhat similar situation, the size of capital that is used depends upon the size of the job. For example, a trench could be dug with low-volume capital (picks and shovels) or high-volume capital (backhoes). A contractor probably would use laborers with picks and shovels to dig a shallow 10-foot-long trench. But a backhoe would be used for a trench 200 feet long and six feet deep.

THE MASS-PRODUCTION ECONOMY

Mass production occurs when firms produce a large amount of a good or service in a certain period. Contrast this with a custom-made production process, in which each customer's good or service is unique. Another type of production process is the batch process, in which a limited number of identical products is made. Although it often is difficult to categorize production processes into these three groups, some examples might help. Mass-produced products include steel, ball point pens, canned peaches, televisions, and most baseball bats. Batch-process items include baseball bats made for professional ballplayers (50 or so specialized bats are made at a time to the players' specifications) and jetliners (from several to 20 specialized planes are made for each airline company). Custom-made items or services include haircuts, portraits, and tailor-made suits.

Take care not to equate mass production with "factory-made." Mass-production techniques indeed include most large factory operations, but they also include commercial farms (generally producing only a few commodities in large volumes), mines, timbering operations, transportation operations (using large trucks, ships, etc.), and electric power production.

Like it or not, firms mass produce or mass market a growing share of goods and services. And a lot of people *don't* like it, preferring the "old-fashioned handmade" operations of small businesses. Witness the rapid growth of micro-breweries in the 1980s, a reaction to the sameness of beers from the major breweries. By 1990, there were 177 micro-breweries in the United States. Also, many shoppers like the atmosphere of "boutiques," which gained popularity in the 1970s.

This section examines two major aspects of the modern mass-production economy, which will explain why it didn't exist prior to the 1800s. First you'll learn about the characteristics of mass production, and then about the role played by mass markets in a mass-production economy.

Characteristics of Mass Production

★5

Most mass-production processes have four major characteristics: 1) specialized, high-volume capital equipment; 2) standardization and interchangeable parts; 3) continuous production processes; and 4) a skilled, specialized labor force. These are not completely independent of each other. Rather, they often complement or depend upon each other. This is indicated by the dotted lines connecting the boxes in the top row of Figure 3-6 on page 74. Use this flow chart to follow the presentation on the next few pages.

■ The first characteristic of mass production reflects the role played by capital. Virtually all large-scale operations use a sizable amount of high-volume capital equipment, which is generally very specialized to fit a particular production process. Some examples: draglines that excavate coal or metal ores, assembly lines that turn out cars, oil tankers that transport petroleum, and blast furnaces that produce steel. Each machine is useless for almost anything besides its intended purpose. Also, today's machines generally produce goods in larger amounts and in less time than the smaller, simpler machines of the past. The following examples illustrate the changes in production processes over the years.

The first wool carding machine, which appeared in 1775, combed wool fibers in one direction so they could be spun into yarn. One person carding wool by hand could produce one pound of carded wool in 10 hours, while someone running a carding machine could produce 120 pounds in the same time.

Before 1883, workers rolled cigarettes by hand, around 300 per hour. Benjamin and James Duke used a machine invented by James Bonsach that rolled 12,000 per hour. The result—cheap cigarettes (and a costly habit).

Before the 1980s, postal workers sorted letters by reading the last two numbers of the ZIP code at the rate of 1,600 letters per hour. The Optical Character Reader now reads all five numbers of the code on typed envelopes at the rate of 10,000 letters per hour.

In 1988, Nucor Corporation made the world's first sheet of steel in its "thin-slab plant." Its new machinery, which eliminated the process of rolling (flattening hot steel), reduced labor time per ton of steel from six hours to 1.5 hours.

★6

■ The second characteristic of mass production involves the concepts of standardization and interchangeable parts. Although often used as synonyms, these words have somewhat different meanings. **Standardization** refers to the identical size, shape, and pattern of *products of different firms.* Some examples: all 60-watt light bulbs made by all bulb manufacturers have bases that fit in every table lamp made by any lamp maker; all lumber firms make two-by-fours the same size; all typing paper in the United States is 8-1/2 by 11 inches; all railroad companies have the same track gauge (size); and all film companies make film that fit in all 35-millimeter cameras.

Without standardization, firms would make much smaller amounts of many products. For example, Sylvania would make 60-watt bulbs with bases of many different sizes—one for each lamp manufacturer. And Kodak would have to make dozens of film sizes to fit the varying film size each camera maker used. Thus, without standardization there would be much less mass production (and more batch-process production).

Interchangeable parts means each part of one unit of *one firm's* product is identical to the respective parts of all other such units produced by that firm. This concept was conceived in France by Le Blanc, promoted by Thomas Jefferson, and introduced by Eli Whitney in 1798 in musket manufacture (and later by Simeon North in pistol manufacture). For example, each flintlock (which held a piece of flint used to fire the powder) Whitney made fit in any of his muskets. Previously, because each barrel, stock, trigger, breech and every other part of the musket had a unique size and shape, each flintlock had to vary in size to match the varying sizes of the other parts before it would fit perfectly. To make these parts interchangeable, Whitney developed the concept of a machine tool. This is a machine (such as a lathe or a drillpress) that cuts or shapes metal or other materials, usually by following a pattern. He was forced to build such machines so he could fulfill his contract with the U.S. Government for 10,000 muskets. Still, progress was slow, and it took him until 1809 to finish the job, partly because his machines weren't perfect. Many parts still had to be filed by hand before they fit perfectly. Whitney's successors at the National Armories in Springfield, Massachusetts perfected his idea.

The next time you change a tire and remove *and replace the wheel nuts at random,* thank Whitney for making life easier for you. And when you buy replacement parts for bicycles or vacuum cleaners, be grateful the parts fit. Or would you prefer to have the old broken parts welded, soldered, or glued together? Even worse, how would you like to pay for expensive, custom-made replacement parts? Until the 1800s, that's the way people did things. It's a main reason why they were poor.

Oliver Terry, a clock maker, also was instrumental in introducing interchangeable parts. In 1807, he received a contract to make 4,000 clock movements (the innards). At the time, 40 to 50 movements per *year* was the ordinary level of output for clock makers. He dramatically increased output by using machines to make clock parts that were interchangeable—first wooden parts and later brass parts. His was the first non-publicly funded use of the interchangeable parts concept. By 1814, he was making inexpensive table clocks, first for $5 and ultimately at $1.25. He later sold his patents to an employee named Seth Thomas, whose firm is still in the business.

But far beyond your convenience, interchangeable parts make possible the production and assembly of products with the aid of machines. Machines depend upon sameness, whether they're machines that make parts or machines that help assemble parts into finished products. Imagine the mess a machine would make if it had to grab and bottle pickles of widely varying sizes (which is why they are still packed by hand). When products are uniform, as in cigarette manufacture, the packing process is a breeze. (The letter-sorting machine mentioned earlier requires *typed* ZIP codes, for handwritten numbers vary too much for machines to read.) Consequently, interchangeable parts vastly increased the potential output possible at individual firms making guns, stoves, pumps, and thousands of other items.

■ The third characteristic of mass production is the **continuous production process**, where production is broken into several steps, with the steps usually taking place in different locations. In addition, raw materials continually flow into the production process while finished products continually exit the process. For example, in grain milling, the cleaning, grinding, and separation of flour from the outer hulls occur in sequence at different locations in the mill. Grain continually flows into the mill, and flour continually leaves the mill. Indeed, it was in corn milling that Oliver Evans first applied this concept in 1785. He built a 300-bushel-per-hour mill that was run by only two men and depended upon conveyors using gravity and water power. By the 1840s, thousands of such mills ground grain at significantly reduced costs for farmers throughout North America.

The continuous production process enhances mass production primarily because it uses specialized machines to aid production. With most products, there are so many steps in production that a single machine could not do all of them simultaneously. Yet several machines, each doing one task and working in sequence, can greatly increase output. However, the continuous production process is not used in all industries, even some with large economies of scale. Growing rice, building a ship, and repairing a car do not involve a constant flow of resources into the production process. In rice growing, for example, seed is planted once a year, so the planter is used only a fraction of the time.

A continuous production process also helps make mass production efficient by allowing for the division of labor. Laborers differ in their aptitude for the various steps or jobs in the production process. The continuous production process allows all laborers to specialize in the jobs in which they have a comparative advantage.

The combination of interchangeable parts, the continuous production process, and specialized capital equipment led to one of the greatest innovations of all time, the moving assembly line. Here, partly finished products are brought to the workers—rather than the workers coming to the product—and a worker assembles only one part of the product. Henry Ford usually gets the credit for adopting this concept in auto production in 1913. He was able to slash the assembly time of the Model T from 12.5 hours to one hour and 33 minutes. This enabled Ford to achieve his goal of a price so low that almost anyone could afford a car. By 1919, the price of his runabout version of the Model T had fallen to $290. It also enabled him to raise his basic wage rate from $2.40 for nine hours to $5.00 for eight hours in January 1914. However, the meat packing industry had used the concept in *disassembling* animals years earlier. As gruesomely described in Upton Sinclair's 1906 book, *The Jungle,* each worker made only one or a few cuts on a carcass before it passed to the next worker.

■ The last characteristic of a mass-production economy is a force of specialized laborers, some requiring a high degree of skills. Examples include machining center operators (who need complex math and computer skills), electronic technicians, and laser operators. However, skilled laborers sometimes are replaced by unskilled laborers following mechanization. This occurred at Whitney's musket factory and Ford's auto factory.

The Role of Mass Markets

The four characteristics of a mass-production economy refer only to the production side of the picture. That is, they result in low production costs because of the large volume of output. But what good is the capacity to produce vast quantities of a good or service if all the output cannot be sold? A mass-production economy also depends upon the existence of **mass markets**, where large numbers of buyers are willing to buy a product.

Two requirements must be met before mass markets can exist. The first is a large number of potential buyers, either in a large domestic population or in a large foreign population.

The second requirement for a mass market is a low product price compared with the average income, so people who want the item can afford to buy it. This is the same as saying that people have high real incomes. Although there is a mass market for pleasure boats in America, there is none in China, even with 1.2 billion people, because Chinese incomes are too low. In turn, four major requirements must be met before a product's price is low relative to income: 1) low production cost; 2) low transport cost; 3) low communication cost; and 4) low marketing cost.

■ First is a low production cost, which essentially requires efficient production as explored in Chapter 2 and so far in this chapter.

■ Second, transportation costs of the product from the factory to the buyer must be low. Otherwise, the buyer will purchase a locally made product with little shipping cost. Local buying is a problem for two reasons. First, the buyer of a local product cannot benefit from any lower *production* costs of a distant manufacturer, who may be more efficient because of better raw materials, more skilled workers, and more know-how. Second, if everyone in the nation bought from local producers, each producer would have a small operation because of the small, local market. Then we would not receive the benefits of mass production—high living standards. The primary value of interstate highways, railroads, dock facilities, and the capital equipment that use them (trucks, freight trains, and large ships) is that these all reduce transportation costs so that manufacturers can achieve mass markets.

■ The third requirement for low price relative to income is low communication cost. Communication is an obvious requirement in any market exchange. It is not difficult or costly for buyers and sellers who live near each other. But mass markets require *distant* markets, requiring long-distance communication. As with transportation, the cost of communicating between distant buyers and sellers must not raise the price so high that only *local* production occurs. Central to a mass-production economy are the telephone, airmail, satellite communication, and the emerging electronic mail system (including fax machines).

■ The final requirement for low price relative to income is a low marketing cost. A low marketing cost often is difficult to achieve in retailing because products usually are sold one unit at a time, with few economies of scale. Consequently, retailers often need to sell items for twice the wholesale price in order to cover the selling costs. There are ways to overcome some of these costs, including self-service stores, "superstores," and scanners that read the bar codes on products.

Incidentally, low transport, communication, and marketing costs often result from the same characteristics of mass production that lead to low production costs. (This is indicated in Figure 3-6 by the dotted line connecting the second row of boxes on the left with the first row of boxes.) For example, "double-bottom" semis and the new three-trailer "trains," oil pipelines, fiber optic (telephone) cables, and computerized inventory control in stores all keep down the cost of business operations.

CONSEQUENCES OF A MASS-PRODUCTION ECONOMY

The 200-plus years since the Industrial Revolution have brought great changes to the economy. Consider some of the major ways our economy differs from that of our ancestors and how it is still changing: 1) higher living standards; 2) a shift from labor to capital; 3) changing relative prices; 4) the appearance of large firms in some industries; and 5) changes in labor markets. Virtually all of these changes stem from the shift to a mass-production economy.

★7

Higher Living Standards

The continuing Industrial Revolution gives us benefits that past generations never dreamed possible. Look around. What do we have that our ancestors did not? Refrigerators and other kitchen appliances, furnaces and air conditioners, TVs and radios, stereo equipment, paved streets, vacations to Disney World and Yellowstone, higher education, cars, indoor plumbing, a longer life span, wall-to-wall carpeting, and hundreds of other things.

Our ancestors could not have afforded such luxuries even if they had known how to produce them. They *had to* concentrate on essentials because just providing their basic needs of food, shelter, and clothing took most of their resources. In 1800, for instance, it required 72 percent of the workforce to grow food for the population, compared with three percent today. Thus, few resources were left to make the luxuries listed above. (Yes, indoor plumbing *is* a luxury. Two-thirds of the world does without it.)

Material abundance resulted from economic changes, including increased specialization and the innovations of interchangeable parts, computerization, and thousands of different kinds of mechanization. These increased the efficiency of resource use, essentially making resources less scarce. Now people can make *more* of the unlimited things they want than with previous production methods. Not all—just more.

Will living standards continue to grow? Will the things now available only to the rich—hot tubs, swanky five-bedroom homes, eating out every week in gourmet restaurants, facelifts, four-car garages filled with luxury cars, yearly trips abroad—be available to most in the future? Why not? That is no more far-fetched than a person of the 1700s or 1800s predicting the lifestyle of today. How can it be done? By doing more of the same—more specialization, more innovation, and more elimination of resource waste. The doom-and-gloom pessimists who predict harder times for future generations have a poor understanding of economic history and economic growth.

A Shift from Labor to Capital

All goods and services require labor, capital, natural resources, and entrepreneurship. In the distant past, labor was the dominant resource used in virtually all production processes, which meant things were usually handmade. Thus, the largest share of the average cost was used to pay the owners of the labor resources—the workers. When producers use such a production process to make a good or service today, economists say its production process is **labor-intensive**.

Because of the countless number of innovations involving mechanization (the replacing of labor with capital), production processes of many goods and services today are **capital-intensive**. This means capital is the dominant resource used in production, so that much of the average cost involves paying for capital—machines, buildings, and tools. Our mass-production economy means that machine-made, rather than handmade, processes dominate the production scene. This is because machine-made methods are cheaper for so many items.

Paving streets with bricks in the early 1900s was very labor-intensive. Modern, capital-intensive concrete paving has made brick streets prohibitively expensive.
(Courtesy of the Wisconsin Historical Society)

Capital-intensive strip mining uses huge machines that have reduced the relative price of strip-mined coal compared with the relative price of coal mined underground with more labor-intensive methods.
(Courtesy of the American Petroleum Institute)

Changing Relative Prices

During inflation most prices increase, but some prices increase more than others. Consequently, economists distinguish between two concepts of prices.

★8

Absolute price refers to the normal concept of price, or the number of dollars it takes to buy something. **Relative price** refers to the amount of some other good or service you could have bought with the money it took to buy item x. Suppose a melon sells for 60¢ and a peach for 30¢. Then a melon costs (or has a relative price of) two peaches, and a peach costs half a melon. (This is not the same as opportunity cost even though it sounds like it. Opportunity cost refers to what you give up from the *best* of the remaining alternatives to x.)

Suppose the price of a melon increases to $1.20 and the price of a peach increases to 40¢. Now a melon trades for three peaches, so the relative price of melons rose from two to three peaches. In contrast, the relative price of peaches fell from one-half to one-third of a melon.

Figure 3-4 shows two examples of changing relative prices, both numerically and with graphs. The first example considers toasters and repairs of toasters in 1970 and 1994. While the absolute prices of both rose, the price of toasters doubled while the price of repairs tripled. The relative price of one toaster equals the number of repairs that can be made for the price of the toaster. In 1970, it was one repair, for each cost $10, but in 1994 it fell to two-thirds of a repair (= $20 ÷ $30). Thus, the relative price of toasters fell. Conversely, the relative price of repairs rose, from one toaster to 1.5 toasters (= $30 ÷ $20). By 1994, a repair

Figure 3-4 Some Examples of Changing Absolute and Relative Prices

Year	Absolute Prices: Toaster	Absolute Prices: Repair	Relative Prices: Toaster	Relative Prices: Toaster Repair
1970	$10	$10	1 Repair	1 Toaster
1994	$20	$30	2/3rds of a Repair	1.5 Toasters
Degree of Price Change →	2x	3x	Relative Price Fell for Toaster	Relative Price Rose for Repair

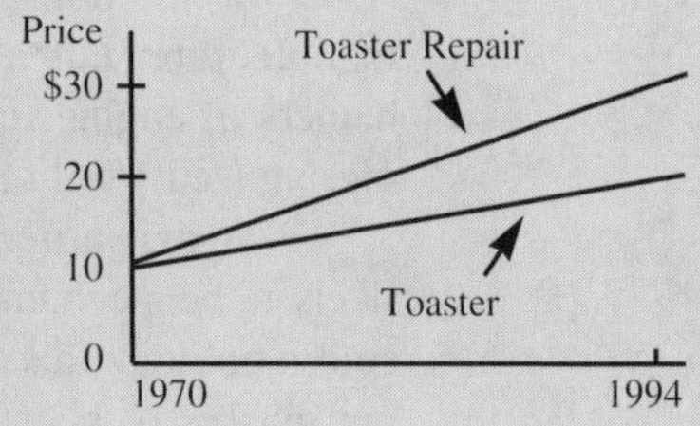

Price
$30
20
10
0
Toaster Repair
Toaster
1970
1994

Year	Absolute Prices: Glass of Beer	Absolute Prices: 6-pack of Beer	Relative Prices: Glass of Beer	Relative Prices: 6-Pack of Beer
1960	30¢	$1.20	1/4th 6-Pack	4 Glasses
1994	80¢	$2.40	1/3rd 6-Pack	3 Glasses
Degree of Price Increase →	2.75x	2x	Relative Price Rose for Glass of Beer	Relative Price Fell for 6-Pack

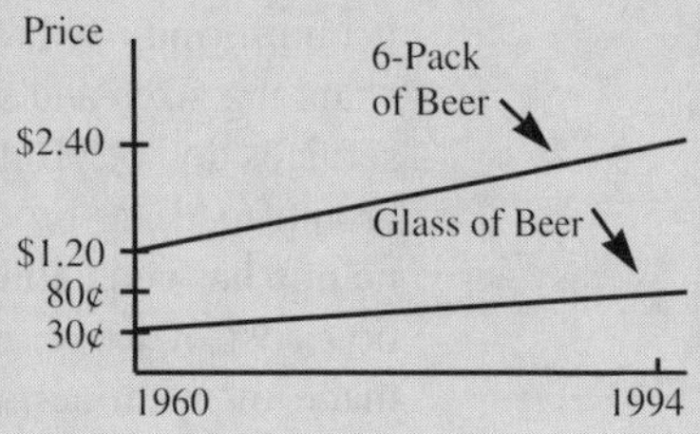

Price
$2.40
$1.20
80¢
30¢
6-Pack of Beer
Glass of Beer
1960
1994

required more toasters to be given up than in 1970—one half of a toaster more. If this continues, sooner or later people will throw away broken toasters and buy new ones instead. Of course, people already do this in our "throwaway" society.

In the second example, the absolute price of a glass of beer served in a bar increased faster than the absolute price of a six-pack purchased in a store. Thus, the relative price of the glass of beer rose from one-fourth of a six-pack (one-and-a-half cans) to one-third of a six-pack (two cans). Conversely, the relative price of a six-pack fell from four glasses to three glasses. Consequently, more people would be expected to drink at home rather than in bars.

The primary reason that the relative price for an item falls is because its production process is more subject to innovation than most other processes. This generally occurs because it is easier to mechanize its production. A firm will mechanize only if it expects lower average costs after mechanization. Thus, the more some item's manufacture is mechanized compared with all other things, the less costly it will be to make compared with all other goods and services. Consequently, its (absolute) price will be lower than if its production process was not mechanized. That is, its relative price will fall.

Conversely, when the relative price for a good or service rises, generally this is because it's difficult or impossible to mechanize or otherwise innovate its manufacturing process. Because costs cannot be cut, its (absolute) price becomes higher relative to more mechanized items. That is, its relative price rises.

Figure 3-5 shows changes in relative prices for an item that is easily mechanized (an air conditioner) and for one that defies mechanization because it lacks product uniformity (engine overhaul). The hypothetical changes over a 24-year period in wages and labor used show why engine overhaul prices do indeed increase so much faster than air conditioner prices.

While both items required 50 hours of labor in 1970, the air conditioner manufacturer cut it to 37.5 hours through mechanization by 1994. But overhaulers of engines cannot do that because each overhaul is unique and not easily mechanized. (All other costs and profit margins are assumed to be unchanged.)

In the earlier case of toasters, the production of new toasters is much more likely to be mechanized than the repair of a toaster. The repair jobs are all unique, so it's unlikely that they can be done more efficiently as time passes. Also, serving glasses of beer has changed very little over time (as proved by *Cheers* and saloon photos of the 1800s). However, "warehouse" retail stores and self-service have significantly increased the efficiency of the marketing of six-packs. Therefore, six-packs have become relatively cheaper than beer served in bars.

As you learned earlier, using machines to produce an item requires product uniformity. Machines that help assemble products cannot deal with constantly changing sizes and shapes of parts. In general, goods possess such uniformity but services do not. But at least part of some goods are not uniform. An example is a broom made of broom corn, a plant that varies so much in height and shape that no one has been able to invent a machine to harvest it. Consequently, the production cost of a broom made of broom corn has risen more sharply than brooms made of machine-made synthetic fibers (which *are* uniform). That spelled the demise of Arcola, Illinois, where 20 firms made brooms in the late 1800s. Today broom corn is grown primarily in Mexico where wages are relatively lower, and only two firms still make brooms near Arcola.

Services generally cannot be mechanized very well primarily because the services each person requires are unique, such as with medical, auto repair, and haircutting needs. Consequently, absolute prices of services generally increase faster than prices of goods. Therefore, relative prices of services generally increase over time while relative prices of goods decrease. To a large extent, that explains why medical and education costs rise so sharply.

Other problems prevent the mechanization of some production processes. Some processes (such as litter pickup) cannot be centralized. Some, such as restaurant services, require human involvement (who wants to be served by a robot?). And some involve limited or unique production, such as art, custom-designed houses, and personal medical equipment. For example, hearing aids cost up to $2,000, largely because each aid must be hand-crafted to fit the particular needs of the patient.

Many changes in our lifestyle over the years are rooted in changes in relative prices. As already noted, we became a "throwaway society" because of escalating repair costs. Like synthetic brooms that replaced natural-bristle brooms, synthetic fibers replaced wool, linen, and cotton in many fabrics. The fax machine is rapidly replacing the hand-delivered message (the mail). Mail delivery defies innovation because mailbox sizes and locations are so variable, forcing stamp prices to skyrocket. Years ago, even men of modest means commonly got shaves in barber shops—an extravagance today. Last, as implied in Figure 3-5,

Figure 3-5 The Effects of Mechanization on Relative Prices

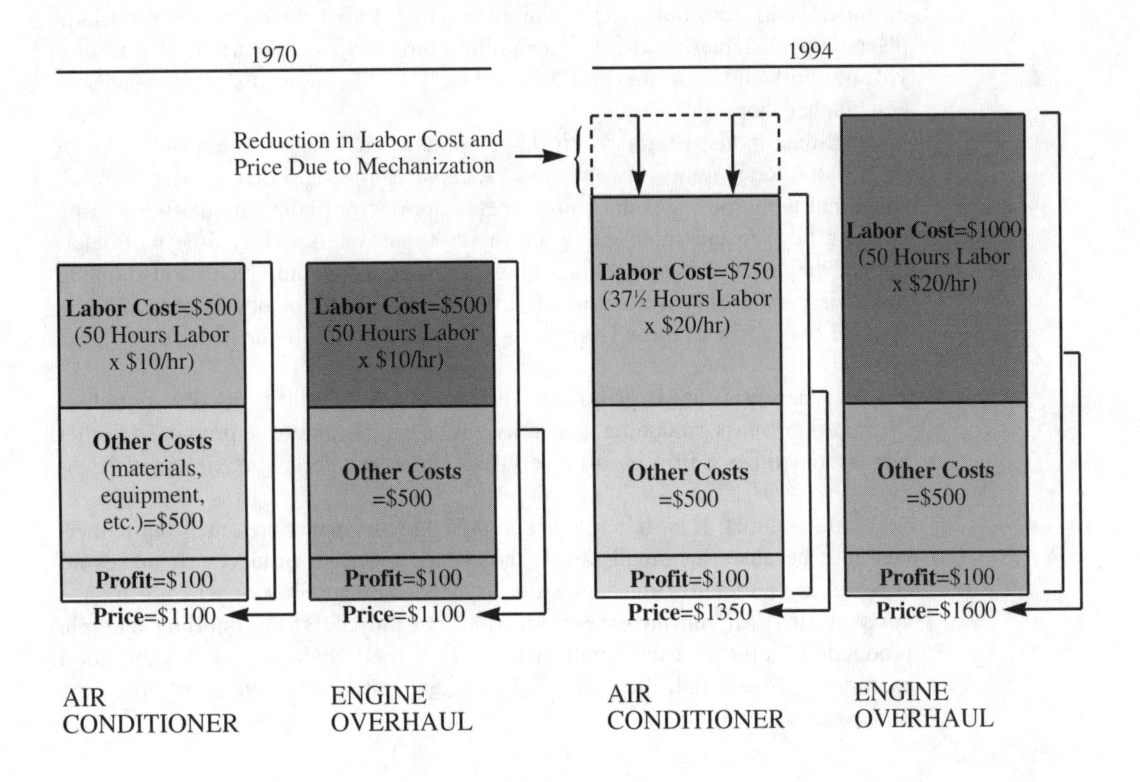

while engine overhauls were common until the 1950s or so, they are rare today. Instead, we melt the worn-out engines and make new ones.

The Appearance of Large Firms in Some Industries

Until the early 1800s, many competing small firms made goods and services. In 1800, for example, about 2,000 shops in the United States made shoes for a population of five million, each with only one or several workers. By 1950, only a few hundred factories produced shoes in much larger plants for a population of 150 million. (By today, most of them have closed, for we import a large share of our shoes.) In the 1800s, each town of any size had several wagon makes, the forerunner of semi-trailer manufacturers. An emigrant in 1877 on his way through Kansas City noticed a dozen different makers in that city alone—very similar but with different nameplates. Today there are only 10 semi-trailer makers in the whole country. In the 1800s, each town with more than a thousand people usually had a brewery, commonly producing only several hundred barrels per year, as compared with breweries today that brew more than eight million barrels per year. Plat maps (which shows all farm boundaries and buildings in rural areas) of Wisconsin in the 1890s show cheese factories about three to five miles apart, so the state had thousands of factories. Today, much bigger plants are 20 to 30 miles apart, and only 195 factories remain. Finally, with massive packing plants now slaughtering two to four million hogs a year, few are needed to provide our pork and ham. In the 1800s and early 1900s, even small towns had several butcher shops.

Some industries today still have the characteristics of these industries of the 1800s. Restaurants, jewelry makers, repair shops, and dental offices are all small and numerous. (Some entrepreneurs are defying conventional wisdom by building huge restaurants, seating up to 1,800 customers. Only time will determine if they will succeed.) Other industries, such as the auto, coal, and shipping industries, have only a handful of firms, each with giant operations. This is because only a few of these large firms are needed to supply the needs of the buyers.

When firms are large but few, it is usually because it is possible to reduce their costs by mass producing, generally with a capital-intensive process. In other words, sometimes a firm must be very large in order to reach maximum efficiency.

In contrast, if an industry is comprised of firms that are small but numerous, it is because this small size is the cheapest way to produce. It makes no sense to get larger, for mechanization is either not possible or will not reduce costs. Firms still can increase production, but they do so by building multiple production facilities, each small in size. Fast food chain restaurants are good examples. To expand, these chains build new restaurants, but all of about the same size.

Changes in Labor Markets

Because of mass production, laborers today work in a world far different from that of their ancestors. Three major differences between the past and present centuries include: 1) changes in skill requirements; 2) a shift from producing goods to producing services; and 3) the creation of new jobs.

■ First, a vast change occurred in skill requirements. Some products that once required great labor skills to make (barrels, wheels, wagons, glass bottles) are made today with unskilled or semi-skilled laborers. This is due to the combination of increased specialization, interchangeable parts, and mechanization. And as noted earlier, changes in lifestyles caused by changing relative prices lead to many changes in the kinds of jobs there are. Jobs have disappeared for many repairmen, broom-corn makers, mail clerks and carriers, barbers, and engine overhaulers. Yet today, many highly skilled people have jobs that didn't exist in the 1800s, including flying aircraft, programming computers, administering and reading x-rays, and operating lasers.

■ Second, jobs producing services dominate today's labor market. In 1800, most people worked in agriculture, while early in this century jobs producing goods were dominant. The inability to mechanize the production of services, while food production on farms and goods production in factories were rapidly

Figure 3-6 A Summary of Relationships in a Mass-Production Economy

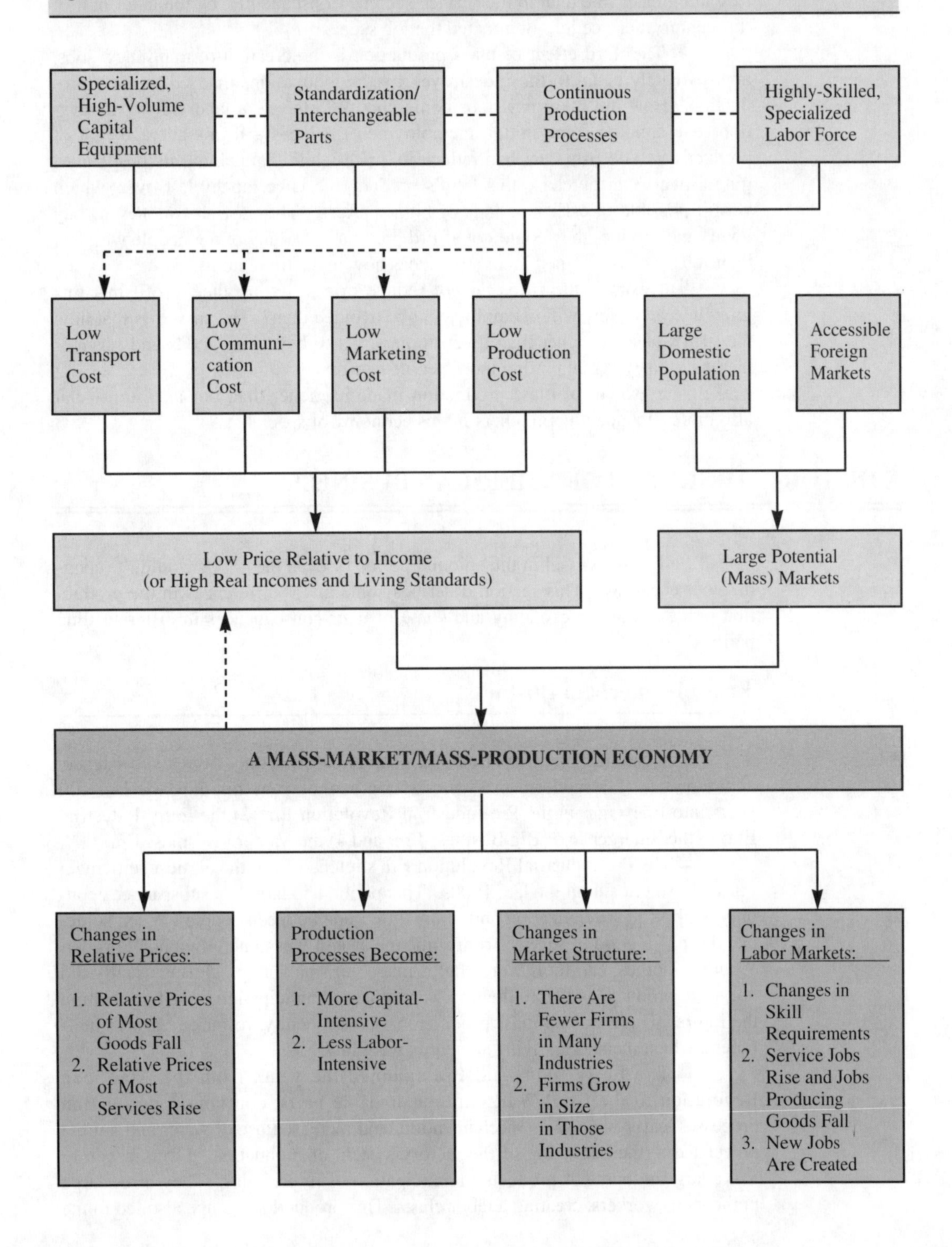

mechanized, forced such shifts. Thus, jobs were "lost" in agriculture and factories at a greater rate than in the service sector. Consequently, by the latter half of this century, service jobs dominated the job scene.

★9

■ The third effect of mass production is the creation of many new jobs, approximately equal to those destroyed by the innovations that led to mass production. How did these new jobs come about? Suppose a labor-saving innovation (one creating some initial unemployment) reduces a firm's average cost of production. The firm can then reduce its price while maintaining its profit margin. Buyers can purchase this firm's product and have money left over, which wasn't possible in earlier periods of higher prices. They use this money to buy goods and services they could not afford previously. Many of the people who lost their jobs because of such innovative ideas now make these items.

But what if the firms do *not* reduce prices, letting their profit margins grow instead? How will unemployment be avoided then? The answer is that now the firm's *owners,* rather than its customers, get to buy more goods and services than previously, again putting more people to work.

The growth of mass production made us richer than our ancestors—but also more dependent upon others in this economy of specialists.

A HISTORICAL SKETCH OF AMERICAN BUSINESS

People who lived in the colonial period or even the 1800s wouldn't recognize our economy. This section describes some major differences in the production processes of the economy and some of their consequences in different time periods.

Eras of American Business

★10

You can trace the transition of the American economy from a subsistence, agrarian state to a modern, mass-production economy by dividing the last 400 years into four eras: 1) the Pre-Industrial Revolution Era; 2) the Early Industrial Era; 3) the Emergence of Big Business Era; and 4) the Modern Business Era.

■ The Pre-Industrial Revolution Era stretched from the earliest settlement in North America until the late 1700s. This period had largely a subsistence economy, with little specialization and, thus, little trade between people. When someone did buy a good or service from someone else, it was generally made to order. Wagons, clothes, and tools were "tailor-made" in small shops. Firms usually did not make products and store them in warehouses in anticipation of selling them in the future. There was no mass production. Consequently, resource use was inefficient, which meant that living standards were low.

■ The Early Industrial Era spanned the years from the American Revolution to the Civil War. Interchangeable parts, continuous production processes, early wide-scale mechanization, and increased use of water and animal power led to the beginning of the factory system of production. Firms began to make large amounts of products in anticipation of future sales. They hired large numbers of workers, creating a labor class. This production change also led to the growth of cities, making exchanges between specialists easier. During this period, early transportation systems began to develop, with roads beginning in the 1810s, canals in the 1820s, and railroads in the 1830s. To gain economies of scale, firms began to grow in size. The high costs of capital equipment led to the growth in the corporate form of business, where many people could participate in ownership by pooling their money. Canals and railroads were the first examples of this, at least on a major scale.

■ However, only a few industries experienced such a transition before the Civil War. Such changes became widespread later on in the third era, the Emergence of Big Business Era, extending from the Civil War to the early 1900s. Giant firms appeared for the first time, especially in steel production. The United States Steel Corporation, formed in 1900 by J. P. Morgan's consolidation of the Carnegie Steel Corporation and several other steel firms, was the first billion-dollar corporation. In 1865, hundreds of small operations produced only 20,000 tons of expensive iron and steel. The new Kelly-Bessemer process made cheap steel on a large scale and resulted in giant firms, with the total output climbing to over seven million tons by 1900.

Consequently, oligopolies (industries with only a few firms) began to appear. Further consolidation into virtual monopolies through the formation of trusts occurred from the 1870s until the end of the century. Capitalists earned enormous profits and often spent their incomes lavishly and conspicuously, creating conflict with the growing labor class. Partly because of this income gap, large numbers of laborers joined unions to improve their welfare.

■ The last era is the Modern Business Era, extending to the present. In this era, businesses developed modern practices of accounting, management, marketing, and advertising. Economies of scale continued to grow in many industries, leading to further business concentration and lessened competition. Small businesses, however, still dominate those goods and services in which mechanization is difficult.

Changes in the production process continue, and they will never stop. Consequently, if you fast-forwarded to the year 2100, you probably would not recognize many of the production processes.

Throughout this era, innovations created fears about employment, labor unrest, class conflict, and reduced competition, along with the growth of monopoly power of big businesses. During the last hundred years, such concern led to legislation regulating business, putting an end to the laissez-faire philosophy of the 1800s. The Interstate Commerce Act of 1887, the Sherman Antitrust Act of 1890, the Clayton Antitrust Act of 1914, the Federal Trade Commission Act of 1914, the Glass-Steagall Act of 1933, the Anti-Merger Act of 1950, and the Small Business Investment Act of 1950 all significantly increased the role of government in business, and all were in response to advances in mass production.

The Future of Production—And the Post-Industrial Economy

Finally, let's glimpse into the future of our economy by noting a few significant innovations and developments of the last few years. Many people are predicting these changes will lead to a so-called post-industrial economy (which a large share would argue is already here). Many people mistakenly believe that it means there won't be many goods produced in the future. That's because we usually associate the word industry with the production of goods. Indeed, for reasons covered in Chapters 2 and 3, a smaller share of all jobs will be involved making goods in the future. But the *total output* of goods will continue to grow. That means those remaining workers producing goods will be highly productive compared with today's workers.

The term "post-industrial" usually implies the production of services, and very often those important to the present "information age." In this age, many jobs deal with creating, transmitting, and processing information. Such information includes news stories, business records and reports, computer analyses, advertising material, and education materials.

Some of the major developments in manufacturing include: 1) just-in-time manufacturing; 2) flexible manufacturing systems; 3) micromachines; and 4) re-engineering.

■ In the last decade or two, several new concepts divided the state-of-the-art factory of the present from that of the 1960s and earlier. One such concept, for which the Japanese receive credit, is just-in-time manufacturing, or *kanban* in Japanese. Instead of warehousing large amounts of parts needed for assembly, suppliers deliver parts immediately before assembly, eliminating costly storage costs.

■ Another new concept, called a flexible manufacturing system, makes efficient production possible without true mass production. Computers direct a series of machines to produce small outputs of different products in batch processes. Seldom-ordered engines, such as a V-8, serve to illustrate this flexible manufacturing system. It even is becoming possible to produce single units of some products—to customize output, in effect—by using modern technology along with equipment usually used in mass production. For example, the Broan Manufacturing Company, which makes more than a million range hoods a year, uses what are called programmable logic controls to produce made-to-order range hoods. These controls, made by Allen-Bradley Corporation, allow Broan to produce hoods 8.7 seconds apart that have completely different shapes, features, colors, and name brands. In another case, the National Institute of Handicapped Research has started a project that will provide orthopedic shoes for people whose feet are different sizes. NASA is involved in the project, in which lasers measure feet "digitally" and computers direct machines to make each shoe a different size so that both fit perfectly.

■ Another new concept, micromachines, promise production that couldn't be done before. The gears, motors, and other components of these machines are so small that they are etched on silicon chips, much like computer chips. In 1988, scientists at the University of California made a motor that was only one-tenth of a millimeter in size. As phenomenal as scientific fiction, machines like these might aid in remote-controlled surgery inside the body without cutting the body open. Other uses include working inside machines and products where hands can't reach and trouble-shooting and repairing in remote or dangerous areas, such as nuclear installations and satellites.

■ Finally, a new term, re-engineering, has been coined in the 1990s to describe what changes are beginning to occur in production that could have dramatic effects on employment, production costs, and living standards.

To start, re-engineering entails a much wider use of work teams, which you encountered in Chapter 2. It also involves "empowerment," where decision-making authority is given to the lowest-level workers as possible—partly because time is saved while waiting for bosses to act (slowly). Finally, and most significantly, re-engineering entails reorganizing assembly lines and offices in countless ways to simplify and speed up work.

Some experts say re-engineering will lead to a loss of a million to 2½ million jobs a year, and a total of 25 million could eventually disappear. This process has just begun, for management consultants claim that no more than 15 percent of firms that produce goods—and very few service firms—have adopted the methods of re-engineering so far. Hardest hit by the job losses are expected to be middle managers of businesses as well as the low-skilled, entry-level workers.

In a decade or two, therefore, skill levels of workers will have to be significantly higher, so a person will find it far more difficult to find a job than today. Some analysts are predicting this to be the biggest social issue in the near future.

Chapter 3 SUMMARY

Firms that mass produce goods and services produce large amounts of output at low costs. This makes relatively low prices possible, which leads to higher living standards.

Firms increase their outputs to larger levels in three ways. First, they can increase a single resource, leaving other resources unchanged. However, such expansion will not continue to increase the efficiency of resource use for long because of a diminishing marginal product. Second, firms can increase all resources at the same rate. If production costs decline with such expansion, firms experience increasing returns to scale. Because of lower production costs, firms tend to become large and engage in mass production. Third, firms can increase all resources at different rates, called an increase in total outlays. If this situation leads to lower production costs, again the firm will probably engage in mass production.

In addition to producing large amounts of output, firms that mass produce also use large-capacity, specialized capital equipment. Mass-production processes depend upon standardization, interchangeable parts, and the continuous production process. Finally, mass production depends upon the existence of mass markets. In turn, such mass markets depend upon efficient transportation and communication systems, low production costs, and low marketing costs.

Besides raising living standards, a shift to a mass-production economy leads to more capital-intensive production techniques, decreases in relative prices of items whose production processes can be innovated, increases in relative prices of other items, such as services, industries dominated by a few large firms, and a labor market increasingly dominated by service jobs.

From colonial times to the present, America shifted from an agrarian economy to a high-tech, industrialized economy. It went through four periods, with mass production dominating the last period. Recent developments in production processes are leading to a "post-industrial economy," including just-in-time manufacturing, flexible manufacturing systems, micromachines, and reengineering.

Chapter 3 RESPONSES TO THE LEARNING OBJECTIVES

1. Output in a production process can be increased by:
   a) increasing the amount of a single resource
   b) increasing the amount of all resources at the same rate
   c) increasing all resources, but each at a separate rate

2. The level of output in a production process where the marginal product falls is the point of diminishing returns.

3. A production process will have:
   a) increasing returns to scale if output increases by more than x percent when all inputs are increased by x percent
   b) constant returns to scale if output increases by x percent when all inputs are increased by x percent
   c) decreasing returns to scale if output increases by less than x percent when all inputs are increased by x percent

4. As a firm increases its level of output, its average cost of production will:
   a) decline if it experiences increasing returns to scale
   b) remain unchanged if it experiences constant returns to scale
   c) increase if it experiences decreasing returns to scale

5. A mass-production economy:
   a) has production processes that are large in scale
   b) makes use of specialized capital equipment
   c) depends upon standardization and interchangeable parts
   d) depends upon the continuous production process
   e) needs mass markets for its products

6. Standardization and interchangeable parts are necessary wherever machines are involved because machines depend upon product uniformity. Well-functioning transportation and communication systems make possible a low cost of marketing to distant markets which, in turn, make mass markets possible.

7. The shift to a mass-production economy has led to:
   a) higher living standards
   b) production processes that are increasingly capital-intensive
   c) decreases in relative prices of items that more readily accommodate mechanization in their manufacture than other items, and vice versa
   d) growth in the size of firms that make products that can be mass produced
   e) increasing domination of the labor market by skilled jobs, with a simultaneous shift from jobs producing goods to jobs producing services

8. Mechanization leads to:
   a) changing relative prices
   b) larger and fewer firms in mechanized industries
   c) the number of firms and laborers that produce services increasing relative to those producing goods

9. Innovation usually reduces the amount of labor and other resources needed to produce items. That results in lower prices for those items, enabling people to buy additional goods and services. Those extra goods and services are usually produced by people who lost their jobs through innovation.

10. The Pre-Industrial Revolution Era was largely agrarian, with any non-agricultural output custom-made in small shops. The Early Industrial Era saw the beginnings of a mass-production economy, but only in a few industries. Transportation and communication systems were poorly developed. The Emergence of Big Business Era witnessed the dominance of the mass production of non-agricultural goods, as well as the establishment of widespread transportation and communication systems. The Modern Business Era extended the mass-production economy, but it also is currently witnessing new managerial and manufacturing techniques.

Chapter 3 LEARNING ACTIVITIES AND DISCUSSION QUESTIONS

1. Do "quick oil and lube" shops have significant increasing returns to scale? If they do, what makes this possible? If they don't, what prevents it?
2. Think of five items that are not mass produced and explain why they are not.
3. Find three examples of standardization and interchangeable parts in your classroom.
4. Why do producers of potatoes find it more difficult to sell at a great distance from where they are located than battery producers?
5. Calculate the relative prices of your school's tuition and one of your favorite foods for today and for 10 years ago. Did they change? If so, why do you think they changed in the way they did?

APPENDIX A THE PRODUCTION FUNCTION

Refer back to Figure 3-1 and Figure 3-2 for a moment. They charted the changes in marginal product and total product as more tons of fertilizer were added to a corn field. Figure A3-1 provides a more general view of a relationship between the inputs of a single resource and the output that results. The curve labelled TP (total product) is called a production function because it shows that production is a "function of" the amount of a resource used to produce it. The curve in the figure shows the production function for only one of the many resources used in the production process, in this case Resource X. There are as many different functions as there are resources that can be varied.

In Figure A3-2, notice that the marginal product curve, labelled MP, rises until it reaches its peak, known as the point of diminishing returns, after which it declines. (Note that the production function, which had been increasing at an increasing rate up to this point, now increases less rapidly.) After MP becomes negative, total product also falls. This is called Stage 3 of the production function. To explain the other two stages requires introducing a new concept, average product. It refers to the amount of output each unit of the variable resource helps to produce, on average. (Generally, labor is considered to be the variable resource, though others could be used.) It is found by dividing total output by the amount of the variable resource used.

Stage 1 of the production function ends where average product reaches its maximum. Graphically, this is the amount of resources used when a tangent line to the production function passes through the origin. It is the point where the amount of output per unit of the variable resource is at a maximum. Stage 2 is the area between that point and the level of inputs where TP is at its maximum.

The first factory in America (on the right), a cotton-spinning mill, built by Samuel Slater in 1790 in Pawtucket, Rhode Island. This water-powered mill employed many single women who lived in the dormitory to the left of the mill.

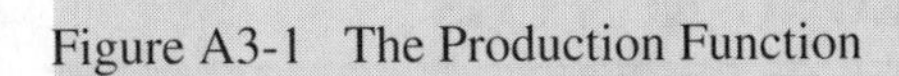
Figure A3-1 The Production Function

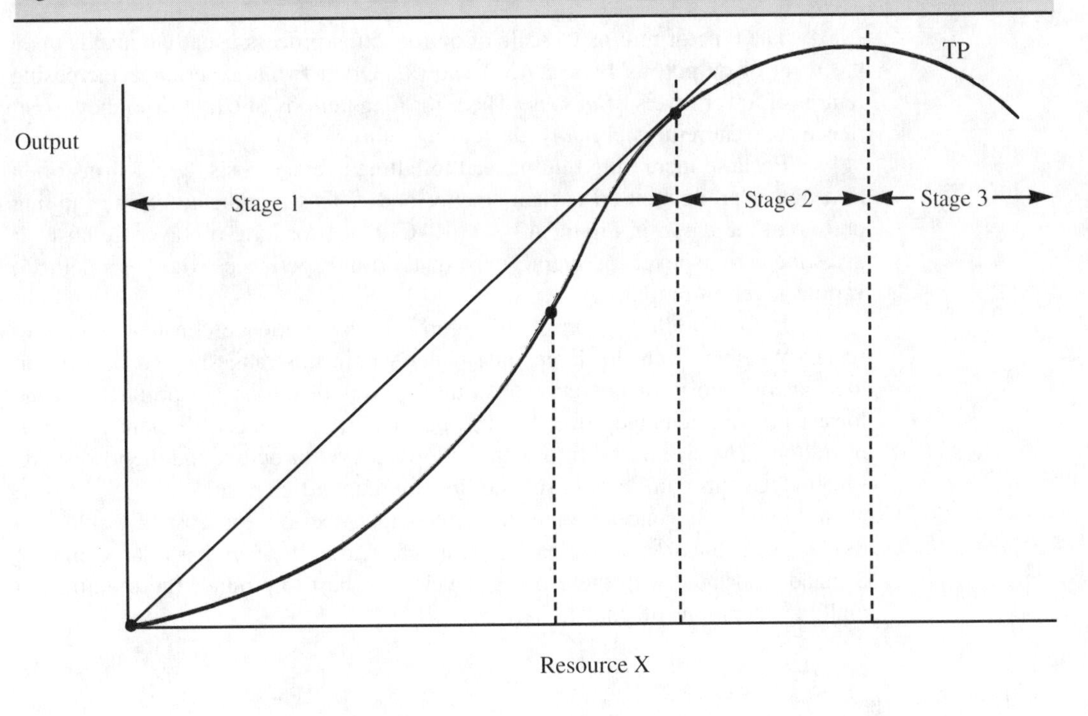

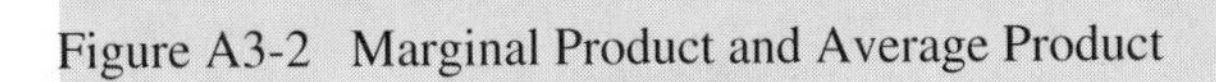
Figure A3-2 Marginal Product and Average Product

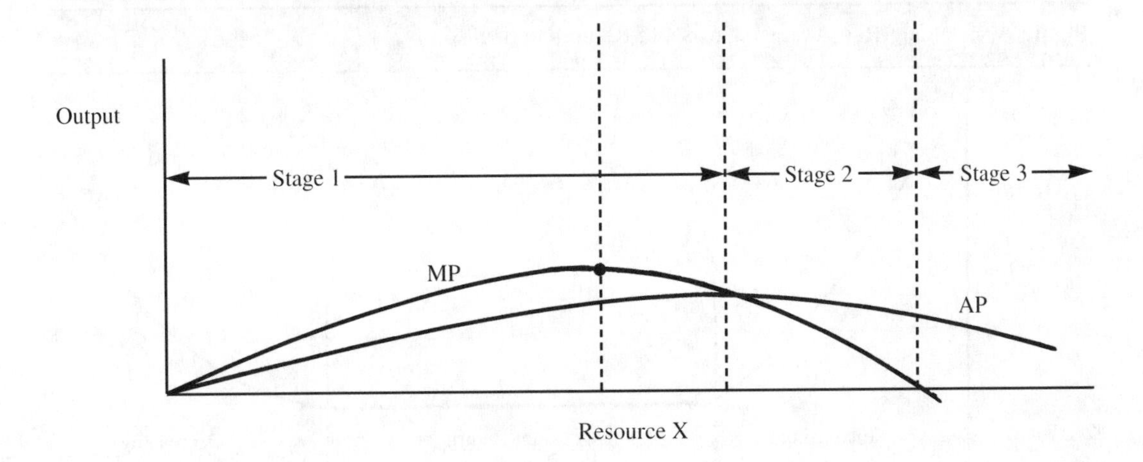

APPENDIX B RETURNS TO SCALE AND LONG-RUN COSTS

The type of returns to scale of a production process usually depends upon the level of output, as Figure A3-3 shows. Often firms experience increasing returns at lower levels of output. Then, for long periods of expansion, they experience constant returns. Finally, decreasing returns set in.

Because increasing returns lead to falling average costs, larger firms often have lower production costs than smaller ones. This is indicated by the falling portion of the curve in Figure A3-3. LRAC stands for long-run average cost. It gives the various levels of average cost that a firm experiences when producing at various levels of output.

In the middle section of the figure, firms experience constant returns to scale. Whether firms are larger or smaller within this range has no bearing on their average costs of operation. As these levels of output are produced at the lowest possible average cost, the firm has achieved its most efficient points of operation. The size of the firm with the lowest level of output and the lowest AC is called the optimum scale of plant or its minimum efficient scale.

Finally, beyond a certain level of output, the average cost of production rises. This is the area of decreasing returns to scale. If a firm has a large enough demand associated with these output levels, it is best to produce these outputs in multiple operations of smaller size.

Figure A3-3 Long-Run Average Costs and Returns to Scale

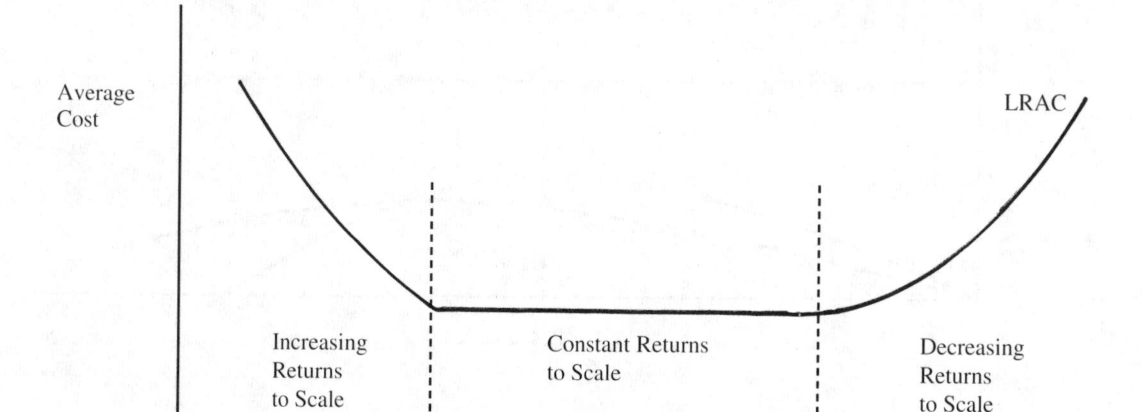

This is a lock on the 185-mile Chesapeake and Ohio Canal, constructed between 1828 and 1850, connecting Georgetown in the District of Columbia and Cumberland, Maryland. Such canals widened the markets for manufacturers by reducing transport costs of their goods.

The Miraflores Locks on the Panama Canal, constructed between 1909 and 1914.

CHAPTER 4

ECONOMIC SYSTEMS

★★★★★ LEARNING OBJECTIVES ★★★★★

1. Explain the purpose of an economic system.
2. Describe the traditional, command, and market economic systems.
3. Explain how each of the Basic Economic Systems answers the three Basic Economic Questions.
4. Differentiate between private and public ownership of resources and give examples of each in the American economy.
5. Describe the two major characteristics of capitalism.
6. Compare pure capitalism with the form of capitalism that exists in the United States and other parts of the world.
7. Describe the two major characteristics of authoritarian socialism.
8. Compare authoritarian socialism with market socialism.
9. Explain the economic meaning of "left" and "right" in the United States and the wider world.
10. Explain the relationship between political parties and the terms liberal and conservative.

TERMS

economic system
Basic Economic Systems
traditional economic system
command economic system
market
private property
private enterprise
public property
public enterprise
capitalism
competition
laissez faire
authoritarian capitalism
authoritarian socialism
communism
centrally directed
Marxist
market socialism
perestroika
mixed economy
liberal
conservative
libertarian

The economic problem—having fewer resources than we need to produce our unlimited wants—forces us to make choices regarding *what* things should be made, *how* they should be produced, and *who* should receive them. These are called the Basic Economic Questions. You learned that a society maximizes its economic welfare by achieving its goals of efficiency, full employment, economic growth, and equitable distribution. It does that by properly answering the Basic Economic Questions.

★1 In this chapter you will see how members of different societies answer these questions. They each use a unique **economic system**—an array of institutions, concepts, and procedures that address the economic problem.

MAJOR CHARACTERISTICS OF AN ECONOMIC SYSTEM

Each country's economic system has two major characteristics. The first is the method used to answer the Basic Economic Questions. The second involves the people who own the resources and produce the goods and services.

★2 There are only three fundamental methods a country can use to answer the What, How, and For Whom to Produce questions. These are the three **Basic Economic Systems**: the traditional, the command, and the market systems. All economies use each of these to a certain extent, but usually one system dominates in a country.

The Traditional Economic System

★3 A nation using the **traditional economic system** answers the Basic Economic Questions the same way each year. The same kinds of goods and services are made (exactly the same style, color, and so on); the same production techniques are used (therefore, there is no innovation); and the same income (and, therefore, the amount of goods and services) goes to each person. Whenever things are done today as before, *specifically because* that is the way they were done before, the traditional economic system is in use.

Although it seems foolish to use a system that guarantees stagnation, it does have a powerful advantage. It guarantees that a society will be safe from failures that might result from innovation. Thus, a decision to follow tradition could be a rational decision to avoid risk in a world of uncertainty. Disaster often has followed innovation. For example, by the mid-1800s, the Irish probably wished they had never changed the answer to What to Produce? to "potatoes rather than wheat" a hundred years earlier. The potato famine, brought on by late blight, a ruinous disease of the potato, led to millions of people dying and millions more emigrating.

Modern industrial societies don't use the traditional system often. Yet, it is used: whenever people buy things (that is, decide What to Produce?) out of habit; when production techniques (How to Produce?) do not change, even though better techniques exist; and when people automatically follow their parents' careers.

The Command Economic System

In a **command economic system**, some individual or group in authority decides what goods and services will be made, how they will be made, and who will get how much of each (their income). These decision makers could be: the whole of society acting by majority rule, appointed or elected officials, or dictators. An ordinary individual has little or no influence in such decisions. In extreme cases, the authority even decides what people will eat and wear, where they will work, travel, and go to school, and how much they will earn.

Every country has at least some elements of a command system. A synonym for a command economy is a central-directed economy because leaders in the (central) government make economic decisions directing or allocating the use of resources. A command economy is also called a planned economy because leaders can plan the use of resources well into the future.

The Market Economic System

A **market** is where people meet to exchange things of value. These include goods, services, resources (such as land or labor), and financial instruments (such as stocks, bonds, and credit).

In a barter system, two things of value are exchanged for each other, such as one good for another good or service. In modern societies, where barter is rare, usually only one thing of value is exchanged for something that *represents* value or, more accurately, represents *the power to purchase* something else of value. That something is money, which gives the holder the power to purchase things of value. Money, in and of itself, has no value. It is useful only when you get rid of it.

A market consists of: 1) a demand side, composed of buyers; and 2) a supply side, composed of sellers. Buyers and sellers voluntarily come to markets to improve their individual economic welfare. Because buyers and sellers seek to improve satisfaction from materialistic goals, they might be considered selfish people. But because such "selfish" moves usually are not designed to hurt others, we might consider most market transactions to be moral. However, although no one is forced to buy or sell anything, well-functioning markets require a certain level of honesty in sellers and buyers.

In a *free* market, buyers and sellers make exchanges voluntarily because exchanges increase the economic welfare of each. Occasionally markets that are *not* free are encountered, where exchanges occur *involuntarily* in "compulsory markets," such as forced labor in a military draft or compulsory community service. Other examples include being forced to wear clothes in public or to attend school until age 16 or 18. These are cases of "restricted markets," where personal freedom is restricted

Opposite to these "compulsory markets" are what are called black markets. These are markets for goods or services that governments forbid to be produced or consumed. Illegally produced alcoholic beverages during Prohibition from 1919 to 1933 was an example. Another is today's market for illegal drugs. Other black markets involve legally sold items, but they are sold at prices other than what the government allows. Examples include concert tickets sold by "scalpers" and food sold at illegally high prices during World War II.

Before exchange voluntarily occurs in free markets, not only must there be buyers and sellers, but there also must be agreement on the rate of exchange—that is, how much of one thing of value trades for the other thing of value. In modern societies, where market participants rarely barter, this rate is known as the price, or the amount of money to be traded for one unit of a good, service, or resource.

Thus, a market exists for an item when there are buyers, sellers, and agreement on a price. If each of these three do not exist for, say, typewriters, then the question, "Shall we produce typewriters?" (a What to Produce question) is answered "no." If all three do exist, the answer is "yes." There is no need to look to the past or to ask the government if it is all right to make or buy typewriters. In a market system, if: 1) some people want to buy something; 2) others want to make it; and 3) a price is agreed upon—it gets made.

How to Produce questions use resource markets for answers. Producers often can make things in different ways by using different resources. For example, manufacturers can stitch coats by hand or with sewing machines. In a market system, the owner or manager of a manufacturing firm examines the price of each resource it could use in making an item. The item is then made in the way that minimizes the cost, which depends upon resource prices. Owners make such decisions in their own self-interests. But this also saves their customers money because lower costs can lead to lower prices. Everyone can win.

The market system answers For Whom to Produce? in a roundabout way. "For Whom" really means who will receive the goods and services, which is determined by income levels. Those having higher incomes will receive more goods and services than others. People, of course, own resources such as labor, land, and capital. These people earn income by selling resources. (Income can be thought of as the power to purchase goods and services, as represented by the money that people are paid.) Thus, in a market system, your income depends upon how many resources you sell as well as the prices of those resources.

This concludes the analysis of the first characteristic of a country's economic system. Next examined is the second characteristic—who owns the resources and does the production. In a modern economy, unlike an economy of self-sufficient individuals, there are two fundamental types of resource ownership: 1) resources can be privately owned; or 2) they can be publicly owned.

Privately Owned Resources

★4

Privately owned resources refer to only capital and natural resources because labor and entrepreneurship always belong to the individual. When there is private ownership of resources—that is, in a system that allows **private property**—only some people own capital equipment or natural resources. Capital equipment could be owned by one person or a group. A group could include several people or thousands, as with ownership of General Motors. It is important to note that the kind of private property considered here involves resources, not consumer goods such as cars, houses, and clothes.

An economy with private property uses the private enterprise system. A **private enterprise** is an organization, usually called a firm, that produces goods and services with privately owned resources in order to improve the economic welfare of the owners. Firms most commonly improve their economic welfare by earning profit, although many firms have additional goals.

Publicly Owned Resources

Public property refers to capital and natural resources that belong to everyone in the society. Public parks, national forests, highways, and public schools are all examples. Individuals cannot sell their share of these resources, possess more than anyone else, or exclude anyone else from using them (with a few exceptions).

Nationalization refers to the takeover of privately owned resources by the public, generally at the central (national) government level. The takeover can be involuntary or voluntary, and the former owners usually receive some payment (but often not, as in revolutions).

The opposite of nationalization is privatization, which occurs when publicly owned resources are sold to private individuals. For example, a city-owned airport such as New York's Kennedy airport could be sold to private investors. In 1992, President Bush made privatization more likely to occur when he issued an executive order allowing states and local governments to sell facilities that were partly financed with federal funds. Privatization also can mean contracting out to private businesses for government services that were previously produced by government enterprises. Examples include garbage pickup, fire protection, and prison operations. Finally, privatization occasionally refers to situations where the government provides a voucher that can be used to buy a good or service at a privately owned business. An example is a school voucher, which is paid for with public tax dollars but can be used to obtain an education in a private school as well as a public one. Sweden began such a system in 1992.

When the public owns resources, **public enterprises** (or government enterprises) produce goods and services with them. The intent is not to improve the economic welfare of individual people through profits as in the private enterprise system, but rather to benefit the entire society. The U.S. Postal Service, public schools, city public works departments, and the U.S. Army are public enterprises.

MAJOR ECONOMIC SYSTEMS

You just learned the two primary characteristics of any society's economy: 1) which Basic Economic System dominates (command or market); and 2) who owns the resources (private individuals or the public). Each characteristic involves an extreme position that a nation can choose. That is, a nation can choose to have either a complete command economy or a complete market economy. Likewise, its resources either can be completely publicly owned, with government enterprises producing all the goods and services, or they all can be privately owned by private enterprises. More realistically, a nation can choose to have any combination of: 1) the command or the market system; and 2) private or public ownership of resources. For example, a country could have three-fourths of its decisions made in markets and one-fourth by the government. Or 60 percent of the resources could be privately owned and 40 percent publicly owned.

In this section we combine both of these characteristics, allowing the placement of all economies into four categories of economic systems: capitalism, authoritarian capitalism, market socialism, and authoritarian socialism. Such categories allow relatively easy comparison of nations' economies. However, no country fits perfectly into any of these categories any more than any country is completely democratic or autocratic. These labels merely mean a country is generally *closest to* one of these models of economic systems.

Capitalism

★5 The economic system of **capitalism**, that of many industrialized nations such as the United States, Canada, and Japan, has two major characteristics: 1) economic decisions about resource use are made in a system of free markets; and 2) privately owned resources are used to produce goods and services by private enterprises or firms.

All people, including owners of firms, face a personal scarcity of time and money. Buyers and sellers alike deal with this problem in market exchanges. Individuals try to maximize their economic welfare by acting in their own self-interest. However, in markets, one seller's gain often causes another seller's loss because the number of buyers is limited. **Competition** refers to the struggles of the market participants for the purpose of maximizing their economic welfare. It is another vital characteristic of capitalism, but it is not a *structural* one as are the two others just mentioned. Competition is not limited to struggles between sellers. Buyers often compete with other buyers for scarce items. Recall from earlier in the chapter that in a *free* market no one has any control over any other market participant or over the price. However, consumers essentially control producers. Producers who don't realize the consumer is king (or "sovereign") in free markets soon become paupers.

It might seem that millions of people, all trying to improve their self-interest, would lead to a destructive free-for-all. In *The Wealth of Nations* in 1776, Adam Smith argued differently. In acting selfishly, he said, each person:

> intends only his own gain, and he is...led by an *invisible hand* to promote an end which was no part of his intention. By pursuing his own interest, he frequently promotes that of the whole society more effectually than when he really intends to promote it.

Thus, selfish people who try to sell things help others, though unintentionally. The reason is that for sellers to become rich, they must be successful at selling. And what sells the best is what buyers want the most—that is, what satisfies them the most.

Sometimes you hear of pure capitalism, in which *no* use would be made of the traditional or command economic system and there would be *no* publicly owned resources. The government neither would produce any good or service nor try to regulate any economic activity. All goods and services—cars, food, education, security (police, etc.), mail delivery, roads, insurance, and so on—would be provided by privately owned firms such as Ford, Del Monte, Pinkerton, UPS, the Blue Ridge Road Corporation, and Allstate. Also, individuals would make economic decisions with no interference by any person or government. People could buy any clothes, drugs, and reading material they wanted, and they could travel anywhere. A government policy that favors such an economy is called **laissez faire**, which means "let the individual be." However, laissez faire does not mean there would be *no* role for government, which, at the least, is needed to issue money. Also, without government private property would be meaningless since each individual would be as free to steal as to buy or sell.

Of course, no country ever has had an economy like that where everyone could do everything they pleased. That would lead to socially unacceptable problems, including pollution, widespread use of automatic weapons in public, and other offensive economic activity, such as bizarre house colors, rampant cocaine consumption, and lewd entertainment. In pure capitalism there also would be no police protection, highways, or public parks. Because such a society is generally unacceptable, people, through government, *do* interfere with the economic decisions of others. Generally this is for the good of the entire society. Yet often such interference is really not to benefit *all* the members of society, but to benefit the ones who interfere. Extremely few people are willing to accept all outcomes of free markets. That is, there are few pure capitalists. Most want to control markets for their own benefit rather than accept free markets.

Authoritarian or Restricted Capitalism

★6

Many nations are called capitalist simply because they have private enterprise systems. But capitalism is not synonymous with private enterprise. Capitalism uses the private enterprise approach to production, along with the *free* market system. Many "capitalist" nations allow private enterprises but have few free markets.

Many of these "capitalist" nations actually have an economic system we might call **authoritarian capitalism**, or, perhaps more accurately, restricted capitalism. Such a system has two major characteristics. First, a nation with such a system has a private enterprise system, as in ordinary capitalism. Second, and in contrast to capitalism, such a nation makes heavy use of the command system to answer the Basic Economic Questions.

Those favoring this system believe that free markets commonly do a poor job of answering the Basic Economic Questions. Often, they say, free markets lead to the making of the wrong goods and services, the use of the wrong production techniques, or an inequitable (unfair) distribution of income. However, they want resources to be privately owned because they believe that private enterprises are more efficient than public enterprises. They believe that huge government monopolies (such as a national steel industry) create such massive bureaucracies that attaining efficiency is impossible.

As with pure capitalism, no such *purely* authoritarian capitalistic economy exists. Nations lie somewhere between the two extremes. Yet there are many examples of nations with *largely* authoritarian or restricted capitalistic systems. National socialism or fascism—of which Nazi Germany was an example—is such a system. Once Hitler came to power, his government dictated much of the production of goods and services, especially those related to the military. Hitler even had a strong influence on the development of a cheap car for the masses, a "peoples (volks) car (wagen)"—the Volkswagen "beetle." Also, what the news media could say or print was largely controlled by the Nazis. But these examples describe only fascism's *economic* system. Its political, religious, and other systems also need description before we have a complete picture, but that is not the intent of this book.

Many countries today, although called capitalist, are really authoritarian capitalistic. Virtually all of Latin America uses the private enterprise system. However, it is difficult if not impossible for many Latin Americans to enter business or certain occupations. Often such restriction takes the form of government red tape, bribery, and the like. In other cases, a rigid class structure prevents upward economic mobility. Equally restrictive is a lopsided political system that denies political power to people with little economic power. As a consequence, a sizable percentage of economic activity is done illegally on the black market. Peru is a good example of an economy with such activity. Taxis, laundries, repair shops, small manufacturers working out of garages and homes, and dozens of other small enterprises constantly risk arrest for such activity. Unfortunately, the small scale of operation of such enterprises prevents the efficiency of mass production. This is a major reason for the failure of such societies to achieve high living standards, in spite of people's willingness to work hard.

South Korea, Taiwan, and Singapore are examples of Pacific Rim nations with authoritarian capitalism that have been more successful economically. An important difference in these countries compared with Latin American countries is the greater ease of entering business.

Another Pacific Rim nation, Japan, is fundamentally capitalistic. But it also has much government involvement, though it is less authoritarian than its neighbors. Its most significant effect is through what is called an industrial policy. Such government policy targets certain industries for expansion and development. The government provides money and other assistance to these industries through various agencies. The best-known of these agencies is the Ministry of International Trade and Industry (MITI), which has been instrumental in the success of Japan's auto and electronics industries.

Two other examples of restricted capitalism occur not because government authorities *directly* restrict economic activity, but because certain individuals are allowed to restrict or alter the activities of others. The first is called unfair competition, which takes many forms. It includes price-fixing by agreements among competitors, false advertising, and below-cost pricing (this enables big firms to drive out smaller ones). The second example of restricted capitalism involves discrimination, which occurs when certain people are denied the right to sell or buy resources, goods, or services in certain markets. For example, for many years it was virtually impossible for blacks or women to enter the medical or legal professions or the construction trades. In many areas, blacks were barred from restaurants and motels until the 1960s.

Finally, a form of authoritarian capitalism that might be called amended capitalism should be noted. Here, although free markets generally are used to answer the Basic Economic Questions, these answers are changed or amended by the government. For example, the income of many people is determined by what they earn in the marketplace *plus* what the government grants them in the form of welfare, subsidies, or tax breaks. Governments also help certain people to increase their incomes by granting privileges that reduce competition between those in particular markets. This includes granting the power to form labor unions or by requiring licenses to enter a profession or business. In these and other cases, justification for such intervention usually centers on the alleged failure of capitalism to provide equity or fairness to people in those markets.

Sweden, Norway, Denmark, Great Britain (until the 1980s), and several other West European nations are examples of significant "amending" of capitalism. Most government intervention into their economies involves For Whom to Produce? (or income distribution). Consequently, these nations often are called welfare states or examples of welfare capitalism. The term capitalism still fits them because a large share of the output of goods and services still is produced by private enterprises. However, many people (incorrectly) call them socialist.

Authoritarian Socialism

Much of the world's population lives in socialist economies. However, there are several forms of socialism, and this section and the next will divide them into two major groups. The first is **authoritarian socialism** (or **communism**). Its first characteristic is the public ownership of resources. In this system, government or public enterprises, rather than private enterprises, produce goods and services. Socialists believe that private property contributes to large and inequitable income differences and, consequently, to conflict between the upper and lower classes.

★7

Karl Marx and Frederich Engels wrote of this class struggle in their *Communist Manifesto* in 1848, a time of revolution throughout Europe. They wrote of the struggle between the workers (the proletariat) and the business owners (the capitalists). Because they thought workers would never get their fair share of the output of any capitalist economy, revolution was the only answer. The *Manifesto* ended with:

> The proletarians have nothing to lose but their chains. They have a world to win. Workingmen of all countries, unite!

In his book *Das Kapital,* Marx argued that capitalists robbed laborers of their output. He maintained that all economic value embodied in products came from the efforts of laborers and that the owners of capital paid workers only a fraction of their value. Thus, he believed that laborers were exploited and would face increasing misery as capitalism developed. Eventually, workers would tolerate their miserable condition no longer and would revolt.

In Marx's vision, after the revolution a "dictatorship of the proletariat" would emerge, in which the workers would exercise control through the state. After all elements of capitalism were wiped out, the state would "wither away," leaving a classless and communistic (communal) society. Once the concept of profit was gone, all economic decisions would be made for the benefit of the community, not necessarily for the individual. This meant a basic change in attitude from self-interest to putting the interest of society first. In such a society, Marx said, workers would produce as much as they could but would consume only what they needed. Thus, the communist doctrine, coined by Louis Blanc: "*from* each according to his ability, *to* each according to his needs."

The Shaker communities of the Northeast, which achieved their peak popularity in the early 1800s, were excellent examples of societies based upon such principles. All actions were to be made in the best interest of the entire community, regardless of the effect on the individual. The Shakers were very industrious and invented many items, not to increase their wealth, but to free up time for worship. Their inventions include the clothespin, the circular saw, the flat broom, and the chair castor.

This brings up the second characteristic of authoritarian socialism: the Basic Economic Questions are answered collectively by a government body that acts for all the members of society. Decisions regarding resource use (What?, How?) and income distribution (For Whom?) are **centrally directed** (answered) rather than individually directed as in a system of free markets. Theoretically, because all decision making and property ownership is communal, the best interests of all are met.

Until the 1989-1992 period, many countries were labelled **Marxist**, including the Soviet Union, East Germany and all the other East European countries, Mongolia, Nicaragua, Angola, and a few others. Today, China, North Korea, and Vietnam still call themselves Marxist. However, none of these nations had (or have, in the case of China, North Korea, and Vietnam) much resemblance to the plan of Marx. Workers, whether on farms, in offices, in factories, or in mines, had little voice in economic decision making. Instead, non-democratically elected officials decided the answers to at least the major economic questions, such as the output level of food, steel, autos, and coal, as well as income levels of all citizens, and sometimes where people worked. These nations still called themselves communist. They still said they wanted to provide an adequate living standard with no major class differences and with freedom from economic hardship for all. Surprisingly, communists said members of their society had more freedom than people in capitalist nations. This was true in that their citizens theoretically had *freedom from* the economic worries of our citizens—unemployment, poverty, and so on. But we, on the other hand, have the *freedom to* engage in economic activities denied their citizens.

Market Socialism

Like pure capitalism, purely authoritarian socialist economies have some severe problems. Because individuals are not rewarded for being exceptionally innovative or productive, such economies do not have high economic growth rates. People with good ideas, which may take great effort to implement, often don't bother with the effort. They also are likely to resent sharing the benefits of their ideas with others, or not being allowed to make many economic decisions for themselves.

★8 However, because many people do prefer the public ownership of resources, a hybrid of capitalism and communism, called **market socialism**, appeals to them. In this system, the public owns the resources (and government enterprises produce things) and the What, How, and For Whom questions rely upon the market system for answers. Oskar Lange, a Polish economist, presented a strong case for a form of market socialism in his 1939 book, *The Economic Theory of Socialism.*

Although firms are government (publicly) owned, government authorities do not decide what goods and services to make. Individual buyers do, acting in their self-interest in markets where the sellers happen to be public enterprises. Yet, although different from capitalistic sellers who own their businesses, the sellers act like capitalists in trying to promote their self-interest. That is because *several* government enterprises make each kind of good or service. The more successful a particular enterprise is, the higher the income for its managers and workers. Therefore, using the market to answer For Whom to Produce? forces managers and workers to be concerned about the answers to the What and How questions—and, supposedly, to serve their customers better in terms of product design, quality, and prices.

As with capitalism, there is little role for government central control in the pure form of market socialism. Even prices are determined without government intervention. There also is much personal economic freedom, which satisfies those who value such freedom. However, no country has ever remotely approached this pure state. Yugoslavia (before it broke up in 1991) often is cited as an example of an economy that came the closest.

A BRIEF HISTORY OF MODERN SOCIALIST ECONOMIES

After World War II, the West, including the United States, Canada, and Western Europe, faced a new enemy or challenge. Communist nations, led by the Soviet Union and China, were a threat to our economic and political systems.

Soviet Premier Nikita Khrushchev, who more than 30 years ago boasted, "We will bury you," stoked the fires of the Cold War. He did not mean it literally or in a military sense, but rather that their *system* would replace ours. The nuclear arms race, the McCarthy communist hunts of the early 1950s, the Korean War, the Vietnam War, the Iron Curtain, and the James Bond films were all part of the antagonism between the communists and the capitalists.

Remarkable changes occurred in many of these nations throughout the 1980s and early 1990s. China, Vietnam, North Korea, and Cuba are the only significant communist economies left—and Cuba is tottering.

The Soviet Union and Its Breakup

The Soviet Union was born in October 1917, when the Bolshevik Revolution, led by Nikolai Lenin, established a Marxist regime in a backward Russia. The revolution was remarkable in that Russia was largely agricultural, not the industrial state of exploited laborers where Marx expected revolt to originate. The spreading revolution and subsequent conquests of other regions and countries ultimately led to the 15 republics of the Soviet Union we knew until the late 1980s. Josef Stalin took over as leader following Lenin's death in 1924 and ruled until his own death in 1953. He was very successful in building the Soviet Union into a modern industrial economy by stressing the production of capital goods and restricting the production of consumer goods. The course and outcome of World War II might have been quite different had the Soviet Union not been our ally.

Later leaders, including Khrushchev and Leonid Brezhnev, did place greater emphasis on consumer goods so that Soviets could live more like people in the West. But although it had abundant natural resources and relatively well-educated laborers, the vast nation did not come close to the living standards of the West. Many people, both inside and outside of the Soviet Union, blamed this on its strong, central-directed economy. Until recently, all major and many minor production decisions came from leaders in Moscow. Factory managers were given production quotas to meet, and they were not allowed to try new production methods. Workers' wages also were determined in Moscow, and it was almost impossible to fire inefficient workers.

In addition, the Reagan administration in the United States began a major military buildup in the early 1980s and also pushed for the Strategic Defense Initiative (or "Star Wars"), a missile-defense system. Many experts believe that the Soviet Union could not afford to match our increases in military expenditure as well as provide the consumer goods its citizens demanded.

In 1985, a new Soviet leader, Mikhail Gorbachev, immediately pushed for reforms in the system to increase efficiency, called *uskoreniye* or accelerated production. In addition to asking workers to work harder, he promoted **perestroika**—a plan for restructuring the entire Soviet economy. In 1986 and 1987, changes were mandated in order to: 1) increase competition between enterprises for the benefit of consumers; 2) shut down inefficient enterprises; 3) consider profits as a measure of success, to be used as managers decide; 4) base salaries partly on the success of an enterprise; 5) appoint managers on the basis of performance; and 6) permit individuals and families to operate privately owned, consumer-oriented businesses in 29 specified areas. The Cooperative Law, passed in May 1988, gave groups of people the right to set up private businesses, much like limited partnerships in the United States. Also in 1988, individual farmers were given the right to lease (but not own) land from the state, to buy equipment, and to hire workers.

The year 1989 was a watershed year for the Soviet Union. Ethnic unrest in several republics and secessionist threats by the Baltic republics of Lithuania, Latvia, and Estonia caused political troubles. Shortages of consumer goods increased, forcing long waits in lines. Boris Yeltsin and other political leaders berated Gorbachev for not "restructuring" fast enough to achieve a market economy. Yeltsin called for mass selloffs of state-owned housing, conversion of state-owned enterprises into joint-stock (private) companies, elimination of government subsidies for such items as sugar and meat, and removal of price controls. On the other hand, Gorbachev faced resistance to *perestroika* from "hard-liners," who wanted to preserve the strong central control of the economy, or even to strengthen it.

In March 1989, Gorbachev pushed through a measure to give farmers the right to own land. The ruble (Soviet currency) was devalued (see page 212) and plans were made for it to be convertible to foreign currencies. Several attempts were made to remove government control of prices, including plans to remove the subsidies given to state-owned enterprises. In March 1990, individuals were given the right to own businesses and produce goods and services without the consent of the state.

Disgusted with the lack of progress, Yeltsin resigned from the Communist Party in July 1990, and several high-ranking followers announced plans to set up an independent party to oppose the communists. In August 1990, Gorbachev decided to work with Yeltsin, and soon afterward they agreed to dismantle the central planning system by early 1992.

In October 1990, Gorbachev and his economist, Stanislaw Shatalin, proposed a 500-day, four-stage plan to move away from the centrally planned, state-ownership economy. First, the budget deficit and the money supply would be cut, and the output of consumer goods and agricultural goods would be increased. Second, prices on about 70 percent of goods and services would be set by competitive forces, and small private businesses would be encouraged. Third, a free market for housing would be established, and a modern banking system would be set up. Fourth, government monopolies would end in many industries, and the ruble would trade freely with other world currencies. Yeltsin attacked the plan as too little and too slow. He threatened to proceed with his own more radical plan for the Russian republic alone. Nevertheless, by November, Gorbachev caved in to the hard-liners and abandoned the plan.

In August 1991, the still-unsatisfied hard-liners tried to oust Gorbachev in a coup. It failed, largely through the efforts of Yeltsin, who faced down tanks at his Moscow headquarters. After the coup, Yeltsin's strength grew, while that of Gorbachev and the hard-liners collapsed. By December 1991, the Soviet Union had broken up into 15 separate republics, 11 of which formed a loose confederation (The Confederation of Independent States, or CIS), and Gorbachev was out of power.

The coup's failure, which removed any significant opposition, allowed Yeltsin and his followers to finally move Russia, the largest of the republics, toward a market economy. Thus, 1992 was a very eventful year for Russia. It also showed the world how difficult it was to do what was never done before—changing an authoritarian socialist economy into a capitalist one.

Yeltsin chose Yegor Gaidar to be his economic minister in this plunge into the unknown. The first shock was the decontrol of most consumer prices on January 1, 1992. Prices zoomed up immediately from 200 to 1,200 percent, the penalty for years of low national output and abundant rubles in Russian pockets. (By the end of 1992, overall prices had risen 2,000 percent and were still climbing at 25 percent per month.) Because wages, still largely set by the government, did not rise, real incomes plummeted and destitutes, beggars, and thieves became familiar sights.

Next, the government allowed the prices of raw materials used by businesses as well as wages to be set by competitive forces. They soon skyrocketed as did, in turn, the production costs of everything. Many enterprises, still state-owned, couldn't raise their prices high enough (for legal or competitive reasons), forcing them to lose vast amounts of money. They began to close their doors instead of operating at a loss, and industrial output plummeted 20 percent in the year. The International Labor Organization estimated that the unemployment rate would be 15 percent or more by the end of 1992. In a country where no one had unemployment compensation, this was traumatic. Moreover, the falling value of the ruble wiped out the value of any savings (the ruble fell from over a dollar to less than a penny in a few months).

In April 1992, many Western nations, including the United States, put together a $24 billion aid package to Russia. This was done partly for purely selfish reasons—no one wants a collapsing economy leading to a civil war where nuclear weapons are exploded. This package took the form of loans to buy scarce consumer goods, to provide humanitarian aid, to defer loan payments, and to stabilize the rate of exchange of the ruble.

The ruble was made fully convertible to other international currencies in August 1992. That was an important move to spur foreign investment in Russia. Until then, a foreign company could not take its profits out of Russia because the ruble profits could not be converted to the company's national currency.

August 1992 also saw the abolishment of the communist distribution system, where state enterprises used to get raw materials from state supplies. Now firms have to obtain supplies by contracting with other firms.

The auctioning off of small shops to private owners began early in 1992. By December 1992, 14,000 shops out of a total of 122,000 had been sold. The privatization of large state enterprises was delayed until late 1992. It was a two-step process, with employees involved first and then the general public. Companies were given two paths to private ownership. First, managers and workers could obtain a 51 percent ownership by paying a certain amount for the shares of the firm. Second, by paying a lower price, they could get a 49 percent ownership and have fewer voting rights. Thus, they would sacrifice control. On October 1, each of 148 million Russian citizens became eligible for a 10,000-ruble voucher that could be used to purchase shares in the approximately 22,000 firms that were being sold. People who didn't wish to purchase shares could sell the vouchers to others who would then use them to buy the shares. By the end of 1992, the rest of the shares of the firms were to be sold for either cash or vouchers. But by July 1993, only 2,620 (or 12 percent) of the enterprises had been auctioned off. This only represented firms with at least 1,000 employees.

In October 1992, Yeltsin issued a decree that permitted the sale of land for these vouchers. However, Russia still will have some public property, including defense plants, pipelines, forest resources, and municipal property.

In November 1992, property rights were given to approximately 100 million Russians who had been holders of small plots of land, usually about 6,400 square feet in size. Almost all workers on state-owned farms had such plots on which they grew food. Many city dwellers also had plots outside of town, often with a country home, called a *dacha.* About one-third of Russia's food was raised on these plots. The new law removed the requirement that a plot had to be held for 10 years after acquisition. It grants free ownership to those with standard-size plots and requires payment for larger plots.

Yeltsin suffered a severe setback in his reform plans in December 1992. He failed in his attempt to have his economic minister, Yegor Gaidar, appointed as prime minister. He was overruled by the Congress of People's Deputies, the legislature established under the former Soviet Union and which was largely comprised of old communists. Many of the deputies were upset with Gaidar's "shock therapy" for the economy, especially the pains suffered by those whose factories were shut down. Yeltsin then accepted a compromise for his prime minister in Viktor Chernomyrdin. Although Chernomyrdin is not opposed to reform, he does not share Gaidar's passion for free markets and private ownership.

In January 1993, Chernomyrdin disheartened many pro-capitalists when he extended price controls on a range of basic goods, including basic foodstuffs and medicines. Profits of manufacturers were limited to between 10 and 25 percent of revenue. He also criticized Gaidar's abandonment of many of the large but inefficient enterprises. Yet, he sought to calm critics by saying, "There is no talk about a backtrack from reforms aimed at a socially oriented market economy. (But) there is another question. How to go forward without breaking your neck?" He did commit himself to privatization, hoping to complete it by the end of 1993.

The most worrisome problem threatening Russia's move forward was hyperinflation, which accelerated to nearly 60 percent in January. Consequently, Deputy Prime Minister for Finance, Boris Fyodorov, announced a plan to curb inflation. The budget deficit would no longer be financed by printing money, and the government would no longer bail out inefficient enterprises.

In July 1993, in an additional bold anti-inflation move that Fyodorov opposed, Yeltsin issued a decree that all ruble currency issued before 1993 was to cease being legal tender (usable as money). Citizens had until August 31 to trade up to 100,000 of pre-1993 rubles for new ones. In effect, the money supply would be reduced, as well as inflationary pressures.

In September 1993, Yeltsin disbanded Russia's parliament, heavily comprised of old communists that resisted his reforms, and called for new elections in December 1993. After barricading themselves in the parliament building for two weeks, Yeltsin used police and tanks to remove them.

It will be years, perhaps decades, before we know if Russia can achieve its transition to capitalism and match the West in living standards. It is not alone in such a transition. Each of its East European former communist neighbors, from East Germany to Bulgaria, is taking a similar route. Even Vietnam is allowing the expansion of private enterprises and freer markets—part of what North Vietnam and the Viet Cong fought to eliminate. In addition, many non-communist economies are shedding themselves of state-owned firms and elements of command in their economies. Mexico has sold 900 state-owned firms. India is struggling to shake off 45 years of red tape, high tariffs, and inefficient state enterprises. Finally, many African nations are selling state-owned assets in a reversal of the nationalization of the 1960s that followed the end of colonial rule.

China, the Last Major Marxist Economy

China was pitifully poor, underdeveloped, and backward when Mao Tse-tung completed his communist revolution in 1949. Mao made great efforts to create a classless society where everyone would make decisions in the best interest of all of China, even if that meant personal sacrifice. In that sense, China came closer to the communist ideal than the Soviet Union did, since the Soviets made heavier use of incentives. China has achieved a dramatic increase in living standards. It is self-sufficient in food production, and its citizens receive free education and medical care. Employment is guaranteed.

Yet, in China's earlier communist years, its citizens suffered great restrictions on their freedoms. People were commonly assigned jobs and careers, often in locations not of their choosing. The Cultural Revolution of the 1960s forced millions of well-educated people to work on farm communes in order to "cleanse them" of non-revolutionary thought. People often were forced to stay in their hometowns because they could not get food ration coupons anywhere else.

The highly antagonistic relationship between the United States and China was a major part of the Cold War. But the relationship greatly improved following President Nixon's trip to China in 1972. It got better after Deng Xiaoping replaced Mao, who died in 1976. Deng instituted many reforms that have moved China away from the communist model. Privately owned small businesses were encouraged, and 27 million people worked in such businesses by 1992. The rural communes were broken up and replaced by private ownership. Workers now are rewarded if they are more productive. State-owned enterprises were granted the power to determine their own prices and output levels.

Consequently, by the late-1980s, China had a much wider variety of goods and services, a rapidly rising living standard, as well as a growing entrepreneurial class with high incomes. However, signs of class struggle, rising materialism, and crime, "decadence," and similar "capitalist problems" gave some leaders second thoughts about such reforms. In October 1988, the Central Committee, China's ruling body, decided to return to somewhat more central control of the economy. The June 1989 massacre of students demonstrating for democratic reforms in Tiananmen Square precipitated even more moves to central control. New tax rules strictly limit the earnings of private business owners. Under "reasonable" profit guidelines, 52 percent of profits go to the state and another 30 percent must stay in a business. By 1990, the government had closed 2.2 million private enterprises. The People's Daily newspaper warned, "Political regimes that are based on private economies breed all forms of corruption."

However, in March 1991, Premier Li Peng said that although China will continue central planning through the year 2000, enterprises will gradually be moved toward the market system. In early 1992, Deng began to campaign hard for further market reforms. The National Party Congress, held every five years, endorsed the reforms in October 1992. However, fearful of sounding like capitalists, the congress adopted a slogan of "Building a socialist market economy"—an economic system no one had ever heard of before, but one which looked suspiciously close to capitalism.

THE ECONOMIC SPECTRUM AND POLITICAL ECONOMY

We tend to use words as labels for philosophies and the people who hold them, especially politicians and those interested in public affairs. Examples include: left, right, middle-of-the-road, moderate, liberal, libertarian, conservative, radical, red, pink, reactionary, Democrat, and Republican. Of course, the terms involve more than economics, but economics dominates their meanings. This section is a brief introduction to them.

The Economic Spectrum

★9

People use the terms "left" and "right" more than any other to differentiate between the economic systems of different countries. Left and right, of course, indicate two directions in which you can move. Similarly, you learned that a nation's economic system has two characteristics that can "move" in two directions. First, resources can become more publicly owned or more privately owned as we travel between countries. Second, the Basic Economic Questions can be answered more frequently with the command system or the market system as we cross borders.

Left and right have somewhat different economic meanings when applied to the world and to the United States, but usually only in degree. A leftist in the United States might not hold the same beliefs as a leftist in Germany. Let us begin by examining what left and right mean in the world approach. Both left and right actually have two uses, as implied above. First, a nation of the left (or a leftist nation) primarily uses government enterprises to produce goods and services. Private property is rare (or even non-existent). Second, a leftist nation makes heavy use of the command system in deciding What? How? and For Whom to Produce? Because the degree to which a nation uses public enterprises (rather than private enterprises) can vary, the degree to which a nation is to the left can vary. Similarly, the degree to which a nation is to the left also can vary with the degree that it uses the command economic system. When we say a nation is to the left of another, we generally mean that it uses more government enterprises to produce goods and services. We might also mean that its government has more of a voice in economic decisions. Of course, this all means that it is an authoritarian socialist economy. But remember that it can vary the degree of authority it exercises.

Conversely, a nation of the right has an economy in which heavy, if not almost exclusive, use is made of the private enterprise system. Less commonly, the term right indicates heavy use of the market economic system, with little government intervention in economic decision making.

Each of the two characteristics that describe an economic system has two extremes. Consequently, there are four primary types of economies on "the economic spectrum." If a nation is not near any of the extreme positions—that is, if it has a fairly equal use of public and private enterprise and neither the command nor the market system dominates—we call it a **mixed economy**.

Refer to Figure 4-1, which helps to show the relationship of each of the economic systems to one another. Note that along the top of the diagram a "left-right spectrum" or continuum appears. Directly beneath the word "Left" are the words "More Use of Public Enterprise," which, of course, is what left means in political economy. Below that, in the main large rectangle, note that both "Market Socialism" and "Authoritarian Socialism" appear. That's because both systems make heavy use of public enterprises. Conversely, below "Right" is "More Use of Private Enterprise." Because both forms of capitalism fit that description, both those terms appear on the right side of the main large rectangle. Now look on the left side of the diagram, where another "left-right spectrum" appears. Here, left means that a nation makes "More Use of the Command System." Of course, that includes nations having authoritarian socialist and authoritarian capitalist systems. Conversely, nations of the right, which make "More Use of the Market System," include nations with market socialist and capitalist systems.

Finally, mixed economies fall in the middle section. Neither the private nor the public enterprise systems dominate those economies, nor do the market or

Figure 4-1 The Economic Spectrum

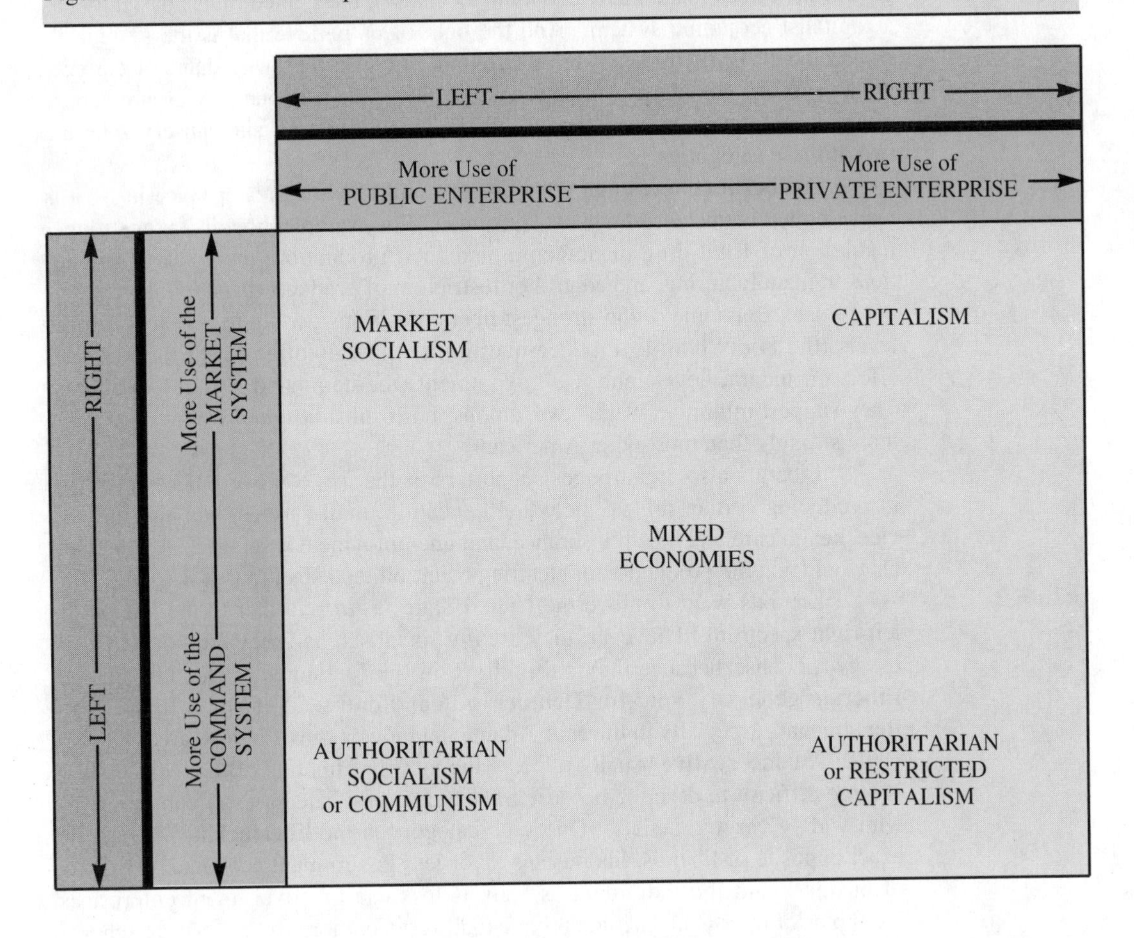

the command systems. As there are no "pure" capitalist or communist economies, all economies are really mixed economies. But the term "mixed economy" is best reserved for nations with a fairly even mix of resource ownership forms and the use of markets vs. central planning. Examples include India, Egypt, and many other less-developed nations. The Canadian health care system is a small example of how a mixed system can be structured. Many medical clinics in Canada are privately owned. However, prices for medical services are set by the government, which also operates the insurance system.

The Political Economy of the United States

Political economy refers to issues and concepts in which politics and economics cannot be separated. Campaign platforms and policy statements of political parties contain heavy reference to economic issues. How, then, do political parties and other groups concerned with our economic system differ on economic issues?

Although the United States does have some public enterprises and the government does make many economic decisions, the United States basically has a capitalist economic system. And the bulk of us believe that is the system we *should* have. But Americans have different views on the exact shape of our economic system. People who wish to change that system in one way or another are often placed in categories and are labelled as such. Liberals and conservatives are two of these categories

A **liberal** believes that government should have a greater voice in what is made, how it is made, and what is consumed. For example, liberals favor stronger regulation of legal drug manufacture and food production, more safety precautions in manufacturing, and control or restriction of products that could be dangerous to use. But some of the strongest liberal positions pertain to people's income levels (the For Whom to Produce question). Liberals often reject the market's effect on income levels and use government (the command system) to alter it. They support minimum wage laws, unions, farm subsidies, and welfare programs more strongly than most other Americans.

Liberals also are stronger supporters of the use of government enterprise in producing certain things, including education, mail service, bus and rail service, health care and health insurance, and unemployment insurance. A few liberals would add the production of electric power, oil, and steel to that list.

★10

Liberals want to move the United States a *little* farther to the left on the left-right spectrum. However, they are *not* socialists, and they are not leftists in the *world* sense because they still believe in the fundamental capitalist model. Liberals generally vote for Democratic candidates. Yet some liberals are Republicans, especially in the Mid-Atlantic and lower New England areas.

A **conservative** usually opposes the views of liberals. But a conservative is more difficult to describe because there are several categories of conservatives, with widely varying beliefs. One such category is the **libertarian**. Almost the exact opposite of liberals, libertarians favor less government economic regulation of business and the individual as well as less use of government enterprises. Examples of their goals include private mail service, more (or all) private schools, and city services contracted to private firms. They also favor eliminating or restricting labor unions, as well as licenses to enter occupations, price controls, and many health, public retirement, and welfare programs. Libertarians want to move us to the right, so they are called right-wingers. Essentially, they believe that we should be more capitalistic. They usually vote either Republican or Libertarian (if their state has a Libertarian party).

Another major type of conservative is the traditional conservative, often simply called a conservative. Like libertarians, most traditional conservatives prefer somewhat less government control of the *economy*. However, many of them want *more* government control over other matters, including religious practices, drug use, sexual practices, abortion, and speech. Their goal is to promote a better society based upon traditional (long-standing) norms and values.

Finally, "moderates" and "middle-of-the-roaders" are not eager to move the nation either left or right. Such people find homes in either the Democratic or Republican parties, and often affiliate with neither. As this group is the largest of all, it is vital at election time, for these people often can be persuaded to move a bit in either direction and thereby swing elections.

A Final Note on Labels

The collapse of communism has introduced confusion regarding the use of left, right, conservative, and liberal because they have the opposite meaning when applied to those changing economies. For instance, the "hard-liners" in Russia (those who oppose moves toward capitalism) are called conservatives and right-wingers. This actually does make sense in that they want to *conserve* the system they had for over 70 years. And those who wish to move toward capitalism, such as Russia's Yeltsin and China's Deng, are called liberals and left-wingers.

Chapter 4 SUMMARY

The purpose of economic systems is to help societies deal with the problem of resource scarcity. All economic systems are based on three Basic Economic Systems: the traditional, the command, and the market systems.

The economies of nations differ in two primary ways: 1) to the degree that their resources are privately or publicly owned; and 2) to the degree to which they use the command and the market economic system.

Capitalism is an economic system that combines the private ownership of resources with the use of the market system to answer the Basic Economic Questions. It is based upon a society of individuals, all seeking to maximize their own economic welfare in a competitive framework. All capitalist societies modify the capitalist model to varying degrees through government intervention. There are some very restricted capitalist economies. Although these are called private enterprise systems, they are not free enterprise systems and are better termed as authoritarian capitalism.

There are several variants of socialism, though all have resources largely or completely owned by the public. Communism or authoritarian socialism makes heavy use of the command system to make economic decisions. Alternatively, market socialism allows the market system to direct resource allocation in most areas, which gives people more freedom in the economy.

The Soviet Union, which existed from 1917 to 1991, was the most important communist economy. It is still in the process of switching to a capitalist economy. China, the other major communist state, is also making strong moves toward a capitalist economy.

Many countries have mixed economies, in which none of these systems dominate. They often have been international pawns in the confrontation between the strongest capitalist and socialist states, such as the United States and the former Soviet Union.

Each nation constantly changes its economic system. In capitalist nations, liberals wish to move their nation further away from the pure capitalist model. Yet, virtually all liberals strongly prefer the basic capitalist model over the socialist model. Conservatives wish to move somewhat closer to the pure capitalist model. However, there are two broad categories of conservatives—libertarians and traditional conservatives. In the United States liberals generally vote Democratic and conservatives generally vote Republican.

Chapter 4 RESPONSES TO THE LEARNING OBJECTIVES

1. An economic system is designed to assist members of society in dealing with a scarcity of resources.

2. In a traditional economic system, all economic decisions are made exactly as they were in the past. In a command system, government authorities make economic decisions about resource use. In a market system, individuals make decisions about resource use in their own self-interest.

3. *In a traditional economic system*: a) goods and services produced today are identical to those of the past; b) production process do not change over time; c) individuals and families have the same incomes over the years. *In a command economic system, government authorities:* a) select the goods and services to be made; b) determine the production processes to be followed; c) establish the income levels of all individuals. *In a market economic system:* a) individuals decide which goods and services to produce by purchasing or refusing to purchase items; b) firms select the production processes by finding the markets with the least costly resources; c) people receive goods and services in relation to what they earned from selling resources in markets.

4. Privately owned resources are owned by one person, several people, or even thousands, but always fewer than the total population. Examples include farmland and the capital equipment of privately owned businesses. Publicly owned resources are owned equally by all citizens in the governmental unit. Examples include city parks, state universities, and federal highways.

5. Under capitalism, resources are privately owned, and economic decisions are made by individuals in a system of free markets, with a minimum of government intervention.

6. In pure capitalism, the government owns no resources and makes no economic decisions. In the United States, various governments own resources, produce some services, and regulate many markets. In other nations, such government involvement is much greater, even when they are still called capitalist economies.

7. Under authoritarian socialism, most or all resources are publicly owned, and most decisions about resource use are made by government authorities.

8. Communist economies have virtually complete government ownership of resources and government production of goods and services. Also, individuals make no major economic decisions in marketplaces. Under market socialism, resources also are publicly owned, but governments make few major decisions about the use of resources, leaving that to individuals in relatively free markets.

9. On a worldwide basis, a "leftist" is someone who prefers a socialist economy, and a "rightist" is someone who prefers a capitalist economy. In the United States, both people on the left and the right prefer capitalism to socialism, but "leftists" want to move the country further away from pure capitalism, and "rightists" want to move closer to pure capitalism.

10. Liberals tend to vote Democratic, and conservatives tend to vote Republican or Libertarian.

Chapter 4 LEARNING ACTIVITIES AND DISCUSSION QUESTIONS

1. Give two examples of how the traditional, command, and market systems are used to answer each of What, How, and For Whom to Produce?
2. List five examples of privately owned property and publicly owned property in your community that is used in producing goods and services. If the ownership were reversed in each case, what would be some of the problems or benefits?
3. Ask five people who are *not* taking an economics class to give the two major structural characteristics of capitalism. How close were they to the correct answer?
4. List five changes that occurred in the economy in your lifetime that might be considered as proof that we are becoming more socialistic. Also, do the reverse. That is, try to prove that we are less likely of becoming socialistic.
5. Ask ten fellow students to categorize themselves as socialist, liberal, moderate, or conservative. Do the results tell you anything about the economy in which they grew up?

CHAPTER 5

DEMAND, SUPPLY, AND PRICES IN MARKETS

★★★★★ LEARNING OBJECTIVES ★★★★★

1. List the major factors that influence how much of a good or service that consumers wish to purchase.
2. Explain why the law of demand is followed by buyers.
3. Compare and contrast elastic and inelastic demands with respect to buyer responsiveness to price changes and the effects on total revenue.
4. Describe what happens when there is a change in demand and list some reasons why it might occur.
5. List the factors that influence how much of a good or service that sellers offer to sell.
6. Explain why the law of supply is followed by sellers.
7. Describe what happens when there is a change in supply and list some reasons why it might occur.
8. Explain why prices tend to change when there are shortages and surpluses.
9. Explain the four reasons why the equilibrium conditions might not be reached.
10. Determine how equilibrium price and quantity will change if there is a change in demand or supply.

TERMS

price
substitute good
complementary good
law of demand
substitution effect
income effect
demand
elasticity of demand
elastic
inelastic
total revenue
change in demand
increase in demand
decrease in demand
law of supply
supply
change in supply
increase in supply
decrease in supply
shortage
equilibrium price
equilibrium quantity
surplus
cartel
price ceiling
price floor

The Basic Economic Questions can be answered with a system of markets, where buyers and sellers of goods, services, and resources come to make exchanges with money in order to increase their economic welfare. The **price** is the rate of exchange of money for one unit of what is sold. For a market to exist for anything, there must be buyers, sellers, and agreement on a price.

How the market system determines prices is the subject of this chapter. You also will learn what makes prices change. First explored is the buyer's side of the market, known as demand, followed by the seller's side, known as supply. Finally, you will learn how the interactions of demand and supply determine price.

The price system provides signals to all participants in a market economy. Such signals direct economic activity, so the price system is at the core of wise decision making in economic affairs.

Supply and demand analysis also explains some paradoxes. For instance, water is one of the most valuable things imaginable. Without it, we die. But the price of a glass of it is virtually zero, proving that price and value are not synonymous.

Finally, supply and demand explains such things as why the whole steer that enters the slaughterhouse gets eaten. You would think that only the best-tasting meat would be eaten, but even the fatty brisket, the brains, the kidneys, and the tongue are eaten. Furthermore, you may be surprised that the price of liver is lower than the price of roast beef (even though a steer has less liver than the meat in its two hind quarters where roast beef comes from).

DEMAND

This chapter covers the markets of consumer goods and services, while Chapter 7 covers the markets for resources. All consumers have limited or scarce income, so they need to get all they can from each dollar. To do so, they bargain with sellers and often compete against other buyers, who also face a scarcity of income.

Factors Influencing the Desire to Buy Goods and Services

★1

Many factors influence how much the buyers (consumers) in a market for a good or service wish to purchase, including: 1) price of the item; 2) benefit provided; 3) population; 4) consumer income; 5) prices of substitutes; 6) prices of complements; and 7) future expectations of price and availability.

■ The first of these factors is the price. Before consumers will buy something, they must believe that the benefit exceeds the cost (which is closely related to the price). Generally, the lower the price, the more consumers wish to buy. The only exceptions are items with snob appeal, such as expensive, showy things that people buy primarily *because* the price is high.

■ The second influence on purchases is the usefulness or the benefit the good or service provides, often called its utility. An item is useful if it provides nutrition, shelter, mobility, recreation, and the like. A consumer buys an item at a certain price if it gives more satisfaction than anything else that could be bought for the same amount of money.

■ The population of the market area is the third factor determining how much of an item consumers wish to buy. Essentially, asking how much all consumers want to buy is asking how many people find that the benefit exceeds the cost. As a rule, the more people there are, the more who will want the item.

■ Consumer income level is the fourth determinant of how much people buy. The greater the income of consumers, the more of *most* items they wish to buy simply because they can afford to—"most" because that's the way it works for what economists call a normal good. But in the case of what is called an inferior good, the more income consumers have, the less they wish to buy of it. Examples of inferior goods include potatoes, acrylic sweaters, cheap cameras with plastic lenses, and other "low quality" products. (Potatoes actually are high in food value, but have traditionally been considered a "humble food.") As incomes or living standards increase, people tend to buy fewer of these items. Instead, they buy imported pasta, wool sweaters, sophisticated 35mm cameras, and other "higher quality" items.

■ The fifth factor influencing consumer purchases is the price of a **substitute good**. A good is a substitute for some other good if it provides approximately the same utility. Steak and pork are substitutes for each other, as are trains and buses, and sweaters and jackets. The higher the price of an alternative or substitute for Good X, the more consumers want of Good X at a specific price for it. For example, let Good X be steak, selling for $3 a pound. If pork initially sells for $2 a pound, consumers might buy 600 pounds of steak. But if the price of pork rises to $2.80 a pound, consumers would buy more steak—perhaps 800 pounds.

■ The sixth factor influencing consumer purchases is the price of a **complementary good**, which is a good used in tandem with another. Typewriters and typing paper are complementary goods, as are cars and gasoline, and CD players and CDs. When the price of a complement rises, consumers tend to buy less of an item. For example, if the price of a CD rises from $16 to $30, fewer people will buy CD players.

■ The seventh factor affecting consumer buying is the expectation of future prices and availability of the good or service. Suppose you need something today and also will need it in the future. If you think the price will soon rise sharply, you may buy enough for now *and* the future. You will also do this if you believe the good will soon go off the market. Conversely, consumers buy less today if they expect the price to drop tomorrow.

The Special Relationship of Price to Consumer Purchases

How much consumers wish to buy of some good or service—what people commonly (but incorrectly) call "demand"—depends upon many factors. Each of these factors can vary, causing "demand" to vary. The following consideration of a particular market assumes that only one of these consumer-influencing factors can vary—the price of the product. All the other factors will have a certain "level"—some assigned income level, length of market period, and so on.

Suppose the market is for apples in a city of 50,000 for one week, that the prices of pears and other substitutes are at some particular level, and that no one expects either the price or the availability of apples to change. Now suppose apples sell for $2 per bushel and that consumers want 500 bushels and have the money to pay for them. However, if the price is $4 rather than $2 and all other influences on purchases remain the same, consumers will ask for less, perhaps only 470 bushels. And at $6, they want 440 bushels; at $8, they want 410 bushels; at $10, they want 380 bushels; and so on. Economists have a special term for each of these specific quantities buyers wish to purchase at specific prices—the quantity demanded. This is what people usually incorrectly call "demand."

Consumers act this way when prices change for almost all goods and services. Economists call this rule that consumers typically follow the **law of demand**. It means that at higher prices, consumers wish to buy less. Conversely, at lower prices, consumers wish to buy more. Thus, price and quantity demanded are inversely related. The law of demand is based on an assumption that all of the other influences on consumers' desire to purchase remain unchanged as the price changes. (This assumption is called *ceteris paribus.*) Consumers obey the law of demand for two reasons: 1) the substitution effect; and 2) the income effect.

★2

■ The **substitution effect** depends upon rational consumers who seek to maximize economic welfare by getting as much satisfaction as possible from each dollar spent. Because there are alternative ways to spend each dollar, consumers need to find the *best* combination of purchases in order to maximize economic welfare. In other words, if a consumer buys something, the benefit must exceed the opportunity cost. Suppose this is true for each of the consumers who want the 500 bushels of apples at $2. Each dollar of the $1,000 spent buys one-half of a bushel, providing a certain level of satisfaction (benefit). Buying pears instead with any of those dollars would provide somewhat *less* benefit. Otherwise consumers would buy the pears. But what if apples double in price to $4 per bushel and nothing else changes, including the price of pears? Then a dollar buys only one-*fourth* of a bushel of apples, so consumers now get less satisfaction from a dollar spent on apples. But as pear prices do not change, neither does the benefit from spending a dollar on pears. *Some* of the consumers who wanted apples at $2 per bushel now find that a dollar spent on apples brings *less* satisfaction than a dollar spent on pears. Such consumers then switch from apples to pears, a substitute good.

■ Consumers also obey the law of demand because of the **income effect**. This means that if the price of a good increases, consumers cannot buy as many goods and services in total. This is a consequence of limited incomes not going as far. The effect of an increase in prices is the same as if consumers suffered a cut in income. They could buy fewer things. For example, when the apple price rises from $2 to $10 per bushel, consumers, facing a scarcity of money (income), can buy fewer things, including apples.

The law of demand shows that the consumer's decision to buy something depends upon the price. In other words, there is a relationship between price and the amount consumers wish to buy. Economists call that relationship **demand**. Thus, demand refers to the relationship between the *various* quantities buyers wish to purchase and the *various* prices that might be charged. Demand does not

Figure 5-1 The Demand for Apples

Price (per bushel)	Bushels of Apples that Consumers Want to Buy (d)
$2	500
$4	470
$6	440
$8	410
$10	380

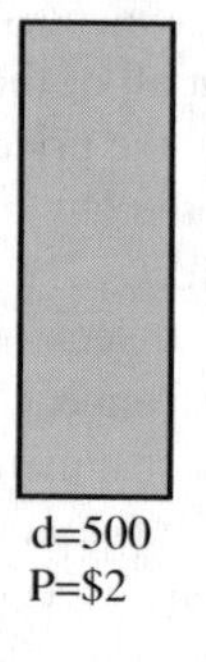

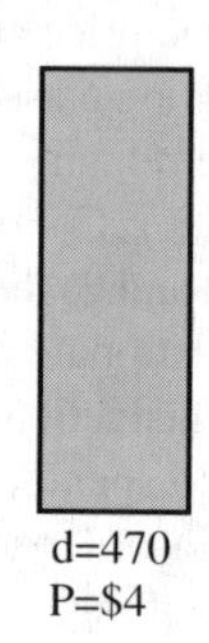

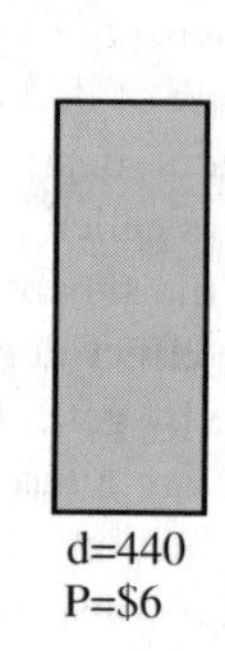

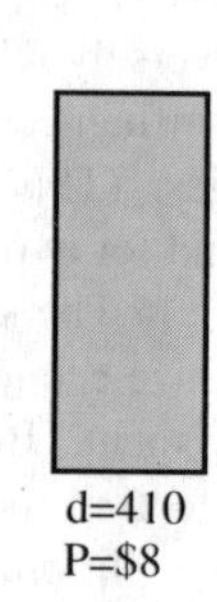

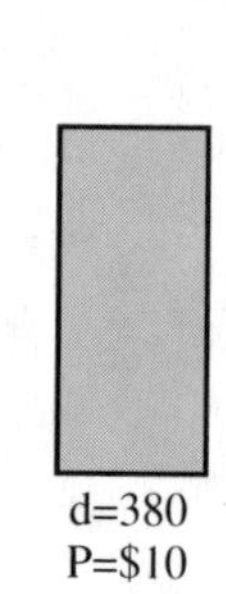

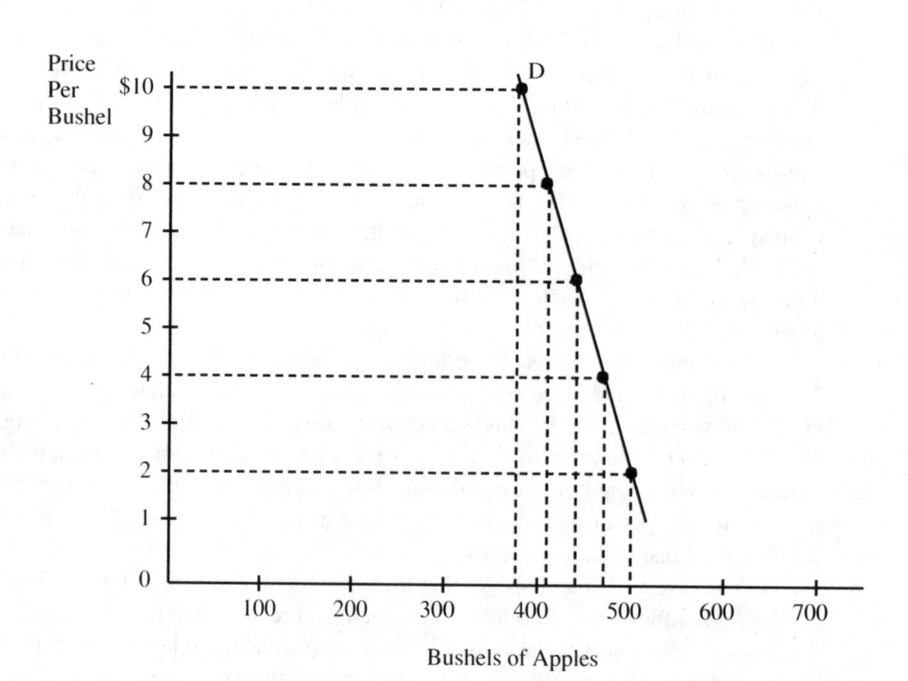

refer to any *specific* quantity. When considering the demand relationship, remember that all other influences on consumer purchases do not change.

Figure 5-1 shows the demand relationship in three different ways. The first way is the demand schedule, where a list of prices appears with a list of consumers' wishes to buy, labelled d. In the example of apples, you see the price and bushel amounts mentioned earlier. These amounts consumers wish to buy depend not only upon the price of apples, but also upon consumers' incomes, the benefits of apples, the length of the market period, and so on. Each influence on the desire to buy (other than the price) *could* change but *doesn't* in Figure 5-1. Each has a specific level or magnitude (for example, the population of the market area being 50,000). Because the magnitude of each influence can vary, the relationship in the demand schedule is only one of many possible relationships.

The second way to show the demand relationship uses diagrams (shown in the middle of Figure 5-1). Suppose there are wooden boxes to hold all the apples people want at each price of $2, $4, $6, $8, and $10. The $2 box needs to hold 500 bushels; the $4 box is smaller because it needs to hold only 470 bushels; and so on. The diagram represents such boxes, where the letter d reflects the amount desired at each price.

The last way to show the demand relationship uses a graph. The price is measured on the vertical axis and the quantity (demanded) on the bottom axis. Notice the five dots on the line labelled D, which graphically represents the demand relationship. Each dot represents two pieces of information, one about the price and the other about the desired quantity. For example, the second dot from the top shows that consumers wish to buy 410 bushels if the price is $8 per bushel. There are thousands of potential points, in addition to the five shown on this line. Connecting all the points gives what is called the demand curve. (Incidentally, demand "curves" can be straight lines.)

Elasticity of Demand

★3

If firms know the demand relationship, they can predict changes in sales if they charge different prices. The **elasticity of demand** refers to the extent consumers change their purchases as price varies. Suppose the price for some good increases. If consumers cut their purchases at a greater rate than the price rises, the relationship is **elastic**. However, if consumers cut purchases by a smaller rate than the price increases, demand is **inelastic**. For example, if the price of sofas rises by 40 percent and consumers buy 60 percent fewer sofas, the demand for sofas is elastic. But if the number of sofas sold falls by only 30 percent, the demand is inelastic.

Businesses need to know the demand elasticity because their sales or **total revenue** (TR) equals the price multiplied by the amount sold. Figure 5-2 shows four possible scenarios with price changes and differing elasticities. In the first case (top left), price rises when demand is elastic. Because the gain in TR from the price increase is less than the loss in TR from the reduced purchases, the net effect is a decrease in TR. However, with an inelastic demand, TR rises, since consumers don't reduce purchases significantly. The situation reverses for price decreases, shown in the bottom two cases. Obviously, a business owner would

Figure 5-2 Changing Prices, Elasticity of Demand, and Total Revenue

Price Changes	Elastic Demand	Inelastic Demand
If the Price Rises by x Percent	1) Consumers Reduce Purchases by More Than x Percent 2) Total Revenue Falls	1) Consumers Reduce Purchases by Less Than x Percent 2) Total Revenue Rises
If the Price Falls by x Percent	1) Consumers Increase Purchases by More Than x Percent 2) Total Revenue Rises	1) Consumers Increase Purchases by Less Than x Percent 2) Total Revenue Falls

like to face an inelastic demand. Then when the price is increased, there will still be lots of buyers.

Changes in Demand

Because the other influences on how much consumers wish to purchase (besides price) can vary in magnitude, there are many possible demand relationships. Take the numbers used in the apple example as the initial relationship. It shows that at different prices, consumers want different amounts of apples. Yet remember that we're assuming a certain level of income, prices of substitutes, and so on. Now let's change the magnitude of one of these factors—the benefits that consumers get from apples.

Suppose the initial demand stems only from the knowledge that apples taste good and provide food value. But if researchers find that apples reduce the risk of cancer, the perceived benefit from apples is higher, and consumers will want to eat more apples. Let's say apples are $4 per bushel. Initially, consumers wanted 470 bushels. (Or, in economists' language, the quantity demanded at $4 per bushel was 470 bushels.) They *could* have requested bushels numbered 471, 472, 489, 520, and so on, but they *did not* because the costs of *those* apples exceeded the benefits. But with the new cancer information, the situation changes for each of the bushels numbered 471 to 550. Now, buyers request 550 bushels at $4 per bushel, or 80 more bushels than before. Similar increases of 80 bushels are made for whatever price apples sell and appear in the demand schedules, the diagrams, and the graphs in Figure 5-3. In each case there is an "old" and "new" request (or quantity demanded) at each price.

★4

What you just saw is a **change in demand**, which occurs when consumers wish to buy a different amount of a good or service *at each price.* Take care to distinguish a change in demand from a change in the amount consumers want *because of a change in the price,* which is known as a change in quantity demanded. A change in demand means consumers want a different amount because some influence *other than the price* changed.

Figure 5-3 An Increase in the Demand for Apples

Price (per bushel)	The Old Amount (bushels) of Apples that Consumers Want to Buy (d-old)	The New Amount (bushels) of Apples that Consumers Want to Buy (d-new)
$2	500	580
$4	470	550
$6	440	520
$8	410	490
$10	380	460

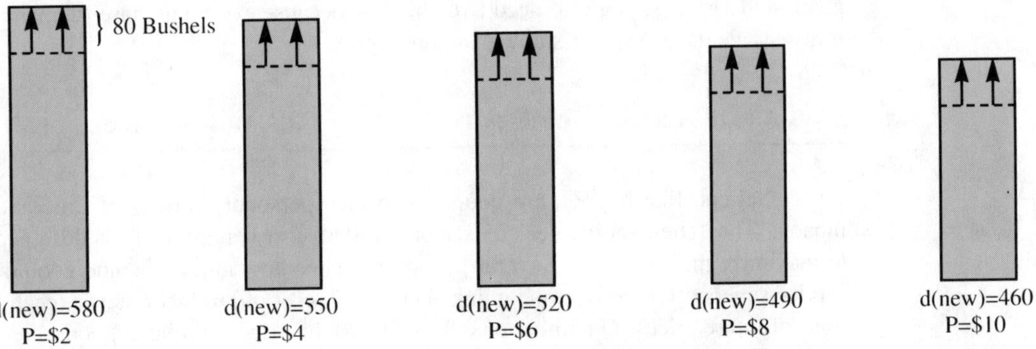

} 80 Bushels

d(new)=580 P=$2
d(new)=550 P=$4
d(new)=520 P=$6
d(new)=490 P=$8
d(new)=460 P=$10

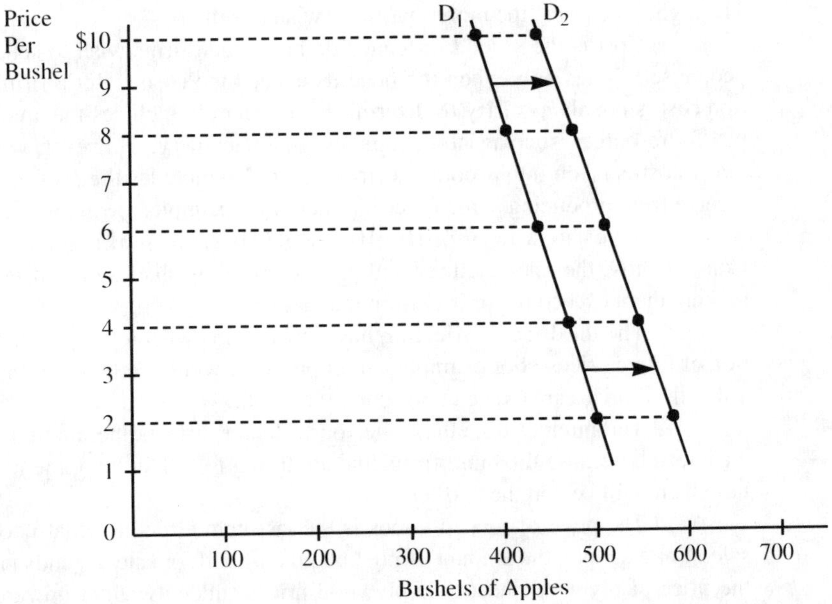

Price Per Bushel
$10
9
8
7
6
5
4
3
2
1
0
D_1
D_2
100 200 300 400 500 600 700
Bushels of Apples

The example above, which links apples to a reduced cancer risk, involves an **increase in demand**. It means consumers want more at each price than before. Demand increases if: 1) the perceived usefulness of the item rises; 2) prices of substitutes rise; 3) prices of complements fall; 4) consumers' incomes rise; 5) consumers expect prices to be higher in the future or that the product will be less available; or 6) population increases. A **decrease in demand** means consumers want less of an item at each price. This results from lower prices of substitutes, higher prices of complements, fewer benefits from the item, lower incomes, expectation of lower future prices, or a lower population.

SUPPLY

Economists often compare supply and demand to a scissors, which requires two blades to cut. To find how the market system establishes prices for goods and services, you also need two "blades" because every purchase (demand) is also a sale (supply). Let's now examine supply.

Factors Influencing the Desire to Sell Goods and Services

★5

Sellers, like buyers, are people who face personal scarcity of time and money. Thus, their selling decisions should reflect cost-benefit analysis designed to maximize their welfare. Several factors influence how much of some good or service sellers offer for sale, including: 1) price; 2) cost of production; 3) expectations of future prices; 4) number of sellers; and 5) the prices of related goods.

■ Because price is a prime factor determining the benefits of selling, price is the first factor determining how much of a good or service firms wish to sell. The higher the price, the more that firms wish to sell.

■ Cost is the second influence on how much firms wish to sell. Rational people sell things only when the benefits exceed the costs. But a firm's production cost is not always easy to determine. It generally includes the amounts firms pay for resources, such as labor, supplies, and machinery. However, when *opportunity* cost is taken into account, a firm's cost also includes the profits it does *not* receive from producing some other product. For example, a window shade manufacturer gives up the opportunity to profit from making canvas tents. Consequently, the manufacturer will produce window shades only if profits from making them exceed the profits from making tents.

■ The third factor affecting how much firms wish to sell is their expectation of future prices. For example, an oil producer would be less willing to sell oil today if oil prices are expected to soar next month.

■ The number of sellers, the fourth factor, affects the amount that firms wish to sell because the more firms that are trying to sell an item, the more of that item there will be "on the market."

■ The price of related goods is the last item affecting what is offered for sale. For example, the amount of pine boards offered for sale depends partly upon the price of plywood sheets. If plywood prices suddenly shoot upward (as they did following Hurricane Andrew), fewer boards will be sent to market. Some pine logs will be made into plywood instead. This is another example of the concept of opportunity cost. Just as *production* costs of a product determine output, so do opportunity costs.

The Special Relationship of Price to Offers to Sell

To most people, "supply" means the combined effect of each of the factors on selling decisions. (Again, as with demand, economists define supply differently, as you will soon see.) As with demand, price receives a special consideration in explaining the supply decisions of firms. In the following example, it is assumed that all other influences on sellers do not vary as the price varies (or *ceteris paribus* again).

Let's again take apples as an example. Suppose that if apples sell for $2 per bushel, growers wish to sell 340 bushels. But if the price is $4 instead, they wish to sell 390 bushels; at $6, 440 bushels; at $8, 490 bushels; at $10, 540 bushels, and so on. (As with demand, economists have a term for each of these specific quantities sellers offer for sale at specific prices—the quantity supplied.)

Notice that sellers do just the opposite of consumers, who follow the law of demand by buying *less* at higher prices. Sellers also act as if they obey an unwritten rule. This rule, called the **law of supply**, holds that at higher prices, firms offer more for sale. Conversely, at lower prices, firms offer less for sale. Thus, price and quantity supplied are directly related. As with the law of demand, this law assumes that all the other influences on the amount offered for sale remain unchanged as the price changes.

★6 The law of supply is followed because different units of a good or service cost different amounts to produce. To understand this, suppose that each tire that could be produced in a certain factory costs the *same* to produce as all others, say $20. If the price of the first tire is $30, the firm wants to sell it, for the benefit (price) exceeds the cost of $20. The same holds true for every other tire that can be made. In fact, this firm would wish to expand its factory to an *infinite* size because each tire makes a profit. (The firm would *wish* to sell an unlimited amount, but how much it *could* sell depends upon demand. The concept of supply refers to sellers' *wishes,* which might or might not equal their sales.)

But such a scenerio would rarely happen. In actual economies, retail firms open only for limited periods. Most McDonald's outlets, for example, do not even try to sell hamburgers at 4:00 a.m. They *could* sell some at that hour, but such sales wouldn't be profitable. Otherwise McDonald's would be open. A hamburger made at that time looks and tastes the same as one made at noon, yet it costs more to make. That's because firms can usually produce at low cost only in large volume. But since the demand for hamburgers is low at 4:00 a.m., the cost is high—so high that the benefit is below the cost.

You will learn in Chapter 6 that, for a given firm size, additional outputs of an item become increasingly costly. The average cost rises so that beyond some level of output, it exceeds the price. Therefore, firms wish to sell no more than that amount of output.

What happens if the price increases? Then firms can afford to produce (that is, produce at a profit) the more costly, larger amounts of output. This explains why there is a law of supply, for as the price increases, the amount offered for sale increases. In summary, *firms obey the law of supply because, at higher prices, they can afford the more costly production techniques of the higher levels of output.*

In short, as the old saying goes, "Money talks." Individuals follow the law of supply as well as firms. You would not sell your favorite tape for $5 if you would give up more satisfaction from the tape than you would gain from whatever else you bought for the $5. But when offered $40, you would surely sell the tape because you "can afford it" (the "it" being the satisfaction you lose from not hearing the music).

Supply is the relationship between price and the amounts of a good or service all firms combined wish to sell. Thus, supply refers to the relationship between the *various* quantities sellers offer and the *various* prices at which the items could sell. (Or, in economists' terminology, supply is the relationship between price and quantity supplied.) Supply does not refer to any *specific* quantity. As with demand, this relationship holds when it is assumed that all other influences on selling remain unchanged.

Consider the apple market again, but this time from the sellers' viewpoint. Figure 5-4 shows the supply relationship in three different ways, with a supply schedule, box diagrams, and a supply curve. Notice that apple growers can produce at least 540 bushels of apples, for they wish to do so at $10 per bushel. But why do they wish to sell only 340 bushels at $2? They *could* produce 200 bushels more, but they don't *want* to because each of these 200 bushels costs more to produce than the first 340 bushels (and more than $2 each). This is because apples differ in size and accessibility, and each tree differs in yield because of genetic makeup, soil conditions, and so on. Such factors influence the cost of apples from different sources. The first bushel picked would be the least costly bushel, the one that came from the tree closest to the packing shed, or with the largest yield or largest apples. Additional bushels would come from more costly apples, those higher on the trees, farther from the shed, and so on. If the price were high enough, trees would even be planted on poor soil, and growers would harvest the apples at the very top of each tree and those that fell and are hidden in the grass. These are very costly apples, but profitable at high enough prices.

The supply relationship assumes: 1) a certain level of costs for each unit of output; 2) given expectations of the future; 3) a given number of sellers; and 4) a given level of prices of related goods. Thus, the relationship is merely one of many that are possible.

Changes in Supply

Now suppose one of these other influences on the amount produced changes—the cost of production, for example. Suppose a new machine can wash, grade, and pack all the apples in one operation, thereby reducing labor needs. It then costs less to market each bushel of apples, both low-cost and high-cost ones. Some apples previously *possible* to grow at, say, $4 per bushel, but *unprofitable,*

Figure 5-4 The Supply of Apples

Price (per bushel)	Bushels of Apples that Producers Want to Sell (s)
$2	340
$4	390
$6	440
$8	490
$10	540

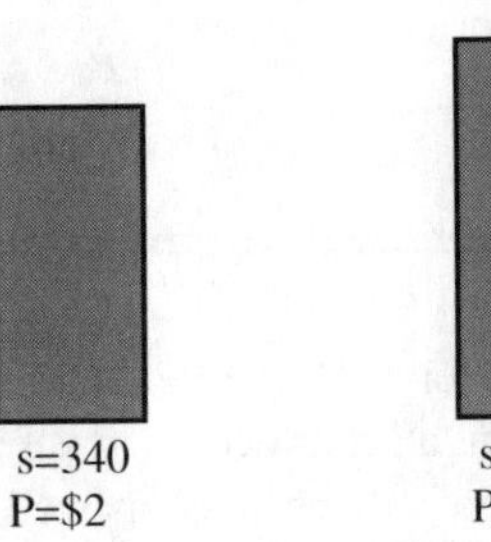

s=340
P=$2

s=390
P=$4

s=440
P=$6

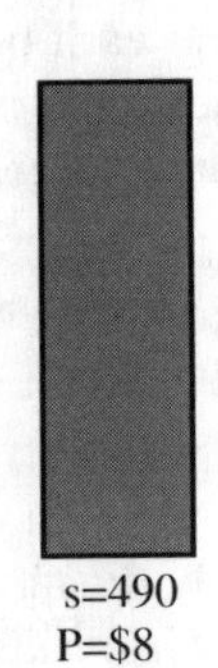

s=490
P=$8

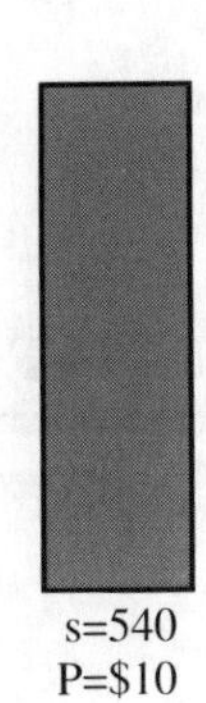

s=540
P=$10

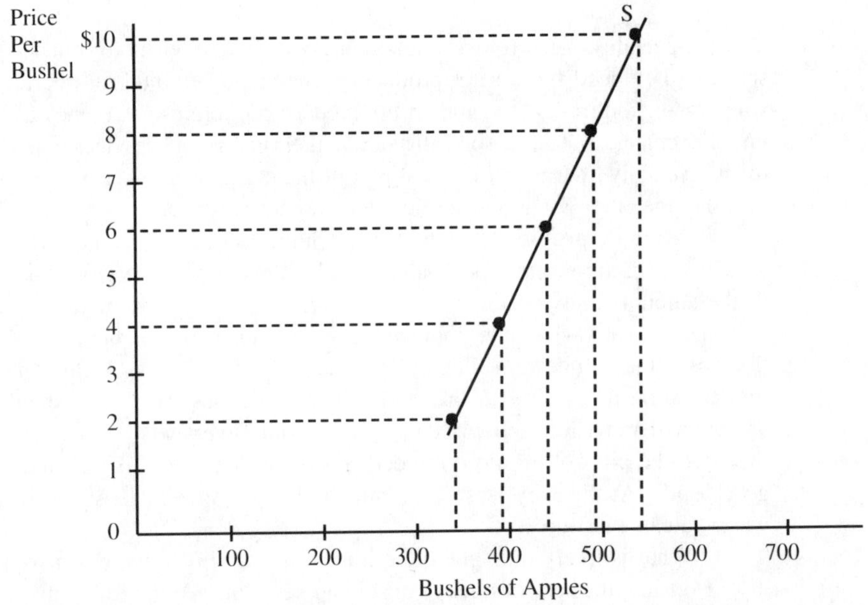

Price Per Bushel

$10
9
8
7
6
5
4
3
2
1
0

S

100 200 300 400 500 600 700

Bushels of Apples

now *are* profitable. This includes bushels 391, 392, and all the way to number 490. What about the remaining bushels that *could* be produced, numbers 491 and above? Because they are so *very* costly (in excess of $4 per bushel), they remain unprofitable, so they are not grown.

Figure 5-5 shows a change in supply in three ways. In each case an "old" or original relationship and a "new" one appear.

★7

A **change in supply** occurs when producers want to sell a different amount at each price. This must be distinguished from a change in desired output *that results from a change in price,* known as a change in quantity demanded. A change in supply occurs when there is a change in any of the influences on desired output *other than the price.* When producers want to sell *more* at each price, there is an **increase in supply**. This occurs if: 1) production costs fall; 2) producers expect lower prices in the future; 3) the number of sellers increases; or 4) other goods that producers were making with their resources decrease in price. The opposite, called a **decrease in supply**, occurs when producers want to sell *less* at each price. This happens when production costs rise, producers expect higher prices in the future, the number of sellers decreases, or other goods that producers were making with their resources increase in price.

DETERMINATION OF MARKET PRICE

So far, several possible prices were considered for both the demand and supply situations. But any exchange between a buyer and a seller occurs in a market at *just one* price. This section explains how that price is determined as well as the prices of all other goods and services.

How Buyers and Sellers Decide to Trade the Same Amounts

Specialists need to exchange their goods and services for other goods and services they need but do not produce. This could be done in a barter system, where one good trades for another, but modern economies use money as a "medium of exchange." Today, specialists trade their goods and services when they sell them. Actually, that is just the first part of the trade. The other part occurs when they buy the other goods and services they do not produce.

A major problem in such an exchange economy is equating: 1) the amounts a certain group of specialists (such as apple producers) wish to sell; and 2) the amounts that consumers wish to buy. These are several factors affecting both the amounts—income, population, price, and so on for buyers and production costs, the number of sellers, price, and so on for sellers. With so many factors affecting the desires to buy and sell, the odds are extremely small that the amount sellers wish to sell will equal the amount buyers wish to purchase. Either there will be piles of unsold (untraded) goods or there won't be enough goods to go around. At the very least, both situations are annoying. At the worst, they waste valuable resources.

What is likely to happen to eliminate these situations in a market economy? Consider the case of piles of unsold apples. Each of the following will make

Figure 5-5 An Increase in the Supply of Apples

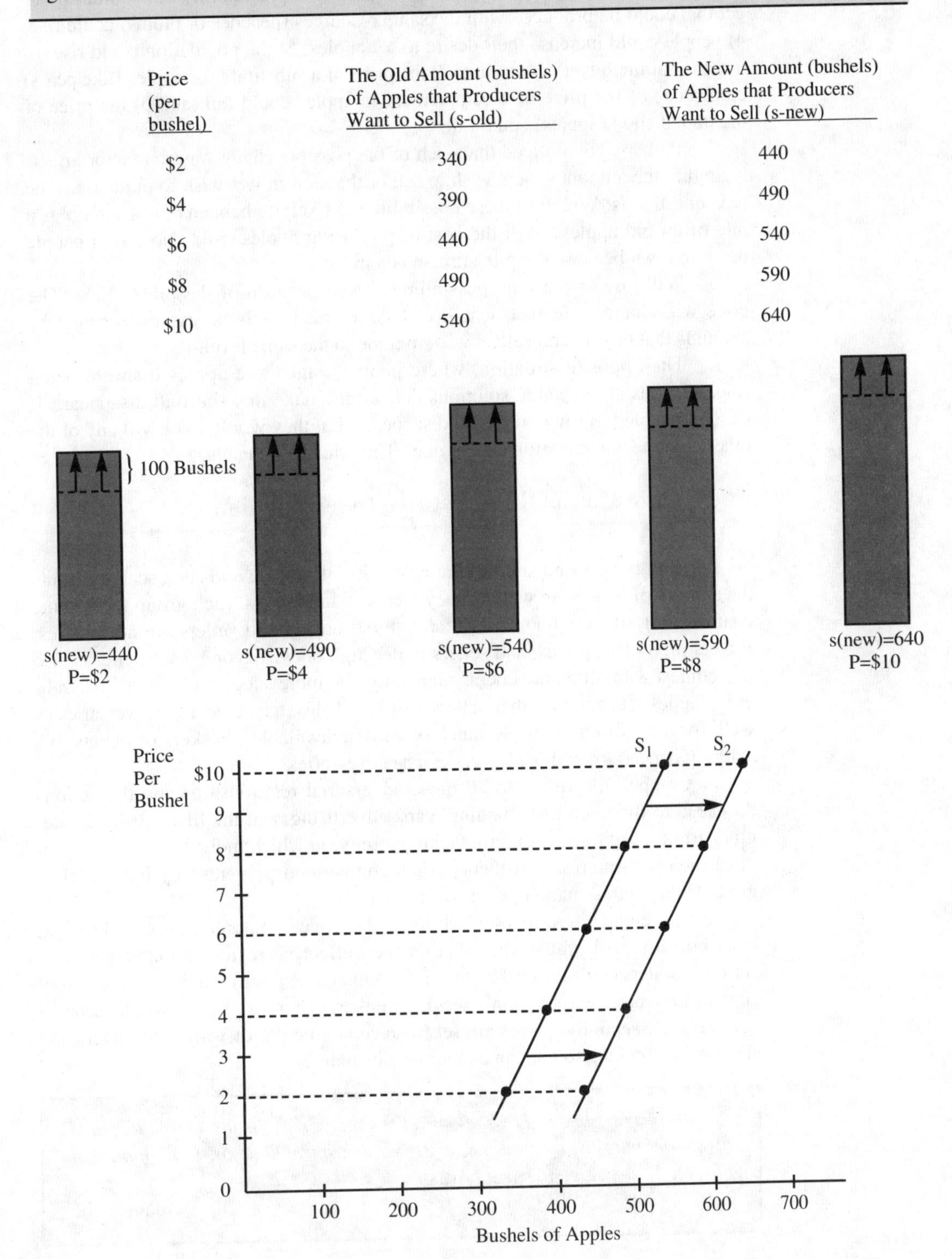

Price (per bushel)	The Old Amount (bushels) of Apples that Producers Want to Sell (s-old)	The New Amount (bushels) of Apples that Producers Want to Sell (s-new)
$2	340	440
$4	390	490
$6	440	540
$8	490	590
$10	540	640

such a pile disappear: 1) production costs of apples could rise; 2) some sellers could go out of the apple business; 3) the price and profitability of a similar product that could be produced with the same resources (peaches or plums) could rise; 4) people could increase their desire to eat apples; 5) the population could rise; 6) incomes of the buyers could rise; 7) the price of a substitute for apples (like pears) could rise; 8) the price of a complement to apples could fall; and 9) the price of the traded good (apples) could fall.

Perhaps you noticed that each of the possible changes was a factor affecting either the amount sellers wish to sell or that consumers wish to purchase. The next question is: Which of these possibilities is likely to happen *because there is* a pile of unsold apples? Will the cost of producing apples rise? No. Will people move to town because the pile attracted them? No.

Will *any* of the nine possibilities result because of the pile? Yes. The price will change. In fact, it will change as much as is necessary to bring the amounts that buyers and sellers wish to trade to the same level.

The opposite situation, where people want more apples than are being sold, also has at least nine solutions that would make that shortfall disappear. If enough people left town, it would disappear—but they won't. Nor will any of the other eight be our salvation except one. The price will change.

The Role of Competition in Price Determination

Both buyers and sellers face a scarcity of income and such scarcity limits the amount of economic welfare they receive. In markets, each group faces some contests that affect economic welfare. First, buyers and sellers are adversaries. Buyers prefer low prices, and sellers prefer high ones. Second, each seller is also in a contest with all other sellers. Generally, the more successful a particular seller is, the less successful other sellers will be. Third, buyers can be adversaries as well, for there often is just so much of an item available. Seekers of tickets to a sold-out concert know how buyers can be adversaries.

Competition refers to all these adversarial relationships and the actions they lead to (price cutting, bidding wars, advertising, and the like). It is an integral part of a capitalist economy facing scarcity, in which individuals seek to promote their self-interest. In theory, such competition prevents any individual or group from gaining market power over others.

In a competitive market, who sets the price? Actually, no one does—at least not alone—because the price is the collective result of many people's actions. Sellers can't set or dictate prices. Otherwise prices would be much higher than they are. Buyers don't set them either, otherwise prices would drop to near zero. Essentially, prices are set in an economic tug-of-war, with buyers and sellers alike seeking to gain an economic advantage.

> *People of the same trade seldom meet together, even for merriment and diversion, but the conversation ends in a conspiracy, against the public, or in some contrivance to raise prices.*
>
> – Adam Smith

Different Price Levels and Their Consequences

If a good or service sells at only one of many possible prices, why that *particular* price? To see why, return to the apple example and consider several different prices. Figure 5-6 brings together the demand for apples from Figure 5-1 and the apple supply from Figure 5-4.

Suppose apples sell for $2 per bushel. Is everyone content with that price? Well, at $2 consumers want 500 bushels. But they can only buy what apple growers wish to sell—340 bushels, so there are a lot of unhappy people who won't get any apples. There is a **shortage**, which occurs when buyers want to purchase more than sellers offer to sell at a certain price. And a shortage creates price instability because of two groups: sellers and buyers.

★8

■ First, individual apple growers notice they are selling all they wish to sell but still have extra customers who don't get any apples. Perhaps, a grower thinks, *some* people who did not get apples might be willing to pay *more* than $2. Some might crave apples so much they would pay $20 a bushel, or some might be "fat cats" with so much money that price doesn't matter to them. On the other hand, some who *did* get apples at $2 are "cheapskates" who would only buy apples if they were $2 or less. What if that grower increases the price to $4? Some people (the "cheapskates") who would buy apples at $2 would not buy any at $4, but perhaps most people would pay the price. Anyway, the grower can afford to lose some customers because there is an excess of them at $2. Essentially, the grower replaces "cheapskates" with "fat cats"—and still sells out of apples, thereby getting more revenue.

If all growers increase their prices to $4, Figure 5-6 shows that consumers now want only 470 bushels, 30 bushels less. Note also that growers now wish to sell 50 bushels more, 390 bushels. These changes, dictated by the law of demand and the law of supply, reduce the shortage to 80 bushels.

■ Customers who could *not* buy apples at $2 make up the second group that forces a price increase when there is a shortage. Not being able to spend $2 in the best way frustrates them. Such a customer might complain to a grower, "Why sell apples to someone else for $2 but none to me when I am willing to pay you *more*—shall we say $4?" It might seem foolish for a buyer to offer more than the going price. Yet, often *some* apples at $4 are better than *no* apples at $2. This is precisely what happens at an auction. The auctioneer never raises the price, but only asks if a *buyer* will raise it. Such adjustments also take place in retail stores and other markets, but it is more evident at an auction. (Remember the Cabbage-Patch-Doll Christmas?)

There is still market instability at $4, for a shortage still exists, though it is smaller. (In general, the lower the price for anything, the greater the shortage will be.) Thus, the price continues to rise until the shortage disappears. This happens at $6 per bushel, when consumers wish to buy 440 bushels and growers wish to sell the same amount. With the shortage gone, there is no force tending to raise the price. The market is at the equilibrium position, which means nothing will change, neither the price nor the amount sold. The **equilibrium price** is the price where buyers want to buy the same amount that firms want to sell. The **equilibrium quantity** is the amount sold at the equilibrium price. Thus, in the apple market, the equilibrium price is $6 and the equilibrium quantity is 440 bushels.

Now suppose the price of apples is *higher*, not lower, than the equilibrium price—say $10 per bushel. Although this sounds great for the growers, they are not completely content. They want to sell 540 bushels, but customers buy only 380 bushels. There is a **surplus**, which means sellers want to sell more than buyers want to purchase at a certain price. Generally, the higher the price for something, the larger the surplus. At $10 the surplus is 160 bushels. As with a shortage, a surplus leads to price changes because of the actions of two groups.

■ First, individual growers sell only a fraction of what they want to sell and see that other growers have customers who *could* be theirs. One grower might say, "How can I get some of my competitors' customers so I can sell *all* that I wish? Perhaps if I reduce my price, apple buyers will flock to my orchard." So that grower does just that, and it works—for a while. However, before long other growers play the same game. It's called competition, and it soon drives the price down to $8, where the surplus is only 80 bushels. The surplus shrinks from 160 bushels for two reasons. First, buyers want more apples at the lower price. Second, growers offer fewer apples for sale—the ones that are no longer profitable to grow.

■ The second group that forces the price down consists of buyers aware of the surplus facing the growers. Such a buyer takes advantage of this "buyer's market" by saying to a grower, "Look, if you don't sell me a bushel of apples at less than $10, I'll find a grower who will." Sooner or later, this forces growers to grudgingly accept lower prices, for the old "half a loaf is better than none" adage is at work. Prices continue to fall so long as there is a surplus, in this case to $6. Now consumers buy all that growers wish to sell. Again the market is at equilibrium.

Figure 5-7 summarizes this entire competitive market price-setting mechanism. Whether the market starts at prices that are "too low" or "too high," it ends up at the equilibrium position.

Markets that Fail to Reach Equilibrium

All markets are *supposed* to work the way this apple market worked. Because of competition, shortages and surpluses force prices to the point that "clears the market"—that is, "clear" of shortages and surpluses. Alas, it doesn't always work like that. Often, the actual market price is either lower or higher than the equilibrium price. Consequently, shortages or surpluses persist for long periods—sometimes forever.

★9

Markets fail to clear for several reasons: 1) ignorance of the equilibrium price; 2) collusion; 3) sellers refuse to raise prices; and 4) government price controls.

■ The first reason markets fail to clear is that sometimes no one knows what the equilibrium price is. No one actually has convenient tables like those in our apple example in order to pinpoint the equilibrium price. Many markets have small surpluses or shortages, caused by prices slightly higher or lower than the equilibrium price. Such situations persist mainly because firms will not change prices, often because changing prices takes time that is too costly to be worthwhile. Also, problems for sellers and buyers caused by the small surpluses and

Figure 5-6 Determination of Price in the Market for Apples

Price (per bushel)	Bushels of Apples that: Consumers Want to Buy (d)	Producers Want to Sell (s)	Shortage or Surplus Condition	Size of the Shortage or Surplus
$2	500	340	Shortage	160
$4	470	390	Shortage	80
$6	440	440	Neither	0
$8	410	490	Surplus	80
$10	380	540	Surplus	160

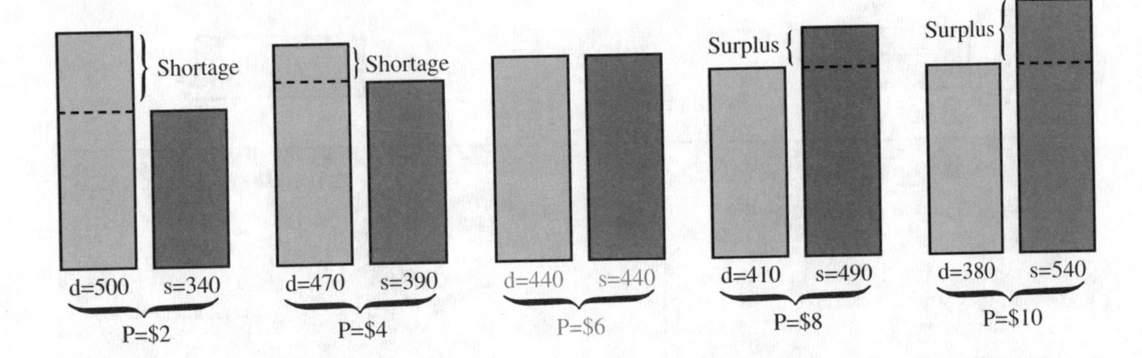

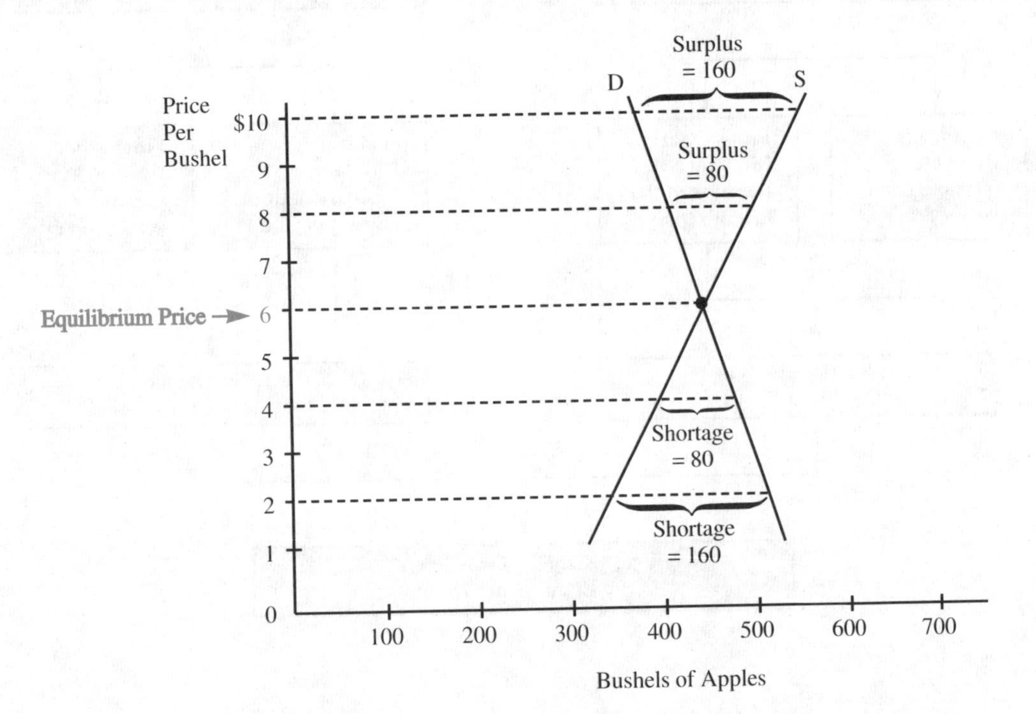

Figure 5-7 How Buyers and Sellers Agree on a Price in a Market

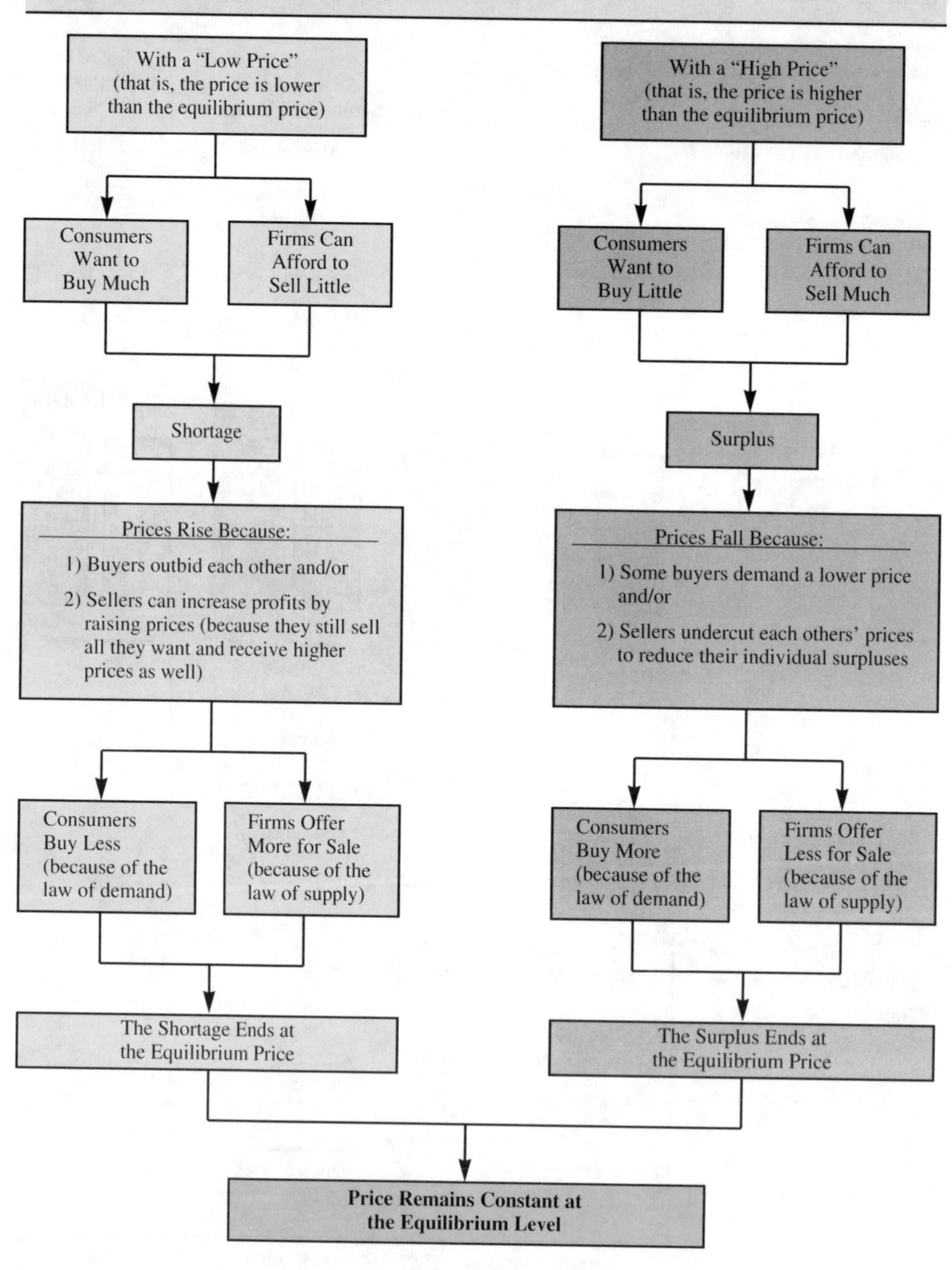

shortages are so slight that no one feels compelled to change prices. An example is a popular sweatshirt that is occasionally out of stock. Finally, often buyers or sellers are not aware of such surpluses or shortages. One such example is a surplus of motel rooms in the form of slightly more unrented rooms than normal.

■ The second reason markets fail to clear involves an agreement between sellers to fix prices, setting them above the equilibrium price. A **cartel** is an organization of such sellers. Because the fixed price, being above the equilibrium, leads to a surplus, the cartel members "share" the surplus. Each cartel member, though wishing to sell more than it can, agrees to limit its production. Consequently, the total output of the cartel shrinks to meet the lower amount that consumers are willing to buy.

The best-known cartel is OPEC, the Organization of Petroleum Exporting Countries. (However, some say it is not a true cartel because it has some non-economic objectives.) Economists often say that cartels such as OPEC usually collapse at some point because individual cartel members have an incentive to cheat on the agreements. For example, a member might secretly offer a lower price through a rebate plan to some favored buyer. Eventually, other cartel members will find out and retaliate, and the cartel will either collapse or become less effective.

Collusion refers to price-fixing agreements between sellers that are prohibited by law. Although cartels are generally illegal in the United States, farmers and fisheries are exempt. Also exempt are laborers, who form unions that operate like a cartel except that the surplus (unemployed laborers) cannot be shared equally by all workers. One either works or does not.

■ The third reason markets don't clear is because sellers sometimes don't take advantage of an opportunity to raise prices when there is a shortage. You probably faced some of the following situations: you couldn't find a popular item at a store; you couldn't buy a ticket to the World Series or a concert; or you couldn't find a parking space. In some cases, the price might have to increase tremendously to match the amount consumers want to buy with the amount sellers want to sell. But it could be done. The most common reason it isn't done is that firms will not risk losing consumer good will. If, for example, a hardware store sharply increases the price of chain saws following a hurricane, consumers might pay the extra amount because they need the saws so urgently. But they might never return.

Another explanation why some sellers do not raise prices when there are shortages is that maximum monetary gain may not be their primary goal. For example: cities do not charge all they could for parking because they also want people to shop downtown; you might not charge a friend as much for something as you would a stranger; and some people feel guilty about charging "whatever the market can bear."

■ The last reason markets fail to clear involves government intervention to help either buyers or sellers. Buyers would like to pay less for things, and sellers would like to get higher prices. If buyers or sellers cannot change the price themselves, they occasionally ask the government for help. Price controls are government laws to establish the market price either below or above the equilibrium price. Such controls fall into two classes: price ceilings and price floors. A

price ceiling is the maximum legal price for something. Because the government's intent is to aid buyers, it sets the price *below* the equilibrium price. (Be careful in using the analogy of a room ceiling. Although a *room* ceiling is "high" or above you, a *price* ceiling is set *low*—at least lower than the equilibrium price.)

Consider again the market for apples. Suppose the government does not want people to have to pay the equilibrium price of $6 per bushel for apples. So it says, "No one can sell apples for more than $4 per bushel." The diagrams and the graph in Figure 5-8 show this situation. In the diagram, any price to the left of $4 is legal. In the graph, any price below the price ceiling limit of $4 is legal. Now suppose apple sellers charge the legal maximum of $4 per bushel. Notice that the "demand box" is larger than the "supply box," indicating a shortage of 80 bushels. The graph indicates a shortage as the horizontal distance between the demand and supply graphs at $4. The shortage occurs because many people want the relatively cheap apples, while growers can profitably produce only a small crop.

Some examples of goods or services with current or recent price ceilings include: oil, natural gas, and gasoline; rent in over 200 U.S. cities; and interest rates for credit. Shortages accompany or accompanied each of these market interventions, and the "energy crisis" of the 1970s was the most dramatic.

A **price floor** is the minimum legal price for something. In some cases it is called a price support because its intent is to "support" prices and prevent them from falling to the equilibrium. (Again, be careful, for although a *room* floor is under or "below" you, a *price* floor is set *high*—at least higher than the equilibrium price.)

Suppose the government wants to help the apple growers by setting a legal minimum of $8 per bushel, well above the competitive equilibrium of $6. The growers' gain in price comes at the expense of the buyers. The diagram in Figure 5-8 shows that if the price is $8 per bushel, 80 bushels of apples remain unsold—a surplus. The graph shows the surplus of 80 bushels as the horizontal distance between the supply and demand graphs at $8. Growers would love to sell lots of these high-priced apples, but consumers refuse to buy many.

Examples of price floors include price supports on many agricultural products (such as wheat, corn, cotton, honey, and milk) that American farmers produce in surplus. There is also a floor for the "price" of labor, known as the minimum wage. Many economists believe that one consequence is a surplus of labor—or unemployment.

Changes in the Equilibrium Position

Some prices—as for salt, pencils, and film—never seem to change much. Other prices fluctuate, often wildly, as for lettuce, gasoline, and corporate stocks. This section explains why one equilibrium price replaces another.

Note in Figure 5-6 that the price where buyers want the same amount as growers wish to sell (440 bushels) is $6 per bushel. This equilibrium condition will remain so long as there is no change in demand or supply. Now let's consider such changes and see the effects on the equilibrium price and quantity. First, the demand will be changed, and second, the supply will be changed.

★10

Figure 5-8 Price Ceilings and Price Floors

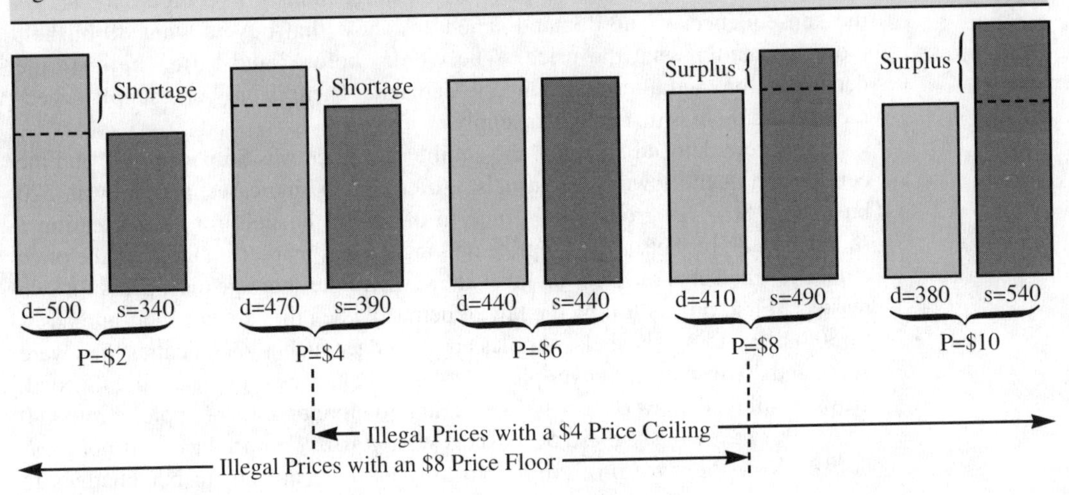

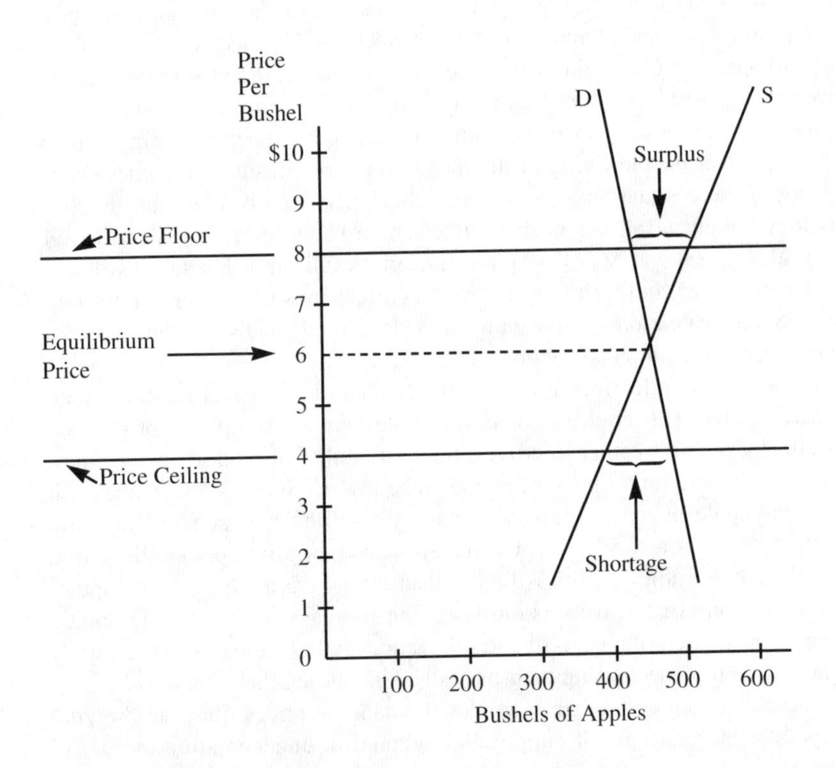

■ Consider an increase in demand for apples, which means consumers wish to buy more apples *even if there is no change in the price*. Figure 5-9 shows the consequences. The demand schedules show that buyers want 80 bushels more, no matter what the price. The words "before" and "after" refer to the demand before and after the change in demand. There is only one supply schedule because there is no change in supply.

Before demand changed, the equilibrium price was $6 per bushel, and the equilibrium quantity was 440 bushels. After demand increases, people want 520 bushels at $6—yet growers continue to offer 440 bushels for sale, creating a shortage of 80 bushels. The $6 price no longer gives market stability, so the price climbs to a *new* market-clearing level at $8, where the shortage disappears for two reasons. First, buyers follow the law of demand when they reduce their purchases by 30 bushels to 490 bushels. Apples are no longer such a good deal as they were at $6, and 30 bushels no longer pass cost-benefit analysis for consumers. Second, growers follow the law of supply by offering 50 more bushels of apples (from 440 up to 490). Previously these 50 bushels were *possible* to produce, but not *profitable*. Now they *are* profitable. So long as there are no further changes in demand, the new equilibrium will remain.

■ The equilibrium price could also increase if the supply decreases. Figure 5-10 shows the effect of such a cutback in supply. The initial equilibrium price is $6 per bushel, and the equilibrium quantity is 440 bushels. After supply falls, growers offer 80 bushels less for sale at each price. The market no longer clears at $6 because there is a shortage of 80 bushels. This is because consumers continue to ask for 440 bushels. Their buying decisions are unrelated to the growers' problems, such as increased costs or bad weather. This shortage leads to a new equilibrium price and quantity of $8 per bushel and 410 bushels.

Equilibrium price might also *decrease* if the demand and supply changes of above are reversed. Consider first a falling demand for apples caused by: people enjoying apples less; pear prices plunging; people expecting a big drop in apple prices; fewer people living in the market area; or consumer incomes dropping. Any of these situations would force consumers to buy less than the 440 bushels they bought at $6 per bushel. Because growers have no reason to sell less, a surplus appears at $6. Consequently, prices fall until this surplus disappears at a new, lower equilibrium price, which corresponds to a lower equilibrium quantity. Such a situation occurs with sale-priced merchandise at the end of a season or when something goes out of style.

Price can also decline in a market because of a surplus caused by an increase in supply. This could occur in the apple market example if: production costs decline; growing weather improves; the profitability of other crops declines; or growers expect the future price of apples to be lower. Such circumstances will *not* affect the apple buyers. They still want only 440 bushels at $6. The extra apple output becomes a surplus. Consequently, the equilibrium price falls, but in this case the equilibrium quantity is higher than it was originally. The computer industry offers one of the best examples of an increase in supply. Dramatic reductions in manufacturing costs due to innovations led to increases in the supply of computers, thereby decreasing their prices and increasing the amount sold.

These and countless other examples of changing prices illustrate the vital role played by the concepts of supply and demand in understanding the world

Figure 5-9 Increasing the Demand for Apples and Its Effect on Price

Price (per bushel)	Bushels of Apples that: Consumers Want to Buy (d) (before)	(after)	Producers Want to Sell (s)	Shortage or Surplus Condition: (before)	(after)	Size of the Shortage or Surplus: (before)	(after)
$ 2	500	580	340	Shortage	Shortage	160	240
$ 4	470	550	390	Shortage	Shortage	80	160
$ 6	440	520	440	Neither	Shortage	0	80
$ 8	410	490	490	Surplus	Neither	80	0
$10	380	460	540	Surplus	Surplus	160	80

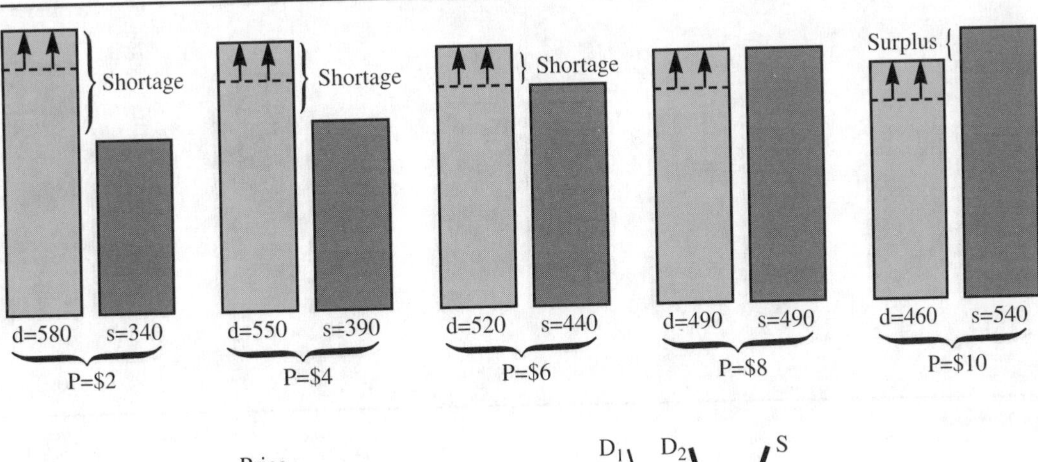

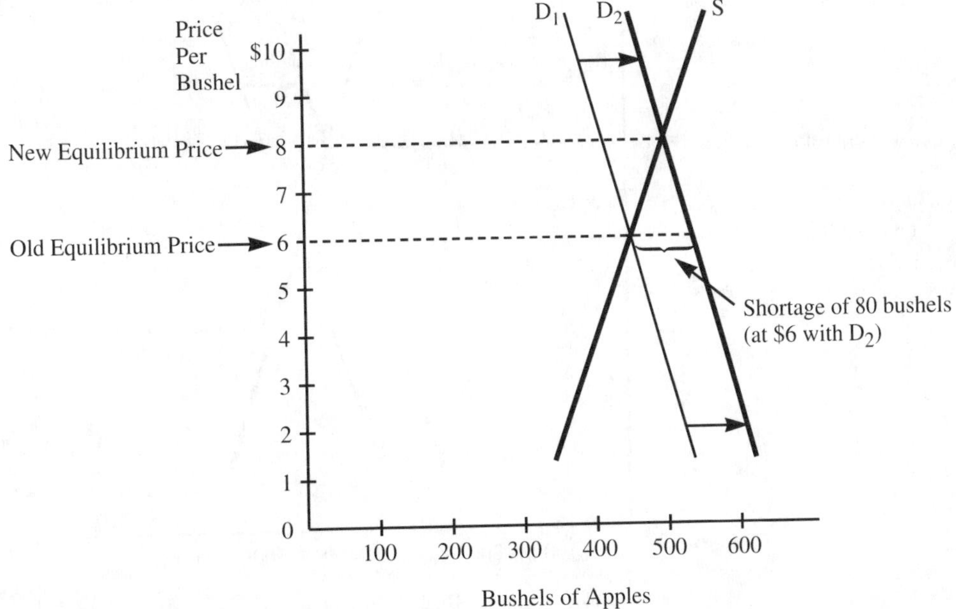

Figure 5-10 Decreasing the Supply of Apples and Its Effect on Price

Price (per bushel)	Bushels of Apples that: Consumers Want to Buy (d)	Producers Want to Sell (s) (before)	Producers Want to Sell (s) (after)	Shortage or Surplus Condition: (before)	Shortage or Surplus Condition: (after)	Size of the Shortage or Surplus: (before)	Size of the Shortage or Surplus: (after)
$ 2	500	340	260	Shortage	Shortage	160	240
$ 4	470	390	310	Shortage	Shortage	80	160
$ 6	440	440	360	Neither	Shortage	0	80
$ 8	410	490	410	Surplus	Neither	80	0
$10	380	540	460	Surplus	Surplus	160	80

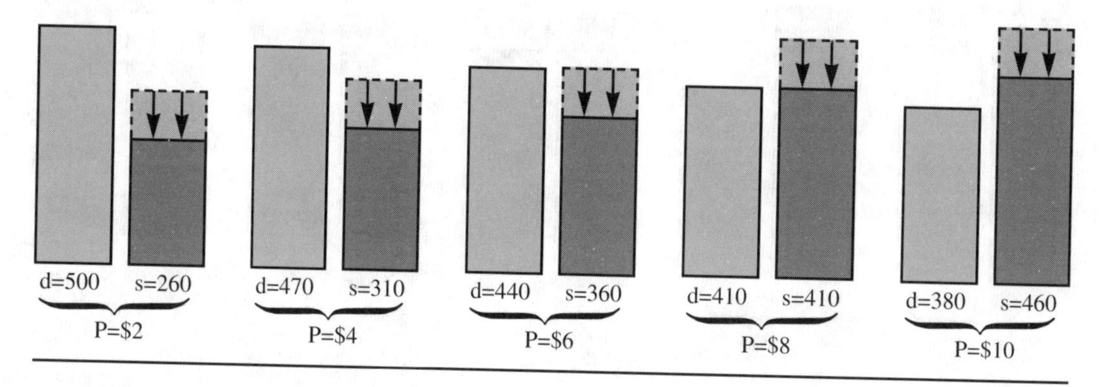

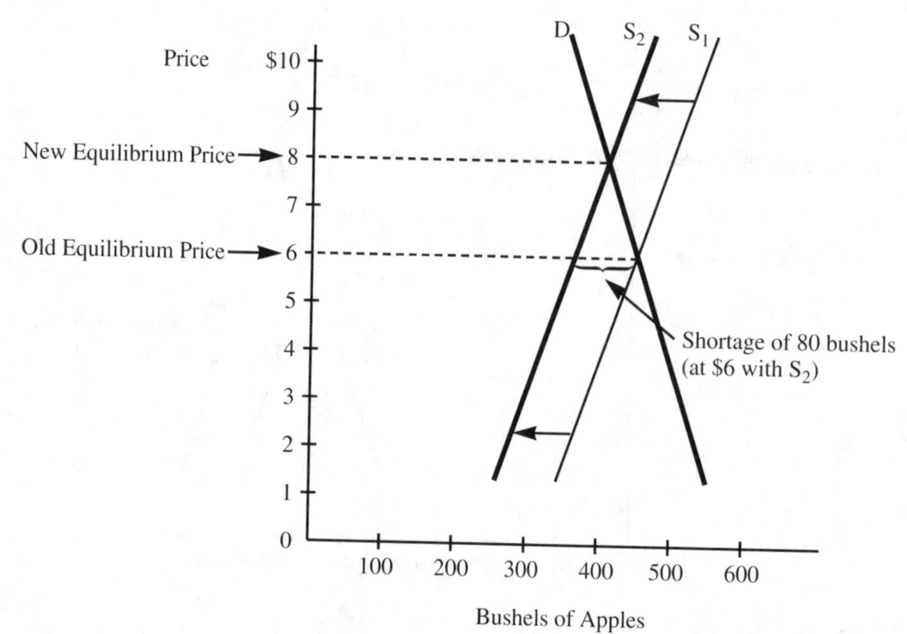

around you—and why that world is changing. You will often be in a stronger economic position if you can predict such price changes *before* they occur.

To conclude this chapter, let's consider the case of the steer that was mentioned at the beginning of the chapter. You might expect to find great shortages of tenderloin steak in meat departments, for a steer has very little of it (a low supply). On top of that, because it's so good and so tender, lots of people want tenderloin (a high demand). And you might expect to find surpluses (that is, uneaten portions) of round steak and other cuts from the abundant hind quarters. Besides, these cuts are tougher and don't taste as good. Finally, you could logically expect either: 1) shortages of liver and tongue because a steer has so little; or 2) surpluses of them because so many people detest them.

If the prices per pound of all parts of the steer were identical, you would indeed see shortages and surpluses of many cuts. But over the years, the price system has established *different* prices for the various cuts. Consequently, there are virtually no shortages. There are also no surpluses, thereby assuring that the whole steer will be eaten.

Chapter 5 SUMMARY

The amount of a good or service traded between buyers and sellers depends upon several things. One of these factors, price, merits special attention. If the amounts that buyers and sellers want to exchange at a given price are not alike, the price will change. In turn, changes in the wishes of buyers and sellers will make these two amounts alike. Once that point of balance, called equilibrium, is reached, there are no further changes in price and the amount traded, so long as demand and supply remain constant.

Buyers follow the law of demand when they buy less of a good or service at higher prices, and vice versa. They do so primarily because of the substitution effect. When an item is costly, substitutes become better things to buy. The income effect also leads buyers to obey the law of demand because higher prices have the same effect as a cut in income, and vice versa.

Sellers follow the law of supply when they offer more for sale at higher prices. They do so primarily because higher prices allow them to profitably produce levels of output that cost more to produce than lower levels of output.

A change in demand means that buyers want to buy either more or less—even though there is no change in price. It is caused by a change in one of the other factors determining how much consumers want to buy, including the usefulness of the item, the prices of substitutes and complements, consumers' incomes, future expectations of price and availability, and population. Similarly, a change in supply means firms want to offer either more or less for sale—even though the price doesn't change. A change in supply will occur following a change in any of the other factors determining how much firms wish to offer for sale, including production costs, expected future prices, the number of sellers, and the prices of other things it is possible to make with the same resources.

Low prices tend to create shortages because buyers want a lot of a low-priced item and sellers can't afford to offer much for sale. Customers who can't buy all they want, along with sellers seeking to increase profits, raise the price up to the equilibrium price. High prices do the opposite because low purchases and high availability create surpluses. Firms undercutting each other's prices plus bargain-demanding buyers force the price down to the equilibrium price.

Several things can prevent the price from moving to the equilibrium level, including government price controls, collusion, ignorance of the equilibrium price, and a reluctance to take advantage of market conditions.

The equilibrium price will increase if demand increases or supply decreases because either of these cause a shortage. The equilibrium price will fall if demand decreases or supply increases because either of these will cause a surplus.

Chapter 5 RESPONSES TO THE LEARNING OBJECTIVES

1. The major factors affecting consumer purchases for an item include the:
   a) prices of the item, its substitutes, and its complements
   b) benefit or satisfaction provided by the item
   c) population
   d) incomes of consumers
   e) prices of substitute goods
   f) prices of complementary goods
   g) expectations of future prices and the availability of the item
2. Buyers follow the law of demand because of the:
   a) substitution effect, for substitute goods provide more benefits per dollar at higher prices, and vice versa
   b) income effect, for buyers' incomes can't buy as many items at higher prices, and vice versa
3. If prices rise by x percent for a good, and if demand is:
   a) elastic, buyers cut purchases by more than x percent and total revenue falls, and vice versa for price deceases
   b) inelastic, buyers cut purchases by less than x percent and total revenue increases, and vice versa for price decreases
4. When there is a change in demand, buyers wish to purchase either more or less at each possible price. This occurs with changes in: satisfaction received from a product, population, consumers' incomes, prices of substitutes and complements, and future expectations of price and availability.
5. How much of an item sellers offer for sale depends on such factors as:
   a) the price of the item
   b) the production cost
   c) the expectation of future prices
   d) the number of sellers
   e) the prices of related goods
6. Sellers follow the law of supply because at higher prices they can afford to produce extra units of output that are more costly to produce than previous units.

7. When there is a change in supply, sellers offer either more or less for sale at each possible price. This could occur because of changes in: production costs, expected future prices, the number of sellers, and the prices of related goods.

8. Prices increase when there are shortages because:
   a) sellers can still sell all they want at the higher prices, thereby increasing their profits
   b) buyers outbid each other in order to gain possession of the item in "short supply"

   Prices decrease when there are surpluses because:
   a) sellers undercut one another in order to sell all they have to offer
   b) buyers refuse to pay the going price when they know someone will sell the item for less

9. Markets might fail to reach equilibrium because:
   a) no one knows exactly what the equilibrium price is
   b) there is collusion among sellers
   c) sellers have other goals besides short-run profit maximization
   d) there are price ceilings or price floors

10. If there is an increase in demand, both the equilibrium price and the equilibrium quantity will rise, and vice versa for a decrease in demand. An increase in supply will lead to a decrease in the equilibrium price and an increase in the equilibrium quantity. A decrease in supply will lead to an increase in the equilibrium price and a decrease in the equilibrium quantity.

Chapter 5 LEARNING ACTIVITIES AND DISCUSSION QUESTIONS

1. Determine if your personal demand for hamburgers, movies, and college tuition would be elastic or inelastic if their prices would increase by 50 percent. Why do these demands have such elasticity?
2. What are some factors that would lead to a decrease in demand for swimsuits? Would they also affect supply? Why or why not?
3. Find three examples each of shortages and surpluses. Why doesn't the price change to clear the market in each case?
4. Why do winning bidders at auctions often not pay as much for the item as they are willing to pay? In such cases, does the value of the item equal the price, or is one larger than the other—both for the winning bidder and the other bidders?
5. Should there be a ceiling on college textbook prices? Why or why not? What would be the consequences, if any?

APPENDIX THE ELASTICITY OF DEMAND

The elasticity of demand refers to buyer response to changes in price. If demand is elastic, a given percentage price change will result in a greater percentage change in purchases. Alternatively, if demand is inelastic, a given percentage change in price will result in a smaller percentage change in purchases.

The Coefficient of Elasticity

The coefficient of elasticity indicates just how elastic or inelastic the demand for a good or service is. It is found by dividing the percentage change in quantity purchased by the percentage change in price, or:

e = (percentage change in quantity)/(percentage change in price)

If these percentages are not known, the coefficient can be calculated by the formula:

$$e = (Q_2 - Q_1)/Q_1 \div (P_2 - P_1)/P_1$$

P_1 refers to the initial price and P_2 to the new price. Q_1 is the initial amount consumers want and Q_2 the amount purchased after the price change. Because demand is an inverse relationship, the coefficient is always negative. However, it is always stated in absolute value form (meaning the minus sign is dropped). If the coefficient is: 1) greater than one, the demand is elastic; 2) equal to one, the demand is unitary elastic; or 3) less than one, the demand is inelastic. (There is a more complex, but also more accurate, version of the formula. The single Q_1 in the numerator is replaced by $(Q_1 + Q_2) \div 2$. The single P_1 in the denominator is replaced by $(P_1 + P_2) \div 2$.)

Suppose consumers want to buy 600 sweatshirts if the price is $12. If the price rises to $15, they want fewer shirts—say only 500. Figure A5-1 shows a demand curve reflecting such desired purchases. The coefficient of elasticity is 0.67, found in either of two ways. First, as the price rose 25 percent ($12 to $15) and the quantity fell by 16.67 percent, then $e = 16.67\% \div 25.0\% = 0.67$

Second, the formula given above can be used to calculate e as follows:

$$e = (500 - 600)/600 \div (15 - 12)/12 = 100/600 \div 3/12 = 1/6 \div 1/4 = 0.67$$

Thus, between $12 and $15, demand is inelastic.

On the other hand, the demand curve in Figure A5-2 is elastic between these prices. Note that for the same 25 percent increase in price, quantity purchased fell 50 percent (600 down to 300), so that $e = 50\% \div 25\% = 2.0$

Essentially, e = 2.0 means the response in purchases to the price change is twice as large as the price change itself.

Figure A5-1 An Inelastic Demand

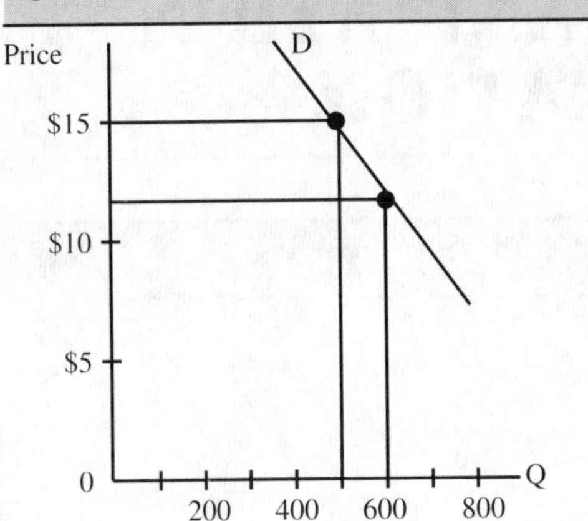

Figure A5-2 An Elastic Demand

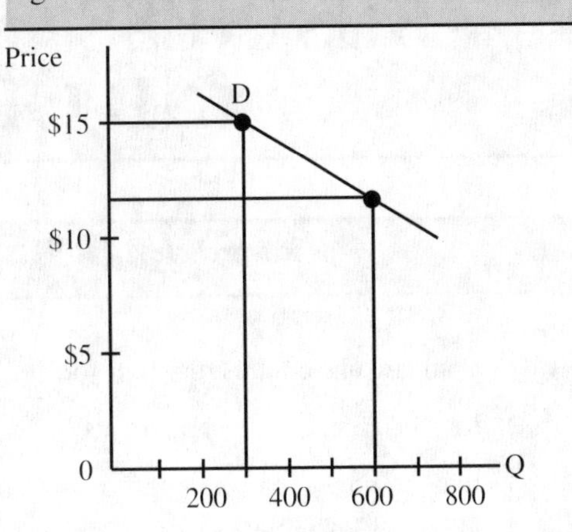

Notice that the demand curve is steeper for the inelastic case than the elastic case. In general, you can say that steeper demand curves imply more inelasticity, but such generalization usually works only in such cases as shown in the figures, where the price and quantity ranges are similar.

If the demand line is horizontal, the demand relationship is called perfectly elastic. Alternatively, a demand line that is vertical means the demand is perfectly inelastic.

Determinants of Elasticity

Four major factors determine the degree of elasticity of demand for a good or service: 1) the number of substitutes; 2) the share of income spent on an item; 3) how necessary the item is; and 4) the length of the market period.

■ The first determinent of demand elasticity is the number of substitutes. The more substitutes a product has, the more elastic the demand tends to be. For example, a certain theater might face competition from a dozen other theaters. A dollar increase in price at the first theater would drive many people to competing theaters. On the other hand, in a small town with little other entertainment, a theater probably wouldn't lose many patrons after a similar price increase.

■ Second, the share of a person's income spent on a product influences elasticity. Something that takes a tiny share of a budget, such as a box of matches, tends to have a very inelastic demand. However, sellers of items such as sailboats and luxury cruises generally find that customers are very price conscious.

■ Third, necessary items such as insulin and work uniforms tend to have extremely inelastic demands. People must pay whatever price is asked. However, when things that people can easily do without, such as novelty items and videotapes, go up in price, their sales drop sharply.

■ Finally, the length of the market period influences price elasticity. Generally, the longer the period of time following a price increase, the more that consumers will reduce their purchases. The OPEC nations found this out the hard way by the early 1980s. Given time to replace their gas-guzzling cars and oil furnaces, consumers used significantly less oil in the long run than they did right after the price increases of the 1970s.

CHAPTER 6

BUSINESS ORGANIZATION AND OPERATION

★★★★★ LEARNING OBJECTIVES ★★★★★

1. Compare and contrast the four forms of business organization.
2. List the components of a balance sheet and an income statement.
3. Explain how to calculate the costs of business operation by using the various methods of measuring costs.
4. Explain the difference between an accountant's and an economist's approach to costs.
5. Compare and contrast the five possibilities for accounting and economic profits and losses.
6. Outline the two roles of profit in a capitalist economy.
7. Compare and contrast the effects of profits and losses on resource allocation in an industry.
8. Compare and contrast the four different market structures.
9. Describe how a firm decides its size of operation.
10. Describe how a purely competitive firm determines its maximum profit level of output in the short run.

TERMS

single proprietorship
unlimited liability
partnership
corporation
limited liability
cooperative
merger
subsidiary
income statement
average cost
total cost
total fixed cost
average fixed cost
total variable cost
average variable cost
marginal cost
marginal revenue
explicit cost
implicit cost
normal profit
economic profit
economic loss
industry
market structure
pure competition
monopolistic competition
barrier to entry
oligopoly
monopoly
optimum scale of plant
short run
long run

In this chapter you will learn about the organization and operation of private enterprises and discover many business terms. Learning the terms and concepts of this chapter will help you understand how the owners of firms face their problem of scarcity and how this affects all of us.

BUSINESS ORGANIZATION

America is a country where you can fulfill the dream of owning your own business. If your innovations increase the efficiency of resource use, you also help relieve the burden of resource scarcity faced by society.

Types of Business Firms

Depending upon how business is defined, America has between 15 million and 20 million firms. Sometimes the distinction between firms and hobbies is fuzzy—as with "weekend farms" and photography "businesses." Retail stores are the most common type of business. There are also 27,000 hamburger outlets and 19,000 pizza parlors, and there are about two million farms.

Businesses generally fall into one of four categories: a single proprietorship, partnership, corporation, or cooperative.

★1

■ The first type of firm is the **single proprietorship** (also called the sole proprietorship). Three of every four firms are proprietorships, but their combined sales account for only 10 percent of the nation's total sales because these firms are usually small.

The proprietor owns the business and in a legal sense *is* the business, keeping all the profits and being liable for its activities. Probably the major reason there are so many proprietorships is that owners get to be their own bosses. A major disadvantage is that the owner faces **unlimited liability** because there is no limit to the amount someone can sue the proprietor. Also, proprietorships usually die with their owners. Another disadvantage is the inability to raise any money beyond the personal credit of the proprietor, thereby limiting the firm's size and its efficiency of operation. Some advantages of the single proprietorship are its ease of formation, flexibility, and being able to avoid the corporate income tax (although the proprietor still must pay personal income taxes on the profits). In addition, government requirements (paperwork and regulations) for single proprietorships are minimal. Proprietorships also face the smallest risk of an income tax audit, as the government finds it more efficient to focus its resources on larger firms.

■ The second business type is the **partnership**, which has multiple owners. Two advantages here are the ability to raise more funds and to attract a wider range of talents. One disadvantage is that each partner usually faces unlimited liability. Another problem is possible friction between partners, which is the main reason why less than one firm in ten is a partnership. Partnerships are most frequent in professions (law firms, accounting firms) and farming.

■ The third form of business is the **corporation**. Although only one in six firms is a corporation, $5 out of every $6 spent in this nation go to corporations. Most big firms are corporations. Technically, a corporation is a "legal person" because, just like a real person, a corporation earns income, pays taxes, can sue and be sued, can own property, and can make contracts, all in the name of the corporation.

Whoever owns a share of corporate stock owns part of the corporation. Most often, there is just one stockholder, but large corporations usually have thousands. Pension funds (organizations that invest the money that corporations and governments have available for their retirees) hold about one-fourth of all stocks. One advantage of the corporate form is **limited liability**, which means stockholders cannot lose more than the amount of money they invested in the firm. Another is the ability to raise large amounts of money to finance the enormous capital purchases of large firms. Corporations also raise money by selling bonds. A bond is a promissory note, so a bondholder is a lender to or a creditor of a corporation. A last advantage of corporations is the possibility of perpetual life, as the stock of deceased stockholders passes or is sold to others.

The corporate form also has disadvantages. Owners suffer "double taxation," for after the corporation itself pays income taxes, the owners also pay taxes on any dividends the corporation distributes. Corporations require more paperwork, from getting the charter (the right to do business from the state) to routine forms and more complex tax returns.

■ The final form of business is the **cooperative** (or co-op), in which the owners are also the people who use the services of the business. If a cooperative is incorporated, it has stockholders and pays dividends in proportion to the amount of business transacted. However, since each owner (or "member") usually has one vote in a democratic process, there is equal control of the operation of the business.

You might know of a food co-op, where members purchase food, often contributing unpaid labor to the business. Co-ops are common in agriculture, where farmers establish marketing cooperatives to sell (and often process) their products. Ocean Spray (cranberries), Sunkist (citrus fruits), and Blue Diamond (almonds) are some examples. Many milk processors are also cooperatives. Farmers commonly use service cooperatives from which they buy supplies and services. The REA (the Rural Electrification Association) is a collection of such co-ops established in the 1930s and 1940s to supply electric power to farms. Credit unions are also cooperatives, where the depositors are the owners. There are more than 14,000 credit unions in the United States.

The Special Terminology of Corporations

The terminology common to corporations is widely used. You already learned what corporate stock is, but corporate stock is of two broad types. Common stock gives the stockholder the right to vote at stockholders' meetings. Each stockholder has as many votes as shares held. Preferred stock, the second type, gives no voting rights to stockholders. However, they have the first claim on profits, which is important in lean years.

A firm known as a private corporation (or a closely held corporation) is one in which all or virtually all the stock belongs to a few people and which no one else can buy. Alternatively, a firm known as a public corporation has many stockholders, and anyone can buy the stock. (Don't confuse this with a *public enterprise* that *everybody* owns, such as the U.S. Postal Service.) Many private corporations start out small and then decide to expand. They often do so by "going public" (letting others purchase stock). Occasionally the opposite occurs, with a small group "taking a firm private" by buying up most or all of the stock. Often the group does this in a "leveraged buyout" (LBO), which means they use "leverage" (credit) for most of the money required.

An ESOP (Employee Stock Ownership Plan) is a mechanism through which employees own shares in the firm where they work. Although many firms sell stock to their employees, ESOPs are unique in that they work through trusts established for the employees. The trust then invests in the company's stock. In recent years, many employees tried to save their jobs in firms that were about to fold by forming ESOPs and buying the firms. There are more than 10,000 ESOPs in the United States.

Stockholders elect directors, who make up the board of directors. The directors' function is to ensure that the returns to the stockholders' investments are maximized. Stockholders hire directors as "watchdogs" because the stockholders might be far away from the firm's operations, ignorant of business operations, or occupied elsewhere. The board, in turn, selects the president, secretary, and other officers who actually operate the firm.

A **merger** combines two or more corporations into one corporation. Generally mergers are of three types: horizontal, vertical, and conglomerate.

- A horizontal merger combines firms that do pretty much the same thing. An example of a firm formed in a horizontal merger is General Motors, which combined several car assembly companies. Another example is the 1993 merger of Russell Stover Candies and Whitman's Chocolates.
- A vertical merger combines firms that are involved in different stages of the production process or the marketing of some good or service. An example is General Motors' purchases of AC Spark Plug Corporation and Fisher Body Corporation (which used to make horse carriages). A special type of vertical merger involves the marketing of a firm's product. Chrysler Corporation's purchase of Dollar Rent A Car Systems Inc. is an example.
- The third type is the conglomerate merger, a combination of unrelated firms. Often called diversified companies, they include LTV, Tenneco, Gulf + Western, and ITT. The reverse of diversification, called divestiture, became increasingly common in the 1980s after many conglomerates fared poorly.

Many people were upset by some mergers in the 1980s that involved "corporate raiders," those intent on gaining a controlling share of a "target corporation" in a "hostile takeover." Generally raiders gain control by offering current stockholders a higher price for the stock than the current market price. Critics say raiders merely want to drive up the price of the stock and sell it at a huge gain. Raiders claim they benefit society by ridding the taken-over firm of bad managers. They offer premium prices for the stock, expecting future dividends to be higher once the new managers increase profits. Or they may hope to coerce threatened managers into buying back shares the raiders purchased, but at a premium above their acquisition cost, a phenomenon known as "greenmail." By 1989, 39 states had laws designed to prevent takeovers. Many managers of target firms try to resist takeovers, often by seeking a "white knight" (a more favorable buyer). They may also force the raider to accept a "poison pill" (a financially disastrous condition following a takeover), such as allowing current shareholders to buy more stock at a large discount. Raiders often finance takeovers by selling corporate bonds. Because the risk of default (non-payment) on these bonds is high, the bonds are called "junk bonds." The bonds pay high interest rates (or yields) to encourage investors to accept this risk.

A **subsidiary** is a company owned by another company, either partly or completely. Miller Brewing Corporation, for example, is a subsidiary of Phillip-Morris, Inc. The subsidiary retains its identity as a corporation, which is not true in most mergers. In the future, the subsidiary could again become completely independent. Fisher-Price Corporation was a subsidiary of Quaker Oats Corporation until Fisher-Price's divestiture in 1989.

A franchiser is a firm that gives another firm, the franchisee, the right to do business in a specified way and area. There are about 2,500 franchisers and 275,000 franchisees in the United States. The franchisee receives guidance, financing, advertising, and other assistance. It pays the franchiser a franchise fee for this plus a share of the sales or profit. Franchises are most common in the fast food business and other small retail operations. But professional sports teams, such as those in the NFL and the NBA, also are corporations that have franchises.

Venture capital is money provided to a new firm that needs it to start operations. Usually the firms are innovators, not copies of existing firms. Among many sources of venture capital is a fairly new type of business firm, the venture-capital firm. There are more than 600 of these firms, with $32 billion invested in thousands of companies. Usually someone in the venture capital firm obtains a position on the board of directors of the new firm. Venture capital is also provided by so-called angels, who are individuals that invest in new firms. There are over one-quarter million of these risk takers.

BUSINESS ACCOUNTING—REVENUES, COSTS, AND PROFITS

In the careful record-keeping that sound business operation requires, two business statements are most critical: 1) the balance sheet or net worth statement; and 2) the income statement.

★2

On the balance sheet, the firm first lists all its assets (what it owns plus other "positives"), including cash, accounts receivable, land and buildings, its inventory of supplies and finished goods, stock owned in other firms, and so on. Next, the firm lists its liabilities (or what it owes plus other "negatives"). These may include accounts payable (bills), accrued (unpaid) wages, loans, and accrued taxes. The difference between assets and liabilities is the net worth or owner's equity. Only what are called stock variables appear on a balance sheet. Like the number of gallons of water in a tank, stock variables are always measured at a *point* in time.

The **income statement**, or the profit and loss (P&L) statement, has three broad sections: 1) revenue; 2) costs; and 3) profit or loss. The P&L statement shows how well the firm did financially for a given period of time. Revenue, cost, and profit or loss are all examples of flow variables. Like water flowing into a tank that is measured in gallons per minute (a *period* of time), they are measured over a period, such as a month, quarter, or year.

■ First, the income statement shows the firm's revenues, or sales, known as total revenue (TR), or total sales. TR equals the price (P) times the quantity sold (Q)—or, TR = P x Q.

★3 ■ Second, this statement shows production expenses or costs. The **average cost** (AC) is the cost of producing just one unit of output, on average. Therefore, a firm's total expenses, or its **total cost** (TC), equals its average cost times the quantity produced—or, TC = AC x Q. Often a firm splits its total cost into two categories, fixed and variable. Its fixed costs, which include such things as property taxes, license fees, and rent, do not change if the firm changes its output. One major cost often (but not always) considered as fixed is depreciation. It reflects a year's share of the purchase price of capital goods that last for more than one year. Adding up the various fixed costs gives the **total fixed cost** (TFC), commonly known as overhead.

If a firm spreads its overhead evenly over each unit of output, each unit's share of the overhead is the **average fixed cost** (AFC). Average fixed cost is found by the formula: AFC = TFC ÷ Q. Suppose a firm makes 20,000 lamps a year and has total fixed costs of $800,000. Thus, its AFC = $800,000 ÷ 20,000, or $40. This means the firm pays $40 per lamp for "fixed resources" (those it need not increase when it increases production). One such resource could be a rented factory. Now suppose the firm adds a second shift in this same factory, boosting output to 40,000 lamps per year. Then the AFC falls to $20 per lamp, as AFC = $800,000 ÷ 40,000, or $20. Essentially, the firm spreads $800,000 over twice as many lamps, which means each lamp's share is half as much. For a given business size (its capital stock), the larger the output, the lower the average fixed cost.

The second category of costs that make up total cost is variable costs. Such costs vary as a firm's output varies. These are the costs of additional "variable resources" a firm needs when it increases output. They include raw materials, labor, and fuel for machines and vehicles. **Total variable cost** (TVC) is the sum of all such variable costs, commonly called operating costs or production costs. If these are spread evenly over all units of output, the result is **average variable cost** (AVC). You find AVC by dividing the total variable cost by the level of production—or, AVC = TVC ÷ Q. Suppose the lamp maker has $1,200,000 in variable expenses when it makes 20,000 lamps a year. Then the AVC is $60, for $60 = $1,200,000 ÷ 20,000. This tells the firm that each lamp cost $60 for operating expenses.

Finally, the same kind of averaging can be done with total costs. Dividing total costs by output gives the average cost—or, AC = TC ÷ Q. You also can find average cost by adding the average fixed cost and the average variable cost—or, AC = AFC + AVC. The average cost of making lamps reflects payment for all the resources needed to make one lamp, on average. Thus, it reflects the efficiency of resource use in making lamps.

One more useful cost concept is **marginal cost** (MC), or the *extra* cost to make an *extra* unit of output. Consider again the lamp maker. At an output of 20,000 lamps, its total cost is $2,000,000 (as TFC = $800,000 and TVC = $1,200,000). If it makes lamp number 20,001, any addition to that $2,000,000 is the marginal cost. Suppose the total cost for 20,001 lamps is $2,000,070. Then the marginal cost is $70 (= $2,000,070 - $2,000,000). So the MC is the difference in the total cost between successive levels of output. However, because fixed costs do not increase as output increases, MC is also the difference in the total variable cost between successive levels of output.

A related concept is **marginal revenue** (MR), the *extra* revenue or sales a firm makes by producing an extra unit of output. If the firm has a total revenue of $2,400,000 when making 20,000 lamps and $2,400,090 when making 20,001 lamps, then its marginal revenue for lamp number 20,001 is $90 (= $2,400,090 - $2,400,000).

Table 6-1 lists all the formulas covered thus far. Table 6-2 presents another example of a producer, which shows a table manufacturer's costs at various daily output levels.

Looking at the average cost column in Table 6-2, notice that AC is lowest at an output of 10 tables, or $150 per table. Therefore, that is the most efficient level of production because the firm is using the least amount of resources to make tables. (Incidentally, the most efficient level of output is not necessarily the most profitable level of output. This should become clear to you on pages 163-164.)

■ The third and last section of the income statement shows whether the firm made a profit or had a loss. That figure appears on the last or bottom line of the statement and is the source of that overused phrase "the bottom line."

Profit can be measured in a number of ways. First, the bottom of an income statement gives the gross income, or profit before any income taxes are paid. If the firm is a corporation, it must pay income taxes on this gross income. The remainder is the firm's net income or net profit.

Second, the net margin method of measuring profit shows what percent of a firm's sales (TR) it earns as net income. The remainder goes to cover its expenses and income taxes. It is found by dividing net income by sales.

Third, the rate of return on equity shows what percent of a firm's equity it earns in net income. It is found by dividing net income by its equity. This method can be likened to the rate of interest you earn on a savings account in a bank.

Fourth, the net income per share shows how much net income a corporation earns for each share of stock. It is found by dividing the net income by the total number of shares held by the stockholders.

Table 6-3 summarizes all the formulas relating to the measure of profit.

Table 6-1 Cost Formulas

TC = TFC + TVC	AC = TC/Q	AC = AFC + AVC
AFC = TFC/Q	AVC = TVC/Q	

Table 6-2 The Various Categories of Costs of a Table Manufacturing Firm

Q	TC	TFC	TVC	AFC	AVC	AC	MC
0	$ 320	$320	$ 0	–	–	–	–
1	600	320	280	$320.00	$280.00	$600.00	$ 280
2	800	320	480	160.00	240.00	400.00	200
3	920	320	600	106.67	200.00	306.67	120
4	1000	320	680	80.00	170.00	250.00	80
5	1050	320	730	64.00	146.00	210.00	50
6	1110	320	790	53.33	137.67	185.00	60
7	1180	320	860	45.71	122.86	168.57	70
8	1260	320	940	40.00	117.50	157.50	80
9	1370	320	1050	35.56	116.67	152.23	110
10	1500	320	1180	32.00	118.00	150.00	150
11	1720	320	1400	29.09	127.27	156.36	220
12	2000	320	1680	26.67	140.00	166.67	280
13	2320	320	2000	24.62	153.85	178.47	320
14	2700	320	2380	22.86	170.00	192.86	380
15	3250	320	2930	21.33	195.33	216.67	550
16	4800	320	4480	20.00	280.00	300.00	1550

Table 6-3 The Formulas Used to Determine Profit

Total Revenue = Price x Quantity Sold or TR = PxQ

Gross Income = Total Revenue - Total Costs

Net Income = Gross Income - Income Taxes

$$\text{Net Margin} = \frac{\text{Net Income}}{\text{Total Revenue}}$$

$$\text{Rate of Return on Equity} = \frac{\text{Net Income}}{\text{Owner's Equity}}$$

$$\text{Profit per Share} = \frac{\text{Net Income}}{\text{Number of Shares}}$$

The business of America is business

– President Calvin Coolidge

Thrift may be the handmaid and nurse of enterprise. But equally she may not. For the engine which drives enterprise is not thrift, but profit.

– John Maynard Keynes

Table 6-4 An Income Statement

Total Sales	**$500,000**
Expenses	
Supplies	$170,000
Wages and Salaries	$148,000
Depreciation	$ 40,000
Utilities	$ 11,000
Legal and Other Professional Fees	$ 3,000
Rent	$ 2,000
Other Expenses	$ 26,000
Total Costs	**$400,000**
Gross Income	**$100,000**
Income Taxes	$ 20,000
Net Income	**$ 80,000**

Net Margin $= \frac{\$80,000}{\$500,000} = 16.0\%$

Rate of Return on Equity $= \frac{\$80,000}{\$600,000} = 13.3\%$

Net Income per Share $= \frac{\$80,000}{50,000} = \$1.60$ per Share

Table 6-4 presents an income statement for a firm with the various measures of profit shown at the bottom. Distributions of dividends to shareholders (not shown in Table 6-4) are usually drawn from net income.

PROFIT AND RESOURCE ALLOCATION

Remember the purpose of economics: to reduce the problem caused by resource scarcity. This occurs when resources are used more efficiently so there are better answers to the Basic Economic Questions. Now you will learn how profits (or the *lack* of them) help maximize efficiency and our economic welfare.

Economic vs. Accounting Profit

★4

Until now it was implied that all costs or expenses require a business to pay money to owners of resources, such as laborers and suppliers. Such costs are known as **explicit costs** and are called that because the paying of money makes it very explicit that the firm gives up something. These are the only costs that appear on an income statement and also the only costs the IRS accepts on tax returns.

Yet every business—or rather its owner—gives up other things of value besides money when operating the business. These are called **implicit costs**. Remember, a cost is anything of value that is given up to gain something else. Suppose that Mr. Edwards, the owner of a radio manufacturing firm, gave up a $60,000-a-year job managing another radio manufacturing firm so he could be his own boss. Since he no longer has that $60,000, it is a real cost for him of making radios. This cost is called implicit wages and is one of the implicit costs of doing business. Here the word implicit means the owner does not pay these costs with money. Another is implicit interest, which is interest given up when money is drawn out of a bank or an investment to be used in a business. Many of these costs can be expressed in money terms, but it's harder to quantify others, such as stress caused by competition, fear of failure, and responsibility. (Implicit costs may be easier to conceptualize if compared to the "loss of sanity" parents experience in raising children. This "loss" is never considered in studies on what it "cost" to raise a child.)

Implicit costs are nothing more than opportunity costs. Economists term the combination of all a firm's implicit costs its **normal profit** (the reason it's called "normal" will be explained shortly). If a firm has enough sales to pay its explicit costs *and* its implicit costs or normal profit, any money left over is called **economic profit**. This situation is shown in the bottom part of Figure 6-1. Note that the economist's explicit costs are identical to the accountant's view of costs in the upper part of the figure.

Alternatively, if there are *not enough* revenues to cover the explicit costs plus the implicit costs, this shortfall is called an **economic loss**. This *economic* profit and loss is different from a profit or loss that appears on the income statement, where it is called accounting profit or accounting loss.

★5

Figure 6-2 shows a firm's five possibilities for accounting and economic profit. Each case represents an increasingly less desirable position, and its position determines whether it will: 1) continue making the item it does; or 2) make some other item or completely close down its operations. The next section on the role of profit explains these decisions in more detail.

■ In the first case, the firm has sufficient revenues to pay all its explicit and implicit costs. Any money left over is its economic profit. This situation means the owners get more benefits from their resources than they could from any other way of using them. Thus, such a firm will keep making whatever it makes so long as it earns this profit. Also, new firms will enter such an industry in order to earn these unusually high profits.

■ In the second case, there are no such "excess" funds, only enough to pay all costs, explicit plus implicit. There is no economic profit, yet no economic loss either. Occasionally a business owner who faces such a situation says, "I'm not making any profit." This can confuse many people, for any accountant or IRS agent will swear that profits are indeed being earned. But these are accounting profits, and in this case they equal the amount of implicit costs. And because business owners consider implicit costs to be just as real as explicit (cash) costs, owners in this situation say they are just breaking even—or are making no profit. But the profit the *owners* are speaking about is *economic* profit.

Figure 6-1 Revenues, Costs, and Profits – Viewpoints of Accountants and Economists

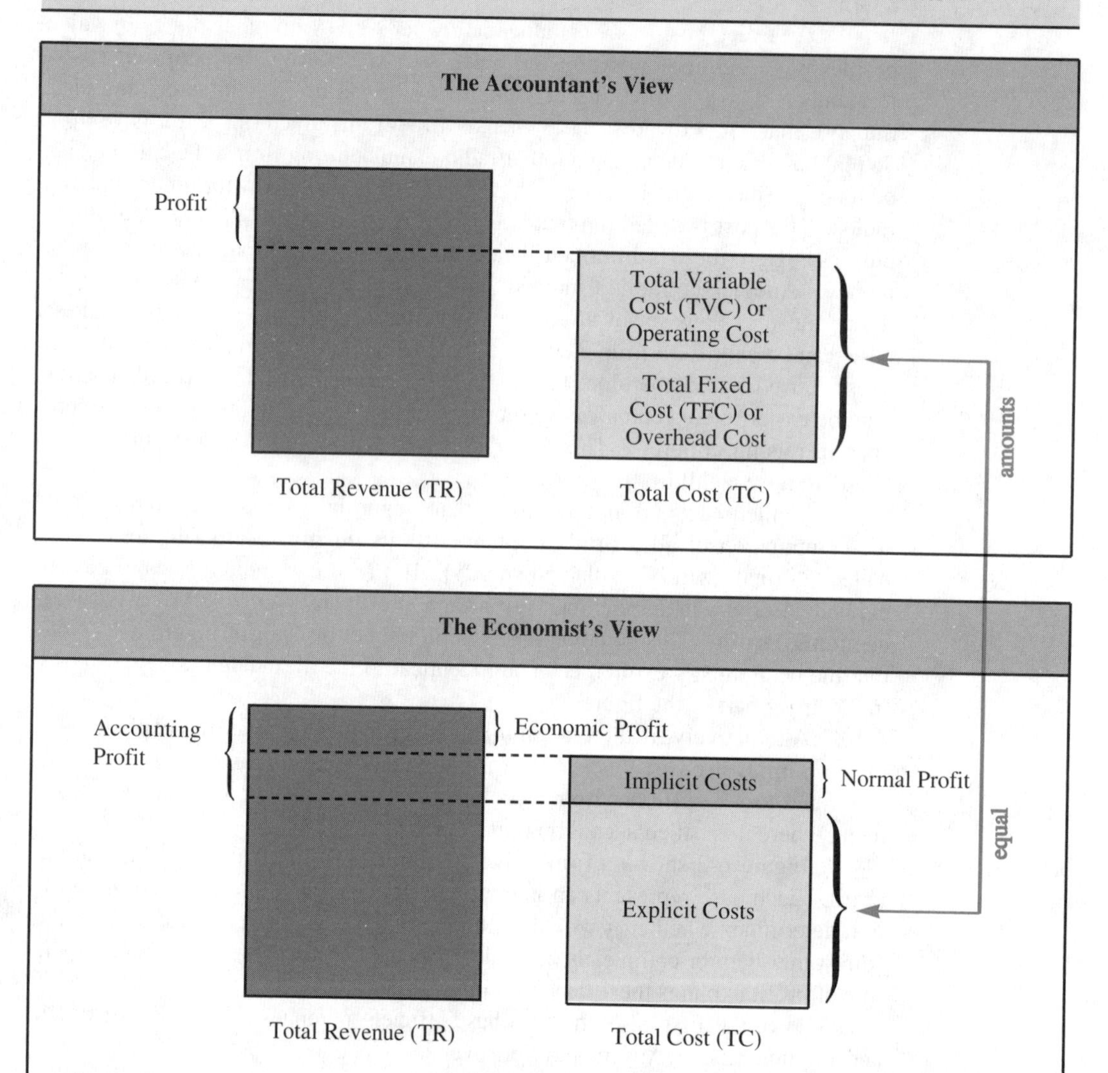

As you saw a few paragraphs above, we say that a firm in this situation is earning only normal profit. The word normal indicates that this is the amount most firms in a competitive industry generally (or normally) earn. The reason they only earn this amount will be explained in the next section. An industry that earns only normal profits and has no economic profits or losses will not attract new firms nor will it lose any.

■ In the third case, there is enough revenue to pay all *cash* (explicit) expenses, plus there is some revenue left over to cover *some* implicit costs. However, the remainder of those implicit costs are *not* covered. That is the *economic* loss the owner suffers. Owners of firms with economic losses could earn more if their resources were employed elsewhere. An owner of a small business

Figure 6-2 Accounting and Economic Profits – 5 Possibilities

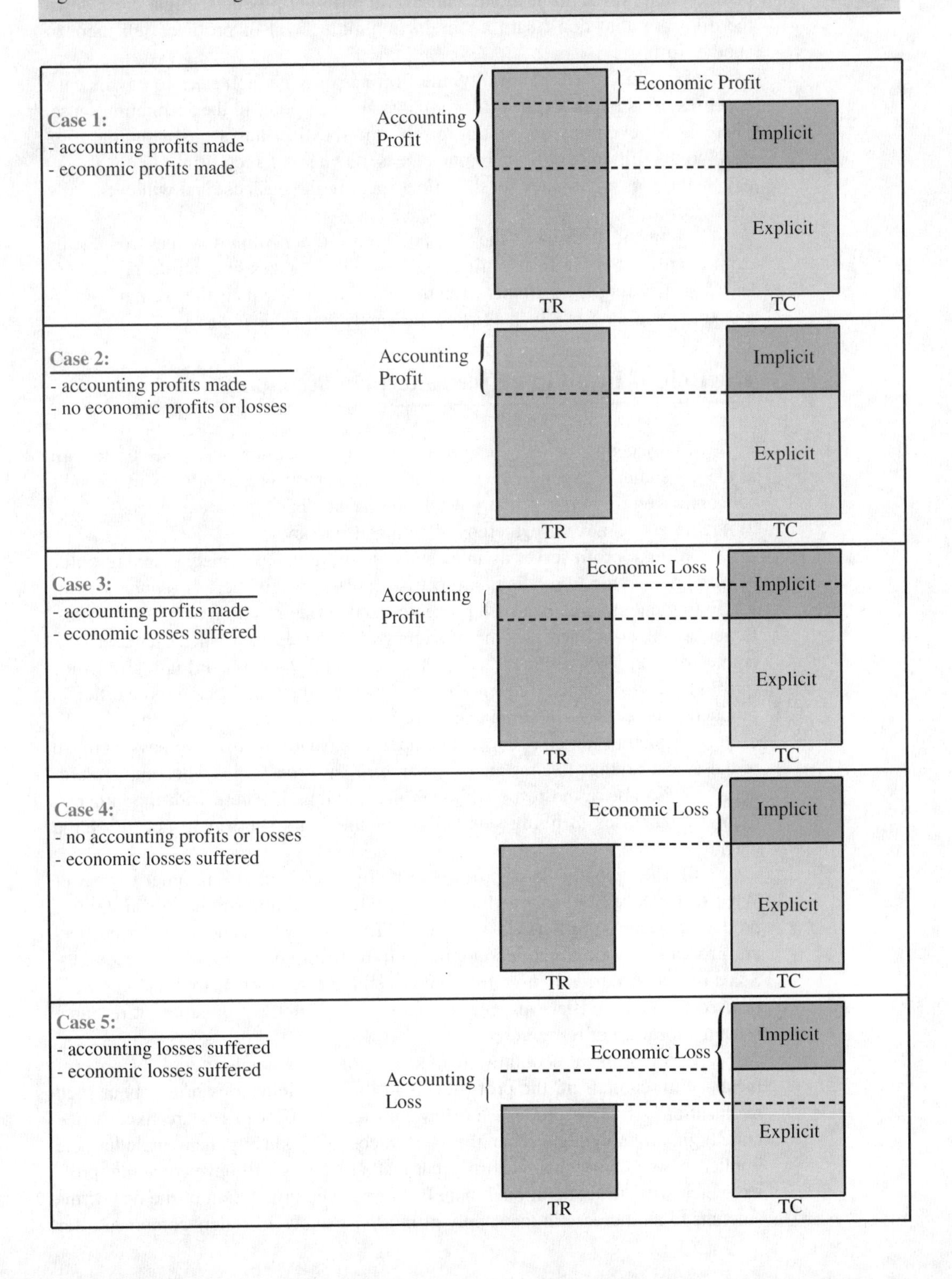

with economic losses might go into another business or line of work. A large corporation that makes not just one, but several different products, might close down the divisions that don't earn a certain minimum level of profit or sell them to another firm.

■ In the fourth possibility, the firm has only enough sales to pay its cash expenses or its explicit costs. It is at its break-even point in the accounting sense. There is not even any accounting profit, and the firm has a big economic loss, equal to the full amount of its implicit costs. Owners of such firms are not able to pay themselves any money for their time spent in the business and will eventually close down.

■ In the fifth case, there is not even enough money to pay for all the explicit costs. As the firm can't pay all its bills, it faces both an economic loss and an accounting loss. In this case, the economic loss equals the accounting loss plus the implicit costs. Such a firm will quickly leave this industry.

The Role of Profit in a Free Enterprise Economy

★6

Many people believe that profit is merely something businesses try to earn at the consumer's expense. But like it or not, profit greatly affects everyone's economic welfare in two primary ways: 1) it is an incentive for entrepreneurs; and 2) it redirects resource use, thereby affecting efficiency.

■ First, profit serves as an incentive to bring the extremely scarce resource of entrepreneurship to production processes. (The "profit" here is *economic* profit.) Entrepreneurs organize such processes, and good ones do it better than others. Better organization increases the efficiency of resource use, which increases economic welfare. When entrepreneurs are successful, their reward is high income (profits), which is the consequence of the lower production costs in more efficient production processes. In a free market economy with strong competition, the efficient entrepreneur (and any copycat competitor) usually is forced to pass on much of these cost savings to consumers. Therefore, *everyone* gains when an entrepreneur can rise above the rest. Although many things interfere with this process, dramatic increases in living standards over the years show it works to a large extent.

■ The second role of profit is to redirect resource use in order to answer What to Produce? or How to Produce? differently. Suppose that too little of a product (say, auto mufflers) is produced. "Too little" means not enough mufflers are produced to maximize economic welfare from society's scarce resources. Some resources currently used to make something else (such as toy trucks) should be used to make mufflers instead. Economists call such a redirection of resource use a reallocation of resources.

★7

In a command economy, reallocation of resources is the job of government. With capitalism, the profit levels in different industries bring about such reallocation. If firms produce too few mufflers, muffler prices are likely to be quite high, probably higher than the average cost of producing them, including the implicit costs. Consequently, firms that make mufflers will have economic profits, which will attract additional manufacturers. The production of the new firms amounts to an increase in the supply of mufflers. Now all sellers combined offer

Figure 6-3 How Economic Profits and Losses Redirect Resource Use

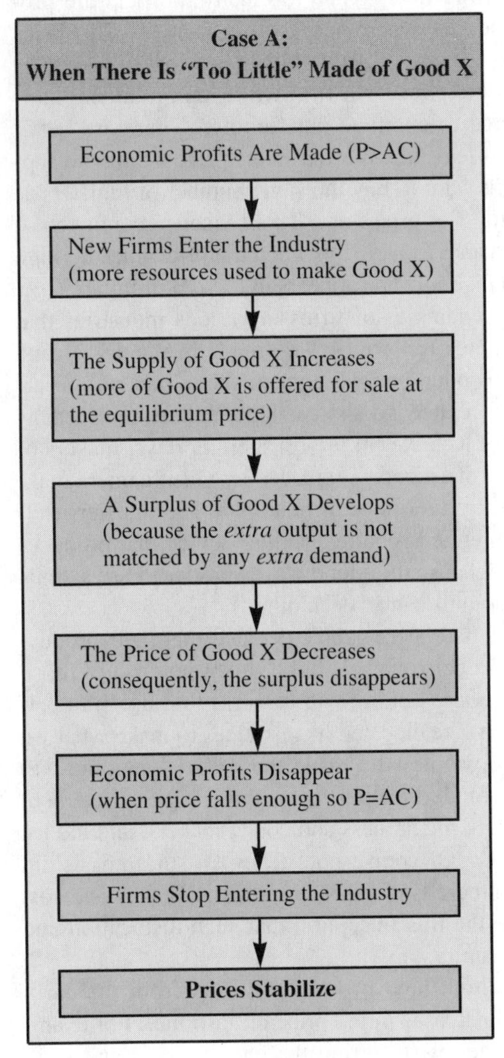

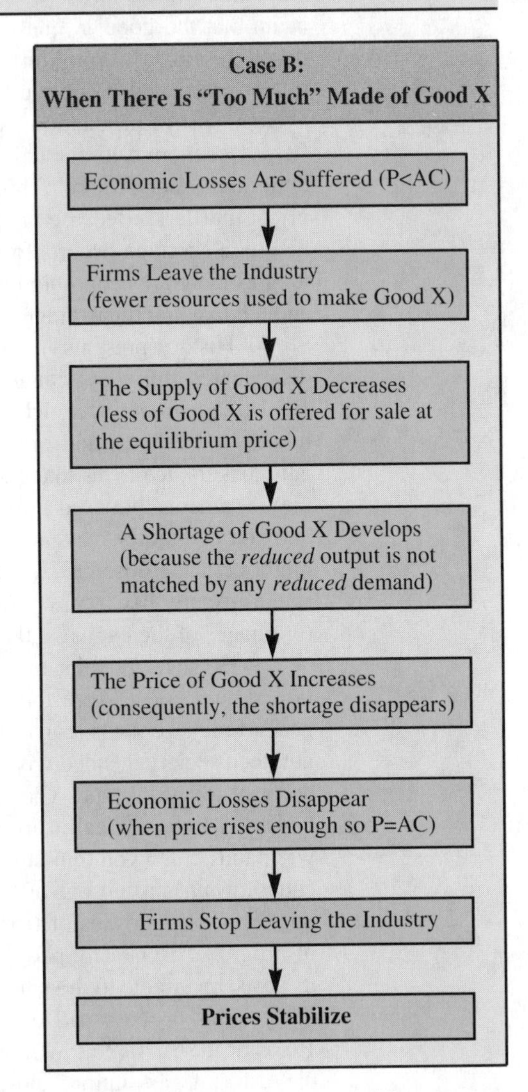

more mufflers at the original price than previously. The higher supply creates a surplus, and the surplus forces the price down. This process of firms entering the industry, increasing supply, and price decline continues until the price equals the average cost. That is because economic profits disappear at that point, as does the incentive for firms to enter the industry. Case A in Figure 6-3 provides a summary of this sequence of events.

Examples of products that have gone through this process are: cotton after Whitney's invention of the cotton gin in 1793; steel after the invention of the Kelly-Bessemer process in the mid-1800s; oil in the 1860s and 1870s; autos from 1900 to the 1920s; refrigerators in the 1930s and 1940s; televisions in the 1940s and 1950s; snowmobiles in the 1960s; fast food restaurants in the 1960s and 1970s; and personal computers in the 1970s and 1980s.

Alternatively, firms might produce too *much* of something, which indicates that the resources used should produce something else instead. Suppose again that the good in question is a muffler. When too many mufflers are produced, muffler firms are unable to sell anywhere near their capacities. This leads to low prices and economic losses—even *accounting* losses in severe cases. The average cost of production exceeds the price. No firm will keep producing mufflers if economic losses are expected to continue indefinitely. There are better opportunities elsewhere. Thus, firms leave the muffler industry, reducing the supply of mufflers. Because people still want to buy the same number of mufflers as before, a shortage occurs, forcing muffler prices up. This sequence continues so long as there are economic losses, which finally stop when the price goes up high enough to equal the average cost. This sequence appears in Case B in Figure 6-3.

History presents noteworthy examples of firms in various industries that disappeared this way: canal companies replaced by railroads in the 1840s and 1850s; cooper shops, which made wooden barrels; corsetmakers; makers of harnesses, horseshoes, and other horse-related goods; carriage makers replaced by auto makers; ice firms that cut ice for iceboxes in pre-refrigerator days; makers of movie cameras that used film instead of videotape replaced by video camera makers; and carburetor makers replaced by fuel injector makers. (The muffler itself might be made obsolete by a computerized sound-canceling device that produces sounds exactly like a car engine's. Because the sound waves produced are a "mirror image" of the engine's, the two sounds cancel each other.)

However popular these items had been, people decided that their production should end. Were those good decisions? Would you want to buy those goods today—corsets, carriages, iceboxes, and movie cameras that use film? If not, then society decided wisely when it reallocated its resources to make what we do want today instead. Clearly, the people who made those decisions (and we) benefited by such reallocation and modernization, even though the adjustment was painful. Do you think the coopers, the harness and corset makers, and the ice cutters *wanted* to go out of business? Of course not. They all suffered, as did owners and employees of firms in hundreds of other industries. That is one cost of progress. But many people have the misconception that such dislocation and its costs are unique to the late 20th century.

This process still occurs. Think how life today differs from the early 1980s or the 1970s following sharp increases in the price of gasoline. For example, a lot of gas stations closed in the 1970s during the energy crisis and were turned into convenience stores, hair-care salons, and muffler shops.

Many firms made successful transitions to new products either when their own products became obsolete or new products were found to be more profitable. One example was the Berlin Whip Company, which switched from concentrating on buggy whips to hand-stitched gloves and mittens. In 1922, it changed its name to the Berlin Glove Company and is still in business. Another example was a Chicago manufacturer that built bicycles called Ramblers. The owner, Thomas Jeffrey, sold his company in 1900. In 1902, he started a new firm that produced Rambler autos instead. In 1916, this company was sold to Charles Nash, who formed Nash Motor Company. Nash merged with Hudson Motor Company in 1954 to form American Motors Corporation, which again produced cars under the Rambler name. Following large losses in the 1970s, Renault Corporation of

France became the major stockholder. Finally, American Motors was absorbed by Chrysler Corporation in 1987, after which American Motors ceased to exist as an identifiable business.

Those affected by resource reallocation sometimes try to stop the process either because they can't make such transitions or are not innovative enough. This happened in the steel industry. In the last 20 to 30 years, per capita use of steel dropped significantly, partly because per capita use of plastic rose several-fold. As expected, steel firms, facing difficult times, did reduce capacity significantly. However, they also tried to limit imports of foreign steel. Agriculture is another example of "overcapacity" that Americans won't allow to shrink (see Chapter 7, pages 189-190).

Competition is often painful for firms, but it is the most important factor in forcing firms to improve themselves. In *The Competitive Advantage of Nations* (1990), Michael Porter writes about his 10-nation study that found competition the main factor in economic success. Tom Peters, in *Thriving on Chaos* (1987), attacks the "If it ain't broke, don't fix it" mentality. Peters, an advocate of competition who also shows extraordinary concern for the customer, notes that many successful firms follow a different philosophy—"If it ain't broke, fix it anyway!" There is always room for improvement.

MARKET STRUCTURE

★8

An **industry** includes all the firms that produce a particular (or closely related) good. There's the auto industry, the garment industry, the beef industry, and so on. (Be careful not to refer to a particular *firm* as an industry, as many people incorrectly do.) **Market structure** refers to the characteristics of an industry: the number and size of firms, the degree of competition and price-setting power of the firms, the similarity of competitors' products, and the ease of entering and leaving that industry. Market structures vary widely, but economists place all industries into one of four major categories: 1) pure competition; 2) monopolistic competition; 3) oligopoly; and 4) monopoly.

■ **Pure competition** is the market structure many economists believe is ideal because, theoretically: 1) buyers can be expected to get the lowest price; and 2) the efficiency of resource use is maximized. An industry in pure competition has many small firms, often hundreds or even thousands. With so much competition, no firm can command a price higher than the rest. Each firm is a "price taker," which means it must accept the "going price." The firms' products are virtually identical, and no firm has more production knowledge than any other. Finally, firms can easily enter and exit the industry because no law, cartel, or other barrier prevents such movement. Consequently, in the long run, there are neither economic profits nor economic losses. But few industries meet these standards. Some that do or come close include: producers of most agricultural commodities; concrete contractors that make drives, patios, and sidewalks; and "greasy spoon" restaurants.

■ **Monopolistic competition** is a market structure characterized by many firms, usually of small size. Their products or their places of business are somewhat different from their competitors'. Each firm has some ability to raise its price above its competitors' prices without losing all its customers. Entry into the industry is sometimes difficult because of a **barrier to entry**, such as licenses, permits, franchises, patents, and copyrights. The fast food industry is a good example of monopolistic competition, for restaurants of different chains are significantly different. Many small-scale retailers and auto repair businesses also are monopolistically competitive.

■ **Oligopoly** is the structure of most "big business." Firms are generally large and few in number. Products are distinctive, usually identified by a brand. Although each firm has much power to manipulate price, competition is occasionally very strong. Sometimes competition exhibits itself in product design, which leads to large advertising budgets that are used to point out advantages of the advertised products. Often there are heavy financial requirements or other barriers to entry. The auto, steel, breakfast cereal, large appliance, and tire industries are all oligopolies.

■ The last structure, **monopoly**, is rarer than people think. In monopoly there is only one firm supplying the output. Thus, it can set price wherever it likes, but its power to do so is limited because people usually don't *have* to buy the product—and don't if the price is too high.

Technically, a single grocery store in a small town is a monopoly, but this example doesn't convey the concept adequately. A true monopolist faces no competitors because of some barrier to entry. Polaroid Corporation is a monopoly producer of instant cameras because of the patents it holds. A public utility, such as a gas or electric company, is called a natural monopoly. Here, certain characteristics of the good or service make multiple production facilities extremely wasteful. Five electric companies would require five sets of wires all over town, creating a costly mess and no extra benefit. States grant franchise rights in specified areas to natural monopolies and establish price-setting power in public service commissions. A structure related to monopoly, called monopsony, means there is only one buyer, such as occurs with the market for U.S. Army tanks.

Figure 6-4 summarizes the major characteristics of each of the four market structures.

BUSINESS OPERATION

This section is a brief introduction to business operations. It covers business goals, determination of firm size, and determination of a purely competitive firm's maximum profit point.

Goals of Business

You might find it difficult to determine the goals of different businesses. One firm might seem to be seeking to maximize sales, another the growth of its scale of operation, and another the returns to its investors or owners. Actually, many firms have a complex mix of goals, some of which may actually conflict. But profit maximization is usually a major goal for most firms.

Figure 6-4 The Four Market Structures and Their Characteristics

MARKET CHARACTERISTIC	MARKET STRUCTURE			
	PURE COMPETITION	MONOPOLISTIC COMPETITION	OLIGOPOLY	MONOPOLY
Product	Homogeneous	Differentiated	Homogeneous or Differentiated	Unique
Number of Firms	Very Many	Many	Few	One
Barriers to Entry	None	Few	Many	Very Many
Control over Price by Firms	None	Some	Much	Complete
Market Power of Firms	None	Some	Much	Complete
Ability to Earn Economic Profit	None	None	Some	Much

Another important and related goal of businesses, especially oligopolies, is market share, a firm's percentage of total sales in the entire industry. Jif peanut butter, for example, accounts for 33 percent of all peanut butter sold. The managers at Jif might, however, believe they need 40 percent to ensure brand loyalty. To achieve that, they might cut price—and sacrifice some short-run profit. Other firms gain market share by stressing quality. They often suffer low profits in the short run because their costs are higher than their competitors' but their sales are not. As customers slowly perceive the benefits of the firm's higher quality, eventually the firm gains sales, market share—and finally, higher profits. The Michelin Company, a French tire manufacturer, followed this strategy when it introduced the revolutionary radial tire in 1946. After decades of low profits, Michelin rose to the top of the industry by the late 1980s.

A final major goal of some businesses is community good will. A business, wanting to be a "good neighbor," might contribute money to local fund drives. Critics of such gifts complain that managers, who often are *not* the owners, give away money that belongs to the stockholders (who *are* the owners) in order to get a "pat on the back" from the community. Good will may be the goal of managers, but the firm's owners will support it only if it is profitable. This is possible if the good will serves as a form of advertising or helps establish consumer loyalty to the firm's product.

Closely related to this good will issue is the issue of whether corporations should be expected to support a wide variety of projects to help society in general, from hospital construction to AIDS research. Advocates of such support say it is the responsibility of firms to aid the society in which they operate. Critics respond that corporations should operate solely for the benefit of their owners (stockholders). And the success of any corporation depends upon how well it serves the customers—and should not depend upon how well it serves the rest of society.

Determining Firm Size or Scale of Operation

In some industries, such as appliance repair and raspberry production, all firms are small. In other industries, such as pencil production, firms are large. This section explains such size differences.

Let's briefly review returns to scale, first covered in Chapter 3. Returns to scale refer to how the level of output changes as a firm increases all of its resources at the same rate. If a firm doubles its resources and consequently *more* than doubles its output, the firm experiences increasing returns to scale (economies of scale). Consider a radio manufacturer. If its total cost is $400,000 when it makes 50,000 radios, its average cost is $8 per radio. Suppose it doubles all its resources, thereby doubling total cost to $800,000. Let's also say that this allows the firm to *more than* double output to 120,000 radios. Then average cost falls to $6.67 (= $800,000 ÷ 120,000 radios).

However, if doubling resources merely allows the firm to double production to 100,000 radios, it experiences constant returns to scale. As output doubles, average cost remains constant at $8 (= $800,000 ÷ 100,000 radios).

★9

Finally, if doubling resources results in an increase in output that is *less than* double, the firm experiences decreasing returns to scale or diseconomies of scale. Now average cost increases with scale increases. Suppose output increases to 80,000 as resources double. Then the average cost will increase from $8 to $10 per radio (= $800,000 ÷ 80,000 radios).

The question facing the radio manufacturer and any other business firm with similar data is: what size operation should it have? It could be large or small, but the firm needs to find its **optimum scale of plant**. This is the plant with the lowest average cost, given some particular demand for its output. Because average cost reflects efficiency, this is the most efficient plant.

In reality, the complex accounting data needed makes finding the optimum size extremely difficult. Because most firms grow from small to larger sizes, they first experience increasing returns to scale, followed by constant returns, and finally decreasing returns to scale. A firm should build larger and larger plants only so long as it experiences increasing returns to scale. (But these larger plants should *not* be built if larger outputs cannot be sold.)

But what if a firm can sell much *more* than its optimum size plant can produce? Should it limit its sales to that output level? Or should it build a bigger plant than the optimum size? The answer is neither. Rather, it should build *multiple* operations of the same optimum size. That is the primary reason for the large number of fast food restaurants. Instead of one or two giant restaurants, smaller places, some belonging to the same chain, are located within a mile or so of each other. Similarly, most electric power companies have several generating plants rather than a single plant because the *generation* of electricity does not involve economies of scale beyond a certain size of generating plant. However, the *transmission* of electricity through wires does, which explains why it is a (natural) monopoly.

For a similar reason, some industries have many firms. Suppose the optimum size operation for some industry can produce only one-thousandth of the demand for the good. Will one firm—a monopoly—have 1,000 plants? Hardly. Rather, there could be as many as a thousand competing firms, each very small. That's how pure competition arises.

Alternatively, suppose the optimum size operation for another industry produces one-fourth of the product's demand. Then this industry will have a handful of firms, each probably of large size. This is basically how economists explain the presence of most oligopolies.

Maximizing Profit in the Short Run

After a firm determines the size of its operation, it must decide how much output to produce. Should it operate at its full capacity or at only a fraction of capacity? You might wonder why a firm would use less than its full capacity. This happens because firms operate both in the short run and the long run. In the **short run**, some of the firm's resources, usually its capital stock, cannot vary. Obviously such factors as plant or store size and the amount of machinery are relatively inflexible. These take months or years to expand. However, the firm usually *can* quickly increase its work force, supplies, and the like—which is how it can vary output. In the **long run**, all resources are variable, so output can be increased by adding capital stock.

★10

How does one firm in a purely competitive industry decide how much to produce in the short run? The answer is determined by the amount that maximizes its profit. Two ways to locate that maximum profit amount will be presented: 1) the total revenue/total cost approach; and 2) the marginal revenue/marginal cost approach.

■ With the first method, it is important to know that a purely competitive firm faces perfectly elastic demand. This means it can sell as much as it wants at the market price, even without advertising. (This actually occurs in the dairy industry and with many other agricultural commodities. Farmers can sell all the milk, wheat, or soybeans they wish at the market price.) Suppose a dairy farm has a barn that, when 200 cows fill it to capacity, enables the farmer to produce 2,200 gallons of milk. But the farmer doesn't *have* to fill the barn, so how much milk *should* be produced? The diagrams in Figure 6-5 for a competitive firm clearly show the answer. They show two approaches to finding the maximum profit point: the total revenue/total cost approach and the marginal revenue/marginal cost approach. Each will be covered in turn.

The worst crime against working people is a company which fails to operate at a profit. – Samuel Gompers, founder of the A.F.L.

The top part of Figure 6-5 uses box diagrams to show only four output levels out of many possibilities. Actually, there are 201 possible levels, since the farmer can have anywhere from zero to 200 cows. The two boxes in each case represent the total revenue (sales) and the total cost for that output level. In the first case, for 200 gallons, the farm has a loss, for costs exceed sales. At 600 gallons, however, costs equal sales, which means the farm is at a break-even point. Adding enough cows to give 1,400 gallons finally produces a profit, as the revenue box now exceeds the cost box. Suppose this is the *most* profitable level of output. The farmer *could* sell more, but if output climbs to 2,200 gallons, losses again occur.

The graphs in the middle of Figure 6-5 show the same thing plus much more. Look first at the line labelled total revenue (= P x Q). The starting point at the lower left corner indicates zero sales with zero cows (or milk produced). Its rise to the right shows that sales increase when the farmer gets more cows and produces more milk. Note that where the total cost curve crosses the vertical axis (where the farm produces no milk), there are costs of $2,000, measured by the distance above the horizontal axis. These are the fixed or overhead costs, including such costs as membership dues in farm organizations and depreciation of the barn and equipment. The total cost line climbs quickly at first, then slowly, and finally, rapidly again. Any such increase in the total cost line represents an increase in variable costs, such as feed bills and vet fees. Variable costs rise at such different rates primarily because of resource "balance and imbalance," as discussed in Chapter 3.

To understand this concept, consider the lamp factory example from earlier. The factory could begin production with only one worker who does all the jobs, but it is unlikely that the worker is a "master" at all jobs. Some jobs, such as polishing, might take this worker a long time to learn. As more workers arrive to boost output, they specialize according to their comparative advantages. Efficiency of resource use increases because of such specialization (division) of labor. As a consequence of higher efficiency, average cost falls. A total cost line that rises more gradually is another way of showing this phenomenon. However, eventually specialization can progress no further, and cost savings stop. Also, "bottlenecks" appear when workers get in each other's way (think of a fast food restaurant at noon). At high output levels in factories, equipment may be overused, minimal maintenance may cause more breakdowns, and the shipping and receiving departments may not have enough room. For these and other reasons, there is an imbalance in resources, which reduces efficiency and raises average costs.

Consider the dairy example again. Combining the total cost and total revenue graphs allows you to see the farmer's profits or losses, but now for *each* level of output, rather than merely four as shown earlier. Any variable measured in dollar amounts, such as revenue and cost, is measured on the vertical axis. Because profit (or loss) is the difference between total revenue and total cost, profit is also measured on the vertical axis. For any particular level of output, profit (or loss) equals the vertical distance between the total revenue curve and the total cost curve. For output below 600 gallons, the farmer suffers a loss, for the total cost line exceeds the total revenue line. At 600 gallons, the farmer breaks even—no loss or profit—for there is just enough revenue to cover costs. Between

Figure 6-5 Finding the Maximum Profit Level for a Firm

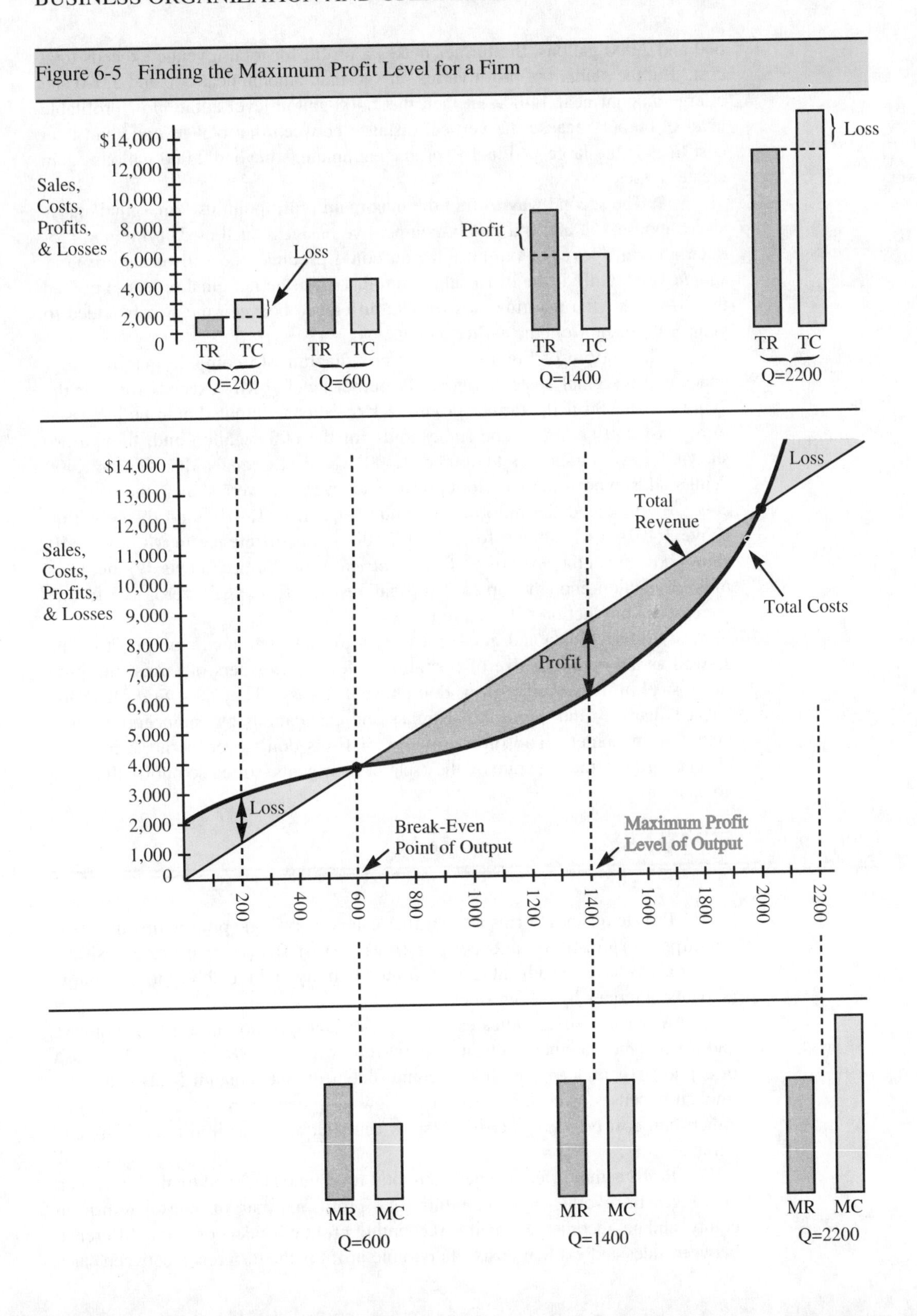

600 and 2,000 gallons, the farmer makes a profit, for total revenue exceeds total cost. But the *amount* of profit varies. It's a small amount near 600 and 2,000 and a large amount near 1,400. In fact, the 1,400-gallon level is the *most* profitable level of output because the vertical distance between the total revenue and total cost lines is the largest. Finally, producing amounts beyond 2,000 gallons again creates losses.

■ The second way to find the maximum profit point uses marginal analysis. Suppose you are in a purely competitive business such as dairying and produce a certain level of output. If you could produce and sell one more unit, *should* you? Only if the *extra* sales from that unit (the marginal revenue) exceed the *extra* cost (the marginal cost). The difference between the two is added to your profit made from the earlier outputs.

The bottom of Figure 6-5 uses box diagrams to compare marginal revenues and marginal costs at four milk output levels. MR exceeds MC for the 200th gallon. So if the farmer produces 199 gallons, output should be increased to at least 200 gallons. The same holds for the 600th gallon and, though not shown, for every gallon up to number 1,400, where MR equals MC. Gallon 1,400 neither adds to nor subtracts from profit. However, if it were shown, the marginal cost would exceed the marginal revenue for gallon 1,401—and every gallon above 1,401—as is shown for gallon 2,200. This difference in MC over MR shows how much the level of profit is *reduced.* If the farmer (unwisely) increases milk production enough—up to 2,000 gallons—profit is again zero, and further increases in production will lead to losses.

With such data and graphs, it is easy to find such maximum profit points as well as the optimum size of operation. However, owners of farms, furniture firms, steel firms, and other firms don't have it so easy. They must *find* such data, but it is hard to find, requiring searches and calculations by engineers, accountants, and managers. Too often, owners of firms don't even bother with such efforts. Instead, they operate by the "seat of their pants," often so poorly that they go bankrupt.

Chapter 6 SUMMARY

Private business firms fit into four categories: single proprietorships, partnerships, corporations, and cooperatives. Most firms are proprietorships. Corporations have the advantages of limited liability and the ability to raise large amounts of money by selling stock.

A balance sheet indicates a firm's financial position at a given moment, and the income statement indicates its position over a period of time. Only cash or explicit expenses appear on an income statement, but economists also consider implicit expenses as costs. A firm can view its expenses from the standpoint of either total cost or average cost. Also, it can split expenses into fixed costs and variable costs.

Profit is the difference between total revenue (sales) and total cost. It can be viewed in several ways, including total profit, net margin, rate of return on equity, and net income per share. Accounting profit considers only the difference between sales and explicit costs. Economic profit is the difference between sales and all costs, including implicit costs.

Profit serves to attract entrepreneurs to the production process and to redirect resources away from or into specific industries. Economic profits in producing a good or service will attract resources to that industry, leading to more firms producing that good or service. Conversely, economic losses will drive firms and resources out of the industry.

Industries and their firms are categorized in one of four market structures in decreasing order of competitiveness: pure competition, monopolistic competition, oligopoly, or monopoly. Firms find their optimum scale of plant by considering the size of demand as well as the existence of increasing, constant, or decreasing returns to scale.

The short run is a period in which the firm cannot change its capital stock. Its maximum profit point in the short run is where total revenue exceeds total cost by the largest amount. That is also the point where the marginal revenue equals the marginal cost.

The long run is a period in which firms can change to any size operation or even go out of business. Also, new firms can enter the industry in the long run. In a purely competitive industry, no economic profits are earned in the long run. Any economic profit draws in new firms, leading to increases in supply, surpluses, and price decreases until all profits are gone.

Chapter 6 RESPONSES TO THE LEARNING OBJECTIVES

1. Single proprietorships are owned by one individual, have the owners subject to unlimited liability, and are easy to form. Partnerships are essentially proprietorships with two or more owners who share the risks, responsibilities, and profits. Corporations are "legal persons" owned by stockholders, each having limited liability. Corporations can have perpetual life and are able to raise large amounts of money. Cooperatives serve the people who own them, are controlled equally by all owners, and operate on a cost basis.

2. Balance sheets list assets on one part, liabilities on another, and net worth or equity last. Income statements are divided into sections on revenues, expenses, and profits or losses.

3. Total cost equals total fixed cost plus total variable cost. Average variable cost equals total variable cost divided by output. Average fixed cost equals total fixed cost divided by output. Average cost equals total cost divided by output. Average cost also equals average variable cost plus average fixed cost. Marginal cost equals the difference in either total costs or total variable costs for two successive levels of output.

4. The accountant views costs as anything that requires the payment of money for resources. In addition to these, the economist includes implicit costs, or things of value given up by the business owner that do not involve the transfer of money to sellers of resources.

5. If there are:
   a) both accounting and economic profits, firms earn more than is necessary to remain in the industry, and new firms enter the industry
   b) accounting profits and neither economic profits nor losses, firms earn just enough to remain in business, and the number of firms in the industry remains unchanged
   c) accounting profits and economic losses, firms can pay their bills but don't earn enough to remain in business, so firms leave the industry
   d) neither accounting profits nor losses and there are economic losses, firms have only enough revenue to pay their bills and no extra for implicit costs, so firms leave the industry
   e) both accounting and economic losses, firms cannot pay all their bills and none of their implicit costs, so firms leave the industry
6. Profit is an incentive or payment for entrepreneurs to organize production processes. Profit also signals that resources need to be redirected to more valuable uses.
7. Profits in making an item lead to additional resources being used to produce it, and losses lead to fewer resources being used to produce it.
8. Pure competition has many small firms producing identical products. Firms cannot influence price, restrict entry into the industry, or have any trade secrets. In monopolistic competition, a fairly large number of firms with somewhat different products often are able to influence market price to some degree. Generally there is freedom of exit and entry into the industry, although sometimes there are some barriers to entry. In oligopoly, a few large firms producing unique products are often able to influence price to a large degree, and there often are barriers to entry. In monopoly, there is only one firm which faces no competition because some barrier to entry prevents it.
9. A firm selects the size of operation that allows it to produce its selected level of output at the lowest average cost, given the size of demand.
10. A firm maximizes its profit by producing the level of output where: a) the difference between the total revenue and the total cost is the greatest; or b) the marginal cost equals the marginal revenue.

Chapter 6 LEARNING ACTIVITIES AND DISCUSSION QUESTIONS

1. Locate a recent example of a merger or a corporate takeover. What were some objections to it?
2. Obtain an annual report from a local company and study its income statement. Do you see any problems for the firm? Are there any reasons for the owners to rejoice?
3. Ask three business owners if they think they are "money ahead" by being in business instead of working for someone else. If not, why do you think they stay in business?
4. Categorize five local industries in each of the four types of market structure.
5. Consider a small business and a big business in your community. Why are these firms of such size?

APPENDIX A GRAPHIC APPROACH TO COSTS AND PROFITS

Table A6-1 repeats the information given in Table 6-2 for a table manufacturer. In addition, there are columns for price, total revenue, and profit. These extra columns will be examined shortly, but first consider how Figure A6-1 is related to the cost information in the table.

The vertical axis measures dollars per unit of output. Thus, the axis could be used to measure AC, AVC, AFC, MC, MR, or price, for these are all stated in terms of one unit of output. First, note that AFC starts out very high because the first few tables have to absorb all the fixed costs. As output (Q) increases, AFC continually falls.

The AC and AVC curves are both U-shaped, which means these measures are higher for both low and high levels of output. The MC curve also follows this pattern, but it starts rising before both AVC and AC rise. Note that as soon as MC crosses the AVC curve, AVC starts upward. The same thing happens to the AC curve. This is similar to the effect increasingly heavy students would have on the average weight in your classroom. If there are 20 students with an average weight of 120 pounds, then if a 21st student who weighs 105 pounds walks in, the average would drop. The same holds if number 22 weighs 107 pounds, number 23 weighs 109 pounds, and so on. Now suppose the 29th student weighs 115 pounds and that the class average is also 115 pounds when (and after) that student enters. If the 30th student weighs *more than* 115 pounds—say 118 pounds—the average would climb. Finally, if each new student after the 30th one weighs more than the average, the class average would continue to climb.

Now consider prices to see how profits can be measured. Figure A6-2 is simplified from Figure A6-1 in that the AVC and AFC curves are gone, for they are not needed to calculate profits. Because it is assumed that the table manufacturer described here is in pure competition, price and marginal revenue are identical. This means the firm can sell as many tables as it wants at the market price. In effect, the line labelled P = MR is the demand curve *for the firm* because it

Table A6-1 Costs, Revenues, and Profits of a Table Manufacturer

Q	TC	AFC	AVC	AC	MC	P=MR	TR	Profit
1	$ 600	$320.00	$280.00	$600.00	$ 280	$220	$220	-$380
2	800	160.00	240.00	400.00	200	220	440	-360
3	920	106.67	200.00	306.67	120	220	660	-260
4	1000	80.00	170.00	250.00	80	220	880	-120
5	1050	64.00	146.00	210.00	50	220	1100	-50
6	1110	53.33	137.67	185.00	60	220	1320	210
7	1180	45.71	122.86	168.57	70	220	1540	360
8	1260	40.00	117.50	157.50	80	220	1760	500
9	1370	35.56	116.67	152.23	110	220	1980	610
10	1500	32.00	118.00	150.00	150	220	2200	700
11	1720	29.09	127.27	156.36	220	220	2420	700
12	2000	26.67	140.00	166.67	280	220	2640	640
13	2320	24.62	153.85	178.47	320	220	2860	560
14	2700	22.86	170.00	192.86	380	220	3080	380
15	3250	21.33	195.33	216.67	550	220	3300	50
16	4800	20.00	280.00	300.00	1550	220	3520	-1280

shows all the combinations of price and quantity buyers will take from this firm.

Note that Table A6-1 also has a column labelled P = MR. If the price is assumed to be $220 per table, the next column, which measures total revenue (TR), reflects the formula TR = P x Q. Finally, as profit = TR - TC, the last column shows the profits for different levels of table output. Note that the firm loses money at low levels of output and at the highest level. Although it makes profit at several different middle levels, it *maximizes* profit if it produces 11 tables. (The firm does equally well at 10 tables, so whether it produces 10 or 11 tables is a matter of indifference). Finally, notice that MC equals MR ($220) at 11 tables. Recall that this is an alternative way to find the maximum profit point. In Figure A6-2 the MC line crosses the MR line at exactly 11 tables.

Because it is not stated in a per-unit-of-output form as are some cost concepts, profit cannot be measured on the vertical axis. However, it is shown as the rectangular, hash-mark area. The area of that rectangle (and the amount of profit) is given by the formula: Profit = (P - AC) x Q as well as by Profit = TR - TC

That's because TR = P x Q and TC = AC x Q, so: Profit = TR - TC = (P x Q) - (AC x Q) = (P - AC) x Q. Because (P - AC) is measured on the y-axis and Q on the x-axis, the profit is measured by (P - AC) times Q—or the length times the width of the shaded rectangle. The AC is shown to be $156.36 if Q equals 11 tables, so the profit margin of $63.64 (= $220.00 - $156.36) multiplied by 11 gives a total profit of $700.

Figure A6-2 shows what can happen in a purely competitive industry in a short-run situation, before new firms have a chance to enter the industry and earn some of these economic profits. Figure A6-3, however, shows the long-run equilibrium situation for the competitive industry. The economic profits in Figure A6-2 draw in new table manufacturers, the price falls to $150, and the typical firm makes no economic profit at all. The firm operates where average cost is at a minimum, corresponding to the point of maximum efficiency of resource use.

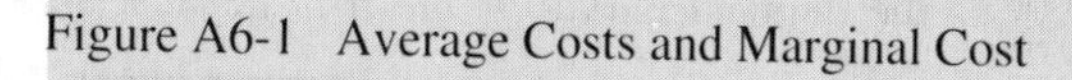
Figure A6-1 Average Costs and Marginal Cost

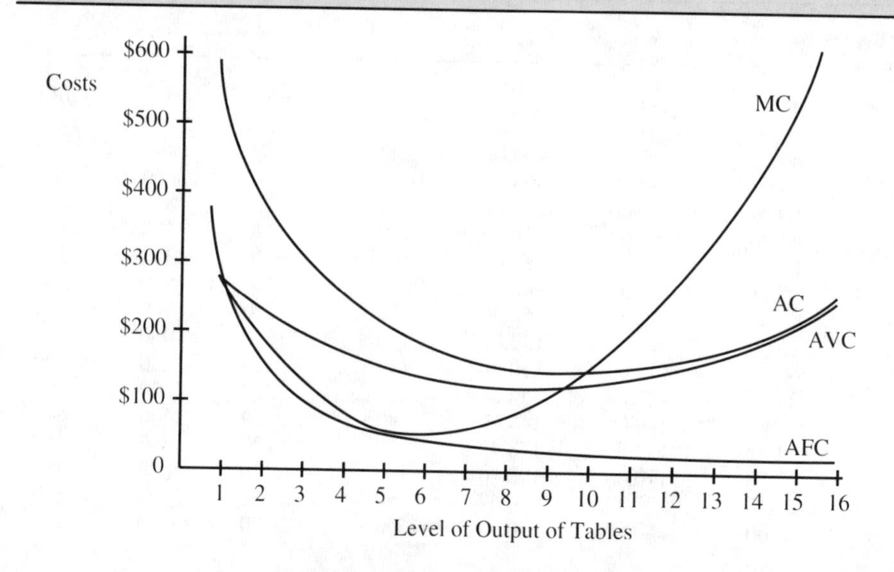

Figure A6-2 Costs, Price, and Marginal Revenue

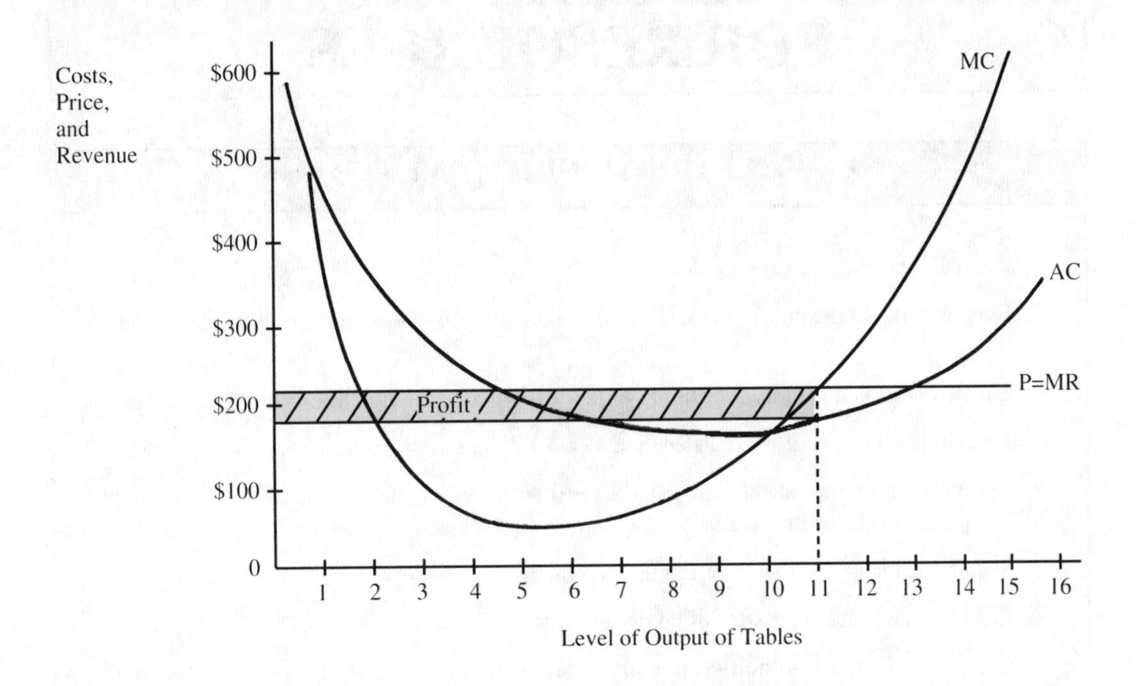

Figure A6-3 Long-Run Equilibrium for a Firm in Pure Competition

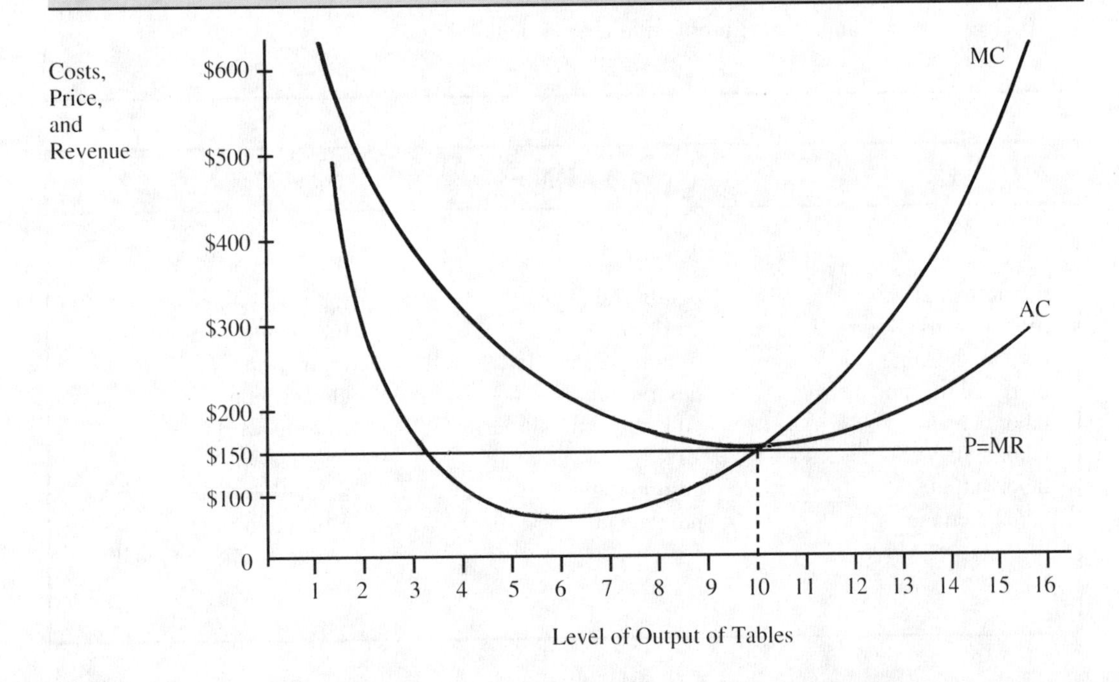

CHAPTER 7

THE MARKETS FOR RESOURCES

★★★★★ LEARNING OBJECTIVES ★★★★★

1. Describe the circular flow model.
2. Explain what is meant by the demand for labor for an occupation and what influences it.
3. Explain what is meant by the supply of labor for an occupation and what influences it.
4. Explain the process of wage determination in a competitive labor market.
5. Compare and contrast the three ways the market wage can be made to exceed the competitive equilibrium wage.
6. Sketch the history of the labor union movement.
7. List the major characteristics of labor legislation.
8. Compare and contrast the two primary types of capital and the methods of financing them.
9. Describe the relationships between economic growth, capital, the interest rate, and the savings rate.
10. Describe the fundamental problem in U.S. agriculture.

TERMS

factor market
product market
derived demand
marginal revenue product
labor demand
labor supply
labor surplus
labor shortage
equilibrium wage
work rule
minimum wage law
labor union
collective bargaining
strike
craft union
national union
industrial union
independent union
injunction
closed shop
right-to-work law
union shop
mediation
arbitration
social overhead capital

Resources are scarce because there aren't enough to produce all the goods and services that people want. This problem is partly solved when people make more efficient use of resources, primarily by increasing resource specialization and by innovation. This, in turn, requires exchanges between specialists.

This chapter describes the markets for labor, entrepreneurship, capital, and natural resources. The first section connects the product and factor markets in the "circular flow." The next two sections examine how workers "sell" labor and employers "buy" labor in both competitive and non-competitive markets. Next is a glimpse of labor unions. The remainder of the chapter covers the markets for entrepreneurs, capital, and natural resources.

THE CIRCULAR FLOW OF ECONOMIC ACTIVITY

★1

Figure 7-1 presents a simplified model of the microeconomy, showing the relationships between small or "micro" parts of the economy, such as laborers, business firms, and consumers. "Circular" refers primarily to money, which flows continually between owners (sellers) of resources and the buyers of resources. Owners include: individuals, such as laborers and landowners; businesses, such as producers of textile machinery; and governments and their agencies, such as the Department of the Interior, which sells off-shore oil leases. Resources "flow to" or are sold to businesses and government enterprises, which convert them into goods and services. The exchange of money for these resources occurs in **factor markets**. The prices in these markets often have special names, such as wage, salary, commission, rent, or the interest rate.

These special prices reflect the income of resource owners, who spend this income on finished goods and services in **product markets**. The money paid for such products becomes income to sellers of these goods and services and is called sales or total revenue. In turn, this revenue provides firms with the ability to buy resources in factor markets. This maintains the continual and simultaneous "flow" of money.

These "flows" of money, resources, and products do not occur at constant rates over time. When they are increasing to particularly high levels, we say we are experiencing prosperity. Declines in the flows mean we are experiencing recession. Finally, activities in any specific market, whether product or resource, can have effects in a multitude of other markets. Thus, a system of markets is a complex array of interrelationships.

THE COMPETITIVE LABOR MARKET

The third Basic Economic Question is For Whom to Produce? It really pertains to income distribution, for our society produces more goods and services for those who have more income. But why do incomes differ, and differ so much, in our society? Explaining these differences is the primary intent of this section.

Many people have a poor grasp of how incomes are determined in a capitalist system. More specifically, they don't know what it is that determines their incomes. People often believe they deserve higher wages than they earn, and

Figure 7-1 The Circular Flow of Economic Activity

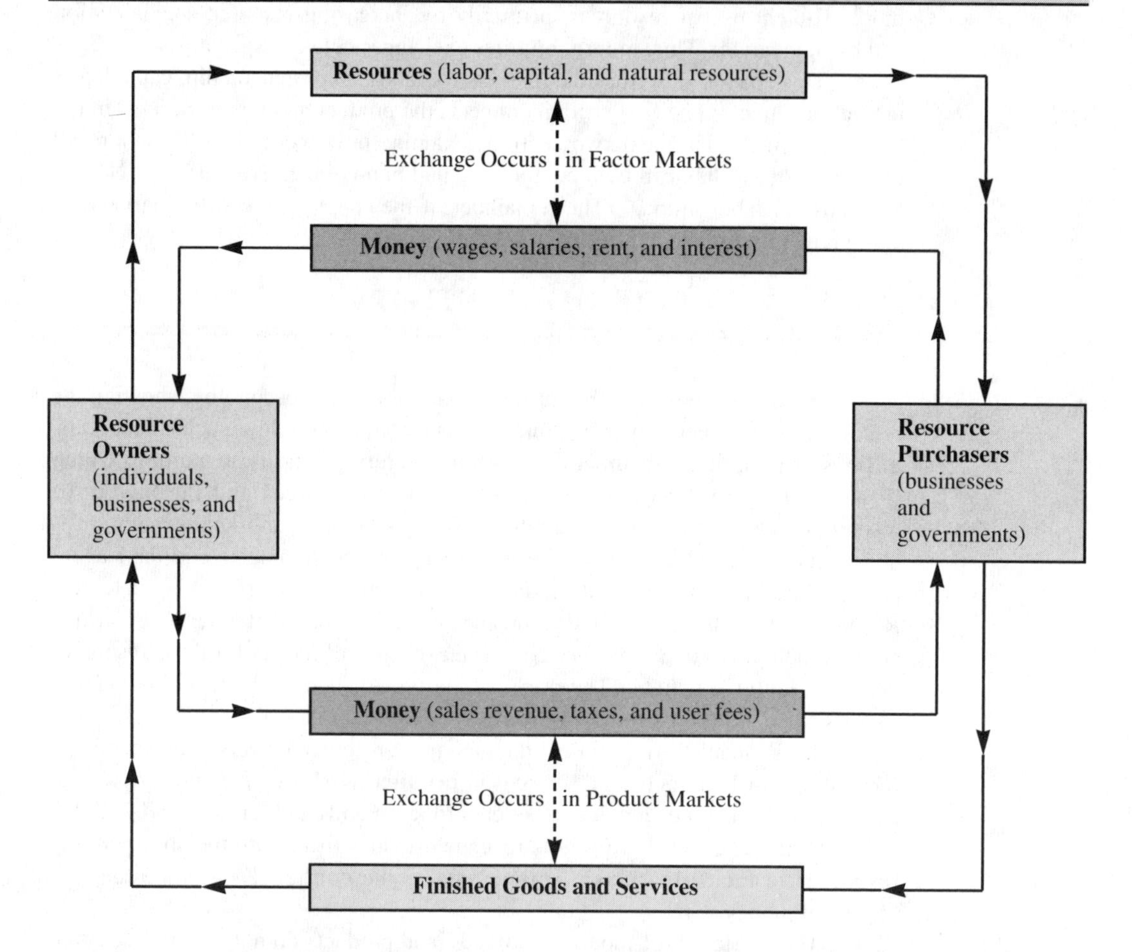

many are resentful because of their "low pay." Part of this poor understanding of income distribution in capitalism is because most of us were raised in "socialist" homes. That is, until adolescence or even beyond, we were given all our basic needs plus many extras—often without being expected to contribute much in return. Although we were constantly told of scarcity of resources (income) by our parents, this is not the same as truly experiencing it as an adult. We seldom associated our parents' income with their productiveness. So it is not surprising that some new employees tell their employers they need x number of dollars per hour because that's what they "need to live." Wages are not determined that way. Let's see how they really are.

In this section it will be assumed that competitive conditions exist in labor markets. Such conditions mean that: 1) no one prevents anyone else from buying or selling labor; 2) no individual buyer or seller can control the price of labor (the wage); and 3) the government is not involved in labor markets. Except in rare cases, these conditions do not exist. But assuming that they do allows us to understand what the main factors are that determine incomes.

The Demand for Labor

Employers are as interested in their self-interest as you are in yours because they face scarcity just as you do. An employer evaluates a particular laborer who applys for a job in much the same way you evaluate a particular shirt you consider buying. The employer wonders if the laborer will provide more revenue than any other laborer—or any other resource, such as a machine. This is like you deciding if one particular shirt is as enjoyable (beneficial) as another—or as another article of clothing.

Several factors determine how many workers with a particular skill an employer wants to hire. Major factors include the wage, the productivity of the laborers, and the price of the firm's good or service. Because the price of the good or service depends in part upon the demand for that good or service, the demand for labor is called a **derived demand**. For example, the demand for glass workers depends upon the demand for glass.

Profit-maximizing firms will hire workers so long as the *extra* money each worker contributes, called the **marginal revenue product** (MRP), exceeds the cost of hiring such workers. The formula for the MRP is:

Marginal Revenue Product = Price x Marginal Product

Remember from Chapter 3 that, because of the law of diminishing marginal returns, marginal product declines as firms hire additional workers. Sooner or later firms will stop hiring workers, for eventually the MRP (the benefit) will be less than the factor cost of hiring workers (the wage).

★2

Therefore, the number of jobs of one type in an industry depends upon three major factors: 1) the wage; 2) the price of the good or service produced; and 3) the productivity of the workers. Remember from Chapter 5 that demand is the relationship between price and how much people are willing to buy. Similarly, **labor demand** is the relationship between the wage and the number of workers all employers combined wish to hire. (Beware of equating labor demand with the number of employees firms wish to hire. Labor demand is the *relationship* between the wage and that number, not the number hired itself.) Each labor market has many possible demands.

Table 7-1 illustrates labor demand for a hypothetical market—that of machinists in the garden tool industry. The table shows the different number of jobs offered (or job openings) by employers at three different wages under three different "strengths" of demand—weak, average, and strong. An average demand for machinists means all occupations, on average, provide these numbers of jobs. For example, at $6 per hour, garden tool manufacturers wish to hire 900 machinists—the average number of job openings expected for all other occupations.

A strong demand for machinists means more jobs are open than in most other occupations. In this case 1,300 machinist jobs are open, compared with 900 for other occupations, on average. A strong demand for labor is created by two main conditions: 1) a high price for the product produced; and 2) high labor productivity. Both lead to a high MRP, and a high MRP means firms can profit by hiring many workers.

Table 7-1 The Demand for Labor Under Varying Conditions

Wage	Number of Jobs Provided by Employers When There Is a: Weak Demand	Average Demand	Strong Demand
$12	100	500	900
$ 9	300	700	1100
$ 6	500	900	1300

In turn, what causes high prices and productivity? A high price is caused by either a strong demand for the product or a small supply of it. Generally, a product with a strong demand is very useful (beneficial) to consumers.

Labor productivity can be high for many reasons, including: good education and training; good physical and mental skills; good work attitudes; a high quantity and quality of capital equipment used by the workers; and a good work environment, such as clean, well-lighted, and pleasantly decorated surroundings.

A *weak* labor demand is caused by the opposite conditions: 1) low product prices; and 2) low productivity. A low price is caused by either a weak demand for the product or a large supply of it. In turn, a product could have a weak demand if it provides little satisfaction to consumers. Therefore, you could expect it hard to find a job producing a product that most people find of little value or even useless, and if you did, you could expect to receive a low income at that job.

Low productivity could result from poor education, minimum skills, poor work attitudes, a low quantity or quality of capital, and a poor work environment. In Table 7-1, a weak labor demand means firms want only 500 machinists at $6, compared with 900 in other occupations, on average.

At a higher wage in Table 7-1, firms want to hire fewer machinists, whether the demand is weak, average, or strong. These inverse relationships between wages and the number of job offerings show that the law of demand applies to labor resources just as it does to consumer goods. Higher wages lead employers to "buy" less labor for two reasons: 1) the substitution effect; and 2) an effect similar to the income effect.

■ The substitution effect occurs when escalating wages prompt firms to replace workers with cheaper alternative resources. These include: 1) capital equipment, such as high-speed drills, bigger trucks, and conveyer belts; 2) natural resources, such as coal, which generates electricity used by labor-replacing machines; and 3) cheaper laborers. Cheaper laborers can be found in various places, such as foreign countries or other parts of the United States where wages are lower. A firm can also find cheaper laborers by subcontracting or "outsourcing" part of its work to firms that hire non-union, lower-paid workers or that have lower costs for other reasons.

Figure 7-2 The Demand for Labor Under Varying Conditions

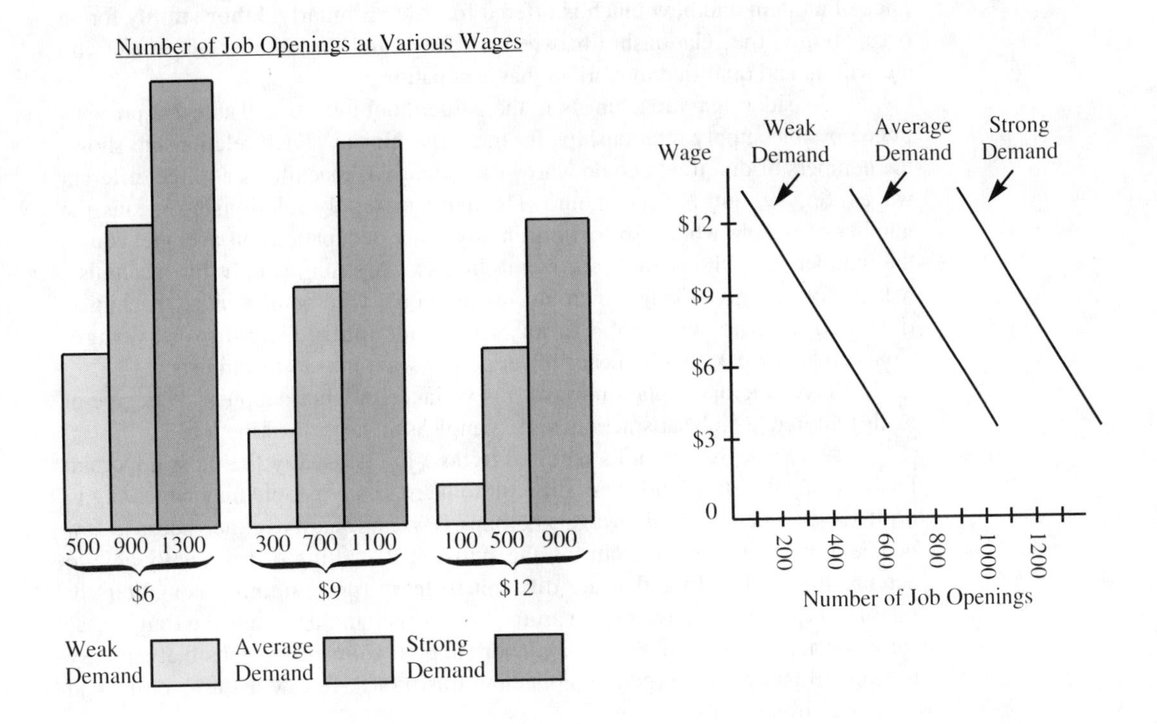

The second reason firms obey the law of demand is similar to the income effect with demand for a good. At higher wages, production costs are higher. In turn, prices will be higher. Since buyers purchase fewer products at higher prices, firms will need fewer employees.

Figure 7-2 provides two alternative ways to view these three labor demand relationships. The bar graphs on the left indicate there are three different levels of job openings for each wage, depending upon the strength of labor demand. The demand graphs on the right show the inverse relationship between wages and job openings.

The Supply of Labor

People will work only if the benefits they receive (wages and any non-monetary satisfaction from the job) exceed the cost. The cost of working at a job for a given period is the satisfaction that could have been received from the best alternative use of that time—perhaps the benefits from an alternative job or a leisure activity.

Several factors determine how many people want to work in any given occupation. These include: the wage of the occupation, the wages of other occupations, the skills required for the occupation, any enjoyment workers get from the job, any negative aspects of the work, the population of the market area, and the ability of qualified workers from elsewhere to move to the market area.

★3 Remember from Chapter 5 that supply is the relationship between the price of an item and how much is offered for sale. Similarly, **labor supply** for an occupation is the relationship between the wage and the number of people who are willing and qualified to work in that occupation.

Consider again machinists in the garden tool industry. Table 7-2 presents three possible supply relationships for these machinists. Each relationship shows the numbers of qualified people who wish to work as machinists at three different wages: $6, $9, and $12 per hour. The average supply relationship means the number of people who wish to work in any other occupation, on average, equals the number who choose to work as machinists. A strong supply for machinists means, for any given wage, there are more people who want jobs as machinists than people who want jobs in any other occupation, again on average. Conversely, a weak supply means fewer people want jobs as machinists.

Three factors explain most of this variance in labor supplies: 1) degree of skills required; 2) job satisfaction; and 3) unpleasant aspects of the job.

■ The degree of skills required to do a job is usually the most important factor of supply. If a job is very difficult to learn, many people may be *willing* to do it for $12 per hour. However, perhaps few can qualify, either because few people are: 1) capable of acquiring the skills; or 2) willing or financially able to acquire the skills. Jobs that are difficult to learn (programming computers or piloting airplanes) or have high learning costs (long and/or expensive training, as for physicians) tend to have a weak labor supply. Conversely, jobs that are easy to learn (flipping hamburgers or collecting trash) or have low learning costs tend to have a strong labor supply.

■ Job satisfaction is the second major factor of labor supply. An enjoyable job tends to draw many people into that occupation. Benefits people derive from the job itself, often called psychic income, include good working conditions, interesting and challenging work, a good work schedule, and prestige and other personal rewards.

■ Any unpleasant aspects of an occupation tend to lead to a weak (small) supply of labor in the field. Such negative factors include boredom, danger, low prestige, a long commute in heavy traffic, stress, job politics, long hours, and hot, smelly, or otherwise undesirable working conditions.

In each of the three labor supply relationships shown in Table 7-2, more

Table 7-2 The Supply of Labor Under Varying Conditions

	Number of People Offering to Work When There Is a:		
Wage	Average Supply	Strong Supply	Weak Supply
$12	900	1300	500
$ 9	700	1100	300
$ 6	500	900	100

people want to be machinists at higher wages than at lower wages. These direct relationships between wages and the number of people wanting to work show that the law of supply applies to labor, just as it does to goods and services. The reason people obey the law of supply for labor is also the same. That is, at higher wages (prices) people are more willing to work at a job (sell labor) because they can "afford to." Consider the average supply case. Although at least 900 people are qualified to be machinists (since that's how many seek jobs at $12 per hour), only 500 want jobs at $6 per hour. The other 400 have things to do, such as other jobs or leisure activities, that provide more benefits. In short, the machinist job costs them too much. However, at a higher benefit of $9 or $12 per hour, more people decide that being a machinist is a good choice.

Incidentally, the law of supply explains the concept of overtime pay. Even if not compelled by law, employers must often pay higher wages to get workers to work longer hours because the extra hours are more "costly" to the workers. The first few hours worked each day force workers to give up relatively unimportant activities, such as the ninth or tenth hour of sleep or some unimportant leisure activity. But the tenth hour of work forces workers to give up very enjoyable (thus, costly) leisure activities. The only way they will come to work is for a higher benefit (wage).

Figure 7-3 shows each of the three machinist labor supply relationships in two ways. The bar graphs show increasing numbers of workers at any given wage for increasingly strong labor supply relationships. Similarly, the labor supply curves for the stronger relationships are farther to the right.

Figure 7-3 The Supply of Labor Under Varying Conditions

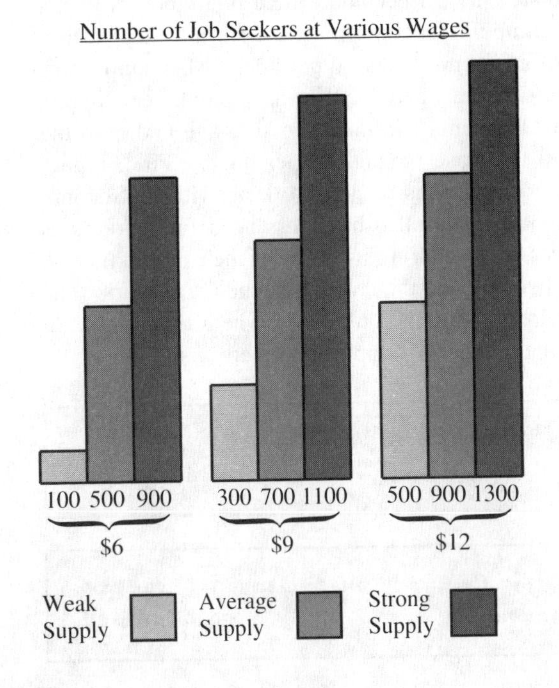

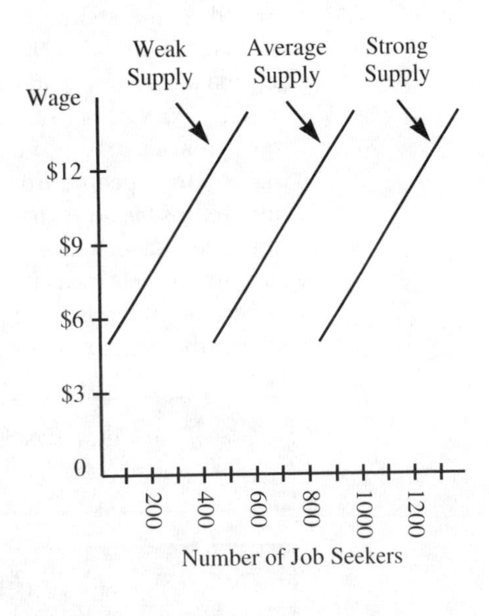

Wage Determination

★4

Wages in labor markets under competitive conditions are determined the same way that prices are determined in product markets. Employers and employees interact in a large "auction" for labor resources. No single individual or firm determines the wage, yet all participants have an influence on it.

Table 7-3 brings together the demand and supply for machinist labor under average conditions, shown in Tables 7-1 and 7-2. The last column shows that there can be either "too many" job seekers, creating a **labor surplus**, or "too few" workers, creating a **labor shortage**.

Table 7-3 "Average Wage" Conditions of Labor Demand and Supply

Wage	Average Demand		Average Supply	Labor Shortage or Labor Surplus
$12	500		900	Surplus of 400 workers
$ 9	700	←equal→	700	No Surplus or Shortage
$ 6	900		500	Shortage of 400 workers

If employers pay machinists only $6 per hour, there is a labor shortage. To end such a shortage under competitive conditions, a firm may try to hire machinists from other firms by offering more than $6 per hour. Also, employees demand higher wages in shortage situations because they have employers "over a barrel." As wages rise, two developments eliminate the shortage and stop the wage from increasing further (in this case beyond $9 per hour). First, higher wages attract people from other occupations or non-work activities. Second, employers substitute cheaper resources and also have less need for workers as production (labor) costs and prices rise, resulting in fewer of their products sold. These two events mean the law of supply and the law of demand are at work. The $9-per-hour wage is the **equilibrium wage**, the only wage where the number of people who wish to work equals the number of people employers wish to hire.

> *Few of us can stand prosperity. Another man's, I mean.*
>
> – Mark Twain

> *The secret of living is to find people to pay you money to do what you would pay to do if you had the money.*
>
> – Sarah Caldwell

Alternatively, if the wage is $12 per hour, more people want the job than there are jobs open (400 more), so there is a labor surplus. Either employers will refuse to pay such high wages or the people who can't find work will offer to work for less. Again, this process sets the laws of supply and demand in action. At lower wages: 1) more jobs open up; and 2) fewer people want them. Eventually the labor surplus disappears at the equilibrium wage of $9 per hour.

Figure 7-4 presents two ways to visualize the wage determination process. On the left side of the figure, each wage considered has a set of box diagrams. The first (blue) box represents the number of job openings and the second (grey) box the number of people who want the job. At $6 per hour, there is an imbalance in these two, representing a labor shortage of 400 workers. There is another imbalance at $12, but this time it represents a labor surplus. Only at $9 per hour is there a balance between the number of job openings and job seekers.

Figure 7-4 "Average Wage" Conditions of Labor Demand and Supply

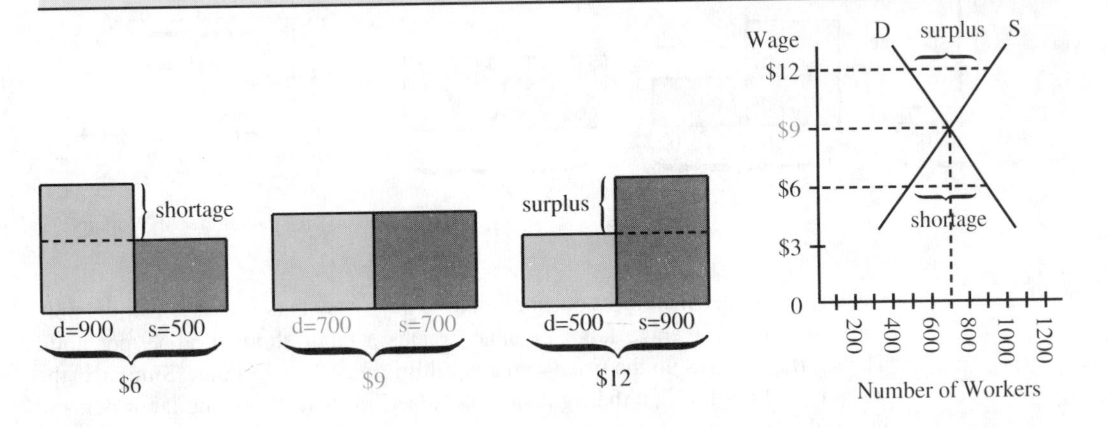

On the right side of the figure, the supply and demand graphs intersect at $9 per hour—the equilibrium wage. At any wage higher than that, such as $12 per hour, there is a surplus of workers. Any wage lower than the equilibrium, such as $6 per hour, leads to a shortage of workers.

If $9 per hour is the equilibrium wage for the average occupation, why do some occupations pay more and some less than that? Because either labor demand or labor supply is different from the average occupation. Figure 7-5 and the left half of Table 7-4 show one reason why an occupation will pay "high

If you don't want to work, you have to work to earn enough money so that you won't have to work. – Ogden Nash

Table 7-4 "High Wage" Conditions of Labor Demand and Supply

Wage	Average Demand		Weak Supply	Strong Demand		Average Supply
$12	500	←equal→	500	900	←equal→	900
$ 9	700		300	1100		700
$ 6	900		100	1300		500

Figure 7-5 "High Wages" Due to an Average Demand and a Weak Supply

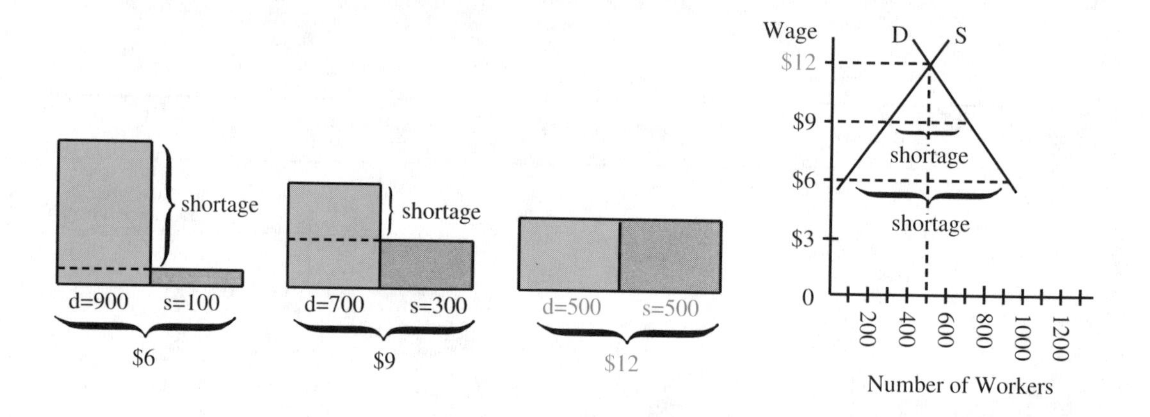

wages" (or higher than most occupations). They show that a weaker labor supply coupled with an average labor demand creates a labor shortage at $9 per hour. The shortage drives up the wage to the equilibrium at $12 per hour. Similarly, the wage is $12 per hour on the right side of Table 7-4, where a strong labor demand is coupled with an average labor supply.

Conversely, Table 7-5 shows why the pay in some occupations is low, at least compared with most other occupations. Such low pay results from either: 1) a relatively weak labor demand, which means there is little competition between employers for the available workers; or 2) a relatively strong labor supply, which means competition between job seekers for the available jobs is relatively strong. Either case leads to a surplus of workers at the $9-per-hour equilibrium wage paid for the average occupation. Because workers at $9 per hour are "a dime a dozen" for such occupations, the equilibrium wage is much lower. In the example, only at $6 per hour do employers want to hire all the people who want jobs in that occupation. Figure 7-6 also shows this second cause of low wages, that of a strong supply.

Figure 7-7 summarizes the conditions leading to wages in one occupation that are higher or lower than in most other occupations. It illustrates that wages in an occupation are directly related to the scarcity of that particular class of human capital.

Table 7-5 "Low Wage" Conditions of Labor Demand and Supply

Wage	Weak Demand		Average Supply	Average Demand		Strong Supply
$12	100		900	500		1300
$ 9	300		700	700		1100
$ 6	**500**	←equal→	**500**	**900**	←equal→	**900**

Figure 7-6 "Low Wage" Due to an Average Demand and a Strong Supply

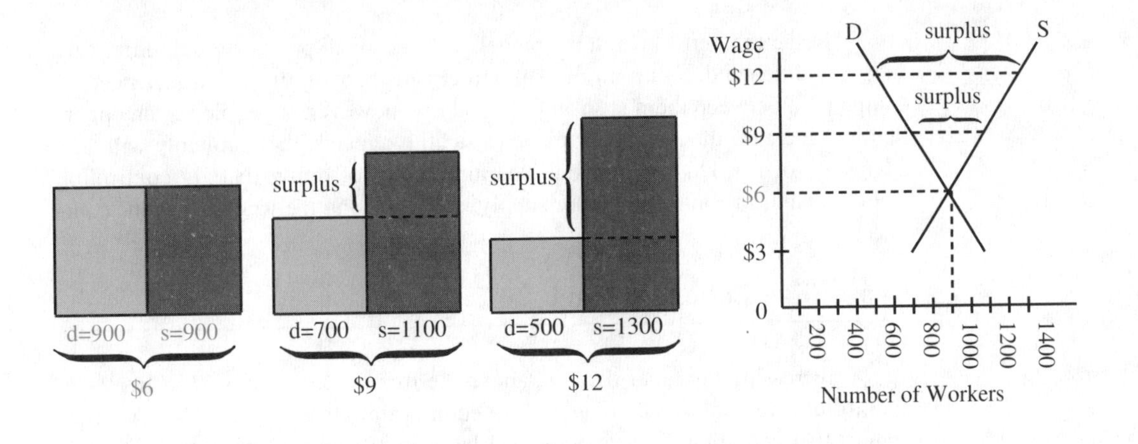

Figure 7-7 Conditions Tending to Make Incomes Relatively Low or High

Determinant of Wages	Determinant of Labor Supply or Labor Demand	Conditions Tending to Make Income for an Occupation Relatively:	
		Low	**High**
Labor Supply	Job Skills Required for the Occupation	Few	Many
	Enjoyable Aspects of the Occupation	Many	Few
	Displeasing Aspects of the Occupation	Few	Many
Labor Demand	Demand and Price for the Product	Low	High
	Labor Productivity	Low	High

Here are some reasons, along with examples, why an occupation tends to be relatively low paying: 1) it requires relatively few skills (fast food service, janitorial service); 2) it has very enjoyable aspects (photography, flower arranging, teaching nursery school); 3) it has few unfavorable aspects; 4) demand for the product is relatively low (professional soccer in the United States); or 5) its workers are relatively unproductive (car wash operations).

Alternatively, an occupation tends to be relatively high paying if: 1) it requires great skills (top entertainers, professional football quarterbacks, corporate executives, physicists); 2) it provides little psychic income; 3) it has very unfavorable aspects (bomb removal and detonation, skyscraper construction); 4) demand for the product is strong (professional football); or 5) the productivity of its workers is high (open pit coal mining).

INCREASING INCOMES ABOVE COMPETITIVE LEVELS

In the theoretical capitalist model, all wages and prices are determined by supply and demand. With all market participants serving their own self-interest, competition between them is strong. In real life, however, if people see an opportunity to increase their incomes above competitive levels, they probably will take advantage of it. This section outlines three ways of doing that: 1) controlling labor demand; 2) controlling labor supply; and 3) raising the wage above the equilibrium level.

Controlling Labor Demand

★5

Increasing the labor demand above the free market level will increase the equilibrium wage above the *competitive* equilibrium wage. Figure 7-8(a) shows competitive conditions in a hypothetical labor market, where the wage is $7 per hour and there are 800 jobs. Figure 7-8(b) shows that a larger, controlled labor demand leads to a $9-per-hour wage and 100 more jobs. In essence, workers seek to increase the competition among employers for the same number of available workers. Workers increase demand for themselves in several ways, including: 1) jurisdiction; 2) work rules; and 3) advertising.

■ First, if workers are in a union, they can demand jurisdiction over certain work, which means only members of that union can do such work. For example, the workers in a school's audio-visual department could insist that only they, not teachers, can operate audio-visual equipment in the classroom.

■ Second, again with union support, workers can push for **work rules**, which are worker-established or -influenced guidelines on how to perform certain jobs. Although the stated purpose of such rules is usually increased worker safety or increased work quality, often the real purpose is the extra work (or "featherbedding") these rules provide. For example, decades after diesel engines made (coal) firemen obsolete, laws still forced railroads to hire firemen.

■ Last, laborers increase labor demand through advertising. Electricians, for example, might take out an ad that shows the danger of tinkering with electrical wires, thus increasing demand for professional electrical service.

Figure 7-8 Raising the Equilibrium Wage Above Competitive Conditions

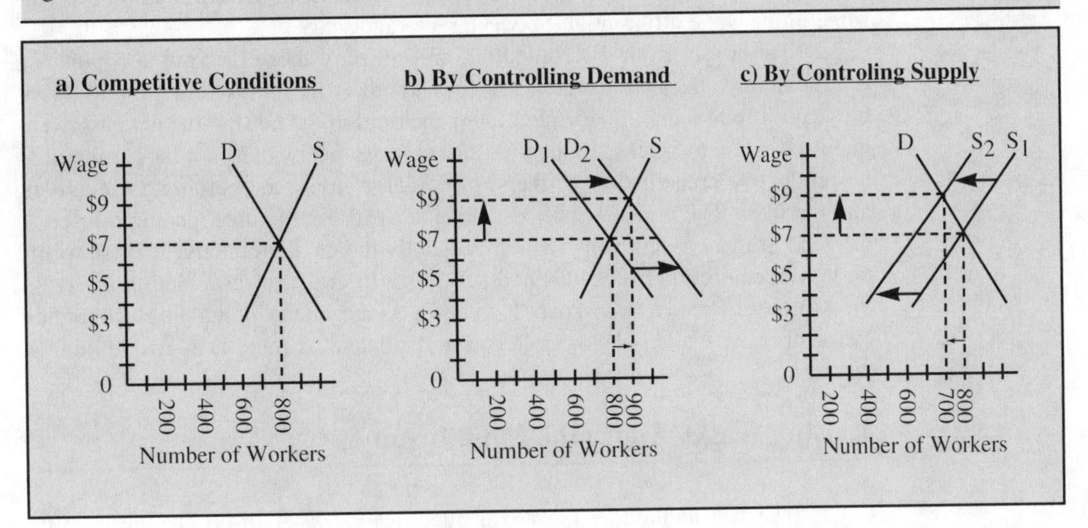

(British coal miners gave a dramatic demonstration of worker effect on labor demand in October 1992. They threatened to bring down the government of Prime Minister John Major after he announced plans to close two-thirds of the nation's publicly owned mines. Closing the 31 mines would have eliminated 30,000 jobs, but Major later reduced the closings to 10, thereby maintaining the demand for coal miners at a higher level.)

Controlling Labor Supply

Workers can also increase their wage by reducing labor supply. In Figure 7-8(c), a reduced supply raises wages from $7 to $9 per hour, but in this case there are 100 *fewer* jobs than under competitive conditions. Simply put, workers seek to eliminate the competition between themselves for the available jobs. The reduced competition creates a labor shortage and, in turn, higher wages. This is accomplished by: 1) raising job qualifications; or 2) discrimination.

■ The first way to control supply is to prevent potential workers from attaining the minimum job requirements by making them more difficult to obtain. Such increased requirements could include: a college degree; age, height, or strength standards; union membership; an apprenticeship period; or a passing score on an entrance exam. If workers who are already employed in an occupation have a voice in job requirements, it is in their best interest to make job requirements difficult for newcomers to attain. For example, the American Medical Association, an organization of physicians, limits licenses for teaching hospitals, thereby controlling the number of new physicians.

■ The second way to control labor supply is through discrimination. If, for example, airline pilots could prevent airline companies from hiring non-whites, non-Christians, or women, only one-third or so of the potentially qualified people could become pilots. (Discrimination could be considered a special case of the first method of controlling supply.) In the past, workers in many occupations "earned" higher incomes because of discrimination. Although laws now outlaw such discrimination, it still occurs to some extent. Discrimination explains some of the wage differentials between races and sexes.

The losers from discrimination are not only those discriminated against. Everyone loses because scarce resources (laborers) are *not* used in the best possible way. If our economy operated today as it did in the not-too-distant past, well-qualified women, blacks, Hispanics, and other groups would not be permitted to be productive construction workers, physicians, engineers, corporate executives, and the like. The effect would be the same as if, for example, people refused to eat food grown on dark soil—which is usually the most productive. There would be less overall output of goods and services. In effect, discrimination *increases* the scarcity of resources. That is *opposite* to the intent in studying economics. Remember the United Negro College Fund slogan: "A mind is a terrible thing to waste."

Raising Wages Above the Equilibrium

The last technique for raising incomes works with no change in either labor demand or labor supply. Instead of letting supply and demand determine the wage, some groups of people set the wage above the equilibrium in one of two

Figure 7-9 The Effects of Minimum Wage Legislation

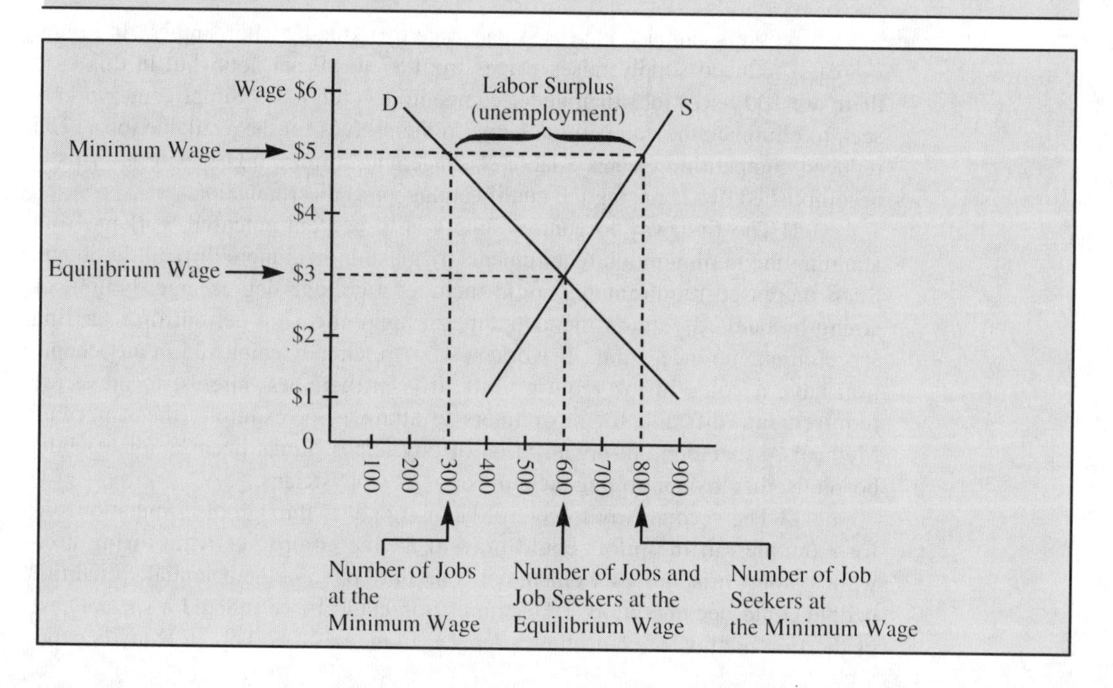

ways: 1) by establishing minimum wage laws; and 2) by allowing collective bargaining between employers and labor unions.

■ First, the government might decide that an equilibrium wage is too low. So it passes a **minimum wage law** prohibiting employers from paying workers less than a certain amount. Although there is much disagreement on the subject, most economists believe the law of demand leads to fewer jobs in occupations that pay the minimum wage. Also, at the higher wage, more people now want the job. Thus, some people who want a job won't get one. Figure 7-9 shows the effects of minimum wage legislation.

■ The second method to raise wages above equilibrium is to give workers the same power as sellers in a cartel. Members of cartels agree not to undercut each others' prices after raising those prices above the equilibrium level. A **labor union** uses the same technique as a cartel. But instead of selling a product, the members "sell labor." Instead of bargaining *individually* for their wages, workers use the **collective bargaining** approach. This means all workers bargain as one through a "bargaining unit." If employers refuse to pay the demanded higher wage, workers can **strike**—which is a refusal to "sell labor."

THE LABOR UNION MOVEMENT

American labor unions have existed in various forms for two centuries. In many respects, unions are remnants of medieval guilds, which were associations of individual craftsmen (shoemakers, silversmiths, gunsmiths, etc.). This section gives a cursory view of union history and characteristics.

Labor Organizations

★6

The first unions appeared in the late 1700s and were unions of localized workers, with no connection to other unions. These were usually **craft unions**, composed of skilled workers in one occupation. By the 1830s, unions began to combine with other local unions, forming federations to gain strength. In the 1850s, many similar local unions combined to form the first **national union**. The Knights of Labor, formed in 1869, was the first widespread national union. It reached its peak membership in the 1880s, when successful rail strikes made it popular. The Knights accepted workers from all occupations, whether skilled or not. This open membership caused problems with the craft unions, which believed they could do better on their own. There were problems within the Knights, too, because members disagreed on goals. Some only wanted to improve their economic welfare within a capitalistic system, while others wanted to revolutionize the whole economic system and move it toward socialism. Such disagreements and other problems led to the Knights' decline.

In 1886, a group of national craft unions founded the American Federation of Labor (AFL). Samuel Gompers was its first president, serving until 1924. He sought immediate gains of better working conditions, higher pay, and shorter hours, but did not get involved in political and economic ideology. Throughout its history, the AFL followed a "conservative" philosophy. That is, it wanted to maintain capitalism, but to get a larger share of the economic pie.

The AFL had little desire to organize unskilled workers. Yet by the 1920s and 1930s, industries that required many unskilled workers, such as steel and rubber, were growing rapidly. Also, mechanization in other industries, such as the auto industry, reduced the need for skilled workers. Eventually, such workers were organized by **industrial unions**, where all workers in one industry, both skilled and unskilled, belonged to the same union. John L. Lewis headed one of these, the United Mine Workers. In 1935, after disagreements with AFL leaders, he and others formed a new federation of industrial unions, the Congress of Industrial Organizations (CIO). After success in the steel and auto industries, the CIO rapidly gained strength. The two federations joined in 1955 to form the AFL-CIO. George Meany, its first president, served until his death in 1980. Lane Kirkland is its current president.

Some national unions, called **independent unions**, do not belong to the AFL-CIO. The National Education Association is a powerful independent union.

Union membership as a share of the total work force is declining. For decades it had been a little over one-fourth of the work force, but it is now about one-sixth and slowly declining.

Labor Legislation

Without government assistance, laborers would have a hard time overcoming their competitive tendencies. Although some court actions and legislation have weakened unions, major legislation over the years has enabled workers to form unions.

★7

- The Sherman Antitrust Act of 1890 was designed to end monopolies in markets for goods and services. However, it was often used to stop unionization because unions were considered to be illegal "conspiracies in the restraint of trade." The Clayton Antitrust Act of 1914 exempted unions from the Sherman Act.
- The Davis-Bacon Act of 1931 requires private contractors to pay "prevailing wages" (which is usually whatever unionized workers receive) on all construction projects that are totally or partly financed by the federal government. It was designed to prevent certain construction firms that had lower-paid, non-unionized workers from competing with unionized firms on construction projects. The president has the authority to temporarily suspend the act.
- The Norris-LaGuardia Act of 1932 eliminated some of the employers' weapons against organized labor, especially the "yellow-dog contract"—in which a worker agreed not to join a union if hired. It also banned the **injunction**, a court order forcing laborers back to work during a strike.
- The National Labor Relations Act (or the Wagner Act) of 1935 gave laborers the legal right to bargain collectively. Until then a firm could fire all its workers who joined a union and replace them with non-union workers. The act set up the National Labor Relations Board (NLRB), which supervises elections and decides which union will represent the workers. The law prohibits firms from interfering in union organizing activity and union administration and from discriminating against union employees. Such actions are called unfair labor practices. However, the act does not cover government employees.

■ The Taft-Hartley Act of 1947 amended the Wagner Act and reduced union strength. The act: 1) outlaws the **closed shop**, where workers are forced to join a union before being hired; 2) allows *states* to pass **right-to-work laws**, which outlaw the **union shop** (where workers must join a union after working for a short period); 3) outlaws some labor practices, most notably featherbedding; 4) prohibits secondary boycotts, in which striking workers pressure a third party not to deal with their employer; and 5) allows the government to suspend a strike with an injunction for an 80-day "cooling-off period" if the strike imperils the national health or safety.

■ The Landrum-Griffin Act of 1959 was designed to eliminate corruption in unions and to promote democratic procedures. It placed tight controls on union finances.

Collective Bargaining and Union Goals

What do union members want? Obviously, higher wages are important, but closely related are fringe benefits, such as health and life insurance, pensions, and vacations. However, higher wages and fringe benefits could cost the union members jobs (because of the law of demand), so the level of employment is also a goal. Consequently, unions occasionally try to delay the introduction of labor-saving devices. A goal that ties wages and employment is for unions to maximize the wage bill, which is the total income received collectively by the members. Finally, unions want better working conditions, better hours, and job security.

A union achieves its goals through the collective bargaining process, in which negotiations occur between management and the union bargaining team. This team, representing the "rank and file" (union members), either: 1) accepts a tentative agreement and recommends it for ratification (acceptance); or 2) recommends a strike to obtain a better agreement. Both actions are voted on by the membership as a whole. After ratification, the entire agreement is written into the contract.

Strikes make headlines, but are relatively rare, or are at least rarer than during the 1950s and 1960s. (Only about 40 work stoppages per year involve more than 1,000 workers.) Labor and management usually reach agreement after long negotiations on dozens of issues. If an agreement cannot be reached, a third party often is called in to assist. Such third-party interventions take one of three forms: 1) fact-finding; 2) mediation; or 3) arbitration. Fact-finding involves a government board that studies the issues and makes suggestions, which do not have to be followed. In **mediation**, the third party listens to the arguments of labor and management and offers non-binding solutions. If all else fails, the bargainers can agree to **arbitration**, after which a jointly-selected arbitrator's recommendations must be followed.

ENTREPRENEURSHIP

Entrepreneurs play a vital role in raising living standards. This section examines that role and why some people want to become entrepreneurs.

The Role of Entrepreneurs

Entrepreneurs fulfill three main roles in the economy: 1) they organize the production process; 2) they increase resource efficiency; and 3) they redirect resource use.

■ The first role of entrepreneurs is the organization of the production process. Specifically, their intent is to produce a good or service with the fewest amount of resources, given a specific production process. In short, their role is to maximize the efficiency of resource use. In turn, this reduces the problems caused by resource scarcity.

■ Closely related is the second role, increasing the efficiency of resource use through innovation. By changing the production process or how something is produced, firms can often produce more than was possible earlier. This increased efficiency of resource use gives rise to the phrase that "entrepreneurs operate in the marketplace for ideas." Entrepreneurs don't actually sell their resources in any market to someone who converts them into goods or services. They use their resources themselves in their *own* businesses.

■ The last role of entrepreneurs is to redirect resource use into or away from various industries where there are insufficient or excess resources—in other words, to increase allocative efficiency.

Some Influences on Entrepreneurship

Many factors determine the number of entrepreneurs—the "supply" of entrepreneurship—in an economy. For example, the education system affects the quantity and quality of entrepreneurs because schools help develop initiative, independence, and organizational skills. Other factors that affect these character traits include parental guidance and peer values.

The number, size, and risk-taking position of financial institutions (banks and the like) also determine how many people take the plunge into business.

The government interacts with entrepreneurs in several ways. First, the tax system determines how much profit entrepreneurs can keep. Many argue that taxing rich, successful entrepreneurs at high rates discourages them and other aspiring entrepreneurs from further innovations that made them rich and the rest of us better off with higher living standards. It's akin to "killing the goose that lays the golden eggs" in the nursery story. Other government influences are bankruptcy laws, government loans to businesses, and technical and other informational assistance to firms.

A relatively new and rapidly growing technique to encourage and assist entrepreneurs is the so-called business incubator. These vary in form, from locations where several tiny businesses share buildings, equipment, and knowledge to where old buildings have been converted to the needs of the new firms and are rented at subsidized rates. Over half of the nearly 600 incubators are sponsored by universities, which use them to make commercial use of what has been learned in their laboratories. Also, corporations often sponsor them as a way of supporting community development.

THE MARKET FOR CAPITAL

Capital is defined as any good used to produce another good or service. Capital, then, is really capital equipment or capital goods—and not money.

Types of Capital

★8

Capital goods generally can be placed into two categories: 1) social overhead capital; or 2) direct capital.

■ **Social overhead capital**, more commonly called infrastructure, includes capital goods involved in providing such services as transportation, communication, energy, education, and public safety. A modern economy based upon specialists who exchange goods and services requires a well-developed infrastructure to function efficiently. Examples of such capital include railroad tracks and roadbeds, power lines, airports, schools, highways, dams, sewer lines, police stations, oil pipelines, dock facilities, and courthouses. Such capital is usually very large and immobile. Often these capital goods do not directly produce other goods or services. A dam, for example, can provide flood control, which in the normal sense is neither a good nor a service. Yet a dam makes possible (or at least facilitates) the production of agricultural crops and improves river navigation by barges and ships. You also learned earlier that some infrastructure, especially when involved with transportation and communication, is essential for mass markets, a vital component of an efficient, mass-production economy.

A relatively new type of infrastructure is called a "data highway." Initially begun on a small scale in the 1960s, it now links millions of computer users in over 35 countries. Users are able to pass messages and browse through a multitude of "bulletin boards." The current system is called Internet, but passage of the 1991 High-Performance Computing Act commits $3 billion to build a new system. That system, the National Research and Education Network (NREN), will have fiber optic cables 100 times faster than Internet's. For example, it will allow anyone anywhere to look at any material in the Library of Congress or to access detailed maps made from satellite photos. Countless other databanks will provide the specialized information that is vital for efficient production in our so-called modern post-industrial information age.

■ A metal-stamping machine is an example of the second category of capital goods. Such goods vary in size from very small to very large, and they can generally be moved from place to place. Because they produce other goods and services more directly, we might call such capital direct capital. Other examples of direct capital include train locomotives and boxcars, office computers, chain saws of logging crews, factories, drill presses, classroom desks and blackboards, taxis, and farm tractors.

Financing of Capital

Most capital goods are expensive, so financing them is a major task. We'll consider social overhead capital first. This type of capital is owned mainly by the public and includes postal facilities and most roads and dams. Private firms also own some, such as railroad rights-of-way and pipelines.

Governments finance their infrastructure in three primary ways. First, governments tax their citizens. Second, governments charge individuals and firms user fees (or user charges) whenever use is made of the capital. A bridge toll is an example, as are airport takeoff and landing fees paid by airlines, and charges to ships using the St. Lawrence Seaway. Third, governments borrow money to purchase capital goods by selling bonds. Governments then collect user charges and/or taxes to repay the bondholders.

Private businesses obtain capital in four primary ways: 1) leasing; 2) retained earnings; 3) equity financing; and 4) debt financing. The first method, leasing, is the only one that doesn't involve ownership of the capital by the user. A lease is a contract giving the firm the right to use capital belonging to someone else for a specified period. The payment for that use appears as an expense on the income statement. Many retail firms lease their stores, some railroads lease boxcars, and some dentists lease their office equipment.

The other three methods of obtaining capital involve ownership. (In these cases, payment for the capital appears as depreciation on the income statement.) The first is financing through retained earnings, which occurs when a firm uses some of its profits to purchase capital. The second method, equity financing, occurs when corporations raise money by selling new corporate stock. The new investors' money increases the firm's equity—hence, the name. Finally, firms obtain funds through debt financing when they borrow money by taking out loans at lending institutions or insurance companies. Corporations also borrow funds by selling corporate bonds and other financial instruments, collectively known as commercial paper.

Capital and Economic Growth

★9

Economic growth is an increase in the amount of goods and services that an economy produces. One way to achieve it is to increase the amount of resources in an economy, including capital. Increasing the capital stock of a nation is also known as capital formation.

When a nation produces capital goods, it is saving for the future. That is, instead of producing consumer goods to be enjoyed in the present, it produces capital goods that will be used to produce consumer goods *in the future*. Many factors determine how many capital goods are produced, including: the expected level of future business activity; business tax rates; the amount and type of government regulation of business; the inflation rate; the level of interest rates; the savings rate; and the number and creativity of entrepreneurs.

Two of these factors deserve elaboration: the level of interest rates and the savings rate. Spending by private business on capital stock, known as investment, tends to rise when interest rates fall. The various capital projects in which firms can invest have different productivities and rates of return (rates of profitability). A firm will invest in a particular project only if it expects the benefit (the extra profits, excluding borrowing costs) to exceed the interest on the loan. Therefore, when interest rates fall, firms will invest in projects that are less productive and which would not have been carried out at higher rates. Consequently, the capital

The Grand Coulee Dam, in Central Washington, was built during the Great Depression in the 1930s, partly to put the unemployed to work. It also provides cheap electric power, flood control, and irrigation water in the semi-arid region. This example of social overhead capital, like many other examples, is publicly owned by U.S. citizens.

This was a toll house on the National Road, also known as the Cumberland Road, now U.S. 40. Built between Cumberland, Maryland and Vandalia, Illinois, a distance of 591 miles. The road was started in 1811 and finally completed in 1852. The road contributed to lower shipping rates, wider markets for products, and hastened the spread of emigration from the Atlantic seaboard over the Appalachian Mountains to the Ohio Valley.

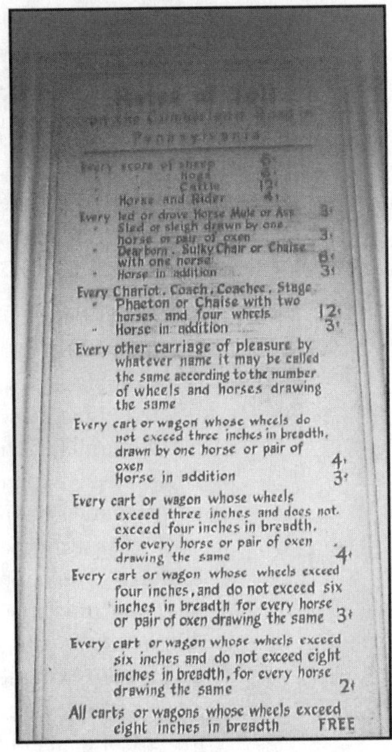

Tariff rates for traffic on the Cumberland Road. Note the higher rates for narrow-wheeled wagons.

> *Our greatest natural resource is the minds of our children.*
>
> – Walt Disney

stock grows. The interest rate, therefore, is a mechanism for dealing with the scarcity of capital. The less scarce these funds are, the lower the interest rate, and the greater the capital stock and economic growth rate.

The savings rate is the other main factor affecting the interest rate. The larger the share of their incomes that people save, the more money there is available for lending. This leads to a lower interest rate because: 1) borrowers have more sources of funds, so they don't have to "bid" as high for credit (pay high interest rates); and 2) lenders, no longer in such a "sellers' market," can't demand such high interest rates. The United States is notorious for its low savings rate, around four or five percent of after-tax personal income. The Japanese save between 17 and 20 percent of their pay. Consequently, Japanese businesses pay much lower interest rates than U.S. firms. In turn, the Japanese have a higher rate of capital formation and a higher economic growth rate.

THE ECONOMICS OF NATURAL RESOURCES

A natural resource is anything found in nature that is necessary to produce certain goods and services. This section first considers natural resources that are unrelated to agriculture. Next covered are agricultural resources and some problems facing the agricultural sector of the economy.

Non-Agricultural Resources

Non-agricultural resources generally fit into four categories: 1) mineral resources; 2) energy resources; 3) forest resources; and 4) waterways. The United States is blessed with an abundance of many of these, providing a primary source of high living standards. Yet some nations, including Japan, Switzerland, and the Netherlands, achieve high living standards with few natural resources. Alternatively, some nations, such as China, Brazil, and Zaire, have abundant natural resources but remain poor.

As technology changes, some natural resources become either more or less useful. For example, iron ore is still a vital resource, but less so than formerly because plastics and other materials often substitute for iron and steel. Alternatively, titanium, a very strong and light metal, once considered of little use, is now extremely valuable to the aircraft and aerospace industries.

People often worry that we will run out of this or that natural resource, but the law of demand usually saves us from such problems. If a resource becomes so scarce that its price climbs sky-high, a substitute resource usually becomes cheaper. A good example was the development of the English coal industry in the 1700s after wood prices rose sharply because the English forests were being cut for fuel. The existence of coal was always known, but wood was always cheaper to use—until then. In turn, the development of Britain's North Sea oil fields led to the demise of its coal industry. For the same reason, the British and the rest of the world need not worry about the depletion of oil. When the price of oil gets high enough, another energy source will eventually substitute for it.

The world became painfully aware of the importance of energy resources in the 1970s after Arab members of OPEC refused to sell oil to the United States and other countries that aided Israel in the 1973 Yom Kippur War. Although the United States is a major oil producer, it has less than five percent of the world's proven reserves of oil. However, the United States is rich in coal deposits, with about one-fourth of the world's total. But burning coal causes environmental damage, especially acid rain. Natural gas, available in abundance, is a much cleaner fuel. Nuclear energy lost favor in recent years because of the growing radioactive waste problem and the Soviet Chernobyl nuclear power plant explosion in 1986. Few rivers are left to dam to create more hydroelectric power, while solar, wind, and other exotic power sources won't have a significant impact for years.

The United States has vast forest resources, covering over 31 percent of its landmass, or 731 million areas, of which 483 million acres are suitable for timber. Our forest lands still amount to 75 percent of the area forested in 1600, and there are more trees now than in 1920. Every year more than two billion tree seedlings are planted. This partly explains why the total amount of wood that is grown per year exceeds our yearly use of wood by over 35 percent. The public owns 28 percent of American forest land, most of it in national forests. Fifteen percent is owned by forest industry firms, and the remaining 57 percent is in non-industry private hands.

The United States is rich in waterways. The Mississippi River system allows inexpensive, high-volume shipping from New Orleans to the Great Plains, the upper Midwest, and as far east as Pennsylvania. Ships from around the world reach as far as Duluth and Chicago via the Great Lakes and the St. Lawrence Seaway. Many other river systems and fine harbors allow firms to achieve mass markets, so vital for marketing the large outputs of the efficient mass-production system.

Agricultural Resources

No other nation has such an abundance of agricultural resources as the United States. Almost one-fourth of our land area grows crops, and another one-third is grassland for livestock. Much of America has fertile soil, a temperate climate, and adequate rainfall. American farmers possess huge amounts of capital resources (tractors, harvesting equipment, and buildings) and human capital resources in the form of farmer education.

Consequently, one American farmer today can feed almost 90 people. More than one-third of U.S. agricultural output is shipped abroad. In 1800, more than 90 percent of the population lived on farms, compared with only two percent today. While it took three hours to produce a bushel of wheat in 1830, it took only seven minutes to produce a bushel in 1960. Because of such advances, the average American in 1990 spent 11.6 percent of after-tax income on food (including the one-third of their meals Americans eat in restaurants). In 1933, food took 25.8 percent of the average person's income (and people cooked almost all their meals at home, without the help we get today from commercial food processors, who do everything from pre-slicing our cheese to making our pancake mixes).

Excess Resources in Agriculture

★10

Unfortunately, this great agricultural resource abundance *and* high resource productivity is connected to all the problems facing farmers today. First, farmers produce far more food than they can sell here and abroad and still earn what many farmers consider inadequate incomes. Thus, America has an *excess* of agricultural resources. Of course, this excess could disappear if people ate more, if more food were sold abroad, or if other uses were found for agricultural products. But food consumption may not increase, given low birthrates and the trend to lighter diets. Second, nations such as Canada, Australia, Argentina, and Western European countries face a similar excess agricultural capacity. Also, many nations American farmers once helped to feed, such as India and Bangladesh, have increased their output and no longer need American food. Simply giving food to poor nations would depress farm prices in those nations, reducing their own farm output. Last, it's unlikely that new uses will be found for crops, with the possible exception of the production of alcohol as a less-polluting substitute for gasoline.

For nearly a century now, these excess resources have led to incomes for farmers that are lower than business ventures that are similar in financial and managerial requirements. Net farm incomes were acutely low in the 1980s, when low prices as well as high fuel costs and high interest rates squeezed farmers on several sides. Land values plummeted, further hurting farmers who used their land for collateral to obtain loans to buy supplies and equipment. Conditions have generally improved in the 1990s, but they still are not rosey.

Firms usually leave industries in which profits are very low, taking the "excess resources" with them. That leads to shortages, then rising prices, and, finally, to adequate profits for the remaining firms. (See Figure 6-3, Case B, page 150.) This does *not* happen in agriculture for two reasons: 1) many agricultural resources are immobile, and 2) farming is a "way of life."

■ Many agricultural resources are immobile and can't be shifted into any other industry. What use is a farm silo except for storing animal feed? Barns, plows, and combines have few, if any, uses outside of farming. Most important, land is completely immobile and has few realistic alternative uses.

■ For many people, farming is a "way of life," not just a business. Many families have lived on the same farms for generations. Farmers tend to feel strong bonds to their land. People who don't live on farms may still feel nostalgic about farming because their parents or grandparents were farmers. Such nostalgia leads to attempts to save the "family farm"—a business owned and operated by the whole family. Since the late 1920s, the government has been trying to prevent the market from working its "solutions" in agriculture.

Government Involvement in American Agriculture

The government assists farmers in five main ways: 1) price supports; 2) target prices; 3) supply restriction programs; 4) credit; and 5) technological research.

■ A price support is a price floor designed to keep farm prices high enough to provide adequate incomes for farmers. The federal government forces food processors to pay prices higher than equilibrium prices to farmers. Of course, this *encourages* more production and *discourages* consumption—creating crop surpluses. The government then purchases these surpluses and stores them, gives them away to the poor, or sends them abroad under the PL-480 Food For Peace program. At various times since 1928, such programs were in force for milk, corn, wheat, cotton, peanuts, and honey.

■ Another program sets a so-called target price for certain crops. A farmer participating in the program obtains a "loan" from the government equal to the amount of output times the target price. If the price of that crop doesn't rise as high as the target price, the farmer doesn't have to repay the loan, and the government then takes the "collateral" (the crop).

■ Supply restriction programs are designed to reduce crop supplies. These include: 1) acreage restriction or "set-aside" programs, which force farmers to reduce acreage of these crops; 2) the Soil Bank of the 1950s and 1960s, which paid farmers *not* to produce anything on some of their land; 3) the Conservation Reserve Program, which is removing up to 45 million acres of erodable land from production; 4) allotment or quota programs, which require permission from the federal government to grow a crop (peanut, cranberry, and tobacco farmers need such permits); and 5) marketing orders, which restrict the sale of commodities by setting quality standards. The government has 47 marketing orders covering 33 products.

Milk is one product for which there is a marketing order. With this order, the government sets the minimum prices to be paid to farmers for milk. Prices vary across the country, with the lowest prices being in Eau Claire, Wisconsin, the center of the dairy industry. The farther from Eau Claire, the higher the price. Initially, this scheme was designed to ensure the production and availability of milk in all parts of the nation. Today, one effect is to subsidize all farmers except those near Eau Claire. The government also boosts milk prices by purchasing about $500 million worth of dairy products annually, mostly butter. It gives most of it away in food programs.

■ The government also assists farmers in the credit markets. For decades the Production Credit Association provided credit at low interest rates to farmers for seed, fertilizer, and other production resources. Similarly, the Farmers Home Administration provided loans for buying land. By the early 1980s, many farmers were in danger of defaulting on their loans. Congress then provided several billion dollars in new money to Farm Credit Services, a new agency that merged the two previous lending institutions.

■ The last farm aid program involves technological research. The Morrill Act of 1862 led to the establishment of land grant colleges and universities in most states. The federal government gave state colleges 13 million acres of unsettled land that it owned, which was then sold to farmers. Money from these sales was used to establish agricultural colleges to teach "agriculture and mechanic arts" and to provide agricultural research. During the last 130 years, such efforts have led to a vast array of discoveries, such as crop breeding, disease control, erosion control techniques—and even rat poison.

Chapter 7 SUMMARY

The circular flow model shows the flows of money that occur between buyers and sellers of resources in factor markets, as well as between buyers and sellers of goods and services in goods markets.

The income received in most occupations depends primarily upon the strengths of the demand for labor and the supply of labor. The labor demand for an occupation depends upon the profitability of hiring workers. Firms determine this profitability by comparing the workers' marginal revenue costs with their factor costs. In occupations where workers are highly productive and/or the product sells for a high price, labor demand tends to be strong, and vice versa. In occupations where few skills are required and the jobs have many favorable aspects, labor supplies tend to be strong, and vice versa. Occupations tend to have higher incomes when there is a strong demand and/or a weak supply. Lower wages are often caused by weak labor demands and/or strong supplies of labor.

People can increase their incomes in an occupation by: 1) increasing the labor demand; 2) decreasing the labor supply; and 3) establishing an income or wage floor. These techniques often require the government to grant special powers to such groups, including the power to form unions, to establish licensing programs, and to raise job qualifications. Unions allow workers to raise their incomes primarily by bargaining collectively with employers.

Entrepreneurs organize production processes, introduce innovations, and redirect resource use. Credit availability, attitudes towards risk, and tax laws are some of the factors that can influence the number of entrepreneurs.

Capital is divided into: 1) social overhead capital (or infrastructure), usually publicly owned; and 2) direct capital, usually privately owned. Publicly owned social overhead capital is usually financed by taxes, borrowing, or user fees. Privately owned direct capital is financed by selling stock, retained earnings, borrowing, and leasing.

The United States has an abundance of natural resources, including coal, gas, many minerals, forest lands, waterways, and farmland.

Chapter 7 RESPONSES TO THE LEARNING OBJECTIVES

1. The circular flow shows how: a) resources flow from resource owners to those who use them in production processes; b) goods and services flow from producers to those who use them; c) money is used to facilitate such movements of goods, services, and resources
2. The labor demand for an occupation refers to the relationship between all the possible wages and the number of people that employers wish to hire. It is influenced by the level of labor productivity and the price of the item the workers produce.
3. The labor supply for an occupation refers to the relationship between all the possible wages and the number of people who are willing to work in that occupation. It is influenced by the skills required for the job as well as by the non-monetary benefits and costs of the job.
4. Labor shortages, associated with relatively low wages, force wages up to the equilibrium wage. Conversely, labor surpluses, associated with relatively

high wages, force wages down to the equilibrium wage. At the equilibrium wage, there are an equal number of jobs and job seekers.

5. The wage for an occupation can be raised above competitive conditions by increasing the demand for labor, decreasing the supply of labor, or by collusion of the employees, who demand wage increases.
6. Early unions were craft unions. The Knights of Labor, the first major national union, organized all workers, regardless of their skill levels. The American Federation of Labor (AFL) was a confederation of national craft unions, and the Congress of Industrial Organizations (CIO) was a confederation of industrial unions. The AFL-CIO was formed when these two merged in 1955.
7. The Sherman Act restricted union activity, especially strikes. The Clayton Act exempted unions from the Sherman Act. The Davis-Bacon Act essentially provided a minimum wage for construction workers on federally funded projects. The Norris-La Guardia Act aided labor by restricting some of management's weapons. The Wagner Act gave workers at privately owned firms the right to bargain collectively. The Taft-Hartley Act reduced the power of unions, especially by restricting the union and closed shops. The Landrum-Griffin Act reduced union corruption and non-democratic leadership.
8. Social overhead capital, which provides a foundation for most production processes, is usually government owned. It is financed by taxes, user fees, and borrowing. Direct capital, used to produce most goods and services, is generally privately owned. It is financed by leasing, stock sales, bond sales, and from retained earnings.
9. Economic growth is directly related to how fast the capital stock grows. In turn, the capital stock grows faster when the savings rate is high and when interest rates are low.
10. The fundamental problem in U.S. agriculture is excess resources. In turn, this leads to low prices and incomes for farmers. These resources do not leave the agriculture industry very readily primarily because most cannot be used elsewhere.

Chapter 7 LEARNING ACTIVITIES AND DISCUSSION QUESTIONS

1. Is there more demand for teachers or for surgeons? How would you prove that? Does that explain the difference in their salaries—or is there some other factor that is equally or more important?
2. In the 1980s, there were two times when there were severe nationwide shortages of nurses. Why do you think the wage didn't rise high enough to eliminate those shortages?
3. Ask five people if they prefer capitalism or socialism. Then ask them: If it were possible to control the labor market you are in to your advantage, would you do so? Finally, ask the people who preferred capitalism and who also would control their markets to reconcile the inconsistency.
4. Ask your parents or grandparents if their views of unions have changed since they were young and to explain any change in their attitudes.
5. Make a list of 10 consumer goods made in your community and another list of 10 capital goods made. Which list was easier to make? What does that tell you about your local economy?

CHAPTER 8

INTERNATIONAL ECONOMICS

★★★★★ LEARNING OBJECTIVES ★★★★★

1. Outline the purposes of exchange and trade.
2. Explain how a nation finds the products in which it has a comparative advantage.
3. Compare and contrast the effects of imports and exports on living standards.
4. Differentiate between the two ways of determining exchange rates.
5. Determine the effects of fluctuating exchange rates on imports and exports.
6. Explain the effects of budget deficits on exchange rates, trade, and employment.
7. Differentiate between merchandise trade deficits and surpluses.
8. List seven objections to free trade.
9. List six obstacles that restrict free trade.
10. Describe the U.S. position in the global economy today.

TERMS

law of comparative advantage
exchange rate
fixed exchange rate
floating exchange rate
merchandise trade deficit
merchandise trade surplus

free trade
dumping
protectionism
tariff
most-favored-nation
quota
voluntary restraint agreement

domestic content and mixing requirement
bureaucratic control
currency devaluation
export subsidy
managed float
gold standard
multinational

The principles of economics apply beyond a nation's borders as well as within them. Each nation faces its own economic problem brought on by the scarcity of resources. Thus far you learned that individuals interact with others to solve their personal economic problems by specializing and exchanging. This chapter shows how such interaction extends beyond national borders. It also shows some of the special relationships and problems arising from international economic interaction.

INTRODUCTION TO THE WORLD ECONOMY

International economics is easier to understand if you draw parallels between different elements of the world economy. This section lists these elements and illustrates how and why they interact, especially during exchange or trade.

Interaction Between Elements of the World Economy

Elements of the world economy—individuals, consumers, resource sellers, producers, regions of a nation, and nations themselves—all interact because it benefits them. Such interaction usually involves exchange or trade. In a sense, individuals who work at different businesses (as specialists, of course) often trade with one another. For example, while buying doughnuts, a person who makes shoes at the Florsheim Shoe Company might encounter a baker wearing Florsheim shoes. Selling doughnuts gives the baker the ability to buy the shoes, and "selling labor" gives the shoemaker the ability to buy doughnuts.

Trade also is said to occur between regions of a nation, but this actually means that many *individuals* from different regions are making trades. For example, individuals (owners and employees of businesses) in the coastal regions of New England ship lobsters to individuals (wholesalers and, ultimately, consumers) in Virginia, North Carolina, Kentucky, and Tennessee. In return, individuals in these states send or "export" tobacco products, furniture, textiles, and other products to individuals in New England.

Finally, it is commonly stated that trade occurs between nations. Again, it is the individuals of nations who trade, rather than the nations themselves. Canada and Spain do not trade, but Canadians and Spaniards do.

What is the Purpose of Trade?

★1 Individuals trade with one another for two main reasons: 1) to obtain certain things that they cannot produce; and 2) to gain the advantages of specialization.

■ First, it is usually impossible to produce the items you want. No one can make an apple pie *totally* "from scratch." You would have to grow an apple tree *and* a cinnamon tree *and* sugar cane, etc. And few people can set their bones if they break them. Finally, residents of Maine can find no natural gas, coal, and petroleum in their state.

■ The second reason for trade is related to specialization. Resources are more efficient when their uses are specialized. Consequently, our living standards increase. Thus, we could say that we trade in order to gain the advantages of specialization—more efficiency and higher living standards.

Everyone agrees that individuals should specialize in what they produce. If not, each of us would be self-sufficient, making everything we consume. And because we would be so inefficient, we would be poor. None of us minds trading with a specialist in our neighborhood or even across town. We engage in such trade when we buy goods and services from our local stores, doctors' offices, or repair shops. Even buying products made in the other side of the state doesn't bother us. Finally, virtually none of us object to buying a good or service produced in an adjoining or even a distant state. For example, someone from East St. Louis, Illinois, would not refuse to buy Budweiser beer made across the Mississippi River in St. Louis, Missouri—or Lone Star beer made in Texas—just because it was brewed in another state.

However, there are a couple of rivers that some Americans do not want to cross in getting their beer—or clothes, cars, televisions, and so on. They are the Rio Grande River and the St. Lawrence River, that is, our Mexican and Canadian borders. Many Americans will refuse to drink Tecate or Corona because Mexicans make it, or Molson or Labatts because Canadians make it. Those Americans do not realize that it is just as wise to have *international* specialization as it is to have local or regional specialization within our nation. The advantage of specialization, increased living standards from increased resource efficiency, does not end at our nation's borders—or any other border.

THE MECHANICS OF INTERNATIONAL TRADE

Certain forces and economic laws direct specialists of the world to trade with one another. How this occurs is the first subject covered in this section, where we'll also consider the consequences of trade, the concept of exchange rates, and the U.S. position in world trade.

How Trade Occurs

★2

How do people in a nation decide what their specialties should be and how to trade? The **law of comparative advantage** is a rule that directs a resource to its proper specialized role. It says a resource has a comparative advantage in producing a good or service when it has the lowest opportunity cost of all other resources.

Opportunity cost refers to the *next best* thing that *could* have been produced with a resource once it is committed to making some good or service. Suppose Americans want some New Year's Eve noisemakers, which American laborers can easily make. However, what if these laborers could also make complex solar equipment? Then the more noisemakers these laborers make, the more solar equipment Americans give up. This forgone solar equipment is the opportunity cost of noisemakers, if you assume that such equipment is the most valuable alternative product they could make. Now assume that laborers in Hong Kong can also make noisemakers but lack the skills to make solar equipment. However, suppose they *can* make toy cars—in fact, suppose that is the most valuable product they can make. Then the opportunity cost of Hong Kong laborers making noisemakers is the value of toy cars they *could* have produced. If it is assumed that solar equipment is more valuable than toy cars, then Hong Kong laborers have a lower opportunity cost when they make noisemakers. That's because Hong Kong-made noisemakers cost Hong Kong residents low-valued toy cars, while American-made noisemakers cost Americans valuable solar equipment. Therefore, Americans should buy noisemakers from Hong Kong. The owners and laborers at the noisemaker firms in Hong Kong can take the money they earn and buy American solar equipment or other American goods.

The Effects of Trade on Living Standards

Many people have misconceptions about how they are affected by imports and exports. Suppose a pollster asked, "Assuming we could increase just one, would you prefer that our nation increase its imports or its exports?" Most respondents probably would choose exports. That's because most people believe exports create jobs for Americans and imports hurt American efforts to maintain high living standards and employment.

★3

Yet, it's the act of *importing*, not exporting, that raises American living standards. Exports are a *cost* to Americans. That's because Americans have to *give the exported goods up* to foreigners to get imports. Thus, the act of exporting *reduces* American living standards. Figure 8-1 illustrates this. Panel (a) shows a situation when the United States has no foreign trade at all. All of the output (shown as a "huge pile of stuff") comes from U.S. resources alone. The standard of living is represented by a "slice" of total output, reflecting the amount of goods and services available for the average person.

Suppose the Portuguese, the Taiwanese, and other foreigners use some of their resources to make things for Americans. These things are exports for the foreigners and imports for Americans. Note in Panel (b) that this *raises* the output available to Americans—and the American living standard. The reverse situation appears in Panel (c), where some American labor, land, machines, and other resources are used to make things for the Portuguese and others. Who benefits from that? *Foreigners* do because *they* have more goods and services. Americans have *less* available output and *lower* living standards.

It might seem ideal to import and not export because living standards could rise to phenomenal heights and no one would have to work. But, obviously, no country has people foolish enough to spend much of their time making things for us without getting something in return. Such people would have little time to produce anything for themselves. But what if Americans give foreigners green pieces of paper in exchange for their goods? Will foreigners accept this paper for goods? Yes—so long as they can exchange that green paper for things from Americans. Of course, these "things" are imports for foreigners (and exports for Americans)—and the green paper is U.S. currency.

A country *must* export. Otherwise imports that raise living standards and provide unattainable items would not be available. In a similar way, when people

Figure 8-1 The Effects of Imports and Exports on Living Standards

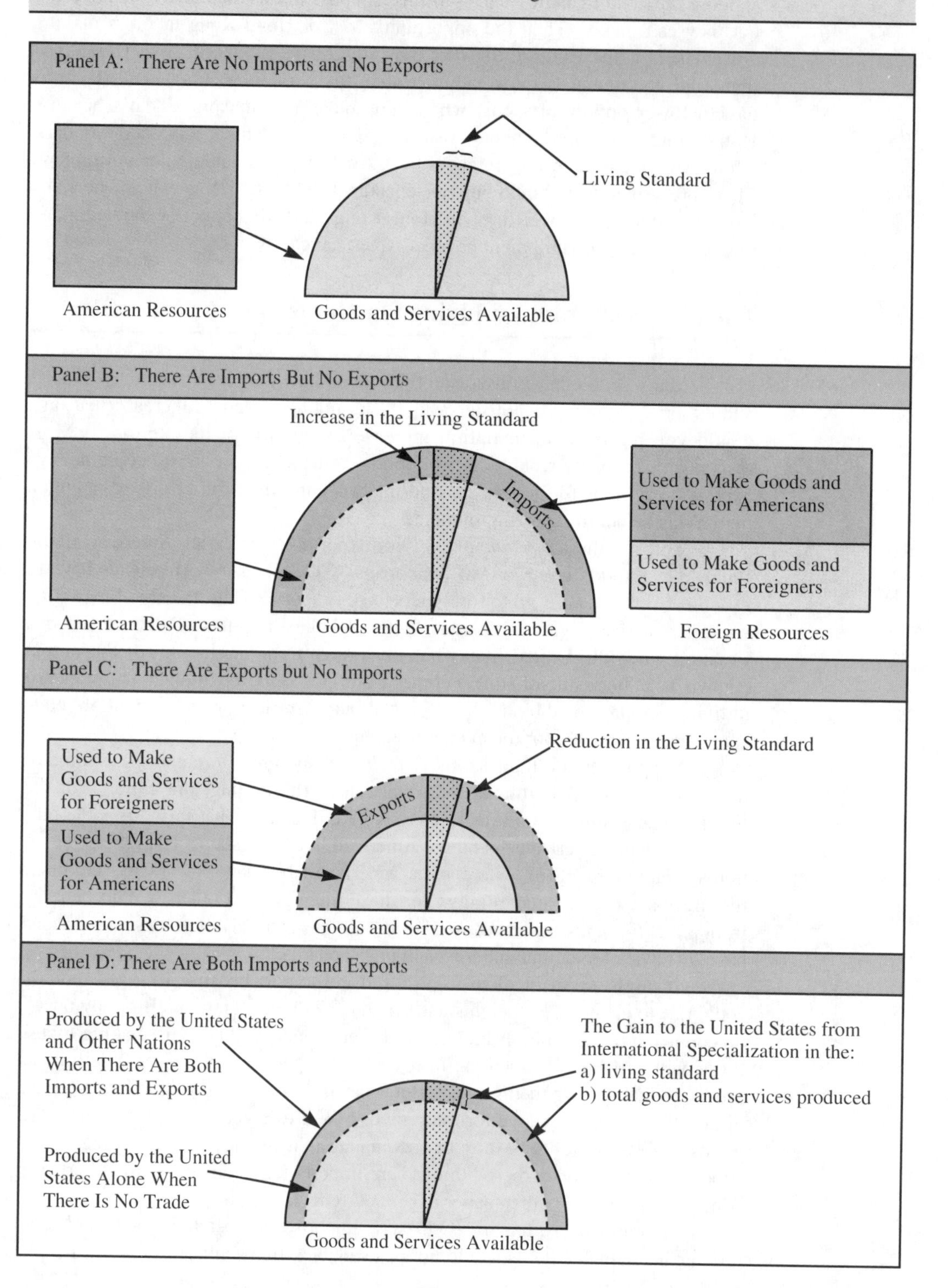

work, they "export" labor services to their employers. They generally don't work because they *want* to, but because they *must* in order to get money with which to buy goods and services (their "imports"). How nice it would be if stores gave customers whatever they wanted for nothing in exchange. But store owners are no more foolish than foreigners.

Many people fear that foreigners will want to sell to Americans but not to buy from them. However, a foreign nation is no more likely to accumulate dollars from selling goods and services to Americans than an individual will accumulate dollars from working without intending to spend them. Foreigners will eventually use those dollars to buy goods and services from Americans. In the long run, exports will equal imports. Similarly, over their lifetimes, the value of what people "sell" (their income) will approximate what they spend (or "import" from others). In the *short run,* however, a nation that exports more than it imports can use the difference to purchase assets abroad, such as land, firms, or financial securities. And this "short run" can extend well beyond a decade in length. (For example, since 1980 foreigners have owned about one percent of U.S. land.) Likewise, in the short-run, an individual can build up considerable savings and other assets by spending ("importing") less than is earned ("exporting").

When two parties trade voluntarily, *both* stand to gain—not one at the expense of another, as is often believed. If both *didn't* gain, why would both *voluntarily* trade? This point is shown in Panel (d) of Figure 8-1, where the United States has both imports and exports. The total output and living standards are somewhat higher than with no trade in Panel (a), but not as good as the dream world of Panel (b). The same situation exists for each nation with which the United States trades.

Foreign Exchange Markets and Exchange Rates

Exchange of one good for another, or barter, rarely occurs between individuals or between nations because the transaction costs are too high (see page 288 for further discussions of transaction costs). Using money for exchanges allows us to trade only one good at a time. Sellers of the good then use the money to buy things they want. *Within* a nation this is no problem, for all individuals use the same "medium of exchange" (money). But the U.S. dollar is *not* money in Sweden—where they use paper notes called kronor (krona for one unit of the currency), and this creates a problem. If J. Peter Grace Jr., head of W. R. Grace & Co., wants to buy a Swedish-made Saab car, he cannot use dollars to buy it because the Saab Corporation will only accept kronor.

The **exchange rate** refers to the amount of one nation's currency that is exchanged for another nation's currency. It is the "price" of foreign currency. Ideally, this exchange of currencies should be of equal *real* value—that is, of equal power to buy goods and services in both nations. Suppose a sugar bowl made in Sweden costs six kronor, while an identical bowl made in the United States costs $1. Because the products are identical, the natural exchange rate, as it is sometimes called, is six kronor to the dollar. Conversely, one krona equals one-sixth of a dollar, or 16.7¢. Actually, this natural rate is found by price comparisons of large numbers of goods, not just one. Purchasing power parity is another commonly used term for this "natural" ratio between currencies, which mirrors the ratio between prices of a collection of identical items in different countries.

★4 Nations use two basic systems to establish exchange rates: 1) the fixed exchange rate system; and 2) the flexible or floating exchange rate system.

■ With a **fixed exchange rate** system, a government decides the rate for which its currency will exchange for other nations' currencies. Governments might try to set these rates at the natural rate, but other objectives could result in a different rate.

■ In a **floating exchange rate** system, rates are determined in the foreign exchange market, where different currencies are traded as in any other market. Before Mr. Grace can buy a Saab, he must buy Swedish kronor with American dollars. Thus, he supplies dollars and demands kronor in the foreign exchange market. (Actually, Mr. Grace would do this through an intermediary, most likely a Saab importer.) This increased supply of dollars depresses the "price" of dollars, or the number of kronor needed to buy a dollar. Similarly, the increased demand for kronor *increases* the "price" of a krona, or the number of dollars needed to buy a krona. When this happens, the dollar depreciates (or decreases in value compared with the krona) and the krona appreciates (increases in value compared with the dollar). Note that the depreciation of any currency means other currencies must have appreciated.

Many factors affect exchange rates by influencing the demand for and the supply of currencies. Besides the currency exchanges needed for trading, currency exchanges are needed to grant foreign aid, for foreign travel, for military spending abroad, and by investors who buy land, stocks, and bonds or build factories or buy firms outside their own countries.

Table 8-1 Exchange Rates Between the U.S. Dollar and the Japanese Yen

Year	Exchange Rates	Change in the Value of the Dollar and the Yen
1987	$1 = 125 yen or 1 yen = 0.80¢	
		- The dollar rose, got stronger, or appreciated - The yen fell, got weaker, or depreciated
1990	$1 = 160 yen or 1 yen = 0.63¢	
		- The dollar fell, got weaker, or depreciated - The yen rose, got stronger, or appreciated
1993	$1 = 120 yen or 1 yen = 0.83¢	

Table 8-1 shows the exchange rates between the U.S. dollar and the Japanese yen that existed at some point in three different years. In 1987, one dollar exchanged for 125 yen. Conversely, it took 125 yen to buy one dollar, so one yen could buy 0.80¢ (note that this is *less than* one cent). By 1990, the dollar bought 160 yen, so the dollar appreciated, or "got stronger" or "rose." Conversely, in 1990 each yen could buy 0.63¢, so the yen depreciated, or "got weaker" or "fell." The reverse happened between 1990 and 1993, when 120 yen exchanged for a dollar and a yen bought 0.83¢. Thus, the value of the yen increased and the dollar "lost" some of its value. However, *within* each nation's borders, there is no effect on the "value" of each currency, or their purchasing power, so long as imported or exported goods or services are not involved.

Most people probably would prefer a strong dollar position over a weak one. "Strong" just *sounds* good—as in a "strong defense." However, the information in Table 8-2 would surprise a lot of these people.

Table 8-2 Prices of American and Japanese Goods at Various Exchange Rates

	Exchange Rates and Year		
	$1= 125 yen (1987)	**$1 = 160 yen (1990)**	**$1 = 120 yen (1993)**
American-Made Pen:			
a) Sold in the United States	$1	$1	$1
b) Sold in Japan	125 yen	160 yen	120 yen
Japanese-Made TV:			
a) Sold in Japan	80,000 yen	80,000 yen	80,000 yen
b) Sold in the United States	$640	$500	$667

★5

The table shows that the Parker Pen Corporation sold a pen in the United States for a dollar in 1987, 1990, and 1993. It also sold the pen in Japan. Parker still wanted a dollar for each pen it sold in Japan, but Japanese buyers had only yen. So Japanese stores charged the equivalent of a dollar—125 yen in 1987. In 1990, the Japanese needed 160 yen to buy the one-dollar pen because the dollar got stronger. Although American buyers of the pen were not affected by the stronger dollar, the Japanese were. Consequently, the Japanese bought fewer Parker pens—and more Pilot pens (a Japanese brand). Thus, the strong dollar (and the weak yen) cost some Americans their jobs—those who produced pens (and other goods). But it *created* jobs for the Japanese, who shipped more pens (and other goods) to the United States. The reverse happened between 1990 and 1993, leading Americans to buy fewer Pilots and more Parkers. That boosted American employment—but reduced Japanese employment.

The bottom half of Table 8-2 shows the mirror image of the pen situation for a Sony TV made in Japan. Sony wants 80,000 yen for each TV, whether sold in Osaka or Omaha. But Omaha buyers have dollars to spend, not yen, and in 1987 they needed $640 to buy Sony's 80,000-yen TV. However, by 1990 they needed only $500, as each dollar traded for 160 yen. Americans responded by buying more Sony TVs—and fewer TVs made in America at Zenith. Again, the stronger dollar hurt U.S. employment. Alternatively, the *weakening* dollar *helped* U.S. employment by 1993.

★6 The most frequently discussed determinant of the strong dollar was the growing federal budget deficit since the early 1980s. Figure 8-2 traces the chain of events that lead to rising U.S. unemployment. Budget deficits (which occur when government spending exceeds taxes) force the Treasury Department to borrow money by selling bonds. This forces up interest rates because more credit is being demanded from savers, creating a shortage of credit. Many foreign savers

Figure 8-2 Effects of Budget Deficits on Imports and Exports

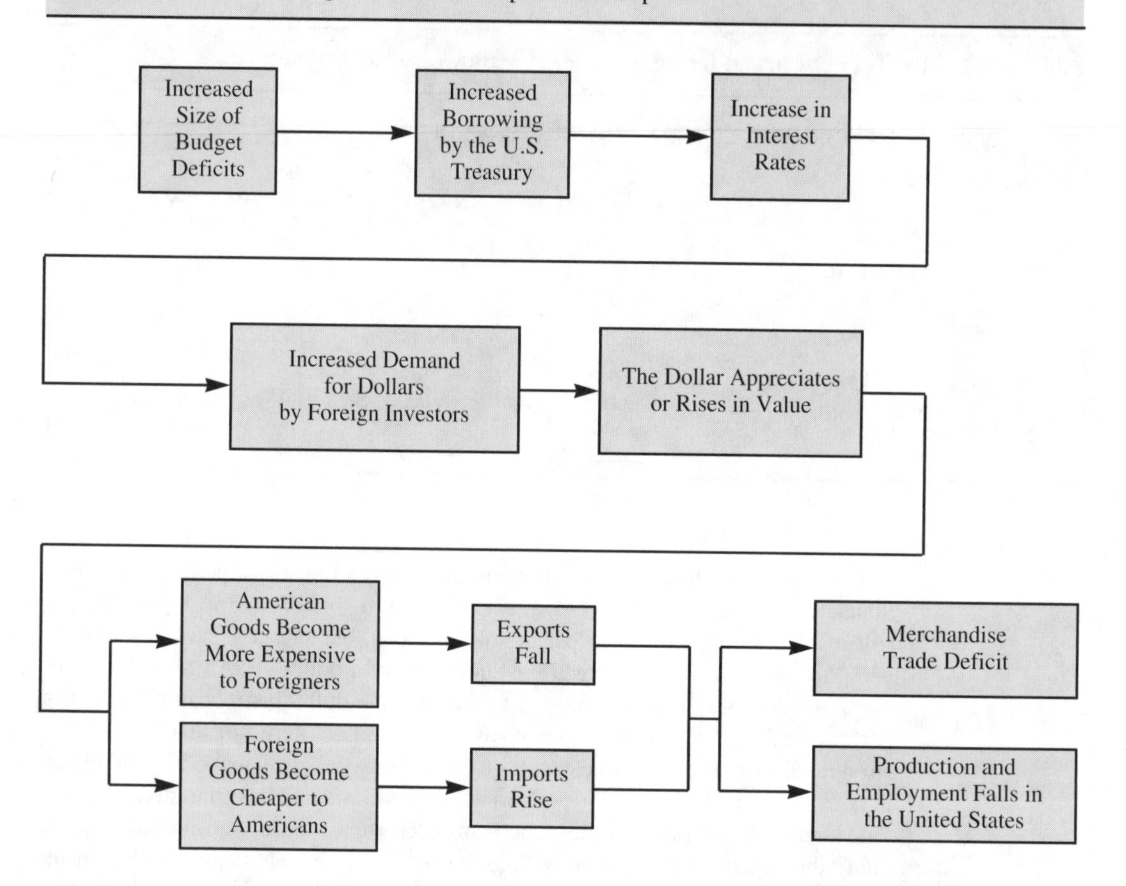

can then earn more interest in the United States than at home. To do that, they convert their currencies to dollars and buy American bonds. This increased demand for dollars makes the "price" of the dollar rise, meaning the dollar appreciates. In turn, American exports fall because foreigners must pay more for American-made goods. Americans also import more of the now cheaper foreign products. The reduced exports and increased imports lead to decreased U.S.

> *No nation was ever ruined by trade.*
>
> – Benjamin Franklin

unemployment and output, as well as a merchandise trade deficit. This shows the intricate connections between economics and politics. If voters want more government spending and lower taxes and politicians oblige them, international economics creates some surprising losers.

America's Position in World Trade

★7 Every year since 1976, the United States has had a **merchandise trade deficit**. This means in each of those years Americans imported more goods than they exported. A merchandise trade deficit is commonly called an unfavorable balance of trade. This is because most people believe the United States should import *less* than it exports. Conversely, a **merchandise trade surplus** (also called a favorable balance of trade) occurs when a nation exports more goods than it imports.

This exposes another misconception about international economics. The merchandise trade deficit doesn't "belong" to anybody, any institution, or any government. And it isn't "bad" or "unfavorable," any more than a merchandise trade surplus is "good" or "favorable." A U.S. mechandise trade deficit merely means Americans have *voluntarily* decided to buy more from abroad than foreigners buy from Americans. No one forces Americans to do this, and if it was so unfavorable, they wouldn't do it.

Many people experience a parallel situation in their personal finances. All people are specialists who trade with others. As noted earlier, purchases from others could be called "imports" and sales to them "exports." The dollar value of a person's "imports" equals spending on consumer goods plus taxes—called "total outlays." The dollar value of that person's "exports" is the same as that individual's personal income from selling resources (working). But a person can have more total outlays than income. How? By borrowing money. Is this "personal trade deficit" and borrowing "bad" or "unfavorable"? Apparently not, for people do so *voluntarily*.

Eventually, people must pay off their personal debts. They do this when they have a "personal trade surplus"—when they spend *less* than they earn. Similarly, foreigners eventually will insist that we send them *more* than they send to us. Of course, that situation would be a merchandise trade surplus. Thus, a merchandise trade deficit will not go on forever, any more than a bank will allow someone to continue borrowing indefinitely.

> *What protectionism teaches us is to do to ourselves in time of peace what enemies seek to do to us in time of war.*
> – Henry George

> *Experience and reflection will develop them the wisdom of exchanging what they can spare and we want for what we can spare and they want.*
> – Thomas Jefferson,
> regarding trade with the Indians
> following the Lewis and Clark expedition.

Figure 8-3 shows these two situations for nations as well as for individuals. A merchandise trade deficit means Americans are currently living "above their means," made possible by foreigners who send us more than we send them. That is neither bad nor good, so long as everyone involved makes decisions voluntarily in what they perceive to be their best interests.

Figure 8-3 Merchandise Trade Deficits and Surpluses and Personal Comparisons

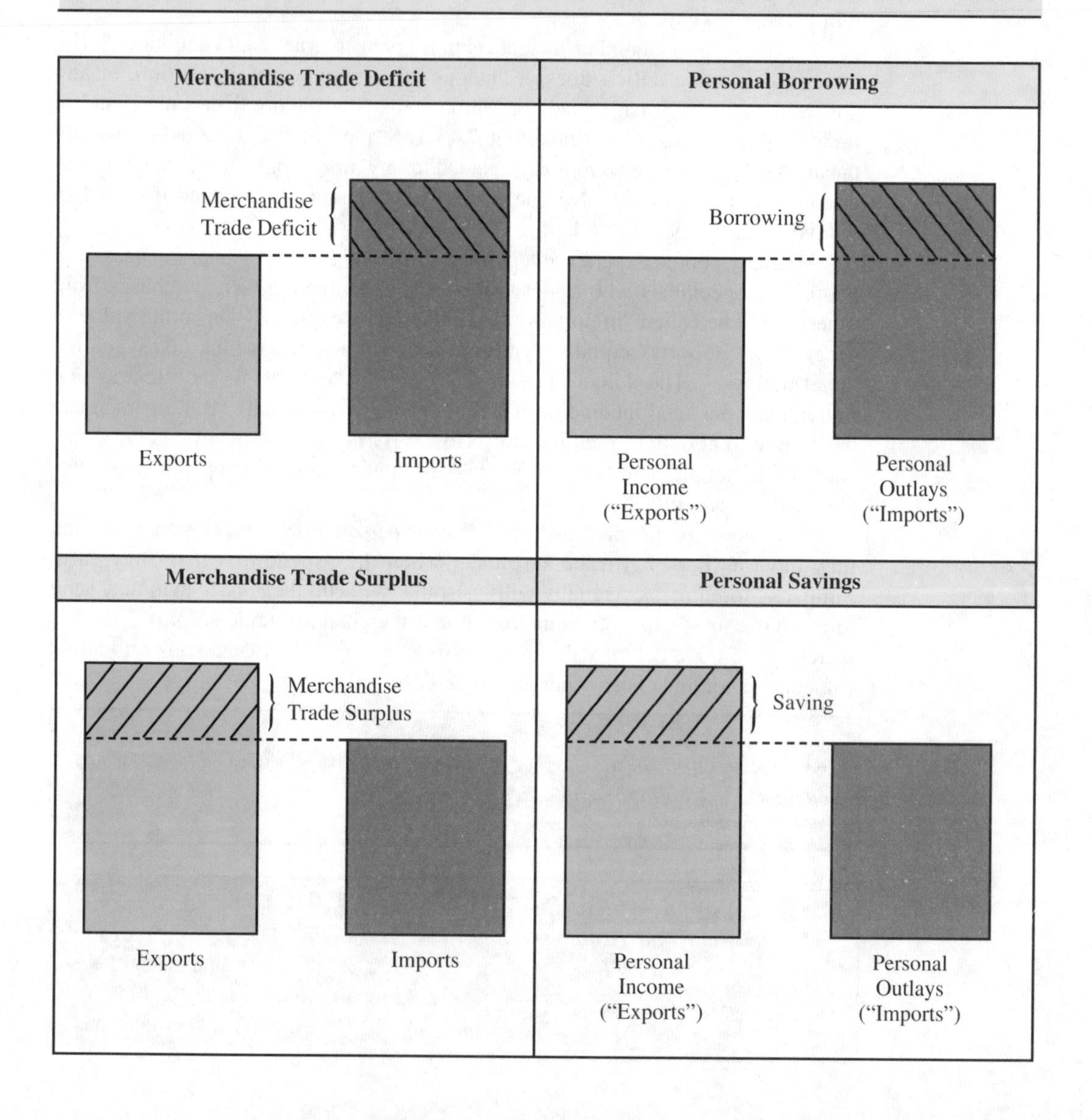

The merchandise trade deficit is often incorrectly referred to as our trade deficit (see the appendix for more detailed explanation). The difference is that the merchandise trade deficit does not include the international sale of services, and the trade deficit does. Such services include accounting, engineering, and legal services, plus the sale of technologies that earn royalties and license fees. They also include spending by foreign visitors. In 1992, the United States sold $59 billion more than it purchased of services. This surplus in services has been growing rapidly and is creating a lot of high-paying jobs in the United States.

Table 8-3 shows the U.S. record of exports and imports of goods (merchandise) from 1970 to the present. From a merchandise trade balance in the early 1970s, the United States developed deep deficits by the mid-1980s. This was partly the result of the strengthening dollar from 1980 to 1985.

Table 8-3 U.S. Merchandise Exports, Imports, and the Merchandise Trade Balance

Year	Exports (billions)	Imports (billions)	Surplus (+) or Deficit (–)
1970	$ 42.5	$ 39.9	+ 2.6
1971	43.3	45.6	– 2.3
1972	49.4	55.8	– 6.4
1973	71.4	70.5	+ 0.9
1974	98.3	103.8	– 5.5
1975	107.1	98.2	+ 8.9
1976	114.7	124.2	– 9.5
1977	120.8	151.9	– 31.1
1978	142.1	176.0	– 33.9
1979	184.5	212.0	– 27.5
1980	224.3	249.7	– 25.4
1981	237.1	265.1	– 28.0
1982	211.2	247.6	– 36.4
1983	201.8	268.9	– 67.1
1984	219.9	332.4	– 112.5
1985	215.9	338.1	– 124.2
1986	223.4	368.4	– 145.0
1987	250.3	409.8	– 159.5
1988	320.2	447.2	– 127.0
1989	361.7	477.4	– 115.7
1990	393.6	495.3	– 101.7
1991	421.7	488.5	– 66.7
1992	448.2	532.7	– 84.5
1993	______	______	______
1994	______	______	______

Sources: *The Economic Report of the President*, 1993; *Federal Reserve Bulletin*, August 1993

Economically, what difference is there between restricting the importation of iron to benefit iron producers and restricting sanitary improvements to benefit undertakers?

– Henry George

Table 8-4 shows the countries and areas of the world where most U.S. trade occurs. Table 8-5 divides both exports and imports into product categories. A consistent bright spot for U.S. exports has been agricultural products, though even they suffered declines in recent years. As any American driver knows, U.S. highways swarm with automotive imports. Ever since the increase in oil prices in the early 1970s, petroleum imports have also been a major foreign purchase. That's because we import almost half of the oil we consume. So, as oil prices rose, so did the number of dollars we spent on oil. (Remember, imports are measured in *dollar* amounts, not physical amounts, such as barrels of oil.)

Trade patterns have changed dramatically in this century. In 1900, the leading U.S. exports were: 1) raw cotton, $242 million; 2) wheat and wheat flour, $141 million; 3) iron and steel, $122 million; 4) hog products, $112 million; and 5) corn, $85 million. The leading imports were: 1) sugar, $100 million; 2) hides and skins, $58 million; 3) chemicals, dyes, and drugs, $54 million; 4) coffee, $52 million; and 5) silk, $45 million. Total exports were $1,499 million, and total imports were $928 million. You can be sure that the trade of the year 2100 will have about the same relation to our trade today as ours does to that of 1900.

OPPOSITION AND BARRIERS TO INTERNATIONAL TRADE

To be able to have high exports so it can have high imports, a nation does not need the best resources of every type. Natural-resource poor Singapore, Hong Kong, and Switzerland prove that, as does the labor-poor but phosphate-rich (and *people*-rich) Pacific island of Nauru. Similarly, you need not have every asset that would help you get rich, such as intelligence, physical abilities, good looks and physique, creativity, and a pleasant personality. Otherwise, how do you explain Roseanne Arnold or Ross Perot? It will help you to bear this in mind as you read this section.

Some people don't want others to have the right to buy and sell whatever they want wherever they want. This section considers why some people want to limit international trade and the ways of limiting it.

Arguments Against Free Trade

★8

Free trade means no individual, group, institution, or government does anything to prevent any exchange of goods and services across international borders. There are seven common reasons for limiting foreign trade: 1) the low wage argument; 2) the employment argument; 3) the infant industry argument; 4) the strategic industry argument; 5) the excessive specialization argument; 6) the unfair competition argument; and 7) the fear-of-foreign-ownership argument.

■ The low wage argument suggests that if Americans buy goods from nations paying low wages, American workers will ultimately have to accept low wages as well in order to compete. But consider what happens when a well-paid attorney hires a teenager for yardwork at $4 per hour. Does the attorney become impoverished? No—just the opposite, for the attorney now has extra time to handle more cases. Similarly, if American workers concentrate on making high-

Table 8-4 U.S. Merchandise Exports and Imports by Area, 1991

Area	Exports Amount (billions)	Exports Percent of Total	Imports Amount (billions)	Imports Percent of Total
Canada	$ 85.0	20.4%	$ 93.0	19.0%
Japan	$ 47.2	11.4%	$ 91.5	18.7%
Western Europe	$116.8	28.1%	$101.9	20.8%
OPEC	$ 18.4	4.4%	$ 33.1	6.7%
Australia, New Zealand and South Africa	$ 11.4	2.7%	$ 6.9	1.4%
Eastern Europe	$ 4.8	1.2%	$ 1.8	0.4%
Other	$132.4	31.8%	$161.2	33.0%
Total	$416.0	100.0%	$489.4	100.0%

Source: *The Economic Report of the President,* 1993

Table 8-5 U.S. Exports and Imports by Category, 1991

Exports Item	Amount (billions)	Percent of Total	Imports Item	Amount (billions)	Percent of Total
Agricultural Products	$ 40.3	9.7%	Petroleum	$ 51.2	10.4%
Industrial Supplies	$101.8	24.5%	Industrial Supplies	$ 80.9	16.5%
Capital Goods	$167.0	40.1%	Capital Goods	$120.7	24.7%
Automotive	$ 40.0	9.6%	Automotive	$ 84.9	17.4%
Other	$ 66.9	16.1%	Other	$151.7	31.0%
Total	$416.0	100.0%	Total	$489.4	100.0%

Source: *The Economic Report of the President,* 1993

value, sophisticated products that enable U.S. firms to pay high wages, U.S. living standards will be higher. Such a strategy depends upon a continuing high level of U.S. human capital in the form of educated and well-trained workers.

■ Bumper stickers that urge people to "Buy American" are rephrasing the employment argument that if Americans buy imports, there will be fewer U.S. jobs. For example, Americans buy 85 percent of their footwear from foreign firms, up dramatically since the 1950s. Consequently, over 800 U.S. shoe factories and suppliers closed down between 1972 and 1992. The federal government's Trade Adjustment Assistance Program assists workers who lost their jobs because of either: 1) imports that hurt their previous employer; or 2) products imported by their previous employer as a cost-cutting measure. It provides benefits for training and relocation.

But the *seemingly* sound employment argument can be attacked in several ways. First, suppose that instead of Americans importing roughly 10 percent of their goods and services, they import 70 or 80 percent. Most people would expect massive unemployment. Yet that is precisely the case in Hong Kong, the Netherlands, Taiwan, Switzerland, and Denmark—with an unemployment rate no higher than in the United States. That is because the more a nation imports, the more it must export to pay for the imports. And more exports create jobs. (Incidentally, U.S. imports rose substantially from $43 billion in 1970 to $390 billion in 1990 with no sign that the unemployment rate was affected.)

The second way to attack the employment argument is to extend it. Suppose it's true that if Americans *can* make a product, it *should* be made in America. This provides U.S. employment, and U.S. employment is more important than foreign employment (to Americans, of course). But just as correctly, Californians could argue, "Why should we buy clothes made in North Carolina when California could employ people in its own garment industry?" So "Buy California" is promoted. Next, a San Diego resident says, "Because jobs in San Diego are more important than jobs in San Francisco, 'Buy San Diego' is my motto." Carried to its extreme, this argument would have every individual producing clothes, food, and other goods just for personal use (where "Buy from Myself" is everyone's motto). Naturally, everyone would be poor because there would be no specialization and economies of scale. But at least everyone would be working, so no one would have to worry about unemployment.

The point is, trade—whether between individuals living next door to each other or between individuals an ocean apart—doesn't affect *overall* employment very much. It merely changes the *type* of employment. Take, for example, the aforementioned Mr. Grace who wants to buy a Saab. The figures in Table 8-6 and the flow chart in Figure 8-4 will help clarify the example.

Suppose again that Mr. Grace decides to buy a Saab that sells for 120,000 kronor in Sweden. The Saab Corporation also will sell the car in the United States—if it receives 120,000 kronor, plus shipping costs (which are ignored in the following calculations). Mr. Grace's first step is to get the kronor. Suppose the exchange rate is six kronor to the dollar (so one krona "costs" 16.7¢). Mr. Grace writes a $20,000 check to someone holding 120,000 kronor. When he does this, he is actually demanding kronor and supplying dollars in the market for foreign exchange. Next, assume that this action lowers the price of the dollar from 6.0 to 5.9 kronor and raises the price of a krona from 16.7¢ to 16.9¢ (= 1 ÷ 5.9).

Table 8-6 The Effects of Fluctuating Exchange Rates

Item	Prices in Sweden (in kronor)		Prices in the United States (in dollars)	
	at 6.0 kronor = $1 & 1 kronor = 16.7¢	at 5.9 kronor = $1 & 1 kronor = 16.9¢	at 6.0 kronor = $1 & 1 kronor = 16.7¢	at 5.9 kronor = $1 & 1 kronor = 16.9¢
Saab Car	120,000 kronor	120,000 kronor	$20,000	$20,339
Coal (1 Ton)	360 kronor	354 kronor	$60	$60
Oil (4 Barrels)	360 kronor	360 kronor	$60	$60

(Actually, such a small purchase would not have this much of an effect, but this would happen if enough of such purchases were made.) The table shows that the *next* Saab buyer will have to pay $20,339—or $339 *more*. The price (120,000 kronor) did not change in Sweden, but, in effect, it rose in the United States. This price increase discourages further imports of Saabs and other Swedish-made goods.

Next, observe what happens to the price of coal mined in the United States. Originally, it cost 360 kronor to buy a $60 ton of U.S. coal. But after the appreciation of the krona, it takes only 354 kronor. Suppose Sweden gets half its energy needs from U.S. coal and half from Saudi Arabian oil. Suppose further that Saudi Arabian oil sells for $15 (or 90 kronor) per barrel and that four barrels of oil equal the energy in one ton of coal. Originally, the Swedes didn't care whether they bought four barrels of oil or one ton of coal because each cost them 360 kronor and provided equivalent energy. But now Mr. Grace's action makes coal cheaper than oil—in kronor only, as no energy prices change in the United States. Consequently, the Swedes buy more coal from the United States, and employment rises at Peabody Coal Company and other U.S. mines. In turn, there is an increased demand for mining equipment made in the United States—draglines from Bucyrus-Erie, power shovels from Link Belt and Koehring, conveyor chains from Rexnord, and huge off-road trucks from Terex. And making these products takes laborers—*American* laborers.

It is obvious to everyone—especially the autoworkers—that Mr. Grace "created" unemployment by not buying a car made by American laborers. It is not so obvious, however, that he "created" employment elsewhere in American industry. Few people make the connection between his car purchase and the new jobs at Peabody, Rexnord, Koehring, and Terex. And this is the effect of only one product—coal. All other American products become cheaper for Swedes as well and have similar employment-creating effects. These new jobholders all owe their jobs to people such as Mr. Grace—who are sometimes called traitors for not "buying American."

Figure 8-4 The Effect of an Increase in Imports on Employment

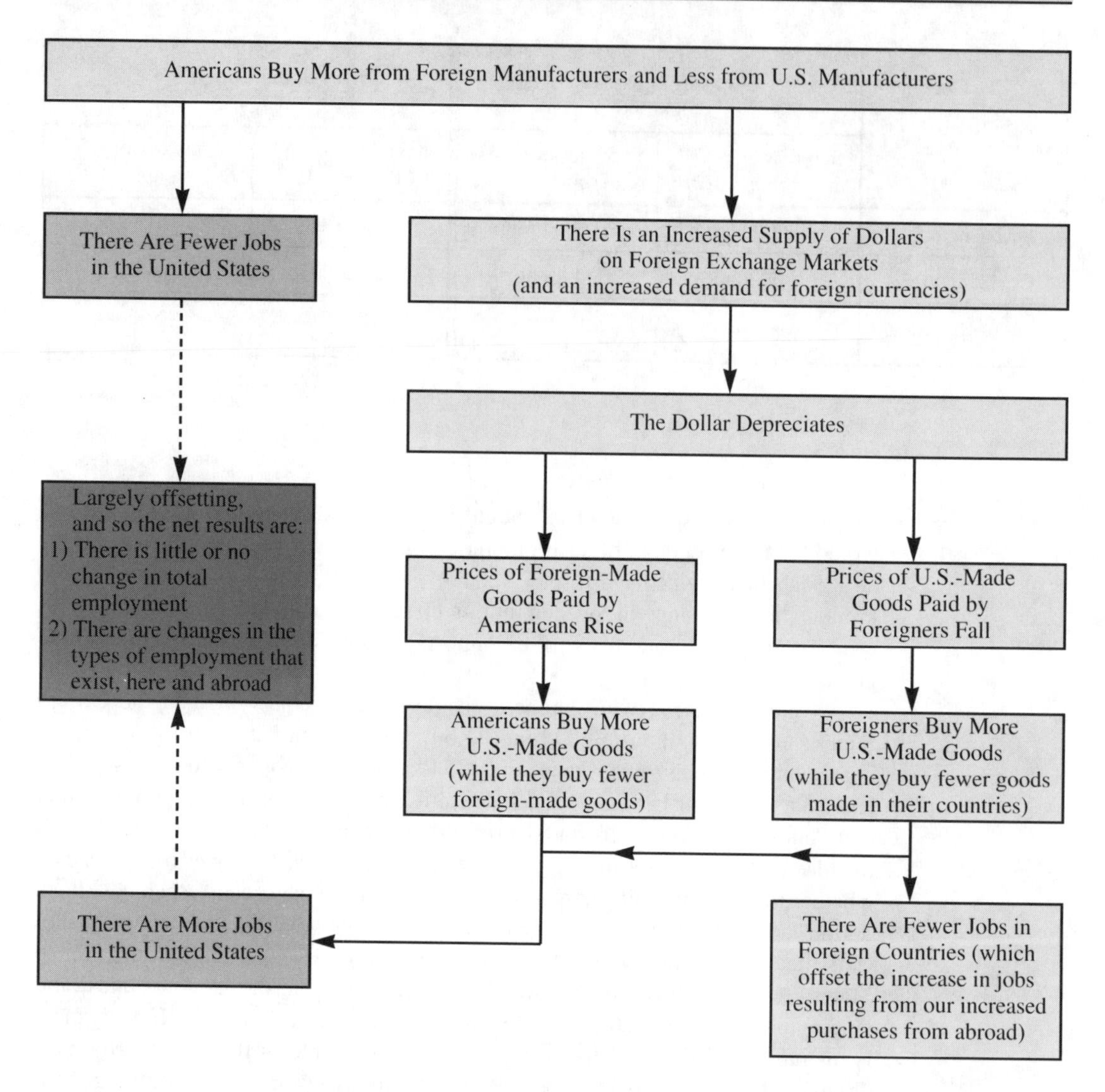

Another employment issue is the common belief that American laborers cannot compete against "cheap foreign labor." That may or may not be true, for it is the *labor cost*—not the wage level—that is most important. Labor productivity also influences labor cost, as shown in the formula:

$$\text{Labor Cost} = \frac{\text{Wages}}{\text{Labor Productivity}}$$

Suppose a worker at the Briggs & Stratton small-engine factory receives \$160 per day in wages and fringe benefits and produces 10 engines per day. Then the labor cost of a American-made engine is \$16 (= \$160 ÷ 10). Suppose a Mexican engine manufacturer pays the equivalent of \$40 per day in pesos to a worker who produces only two engines per day. The labor cost of the Mexican-made engine is $20 (= $40 ÷ 2)—more than the American-made one—in spite of the advantage of "cheap labor." This is not unrealistic. Because they often have better machines, better training, and better work attitudes, American workers often do produce goods at lower costs than many low-paid foreigners. These are the products the United States *cannot* import more cheaply from "low-wage" countries.

However, these advantages are not as important in producing other products, those which are difficult or impossible to mechanize, such as shoes and products requiring much assembly (such as electric motors). These are the products where jobs will be going abroad.

■ In the infant industry argument, an "infant industry" is one so new that economies of scale have not yet been attained. Nor are workers and managers yet at peak efficiency. It is believed that if the industry is given some protection from foreign competition, it can eventually compete in international markets. The United States sought to promote its own industries in 1816 when it enacted its first protective tariff.

■ According to the strategic industry argument, products that are vital for our national security should be produced here. Such products include armaments, steel, petroleum, and U.S. Navy ships. Many economists say this is the best or the most justifiable argument against free trade. The argument was vital to passage of the Jones Act of 1920, which requires that all ocean shipping between U.S. ports be done with American-built, -owned, and -crewed ships. The intent was to provide a reserve fleet of ships for the military in wartime.

■ The fifth argument against free trade is that it leads to excessive specialization and dependence on one or a few products. The loss of 30,000 Swiss jobs in the watch industry after the introduction of quartz watches in the 1970s is one example of a failure to diversify.

■ The sixth objection to free trade is that it leads to predatory or unfair competition. Suppose Country A sells its refrigerators below cost in Country B, which also makes refrigerators. Eventually, the firms in Country B might be forced to shut down. Country A then has a monopoly and can charge much higher prices in Country B. Selling a product for a lower price abroad than at home or below production cost (which includes a 10 percent markup for overhead and 8 percent for profit) is called **dumping**. It is outlawed by the Tariff Act of 1930. However, sometimes firms sell cheaper abroad than at home not to eliminate competition, but to gain economies of scale from larger output and sales.

■ The fear-of-foreign-ownership argument stems from the fact that any deficit in the current account (which includes but is slightly broader than the merchandise trade account, see Appendix) will be balanced by an identical surplus in the capital account. The capital account includes purchases of U.S. firms, property, and bonds by foreigners, as well as the purchases of foreign firms, property and so forth by U.S. citizens. Therefore, an increasing portion of the U.S. economy has become foreign-owned in recent years. Fears of foreign owners operating against the interests of U.S. workers or consumers are probably misplaced. But, more troubling, these investments give foreigners a permanent claim on future U.S. output. When Honda makes profit from its U.S. plants, it does not need to send more yen to receive U.S. products. Honda already has the dollars and, assuming the operation remains successful, will continue to receive dollars into the indefinite future. This problem might not seriously affect the United States for many years, but many less-developed countries who received loans and investment from the United States during the 1950s and 1960s have found they cannot afford to give up the vast quantity of production required to pay off the loans or to turn U.S. investors' profits into real goods. Nevertheless, the International Monetary Fund has frequently required these countries to lower their standard of living in order to pay the loans, just as your personal loans eventually must be paid.

Obstacles to Trade

In order to reduce imports, governments interfere in the markets for internationally traded goods in various ways. This interference is called **protectionism** because its intent is to protect some elements of the economy from foreign competition. Thus, the policy of protectionism is opposite to that of free trade. Six commonly used protectionist measures include: 1) tariffs; 2) quotas; 3) domestic content and mixing requirements; 4) bureaucratic control; 5) currency devaluation; and 6) export subsidies.

★9

■ The most commonly used protectionist measure is a **tariff** or duty, which is a tax on an imported good. For example, a 20 percent tariff would increase the price of an imported $40 German clock to $48 (= $40 x 1.2). If a comparable American clock sells for $44, then sales of the American manufacturer would rise after such a tariff is levied. In the past, the United States commonly had tariffs above 50 percent. The 1828 Tariff of Abominations (65 percent duty) and the Smoot-Hawley Tariff of 1930 (60 percent) were the highest tariffs in U.S. history. In recent decades, the concept of free trade has been increasingly accepted, and tariffs are much lower. Nations that are granted the lowest tariff rates for imports to the United States receive what is called **most-favored-nation** status.

■ The second obstacle to trade is a **quota**, which is a physical limit on the amount of imports of a specific item. For example, the United States limits the amount of sugar imports in order to aid American sugar cane and sugar beet growers. When a country refuses to import any amount of an item, it imposes a special kind of quota called a ban. Japan, for example, has banned foreign rice since 1971. Japanese consumers, forced to buy the rice of very inefficient, small-scale Japanese farmers, pay up to six times the world average. The United States is almost as strict about dairy products, allowing only 1.5 percent of our supply to come from abroad. Worse yet, only 0.1 percent of the ice cream we consume can be imported, and only five countries can sell theirs here. In 1988, only New Zealand and Denmark did—576 gallons and 12 gallons, respectively.

> *To introduce a tariff bill into Congress or parliament is like throwing a banana into a cage of monkeys. No sooner is it proposed to protect one industry than all the industries that are capable of protection begin to screech and scramble for it.*
>
> – Henry George

Voluntary restraint agreements are very similar to quotas, except that a foreign nation voluntarily agrees to limit how much it sends abroad. It does that to avoid an even stronger quota that the importing nation might impose. For example, in 1981 the Reagan administration persuaded Japanese auto manufacturers to voluntarily limit their shipments of cars to America. Congressional action was threatened if such limits were not imposed. In 1982, the steel industry received protection from 29 foreign steel producers that agreed to reduce the import share of total U.S. steel usage from 26 percent to 20 percent. The agreements extended until March 31, 1992.

However, such actions don't always work the way they're intended. The Economic Policy Institute, a private think-tank, calculated that such restriction on steel imports cost the American economy almost $1 billion annually in the 1980s. Also, according to the International Monetary Fund, by 1985 the auto quotas had transferred up to $10.5 billion from the U.S. economy to the Japanese auto industry because Japanese firms were able to raise prices significantly. U.S. auto makers, facing less competition, were also able to raise prices much more than otherwise. Employment in the U.S. auto industry did rise, as was hoped. However, it was estimated that the cost to the U.S. economy was between $110,000 and $145,000 over a three-year period for *each* job gained.

■ **Domestic content and mixing requirements** constitute the third obstacle to trade. In this country, these require a U.S. industry to use a minimum percentage of U.S.-made parts in the final product. U.S. labor unions have long pushed for laws that would force automakers to use a minimum share of U.S.-made parts.

■ The fourth obstacle to trade is **bureaucratic control**, or "red tape" that makes importing difficult. Such bureaucracy raises marketing costs and the price as well, so fewer imports are purchased. For example, the Japanese have extraordinarily strict controls on food imports, so that only "perfect" fruits and other foods pass inspection. Likewise, for 470 years (until 1987) the Germans protected their breweries by insisting that beer sold in Germany be made of only malted cereals, hops, water, and yeast. This, they said, was to protect Germans from "inferior beer" and harmful preservatives (one must wonder what protected them from the *alcohol*).

Japan is also involved in another protectionist measure that is related to bureaucratic controls. Critics charge that the reason many major Japanese firms work closely with each other is to prevent foreign firms from doing business in Japan. For example, a Japanese auto maker would only buy parts from a Japanese firm in its "network" group of firms. These groups are called *keiretsu* and are resented by U.S. and other Western firms.

■ The fifth trade obstacle is **currency devaluation**, a government-sponsored depreciation of its currency. For example, if Spain devalues its peseta, Americans might receive 120 pesetas for a dollar rather than the current 100. Then, in effect, prices of Spanish goods sold here would fall to 0.83 of their original levels (= 100 ÷ 120). Consequently, Spain would export more to the United States. Also, Spaniards would pay 20 percent more for imports, so their imports from the United States would fall.

■ **Export subsidies**, the last interference in trade, are designed to boost exports by reducing the prices foreigners pay for a nation's exports. With a direct subsidy, the government makes up the difference between a producer's selling price and the lower purchase price paid by the importer. The United States subsidizes grain shipments abroad through the Export Enhancement Program, costing about $1 billion a year.

There are also indirect subsidies that help firms sell their products abroad, including government-financed trade missions and fairs, help provided by embassy staff, and research support. For example, the U.S. Government gives industry, associations, and companies about $150 million a year to promote 66 U.S. foods and farm products abroad through the Market Promotion Program—(including $11 million for wine, $7 million for Alaskan seafood, and $5 million for prunes).

Trade restrictions create winners and losers. Laborers and manufacturers in protected industries win from trade restrictions if the restrictions help them compete against foreign competition. But consumers lose when denied the cheaper foreign goods, and taxpayers lose if they pay for export subsidies. The World Bank estimates that the combined protectionist measures of the United States, Western Europe, and Japan just for agricultural goods cost consumers and taxpayers $100 billion each year. But trade restriction is not a "zero-sum game"—the winnings do not equal the losses. When there is less specialization and trade, the world as a whole has lower living standards because less efficient producers make the products. *Total* employment in each nation and the world is probably about the same with or without trade.

International Agreements Relating to Trade

In the past few decades, many nations made agreements to promote trade. Much of the impetus for such efforts came from the disastrous 1930s, when world trade virtually ceased, as each nation protected its own industries in the worldwide Great Depression.

In 1944, the Bretton Woods Accord sought to promote a free flow of trade by establishing an orderly system of exchange rates. It aimed to: 1) establish a set of rules to maintain fixed exchange rates; 2) ensure that any change in exchange rates would occur only if there were long-term balance of payments deficits or surpluses (see Appendix); and 3) guarantee that such changes would not lead to currency devaluation. The International Monetary Fund (IMF) was established to carry out the Bretton Woods Accord. The IMF worked to ensure that nations maintained fixed exchange rates, and it consulted with nations if they wanted to change the rates. It also lent funds to nations with balance of payments deficits.

By the 1970s, various problems, including U.S. inflation and its balance of payments deficits, led to an abandonment of the Bretton Woods Accord and fixed exchange rates. This was partly precipitated by President Nixon's decision to stop guaranteeing payment of U.S. international transfers in gold, which ended the link between the dollar and gold. By the mid-1970s, most Western industrialized nations had adopted a floating exchange rate system. The Jamaica Agreement of 1976 amended the IMF charter to ratify this move and to de-emphasize gold as a basis for settling international accounts.

However, the strong fluctuations in exchange rates during the 1980s led to a disenchantment with floating exchange rates. Many nations began to order their central banks (see page 294 to learn about central banks) to buy and sell currencies in order to influence the exchange rates. A good example was the 1985 agreement by Western nations to weaken the U.S. dollar. Such a system of partly managed exchange rates is called a **managed float** (or a "dirty float"). Some people want to go further and return to a form of the **gold standard**, in which each nation would have its currency convertible into a fixed amount of gold. Consequently, there would be no change in exchange rates. Much of the world used such a system from the late-1800s to the 1930s.

A more direct approach to trade promotion was the post-war General Agreement on Tariffs and Trade (GATT). Under GATT, nations agree to meet periodically to negotiate reductions in tariffs. There were three periods of such reductions. The first was the Kennedy Round, extending from 1972 to 1977. The Tokyo Round began reducing tariffs in 1981. The Uruguay Round was to have ended deliberations on further reductions in 1990, but major disagreements extended the talks until 1993.

The Uruguay Round was primarily intended to reduce trade restrictions on agricultural goods. But many of Europe's 10 million farmers (especially the French) opposed the proposed cuts in their export subsidies, part of Europe's 30-year-old Common Agricultural Policy. The talks broke down over a failure to agree how to resolve the conflict. The Uruguay Round also addressed trade restrictions on "intellectual property" (patents and copyrights), services (such as telecommunications), and textiles. Other issues addressed included foreign investment, export subsidies, and the role of less-developed nations in GATT. The Uruguay Round of trade liberalization was expected to increase world trade by $200 billion a year.

In 1987, the United States and Canada agreed to form a North American free-trade area. The agreement will eliminate tariffs and reduce other trade barriers over a 10-year period, ending on January 1, 1999.

In August 1992, it was announced that Mexico was to be part of this North American free-trade area. The pact, known as the North American Free Trade Agreement (NAFTA), had to be ratified by the legislatures of all three countries before its implementation.

NAFTA will eliminate tariffs and other barriers to trade and investment over a 15-year period, but many are scheduled to be eliminated much earlier, starting January 1, 1994. U.S. and Canadian banks, until now barred from Mexico, will be allowed to establish Mexican subsidiaries. Mexico will also allow foreigners to invest in its trucking firms, and foreign trucks and buses with international cargo will be allowed to travel in Mexico. It is likely that Mexican firms will be able to sell much more in the United States and Canada than they do now, and that is a major concern of American and Canadian firms and their employees.

In 1989, the United States established a new type of agreement, called a bilateral consensus agreement, with major foreign steel suppliers. Its purpose is to restrict subsidies of foreign steel industries, and it provides for dispute-settlement procedures that include arbitration.

In June 1990, Japan and the United States established a trade pact, called the Structural Impediments Initiative. As conditions of the pact, Japan promised to: 1) widen its markets for our exports; 2) use more of its financial capital domestically; 3) spend more on public works; 4) strengthen its antitrust policy; and 5) streamline its very inefficient distribution (marketing) system. The United States agreed to: 1) reduce its budget deficit; 2) increase its savings rate and reduce consumer debt; 3) boost worker training, especially in science and math; 4) increase spending on research and development; 5) reduce the cost of financial capital for corporations; 6) reduce export controls and liberalize import restrictions; and 7) maintain non-discriminatory treatment of Japanese investment in the United States.

Most European nations formed a free-trade pact that was implemented by the end of 1992. All forms of trade restrictions between the participants were eliminated. However, many Europeans hope they can go much further and form stronger economic and even political unions. Efforts are being made to replace all European currencies with a single new currency. The Maastricht Treaty, if ratified, is to entail all these agreements. But serious problems are faced by such unions, so perhaps only the free-trade aspect will come to fruition.

THE UNITED STATES IN THE GLOBAL ECONOMY

Americans must face the fact that old, as well as new, foreign competitors are economically stronger today. We must be aware of these competitors and how American workers and firms can deal with that competition. We must also be aware of how increasingly interdependent all nations of the world have become.

The Concept of a Global Economy

People who traveled abroad decades ago knew they were in a foreign country, for products and stores in other countries had unfamiliar names. But if you travel today to England, Germany, the Philippines, or Japan, you will see factories with GM, GE, and Johnson & Johnson signs. You can buy a Big Mac in many countries and Coke virtually anywhere in the world. Also, foreigners visiting here recognize their own firms' products, stores, and factories, such as Bic, Nestle, Shell, Nissan, and Benetton. Sometimes it's hard to tell where a product comes from. Today a car may have French tires, a German engine, a Brazilian steering wheel, and Japanese paint.

Part of the reason for the blurring of national *economic* boundaries is the growth in the importance of the **multinational** (or multinational corporation). Although such a firm's headquarters might be in New York or Bonn or Tokyo, its stockholders live everywhere. It manufactures products in several nations—and it holds allegiance to no nation. It markets its products everywhere, and it might own a dozen subsidiaries in a dozen nations. Each subsidiary could be a multinational itself. Multinationals even act as quasi-governments because they engage in education (of their work force), road construction and other infrastructure projects, and long-run planning of resource use.

Many people fear multinationals because of their size and to what that might lead. Their economic size gives them great political power to change whole cultures. For example, many people wonder if the world really should be

"McWorlded," so that one can never really escape the United States by traveling abroad. Others fear the effects of multinationals on employment. They question whether a firm should be able to move production to plants abroad so readily, thereby disrupting the lives of those dependent upon the status quo.

Competition in the New Global Economy

★10 By the early to mid-1980s, increasing imports and trade deficits raised concerns about America's competitive strength. Studies everywhere examined why U.S. workers were (supposedly) less productive than foreign workers, why U.S. firms were so poorly managed, and why U.S. products were so shoddy. By the 1960s, the United States was losing markets to firms in the rebuilt nations of wartorn Europe (Volkswagen of Germany, for example). Later competitors were the Pacific Rim nations of Japan, Korea, Taiwan, and Singapore. Even less-developed nations, including Argentina and Brazil in farm products, now give American firms competition in many areas. Finally, the formerly communist nations of Eastern Europe provide new challenges to American firms.

Many controversial ideas have been proposed to meet these challenges. One position is to regain the strong export position the United States once held in the manufacture of autos, steel, textiles, and so on—the so-called basic industries—through a policy known as reindustrialization. This requires massive investment in new facilities and manufacturing processes. It also involves new managerial structures, such as the Japanese approach to industrial organization. This approach owes much to D. W. Demming, an American who went to Japan as an advisor after World War II. He stressed attention to detail and quality products. Many people believe that the United States can eventually regain its competitive advantage in these industries.

Critics say this is folly, that America must allow these basic industries to wither away. They agree that these industries might have a slight *absolute* advantage in production. But they argue that maintaining such industries prevents the United States from focusing on industries where America has a *very large* absolute advantage. Those are the industries where the United States has a *comparative* advantage. Compared with the Koreans, for example, U.S. engineers, machinists, and electronics specialists are much more plentiful and adept at making high-technology hospital equipment. An example: machines that make computerized axial tomographs, called CAT scanners, used in medical diagnosis. To use these same Americans to manufacture autos, a relatively simple task, would be wasteful because they could then *not* make CAT scanners. Critics of the basic industry approach maintain that future American exports will include many highly advanced products, such as medical equipment, lasers, synthetic materials to replace steel and other metals, computers, robots, holographic equipment, word processors and other communication/information-processing equipment, and high-speed transport equipment.

All of these products have something in common. They are high-technology products. Promoters of these industries say it is no wiser for Americans to produce all their own autos than it is for Jack Smith, chairman of General Motors, to tune his own car. Highly productive people have better things to do with their time and talents. In both cases, what is given up is the ability to produce more "complex" things that earn a very high income, which can be traded for "simple" things made by others. Let Smith manage General Motors—and let Americans produce high-technology products.

Incidentally, the Japanese are looking ahead to the day when they will not be assembling autos or even producing many of the parts. They reason that the talents of their highly educated workforce are wasted on relatively simple tasks, such as auto asssembly. They will continue to do the more complex parts of auto manufacture, such as design, engineering, and marketing. Thus, they are building auto assembly plants around the world in areas where workers aren't so well trained—such as in the United States (though not for this reason alone).

Whether the future will bring more or less trade and specialization—and more production of "basic" or high-tech goods in the United States—is not clear. As mentioned earlier, whether we can compete successfully in the markets for high-tech goods depends heavily on the skills of the American people. If our education system does not improve, we will fail in those markets. Then our more poorly educated workers will only be qualified to produce products that are relatively simple to make. Correspondingly, their incomes will be relatively lower. Americans will also help decide trade issues through their elected representatives. And how we decide depends largely upon how well we understand economics.

Chapter 8 SUMMARY

Trade occurs primarily to gain the increased efficiency of resource use that comes from specialization. The principle works equally well whether the trade is between individuals in a country or between individuals in different nations. A nation should specialize in producing products in which it has a comparative advantage. The act of exporting reduces a nation's living standard, but exports give it the capability of importing, which raises its living standard.

Nations have the value of their currencies established against other currencies in either a fixed exchange system or a floating exchange rate system. If a nation's currency appreciates, its citizens will pay less for imports, and foreigners will pay more for its exports. Alternatively, if its currency depreciates, its citizens will pay more for imports and foreigners will pay less for its exports. Exchange rates fluctuate for many reasons, a primary one being a large budget deficit, which tends to make a currency appreciate. A nation has a merchandise trade deficit when it imports more goods than it exports, and vice versa for a merchandise trade surplus.

Some people object to free trade because they believe it: 1) brings lower wages; 2) causes unemployment; 3) doesn't allow new industries time to become efficient; 4) imperils the national security; 5) leads to overspecialization; 6) leads to unfair competition; and 7) leads to foreign ownership of resources in our country. Some obstacles to free trade include: tariffs, quotas, domestic content and mixing requirements, bureaucratic controls, currency devaluation, and export subsidies.

International trade was been promoted by the Bretton Woods Accord of 1944 as well as the General Agreement on Tariffs and Trade (GATT). All of North America will become a free-trade zone if NAFTA is ratified.

The structure of the global economy is changing so that the United States has new, strong competitors in many products. This has led to calls for protectionism as well as for restructuring our own economy so that American firms can compete more effectively in the world economy.

Chapter 8 RESPONSES TO THE LEARNING OBJECTIVES

1. People trade with each other:
   a) to obtain the things they cannot produce themselves
   b) to gain the increases in resource productivity and living standards that result from resource specialization
2. A nation has a comparative advantage in producing an item if it has the lowest opportunity cost of all nations that produce it.
3. Imports raise a nation's living standard because they raise the amount of goods and services available. Exports reduce a nation's living standard because they are goods and services given up to foreigners. Essentially, a nation exports in order to gain the ability to import.
4. Exchange rates can be determined by:
   a) governments in a fixed exchange rate system
   b) the supply of and the demand for currencies by individuals in a freely floating exchange rate system
5. If a nation's currency:
   a) appreciates, its exports become more expensive and its imports become cheaper
   b) depreciates, its exports become cheaper and its imports become more expensive
6. Budget deficits lead to a nation's currency appreciating because the higher interest rates caused by the deficits increase foreign demand for the currency. The appreciating currency leads to higher prices for exports and lower prices for imports. Consequently, exports fall and imports rise, both of which lead to less domestic production and employment.
7. When there is a merchandise trade deficit, a nation imports more goods than it exports. A merchandise trade surplus means that it exports more goods than it imports.
8. Some objections to international trade include:
   a) the belief that trading with low-wage nations reduces domestic wages
   b) the belief that trading with low-wage nations causes domestic unemployment
   c) the argument that domestic industries need time to become competitive
   d) the argument that a nation needs certain strategic industries
   e) the belief that dominance of one industry makes a nation susceptible to economic disaster in the event of a decline in that industry
   f) the belief that some foreigners engage in unfair competition
   g) the fear of having foreigners owning domestic firms and resources

9. Free trade is blocked by tariffs, import quotas, bureaucratic controls, export subsidies, and currency devaluations.
10. The United States is losing or has lost its dominance in many industries, including autos, electronics, and machinery. It still is a formidable competitor in "high-tech" industries and in agricultural goods.

Chapter 8 LEARNING ACTIVITIES AND DISCUSSION QUESTIONS

1. Three hundred years ago, our ancestors made virtually all their own goods and services, but today we buy most of them from others. If someone had predicted that to our ancestors, what might they have predicted our unemployment rate would be today? Would they have erred? If so, how?
2. An individual who decides to work longer hours and a nation that exports more goods and services are both giving up more (that is, they experience increasing costs). Why do you suppose most people do not see the similarity?
3. Find the exchange rate of the dollar for the German mark for today as well as a year ago. Can you explain any difference in the rates?
4. Ask some people if Americans should be in debt to foreigners. Do you agree with their positions? Why or why not?
5. Ask three people if they believe in completely free trade: 1) between nations; and 2) between the 50 states. Did anyone answer "yes" to one question and "no" to the other? Why?

APPENDIX MEASURES OF INTERNATIONAL MONEY FLOWS

The merchandise trade balance covered earlier is only one measure of the flows of money across international borders. Money also crosses borders: when people travel, invest, or send money gifts abroad; when governments send foreign aid or carry on military operations abroad; and when individuals and firms purchase services abroad, such as insurance, banking services, and shipping. Therefore, the United States has four "balances" to consider: 1) the merchandise trade balance; 2) the balance of trade; 3) the balance on current account; and 4) the balance of payments. Figure A8-1 shows all these balances by comparing bar graphs of the various money flows into a country, called credits, and money flows out of a country, called debits.

■ The first credit is the value of exports of goods, which gives Americans money to spend. Offsetting this is the debit of imports of goods, and the difference between these is the merchandise trade balance (a surplus in this case).

■ Next are services Americans sell to foreigners, including: insurance, consulting services, banking and all other business services; the money foreign tourists spend in the United States; and the interest and dividends paid to Americans on U.S. loans and investments abroad. Offsetting this is a debit for the same kinds of services foreigners provide to Americans. The balance of trade refers to the difference between the addition of exports of goods and services and the addition of imports of goods and services, or in formula form:

Figure A8-1 The Balance of Payments

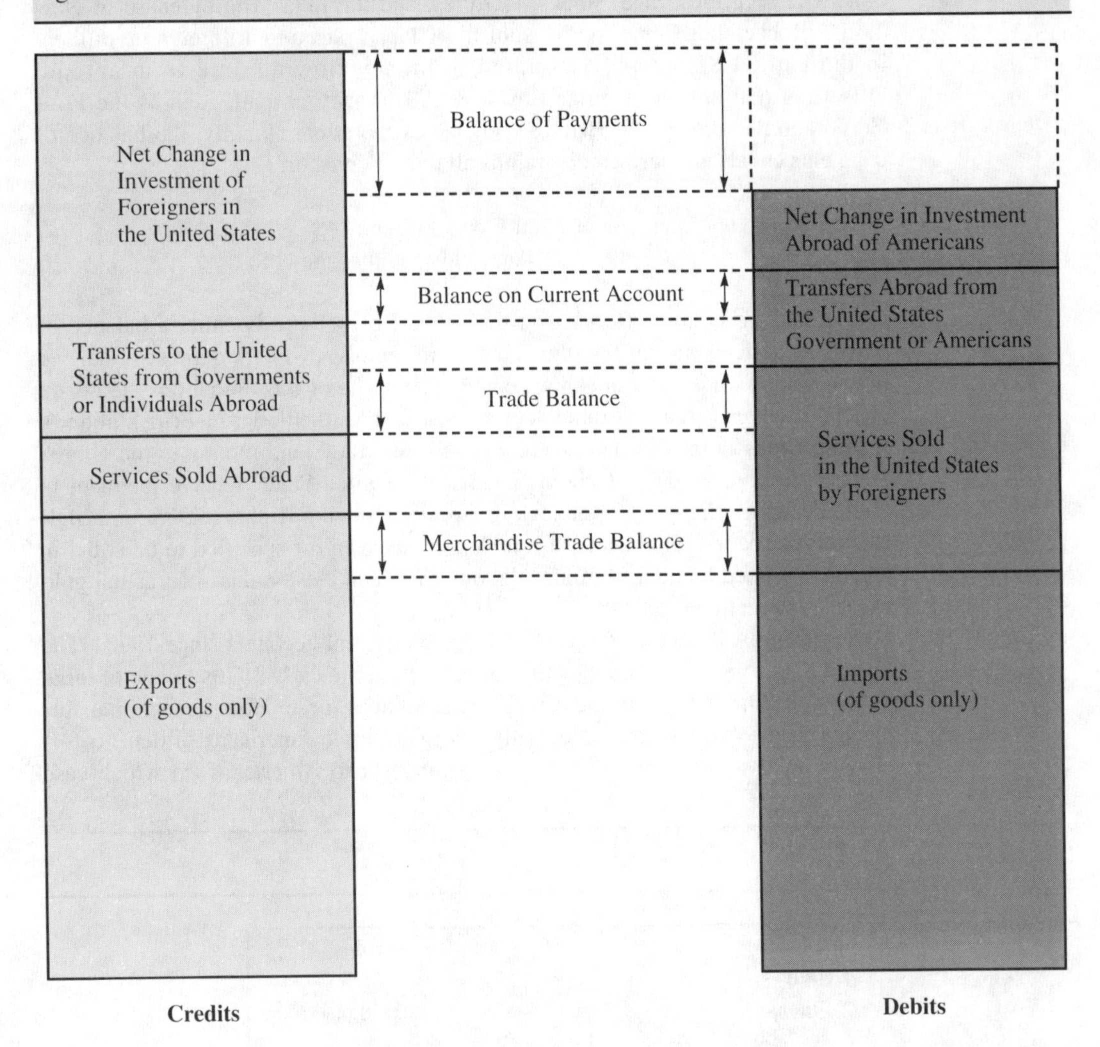

Balance of Trade = (Exports of Goods and Services)
- (Imports of Goods and Services)

In Figure A8-1 this difference is negative, so there is a trade deficit. (If the difference were positive, there would be a trade surplus.)

■ The next credit is any money the U.S. Government receives from any foreign government plus any money gift sent by individuals in foreign countries to Americans. Offsetting that is a debit for any similar money sent abroad. Adding the three sets of credits and subtracting the total from the three sets of debits gives the nation's balance on current account. In the case shown, there is an actual *imbalance*, or a deficit, because there are more debits than credits.

■ The last credit involves any change in money that foreigners invest in American securities, land, stocks, factories, and the like. The purchase of New York's Rockefeller Center by Mitsubishi of Japan raised total foreign investment in the United States and amounted to money flowing here from abroad. Offsetting that are any similar flows of U.S. money abroad, such as the Ford Corporation's purchase of Britain's Jaguar Corporation. Finally, the balance of payments equals all these credits minus all these debits, or:

Balance of Payments = Total Flows Into the U.S.
(-) Total Flows Out of the U.S.

If there is any difference in these two flows, there is either a balance of payments deficit or a surplus (the situation in Figure A8-1). A deficit is financed in two ways. First, foreign central banks hold some of this amount as claims on official reserves (usually "sound" currencies, such as the dollar or British pound). If these banks do not demand payment, in effect they lend money to the United States. Second, holders of claims against the United States receive payment in gold, foreign exchange (currencies), or Special Drawing Rights (SDR). An SDR is a sort of "paper gold" because it is denominated in (or specified to be equal in value to) a fixed amount of gold. Nations can trade these rather than actual gold to settle international accounts.

Table A8-1 shows the U.S. balance on current accounts since 1970. The United States moved from a position of balance in the early 1970s to one of large deficits, which continue to the present. Essentially, these deficits mean that foreigners lend to Americans. Normally that would put Americans in debt to foreigners, unless foreigners were previously in debt to Americans (in which case

Table A8-1 U.S. Balance on Current Account

Year	Surplus (+) Deficit (–) (billions)	Year	Surplus (+) Deficit (–) (billions)
1970	+ 2.3	1982	– 9.1
1971	– 1.4	1983	– 46.6
1972	– 5.8	1984	– 107.0
1973	+ 7.1	1985	– 116.4
1974	+ 2.0	1986	– 141.4
1975	+ 18.1	1987	– 160.7
1976	+ 4.2	1988	– 128.9
1977	– 14.5	1989	– 110.0
1978	– 15.4	1990	– 99.3
1979	– 1.0	1991	– 3.7
1980	+ 1.9	1992	– 62.5
1981	+ 6.3	1993	____

Sources: *The Economic Report of the President,* 1993
Federal Reserve Bulletin, August 1993

their debt to us would then be smaller). Indeed, foreigners were in debt to Americans until early 1985. Table A8-2 shows that until that point, Americans held more assets abroad than foreigners owned assets in the United States. This means the United States was a creditor nation. But after 1985, the United States became a debtor nation, which means that, collectively speaking, Americans are now in debt to foreigners. However, that doesn't mean you *personally* owe anything to any foreigner. (On the other hand, you *are* personally in debt because of the federal *budget* deficit, which is covered in more detail in Chapter 10.)

Americans receive credit from foreigners in several ways. First, we receive direct investment, which includes such things as the Honda Corporation's car and motorcycle factories in Ohio and farmland purchased by foreigners. Second, foreigners purchase U.S. Treasury securities, which are bonds the federal government sells when it spends more than it collects in taxes. Third, foreigners purchase bonds sold by state and local governments. Finally, foreigners buy stocks and bonds in U.S. corporations.

The United States was in this position before. A hundred years ago, wealthy Europeans invested heavily in U.S. manufacturing firms, railroads, and mortgages for farmland in an expanding U.S. agriculture. They (correctly) believed the U.S. economy had a healthy future. This money provided an incredible impetus for U.S. economic development, which propelled the U.S. economy to the top of the world.

Many people see benefits in this debtor position. Interest rates are lower because of foreign credit. This encourages spending on research and development and innovative capital, thereby raising U.S. living standards. In addition, the U.S. public debt is cheaper to finance because of these obliging foreigners. Yet many people find it uncomfortable to owe money to others, no matter what the benefits.

Table A8-2 International Investment Abroad and in the United States

Year	Foreign Assets Held by Americans (billions)	U.S. Assets Held by Foreigners (billions)	Net International Investment Position of U.S. (billions)
1980	$ 606.9	$ 500.8	$ 106.0
1981	719.6	578.7	140.9
1982	824.8	688.1	136.7
1983	873.5	784.5	89.0
1984	895.9	892.6	3.3
1985	949.7	1061.1	(–)111.4
1986	1073.3	1341.1	(–)267.8
1987	1169.7	1548.0	(–)378.3
1988	1253.7	1786.2	(–)532.5
1989	1413.0	2076.8	(–)663.8
1990	1924.8	2216.7	(–)291.9
1991	1998.4	2363.2	(–)364.8
1992	2003.4	2524.7	(–)521.3

Source: *Economic Report of the President,* 1993

CHAPTER 9

PROBLEMS IN A MARKET ECONOMY

★★★★★ LEARNING OBJECTIVES ★★★★★

1. Differentiate between private costs, external costs, private benefits, and external benefits.
2. Explain how resource allocation is affected by negative externalities and positive externalities.
3. Outline three methods of preventing or reducing external costs.
4. Outline two methods of dealing with the problem caused by external benefits.
5. Outline the two characteristics of social goods.
6. Explain why social goods are not produced in a capitalist economy.
7. Identify the causes and consequences of imperfect competition.
8. Outline the methods the government uses to deal with imperfect competition.
9. Explain why income inequality exists in a market economy.
10. List the three methods the government uses to redistribute income.

TERMS

externality
negative externality
positive externality
external cost
private benefit
private cost
social cost
external benefit
social benefit
subsidy
social good
private good
income
income distribution
wealth
wealth distribution
present value
income redistribution program

The scarcity of resources forces us to use them only if the gain (benefit) exceeds what is given up (opportunity cost). People do this (and thus maximize their economic welfare) by correctly answering the three Basic Economic Questions: What to Produce?, How to Produce?, and For Whom to Produce? The purpose of an economic system is to answer these questions. In the United States, we use the capitalist economic system, where resources are privately owned and where economic decisions and exchanges are made in a system of free markets. Most of us believe this system achieves the economic goals of efficiency, economic growth, and equity better than any other system.

However, these goals are not always met in a capitalist system because of four problems, often called market failures: 1) externalities; 2) the failure to produce social goods; 3) imperfect competition between businesses; and 4) an unacceptable distribution of income. Most people believe that government should correct the damage caused by these problems, or prevent them in the first place. This chapter explains these problems and gives examples of where they tend to occur.

EXTERNALITIES

An **externality** is any effect, good or bad, that someone else experiences when a person acts out an economic decision that involves the use of resources or the consumption of a good or service. Externalities are sometimes called neighborhood effects because "those in the neighborhood" are affected when someone does something. Occasionally they are called spillover effects because often the effects of our decisions "spill over" onto others. Externalities are of two types: 1) when bystanders to the act suffer bad effects (or costs), there are **negative externalities**; and 2) when bystanders receive benefits, there are **positive externalities**.

Negative Externalities

★1 Another term for a negative externality is **external cost**. It is a cost of resource use that is not paid by the decision maker. For example, when an airliner takes off from Boston, people in Boston give up some peace and quiet and some clean air. Candy wrappers thrown on a sidewalk, unexpected noise from firecrackers, a traffic jam after an accident, chatter outside a classroom, a house with peeling paint, pets that roam in the neighborhood, smoke from factories, nuclear fallout from bomb tests, and people walking the streets in grubby clothes are other examples that involve external costs.

The innocent bystanders are the losers. If you do something that creates an external cost and do nothing to compensate the one who suffers, the effect is the same as if you would insist that the stranger next to you at a restaurant pay part of your bill. The stranger gains nothing—but suffers some costs.

Why do those creating external costs commit these acts and expect others to pick up a share of the tab? It's because people often make decisions with only themselves in mind. People generally act when *their* benefits, known as **private benefits**, exceed *their* costs, known as **private costs**. Each of these decisions is considered to be a good private decision because it makes *the individual* better off.

A more technical reason for externalities stems from the fact that the property rights to the use of some resources are not well defined. Consider the air above Jim's yard. Is it his? If so, he can fill it with trees. But what if his towering trees block the sunlight needed to help his neighbor Joe's garden grow, or prevents the refreshing summer breeze from cooling Joe or chasing away the mosquitos, or prevents Joe from ever seeing a sunset from his own yard? These "neighborhood effects," or externalities, are very clear here, and it is clear why they exist. It's either because: 1) Jim doesn't care about Joe's well-being; or 2) it was never made clear who owns the air above Jim's yard, so Jim acts as though *he* does.

For another example, consider someone riding a skateboard on a sidewalk. If someone else is disturbed by the skateboarder, external costs enter the picture. In Figure 9-1 the external costs are on top of the private costs. The addition of private and external costs is the **social cost**—what everyone combined in society gives up when someone uses resources. The social cost exceeds the benefits of the skateboarder. Even though the skateboarder is better off when enjoying the skateboard, society as a whole is worse off. A good *private* decision turns out to be a bad *social* one. The word "bad" means members of society as a whole (including the skateboarder) have more to lose than they will gain from this decision. Realistically, it is impossible to measure the costs and benefits accurately, partly because they involve value judgments.

The two diagrams on the top right show a situation where someone else enjoys skateboarding much more than the first skateboarder, as evidenced by the bigger private benefits. Now the private benefits *do* exceed the social cost, so riding the skateboard is a good private decision *and* a good social decision. Essentially, the rest of society should accept a little nuisance so that someone who truly loves skateboarding can do so.

★2

The major consequence of negative externalities is excessive production (or consumption) of products that produce external costs. Thus, resources are misallocated, which means too many resources are used to produce things that have external costs. For example, the skateboard of the first rider made the members of society collectively worse off, so What to Produce? is answered incorrect-

Figure 9-1 Negative Externalities or External Costs

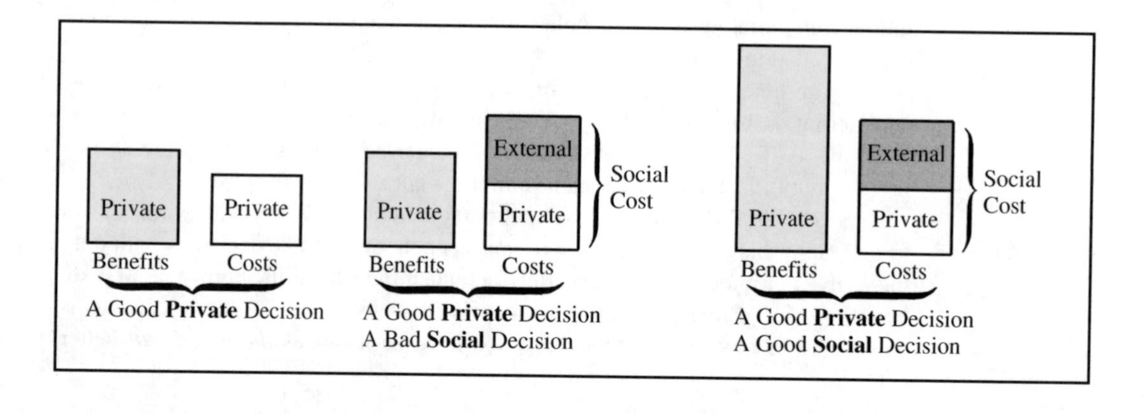

ly. Society would be better off if the board didn't exist. However, producing the board for the second skateboarder *is* a good decision. Thus, *some* skateboards should be produced—but fewer than are produced in a free market. In general, lesser amounts of products that have external costs should be produced.

Sometimes external costs are felt at a distance or at some time in the future. Acid rain, caused mainly by burning coal in power plants, is a good example. The lakes of the Northeast and Canada are becoming more acidic, partly because of coal burned in the Midwest.

Another devastating external cost might be the flooding of the world's coastal cities as a result of the destruction of tropical rain forests. These forests consume much carbon dioxide when their trees manufacture sugar, so after they are cut, the concentration of carbon dioxide in the atmosphere increases. It is increased still more by the burning of fossil fuels such as coal, oil, and natural gas. The problem is that carbon dioxide creates a "greenhouse effect." After sunlight strikes the earth and warms it, the warmed earth then emits infrared (heat) rays that the carbon dioxide prevents from escaping into space. So the infrared rays heat the atmosphere. Consequently, global temperatures are expected to rise—perhaps eventually melting the polar ice caps and raising sea levels and turning the Midwest into a semi-desert.

Destroying tropical rain forests also robs us of potential medical discoveries in tropical plants. More than half of the world's plants live in these forests, and many have yet to be identified, much less studied for their usefulness. Unfortunately, many species will become extinct before identification. Thus, cures for cancer, AIDS, or aging diseases might be literally cut out from under us because of the economic decisions in the tropical countries.

A rain forest in Costa Rica, with some trees over 150 feet tall.

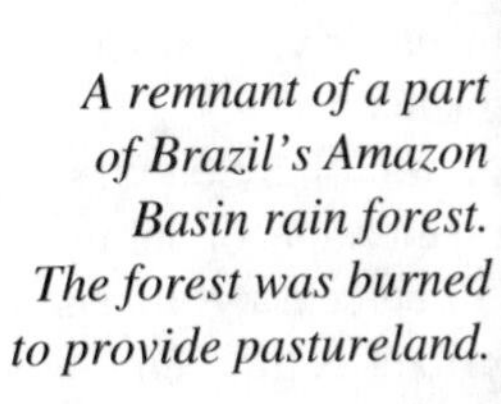

A remnant of a part of Brazil's Amazon Basin rain forest. The forest was burned to provide pastureland.

Preventing or Reducing External Costs

★3

How can such resource misallocation be limited or stopped by limiting or stopping the production of goods or services with external costs? There are several ways: 1) internalize external costs; 2) prohibit acts that cause external costs; and 3) reward good behavior.

■ Internalizing external costs means whoever causes the external costs must pay the equivalent of these costs (or at least part of them), usually to the government. Such payments usually take the form of special taxes. Examples include "sin taxes" on alcoholic beverages and tobacco products. Figure 9-2 shows that the tax increases the private costs to the point where there are more costs than benefits for the individual. This process doesn't stop *all* acts that have external costs. For example, a steep tax on whiskey would stop someone from buying whiskey only if that person had costs and benefits as shown in the boxes. For another person, the benefits might still exceed the costs, so that person still buys the whiskey. But the intent is not to stop all acts that have external costs, merely some.

Figure 9-2 How to Discourage Acts that Have External Costs

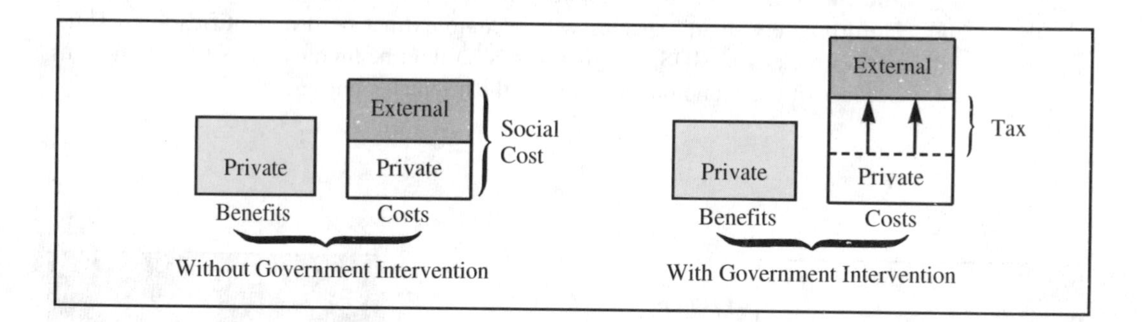

In 1990, France became the first nation to tax air pollution when it imposed a 150-franc (about $27) tax per ton of sulfur dioxide. Another use of taxes to curb externalities is Wisconsin's exclusion of cloth diapers and diaper services from the state sales tax, while disposable diapers, which are not only non-recyclable but also create unsanitary landfills, are taxed.

■ The second way to curtail the problem of external costs is to prohibit the act itself. Examples include: the ban on the production and consumption of alcoholic beverages during Prohibition in the 1920s; anti-noise ordinances; laws prohibiting drunken driving, littering, and pollution; speed limits; and rules on yard and home maintenance.

A variant of prohibition was made part of the Clean Air Act of 1990. The act requires that emissions of sulfur dioxide (a contributor to acid rain) by public utilities be cut 50 percent by the end of the century. But plants that pollute less than their prescribed ceiling amounts can sell "pollution allowances" to other plants that exceed their amounts. This "market approach" provides a less expensive way for some utilities to meet pollution-reduction requirements as compared with investing in costly new equipment, while still resulting in the same amount of pollution reduction in total.

■ A third way to reduce external costs, although rarely used, discourages "bad" behavior by rewarding "good" behavior—much as a parent who pays a child for good grades. This amounts to a bribe. For example, governments could give awards for spotless driving records or pollution-free factories.

Positive Externalities

With a positive externality, also known as an **external benefit**, some of the benefits of using resources go to someone other than the one who decides to use the resources. Some examples: flowers in someone's *front* yard that please passersby (*back* yard ones can't be seen); perfume or attractive clothing, which please people in contact with the wearer; and your education, which benefits those who touch your life.

Usually someone who uses resources that benefit others doesn't care that others will receive any benefit. But such indifference can lead to a misallocation of resources. Thus, society fails to maximize its economic welfare because people answer What to Produce? incorrectly.

Suppose Dawn is deciding whether to attend her freshman year of college. Among the resources needed to educate her are some labor (teachers and staff) and some capital (desks, school equipment, and supplies). Suppose she must pay the full cost of these resources, $6,000 per year, which would be her private cost. She then considers how much she would benefit from the education, including her future income potential, the satisfaction of learning, and more social opportunities. Suppose she calculates this to be worth $4,000 per year, which means $4,000 is the most she would pay for the education. "It's not worth it," she says, and looks for a job instead. The diagram on the left side of Figure 9-3 illustrates this.

However, Dawn hasn't considered the *external* benefits the rest of society would get if she goes to college. These include cheaper and higher quality goods or services made by a better-trained worker (Dawn). She might become a better

Figure 9-3 Positive Externalities or External Benefits

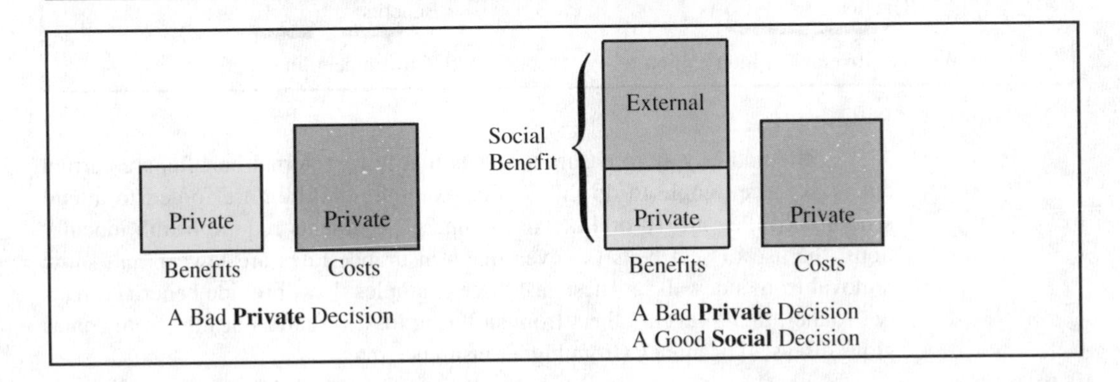

citizen because of her increased knowledge of government and economics and might be better company for her friends. The diagram on the right side of Figure 9-3 shows that these external benefits exceed Dawn's private benefits. The addition of these two benefits is called the **social benefit** of her education—what society *as a whole* gains.

Because the social benefit exceeds the cost of Dawn's education, it is best for society if she goes to college. If people would decide whether to go to school solely on the basis of *their* benefits and costs, many wouldn't go, and society would provide fewer educational services than it should. Generally, not enough goods and services that have external benefits are produced in a capitalist economy.

Encouraging Acts with External Benefits

★4

In order to make people do things that provide external benefits, governments occasionally become involved in people's lives. Governments do this by: 1) subsidizing people; and 2) coercion.

■ A **subsidy** can take the form of a payment you receive from the government for which you did nothing to earn or of the government paying some bill for you. For example, the state might pay for 60 percent ($3,600) of Dawn's education cost, leaving her to pay only $2,400. Consequently, she will go to school, for $2,400 is less than the $4,000 in benefits she receives. Figure 9-4 shows how subsidies change behavior, such as Dawn's. Education is subsidized primarily because everyone benefits from a better-educated public.

Figure 9-4 How to Encourage Acts that Have External Benefits

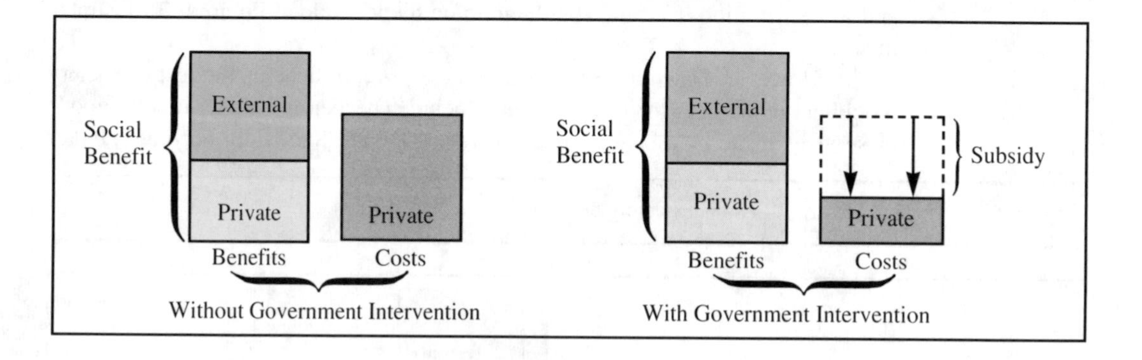

■ Another way to ensure that acts that have external benefits are carried out is to force people to do them. For example, children are forced to attend school until they are 16 or 18. Also, some governments require health inoculations, the use of seat belts (so everyone's insurance rates are lower), and snow removal from sidewalks. These last three examples don't provide benefits directly. Rather, they prevent others from suffering losses, such as health (from contagious diseases) or money (from higher insurance rates).

Such coercion bothers many people, who say, "I should have the freedom to decide if I want to wear a seat belt (get inoculated, wear a motorcycle helmet, have smoke alarms, and so on)." While these protests make sense, nobody lives unconnected to others. So long as most people want to be in insurance pools to cover their medical bills, there is at least some justification (but perhaps not enough) for restricting behavior that threatens the insurance "kitty."

To conclude, this section dealt only with individuals' decisions that had external costs or benefits. The concept also applies to other economic units, such as businesses and government agencies. For example, the Occupational Safety and Health Administration (OSHA) and the Federal Deposit Insurance Corporation (F.D.I.C.) were established to deal with problems caused by externalities of business.

SOCIAL GOODS

★5

The second problem of a market or capitalistic economy also leads to wrong answers to What to Produce? **Social goods** (or public goods) have two characteristics that distinguish them from other goods (or **private goods**): 1) they are non-rival; and 2) they are non-exclusionary.

■ Non-rival means that even if you consume more of some good, there is not any less of it for others to enjoy. A lighthouse is non-rival. If the Thompsons go sailing and use a lighthouse for navigation, they do not interfere with anyone else who wants to use it. On the other hand, your notebook is *not* non-rival (it is rival). If your friend uses a sheet of paper from it, there is less for you to use.

■ To say a good is non-exclusionary means no one can be prevented from using it. The lighthouse is non-exclusionary, for no one can stop the Thompsons from seeing the light so long as everyone else can. Your notebook is *not* non-exclusionary. You don't have to let anyone use your paper. Other non-exclusionary goods include emergency weather sirens, civic holiday decorations, and road signs.

Thus, the lighthouse, the sirens, the decorations, and the signs are social goods, and the notebook is a private good. Other social goods (or services) include national defense and the military equipment that helps provide such defense, street lights, highways, public fireworks displays, and city parks.

★6

However, in a purely capitalist economy, few people would buy such goods, partly because of the "free-rider effect." This means if one person buys such a good—say, the lighthouse—everyone else can use it for free. If the Thompsons buy it, they would resent such "free-riders"—so much that they wouldn't buy it in the first place. However, the main reason that social goods are not produced in a capitalist economy is that they are generally too expensive for one person to buy. Consequently, all members of society buy them collectively. Usually, governments purchase such goods, such as schools and roads from the private enterprises that actually produce them. However, the governments often maintain these goods. But, as noted in Chapter 4, there is a trend toward privatization, with more private businesses maintaining public goods under government contract.

IMPERFECT COMPETITION

Economists generally believe the ideal market structure is pure competition, where many small firms provide so much competition that firms make only normal profit and not "excessive" or economic profit. But monopolistic competition, oligopoly, and monopoly are all types of imperfect competition that commonly exist in our economy. This is a problem because it reduces economic welfare by forcing the wrong answers to What to Produce? and For Whom to Produce?

Causes and Consequences of Imperfect Competition

★7

In an industry with imperfect competition: 1) firms can determine market price to some extent; 2) competitors' products differ from each other; and 3) firms tend to be large and few. There are two major reasons for imperfect competition. First, the production processes of some goods and services are subject to economies of scale, meaning firms must become large in order to be efficient. Therefore, only a handful of firms are needed to meet market demand. Second, some industries have barriers to entry that restrict the number of competitors. These include patents, licenses, permits, copyrights, and control of an essential resource, such as a rare mineral ore. Another barrier is brand proliferation, which occurs when each firm has many brands of similar products, such as cigarettes and breakfast cereals. This forces a new competitor to spend a great deal of money to fight all these established brands of products.

A final barrier is government regulation that is intended to protect buyers of goods or services. Local, state, and federal regulatory boards are to determine which firms meet standards set by law. But often these boards are dominated by members of the industry that are regulated, and they may reject firms that are potential new competitors—not to protect the public from bad products, but to protect the turf of established firms.

Imperfect competition has two primary negative social consequences: 1) prices and profits are higher than in pure competition; and 2) less than the optimum level of output is produced.

■ Prices tend to be higher with imperfect competition than when firms are purely competitive. This creates somewhat higher profits for the imperfectly competitive firms. They even earn economic profits (income in excess of normal profit). However, these higher profits don't attract competing firms and resources as theory predicts. In turn, stockholders receive higher dividends. Therefore, society incorrectly answers For Whom to Produce? The higher prices reduce the amount of goods and services consumers receive from their limited incomes. And the higher dividends increase the amount of goods and services stockholders can buy. So, the competitive market's answer to For Whom to Produce?—the answer assumed to be best—is not achieved.

■ A second negative social consequence of imperfect competition is that the output level of each good and service is less than the optimum amount for society. What to Produce? refers to which of the goods and services that *could* be made with scarce resources *should* be made. Equally important, it refers to the quantity. There is only one "right amount" that maximizes the economic welfare of everyone combined. The reason this amount isn't always produced involves the law of demand. Because prices are higher in imperfectly competitive industries, buyers purchase less than the optimum amount of the goods and services of these firms.

Government Responses to Imperfect Competition

★8 There are several ways to reduce the amount of imperfect competition or its negative consequences: 1) antitrust legislation; 2) higher tax rates for larger firms; 3) special help for small businesses; and 4) price regulation.

■ Trusts were firms that operated an industry of many firms as a monopoly because all firms placed their operations "in the trust" of the new firm. Standard Oil of Ohio, formed in 1870 by John D. Rockefeller, led to the first trust. By 1877, Rockefeller controlled 95 percent of all oil refineries. In 1879, he consolidated 27 firms into the Standard Oil Trust. In the next two decades, many other industries established trusts. The Sherman Antitrust Act of 1890 outlawed any "restraint of trade," meaning any effort to control any market to gain monopoly power, including trusts. The Clayton Antitrust Act of 1914 and subsequent laws sought to promote competition between firms. The reasoning behind such laws is that, with strong competition, prices reach equilibrium levels and profits are only high enough to keep businesses in operation.

■ The government taxes large firms (supposedly the imperfectly competitive ones) at higher rates than smaller firms, ranging from 15 to 35 percent of their income. Also, small firms can choose to do business under the Sub-Chapter S Corporation form ("S" stands for small). These corporations pay no corporate income tax at all. However, the stockholders pay personal income taxes on their earnings.

■ The Small Business Administration (SBA) provides loans to small businesses that can't get loans elsewhere. Many states offer workshops, seminars, and university extension programs to help people start and operate small businesses. Many states also provide venture capital and "incubation centers" to help innovative entrepreneurs begin businesses. Finally, in the interest of competition, governments occasionally provide subsidies to keep some businesses alive. For example, for many years the federal government provided subsidies to air carriers. Another example is the SBA's set-aside program, which since 1968 has given small firms a break in bidding against large firms for federal government projects. Currently, about 4,000 companies are in the program, which is open to owners who are socially disadvantaged, especially minorities.

■ You learned in Chapter 6 that natural monopolies, including public utilities, have their prices regulated or approved by state public service commissions. The first major federal government regulation of prices of particular firms or industries involved railroads. The Interstate Commerce Act of 1887 created the Interstate Commerce Commission (ICC), partly to regulate shipping rates on traffic that crossed state borders. The most recent law was the cable television regulation law passed in 1992. It gives power to the Federal Communication Commission (FCC) to determine "reasonable rates" for basic cable services as well as to set service standards. The FCC began to exercise that power in 1993.

INCOME DISTRIBUTION AND POVERTY

The last problem of a market economy, an unequal distribution of income, is probably the easiest to see. Although many Americans are well-off and some live in opulence, a short drive brings you face-to-face with poverty. You see people living in shoddy houses, with worn clothing, and without adequate health care. Many people believe our income distribution is so unequal that it is unfair.

Income and Wealth Distribution

Income distribution—how many goods and services each person receives—is actually the answer to For Whom to Produce? Recall that a scarcity of resources means most people won't get all the goods and services they want. The goods and services produced can be distributed in an infinite number of ways, and only one way provides the maximum welfare for everyone combined. Finding that distribution is, therefore, an impossible task.

Two main financial measures are used to compare members of society: income distribution and wealth distribution. **Income** is the amount of goods and services you get in some time period, such as a year. In modern societies, income is measured with money, which is used to trade for goods and services. Most people earn their income, which means they sell (trade) something of value—usually resources—for money. People can also receive income in the form of gifts, welfare payments, capital gains, or lottery winnings. **Income distribution** refers to how much income flows to each member of society in relation to what other members have. However, usually only earned income is considered.

Wealth refers to how much power you have to purchase goods and services at any given moment—not over some period, as with income. Your wealth is usually measured by equity or net worth, the difference between your assets (what you own) and liabilities (what you owe). Sometimes wealth is measured by assets alone. **Wealth distribution** refers to how much wealth different members of society have in relation to all the others.

Another way of measuring wealth involves the concept of **present value**, which is the value today of an asset that will be received or yield income in the future. Suppose someone is to pay you $1,080 one year from now and that the interest rate is eight percent. If the person offered to pay you $1,000 today instead, would you accept? In terms of money consideration (excluding tax considerations), you would be indifferent because you could put the $1,000 in the bank and earn $80 interest in a year and end up with $1,080 anyway. Thus, the present value of $1,080 to be received a year from now is $1,000. Consequently, a more realistic measure of wealth includes the value of property you have at the moment plus the present value of future earnings.

The most common way to measure both income and wealth distribution is to divide the nation into groups of equal numbers of people or families. Let's consider income distribution first. Suppose you line up all American families, with the lowest-income family on one end and the family with the highest income on the other. Assume that there are 100 million families, split into five groups of

20 million families each. The poorest 20 percent of all families, or 20 million of them, all fit in the first group. The next poorest is the second group and so on until the fifth group, which has the 20 million families with the highest incomes. Next, add up the total income in each group. Finally, find what percent of the nation's total income each group earned. The difference in these percentages show the inequalities of income distribution. Table 9-1 gives such income distribution figures for the United States. (Incidentally, the top five percent of families generally receive between 17 and 18 percent of all income.) These figures, however, do not include welfare and other government payments, which primarily help the poor and make income distribution somewhat less unequal.

Table 9-1 The Distribution of Money Income of Families by Income Class, 1990

Income Class	Percent of Total Income Earned by Group
Lowest Fifth	5.2%
Second-Lowest Fifth	11.5%
Middle Fifth	17.5%
Second-Highest Fifth	24.3%
Highest Fifth	41.5%

Source: *The Statistical Abstract of the United States,* 1993

In the 1960s, the United States officially began defining poverty in terms of specific income levels. Take, for example, a family of two adults and two children. The government first finds what a family of four needs to spend on food at a "minimum diet level" for a year. It then multiplies that figure by three to get the official poverty level. Table 9-2 shows the official poverty levels for an urban family of four since 1960. The large increase in the poverty level is due primarily to inflation. The table also shows the percentage of all American households, as well as white and non-white households, that fell below the poverty level since 1960. The figures include welfare and other government cash grants, but not in-kind incomes (goods and services given directly to people).

Similar procedures are used to measure wealth distribution, which is much more unequal than income distribution. In 1989, for example, the richest one percent of households held 37 percent of all assets. The richest 10 percent held 68 percent of the assets, while the remaining 90 percent held only 32 percent.

Methods of Distributing Income

★9 Income is measured as the number of dollars flowing to a person during a year, and that depends mainly upon two things: 1) the price of the resource (or resources) sold; and 2) the amount of resources sold. Consider labor. The wage of any occupation (the "price" of labor) depends upon the demand for and the supply of that labor. This reflects an industry's need to hire such workers and

Table 9-2 Poverty Level (for a family of 4) and Percent of Families in Poverty

Year	Poverty Level	Percent of Families in Poverty			
		All	White	Black	Hispanic
1960	$ 3,022	18.1%	14.9%	n.a.	n.a.
1970	$ 3,968	10.1%	8.0%	29.5%	n.a.
1980	$ 8,414	10.3%	8.0%	28.9%	23.2%
1985	$10,989	11.4%	9.1%	28.7%	25.5%
1986	$11,203	10.9%	8.6%	28.0%	24.7%
1987	$11,611	10.7%	8.1%	29.4%	25.7%
1988	$12,092	10.4%	7.9%	28.2%	23.7%
1989	$12,675	10.3%	7.8%	27.8%	23.4%
1990	$13,359	10.7%	8.1%	29.3%	25.0%
1991	$13,942	11.5%	8.8%	30.4%	26.5%
1992	$14,335	11.7%	8.9%	30.9%	26.2%
1993	_____	_____	_____	_____	_____
1994	_____	_____	_____	_____	_____

Sources: *Economic Report of the President,* 1993; *Census Bureau Reports*

how many people can and want to do such work. Under competitive conditions, the wage paid will be the equilibrium wage. But a laborer's income depends not only upon the wage, but also on how many hours that laborer works in a year—that is, the amount of resources sold. Similarly, you can find the income of the owner of a gravel pit by multiplying the price of gravel by the amount sold (and subtracting expenses).

Very few people accept what the free, competitive marketplace gives them when they have the opportunity to get more. People raise their incomes above competitive conditions by controlling labor demand and supply, colluding (price-fixing), collective bargaining, and discriminating.

Reducing Income Inequality

Does the American economic system give the best answer to For Whom to Produce? Even if the United States had pure capitalism, with highly competitive markets, would that system give the "best" answer? Few people would answer yes to either question. They believe that some people should have more income and some people less income than what they earn by selling resources at equilibrium prices.

Equity, one of society's economic goals, means everyone should have a fair share of the goods and services produced. However, defining "fair share" is difficult because it involves value judgments and personal philosophies. Probably a majority of people believe that everyone has a *right* to the basic necessities of life—food, shelter, clothing, education, and medical care. Whether people *earn* any income to pay for them is not relevant in this philosophy. Nor is there much connection between the amount of goods and services they produce and the amount they consume—at least for basic needs.

An opposing philosophy holds that a person's consumption of goods and services should depend upon that person's production of goods and services. If you work a lot and produce a lot, then you will have a lot of goods and services as well. But if you produce little, you will have few goods and services to consume. Followers of this philosophy say this promotes the greatest effort from individuals and maximum efficiency. They say people should have the right *to pursue* happiness (as stated in the Declaration of Independence), but not the right to happiness itself (in the form of goods and services). They would grant everyone the right to compete in the pursuit of income along with all others in all markets. Essential to that right is a "level playing field" for all market participants, which means the only thing that should matter in market transactions is productivity. That is, people who try to sell goods, services, and resources (their labor or other talents) *should be* discriminated against (meaning no one buys from them) if they are less productive than others. However, people should *not* be denied the opportunity to sell resources (be discriminated against) because of their race, sex, creed, or any other reason. Indeed, most Americans approve of government intervention to prevent these other kinds of discrimination.

★10 Most people support at least some government involvement in answering For Whom to Produce? Governments do this in three general ways: 1) direct intervention into markets; 2) raising productivity; and 3) direct payments.

■ First, governments sometimes intervene directly in resource or product markets, generally to raise prices and the income of the seller. Examples include minimum wage legislation, the legalization of collective bargaining and cartels in agriculture, farm price support programs, affirmative action programs, and minimum-markup laws for retailers.

■ Second, governments seek to raise the productivity of certain resources. In turn, this causes the demands for these resources, as well as their prices, to increase. Examples include retraining programs for laid-off workers, small business management workshops, and agricultural research. Another example is Head Start, a federal program that provides up to two years of preschool for 600,000 poor children.

■ Third, governments raise some people's income directly with payments, either with cash or in-kind income (goods and services). Collectively, such programs are called **income redistribution programs** because such income payments come from someone else's income in the form of taxes.

These programs generally involve direct payments to individuals, although occasionally business firms receive such payments. The most widespread program is Medicaid, which covers almost 30 million people and provides medical care to the poor. Child nutrition (free lunch) programs in public schools serve around 25 million children. Aid to Families with Dependent Children (AFDC) provides assistance to low-income families with children. In 1992, about 13 million people benefited from the program, which cost the federal government about $15 billion. Supplemental Security Income (SSI) provides benefits to almost five million people who are old, blind, or disabled. The Social Security Administration is responsible for SSI. The Food Stamp Program, administered by the U.S. Department of Agriculture, sells or gives away food stamps, which people use like cash to purchase food. In 1993, 27 million people received food stamps, worth an average of about $70 a person per month, with a family maximum of $370 for four people. The program, which costs about $18 billion a year, calculates food stamp benefits according to a family's size and income (individuals also can qualify). In 1993, a family of four was eligible for food stamps up to an annual net income of $13,956. Finally, most local communities provide what is commonly called General Relief to those who receive an inadequate income and may not qualify for other programs. Such government relief programs were virtually unknown before the 1930s, and many had their start in the 1960s.

The Job Opportunities and Basic Skills (JOBS) program, created as part of the 1988 Family Support Act, requires able-bodied AFDC recipients who are parents of children over age three (age one at state option) to participate in work, education, or training programs. Recipients receive child-care help and transportation. The program requires that 20 percent of eligible parents be in the JOBS program by 1995. Starting in 1994, one adult in a two-parent AFDC household must look for a job. If none is found, 16 hours of community service work must be done each week. Young parents can work toward a high school degree instead. States will be required to increase child support collection from absent parents.

The next chapter shows that "there is no such thing as a free lunch"—a favorite saying of economists. It means that any decision about scarce resources involves a cost. When the government is involved in such decisions, someone usually has to pay taxes to cover the costs. All four problems of capitalism covered in this chapter require government intervention—and thus require that citizens pay taxes to solve them.

We in America today are nearer to the final triumph over poverty than ever before in the history of any land. The poorhouse is vanishing among us.

– Herbert Hoover, 1928

If a free country cannot help the many who are poor, it cannot save the few who are rich.

– John F. Kennedy

A miser grows rich by seeming poor; an extravagant man grows poor by seeming rich.

– William Shakespeare

Poverty is not dishonorable in itself, but only when it comes from idleness, intemperance, extravagance and folly.

– Plutarch

Chapter 9 SUMMARY

Four major problems appear in capitalistic economies: 1) externalities; 2) social goods are not produced; 3) imperfect competition; and 4) an unequal distribution of income.

The first type of externality imposes external costs on people, and it results in excess production of products causing the externalities. Negative externalities can be reduced by: 1) internalizing the external cost; 2) prohibiting production of goods with external costs; and 3) bribing people. Positive externalities provide external benefits to people. But there is not enough production of goods and services that have external benefits. To encourage production of items with external benefits, the government: 1) provides subsidies; and 2) forces people to do things that provide external benefits.

Social goods have two characteristics. First, they cannot be denied to anyone. Second, if you increase the amount you use, there is not less for others. Because no individual will buy social goods, governments purchase and provide them. Social goods include such things as roads, police protection, and weather sirens.

Some industries are imperfectly competitive, which is due primarily to increasing returns to scale and barriers to entry. Prices and profits in such industries tend to be higher, and outputs are less than socially desirable. The government attempts to offset these negative aspects with antitrust laws, differential tax rates, and special aid to small businesses.

People sell resources at widely different prices, and some people don't sell many resources. Consequently, the income and wealth distribution in a capitalist economy is unequal. The government reduces such inequality by: 1) raising the prices of the resources sold by the poor; 2) raising the productivity of the poor; and 3) giving the poor money or goods and services.

Chapter 9 RESPONSES TO THE LEARNING OBJECTIVES

1. Private costs are those borne by the one who decides how resources are to be used. External costs refer to anything given up by other people because of that decision. Private benefits are those received by the decision maker. External benefits are benefits received by anyone other than the decision maker.

2. When an item has negative externalities, too many resources are allocated to making it, meaning that too much of that item is produced. If an item has positive externalities, too few resources are allocated to making it, meaning that too little of that item is produced.

3. External costs can be reduced by:
   a) fines and taxes, which internalize external costs
   b) prohibition of acts that create external costs
   c) bribes for behavior that have no external costs

4. Activities that result in external benefits are encouraged by subsidies. In addition, people are forced to carry out some activities in order for others to derive external benefits from such activities.

5. Social goods are:
   a) non-rival, which means that if someone uses more of them, there is not less available for others
   b) non-exclusionary, which means that no one can be denied access to them

6. Social goods are not produced in capitalist economies because of the free-rider effect and because they are often too expensive for one person to purchase.

7. Imperfect competition is caused by increasing returns to scale and barriers to entry. Its consequences include higher prices, higher production costs, and less than the optimal amount of resources used to produce an item.

8. The government responds to imperfect competition with antitrust legislation, differential tax rates for larger and smaller firms, and special help for small businesses.

9. Income inequality is the result of people selling different amounts of resources and at different prices, as well as luck.

10. The government redistributes income by raising:
    a) prices of certain resources
    b) incomes of certain individuals
    c) the productivity of certain resources

Chapter 9 LEARNING ACTIVITIES AND DISCUSSION QUESTIONS

1. Think of five things you have done that imposed external costs on others. Why did you do them?
2. Make a list of three things people do that produce positive externalities that, in your opinion, the government should subsidize.
3. Can you think of times when social goods, which are usually non-rival and non-exclusionary, are *not*? Why is that?
4. Do you think your local power company should face competition? Why or why not?
5. Critique this statement, "The rich get richer and the poor get poorer."

APPENDIX A INTERNALIZING EXTERNAL COSTS

A supply curve for a product shows the relationship between the prices of the product and the amounts that firms find profitable to offer for sale. Because a product is profitable when the benefit of producing it (its price) exceeds its cost, the supply curve is also a reflection of production costs. However, supply curves reflect only the *private* costs paid by the firm. External costs are ignored.

Figure A9-1 shows a hypothetical supply curve for whiskey that reflects only private costs, labelled S_{PC}. Given the demand curve as shown, the price of a quart of whiskey is $10 and the quantity purchased is 1,500 quarts. Suppose the government estimates there is an external cost of $5 for each quart of whiskey consumed, on average. Also, suppose it imposes a tax of $5 per quart, to be paid by distillers. The distillers can view the effect in two ways. First, they might say they can now profitably produce only 1,000 quarts, rather than 1,500, at $10 per quart. The other 500 quarts earned low profits before the tax—so low that the tax now completely wipes out the profits. Thus, the supply curve appears to shift to the left by 500 quarts. Second, distillers might say they will continue to produce 1,500 quarts, but only if the amount of the tax is matched by a price increase. In this case, it appears that the supply curve shifted up by $5. Whatever viewpoint you choose, there is a new supply curve. It is labelled S_{SC} because it reflects all the costs of the whiskey, private plus external, which together equal social costs.

This shift in the supply curve, coupled with a constant demand, leads to a shortage of 500 quarts of whiskey at $10. As a result, the price rises to a new equilibrium price of $13. Thus, the consumer, not the distillers, pays most of the tax (60 percent). This is called tax shifting because firms shift (some of) the tax onto consumers. Many people believe this is the way it should be because the drinkers, not the producers, create external costs with their behavior.

Finally, notice that consumption fell from 1,500 quarts to 1,300 quarts after the price went up. That is the reason for internalizing external costs—to reduce the amount of the "problem good" that is produced and consumed.

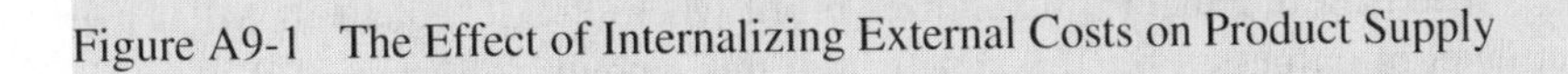
Figure A9-1 The Effect of Internalizing External Costs on Product Supply

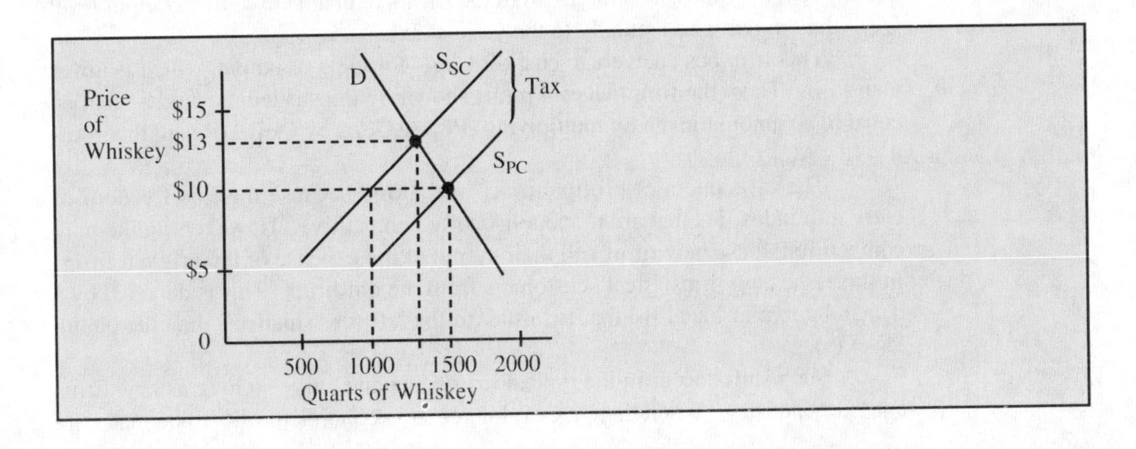

APPENDIX B MONOPOLISTIC COMPETITION

Recall that there are four primary economic differences between pure competition and imperfect competition. In an industry where there is imperfect competition: 1) prices are higher; 2) production costs are higher; 3) firms operate at less than the optimum output level; and 4) there are excess resources in the industry. The first three can be seen graphically in Figure A9-2. The graphs depict the situation for a typical firm in an industry in monopolistic competition. The first figure shows the short-run situation, where economic profits are made. The second shows the long-run situation, where no economic profits are made—only normal profits. (In the cases of oligopoly and monopoly, economic profits often *are* made in the long run.)

There are no differences in the AC (average cost) and MC (marginal cost) curves for purely competitive firms and imperfectly competitive ones. But notice in Figure A9-2 how the demand curve for the monopolistically competitive firm slopes downward. (Refer back to Figure A6-2, page 164. Notice that the demand curve for a firm in pure competition is horizontal. That's because it can sell all it wants at the market price.) Imperfectly competitive firms must lower their prices if they want to sell more. Thus, their demand curves slope downward, showing an inverse relationship between quantity sold and prices.

Another distinction from A6-2 is the MR (marginal revenue) function. For a purely competitive firm, it is horizontal, and the MR is always equal to the price, which means one extra unit of output sold brings in an amount of extra or marginal revenue equal to the price. But an imperfectly competitive firm that sells an extra unit brings in an amount of MR that is *less* than the price. This might seem puzzling, for if a product sells for $8, shouldn't an extra unit sold yield marginal revenue of $8? No, for the firm must reduce the price on *all* units sold. Because it could have sold all the units except the last one at a price *greater* than $8, the firm loses some revenue on each unit previously sold at the higher price. This loss offsets the *gain* in revenue made by selling the extra unit at $8. The MR line depicts the net effect of this gain and loss for each unit of output.

The firm in Panel (a) maximizes profit where its MC equals its MR—that is, at level of output Q_{SR}. It is able to sell this amount at a price of P_{SR}. This price is found by moving straight up to the firm's demand curve from output level Q_{SR}, then moving horizontally to the vertical axis.

This firm has an average cost of AC_{SR} for Q_{SR} of output, which is lower than P_{SR}. Thus, the firm makes a profit shown by the shaded rectangle—that is, equal to an amount given by multiplying (P_{SR}-AC_{SR}) by Q_{SR}. (Recall that profit = (P - AC) x Q.)

These (economic) profits attract new firms because there is freedom of entry into industries that are monopolistically competitive. However, unlike pure competition, these new firms sell their output at the expense of the original firms. In short, the new firms "steal" customers from the old firms. This is depicted by a demand curve in Panel (b) that is farther to the left (or "smaller") than the one in Panel (a).

Such shifts occur in the typical firm's demand curve so long as new firms enter the industry. When there are no longer any economic profits to be made, no

Figure A9-2 A Firm in Monopolistic Competition

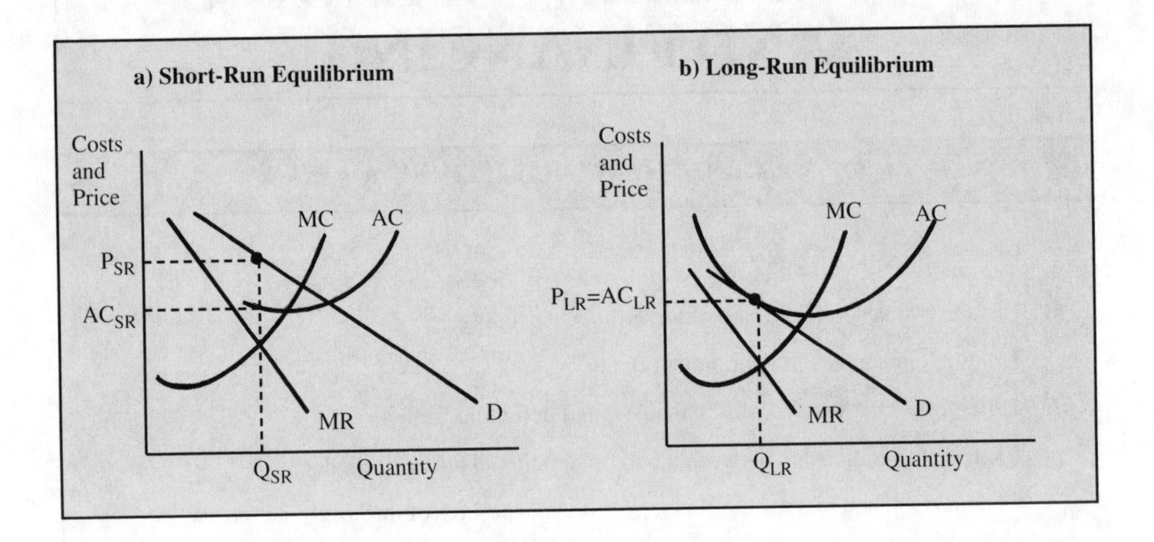

new firms will enter and the demand curve will stabilize. Panel (b) shows this final, or long-run, situation of monopolistically competitive industries.

Again, the typical firm produces an output where MC equals MR—this time Q_{LR}. It can sell this amount at a price of P_{LR}, and it faces an equivalent amount of costs of AC_{LR}. Thus, the firm makes no (economic) profit—only normal profit.

Now you can see the three economic differences from the purely competitive model. First, the price is higher for the firm in monopolistic competition. Remember that in pure competition the price is equal to the AC at the level of output where AC is at a minimum. (Refer back to Figure A6-3, page 164, to see this.) Second, the AC is higher for the firm in monopolistic competition, for its AC at the point of maximum profit is not at the lowest possible amount—as it is for purely competitive firms. Third, because the output level for the monopolistically competitive firm is not where resources are used most efficiently—that is, where AC is the lowest—the firms operate at less than the optimum level of output. Consequently, more firms are needed to produce the output that is demanded. Thus, the resources used by these additional firms are wasted, adding to the scarcity problem that already exists.

CHAPTER 10

GOVERNMENT SPENDING AND FINANCING

★★★★★ LEARNING OBJECTIVES ★★★★★

1. List the two general purposes of government spending.
2. List the four sources of government financing.
3. Differentiate between surplus, balanced, and deficit budgets.
4. Explain the relationship between a budget deficit and government debt.
5. Compare and contrast the absolute and relative measures of the size of governments.
6. Differentiate between the benefits-received and the ability-to-pay principles.
7. Explain the difference between horizontal and vertical equity.
8. Determine whether a tax is regressive, proportional, or progressive.
9. Sketch the history of the income tax.
10. Explain how the federal government determines the amount of income tax one is to pay.

TERMS

transfer payment
total outlays
user fee
total receipts
total funding
budget deficit
balanced budget
budget surplus
public debt
benefits-received principle
ability-to-pay principle
horizontal equity
vertical equity
regressive tax
proportional tax
progressive tax
taxable income
deduction
exemption
marginal tax rate

All societies face a scarcity of resources, and this forces them to establish economic systems to answer the Basic Economic Questions. One of these systems is capitalism, the basis of our economy. However, because capitalism is associated with the four problems studied in Chapter 9, governments with capitalist systems try to solve them. And that takes money (taxes). No wonder Benjamin Franklin said, "There is nothing certain but death and taxes."

PURPOSES OF GOVERNMENT SPENDING

You might wonder why governments should spend any money at all. Couldn't individuals buy everything they need from private enterprises? And couldn't scarce resources be used as efficiently as possible by using the market economic system, which requires no government intervention? Who needs the government?

★1 But recall the four classes of problems of a market economy that lead to government intervention: 1) externalities; 2) the failure of capitalism to provide social goods; 3) imperfect competition; and 4) an unequal distribution of income. To prevent these problems or to deal with their effects, governments spend money. For accounting purposes, government spending is split into two categories—first, purchases of goods and services, and second, spending on transfer payments.

Purchases of Goods and Services

In this first spending category, the government receives goods, services, or resources when it spends money. This is not the case with transfer payments, covered in the next section.

The largest share of government purchases of goods and services involves social or public goods. The federal government is involved in constructing highways, buying F-16 fighters for the Air Force, hiring toxic waste site inspectors, building flood control dams, paying for trucks for the Forest Service, and buying land for new national parks. State and local governments purchase street lights and the electricity for them, school buildings, sanitation trucks, and flowers for boulevards. Governments also buy resources to produce private goods and services that most Americans prefer to have the government produce. These include postal service, Amtrak passenger train service, and unemployment insurance. Thus, governments buy postal trucks and buildings, trains, and the like. They also hire administrators, postal clerks, secretaries, train conductors, and many more employees.

Externalities also lead governments to buy goods and services. School buildings, teachers, and library books are resources used in providing education, and education provides external benefits. Similarly, public health services pro-

> *Government, like dress, is the badge of lost innocence.*
>
> – Thomas Paine

vide immunizations, which indirectly protect everyone. Negative externalities are more common and require much government expenditure for such uses as law enforcement staff and equipment, pollution-monitoring staff and health department equipment, and staff and facilities for municipal zoning departments.

Finally, market imperfections require government spending. The U.S. Department of Justice hires lawyers, economists, accountants, and secretaries to determine if proposed mergers would significantly reduce competition. The Small Business Administration provides resources and loans to aid small businesses. Federal and state agencies watch for cases of price-fixing, false advertising, and other "unfair competition" practices and illegal discrimination in markets.

Transfer Payments

The fourth problem of a market economy, an inequality of incomes, leads government to reduce the difference in the amount of goods and services poorer and richer people can buy in a purely market economy. A redistribution of income refers to efforts to reduce income inequality.

Governments use two broad ways to redistribute income: 1) transfer payments; and 2) differential tax payments.

■ In the first case, governments give certain people money, goods, or services—called **transfer payments**. Essentially, the government transfers wealth from some people to other people. People who receive transfer payments are not required to provide anything to the government or do anything for them in return.

Generally, transfer payments involve paying money, called cash grants, to recipients. Some examples are unemployment compensation, subsidy payments to farmers, welfare payments, student grants, and Social Security payments. A second type of transfer payment is in-kind income, obtained when a person receives a good or a service rather than money. Such income includes free or partly free medical care (Title 19, for example), food (such as surplus dairy products) as well as food stamps, housing (federal and local projects), and home repairs. Sooner or later virtually everyone receives a transfer payment, but poorer people generally receive more of them.

In recent years, the word entitlements has come to be virtually synonymous with transfer payments. It stems from the belief that people are entitled to certain benefits from the government as prescribed by law, including Social Security and welfare. But, actually some transfer payments, such as business subsidies, are not classified as entitlements.

■ The second way to redistribute income is to have poorer people pay less money in taxes than richer people. Consider defense spending. Dividing the total defense budget by the entire U.S. population gives a per capita figure of around $1,120 for 1993. Yet a poor person doesn't pay anywhere near that, and rich people usually pay much more. Thus, poorer people have a somewhat greater ability

> *The point to remember is that what the government gives it must first take away.*
> – John S. Coleman

to buy goods and services for their own use with the money they "save" by not paying the full $1,120—and the rich have less.

Figure 10-1 uses two hypothetical people to show how these two income redistribution programs work. Person A has more earned income (or gross pay) than Person B by a wide margin. First, note that A pays much more taxes than B. Second, note that part of A's taxes go to B in the form of transfer payments—both cash grants and in-kind income. (Although the diagram doesn't show it, some of B's taxes return to B as transfer payments, and some also go to A as transfer payments—yet these amounts are small when compared with the transfers shown.) At the end of this process, A still is better off than B. However, the difference is not nearly as large as it would be without income redistribution programs.

Figure 10-1 How the Government Redistributes Income

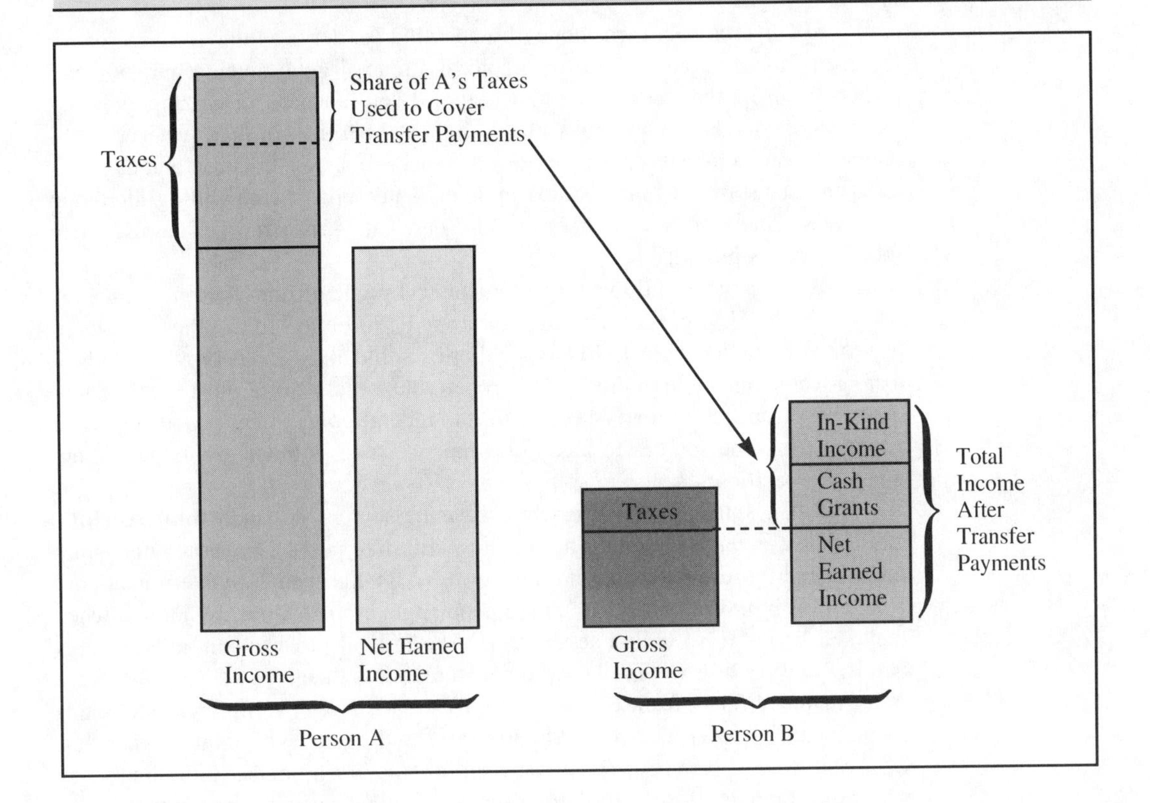

Total Outlays

Adding government spending on goods and services to the amount of transfer payments equals **total outlays**. Taken literally, this refers to the total amount of money "laid out" for all government programs combined. When you hear the term "government budget" on the news, it usually refers to total outlays.

THE FUNDING OF GOVERNMENT

If the government is to spend money, it must first get some. This section surveys major sources of its money and also addresses budget policy.

Sources of Government Finance

★2

Governments obtain money from dozens of sources, but most fit into four categories: 1) taxes; 2) earnings; 3) other governments; and 4) borrowing.

■ Tax receipts are the largest source of revenues for most governments. There are taxes on income, real estate property, estates, imports (tariffs), the dollar amount of purchases (sales taxes), and the actual amount of a good purchased (excise taxes, such as taxes on tobacco products, alcoholic beverages, and gasoline).

■ Governments earn money by charging for services they provide or for the use of their resources. For example, the federal government charges barge owners for using the locks on the Mississippi River, ranchers for grazing their cattle on federal lands, and patrons of the U.S. Postal Service for mail service. Also, publicly owned colleges charge tuition, state parks charge admission and camping fees, and state-owned liquor stores in some states profit from selling alcoholic beverages. Many of these sources of money are called **user fees**, as the users pay for the services provided.

■ Only states and local governments get money from other governments. (However, the U.S. government did get around $50 billion from other nations to pay for its costs in the 1991 Gulf War.) For example, most states provide funds to local governments. Often this is for "property tax relief," since most local financing comes from the property tax. Also, the federal government provides a wide variety of funding sources to local governments, such as block grants, which are given for specific uses.

■ The total of these first three revenue sources is called **total receipts**. Often that is enough to equal total outlays. But like people, governments sometimes spend more money than they take in. Also like people, governments are able do this by borrowing. But unlike people, governments borrow money when they sell bonds (also called securities). The federal government sells savings bonds, Treasury bills (or T-bills, which mature in less than a year), Treasury notes (with maturity dates from two years to 10 years), longer-term Treasury bonds (which mature anywhere from 10 to 30 years), and a few less common securities. State and local governments borrow by selling municipal bonds. Individuals buy government bonds, as do corporations, banks, insurance companies, mutual funds, foreigners, and even other governments. **Total funding** refers to the addition of all four sources of financing, and it equals total outlays, as shown in the box on the right side of Figure 10-2.

> *The American Republic will endure until the politicians find they can bribe the people with their own money.* – Alexis de Toqueville, 1831

Figure 10-2 Government Spending and Funding

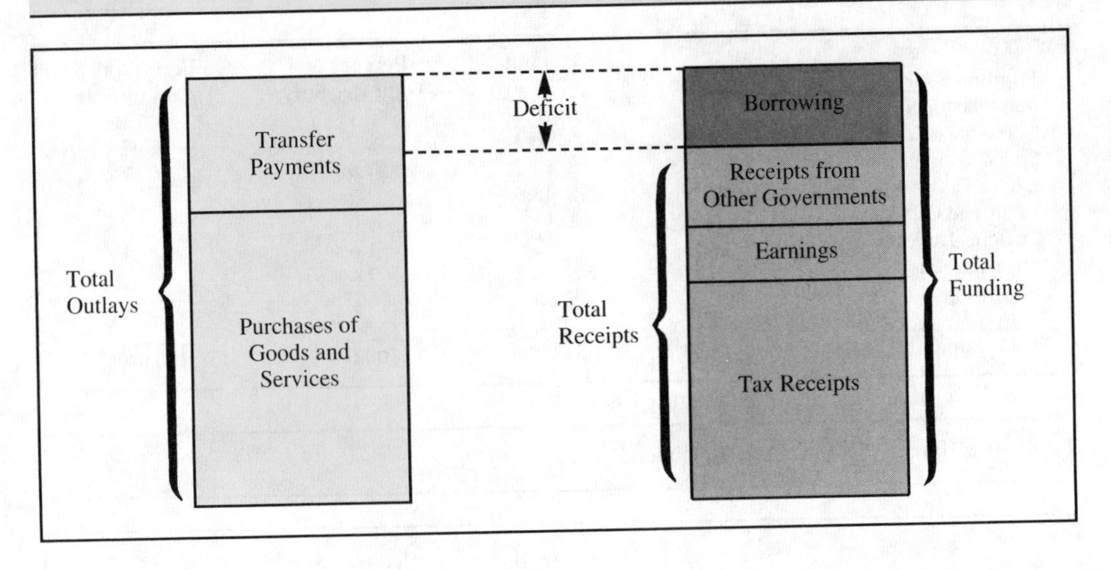

The Financing Record of Governments

The following three tables show sources of money for various governments. Table 10-1 shows that the federal government receives the largest single amount of money from the individual income tax, followed by F.I.C.A. taxes (Social Security taxes). The dollar amounts collected are shown in the second column and the share of total receipts in the third column. The last column shows the percentage that each funding source contributes to the federal budget.

The sources of funding for all 50 states combined are shown in Table 10-2. Revenue from other governments, especially the federal government, contributes the largest single source of money. Sales taxes and individual income taxes are usually next in the order of importance. Several states have no income tax and some have no sales tax.

Table 10-3 lists the sources of revenue for all U.S. city governments combined. It does not include other local governments, such as counties, townships, villages, and school districts. Money coming from other governments is the largest single source of funding for most cities. The largest single tax is usually the property tax—most often just for real estate property.

> *Everything now seems to be under federal control except the national debt and the budget.*
> – Bob Goddard

Table 10-1 Federal Financing for Fiscal Year 1992

Funding Source	Amount (in billions)	Percent of Total Receipts	Percent of Total Funding
Individual Income Tax	$476.1	43.7%	34.5%
Corporate Income Tax	$100.3	9.2%	7.3%
Social Insurance	$413.2	37.9%	29.9%
Excise Tax	$ 45.6	4.2%	3.3%
Estate and Gift Tax	$ 11.1	1.0%	0.8%
Customs Duties	$ 17.4	1.6%	1.3%
Miscellaneous	$ 26.5	2.4%	1.9%
Borrowing	$290.3	—	21.0%
Total Funding/Outlays	**$1380.5**	**100.0%**	**100.0%**

Source: *Federal Reserve Bulletin,* August 1993

Table 10-2 Financing of State Governments in 1990

Funding Source	Amount (in billions)	Percent of Total Funding
Individual Income Tax	$ 96.1	14.3%
Corporate Income Tax	$ 21.8	3.2%
Excise Tax	$ 28.1	4.2%
Sales Tax	$ 99.7	14.8%
Property Tax	$ 5.8	0.8%
Other Taxes	$ 19.3	2.9%
Licenses	$ 18.8	2.8%
Charges and Miscellaneous	$ 90.6	13.5%
Revenue from Other Governments	$126.3	18.8%
Other Sources	$125.6	18.7%
Borrowing	$ 40.5	6.0%
Total Funding/Outlays	**$672.6**	**100.0%**

Source: *The Statistical Abstract of the United States,* 1993

Table 10-3 Financing of Cities, 1990

Funding Source	Amount (in billions)	Percent of Total Funding
Property Tax	$ 35.0	17.6%
Sales Tax	$ 19.2	9.6%
Other Taxes	$ 14.6	7.3%
Revenue from Other Governments	$ 45.3	22.8%
Charges and Miscellaneous	$ 44.2	22.3%
Other Sources	$ 40.5	20.4%
Total Funding	**$198.8**	**100.0%**

Source: *The Statistical Abstract of the United States,* 1993

Combining Spending and Funding

★3 In Figure 10-2 the amount of money borrowed equals the amount of the deficit, shown as the distance between the dotted lines connecting the two box diagrams. A **budget deficit** equals the excess of total outlays over total receipts in a fiscal period (a year for most governments). A government finances a deficit by selling bonds (securities). Do not think the deficit is caused by transfer payments just because they are shown as the top part of the total outlays in the box on the left side of Figure 10-2. Spending for goods and services are equally important in creating the deficit.

When total outlays equal total receipts, the government has a **balanced budget**. Laws require many local and state governments to balance their budgets, and there is much support for a constitutional amendment to force the federal government to do so. Thomas Jefferson proposed an even stronger measure in 1798 that would have prohibited the federal government from borrowing money. Current proposals for amendments usually allow for special situations where borrowing and deficits could occur.

If a government has more total receipts than total outlays, the difference is a **budget surplus**. The government can use this money to pay off any debt incurred in earlier years, or it can save it for use in future years. Prolonged surpluses generally lead to either increased spending or lower tax rates.

Deficits and Debt

Many people confuse the words deficit and debt. Deficit refers to a shortfall of total receipts compared with total outlays over a *period of time,* usually a year. Debt refers to how much the government *owes* at some *point in time.* However, the federal government has several accounting methods that define debt differently. The most commonly used concept is the **public debt** (often called the national debt), which covers only the borrowing of the U.S. Treasury. It excludes borrowing by independent federal government agencies, such as the Tennessee Valley Authority and Farm Credit Services. Congress sets a maximum limit on the public debt, and it periodically raises the limit because of continuing deficits.

The public debt equals the value of all outstanding government securities—all the Treasury bonds, bills, and notes not yet "cashed in" or matured. Table 10-4 shows the amount of the various federal securities outstanding, as well as each one's share of the total.

★4 The level of the public debt can be found by adding all the deficits of past years and then subtracting all past surpluses from that amount. Thus, the effect of a budget deficit is to increase the public debt, while a budget surplus decreases the debt.

The public debt can be viewed in two ways. First, the *gross* public debt is the total amount of money the federal government borrowed from all sources. But around one-fourth of such borrowing is from various government agencies and branches, such as the Federal Reserve Banks and the Social Security Administration. Second, economists often prefer to focus on the *net* public debt, which counts only the debt held by private individuals and firms.

Table 10-4 Interest-Bearing Public Debt of the Federal Government, 1992

Debt Instrument	Amount Outstanding (in billions)	Percent of Total Debt
Treasury Bills	$ 657.7	15.8%
Treasury Notes	$1608.9	38.5%
Treasury Bonds	$ 472.5	11.3%
U.S. Savings Bonds	$ 135.9	3.3%
Other Non-Marketable Securities	$1302.0	31.1%
Total Gross Public Debt	**$4,177.0**	**100.0%**

Source: *Federal Reserve Bulletin,* August 1993

The public debt is largely an internal debt, which means Americans owe the debt largely to other Americans. But two points must be made here. First, only some Americans own the debt (that is, they hold bonds), so paying it off would require a substantial adjustment in individual financial positions. Money would flow from those without bonds to those with bonds. Second, the debt is more of an external debt than it used to be. That means Americans owe a growing share of it to foreigners, who in recent years used money from their trade surpluses with the United States to buy U.S. Government securities.

U.S. Deficits and the Public Debt

Figure 10-3 shows U.S. budget deficits and surpluses since 1960. There were budget surpluses in only two of these years, 1960 and 1969. In all other

Table 10-5 Ownership of the Gross Public Debt, 1992

Holders of Securities	Amount (billions)	Percent of Total
U.S. Government Agencies and Trust Funds	$1,047.8	24.1%
Federal Reserve Banks	$ 302.5	7.2%
State and Local Governments	$ 520.3	12.5%
Individuals	$ 263.9	6.3%
Commercial Banks	$ 292.0	7.0%
Money Market Funds	$ 80.6	1.9%
Insurance Companies	$ 183.0	4.4%
Other Corporations	$ 192.5	4.6%
Foreign	$ 512.5	13.3%
Miscellaneous	$ 781.9	18.7%
Total	$4,177.0	100.0%

Source: *Federal Reserve Bulletin,* August 1993

Figure 10-3 Federal Budget Deficits and Surpluses Since 1960

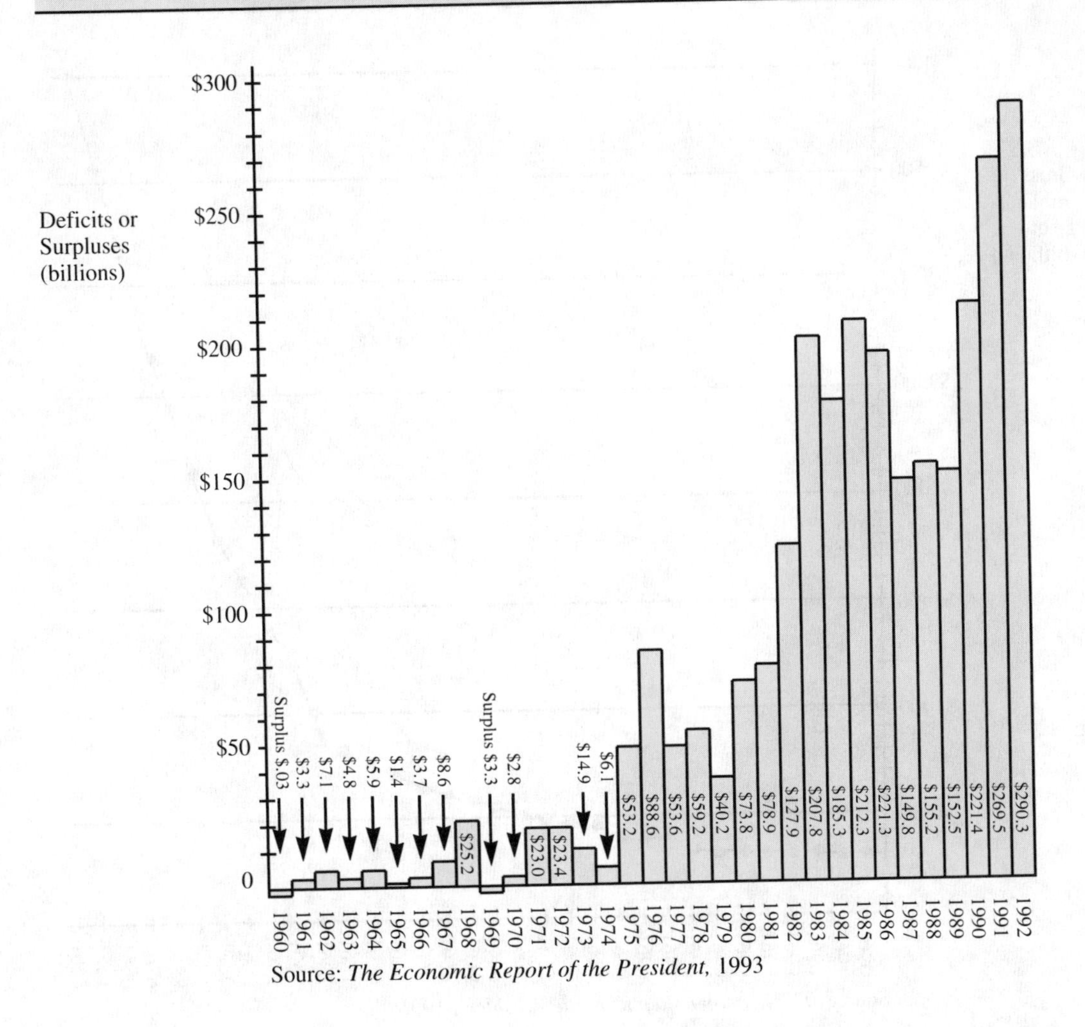

Source: *The Economic Report of the President*, 1993

years there were deficits, and they were especially large since the 1980s. Figure 10-4 indicates that as deficits rose sharply since the 1980s, the public debt rose, too.

Table 10-5 shows the recent status of the gross public debt and who owns that debt—that is, who holds those securities. It is now over $4 trillion, which means each U.S. citizen's share of it is approaching $16,000.

The only time the federal government did *not* have a debt was in 1835, when $37 million was in the treasury. Henry Clay quickly pushed through a bill that President Jackson signed, giving the money to the states.

> *A national debt, if it is not excessive, will be to us a national blessing.*
>
> – Alexander Hamilton

Figure 10-4 The Public Debt Since 1960

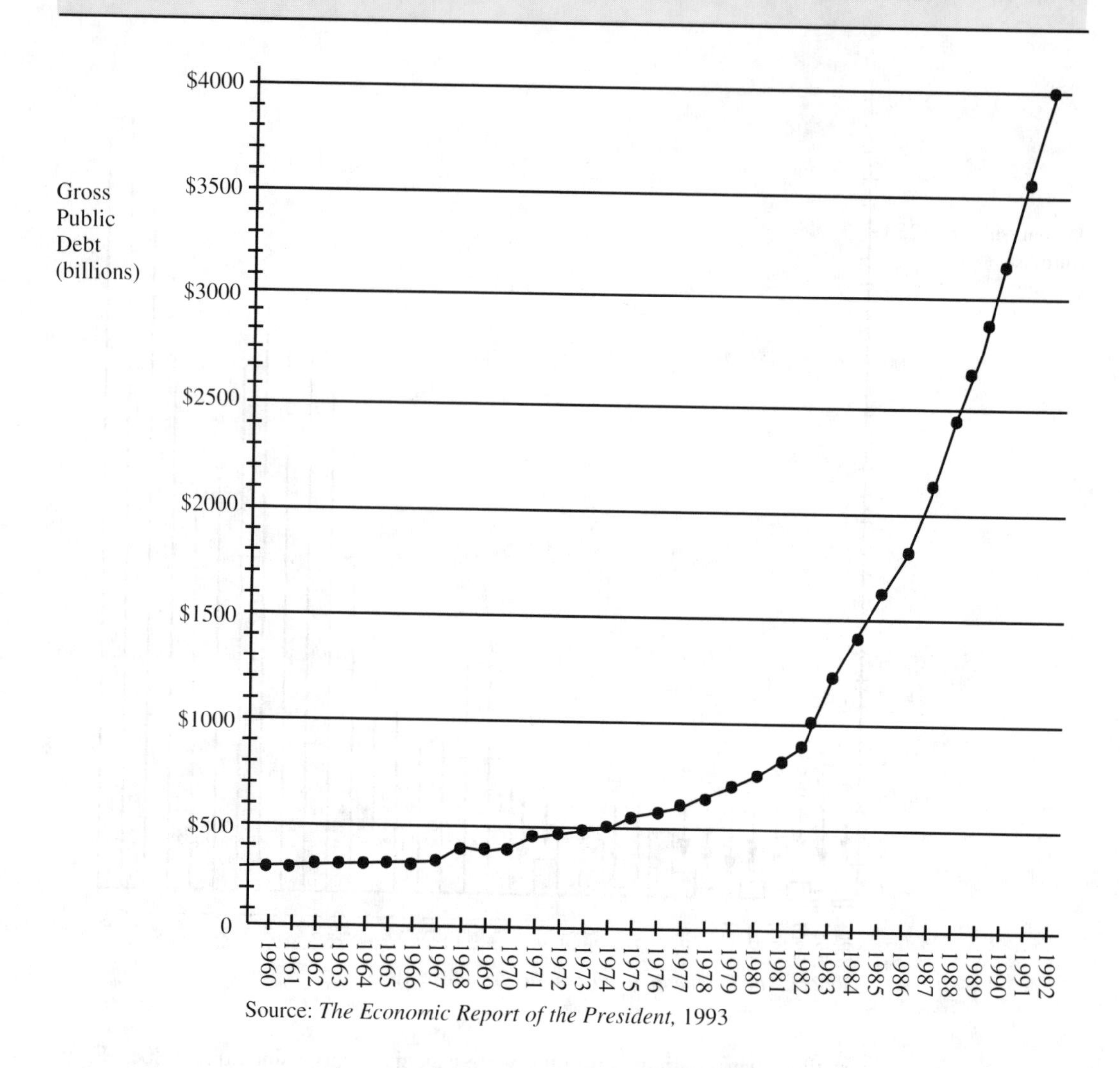

Source: *The Economic Report of the President,* 1993

THE SIZE OF GOVERNMENT

No one doubts that government plays a major role in the economy. In this section, we'll first study several ways to measure that role and then the actual data on government activity in recent periods.

Measuring the Size of Government

Three common measures of the size of government are: 1) the number of government employees; 2) the amount of spending the government does (this may include transfer payments); and 3) the amount of taxes collected.

But such measures can be misleading if the size of government is compared over long periods. Over time the population grows, along with living standards, prices, and several other important variables. Obviously, the various measures of government grow along with these other variables. This point tends to be misunderstood by people who complain that government has grown too much.

★5

To avoid this misleading interpretation, the three measures of government are viewed in two ways: the absolute approach and the relative approach. Absolute measures of government include: 1) the *number* of government employees; and 2) the *dollar amounts* of either spending or taxes. Relative measures of government include: 1) the *share* of the work force working for the government; 2) government spending and taxes as a *share* of some measure of the nation's income, such as the GDP (gross domestic product). These relative measures help determine if the government is getting "out of balance" with other sectors of the economy.

Table 10-6 shows both absolute and relative measures of all civilian government employment. The number of employees (including part-timers) gives an absolute measure, and the percentage of total employment gives a relative measure.

Government Spending and Taxes

The next few tables and charts combine the other two methods of measuring government's size—spending and taxes. Figure 10-5 shows a trend of increased involvement in the economy by the federal government since 1960, when total outlays were around 18 percent of GDP. Total outlays increased to around 22 to 24 percent of GDP by the 1980s, and to over 25 percent by the 1990s. In the late 1920s, the figure was only three percent.

The line for total receipts shows they have stayed between 18 and 20 percent since the early 1960s. Using this measure of government, you might conclude that the government has not grown since the 1960s. But a better measure of the government's importance in the economy is what it is *spending* (basically,

Table 10-6 Government Employment in Absolute and Relative Terms

	Number of Civilian Employees (in thousands)				Percent of Total Civilian Employment		
Year	Federal	State & Local	Combined	Year	Fiscal	State & Local	Combined
1950	2,117	4,285	6,402	1950	3.6%	7.3%	10.9%
1960	2,421	6,387	8,808	1960	3.7%	9.7%	13.4%
1970	2,881	10,147	13,028	1970	3.7%	12.9%	16.6%
1980	2,898	13,315	16,213	1980	2.9%	13.4%	16.3%
1985	3,021	13,669	16,690	1985	2.8%	12.8%	15.6%
1990	3,105	15,263	18,368	1990	2.6%	12.9%	15.5%

Source: *The Statistical Abstract of the United States*, 1993

Figure 10-5 Federal Government Outlays and Receipts as a Percent of GDP

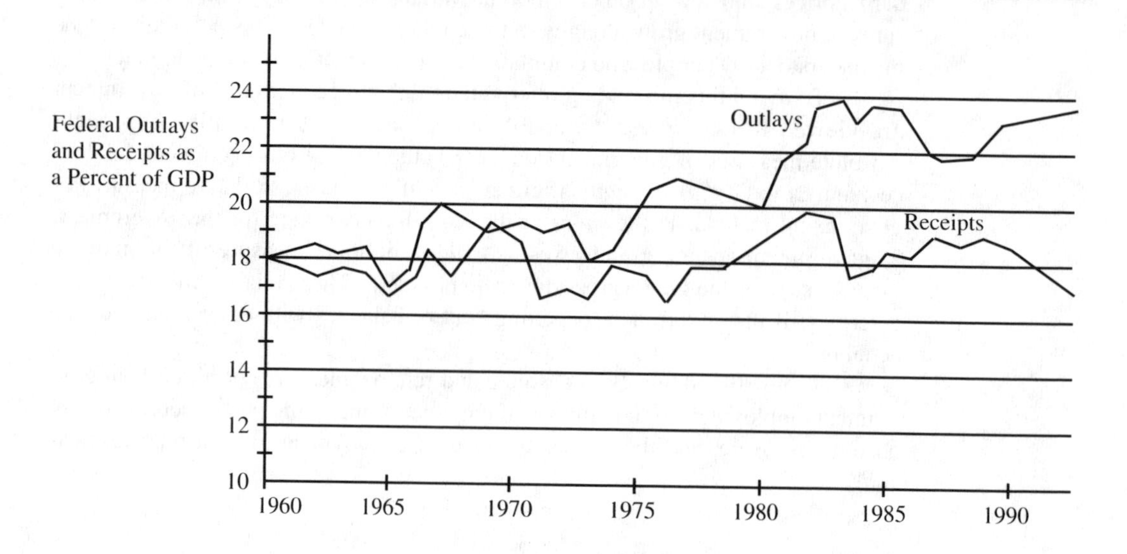

how much of society's resources it impacts). It can increase its spending with the same total receipts by borrowing. The divergence of the two lines on the chart indeed implies growing budget deficits, especially since the 1970s.

Table 10-7, showing total outlays, also considers state and local spending as well as federal spending since 1929. The left side of the table gives dollar

Table 10-7 Total Outlays of the Federal, State & Local, and All Governments Combined

	Total Outlays (in billions)			**Total Outlays as a Percent of GDP**			
Year	Federal	State & Local	All Governments	Federal	State & Local	All Governments	GDP (billions)
1929	$ 2.7	$ 7.8	$ 10.3	2.6%	7.5%	9.9%	$ 103.9
1940	$ 10.0	$ 9.3	$ 18.5	10.0%	9.3%	18.4%	$ 100.4
1950	$ 41.2	$ 22.5	$ 61.4	14.3%	7.8%	21.3%	$ 288.3
1960	$ 93.9	$ 49.9	$ 137.3	18.2%	9.7%	26.6%	$ 515.3
1970	$ 207.8	$134.0	$ 317.4	20.5%	13.2%	31.3%	$1015.5
1980	$ 615.1	$432.3	$1047.4	22.5%	15.8%	38.3%	$2732.0
1985	$ 984.9	$656.2	$1641.1	24.6%	16.4%	41.0%	$3998.1
1990	$1270.1	$972.7	$2242.8	23.0%	17.6%	40.6%	$5524.5
1991	$1323.0	____	____	23.3%	____	____	$5677.5
1992	$1380.7	____	____	23.2%	____	____	$5950.7
1993	____	____	____	____	____	____	____

Source: *Statistical Abstract of the United States,* 1993

amounts of spending—an absolute measure. The right side gives spending as percentages of GDP—a relative measure of government's size. (The columns for all governments combined do not add up to the columns of the federal plus the state and local combination. This is because federal grants-in-aid money sent to states is excluded from total spending so that the money is not counted twice.)

The table shows some interesting points. Notice the figure for federal spending in 1929, $2.7 billion. That figure, which covered an entire *year* in 1929, was less than the amount that the United States spent *each day* in 1993. Of course, because of inflation's effect on the dollar's purchasing power, these dollars were not the same. Still, the increase is extraordinarily large. The United States now spends around $47,000 *every second.* In George Washington's administration, it took 12 *days* to spend the same amount.

Second, notice that until the 1930s the federal government spent less money than all state and local governments combined. The current federal dominance does not show any sign of reversing.

The second to the last column in Table 10-7 reveals the percentage of GDP spent by all governments combined. This figure rose from 9.9 percent in 1929 to more than 40 percent today. More than any other measure of government's size, this column shows why government takes a much larger "bite" from paychecks today than in the past.

The Federal Budget

Table 10-8 divides total outlays of the United States into 18 categories or "functions." Congress acts upon most of these functions separately when formulating the budget for the next fiscal year, which extends from October 1 to September 30. For example, Congress acts on separate transportation and defense budget bills. The president initially proposes the budget to Congress around February 1, giving Congress until October 1 to pass it for the president's signature.

National defense recently surrendered its hold on first place in federal spending to Social Security/Medicare. The third largest item, interest on the national debt, grew rapidly in recent years. This was due to the rapid escalation in the public debt, coupled with relatively high interest rates in the 1970s and 1980s. The last major item in the budget is income security. This includes federal employee retirement programs, housing and food assistance for the poor, and unemployment compensation.

State and Local Government Budgets

Federal and state governments are involved in quite different areas of the economy. Generally, the major concern of states is education. Table 10-9 shows that over one-third of state spending goes toward education, with public welfare holding second place at about one-fifth of total outlays. Highways, health, and hospitals are other major areas of state spending.

Table 10-8 Federal Budget, Fiscal Year 1993

Function	Amount (billions)	Percent of Total Outlays
National Defense	$ 298.4	21.5%
International Affairs	$ 16.1	1.2%
Income Security	$ 197.9	14.2%
Health	$ 89.6	6.5%
Social Security and Medicare	$ 406.6	29.3%
Veterans Benefits and Services	$ 34.1	2.5%
Education, Employment, and Social Services	$ 45.2	3.3%
Commerce and Housing Credit	$ 9.8	0.7%
Transportation	$ 33.8	2.5%
Natural Resources and Environment	$ 20.0	1.5%
Energy	$ 4.5	0.3%
Community and Regional Development	$ 7.9	0.6%
Agriculture	$ 15.0	1.1%
Interest on the National Debt	$ 199.4	14.4%
Science, Space, and Technology	$ 16.4	1.2%
General Government	$ 12.9	1.0%
Administration of Justice	$ 14.5	1.1%
Offsetting Receipts	(–)$ 39.3	(–)2.9%
Total Outlays	$1,380.7	100.0%
Total Receipts	$1,090.5	
Deficit	$ 290.2	

Source: *Statistical Abstract of the United States,* 1993

Table 10-9 State Government General-Purpose Expenditures, 1990

Function or Purpose	Amount (billions)	Percent of General Expenditure
Education	$184.9	31.2%
Public Welfare	$105.0	17.7%
Highways	$ 44.2	7.5%
Health and Hospitals	$ 42.7	7.2%
General Control and Administration	$ 8.4	1.4%
Corrections	$ 17.3	2.9%
Natural Resources	$ 9.9	1.7%
Police Protection	$ 5.2	0.9%
Employment Security	$ 3.0	0.5%
Housing and Community Development	$ 2.9	0.5%
Miscellaneous	$168.7	28.5%
Total (General Expenditure)	**$592.0**	**100.0%**

Source: *Statistical Abstract of the United States,* 1993

DETERMINING WHO SHOULD PAY THE TAXES

After citizens decide that their government should spend money to solve economic problems, they must decide how much of the total outlays each person should pay for. This section introduces major factors in that decision.

Principles of Taxation

One way to decide each person's tax is to divide the budget by the population served by that government. That amount is what each person would owe, even children and retired people. For example, the roughly $1,500 billion federal budget would be spread evenly over roughly 260 million Americans—about $5,770 a person. Obviously, no one would suggest such a system, and governments actually charge each person a *different* level of taxes. To do this, a government must establish taxes that are based on specified ways that people differ from each other. Such a basis is called a taxing principle.

★6 Characteristics in which people differ include age, income, value of real estate owned, amount of spending per year, number of children, how often they use government services, and the amount of money they give to charity. These characteristics are used in one or the other of the two most common taxing principles: 1) the benefits-received principle; and 2) the ability-to-pay principle.

■ The first taxing principle is the **benefits-received principle**. With this principle, the more services (benefits) you receive from the government, the more you must pay in taxes, regardless of your income, wealth, or age. This is how people pay for goods and services purchased from private businesses. For example, everyone pays the same price for a loaf of bread, whether poor or rich, young or old.

User fees are based on this principle, and some examples are: bridge tolls; tuition (the more classes you take, the more you pay); stamps (the more letters you send, the more postage you pay); and the gasoline tax (the more you use the roads, the more gasoline you buy and taxes you pay).

■ Yet, most people believe that payment for most of the services that governments provide should not be based on the benefits-received principle. They believe that taxes should be levied (charged) with the **ability-to-pay principle**. Then people who are more "able to pay" taxes would pay more than those who are less able. This principle is more difficult to implement, for how is "ability to pay" determined?

That ability could be indicated by your income. The more you earn, the more taxes you should be able to pay. Or wealth could indicate that ability, or some part of your wealth, such as the value of real estate. Of course, governments use both of these—income in the income tax and wealth in the property tax. Governments also use other factors to determine ability to pay and, in turn, to adjust taxes of certain people. The number of your dependents, for example, influences your income taxes.

Seeking Equity in a Tax System

★7

Equity in taxation, meaning the fairness in the way taxes are levied, is an important objective of tax-bill writers. Their goal is a tax system that treats all taxpayers equally (equitably). A tax has **horizontal equity** when taxpayers in the same general economic situation (income, wealth, needs) pay about the same amount in taxes. A tax achieves **vertical equity** when taxpayers in higher economic positions pay more taxes.

But when a government tries to determine *what* to equalize, it runs into a problem. There are three major items or tax payment criteria that tax-bill writers could equalize: 1) dollars paid in taxes; 2) the percentage of income paid in taxes; and 3) the cost or burden of paying taxes. The problem is that it is impossible to equalize more than one of these at a time with any tax.

Any parents of a clever, calculating child will recognize this problem. Suppose the Larsons have two children: Shawn, age eight, who weighs 60 pounds; and Jean, age five, who weighs 40 pounds. If Grandma Larson sends a 100-piece bag of candy for the kids to share, how does Mom divide the 100 pieces of candy "fairly"? Most kids (and parents) would say each should get half, or 50 pieces.

Luckily for most parents, virtually all kids accept that—but not Shawn. He argues, "Seeing that I weigh 60 pounds, when you give me 50 pieces, I get only 0.83 pieces of candy for each pound of my body (50 pieces ÷ 60 pounds). But Jean gets 1.25 pieces for each of her pounds (50 pieces ÷ 40 pounds). That's not fair because 1.25 is more than 0.83. I should get more candy so that our 'candy-per-pound' amounts are equal. If you give me 60 pieces and Jean 40 pieces, we'll each get one piece per pound of body weight—and I'll be happy." (How happy do you suppose *Jean* will be?)

Figure 10-6 illustrates a similar impossibility of satisfying every taxpayer. One taxpayer earns only $10,000 per year, while another earns $30,000 per year. Suppose the tax considered is the income tax. A different tax payment criterion is equalized in each of three cases.

■ In the first case, each taxpayer pays the same dollar amount, $2,000. The blue boxes beside the $2,000, connected by dotted lines, show this equality graphically. Such a tax system satisfies people who believe that if everyone gets the same amount of goods and services from the government, everyone should pay the same number of tax dollars (in other words, the benefits-received principle).

However, the poorer person pays 20 percent of income in taxes, while the other person pays only 6.7 percent, indicated by the difference in box sizes. Also, there is a difference in the cost or burden of paying taxes—the *opportunity* cost, that is. That burden is found by asking how each taxpayer *would have* spent the money if the taxes did *not* have to be paid. A poor person would obviously use the money to buy $2,000 worth of food, shelter, clothing, and the like—necessities. A typical person earning $30,000 would already have life's basic needs covered, so that person could spend the $2,000 on some luxuries, perhaps a summer vacation. According to the law of diminishing marginal utility of income, $2,000 of luxuries give less satisfaction than $2,000 of necessities. (This law is essentially an extension of the law of diminishing marginal utility covered in Chapter 16,

Figure 10-6 Achieving Equity in Taxation by Equalizing Different Criteria

Tax Payment Criteria Used	Tax Payment Criteria	Taxpayer With an Income of $10,000	Taxpayer With an Income of $30,000
Equal Dollar Amounts Paid in Taxes	Taxes Paid →	$2,000	$2,000
	Percent of Income Paid in Taxes →	20%	6.7%
	The Cost or the Burden of Taxes →	Necessities Forgone	Some Luxuries Forgone
Equal Percentages of Income Paid in Taxes	Taxes Paid →	$2,000	$6,000
	Percent of Income Paid in Taxes →	20%	20%
	The Cost or the Burden of Taxes →	Necessities Forgone	More Luxuries Forgone
Equal Cost or Burdens of Paying Taxes	Taxes Paid →	$2,000	$9,000
	Percent of Income Paid in Taxes →	20%	30%
	The Cost or the Burden of Taxes →	Necessities Forgone	Many Luxuries Forgone

page 383.) Thus, the box size for the taxpayer with a $30,000 income is smaller.

■ The second case satisfies those who believe that everyone should pay an equal percentage of income in taxes. Such a tax is commonly called a flat tax (because the *rate* is constant or "flat"). If the poorer taxpayer still pays $2,000 in taxes, or 20 percent of income, the $30,000-income taxpayer needs a tax bill of $6,000 to have a similar 20 percent rate. The dotted lines between the boxes, which signify equality, shift down to the middle set of boxes, shaded blue. But now the top set must be unequal. Now those people who want to equalize *taxes paid* will be unhappy. The bottom set also is still unequal. That's because although $6,000 involves more lost satisfaction than $2,000, it still comes from luxuries, and it still falls short of the benefits provided by $2,000 of necessities.

■ In the last case, these costs or burdens of paying taxes are finally equalized. The $9,000 in taxes cut so deeply into the middle-class taxpayer's "luxury budget" that this person finally gives up as much satisfaction as the poor person who gives up $2,000 of necessities. Thus, the last set of boxes, shaded blue, is equal. The $9,000 paid by the middle-class taxpayer results in a 30 percent tax rate. But now both the people who want an equal tax *rate* and those who want equal tax *payments* are unhappy.

With such different viewpoints on what is fair, it's no wonder many people say taxes are "unfair." And because such viewpoints are value judgments, everyone is right—even though they disagree.

★8 A common way of determining the fairness of a tax is to determine if it is regressive, proportional, or progressive. Figure 10-7 illustrates these three types of taxes. With a **regressive tax**, the percent of income paid in taxes decreases (regresses) as income rises. That is, poorer people pay a higher percentage of their incomes in taxes than richer people. A **proportional tax** takes the same percentage or proportion of everyone's income. A **progressive tax** takes a larger percentage of the incomes of higher-income taxpayers.

Consider again the two taxpayers from the previous example, with incomes of $10,000 and $30,000. The figures below the diagrams give an example of each of the three types of taxes. In the first case, showing a regressive tax, the percentage of income paid in taxes drops from 20 percent for the poorer taxpayer to 10 percent for the one earning $30,000. The pie charts show this effect graphically. The inner circle represents the $10,000 income. The slice of that income paid in taxes, one-fifth or 20 percent, is denoted by the wavy area. The outer circle represents $30,000 of income, and someone with such an income has a narrower slice or bite taken in taxes, as the dotted area indicates. However, the total dotted area is greater than the wavy part of the diagram, indicating that the taxpayer who earns $30,000 pays more *dollars* in taxes, in spite of a smaller tax *rate*.

With a proportional tax, shown in the center, both taxpayers have the same angle of "take" by the government. However, the higher-income person pays triple the number of tax dollars. In the progressive case on the right, the angles are again unequal, but now the higher-income taxpayer pays a larger percentage of income in taxes than the person with a lower income.

User fees and excise taxes are usually regressive because rich people generally don't pay much more in *dollar amounts* for such taxes than lower income groups. A general sales tax, which covers most items purchased, is also regressive. Even though everyone pays the same percentage of the *purchase price* in sales taxes, the percentage of *income* taken by the tax falls as income rises. That is because poor people usually spend all of their incomes, but people with higher incomes save some of theirs. Thus, they avoid sales taxes on that part of their incomes that is not spent. To deal with this regressiveness problem, many states have selective sales taxes, which do not tax food and other necessities. This makes the tax less regressive because now a large part of a poor person's income

Figure 10-7 Regressive, Proportional, and Progressive Taxes

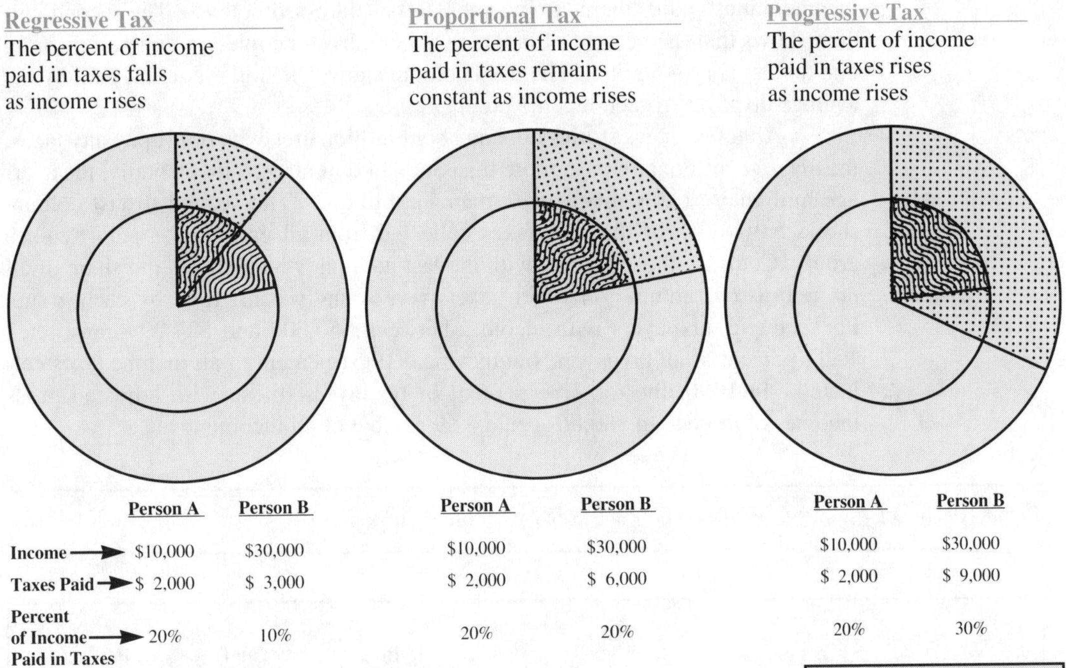

Note: a) The area or size of each circle indicates each person's level of income.
b) The angle of the "slice" of each person's income indicates the *percent of income* paid into this tax.
c) The area *of that "slice"* indicates *the dollar amount* of taxes each person pays.

Taxes Paid by Person A | Taxes Paid by Person B

(the part used to buy necessities) is not taxed.

The only specific tax that is proportional is the F.I.C.A. tax, which supports Social Security and Medicare. Yet it is only proportional up to a certain level of income—$57,600 for 1993, $__________ for 1994, and $__________ for 1995. The tax rate for support of the retirement fund (which people know as "social security") plus the disability income fund is 5.20%. No one pays that tax on any income in excess of the maximum listed. However, the Medicare tax rate is 1.45 percent of incomes extending to $135,000. Essentially, then, the F.I.C.A. tax becomes regressive at income levels higher than these maximum taxed levels.

> *Don't tax you. Don't tax me. Tax that fella behind the tree.*
> – Senator Russell Long

The federal income tax is the best example of a progressive tax. Table 10-10 shows some interesting income tax data. The first column divides taxpayers into various income categories, based on adjusted gross income (equal to gross income minus "adjustments to income," to be addressed below). The second column shows that the percent of income paid climbs as people get richer, indicating that the tax is progressive. The third column shows the dollar amount paid by the average taxpayer in each income group.

Although news stories abound about millionaires who don't pay any taxes, the *average* millionaire pays more than $600,000 in taxes. (Incidentally, the average millionaire earns much *more* than $1 million.) The second to last column shows how much of the total taxes collected from all groups was paid by each group. Compare those figures with the last column, which shows the share of all tax returns (for returns on which taxes were actually paid) filed by each group. For example, taxpayers with incomes between $50,000 and $74,999 constituted 12.17 percent of all taxpayers, but they paid 19.51 percent of all income taxes collected. In 1990, the top five percent of taxpayers (those with adjusted gross incomes of more than $80,867) paid 42.9 percent of all income taxes.

Table 10-10 Payment of Federal Income Taxes by Income Class, 1990

Income Class (as measured by adjusted gross income)	Tax as a Percent of Adjusted Gross Income	Average Taxes Paid per Taxpayer	Combined Taxes Paid by All Taxpayers (billions)	Percent of Total Income Tax Receipts Paid by Income Class	Percent of Total Tax Returns Filed by Income Class
Less than $1,000	N.A.	$ 120	$0.2	0.02%	0.81%
$1,000-$2,999	4.7%	$ 89	$0.2	0.04%	2.24%
$3,000-$4,999	4.0%	$ 161	$0.3	0.08%	2.41%
$5,000-$6,999	3.6%	$ 219	$0.8	0.17%	3.87%
$7,000-$8,999	5.3%	$ 419	$1.5	0.34%	4.02%
$9,000-$10,999	6.3%	$ 626	$2.3	0.52%	4.10%
$11,000-$12,999	6.8%	$ 818	$3.2	0.71%	4.33%
$13,000-$14,999	7.2%	$ 1,012	$4.1	0.92%	4.54%
$15,000-$16,999	7.3%	$ 1,167	$4.8	1.08%	4.62%
$17,000-$18,999	7.6%	$ 1,376	$6.1	1.36%	4.92%
$19,000-$21,999	8.4%	$ 1,720	$10.6	2.37%	6.87%
$22,000-$24,999	8.9%	$ 2,085	$11.3	2.52%	5.95%
$25,000-$29,999	9.7%	$ 2,653	$20.6	4.60%	8.63%
$30,000-$39,999	10.7%	$ 3,708	$45.3	10.13%	13.54%
$40,000-$49,999	11.4%	$ 5,090	$44.9	10.03%	9.80%
$50,000-$74,999	13.3%	$ 7,986	$87.2	19.51%	12.17%
$75,000-$99,999	15.9%	$ 13,563	$44.4	9.92%	3.65%
$100,000-$199,999	19.0%	$ 24,865	$57.8	12.94%	2.59%
$200,000-$499,999	23.1%	$ 67,544	$43.4	9.71%	0.20%
$500,000-$999,999	24.1%	$161,017	$20.9	4.68%	0.15%
$1,000,000 or more	24.2%	$616,495	$37.3	8.35%	0.07%
			$447.2	100.0%	100.0%

Source: *Statistics of Income Bulletin,* Summer 1992, Internal Revenue Service

THE INCOME TAX

The federal income tax is the largest single tax, and this section briefly outlines its history and structure.

History of the Income Tax

★9 The federal income tax first appeared with the Revenue Act of 1861, when money was needed for the Civil War. Amended in 1862, it taxed incomes between $600 and $10,000 at three percent, and higher incomes at five percent. It ended in 1872 as revenue needs dropped.

Congress enacted another income tax in 1894, but the Supreme Court declared it unconstitutional because it was not apportioned according to the population in each state. But the idea survived, and in 1913 the 16th amendment to the Constitution led to the enactment of the modern income tax, which began in 1916. However, its early effect was negligible, for by 1918 only five percent of income earners paid any income tax. The number of taxpayers rose from four million to 43 million during World War II. Withholding of taxes by employers began in 1943 to ensure payment of a growing tax liability.

The income tax, especially tax rates, changed significantly in the last several decades. The Economic Recovery Tax Act of 1981 was designed to stimulate economic growth through major cuts in tax rates. The Tax Reform Act of 1986 had two primary goals: 1) a tax that was much less complicated to calculate; and 2) substantial rate cuts that would encourage economic activity—especially entrepreneurial activity.

Structure of the Income Tax

★10 The term "income tax" is a misnomer because only a part of your income is taxed, and that amount is called **taxable income**. To arrive at taxable income, you must first subtract from your total income any "adjustments to income" (such as alimony payments, IRA contributions, and penalties for early withdrawal of savings from a CD) to get your adjusted gross income. (See IRS Form 1040 for more specifics.)

Next, your **deductions** are subtracted from this figure. You can determine your deductions in one of two ways: 1) using the standard deduction; or 2) itemizing deductions. Most people take the standard deduction, which for 1992 was $6,000 for a married couple and $3,600 for a single taxpayer. The corresponding figures for 1993 were $______________ and $______________, and for 1994, $__________ and $__________. Other people itemize deductions if they can exceed the standard figure. This involves adding up a long series of items, including state and local taxes (excluding sales taxes), charitable contributions, medical expenses, casualty and theft losses, and interest on a home mortgage or home-equity loan.

Finally, **exemptions** are subtracted. One exemption is given for each taxpayer and for each of the taxpayer's dependents. Exemptions rise each year, based upon the inflation rate. For 1992 they were $2,300, for 1993 $_________, and for 1994 $__________. After the exemptions are subtracted, the remainder is taxable income.

To ensure that the income tax is progressive, taxable income is not all taxed at the same rate. Taxable income is divided into categories, called brackets. Each bracket has its own tax rate, and higher brackets (those "holding" your higher levels of income) have higher rates. The **marginal tax rate** is the percent of an extra dollar earned that you would then pay in taxes. When people say they are "in" a certain tax bracket, they are referring to the marginal tax rate. Do not confuse this rate with the *average tax rate,* which is the percentage of *all* income earned, on average, that you pay in taxes. This is found by dividing your income taxes by your total income and expressing it as a percentage.

There are currently five income tax brackets. The tax rates on income in those brackets are 15, 28, 31, 36 and 39.6 percent.

The hardest thing in the world to understand is the income tax.

– Albert Einstein

The income tax has made more liars out of the American people than golf has. Even when you make a tax form out on the level, you don't know when it's through, if you are a crook or a martyr.

– Will Rogers

The art of taxation consists in so plucking the goose as to get the most feathers with the least hissing.

– Jean Baptiste Colbert

The Eiffel Tower is the Empire State Building after taxes.

– Anonymous

Chapter 10 SUMMARY

Governments spend money in order to purchase goods and services for their citizens as well as to transfer wealth and income between their citizens. Governments get money from taxes, earnings, other governments, and borrowing. A budget deficit means that total outlays exceed total receipts, and vice versa for a budget surplus. A government goes into debt when it borrows money to finance a deficit. The U.S. Government ran very large deficits during much of the 1970s and 1980s.

The size of a government can be measured either: 1) absolutely, or in dollar terms; or 2) relatively, or in percentage terms when compared with another figure, such as the GDP. There has been substantial growth in both such measures for virtually all governments since the 1930s.

The benefits-received and the ability-to-pay principles are used to determine who should pay for government expenditures. A major goal in setting taxes is to achieve horizontal and vertical equity. Tax-bill writers attempt to achieve equity in taxation by equalizing: 1) the dollar amount of taxes paid; 2) the percentage of income paid in taxes; or 3) the burden of paying taxes. A progressive tax is one that taxes those with higher incomes at a higher tax rate than those with lower incomes. Alternatively, a regressive tax takes a larger share of a poor person's income. A proportional tax takes the same share of everyone's income.

The income tax is a progressive tax. After subtracting their exemptions and deductions, people pay different tax rates for different categories or brackets of their income. Income in higher brackets is taxed at higher rates. The 1986 Tax Reform Act was designed to introduce more fairness to the system by eliminating or reducing many tax breaks. Tax rates for higher-income taxpayers were raised in 1993.

Chapter 10 RESPONSES TO THE LEARNING OBJECTIVES

1. Government spending pays for goods and services and for transfer payments.
2. Governments finance their budgets:
   a) with taxes
   b) with earnings from services they provide
   c) with receipts from other governments
   d) by borrowing, which is done by selling bonds
3. A government budget:
   a) has a surplus when total receipts exceed total outlays
   b) has a deficit when total outlays exceed total receipts
   c) is balanced when total outlays equal total receipts
4. A budget deficit refers to the shortfall of total receipts compared with total outlays over a year's time. It also equals the amount that is borrowed that year. Government debt refers to how much money that was borrowed in the past that has not yet been repaid. The debt level refers to a point in time.

5. An absolute measure of government spending refers to the dollar amount of spending. A relative measure of spending refers to the percentage of the GDP that government spending represents.
6. With the benefits-received principle, the more services you receive from the government, the more taxes you pay. With the ability-to-pay principle, the amount of taxes you pay increases with your income and/or wealth.
7. Horizontal equity means that people in similar financial situations pay about the same amount in taxes. Vertical equity means that people in better financial situations pay more money in taxes than those in worse financial situations.
8. After finding the incomes and taxes paid into a certain tax for two or more people, calculate the percentage of income each person pays in the tax. If the percentage:
   a) falls as incomes rise, the tax is regressive
   b) remains constant as incomes rise, the tax is proportional
   c) rises as incomes rise, the tax is progressive
9. The first U.S. income tax was used to finance the Civil War. The present income tax began in 1916, but it wasn't until World War II that most people paid significant amounts of tax. Two major tax overhauls in the 1980s reduced tax rates, the number of deductions, and the number of brackets.
10. You pay tax on your taxable income, found by subtracting from or adding to the gross pay with the "adjustments to income." Next, the amount of the deductions and exemptions are subtracted, and the result is your taxable income.

Chapter 10 LEARNING ACTIVITIES AND DISCUSSION QUESTIONS

1. List 10 things the government purchases today that it did not buy 50 years ago. Considering such purchases, were the "old days" better or worse?
2. List five examples of user fees in yourcommunity.
3. What is your share of the national debt? If you have savings bonds in excess of that, are you still in debt to the other bondholders? Explain your answer.
4. Ask five people if taxpayers should: 1) pay equal amounts of taxes; 2) pay equal percentages of income paid in taxes; or 3) have equal burdens when paying taxes. If you note a connection with their answers and their economic position, can you explain the connection?
5. Is the income tax fairer since the two new brackets were added in 1993? Why or why not?

CHAPTER 11

INTRODUCTION TO THE MACROECONOMY

★★★★★ LEARNING OBJECTIVES ★★★★★

1. List the three major macroeconomic goals.
2. Explain how GDP is calculated and what factors influence its size.
3. Differentiate between actual GDP and potential GDP.
4. Explain how to calculate the inflation rate by using a price index.
5. Differentiate between current GDP and real GDP.
6. Explain how to calculate real GDP by using a price index.
7. Describe the three approaches to GDP.
8. Explain how to calculate the unemployment rate.
9. Compare and contrast the three categories of unemployment.
10. Explain how full employment is related to potential GDP.

TERMS

gross domestic product
GDP per capita
potential GDP
actual GDP
price index
Consumer Price Index
inflation rate

real GDP
current GDP
economic growth rate
consumption
investment
government spending
net exports
labor force

employed
unemployed
unemployment rate
discouraged unemployed
frictional unemployment
structural unemployment
cyclical unemployment
full employment

We know the economy can't provide us with all the goods and services we want because resources are scarce. You learned concepts that explain how individual consumers, firms, or government agencies deal with scarcity. That part of economic theory, called microeconomics, concerns small sectors or individual units of the economy (firms, consumers, laborers, and so on). Microeconomics studies such things as how consumers maximize satisfaction, how firms maximize profits, how society should use public resources, how the price of a particular product is determined, and how worker productivity in a factory increases.

The next five chapters show how society deals with scarcity in a larger sense. This subject, called macroeconomics, studies large (macro) sectors of the economy and their relation to the nation's economic goals and the condition of resource scarcity.

MACROECONOMIC GOALS

★1

Our society has three main macroeconomic goals: 1) full employment; 2) price stability; and 3) economic growth.

■ If full employment is not achieved, the effect is the same as if labor resources were even more scarce than they already are or were used inefficiently. Full employment also leads to fewer social problems, such as crime and poverty.

■ Price stability means there is no or little inflation or deflation (where prices fall). When future prices are known, businesses are more willing to invest in capital equipment and innovations that will pay off in the future. Also, the purchasing power of incomes will not erode if prices are stable.

■ Economic growth allows living standards to grow. It occurs in various ways, including an increase in resource productivity and the development of new resources.

THE MEANING OF MACROECONOMICS

Much of the news about economics deals with macroeconomic topics: unemployment, recession, inflation, interest rates, economic growth, tax policy, fiscal policy, and monetary policy. These topics are called macroeconomic variables. This chapter introduces most of these variables. Chapter 12 introduces others, which are associated with money. Chapters 13-15 focus on two aspects of such economic variables: 1) the relationships between the variables; and 2) how the government tries to influence these variables. As is always the purpose in economics, we study macroeconomics to find out why the economy is not providing the greatest economic welfare, given our scarce resources—and then to make certain that it does.

An Introduction to Some Macroeconomic Variables

As a brief overview of this chapter, this section introduces some major macroeconomic variables (noted in italics). The *total output* of goods and services refers to the combined yearly output of all business firms and government enterprises. *Gross domestic product* is an indirect measure of that output. The *standard of living* refers to the output of goods and services available for each person, on average. *Economic growth* measures how fast the output of goods and services grows. *Total spending* deals with the demand for output. The *inflation rate* measures price increases. Also covered are some labor statistics, such as the *labor force,* the *unemployment rate,* and *labor productivity*.

GROSS DOMESTIC PRODUCT

Many people always seem to be measuring things: blood pressure, weight, income, their cars' MPG, and so on. People measure what is important to them, and they hope the measurements show they are closer to their goals.

Defining and Determining Gross Domestic Product

The ultimate economic goal of society is that all its members get all the goods and services they want. Because the scarcity of resources prevents this, the government measures how much *is* produced in a year—an indication of how close society is to achieving that ultimate goal. But how is that done? How is it possible to measure the output of trucks, strawberries, rock concerts, helium gas, and bread at one time? Because goods and services are different, their outputs can't be added—that is, they can't be measured directly.

★2 However, it is possible to *indirectly* measure the combined output of unlike goods and services by using a common denominator for them. That common denominator is the dollar. Each year just so many toasters are produced, and firms sell them for a certain amount of money (or dollars). The same is true for haircuts, cars, and lawn mowers. Adding up the dollar amounts of every good and service gives an indirect measure of the physical amount of things produced. Thus, that dollar amount reflects the physical output of goods and services.

However, counting or measuring the same good twice must be avoided, for that would overstate output. Such a double-counting error would occur if the value of the steel used to produce a car were counted, and then that same steel were counted in the value of the car. The dollar value of a car includes the cost of all its components, including steel. The intent is to add up the dollar value of *final* goods, or goods that are ready for use. All other goods are called intermediate goods. All the goods in retail stores are final goods, as are concert tickets, computers, factory robots, insurance policies, and visits to the doctor. Intermediate goods include such items as coal, steel, sugar cane, lumber, and computer chips.

Gross domestic product (GDP) is the market value of all final goods and services produced in a year with resources located in the United States. It does not matter if the resources are owned by Americans or by foreigners. For example, the value of Honda cars produced in Ohio by Japanese-owned capital (the factory and the machines in it) is part of GDP of the United States. Also, the income earned working in the United States by Canadians is included in GDP because their income reflects the value of goods and services they produce in the United States.

Until 1991, the value of total output was measured with a variable called gross national product (GNP). That reflected the production of goods and services by resources that were supplied by U.S. residents, wherever they resided. For example, a dam built in Paraguay by Bechtel Corporation, a U.S. firm, would have been included in GNP if Bechtel equipment and American laborers did all the work. The difference between GDP and GNP is only about $30 to $50 billion a year, which is relatively small when compared with the roughly $6,000 billion total. The formula relating the two measures is:

GDP + Income Earned from American Resources Located Abroad
- Payments to Foreigners for Their Resources Located in the United States
= GNP

We can think of GDP as the summation of each final good's price multiplied by its output. To illustrate, we could multiply the price of gasoline by the number of gallons produced, add that to the price of haircuts multiplied by the number of haircuts given, and so on. Figure 11-1 shows the relationship of GDP to output. Imagine that the box labelled GDP is filled with enough dollars to equal the value of all the final goods and services produced in a year. (That production is represented by the "pile" of output on the left.) Because it is impossible to measure that "pile" directly, it is measured indirectly by GDP, which *reflects* total output.

Figure 11-1 The GDP — Its Relationship to Production

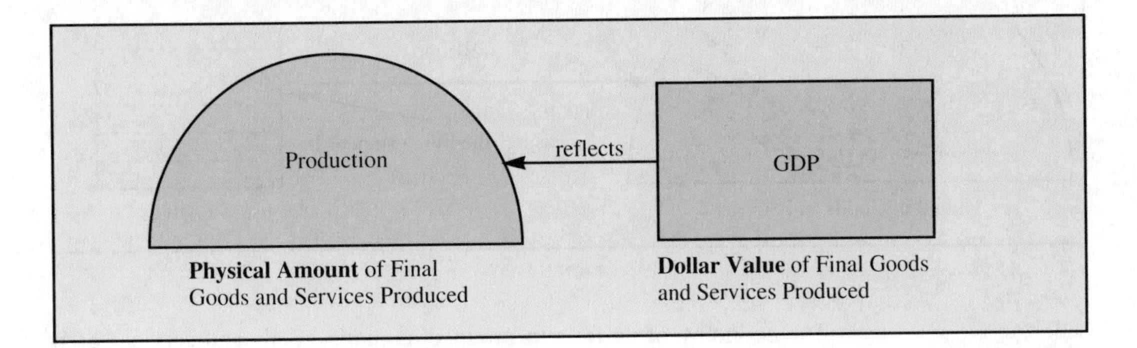

GDP does not include all of the nation's output, only the goods and services the government can measure. These include goods and services sold in legal transactions in marketplaces (stores, auto dealerships, and so on). But GDP misses all output from the "underground economy." This includes work some people do for unreported cash to avoid income taxes (as when plumbers do work "on the side"), illegal drug production and sales, and under-reporting of sales by retailers. Some economists believe such output is equal to one-tenth of GDP or more. Often "underground" activity is legal, such as cutting a neighbor's grass or delivering newspapers.

In addition, production (work) people do for themselves doesn't appear in GDP. Those who paint their own houses, cook their own food, clean their own homes, build model airplanes, sew their own clothes, and grow their own vegetables do not have this output included in GDP. This problem of understating output by using the GDP is relatively large for poor nations, where many people produce their own food, shelter, and clothing.

Consequently, GDP only approximates total output. The Department of Commerce reports GDP for each quarter of a year and then again for the entire year. However, the quarterly report is stated at a yearly rate. For example, if the value of output was $1,600 billion in the third quarter, the report would state that "goods and services, as measured by GDP, were produced in the third quarter at a rate of $6,400 billion per year" (= $1,600 billion x 4).

GDP per capita refers to the value of goods and services produced in a year for each person, on average. It is found by dividing GDP by the population. This gives an indirect measure of the living standard, which is the *physical* amount of output available to the average person. This concept appears in diagram form in Figure 11-2, where a "slice" of both GDP and output refers to a "one-person slice of the population."

Figure 11-2 The GDP Per Capita and the Living Standard

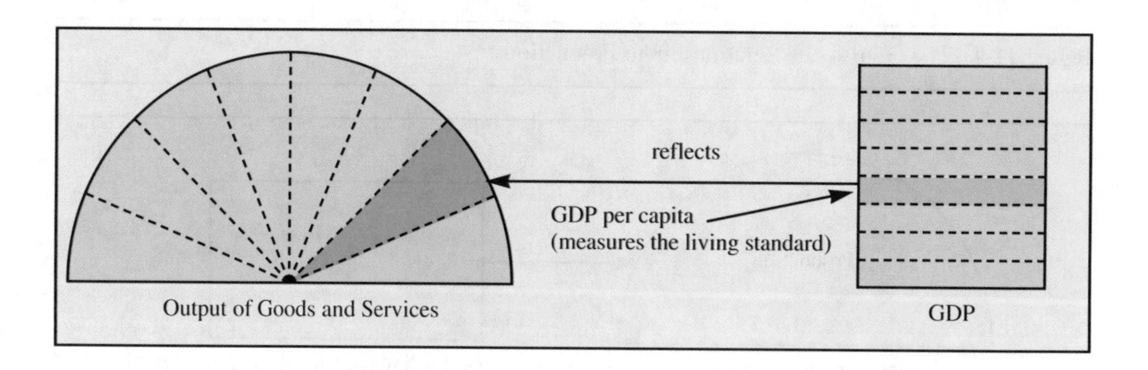

★3 The economy often fails to produce as many goods and services as it could. **Potential GDP** refers to the dollar value of *potential* output, that is, the total output of goods and services when all the resources are fully used. Potential GDP might not be reached because, for example, many laborers could be out of work or many factories could be operating at less than full capacity.

Actual GDP refers to the value of goods and services actually produced in a year. If less than the potential output is produced, potential GDP exceeds actual GDP, as illustrated in Figure 11-3. The *difference* between the two "piles" of output on the left or the two rectangles reflecting GDP on the right both indicate the degree of unused resources in the economy—unemployed laborers, factories with idle machines and inactive shipping departments, restaurant grills not being used much, and idled coal and iron mines.

Figure 11-3 The Concepts of Potential and Actual GDP

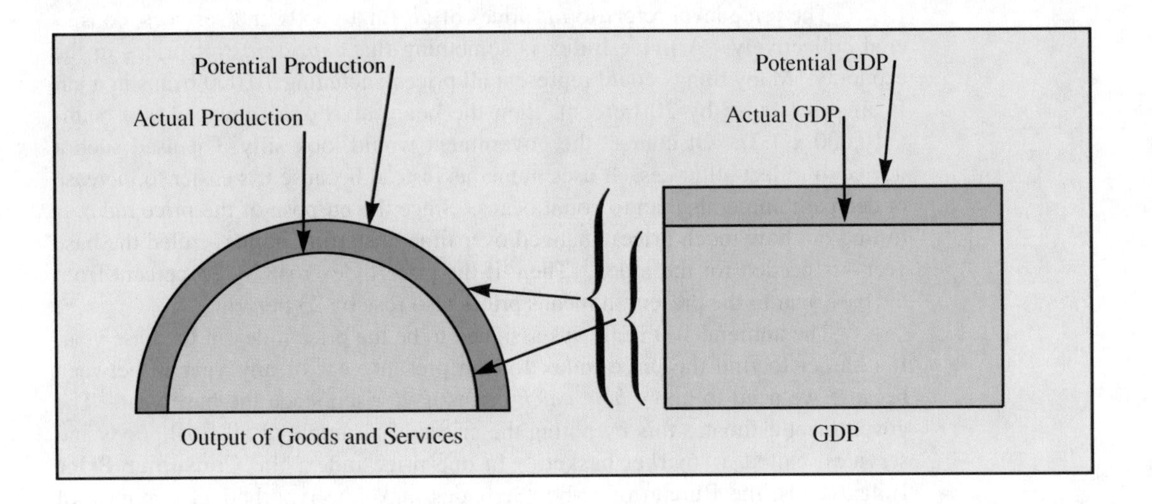

Problems in Using GDP When Prices Change

If the device used to measure output changes in some way, what happens? An analogy might help. Suppose that you dent a teaspoon so that it holds only two-thirds as much as it did before. If it's your only spoon, what do you do when a cake recipe calls for two teaspoons of baking powder? You must adjust your procedure to ensure an accurate measure, so you should now use *three* "teaspoons"—of the bent one, for $2 = 3 \times 2/3$.

A similar problem exists when measuring total output with the GDP. The "measuring device" for output (the dollar) changes in "size" (what it can buy) every time prices in general rise or fall. If we want a change in GDP to reflect only the change in the output of goods and services, there is a problem in measuring. Suppose total output does *not* increase from one year to the next but that prices *do* by 10 percent. Then GDP also rises by 10 percent.

How can GDP rise if output doesn't? This is possible because *two* factors determine GDP: 1) the output of goods and services; and 2) their prices. To solve this measurement distortion problem caused by changing prices, GDP must be adjusted—just like the baking powder measure had to be adjusted when the spoon was dented. It is necessary to "factor out" the price change or adjust GDP so that it reflects output alone. This is done with a simple mathematical equation. But first it is necessary to construct a measure of the price level, just as it was necessary to determine how much the teaspoon was dented. Then we will know just how much to adjust GDP in order to eliminate the effects of price changes on GDP, leaving only the effects of output changes.

Constructing a Price Index

The price level refers to *all* prices of *all* final goods and services, considered collectively. A **price index** is something that *represents* all prices in the economy. Many things could represent all prices, including 10,000 beans in a jar. If all prices rose by 20 percent, then the bean jar should have 12,000 beans (=10,000 x 1.2). Of course, the government would look silly if it used such a device to reflect all prices. It uses numerals instead because it's easier to increase or decrease numerals than to count beans. Since the purpose of the price index is to find out how much prices changed over time, a starting point—called the base year—is needed for the index. Then, if the price index rose by 23 percent from the base year to the present, it means prices also rose by 23 percent.

The numeral 100 is always assigned to be the price index in the base year. It's harder to find the price index for the present year or any year in between because we need to know *how much* prices have risen since the base year. The government estimates this by noting the prices of a sample of all final goods and services, called a "market basket." In one price index, the **Consumer Price Index** (CPI), the Bureau of Labor Statistics makes a hypothetical purchase of some 400 items that typical urban wage earners buy. It includes more of some things than others (perhaps five gallons of milk, but only two shirts) to better reflect true buying patterns. Suppose this "market basket" costs $1,000 in the base year. (The government currently assigns the two-year period from 1982 to 1984 as the base "year.") If those same items cost $1,300 (30 percent more) today, then prices in general rose 30 percent since 1982-84. The price index is used to determine the "cost of living." This refers to the amount of money people need to buy the things they typically buy. If the price index rises, you can assume it costs more to live—that is, to buy things in general.

The government has several other price indices: the implicit price deflator (or GDP deflator), which is used to adjust GDP for price changes; the Producers' Price Index, which reflects wholesale prices; and various partial indices, such as the housing price index, which reflects only housing costs.

Calculating the Inflation Rate

A price index can be used to calculate the inflation rate as well as to adjust GDP and other economic variables for price changes. Inflation is a condition of persistent increases in the price level. The **inflation rate** is the percentage increase in the price level from one year to the next. For example, the 3.1 percent inflation rate for 1991 means that, on average, prices were 3.1 percent higher on December 31, 1991, than they were on December 31, 1990.

★4 The inflation rate is calculated between two consecutive years (called Year 1 and Year 2) with this formula:

$$\text{Inflation Rate} = \frac{\text{Price Index in Year 2} - \text{Price Index in Year 1}}{\text{Price Index in Year 1}} \times 100$$

The government actually measures prices monthly and then reports the inflation rate for that month, but on a yearly basis. It assumes that prices will continue to increase in the 11 months that follow at the same rate they did in the month checked. For example, suppose the CPI was 120.0 in July 1990 and 120.6 in August 1990. Thus, the CPI rose 0.5 percent in one month, as 0.5 = (120.6 - 120.0) ÷ 120. Multiplying 0.5 percent by 12 (months) gives a six percent annual inflation rate on the basis of the July to August record (ignoring compounding effects).

It is also possible to look at price indices over many years and tell how long it took for prices to double, triple, quadruple, and so on. Suppose you want to know when prices were only one-third of what they are today. First, you must find the price index for the present. Second, divide that price index by three. Finally, take the quotient you found in the second step and locate the year when it was the price index. For example, if today's price index is 180, then dividing it by three gives us 60. If the price index was 60 in 1971, then we can say that prices rose threefold since 1971 or that prices in 1971 were one-third as high as today's prices. Then, when people say that today's dollar is only "worth 33¢," they're equating the purchasing power of today's dollar to that of 33¢ in 1971.

Adjusting GDP for Price Changes

★5 GDP reflects both the output of goods and services as well as the price level. If, over time, only the output changes, there is no measuring problem—any change in GDP came solely from the output change. But since prices usually *do* change, it is necessary to separate out the price changes from the GDP change. Once this is done, there is a special name for GDP—**real GDP**. (It is sometimes also called by two other names: constant dollar GDP and GDP adjusted for inflation.) Real GDP is the most accurate measure of the production of goods and services. ★6 The GDP figure the government actually measures is **current GDP**, also called nominal GDP. Real GDP is calculated with the following formula:

$$\text{Real GDP} = \frac{\text{Current GDP}}{\text{GDP Deflator}} \times 100$$

(Remember from earlier that the GDP deflator is a price index.) Suppose current GDP doubled during some period. Real GDP would also *tend* to double—but it wouldn't change at all if prices also doubled during the period.

The examples in Figure 11-4 of possible price and output changes help illustrate this more clearly. The diagrams show three different combinations of changes in output and price level between two periods, called Period 1 and Period 2. Using numbers and diagrams, this example measures four variables: 1) the price level (measured by the GDP deflator); 2) the output or production level (measured by "production units," an imaginary device that allows us to add up apples and oranges and everything else); 3) current GDP; and 4) real GDP.

Figure 11-4 The Effects of Price and Production Changes on Current and Real GDP

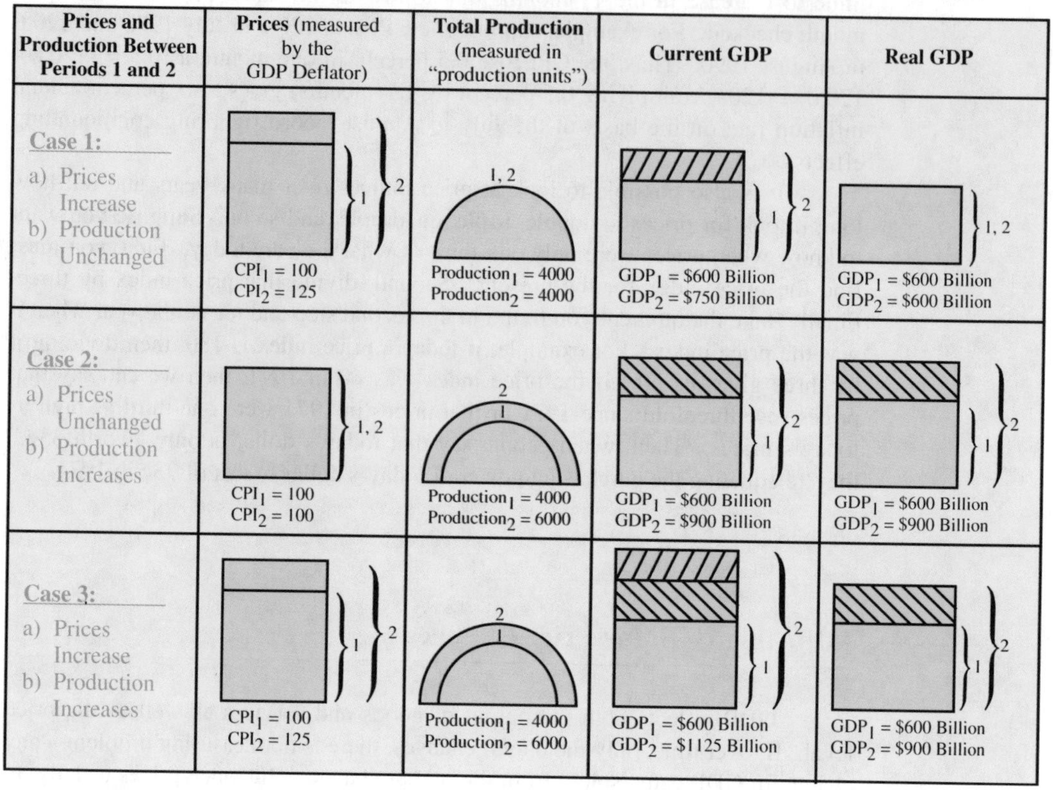

Prices and Production Between Periods 1 and 2	Prices (measured by the GDP Deflator)	Total Production (measured in "production units")	Current GDP	Real GDP
Case 1: a) Prices Increase b) Production Unchanged	1; 2 $CPI_1 = 100$ $CPI_2 = 125$	1, 2 $Production_1 = 4000$ $Production_2 = 4000$	1; 2 GDP_1 = \$600 Billion GDP_2 = \$750 Billion	1, 2 GDP_1 = \$600 Billion GDP_2 = \$600 Billion
Case 2: a) Prices Unchanged b) Production Increases	1, 2 $CPI_1 = 100$ $CPI_2 = 100$	2; 1 $Production_1 = 4000$ $Production_2 = 6000$	2; 1 GDP_1 = \$600 Billion GDP_2 = \$900 Billion	2; 1 GDP_1 = \$600 Billion GDP_2 = \$900 Billion
Case 3: a) Prices Increase b) Production Increases	1; 2 $CPI_1 = 100$ $CPI_2 = 125$	2; 1 $Production_1 = 4000$ $Production_2 = 6000$	2; 1 GDP_1 = \$600 Billion GDP_2 = \$1125 Billion	2; 1 GDP_1 = \$600 Billion GDP_2 = \$900 Billion

The first case shows what happens when production does not change from Year 1 to Year 2. However, prices *do* change. They rise by 25 percent. Thus, the GDP deflator rises 25 percent (from 100 to 125). Reflecting this, the box representing prices in Year 2 is 25 percent larger than the box for Year 1. The production is 4,000 units for both years, so their "piles" (of output) coincide perfectly. Current GDP grew by 25 percent, from \$600 to \$750 billion, because only one of the two possible influences on it (prices) grew. Using the formula for real GDP, note that in Year 2 it is unchanged at \$600 billion. In Year 1, real GDP = (\$600 ÷ 100) x 100 = \$600 billion. In Year 2, real GDP = (\$750 ÷ 125) x 100 = \$600 billion. Finally, the boxes representing real GDP for both years coincide perfectly. So the increase in current GDP is merely an illusion—it does not reflect any output change.

In the second case, production *does* increase, but prices *don't*. Therefore, the GDP deflator remains at 100, while output jumps from 4,000 to 6,000, a 50 percent climb. Consequently, the boxes representing price levels are the same, but the production "pile" climbs 50 percent. Current GDP increases by 50 percent as well, from \$600 to \$900 billion, reflecting changing output and stable prices.

Finally, real GDP climbs at the same rate as current GDP. So if the output of goods and services increases by 50 percent, real GDP should also increase by 50 percent.

In the third and most realistic case, both prices and output increase by Year 2. It is assumed that prices rise 25 percent and output increases 50 percent. Current GDP increases to $1,125 billion. Note that the hash marks, denoting the increases, are different. That's because there are two factors pushing up current GDP—price increases and production increases. Real GDP merely rises to $900 billion—just as it did in the second example when only output increased. The $900 billion figure results from the formula, as ($1,125 ÷ 125) x 100 = $900 billion.

Newspaper articles often refer to both current GDP and real GDP. Real GDP is always reported as less than current GDP for the reason you just saw. Such articles refer to the **economic growth rate**, which is the percentage increase in real GDP during the year (although it is also measured on a quarterly basis). Comparing outputs of two different years requires using real GDP because it avoids the distortion caused by price changes.

Such procedures that adjust for price changes also work for the measure of the living standard, GDP per capita. Because real GDP is the best measure of output, real GDP per capita is the best measure of the living standard because it reflects the amount of goods and services produced per person.

Table 11-1 shows actual GDP for selected years, shown in current dollars and in constant dollars (dollars with the purchasing power of 1987 dollars). It also indicates real GDP per capita. From these figures it is clear that the living standard rose approximately threefold since 1930.

Table 11-1 GNP and GDP Figures for Selected Years (in billions)

Year	Current GNP	Current GDP	Real GNP (1982 dollars)	Real GDP (1987 dollars)	Real GNP per Capita (1982 dollars)	Real GDP per Capita (1987 dollars)
1930	$ 90		$ 710		$ 5,796	
1940	$ 100		$ 773		$ 5,852	
1950	$ 288		$1,204		$ 7,905	
1960	$ 515	$ 513	$1,665	$1,971	$ 9,214	$10,909
1970	$1,016	$1,011	$2,416	$2,874	$11,780	$14,016
1980	$2,732	$2,708	$3,187	$3,776	$13,990	$16,581
1985	$3,998	$4,039	$3,585	$4,280	$14,981	$17,948
1986	$4,209	$4,269	$3,677	$4,405	$15,226	$18,305
1987	$4,524	$4,540	$3,854	$4,540	$15,776	$18,698
1988	$4,881	$4,900	$4,024	$4,719	$16,308	$19,260
1989	$5,248	$5,251	$4,144	$4,838	$16,656	$19,560
1990	$5,525	$5,522		$4,878		$19,518
1991		$5,678		$4,821		$19,079
1992		$5,951		$4,923		$19,276
1993		—		—		—

Sources: *The Economic Report of the President, 1993; Survey of Current Business,* June 1993

The Expenditure Approach to GDP

★7

There are several ways to measure GDP: 1) the production approach; 2) the income approach; and 3) the expenditure approach. The production approach, which was used earlier in the chapter to introduce GDP, adds the value of the production of all final goods and services to arrive at GDP. The income approach adds the income people earn while producing goods and services. The expenditure approach assumes that total spending for goods and services must equal the value of goods and services produced—that is, GDP.

The reason all three approaches are acceptable is that money received by people (income) ultimately comes from sales (revenues) of items that people wish to consume (goods and services). In other words, each appeals to the idea that every purchase is a sale (money changes hands) and people give money to get some good or service in exchange.

Total spending (or expenditures), often called aggregate demand, can be divided into four categories or components: 1) consumer spending; 2) investment spending; 3) government spending; and 4) net exports.

- Consumer spending or **consumption** (C) includes all spending on consumer goods—those goods consumers buy to satisfy personal needs and wants, including food, clothing, cars, records, movies, and school supplies. It usually accounts for 60 to 70 percent of all the output produced.
- Investment spending or **investment** (I) has three components: 1) expenditures by privately owned businesses for capital equipment, such as machinery, tools, and office computers; 2) spending on building construction in the private sector for homes and for such business structures as offices, factories, warehouses, and pipelines; and 3) an adjustment for business inventories. Here's an example to help you understand this third component. Suppose the Acme Shoe Company had a $60,000 inventory of finished shoes on January 1, 1993. On December 31, 1993, Acme Shoe had $80,000 worth of shoes, a difference of $20,000. But that $20,000 worth of shoes was in the warehouse, so clearly no one had bought them. However, the Commerce Department acts as if the shoe company bought these shoes from itself. The government uses this procedure to account for all the nation's production of goods and services. Alternatively, a firm could end a year with *fewer* inventories than it had at the beginning. To avoid the misleading assumption that spending exceeded output, a negative figure is used for this third component of investment spending. Investment spending accounts for about 10 to 20 percent of total output. (This definition of investment differs from "personal investment" in stocks, bonds, real estate, or commodities, and the two definitions should not be confused.)
- **Government spending** (G) includes the part of government budgets used to purchase goods and services. This includes spending on military supplies, government buildings, and equipment for public schools. This government spending (federal, state, and local combined) accounts for between 20 and 30 percent of total production. It does *not* include spending on transfer payments because the government receives no goods or services whenever such payments are made.

■ **Net exports** (X-M) measure the difference between exports and imports. Exports (X) reflect spending by foreigners for (part of) our output, so it's similar in that respect to C, I, and G. However, some part of purchases by U.S. consumers, businesses, and governments are on foreign-made products. These are our imports (M), and they must be subtracted from the spending on C, I, G, and X so that there is an accounting balance between the value of *our* output and total spending on that output. Compared with C, I, and G, net exports are small and will not be considered in the following chapters.

The following formula for GDP sums this all up. It shows that the value of total output (GDP) is equal to total spending on that output:

$$GDP = C + I + G + (X - M) = \text{Total Spending}$$

Table 11-2 shows these four components of the GDP for 1992.

Table 11-2 Total Spending Components of GDP, 1992 (in billions)

GDP	=	Consumer Spending	+	Investment Spending	+	Government Spending	+	Net Exports
$5,945.7		$4,093.9		$769.7		$1,114.8		(-)$32.7

Source: *Federal Reserve Bulletin,* August 1993

LABOR IN THE MACROECONOMY

In Chapter 7 you studied labor from a microeconomic perspective. The chapter explained wage determination, productivity of individual workers and occupations, and other aspects of labor. This chapter focuses on labor resources from a different, broader perspective.

The Labor Force

Figure 11-5 categorizes the entire population in various ways. At the top, the rectangle extending the whole width of the chart represents the entire population. The population is then divided into two groups, those in the labor force and those outside the labor force. The **labor force** includes everyone who has a job or is actively looking for a job. People not in the labor force include those not employed and not looking for work. This includes anyone under age 16, retired people, homemakers, most college students, and those in institutions, such as hospitals or prisons.

Figure 11-5 The Labor Force

<table>
<tr><th colspan="9">TOTAL POPULATION</th></tr>
<tr><td colspan="3">Labor Force</td><td colspan="6">Persons Not in the Labor Force</td></tr>
<tr><td rowspan="2">Armed Forces</td><td colspan="2">Civilian Labor Force</td><td rowspan="2">Persons Under 16 Years of Age</td><td rowspan="2">Retired Persons</td><td rowspan="2">Home-makers</td><td rowspan="2">Persons in Institutions</td><td rowspan="2" colspan="2">Other</td></tr>
<tr><td>Employed</td><td>Unemployed</td></tr>
</table>

The labor force has two components: 1) the armed forces, including all military personnel; and 2) the civilian labor force. The civilian labor force is divided into the employed and the unemployed. Each month the government surveys 55,000 households and classifies someone as **employed** if that person is between the ages of 16 and 65 and worked one hour or more in the previous week. It classifies someone as **unemployed** if that person did not work the previous week but looked for work. "Looking" includes reading the employment ads, filling out an application, or stopping at an employment office. Someone does not have to collect unemployment compensation to be classified as unemployed.

★8

The **unemployment rate** is the percentage of the labor force that is unemployed. The government reports this figure monthly as well as yearly. The rate is determined with the formula:

$$\text{Unemployment Rate} = \frac{\text{Number of Unemployed}}{\text{Labor Force}} \times 100$$

Many people who want a job stop looking when they can't find one after a long search. The government calls the people who have stopped looking the **discouraged unemployed**. Officially, these people are not classified as unemployed. That's because the government can't always tell which people who are not working would actually work if offered a job. For instance, some homemakers and retired people would work if offered nice jobs at high enough wages. Should these people also be classified as unemployed? No. Thus, the government says you must be looking for a job to be considered unemployed. Table 11-3 shows some labor statistics from 1950 to the present.

A problem with the unemployment rate is that it does not reflect the degree of *underemployment* that exists. This refers to people who are employed in positions below their job skills. It includes cab drivers with college degrees and laid-off machinists who flip hamburgers.

Types of Unemployment

★9

Although there are many reasons for unemployment, economists fit unemployment into three categories: 1) frictional unemployment; 2) structural unemployment; and 3) cyclical unemployment.

Table 11-3 Selected Labor Statistics

Year	Population (millions)	Labor Force (millions)	Number of Unemployed (millions)	Unemployment Rate
1950	123.2	63.4	3.3	5.2%
1960	180.7	71.5	3.9	5.4%
1970	205.1	84.9	4.1	4.8%
1980	227.7	108.5	7.6	7.0%
1981	230.0	110.3	8.3	7.5%
1982	232.3	111.9	10.7	9.5%
1983	234.5	113.2	10.7	9.5%
1984	236.7	115.2	8.5	7.4%
1985	238.8	117.2	8.3	7.1%
1986	241.0	119.5	8.2	6.9%
1987	243.8	121.6	7.4	6.1%
1988	246.3	123.4	6.7	5.4%
1989	248.8	125.6	6.5	5.2%
1990	251.4	126.4	6.9	5.4%
1991	252.7	126.9	8.4	6.6%
1992	255.4	128.5	9.4	7.3%
1993	______	______	______	______
1994	______	______	______	______

Source: *The Economic Report of the President,* 1993

■ **Frictional unemployment** means that "friction" in the economy prevents everyone from working all the time. Some jobs are seasonal. Some people have just entered the work force and have not yet selected a job. Some workers have voluntarily changed jobs but haven't started their new ones yet. Finally, some workers aren't aware of available jobs for which they are qualified.

■ **Structural unemployment** refers to unemployment stemming from the changing structure of the economy. It occurs when jobhunters don't have the skills required for the available jobs. Some reasons for structural unemployment include: a new machine that is cheaper than laborers ("technological unemployment"); a sharp drop in demand for a product (slide rules, for example); or fewer jobs for the uneducated or extremely unskilled (the "hard-core unemployed").

■ **Cyclical unemployment** occurs during recessions or downturns in the economy that affect almost all industries. Such unemployment is potentially the largest of the three, and during the Great Depression of the 1930s it hit more than 20 percent of the labor force. In prosperous times it hardly exists because firms can't find workers to fill all job openings.

★10

If the economy succeeds in creating jobs for everyone *except* the frictionally unemployed and the structurally unemployed, it is said to be at **full employment**. The economy will achieve potential GDP if it is at full employment. In the 1960s, this condition corresponded to an unemployment rate of about three or four percent. Today most economists say full employment means an unemployment rate of around five or six percent. Economists blame this increase on: an increase in required job skills while individual education levels decline; a greater share of the labor force made up of women and teenagers, who have relatively fewer job skills; and the growth of government assistance programs, which provide sources of income other than employment.

Another term, labor productivity, refers in macroeconomics to the efficiency of a very large group, sometimes even the entire labor force. In microeconomics it refers to a specific worker or a small group of workers. Recall from Chapter 3 that service workers generally have lower rates of productivity growth than workers producing goods.

The government reports the changes in productivity each quarter, especially for the non-agricultural private sector. These figures are indicators of the likelihood of U.S. success against foreign competition in the marketplace and against inflation. Table 11-4 presents the figures for yearly labor productivity growth in the private, non-agricultural sector of the economy.

Table 11-4 Annual Changes in Labor Productivity in the Non-Farm Business Sector

Year	Percent Change
1980	-0.4
1981	1.0
1982	-0.6
1983	3.3
1984	1.8
1985	0.5
1986	1.6
1987	0.9
1988	1.4
1989	-0.7
1990	-0.9
1991	0.5
1992	2.8
1993	____
1994	____

Sources: *The Statistical Abstract of the United States,* 1993
Monthly Labor Review, August 1993

Chapter 11 SUMMARY

Macroeconomics studies large sectors of the economy, such as the labor force, total output, the price level, and interest rates. The major macroeconomic goals are full employment, price stability, and economic growth. When achieved, each of these goals reduce the problems caused by a scarcity of resources.

Gross domestic product indirectly measures the yearly output of final goods and services. Comparing GDP of two or more years is difficult because prices often rise over time. The problem is that price increases raise GDP just as increases in production do. Real GDP more accurately measures output because the inflationary effects are removed. Real GDP per capita is a measure of the living standard because it measures yearly output per capita.

The price level is measured or represented by a price index. A price index is calculated by comparing the cost of a given amount of goods and services in several time periods. The inflation rate is the percentage change in the price index in a year. The price index is also used along with current GDP to calculate real GDP.

GDP can be found by: 1) adding the value of all goods and services produced; 2) adding the incomes people get from selling their resources; and 3) adding the amount of purchases of all spenders. In the expenditure approach, GDP equals the amount of consumer, investment, and government spending plus the difference between exports and imports.

The labor force includes the employed and the unemployed. The unemployed include those out of work and those looking for it. The unemployment rate is the percentage of the labor force that is unemployed. The unemployed are categorized as frictionally, structurally, or cyclically unemployed.

Chapter 11 RESPONSES TO THE LEARNING OBJECTIVES

1. The major macroeconomic goals are full employment, stable prices, and economic growth.

2. The GDP is found by adding the dollar value of all final goods and services produced in a year. Its size is determined by the level of production and the level of prices.

3. The actual GDP is the value of goods and services that are produced, while the potential GDP is the value of goods and services that could be produced if there were full employment. If, indeed, there is full employment, the actual GDP equals the potential GDP.

4. The inflation rate is found by calculating the percentage increase in the price index over a year's time.

5. The current GDP is the value of output calculated by using prices that existed in the year the output was produced. The real GDP is the value of a year's output calculated with a dollar having the purchasing power of the base year of the price index. The real GDP can be thought of as the current GDP after adjusting for inflation.

6. The real GDP is found by dividing the current GDP by the price index, then multiplying that figure by 100.

7. The production approach to the GDP adds the value of production of all final goods and services. The income approach adds the earned income of people. The expenditure approach adds the spending done on: a) consumer goods and services; b) capital goods, construction, and business inventories; and c) goods and services received by governments.

8. The unemployment rate is found by dividing the number of unemployed by the size of the labor force and expressing the rate as a percentage.

9. Frictional unemployment stems from "friction" in the economy that prevents everyone from working all the time, such as seasonal unemployment. Structural unemployment results from a change in the structure of the economy, such as a job skill becoming obsolete. Cyclical unemployment occurs when there is a recession.

10. The maximum possible output of goods and services is produced at full employment. The value of such output is the potential GDP.

Chapter 11 LEARNING ACTIVITIES AND DISCUSSION QUESTIONS

1. Calculate how much living standards have increased since you were born.
2. Calculate how much prices have risen since you were born.
3. Why aren't homemakers and prisoners considered to be in the labor force?
4. Recalculate the real GDP for 1970, 1980, and 1990 if the GDP deflator index was: a) twice as high; and b) half as high as it really was. (Hint: You don't have to know the actual index number.)
5. Which do you believe is more important—full employment, price stability, or economic growth? Did your own economic position influence your answer? How so?

APPENDIX NATIONAL INCOME ACCOUNTS

Although GDP is a good first step in measuring the macroeconomy, there are other measures of elements of the macroeconomy besides GDP. In the 1930s, economist Simon Kuznets established a way of connecting all these measures in what is known as the national income accounts. Table A11-1 shows the major elements of these accounts and their interrelationships.

The accounts start with GDP, the value of all final goods and services produced. Depreciation, also called capital consumption allowances, is subtracted from GDP to give the net domestic product (NDP). Depreciation reflects the wearing out of capital. So the amount of capital produced each year to replace old capital is subtracted from GDP to give a more accurate view of the *additional* goods and services available as compared with the previous year.

Next, indirect business taxes, including sales, property, and excise taxes, are subtracted from NDP. The remainder is national income (NI), which equals the payments to the factors of production—wages and other employee contributions, interest, rent, and profits. GDP and NDP are fundamentally different concepts from NI in that they measure the value of production, while NI measures the amount of income earned. Because depreciation and indirect business taxes don't represent any person's income, they must be subtracted from GDP to arrive at NI.

However, NI does not include all the income people have available to them. Five adjustments must be made before arriving at that figure, which is known as personal income (PI). Three items are subtracted from NI and two are added to it. The first to be subtracted is corporate savings. Although owners of corporations earn profits, the part of profits that remains in the corporate accounts (savings, checking) is not available for spending by the firms' owners. The same thing holds for income taxes corporations pay. Finally, Social Security taxes also represent money that is not (immediately) available to people, even though the taxes are paid with income people earned from selling resources.

Conversely, transfer payments add to the income people receive from selling resources, so they are added to NI. Interest earned on government bonds is also added to NI because it is income to people and was not counted in national income as interest income to resource owners.

Although personal income represents all the flows of money to people, it still does not indicate what they can spend. To find that amount, known as disposable income (DI) or disposable personal income, personal taxes must be subtracted. These are the various taxes paid by individuals for personal income taxes, property taxes, sales taxes, and the like. Finally, personal consumption expenditures (C) are subtracted from disposable income, leaving personal savings (S) as a residual. The consumption figure (C) includes interest payments on loans that individuals took out. Thus, it does not reflect a pure measure of the amount of goods and services purchased in the normal sense.

Table A11-1 The National Income Accounts

	GDP (Gross Domestic Product)
	minus Depreciation
=	**NDP (Net Domestic Product)**
	minus Indirect Business Taxes
=	**NI (National Income)**
	minus Corporate Savings
	minus Corporate Income Taxes
	minus Social Security Taxes
	plus Transfer Payments
	plus Interest Paid by Governments
=	**PI (Personal Income)**
	minus Personal Taxes
=	**DI (Disposable Income)**
	minus Personal Consumption Expenditures
=	**S (Personal Savings)**

CHAPTER 12

MONEY AND BANKING

★★★★★ LEARNING OBJECTIVES ★★★★★

1. Describe the two alternative methods of exchange.
2. Describe money.
3. List the three functions of money.
4. List the five characteristics something must have before being accepted as money.
5. Describe the organization of the Federal Reserve System.
6. Compare and contrast the four financial intermediaries.
7. State the purpose of the Monetary Control Act of 1980 and the Garn-St. Germaine Act of 1982.
8. Explain how banks create money.
9. List the three ways in which the Federal Reserve controls excess bank reserves and the money supply.
10. Describe both types of open market operations.

TERMS

barter
double coincidence of wants
transaction costs
purchasing power
medium of exchange
store of value
standard of value
monetary aggregate
electronic funds transfer
debit card
Federal Reserve System
central bank
financial intermediary
commercial bank
savings and loan
savings bank
credit union
required reserves
reserve requirement
excess reserves
deposit multiplier
discount rate
open market operations
federal funds rate

Although a primitive, subsistence economy can function without money, a modern economy can't. In this chapter you will learn what money is (you might be surprised) and how it helps to alleviate the economic problem caused by a scarcity of resources. You will also learn about the Federal Reserve System, the commercial banking system, and how both of these affect the money supply.

MONEY—THE CONCEPT AND ITS MEASURE

What is money, the stuff people *say* they want so much—but then get rid of as fast as they can when they get it? It is a strange item indeed. Money is probably the only thing that is useless—*until you get rid of it.* (Think how useless a pocketful of money would be to someone shipwrecked on a desert island where there is nothing to buy.)

The Concept of Money

Money plays an important role in achieving specialization and raising living standards. Each person specializes in producing some good or service in order to increase the efficiency of resource use, which, in turn, promotes higher living standards. But this leads to individual specialists producing vastly more of a product than each needs—but having little or nothing of whatever else is needed. Thus, specialization forces specialists to exchange their products.

★1

There are two ways of trading: by using the barter method and by using money. **Barter** is a system in which one person provides a good, service, or resource to another in exchange for some other good, service, or resource. Such trade requires that there be a **double coincidence of wants**, which means each person has what the other person wants and wants what the other person has. That would be a rare occurrence. For example, if you tried to trade some surplus pencils for an Eric Clapton disc, it could take years to make a trade. Economists call the time plus other things of value that are given up when making exchanges **transaction costs**. People who hate to spend time shopping and to endure crowds know about such costs. When people do comparison shopping to find the best deal, they deliberately increase their transaction costs. Whether that is a wise activity depends upon what they gain (in saved money) compared with the value of their time.

Throughout much of history, such high costs discouraged people from specializing. Instead, they were self-sufficient, producing most of their own needs. Because they did not have the advantages of specialization, they generally were poor, often living at a subsistence level. Frontier settlers were prime examples.

But thousands of years ago, an idea took hold that is still useful. A person who knew the value of specialization might have suggested: "Why not become a specialist and give your surplus to another specialist (say, John) in exchange for something you *don't* want, but which any other specialist (say, Bob) would in turn take from you in exchange for what Bob has? That would eliminate the need to fulfill a double coincidence of wants. Then you would not have to spend time finding somebody who has what you want, *plus* who wants what you have. You merely give such people what they *don't* want—money." (We know people don't want money itself because they part with most of it as soon as they get it.)

Figure 12-1 illustrates the differences in these two systems of exchange. Suppose John produces nails and wants some cheese. In a barter system, he needs to find a cheese maker who needs some nails. Note that there are five cheese makers with whom John can trade—Mary, Bob, Chris, Shawn, and Elaine. But

Figure 12-1 Trade in a Barter System and a Money System

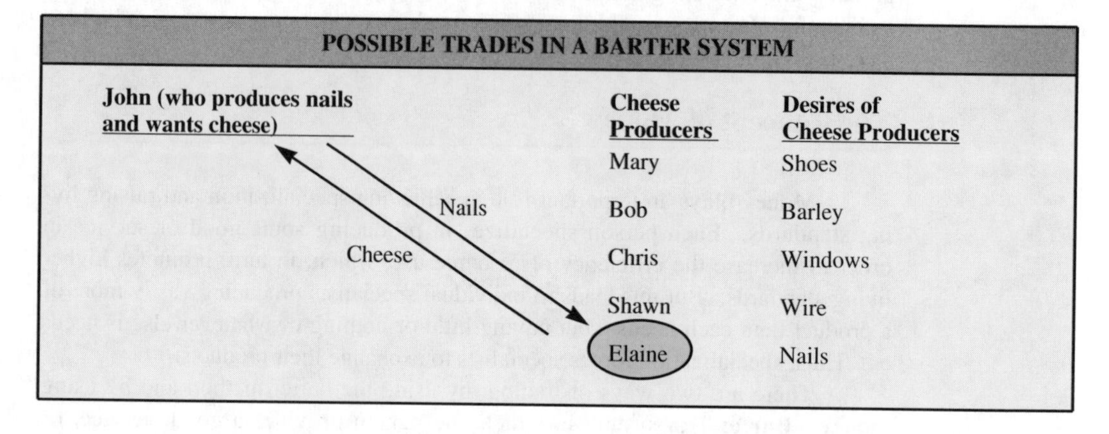

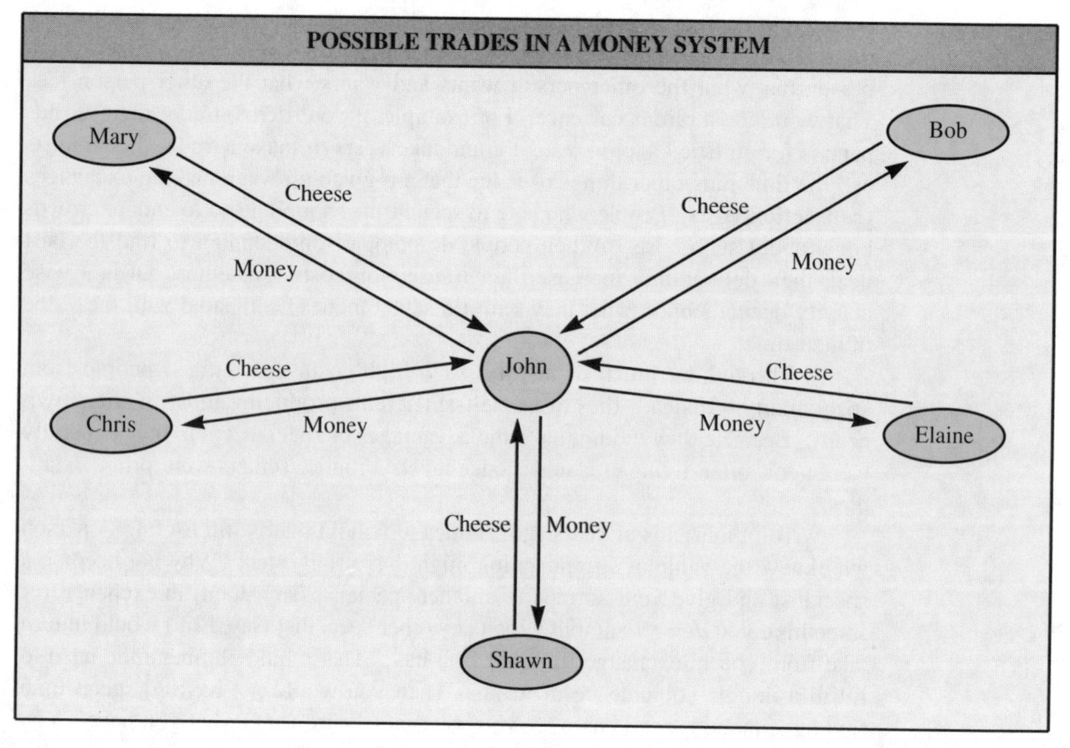

note further that each of them wants different products. Only one (Elaine) wants nails. Thus, for John to make a trade, he needs to first find someone like Elaine and, second, they need to agree on how many nails to trade for each pound of cheese.

In the lower half of Figure 12-1, showing a money system, there are *five* possible trading situations, for John no longer needs to find someone who wants nails. Not only is it easier to find a trading partner, but John is also more likely to come up with a *better* trade because Elaine now has competition.

Money is a great invention because it makes exchanges so easy to make that they *are made*. By reducing transaction costs, money makes it more likely that people will be specialists, thereby reaping the rewards of greater efficiency and higher living standards.

Suppose that Jane, a beekeeper, could use some of the cloth produced by Steve. Before people used money, someone in Jane's situation could get Steve's cloth only if Steve wanted some honey.

Honey and cloth are useful (beneficial), so Jane and Steve are producing things of value to themselves or to others. Jane and Steve can use only a little of the honey and cloth they make. But they make more than they need because this increases their ability to trade for other items. By making more honey and cloth, Jane and Steve gain the power to purchase more of other things. That is, by increasing their production, they increase their **purchasing power**.

★2

In a barter economy, people store purchasing power *in the things* they make. Jane and Steve would have had their purchasing power stored in the honey and cloth in their storage rooms. But in a modern economy, people store purchasing power *in the money* they earn by producing things. (They also store it in other assets that can be "denominated" or measured in money terms, such as corporate stocks and silver bullion.) Money, then, is a *representation* of purchasing power—the power people earn by producing things (really, by selling resources used to make things).

★3

Money has three functions, serving as: 1) a medium of exchange; 2) a store of value; and 3) a standard of value.

- As a **medium of exchange**, money replaces one of the goods needed for exchange. With barter, Jane got cloth from Steve only if he wanted honey. One good exchanged for another. Money eliminates the need for a double coincidence of wants.
- Money is a **store of value** because, when you hold on to money, you have the power to purchase goods or services whenever you want. You store value in it, just like pioneers stored value in the granaries they filled with grain to eat until the next harvest.
- Money is a **standard of value**, allowing people to know how much more one thing is worth than another thing. A "unit of account" makes such comparisons possible. In the United States, it is the U.S. dollar; in Mexico, the peso; and in China, the yuan. Thus, a $70 price tag on a radio means that the radio has a value equal to the combined purchasing power of 70 units of account (dollars).

These three functions are not independent of each other. For example, if prices rise extremely rapidly, money will be useless as a store of value. People would resort to barter for many exchanges, and money would cease to be used as a medium of exchange.

Characteristics of Money

Many things could represent purchasing power, and many things have in the past, including gold, silver, bronze, and even stones. Early American colonists, lacking coined precious metals and significant local sources of ore, used commodity money—literally, things. They used rice, dried fish, tobacco, sugar, beaver skins, and molasses as mediums of exchange. Pennsylvania residents in the late-1700s even used whiskey as money.

★4

Before people will accept something as money, it must meet several criteria that enable it to be a good medium of exchange. First, money should be portable. Carrying it around should be no problem (radioactive plutonium wouldn't work). Second, money must be durable (eggs wouldn't work). Third, money must be uniform—that is, all units (of a certain denomination) must have identical purchasing power (pumpkins fail this test). Fourth, money must be finely divisible so that it can buy things of small value, such as candy and safety pins (which explains why our unit of account is divided into 100 parts, or cents). Fifth, money must be scarce or rare. This ensures that it takes only a little of it to buy something. (Otherwise sand would have worked as well as gold did for so long. They were both uniform, durable, finely divisible, and portable—but sand wasn't rare and gold was. It might have taken a ton of sand to buy a dozen eggs.)

The Money Supply

What is (or should be considered) money in the United States? This might seem like an easy question, but at times even economists disagree on the answer. Remember, money is something that represents purchasing power (a store of value). This includes, of course, coins, paper money, and what is in our checking accounts. But what about the bonds people hold or what is in their savings accounts—don't people call that money, too? Is it? Well, yes and no.

You see, money is not only a representation of purchasing power (a store of value). It is also a medium of exchange. This means that before anything is used as money, businesses must readily accept it as an exchange for goods or services. Likewise, laborers and other sellers of resources must readily accept it. But people can't make exchanges with assets such as bonds or savings account "money." Nor can they make trades with foreign currency, stocks, or their life insurance cash values, even though they store value in these assets. Economists call some of these assets "near money." They are assets that serve as a store of value, cannot buy things, but can easily be changed into a *spendable* asset—money. In general, economists use the concept of liquidity to judge how close something is to money. Cash and checking account money can be spent at any time, so they are fully liquid. But you may have to visit your bank to get money from a savings account, so that money is less liquid.

To deal with this money definition problem, the government has four classifications of money: M1, M2, M3, and L. Each of these money measures, called **monetary aggregates**, has its own purpose. Here the concentration will be on M1, the most liquid form of money, which consists of: 1) currency; 2) non-bank travelers checks; and 3) checkable deposits.

■ All coins from pennies through the dollar coin constitute what is called fractional currency, which represents only two to three percent of M1. Fractional currency ensures that American money fulfills the divisibility characteristic of money.

Paper money is the second component of currency. A piece of U.S. paper money is called a Federal Reserve Note and is printed by the Treasury Department's Bureau of Engraving and Printing. The 12 Federal Reserve Banks (explained on page 297) distribute currency to the commercial banks. Each reserve bank has its "own" currency, as noted by the seal on the left front of each bill and the number on each corner. Every Federal Reserve District has its own letter and number. Paper currency accounts for 25 to 30 percent of M1.

However, M1 includes only currency held by people or businesses. Currency in banks is *not* money, strange as that seems. In fact, such currency has special names—vault cash or till money. Why is vault cash not money? Suppose you had $300 of money (purchasing power) in your checking account (which also is part of M1). You then write out a check for $100 in "cash" at your bank. After the teller gives you $100 in currency, you still have only $300 in money—$200 in checking plus $100 in currency. You merely *changed the form* of your money. So if $100 of checking account money disappeared when your balance dropped from $300 to $200, then $100 in vault cash must have *become* money at the same instant. That instant is when the teller gives you the currency. It doesn't change its physical appearance when the teller hands it to you, but what it *is does* change. It changes from green paper to a representation of purchasing power—money. Consequently, no one can steal money from a bank—because it has none!

■ Non-bank travelers checks also are money. Companies such as American Express issue such checks, which are usually just as easy to spend as cash. However, checks issued by banks such as the Bank of America are not included in M1, since these checks are already included in the banks' own checking accounts.

■ The amount of money in the form of checkable deposits is the largest component of money, usually including more than 70 percent of M1. A checkable account holds money that can be withdrawn or transferred to someone by writing a check. For large purchases or mail payment, a check is the most convenient and the safest way to pay. Deposits in checkable accounts are called demand deposits at commercial banks, negotiated orders of withdrawal at savings and loans, and share drafts at credit unions.

Checking account money is a bit abstract. *Where is* the money that is in the checking account? In your checkbook? The bank? Actually, it's *nowhere.* Remember, having money merely means you have *the power* to purchase things. You can't see or feel purchasing power—it's just "there." That's why paper money really isn't purchasing power *itself.* It merely *represents* this intangible thing called purchasing power. The purchasing power you have in your checking account is represented with numbers (rather than with metal or paper). Those numbers are not really in your checkbook—nor in the bank. They're just "there," for numbers are intangible. When Christy writes a $20 check to Stacey, Christy merely tells her bank to transfer 20 units of account of purchasing power ($20, that is) to Stacey. Then Stacey can place that purchasing power in currency form or in demand deposit form. Therefore, the check itself is not money. It is merely a form of communication between the check writer and the bank. To see this more clearly, note that the writing on a check is a sentence. If you wrote a $40 check to AT&T, it would read. "Pay to the order of AT&T $40." Your signature, on record at the bank, proves that you indeed ordered the bank to make the transfer.

Someday moving electrons (or electricity), a new form of communication between the depositor and the bank, will replace most checks. With **electronic funds transfer** (EFT), you instruct your bank to transfer purchasing power (money) from your account to some store's or other account with electronic rather than written communication. This is more efficient in several ways. It saves a vast amount of paperwork (by store clerks, mail carriers, and bank employees). It allows you to "write electronic checks" everywhere (not just where people know you). Before the transaction is completed, the electronic system informs you if there is enough money in your account to cover the purchase. Thus, you can no longer write a "bad check" and "cover it" before the check reaches your bank and your account is debited.

Such transactions are already being made by people who have **debit cards**. These look like credit cards but function as money. It might surprise you, but credit cards are not money because you can't buy anything with them. You can only *take possession* of goods by using credit cards. You actually buy the items you charged when you pay off your bill from the credit company. In 1991, according to the Nilson Report newsletter, 0.4 percent of store purchases were made by debit cards, and the figure is expected to climb to 2.7 percent by the year 2000.

M2 includes everything in M1 plus savings account deposits, time deposits (such as CDs, or certificates of deposit) up to $100,000, money market mutual fund shares and deposit accounts, plus overnight repurchase agreements. The other aggregates, M3 and L, differ in that they include other near monies (government banks, SDRs, etc.) in addition to the components of M1 and M2. Note that the other measures of money include M1 and less liquid forms of money, such as savings accounts. Generally, economists focus just on M1 because the various measures move together. However, at some times, as in the 1970s and 1980s, financial innovations cause the other measures of money to

Table 12-1 Monetary Aggregates

Monetary Aggregate (or component of)	**Amount in Billions** (in December)				
	1990	**1991**	**1992**	**1993**	**1994**
M1	$ 826.1	$ 898.1	$1026.6	____	____
Currency	$ 246.8	$ 267.3	$ 292.4	____	____
Demand Deposits	$ 277.1	$ 289.5	$ 340.9	____	____
Other Checkable Deposits	$ 293.9	$ 333.2	$ 385.2	____	____
Travelers Checks	$ 8.3	$ 8.2	$ 8.1	____	____
M2	$ 3339.0	$ 3439.8	$3503.5	____	____
M3	$ 4114.9	$ 4171.0	$4173.5	____	____
L	$ 4965.5	$ 4988.1	$5059.2	____	____

Source: *Federal Reserve Bulletin,* August 1993

move far more quickly than M1. One of those changes, the development of money market mutual funds, is discussed below, but life will be simpler if we focus mainly on M1.

Table 12-1 lists the actual amounts of each of these monetary aggregates. It also shows the share of M1 that each of its components represents.

THE FED, THE COMMERCIAL BANKING SYSTEM, AND CONTROLLING THE MONEY SUPPLY

The Federal Reserve System

In the 1800s and early 1900s, there were many serious monetary problems. One problem was the lack of a uniform national currency. From the 1830s through the 1850s, state-chartered banks each printed their own currency. Although their currencies were supposedly redeemable or convertible into gold, many of the banks had "offices" in the vast forests of the newly settled areas to avoid such redemption of the overprinted currency. They were called "wildcat banks" because they were often located where "there were more wildcats than people." By the early 1860s, there were 7,000 different state bank notes in circulation plus 5,000 counterfeit notes. Because each note had a different value (purchasing power), large city banks often hired specialists to keep track of such values. They were called bank tellers, as they were to "tell" the value of different currencies.

Another problem was caused by the rapid increases and decreases in the availability of credit, which led to frequent financial panics and depressions. Following one of these, the Panic of 1907, the National Monetary Commission was formed to study this problem.

As a result, the **Federal Reserve System**, commonly called the Fed, was established by the Federal Reserve Act of 1913. It controls the banking system and provides an "elastic currency," or a money supply that changes with the needs of the economy. The Fed is a **central bank**, or a "bankers' bank," which provides commercial banks financial services, just as individuals receive such services from commercial banks. Other nations also have central banks, such as the Bank of England, the Bank of Japan, and the Bundesbank (Germany).

★5 The Fed consists of the Board of Governors, 12 Federal Reserve District Banks, the Federal Open Market Committee, and three advisory committees. The seven members of the Board of Governors are appointed by the president and confirmed by Congress for 14-year terms. One member is appointed to a four-year term as chairman. Alan Greenspan took over the position in 1987 and was reappointed in 1991. The chairman is often called the second most powerful person in the country—and in terms of economic power, may be the *most* powerful.

Money is a lot like manure. Spread it around and it does a lot of good, but pile it in one place and it smells like hell. – Clint Murchisen

A state bank note of the "wildcat banking" period, issued by the Tecumseh Bank of Michigan.

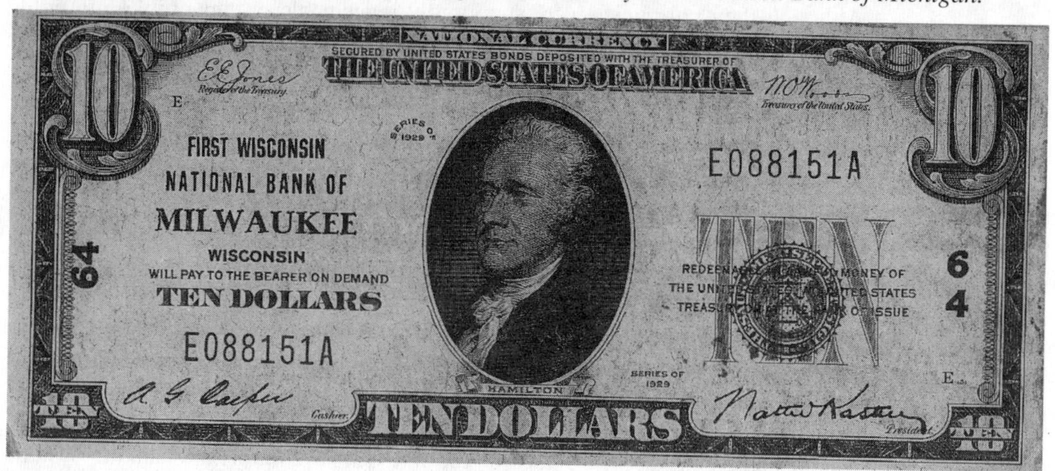

A national bank note (or national currency). The 1863 National Banking Act let each national bank issue its "own" currency.

Confederate currency issued by the Confederate States of America.

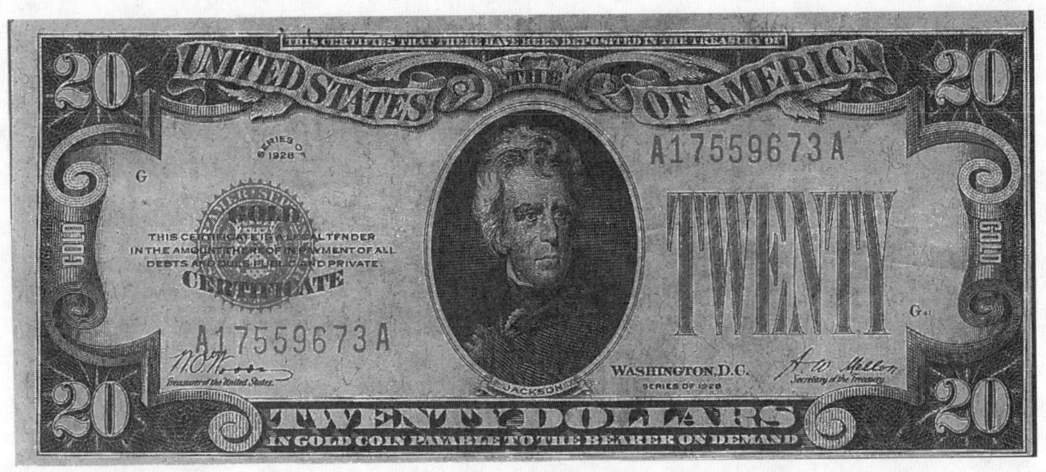

Gold certificates like this could be exchanged at the U.S. Treasury for gold until 1933.

An early version (1890) of silver certificates, which could be exchanged for silver at the Treasury.

The last version of silver certificates, which could be exchanged for silver coin until 1967.

The 12 Federal Reserve District Banks serve and control commercial banks in those districts. These banks (followed by their offical district numbers) are in Boston (1), New York City (2), Philadelphia (3), Cleveland (4), Richmond (5), Atlanta (6), Chicago (7), St. Louis (8), Minneapolis (9), Kansas City (10), Dallas (11), and San Francisco (12). The commercial banks own these facilities. All federally chartered banks must belong to the Federal Reserve System, and state chartered banks can join if they wish.

The Federal Open Market Committee consists of the seven Fed board members plus the presidents of five of the District Banks. This committee directs the purchase and sale of government securities in order to control the money supply (addressed in more detail shortly).

The three advisory committees include: 1) the Federal Advisory Council, a 12-member body that advises the Board of Governors on economic and banking issues; 2) the Consumer Advisory Council that represents consumers and institutions that finance them; and 3) the Thrift Institutions Advisory Council, which provides information and views on the special needs and problems of thrift institutions. It consists of one member from each of the 12 districts.

The Fed has several roles. First, its most important role is controlling the money supply. If Fed members believe that the economy needs more (or less) total spending, they increase (or decrease) the money supply with tools examined in the next section. Its second role is to clear checks—to transfer funds between banks when one party writes a check to a second party who banks elsewhere. To keep better track of money and keep the banking system honest, the Fed was given the power during the 1980s to clear all checks (which it did not do before), even those at credit unions. Third, the Fed holds the reserves that commercial banks must keep on hand to meet any heavy withdrawals by depositors. Fourth, the U.S. Treasury deposits its money with the Fed (from tax collections and other activities) and also sells its securities through it. Fifth, the Fed regulates commercial banks through a series of rules on banking practices. Sixth, the Fed issues new currency to commercial banks and collects and destroys worn or "mutilated money." Seventh, the Fed occasionally influences foreign exchange rates by buying or selling currencies of other nations. This is done in coordination with the U.S. Treasury, so it is not an independent function of the Fed.

The Fed doesn't control the money supply directly. Rather, it controls it indirectly by managing certain aspects of the banking system. Before considering how the Fed does this in detail, you must understand more about the private commercial banking system.

The Commercial Banking System

In the past, when economies were primarily local and small, a person who needed to borrow money generally did so directly from someone who had saved significant amounts of it earlier. The loan amounted to an exchange of purchasing power (money) between a saver and a borrower.

Today, only a tiny fraction of loans are made in this way. The complexity of our economy and the growth in the size of loans to finance large industrial and other projects requires the pooling of the savings of thousands of people. This pooling and the subsequent granting of loans is carried out by **financial interme-**

diaries, businesses that act as middlemen between savers and borrowers.

★6 Historically, financial intermediaries fell into two categories: commercial banks and thrifts. A **commercial bank** is defined by law as a firm that: 1) provides checking accounts; and 2) makes commercial (business) loans. There are about 11,000 commercial banks, and they are either nationally chartered by the Comptroller of the Currency (a U.S. Treasury agency) or state-chartered. Banks that are Fed members are regulated by the Fed, and non-member state banks are regulated by state banking boards. Bank deposits are insured up to $100,000 by the Federal Deposit Insurance Corporation (F.D.I.C.), an agency of the federal government.

There are three types of thrifts: 1) savings and loans; 2) savings banks; and 3) credit unions. They are called thrifts because most of the savers are (thrifty) individuals with relatively small accounts. However, several acts of the federal government have blurred the distinctions between banks and thrifts. (These will be covered in the next section on the savings and loan crisis.)

■ A **savings and loan** (S&L), the first type of thrift, was originally designed to provide credit to home buyers. In fact, until recently savings and loans were limited by law to home mortgages. There are about 3,000 S&Ls, half federally and half state-chartered. They are regulated by the Office of Thrift Supervision, a branch of the U.S. Treasury. Deposits up to $100,000 are insured by the Savings Association Insurance Fund.

■ The second type of thrift is the **savings bank**, also called a mutual savings bank. There are about 800 of these, concentrated in five Eastern states. They are operated as cooperatives, which means the depositors are the owners. These banks are regulated by the Federal Reserve Board, and deposits up to $100,000 are insured by the F.D.I.C. Recently, many S&Ls in the nation were converted into savings banks, partly to avoid regulation by the Office of Thrift Supervision and the associated examination fees.

■ The last type of thrift, the **credit union**, is a cooperative formed by members who work in the same firm or government agency or belong to the same union. The first was formed in 1909, and there are more than 14,000 today. Most are federally chartered, and these are regulated by the National Credit Union Association. Deposits up to $100,000 are insured by the National Credit Union Insurance Fund.

The Savings and Loan Crisis

The problem now facing many of the nation's savings and loan associations is being called the worst financial crisis in America's history. Undoubtedly this is because of the bailout cost estimates, which started at about $40 billion in 1984 and reached hundreds of billions by 1990. How did we get into such a mess?

> *Rags make paper; paper makes money; money makes banks; banks make loans; loans make poverty; poverty makes rags.* – Jacob Coxey

It started with the rising interest rates of the late 1970s. These were a consequence of the high inflation rates of the period. Savings and loans (as well as banks) were limited by the Fed in how much interest they could pay to savers. They were allowed to pay 0.5 percent more than banks paid. (The intent was to ensure that S&Ls could attract funds needed by home buyers.) In the late 1970s, money market mutual funds arrived on the scene. The non-bank firms that offered these funds paid very high interest rates (commonly above 12 percent). Even though deposits in these firms were not insured, much money was withdrawn from S&Ls and placed in these funds. Besides suffering from shrinking deposits, many S&Ls were hurt by loans they made in the 1950s and 1960s. Many of the loans were 30-year home loans at fixed rates between six and eight percent. Since these wouldn't be paid off until between the mid-1980s and the turn of the century, S&Ls had a smaller income than if they had protected themselves with escalator clauses, which allow them to raise rates.

★7 In 1980, partly to help the S&Ls remain in business, Congress passed the Monetary Control Act. It allowed S&Ls to pay whatever interest rates they wanted (after a phase-in period to April 1986). It also allowed S&Ls (and other financial institutions) to pay interest on checking accounts.

But that act didn't solve their problem of declining profits that resulted from low income on home mortgages and increasing costs of borrowed money. In 1982, the growing number of insolvent (bankrupt) S&Ls led Congress to pass the Garn-St. Germaine Depository Institutions Act. The act allowed S&Ls to offer higher-paying money market deposit accounts and to make loans in a wide range of areas to consumers and businesses, rather than only in home mortgages. It also made it easier for S&Ls to merge (so the weaker partners could survive).

By the 1980s, a combination of factors led to wholesale bankruptcies of S&Ls (especially in the Sun Belt) and to subsequent government bailouts. First, funding was cut sharply for the Federal Home Loan Bank Board, the primary regulator of the industry. Second, 100-percent insurance on depositors' accounts invited unwise risks by S&L managers (and people were allowed to have multiple accounts, each one insured to $100,000). If the loans the managers made weren't repaid, depositors couldn't lose. So in their battle to stay alive, many lenders put money into very risky ventures, including real estate—just when the real estate boom was ending. Many also invested in junk bonds, which nose-dived in 1989 and 1990. Third, fraud and use of an S&L's deposits by managers for lavish personal expenses further weakened many S&Ls. Fourth, several powerful politicians were accused of either dragging their feet in dealing with these problems or of helping executives of troubled S&Ls in return for campaign money.

In 1989, Congress passed Public Law 101-73 to deal with the crisis. It had three main components. First, it required S&Ls to have at least 70 percent of their loans in home mortgages and other residential loans. Second, the previous insurer of depositors' funds, the Federal Savings and Loan Insurance Corporation (F.S.L.I.C.), was replaced by the Savings Association Insurance Fund (S.A.I.F.). Third, the Resolution Trust Corporation (RTC) was formed to bail out failed S&Ls. Under the bailout plan, the U.S. Treasury will sell $50 billion in 30-year bonds. The funds obtained will be used to buy the failed S&Ls and liquidate (sell) the properties to which the S&Ls lent money. By 1992, according to the Southern Finance Project (a private think tank), the RTC was selling properties for only 55 percent of the value they were assigned when the S&Ls lent money for them. Apartment buildings brought 68 cents on the dollar, hotels 77 cents, and undeveloped land only 36 cents.

How Banks Create Money

One of the more baffling things about economics is how banks create money. To understand this, remember that coin and paper currency account for only about one-fifth of our money and that the U.S. Treasury makes that form of money. Checkable deposits make up most of the rest. And such money is possible because of the banking system, especially because of the ability of banks to make loans.

Hundreds of years ago, there were no banks. Many people saved their money (often gold) at home. But goldsmiths commonly stored other people's gold in their vaults for a fee. Over time the receipts given by the goldsmiths to "depositors," rather than the gold itself, became the medium of exchange. It was said that the receipts were "as good as gold" because they were "backed by gold." Eventually the goldsmiths realized they could lend out some of the gold, for it was unlikely that all "depositors" would want to draw out their gold simultaneously. The borrowers of the gold could then use it to buy things. Now, did the total value of the savers' money (gold) deposits drop because of such loans? No. And because the loans *added to* the purchasing power of the original money supply, the money supply increased. Eventually, instead of charging a fee to depositors, goldsmiths *paid* a fee—interest—in order to get more people to deposit (save) their money.

★8 It isn't all that different today. Suppose you receive a check for $1,000 and open a checking account with it. Because of your deposit, your bank can now make a loan. However, the Fed requires banks to keep a certain share of such deposits as part of its **required reserves**, and they cannot make loans based on this share of those deposits. The **reserve requirement** is the percentage of such deposits the bank must keep on reserve, either in the bank vault or at the Fed. (It is called the reserve ratio when expressed in decimal form.) Suppose that it's 20 percent of your $1,000 deposit, or $200. Thus, the bank is free to lend an amount of money equal to the difference, or $800, to Susan, who wants a new stereo system. The bank either sets up a checking account for Susan, putting the $800 into it, or gives her a cashier's check. If she has a new checking account, she can write $800 worth of checks, so the $800 is money. She can also use the cashier's check to buy the stereo or anything else, so it, too, is money. Either way, where did the money come from? From *your* checking account? Well, how much is in your account now, assuming that you didn't spend any of it—$200 or $1,000? The answer is $1,000.

So, where did Susan get the $800 for her stereo? After all, you still have all your $1,000 in your account. Almost magically, the bank "created it" from out of nowhere! Banks have such power. That's why it's important to grasp the concept that money is a *representation* of purchasing power. So if Susan has more purchasing power (represented by money) and you don't have any less, then the bank must have created the money, thereby increasing the amount of purchasing power in the economy. This process repeats itself when Susan buys the stereo and the dealer deposits the $800 check. The dealer's bank can now lend 80 percent of $800, or $640. After many such "cycles," your original $1,000 deposit leads to a *multiple* increase in the money supply. The reason that coins and currency are only about one-fifth of M1 is because they lead to the creation of demand deposits which, in turn, lead to the creation of even more demand deposits. (It's like two people who ultimately create a family of 100 people, but only make up two percent of the family themselves.)

Often banks make fewer loans than they are allowed to make on the basis of their depositors' money. This difference between what banks can lend and what they have already lent is called **excess reserves**, or the reserves banks have in excess of their required reserves. Because excess reserves are capable of creating new money, the Fed controls their amount in order to control the money supply. The **deposit multiplier** refers to the number of times the money supply could expand if all excess reserves were lent. It is found by:

$$\text{Deposit Multiplier} = \frac{1}{\text{Reserve Requirement}}$$

In the bank example above, where Susan got her loan, the deposit multiplier is five (= 1/0.2).

The Fed's Control of Bank Reserves and the Money Supply

★9

The Fed controls these excess reserves and, in turn, the money supply, with three main techniques or tools: 1) the discount rate; 2) the reserve requirement; and 3) open market operations. Excess reserves give banks the ability to increase the money supply by using these reserves as the basis for additional loans. Thus, when excess reserves are increased, the money supply can grow faster. Conversely, when excess reserves are decreased, the money supply can't expand as fast.

■ The **discount rate** is the rate of interest the Fed charges its commercial bank members when it lends them additional reserves. When you put money in a checking or savings account, the bank can use your money (purchasing power) to create more purchasing power in the form of a loan. The Fed gives your bank another method of creating purchasing power through loans when it lends the bank these reserves. However, the Fed doesn't actually lend the bank any *money*—only what are called reserves. These reserves represent the ability to create purchasing power when your bank makes a loan. That purchasing power, in the form of a demand deposit, *is* money.

In reality, banks seldom borrow reserves from the Fed. When they do, it's usually because they find that they don't have sufficient deposits with the Fed plus vault cash (the two together are called legal reserves) to meet the reserve requirement. (Reserve requirements must be met with legal reserves.) This could occur if several major depositors at a bank withdrew their funds at a time when the bank had few or no excess reserves.

The reason the Fed changes the discount rate usually is not to change the amount of borrowing but to send a message to lending institutions. The message is that the Fed has either expanded or contracted bank reserves in alternative ways. Usually these actions coincide with moves in interest rates in financial markets.

■ Changing the reserve requirement is the second method the Fed uses to control bank reserves. Figure 12-2 shows a bank that initially had $100 million in deposits from saving and checking account deposits. If the reserve requirement is 20 percent, then the bank must have $20 million in required reserves. Thus, it can make $80 million in loans. But if it made only $60 million in loans so far, it has excess reserves of $20 million. Suppose the Fed reduces the reserve requirement to 15 percent. Then the bank needs only $15 million in required reserves, leaving $85 million that it can lend. Because it lent only $60 million so far, it has $25 million in excess reserves, an increase of $5 million. This change appears in the diagram on the right. The middle diagram shows the reverse, where the Fed raises the reserve requirement to 25 percent. Since the bank now needs $25 million in required reserves, it is left with only $15 million in excess reserves.

Figure 12-2 Changing Bank Reserves by Changing the Reserve Requirement

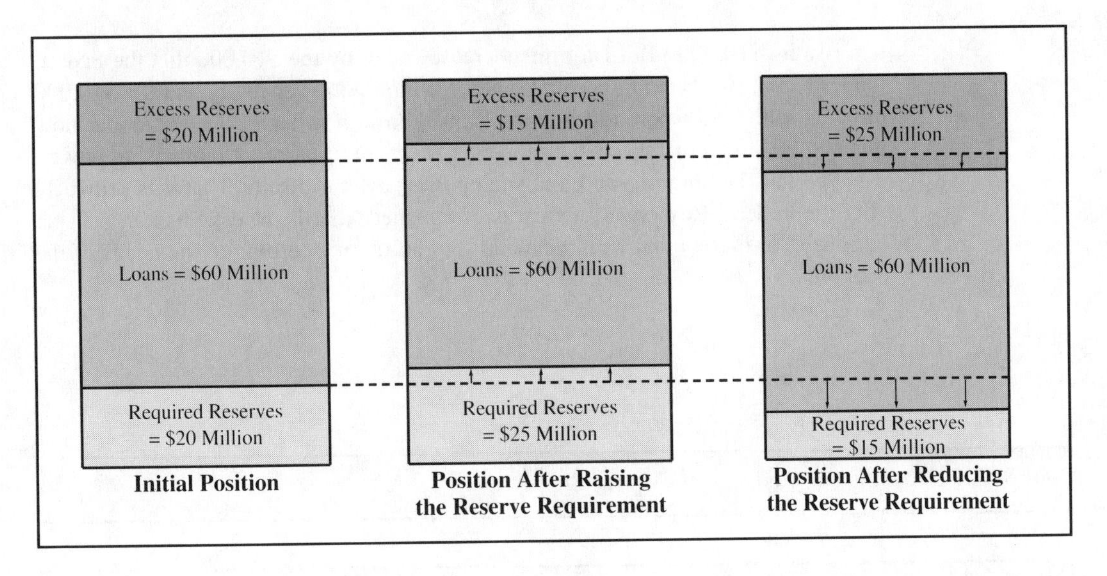

★10

■ The last method for changing excess bank reserves is **open market operations**, referring to the Fed's purchases and sales of federal government securities the Treasury sells to finance the budget deficit. Often the initial buyers of these securities decide not to hold them to maturity, so their brokers find buyers for the securities. You can follow each of these steps in Figure 12-3. Suppose you buy a $10,000 T-bill from some individual through a broker. What happens to the total excess reserves in the entire banking system as a consequence? Nothing, for although your bank has $10,000 less in total reserves after you write a check to the broker, the seller's bank has $10,000 more after the seller deposited your check. These effects on reserves cancel each other.

But suppose the Fed buys that T-bill instead. The Fed's $10,000 check is deposited in the original bondholder's bank, so reserves in the entire banking sys-

Figure 12-3 The Deficit and Money Creation by the Fed

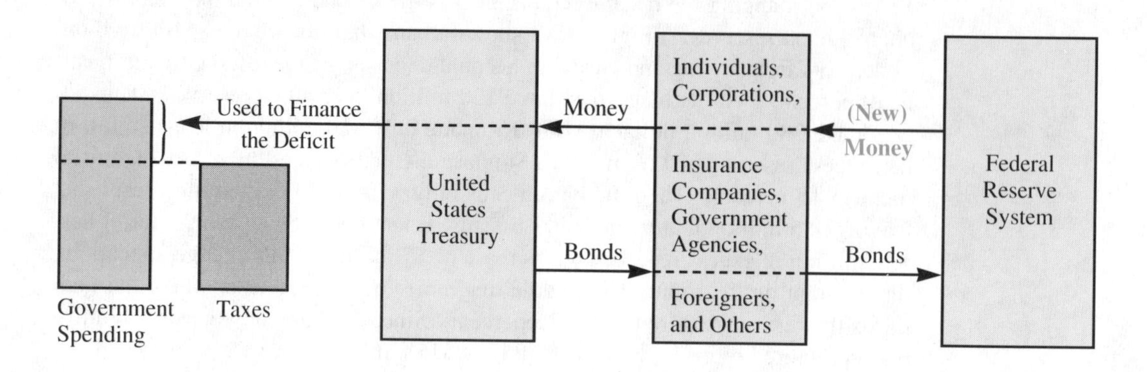

tem rise by $10,000. But isn't this increase offset by the $10,000 that the Fed no longer has in its checking account? No, for the Fed never really had the $10,000 to begin with. So where did it come from? From nowhere! If you wonder how that can be, just remember what money is—a representation of purchasing power. The Fed has the authority to grant such power, even to itself. That was primarily why the Federal Reserve System was established, that is, to establish an "elastic currency" or money that would expand (or contract) according to the needs of the economy.

Figure 12-4 How the Fed Reduces the Money Supply

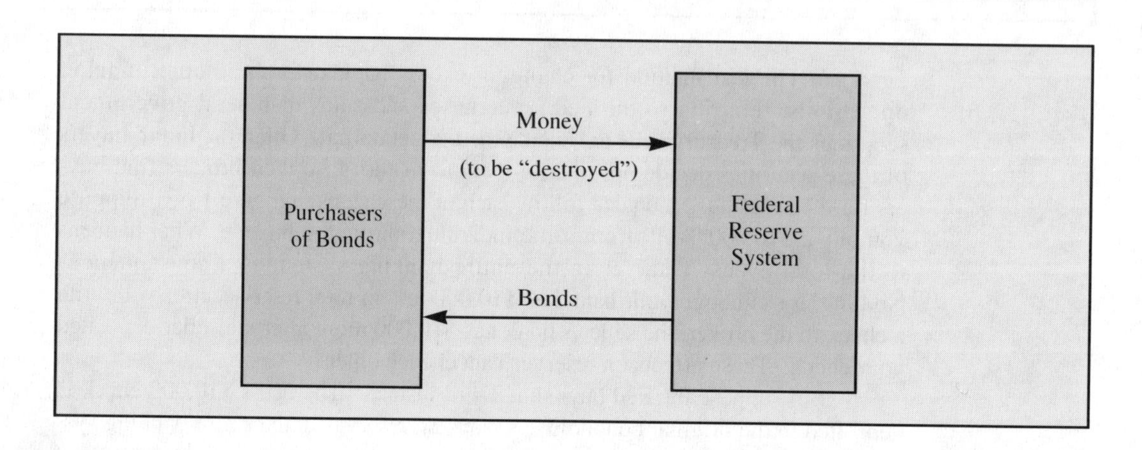

Alternatively, suppose the Fed *sells* you a bond. If you write the Fed a check for $10,000, your bank's total reserves drop by that amount, leaving the bank less to lend. What does the Fed do with the $10,000? The Fed acts as if it never got the check. It neither spends it nor adds it to any savings or checking account. The money—$10,000 worth of purchasing power—simply vanishes. You surely couldn't do that with gold. See Figure 12-4 for an illustration of this.

The Fed determines whether to expand or contract bank reserves by observing the **federal funds rate**. That is the interest rate on so-called federal funds, or excess reserves that commercial banks lend to each other. This rate gives the Fed an indication of the availability of credit in the entire economy and, consequently, of the likelihood of increased loans and spending. If there are few excess reserves, there is little credit available and the federal funds rate will be high. Alternatively, a low rate indicates ample excess reserves and availability of credit.

Following this introduction to money, the next two chapters are concerned with problems of the macroeconomy. Often these problems have to do with the money supply. Finally, Chapter 15 explains, among other things, how the Fed uses changes in the money supply to deal with these problems.

Chapter 12 SUMMARY

Money is an indirect consequence of specialization. When we specialize the use of our resources to increase productivity, we need to exchange goods and services with each other. Producing goods and services give specialists the power to obtain other goods and services through exchanges. One way to exchange, though inefficiently, is with a barter system. Modern economies need a medium of exchange, or money, to make exchanges efficiently, which means with low transactions cost. Money is a representation of purchasing power, and it serves three functions, as: 1) a medium of exchange; 2) a store of value; and 3) a standard of value. Anything used as money needs to be portable, durable, uniform, finely divisible, and scarce.

The U.S. Government has four classifications of money. The most important, M1, consists of currency, checking account deposits, and travelers checks. Savings accounts and other assets are called near money.

The Federal Reserve System's primary functions involve regulating commercial banks and controlling the money supply. It consists of the Board of Governors, the District Banks, member banks, the Federal Open Market Committee, and three advisory boards.

Financial intermediaries, which connect savers and borrowers, include commercial banks, savings banks, savings and loans, and credit unions. They are either federally or state chartered, are regulated by federal and/or state agencies, and have their deposits insured by the federal government.

The savings and loan crisis developed in the late 1970s and in the 1980s, starting with high interest rates and low income. Several government acts sought to make S&Ls more competitive, but it also led to reckless management and many failures. The government bailout of the industry is expected to cost several hundred billion dollars.

Commercial banks create money when they make loans that are made possible with bank deposits. They are required to keep a small share of deposits either at the Fed or in their vaults. Reserves held by banks in excess of their required reserves are called excess reserves and represent a potential increase in the money supply.

The Fed controls excess bank reserves and the money supply by changes in the discount rate and the reserve requirement and through open market operations. When excess reserves are increased by cuts in the discount rate and the reserve requirement or by the purchase of government securities, the money supply expands, and vice versa.

Chapter 12 RESPONSES TO THE LEARNING OBJECTIVES

1. Things of value can be exchanged in:
   a) a barter system, where two things of value are exchanged for each other
   b) a money system, where one thing of value is exchanged for a medium of exchange that usually has no value but can be traded again for something of value

2. Money is anything that represents the power to purchase goods and services and is used to exchange for them.

3. Money functions as a medium of exchange, a store of value, and a standard of value.

4. Anything used as money should be durable, finely divisible, uniform, portable, and rare.

5. The Federal Reserve System consists of the Board of Governors, the 12 Federal Reserve District Banks, the member banks, the Federal Open Market Committee, and three advisory councils.

6. Commercial banks accept checkable deposits and make commercial loans. Historically, thrifts could not, including savings and loans, savings banks, and credit unions. But they began to do so in the 1980s. S&Ls concentrate on real estate loans. Credit unions operate through sources of employment and operate on a cooperative basis.

7. The Monetary Control Act was primarily designed to allow savings and loans to better compete with other financial intermediaries by paying higher interest rates. The Garn-St. Germaine Act was also intended to aid S&Ls by allowing them to invest in a wider variety of areas besides real estate.

8. Banks create money when they establish a demand deposit made possible by the excess reserves. This demand deposit becomes part of the money supply.

9. The Fed changes the money supply indirectly by changing the amount of excess reserves there are in the commercial banking system. More of such reserves lead to more loans and, in turn, a larger money supply, and vice versa. The Fed controls excess reserves by: 1) changing the discount rate; 2) changing the reserve requirement; and 3) by buying and selling government securities in open market operations.

10. Expansionary open market operations involve the Fed purchasing government securities from individuals and others that had previously been purchased from the U.S. Treasury. The effect is to increase excess reserves. Contractionary open market operations involve the sale of government securities by the Fed to individuals and others. Such sales reduce the level of excess reserves.

Chapter 12 LEARNING ACTIVITIES AND DISCUSSION QUESTIONS

1. Try and make a hypothetical barter trade with some item you own, a trade you actually would be willing to make. Next, try and sell that same item for a price that is acceptable to you. Keep track of the total time each trade took. Was there any difference in time? Why?
2. Calculate the percentages of your "personal" M1 that are in the form of coin, paper currency, checking account money, and travelers checks. How close are your figures to the actual M1?
3. Ask five people where they have their checking accounts and savings accounts and why they chose those financial intermediaries. Do you see a pattern?
4. In what sense is counterfeit money actually money, and in what sense is it not?
5. If you state that you "made more money" this year than last year, does that mean M1 is bigger this year than last year? Reconcile your answer to your statement.

CHAPTER 13

MACROECONOMIC ACTIVITY AND RECESSION

★★★★★ LEARNING OBJECTIVES ★★★★★

1. Compare and contrast the four phases of the business cycle.
2. Identify the components of the macroeconomic model.
3. Explain the relationships between the variables in the macroeconomic model.
4. Describe the appearance of an economy that is in macroeconomic equilibrium.
5. Describe the two conditions necessary for an economy to reach equilibrium.
6. List the three major and seven additional events that occur during a recession.
7. Explain why recession occurs.
8. Indicate the three causes of a decline in total spending.
9. Explain why consumer, investment, and government spending decline.
10. Explain how a recession can be avoided if something occurs that tends to cause a recession.

TERMS

business cycles
prosperity
recession
contraction
trough
depression
recovery
expansion
personal income
disposable income
macroeconomic equilibrium
equilibrium GDP
leakage
injection
growth recession
econometric model

One way people deal with the economic problem caused by the scarcity of resources is to specialize. Although specialization increases efficiency and, consequently, living standards, it also forces specialists to exchange with each other. But sometimes people have trouble finding others with whom to trade. Under such circumstances, for instance, business owners (and, in effect, their employees) don't sell as much as they would like (that is, they don't trade many goods or services for money). And many people who wish to sell their time for money (that is, they want to work) can't find anyone to employ them. This inability to trade results in idled resources and, thus, reduced living standards. This is what business cycles—the topic of this chapter—are all about.

BUSINESS CYCLES

The subsistence economy of the distant past changed very slowly over time. Each year all families produced about the same amount of whatever they needed the most and had time and ambition to produce. Consequently, the "gross domestic product" of these early economies changed little. Their "GDP" was the total output of goods and services of all families combined. It increased mainly because the population grew and because occasional innovations increased the efficiency of resource use. However, because these people didn't specialize much, they remained poor by today's standards.

Specialization and exchange gradually became more common. When this happened, people produced goods and services for others rather than just for themselves. So long as people made exchanges by bartering, the economy remained similar to earlier times. People still needed about the same amount of the same things each year from the few people with whom they traded. Production didn't change much, except to the extent that weather affected agricultural output.

When the use of money made bartering obsolete, relationships between specialists changed. Instead of two specialists agreeing on an exchange and then making their respective products, now products were made *in anticipation of* exchanges (sales). Today when trading is very active for most people, the economy is said to be in prosperity. When trading slows down, the period is known as recession.

Phases of the Business Cycle

Records from as long as 150 years ago tell about prosperity and recession. Because the good and bad times alternated, the economy experienced what economists call **business cycles**. However, although the word "cycles" implies *regularity* of change, business cycles are anything but regular. Prosperity can last a decade—or only a year—as can recession.

★1 A business cycle has four phases: 1) prosperity; 2) recession; 3) trough; and 4) recovery. Figure 13-1 illustrates these phases.

Figure 13-1 The Business Cycle

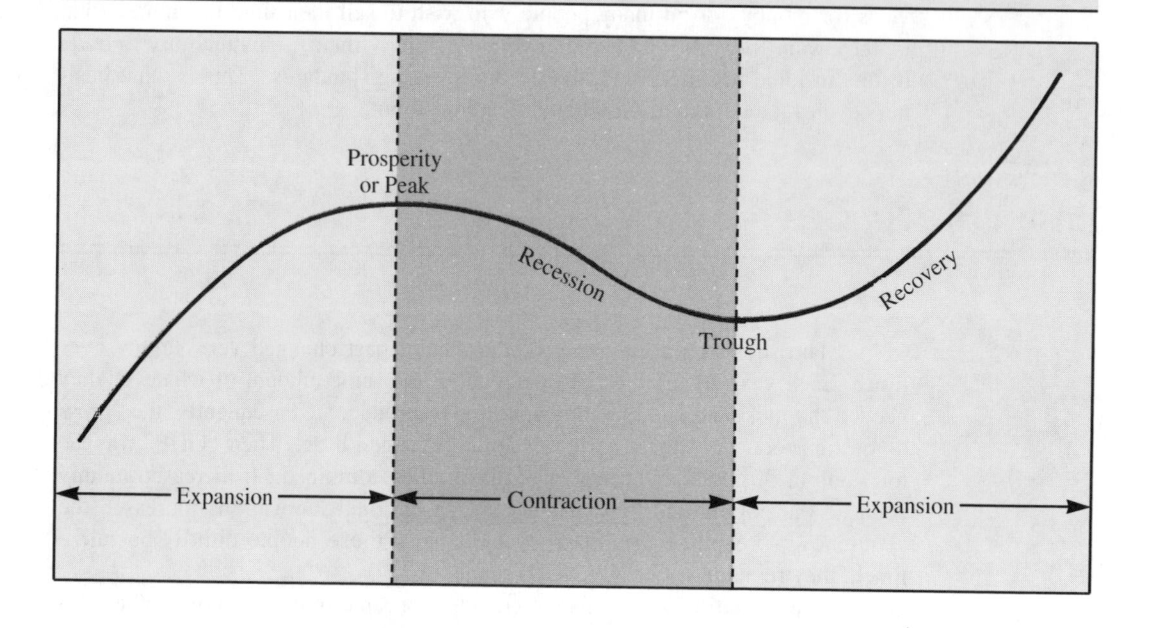

Prosperity means a high percentage of individuals and businesses succeed in selling (trading or exchanging) their resources and products. Jobs are easy to find. Most firms can sell any product or service they make, and it is relatively easy to become prosperous. If times are exceptionally good, the economy is said to be experiencing a boom. Another word for the prosperity part of the cycle is "peak."

> *Take care to be an economist in prosperity; there is no fear of your not being one in adversity.*
> – Zimmerman

> *An economist is the fellow who'll figure out tomorrow why the things he predicted yesterday didn't happen today.*
> – Anonymous

> *Some economists can't predict exactly when a business slowdown will occur, but we can – 4:15 most days, 3:30 on Fridays.*
> – Anonymous

■ Sooner or later the economy "cools off" or enters a **recession**, a time when many macroeconomic variables decline (recede). Businesses sell less and, in turn, cut production. Consequently, employment drops and job openings are rare. Years ago people called this a "bust" period (like an expanding bubble that "busted"). If conditions got bad very quickly, the frightened firm owners, investors, and employees panicked (partly because there were no government programs, such as unemployment compensation, to ease the burden). Such periods were known as panics, such as the Rich Man's Panic (1903) and the Panic of 1907. Finally, such a period was called a **contraction** because the whole economy seemed to contract or grow smaller.

■ The next phase of the business cycle is the **trough**. As with an ocean wave, the trough refers to a low point—specifically, the worst point of the business cycle. Business sales and employment drop to their lowest point. Years ago people called this condition a **depression**, but today economists refer to it as a trough. Today the term depression refers to a very bad recession. For instance, if the unemployment rate remained above 10 percent for several years, we would say the economy was in a depression. The last such depression was the Great Depression, lasting from 1929 through 1941.

■ When there is significant improvement in sales, employment, and other variables, the economy enters the **recovery** phase of the cycle. Like a patient recovering from surgery, an economy in recovery is still in relatively poor shape. But sooner or later the economy returns to the prosperity phase. The period starting with the recovery and extending throughout the prosperity period to the next peak is called the **expansion** because the economy "expands" in size (more output, employment, and other positive trends).

A MACROECONOMIC MODEL

An economic model simplifies the way a certain part of the economy operates. All the variables, elements, and inter-relationships don't appear in the model—just the main ones. Economists build models to get a clearer picture of how the major elements of the economy interact.

★2

Figure 13-2 is a model of the macroeconomy that can be compared to the circular flow model of the microeconomy in Figure 7-1, page 167. It illustrates the connections between total spending, production, employment, income, taxes, savings, and spending by consumers, investors, and governments. When you examine the model, keep in mind these assumptions: 1) there is no foreign trade; 2) there are no transfer payments—thus, people earn all their income; 3) the money supply remains constant; 4) the amount of resources and the level of resource efficiency remain constant; 5) all governments balance their budgets; 6) businesses pay no taxes—thus, all business income flows to the owners; and 7) financial institutions lend out all savings for investment spending, so consumers pay cash for their purchases. (These assumptions *can* be dropped, and the first one will be later on. This artificial simplicity makes it easier to understand the major relationships in the macroeconomy and how recession happens.)

Figure 13-2 A Model of the Macroeconomy

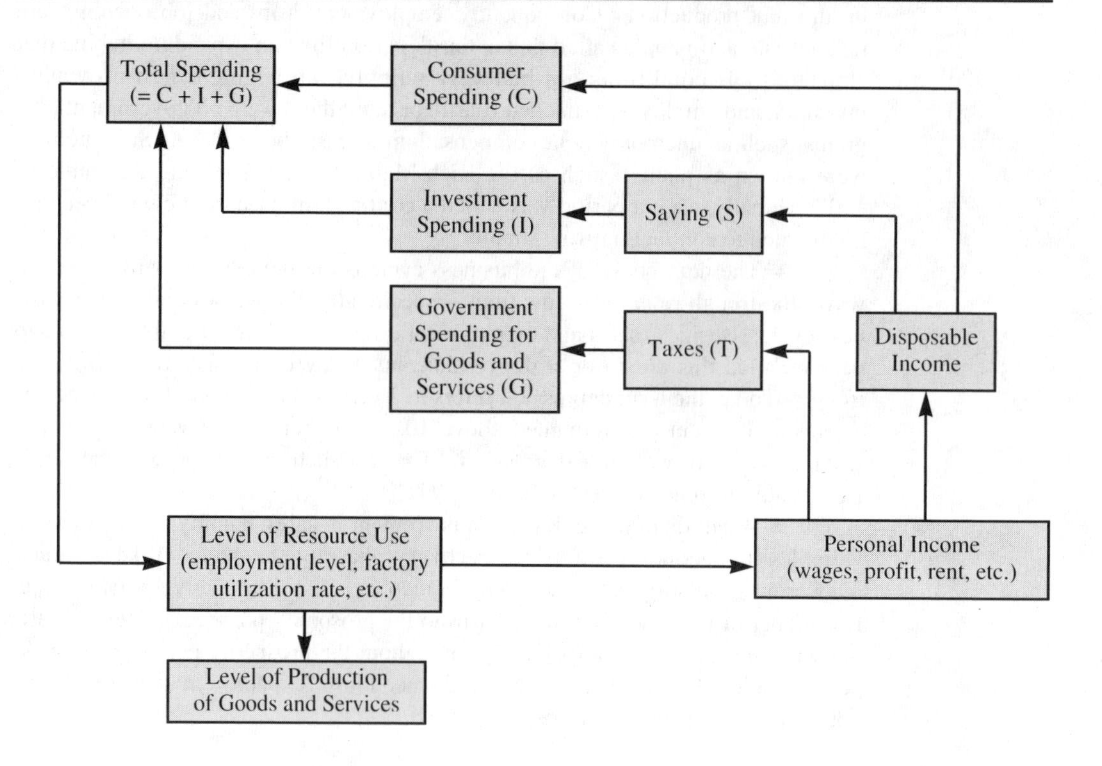

★3

In examining the model, it's best to start at the top left, with total spending. (Total spending is often called aggregate demand—that is, the sum of the demands for all final goods.) Total spending is the GDP from the expenditure approach, composed of expenditures by consumers (C), investors (I), and governments (G). Net exports (X - M) do not appear because it is assumed there is no foreign trade. Total spending is the main influence on the next component in the model, the level of resource use. This "level" refers to how many workers businesses hire, how many supplies they buy, and how many factories they build. The higher total spending is, the more resources firms will buy. Firms want these resources in order to produce goods and services. As resource use increases, so does the level of production of goods and services.

People sell resources in order to earn income. Thus, the more resources they sell, the greater is their **personal income**, including: 1) wages, salaries, and commissions paid to laborers; 2) interest paid to owners of capital; 3) rent paid to owners of natural resources; and 4) profits paid to entrepreneurs. (The government calculates personal income each month, but the government's figure differs from the model in that it includes transfer payments.)

In the model, personal income is divided into two parts—taxes and disposable income. Taxes allow governments to spend money on goods and services.

Next, government spending (G) becomes part of total spending (the starting point). **Disposable income** refers to that part of personal income that people are free to "dispose of," the part they retain after paying taxes. People "dispose of" their income either: 1) by consumption, or spending on consumer goods (C); or 2) by saving (S), or not spending all or part of their income. Consumption provides the second leg of the total spending composite. The final leg is investment spending (I), including spending for capital goods, construction of buildings, and any change in inventories. It is assumed that firms borrow money for such spending or use their savings (such as retained earnings from their profits).

Now that you are familiar with the basic model (Figure 13-2), let's consider what else influences the three components of total spending.

■ First—consumer spending. Besides disposable income, consumer confidence in the economy's future is another major determinant of consumption. If people expect a recession, they will spend less now in order to have some money for the bad times ahead. Interest rates and the availability of credit also determine how much consumers spend. Lower interest rates and readily available credit encourage consumers to spend.

■ Second, interest rates, along with expectations of future sales and profit, determine investment spending. Predictions of good times ahead cause investment spending to rise because firms want to be ready with new capital equipment and factories when people start buying at a faster rate. Conversely, firms spend less on capital if they expect lower sales of their products in the future. Tax laws favoring business expansion stimulate investment spending. Finally, government regulation and "red tape" often discourage capital spending by businesses.

■ Third, government spending depends not only upon tax receipts, but also upon how much governments can borrow. In turn, borrowing by governments depends upon interest rates, the political acceptability of deficits, and legal or constitutional restrictions on such borrowing.

Let's return to the simpler economy of the macroeconomic model in Figure 13-2. We can now use this model to show how an economy gets into recession or inflation. However, before using the model to illustrate recession or inflation possibilities, we must first consider macroeconomic equilibrium, a condition where there is neither recession nor inflation.

THE MACROECONOMY IN EQUILIBRIUM

You are already familiar with equilibrium on the microeconomic level. The equilibrium price for a good is the price that balances consumers' desires for that good with the amount firms offer for sale, an amount called the equilibrium quantity. Now a similar situation is examined for the economy as a whole—the macroeconomy.

The Meaning of Macroeconomic Equilibrium

★4

Macroeconomic equilibrium means certain macroeconomic variables don't change over time. The variables are those in the macroeconomic model, including total spending, the amount of production of goods and services (GDP), personal income, and employment. Several forces tend to increase or decrease each variable, but in equilibrium these forces balance each other. Thus, each variable does not change. So **equilibrium GDP** is the level of GDP that does not change over time because all the forces that influence it are balanced. (This view of equilibrium is called static equilibrium, where an economy does not grow. More sophisticated analysis involves the study of dynamic equilibrium, where growth can occur. It is not the intent of this book to present such in-depth analysis.)

The beginning of this chapter focused on macroeconomic equilibrium in a subsistence, non-exchange economy, where almost everyone produced the same things each year and in the same amounts. Thus, the collective output of the members of society—their "GDP"—did not change either.

To keep things simple, we will proceed as if equilibrium occurs only when there is no inflation and no unemployment. This allows us to ask what changes would lead the economy into inflation or unemployment. However, as you will discover in Chapter 15, "Keynesian" economists believe that equilibrium can exist when there is unemployment or inflation and that government intervention is then required to solve these problems. The analysis is not much different in the Keynesian case, but you should be aware that equilibrium does not always mean there is no inflation or unemployment.

Conditions Under Which Equilibrium Occurs

Before proceeding, we must make another assumption about price levels in the model. "Price level" refers to the consideration of all prices simultaneously, as measured by a price index. It is assumed that in equilibrium there is only one price level. That is, prices in general don't rise (inflation) or fall (deflation).

GDP reflects the production of all businesses combined. Why would these firms produce the same amount each year, which they do in equilibrium? Think of why businesses produce anything at all. To sell their products and make a profit, of course. As you've learned, when customers buy more than previously, firms usually expand output. When customers buy less than previously, firms usually cut back on output.

Therefore, if a firm neither expands nor cuts back on output this year, apparently the managers think they can sell the same output as last year—no more and no less. This is because customers want to buy the same amount as last year. Now suppose that all firms are in this situation. Suppose further that the combined sales of all firms last year equaled the value of what they produced. Thus, their warehouse inventories neither increased nor decreased. Then the total output of the nation this year will not change from last year's level, for if total spending doesn't change, firms will not change output.

Look at what problems happen if that output *does* change. First, if output expands and spending does not, firms store the extra output in warehouses—a costly procedure. Alternatively, if firms cut back on output while customers still want the same amount of goods and services, the firms must remove products from their warehouse inventories. Eventually, some customers won't get all they want to buy. Because this annoys customers and means profit opportunities are lost, firms try to avoid this situation. Thus, if total spending remains constant, firms neither expand nor contract output to avoid these problems.

★5 Therefore, for an economy to reach macroeconomic equilibrium, it is necessary for total spending to equal the total value of goods and services produced, given a particular price level.

An important question is: How does total spending remain constant? A constant level of total spending is a part of macroeconomic equilibrium, along with a constant level of total production. Total spending equals the combined spending of consumers (C), investors (I), and governments (G). It's easy to imagine constant "spending" in a simple subsistence economy of the past. Of course, with no money and exchanging, those people didn't spend any money. But they did spend *time and effort* to make things, the counterpart of today's consumer spending. Their efforts ("spending") didn't change yearly because their needs didn't change.

Two main elements of today's economy, savings and taxes, pose potential problems for the stability of total spending. Economists refer to savings and taxes as **leakages** (that is, they "leak out" of the spending flow). That's because resource earners: 1) save some of the income they earn in order to buy goods and services *in the future;* and 2) use some of it to pay taxes to support the government. In other words, people don't spend all of *today's* income for goods and services received *today.*

Does the fact that people don't spend all their income mean that total spending drops each year? No, for someone else spends the part they don't spend. Savings usually are not placed in cookie jars, but in banks and other financial institutions. In turn, these savings give financial institutions the ability to make loans so firms can purchase capital equipment and individuals can build homes. So long as *all* savings dollars find their way into investment spending, total spending will not fall just because some personal income "leaked" out of the normal spending stream.

Similarly, the taxes people pay don't just remain in government treasuries. Governments spend that money as fast as possible, it seems. Thus, *total* spending can be the same as if people spent all their income themselves as soon as they earned it. What differs is that government spending is now part of total spending, making the consumer component smaller. So long as government spending equals taxes, the tax leakage won't cause total spending to fall.

A related term to leakages is **injections**, which refers to investment spending and government spending. It means "idled" money is "put to use" in purchasing goods and services—or money is "injected" into the "spending stream." (Note that this is not *new* money created by the Federal Reserve System. See pages 302-303 for an explanation.)

Macroeconomic equilibrium is achieved if the combined injections equal the combined leakages—that is, if savings plus taxes equal investment spending plus government spending. In equilibrium, owners of resources use all the money they earn producing goods and services to purchase that same amount of goods and services. The value of those purchases equals what they spend on consumer goods plus their savings and taxes. If total spending matches the value of production, firms will continue to produce the same amount, so there is equilibrium.

Suppose the economy has a potential GDP of $2,000 billion. Suppose further that there is full employment, with 95 million people working out of a labor force of 100 million. Thus, the unemployment rate is five percent. Labor and the other resources produce $2,000 billion worth of output, which creates a similar $2,000 billion income for resource owners. They, in turn, must pay $300 billion of this in taxes, leaving a disposable income of $1,700 billion. If people save $200 billion of that, the remaining $1,500 billion is spent on consumer goods. Finally, suppose the government spends all the $300 billion it collects in taxes and investors spend an amount equal to the $200 billion of savings. Then total spending is $2,000 billion, for C ($1,500) plus I ($200) plus G ($300) equals total spending. The economy is in equilibrium, for firms again produce the same $2,000 billion of output they originally did. Figure 13-3 summarizes these events.

Figure 13-3 Equilibrium Conditions

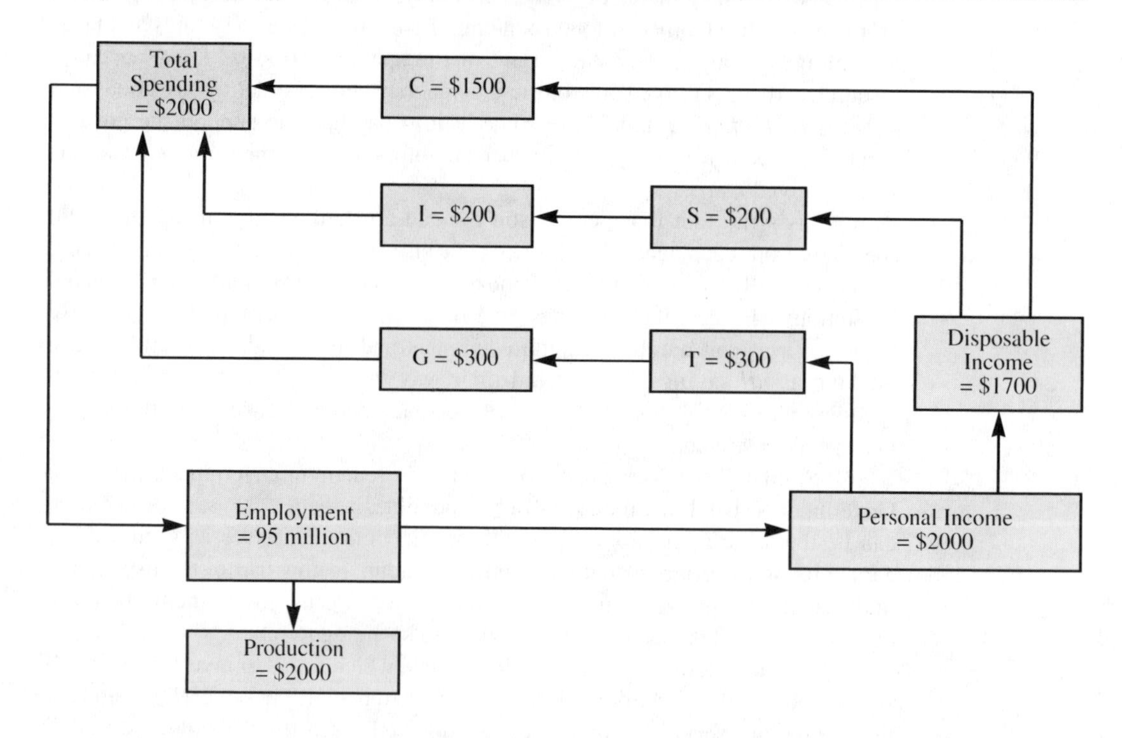

Incidentally, for equilibrium to occur, it is *not* necessary for investment spending to equal savings and for government spending to equal taxes—as it does in Figure 13-3. It is only necessary that investment and government spending *combined* (I + G) be equal to savings and taxes *combined* (S + T). This situation, when I + G = S + T, can also occur when investment spending exceeds savings—so long as taxes exceed government spending by the same amount. Using a numerical example, let I = $220, G = $280, S = $180, and T = $320—all in billions of dollars. Then I + G = S + T, for $220 + $280 = $180 + $320—or $500 billion on both sides of the equation.

This example may seem silly or irrelevant, but it helps illustrate an important phenomenon known as crowding out, where the government finances a deficit by taking savings that would otherwise have gone to private investment. We say "taking" savings because the government, unlike private investors, can pay *any* interest rate required to finance the deficit. Recall from earlier that the government borrows money to finance a deficit when it sells bonds. When the government competes with private investors for savings, it will increase the interest rate as high as is necessary to assure that the government will be able to sell its bonds. Thereby, private investment spending financed with borrowed money will be reduced (there is more about this in Chapter 15). Of course, the government just runs up a bigger deficit in doing so.

INTRODUCTION TO RECESSION

The preceding section is imaginary. Its assumptions and the equaling of injections and leakages rarely if ever happen. But you didn't read those pages in vain, for they will help you understand why recession occurs. Remember the purpose of models—to simplify the world so the primary relationships can be seen more clearly.

This section describes a recession, explains how economists predict recessions, and examines the causes of recessions.

An Economy in Recession: Some Major Events

★6

Remember, certain economic variables "recede" in a recession. That is, economic conditions decline. Three central events indicate that an economy is in a recession: 1) total spending falls; 2) production falls; and 3) employment falls.

■ First, total spending decreases immediately preceding and during much of a recession. The drop can come from decreases in consumer spending, investment spending, or government spending, or a combination of these. Each causes firms to lose sales.

■ Second, production of goods and services declines. Firms respond to lower sales by either cutting back on output or stopping production completely. This is reflected in a fall in real GDP. In a typical recession, real GDP falls from one to three percent per year. In major depressions in the 1800s and in the 1930s, output often fell more than 10 percent. Generally, the economy is considered to be in a recession if real GDP falls for at least two consecutive quarters. However, real GDP could fall for only one quarter, then rebound for a quarter, only to fall again in the third quarter. If several other measures of the economy were unfavorable, this might still be called a recession. Most economists depend on a group of seven in their profession at the private National Bureau of Economic Research to determine when recessions start and end.

■ Third, employment falls and the unemployment rate increases during recession. However, because many people drop out of the labor force when jobs are scarce, the unemployment rate doesn't climb as high as we might expect. At any rate, jobs are much harder to find, layoffs are more common, and the "quit rate" drops (meaning people are less likely to quit their jobs).

Figure 13-4 The Unemployment Rate Since 1960

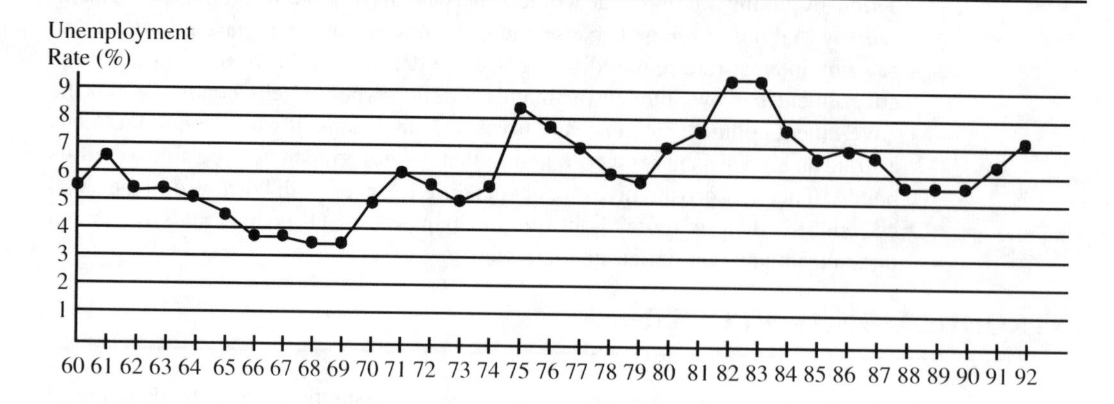

Figure 13-4 shows the unemployment rate dating back to 1960. Since 1960, recessions occurred in 1960, 1970-71, 1974-75, 1980, 1982, and 1990-91—as evidenced by the increases in unemployment rates. An increase in the unemployment rate can tip a presidential election away from the party in power. Such was the case in 1960 (which helped Kennedy against Nixon), 1976 (which helped Carter against Ford), 1980 (which helped Reagan against Carter), and 1992 (when a sluggish recovery was a major factor in Clinton's defeat of Bush).

Growth recession describes a situation when real GDP does *not* fall, but the unemployment rate rises nevertheless. The economy continues to grow, including employment, but not enough to keep the *percentage* of those unemployed from rising.

Additional Occurrences of a Recession

Several other economic conditions indicate that a recession is at hand: 1) the inflation rate falls; 2) wages rise slowly; 3) businesses cut costs sharply; 4) interest rates fall; 5) transfer payments rise; 6) tax collections fall; and 7) the budget deficit increases. Each of these is a consequence of one or more of the three major events considered above.

■ First, the inflation rate drops during a recession. (Be careful. A falling *inflation rate* doesn't mean *prices* fall. It just means they don't rise as rapidly as before. However, in steep recessions or depressions, the price level *might* actually fall, but this is rare. That situation is called *de*flation.) Very often in strong prosperities preceding a recession, there are sharp increases in the demand for many goods and services. If firms cannot expand rapidly enough to meet these increased demands, shortages appear. Consequently, prices of many items increase. But in the recession following prosperity, demands for goods and services don't increase as much. In fact, they usually fall. Thus, there are fewer and smaller shortages (even many *surpluses*), leading to smaller price increases and less inflation.

■ Second, wages (and other resource prices) don't increase as much during a recession for similar reasons. In prosperous times, firms fight for the available workers by rapidly bidding up wages. In recession, with so many people seeking work, those who do hold jobs don't get such rapid wage increases as they did during periods of widespread labor shortages.

■ Third, businesses make sharp reductions in expenses during a recession. They do this to maintain their profit margins, which fall along with sales during recession. However, even reduced expenses can't save firms that have severe sales drops or were in financial difficulty before the recession. Thus, business bankruptcies increase sharply during a recession.

■ Fourth, interest rates fall. An interest rate is a price—the price of credit. Recall that surpluses lead to falling prices and that surpluses are caused by either a decrease in demand or an increase in supply. During a recession, the demand for credit decreases because businesses and individuals take out fewer loans. Businesses see poor prospects for new ventures or for any new equipment paying for itself. Also, individuals fear they won't be able to repay their consumer loans if they lose their jobs.

■ Fifth, transfer payments rise sharply. The government receives more requests for assistance because of rising unemployment, reduced work hours, possibly reduced wages, and the like.

■ Sixth, the government takes in fewer tax receipts. Income tax collections are down because fewer people are working or getting overtime pay. Sales tax collections are down because sales are off in the recession.

■ Seventh, rising transfer payments and falling tax receipts combine to create the last event of a recession—a growing budget deficit. For example, budget deficits rose in the 1930s in spite of President Roosevelt's effort to balance the budget—which was a "plank" in the 1932 Democratic Party platform.

Economic Forecasting

Just as we try to predict the weather, many people try to predict the future of the economy. The Department of Commerce calculates its Composite Index of Leading Indicators to do just that. For this index, it uses 11 economic variables, ones that "lead" the rest of the economy. This means the variables either move up or down *before* most other macroeconomic variables. They are: 1) stock prices; 2) building permits; 3) the length of the manufacturing workweek; 4) price changes for "sensitive" or key raw materials; 5) orders for new business equipment; 6) changes in the money supply; 7) the number of manufacturing layoffs; 8) length of delivery time for goods; 9) consumer confidence; 10) new orders for consumer goods; and 11) the number of unfilled orders for durable goods. (Durable goods, such as autos, furniture, and large appliances, usually last for a long time. Non-durable goods, such as food, paper products, and toiletry articles, usually have shorter lives.)

Economists also try to predict the economic future by constructing mathematical models with equations that describe the relationships between major macroeconomic variables. The models are called **econometric models**. Using dozens and even hundreds of such equations, these model builders enter certain data (such as the money supply and tax rates) and let a computer predict the future of such variables as GDP, interest rates, and income growth.

CONDITIONS AND CAUSES OF RECESSION

Suppose the economy has been at full employment for several years. In other words, actual GDP equals potential GDP. Firms produce all they can because consumers, investors, and governments want to buy all that output. So why would firms produce less—causing a recession?

General Conditions Leading to Recession

Remember that firms produce goods and services because somebody buys their output. So when customers decide to buy less than before, firms produce less. More precisely, total spending on goods and services (C + I + G) declines. But why? Recall that when the economy was in equilibrium, total spending did *not* decline (or rise either). The reason was that leakages (savings and taxes) equaled injections (investment and government spending). Essentially, investors and governments spent all the "unspent" income.

★7

But now total spending *does* change—it falls. Apparently leakages no longer equal injections. In fact, leakages exceed injections. Simply put, the total of people's savings and taxes exceeds the amount of that money used to buy capital goods and buildings and goods and services for the government. Thus, the difference between leakages and injections amounts to "unused money," which drags the economy down. The next section shows how such a condition can arise.

To summarize, there are two general conditions necessary for recession. First, total spending must fall. Second, for total spending to fall, leakages must exceed injections.

Causes of a Decline in Total Spending

★8

Look again at the circular flow model under equilibrium conditions in Figure 13-3 on page 315, where the economy is at potential GDP, or full employment. The situation will now change as the economy in the model moves into recession. This can occur for two reasons: 1) leakages increase; and 2) injections decrease.

■ Suppose everyone decides to save more than before—say, collectively, $250 billion rather than $200 billion. Suppose that at the same time the government raises taxes from $300 billion to $350 billion, leading disposable income to fall to $1,650 billion. Then consumer spending will drop to $1,400 billion. Consequently, what happens to total spending? It depends upon what happens to investment and government spending. If they stay at $200 billion and $300 billion, respectively, then total spending drops to $1,900 billion (= $1,400 + $200 + $300). Figure 13-5 shows this, and the S and T boxes are shaded grey to indicate the cause of the recession.

(In reality, if the government would raise taxes by $50 billion, C would fall by less than $50 billion. That's because some of the $50 billion that was taken from people would have been saved and not spent. However, because it would be a small amount, it will be ignored here.)

Figure 13-5 Recession Caused by an Increase in Leakages

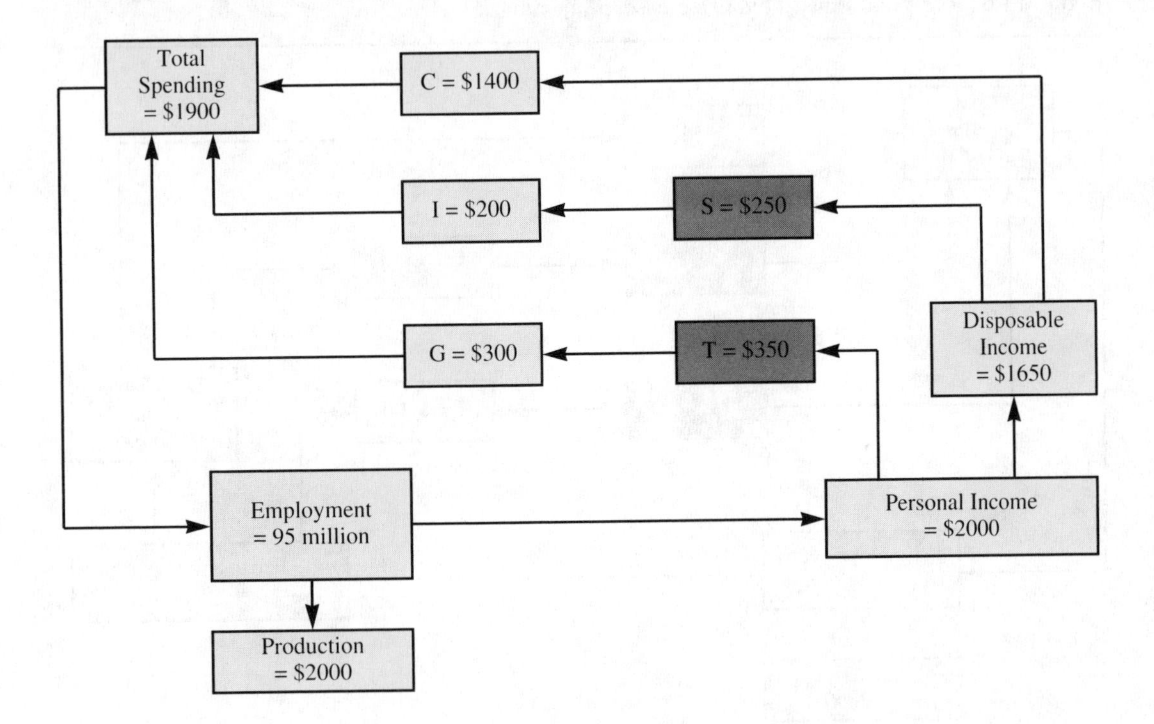

Next, what happens to employment and production when savings and taxes increase? Probably nothing—initially. First, business owners may not be aware of the increase in savings. Even if they are, they won't lay off workers immediately, since they do not know if the downturn is temporary or long term. If firms lay off experienced, productive workers, the workers might not be around to rehire when good times return. So firms wait as long as possible before cutting back on production and employment. After they do cut back, spending and production eventually might come into balance at a new equilibrium level, but lower than $2,000 billion.

Employment is nature's physician, and is essential to human happiness.

– Galen

■ The economy can fall into a recession even when taxes and savings do *not* rise. This alternative route involves injections. Suppose investment falls to $150 billion and government spending falls to $250 billion. Again, total spending falls to $1,900 billion (= $1,500 + $150 + $250). Even though total spending falls for a different reason than increased leakages, the effect would be the same—production would fall, millions of people would be out of work, and total income would be down. The first stage of this scenario appears in Figure 13-6, where again the causes are shaded grey—but this time they're the I and G boxes.

Figure 13-6 Recession Caused by a Decrease in Injections

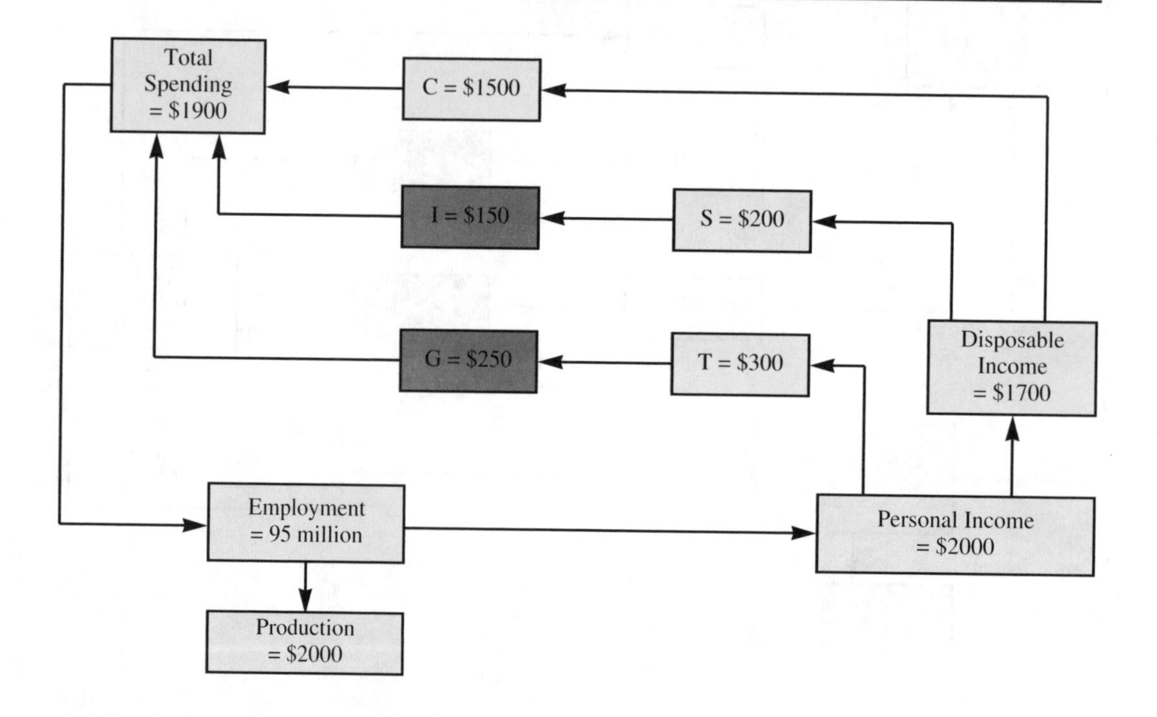

Figure 13-7 From Prosperity to Recession

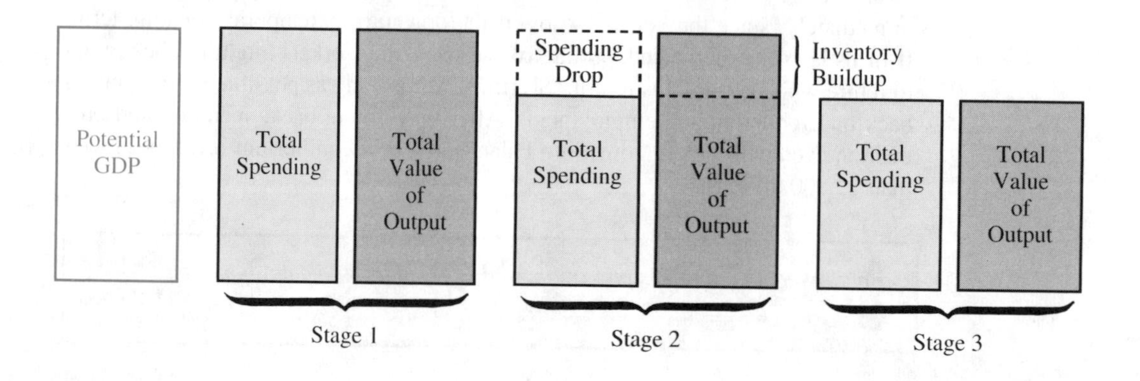

Figure 13-7 presents this same sequence leading to recession in another way. The box on the far left represents potential GDP, equal to $2,000 billion. In Stage 1—the initial equilibrium—total spending and production are both $2,000 billion, so the boxes representing them match the potential GDP box. Stage 2 shows conditions immediately after a drop in total spending, caused by either an increase in leakages or a decrease in injections. Total spending drops below the value of output of goods and services, so firms put the excess in warehouses. In Stage 3 the process is complete because total spending and production match—but at less than the full employment level of output.

Reasons Why Leakages Increase

Rising savings and taxes cause problems, but why should they rise? In other words, what ultimately causes the recession? This section deals with these two causes in turn.

★9 ■ First, consider the increase in savings. More than anything else, people's confidence in future economic conditions influences how much they save today. If most people expect economic hard times a year from now, they will save more today than if they expect prosperity. Many won't buy expensive items they can delay, such as cars, large appliances, furniture, and other durable goods. Forecasters pay close attention to sales of durable goods to predict the future of the economy.

As you can see, recessions often are caused by self-fulfilling prophecies. People expect bad times, so they make fewer purchases now. Eventually this *creates* bad times.

Many events can create a widespread fear of the future. One is a major stock market decline. The stock market crash of 1929 helped turn an ordinary recession into a major depression that lasted until 1941. People reasoned that because the market collapsed, the whole economy would go sour by 1930 or 1931. To protect themselves against the future, many people decided to fix their old Model T Fords rather than buying new Model A Fords. As a result, the Ford Motor Company and its employees suffered, as did hundreds of thousands of other manufacturers and millions of their employees.

The worse the Depression became, the more that people feared the future. In his 1933 inaugural address, President Roosevelt warned people, "The only thing we have to fear is fear itself." A goal of his frequent "fireside chats" on the radio was to reduce such fears with his calming, fatherly manner.

The stock market crash of October 19, 1987, and the market's turmoil in the following months created anxiety among producers and retailers. One problem in such a period is that many months have to pass before consumer reactions are known. The economy could be in a recession for months before anyone was aware of it. In this case, those who expected a sharp recession in late 1987 or early 1988 were wrong. The consumer, ever unpredictable, baffled the experts by continuing to spend at high levels.

There are several organizations that measure consumer confidence in the economic future. One of these is the Conference Board. Its measures show that confidence nosed downward in mid-1990 (immediately preceding the recession) and didn't rise until late 1992 (a few months too late to save President Bush).

This record-length sour outlook was a main contributor to the sluggish recovery—and the blame was then laid on Bush.

Another reason for an increase in the savings rate is an increase in interest rates. When interest rates rise, people tend to buy fewer products now so they can buy more later with their interest income. So there is an increase in the volume of deposits into savings accounts and other interest-earning accounts.

■ An increase in taxes is the second leakage that can cause a recession. The most likely reason for an increase in taxes without a corresponding increase in government spending is a drive to sharply reduce the federal budget deficit.

Reasons Why Injections Decrease

The other two causes of recession involve a decline in either investment spending or government spending. Investment could fall for several reasons: 1) expectations of lower profits; 2) increased interest rates; and 3) irregularity of innovations.

■ First, if business owners believe profits will fall in the future, they will invest less in capital equipment. If they expect their sales will fall, they also will expect lower profits—and they will expect lower sales if they believe that the events just covered will happen.

■ Second, investment spending is likely to fall if interest rates rise. Many firms finance capital expenditures with loans. Thus, higher finance charges discourage such purchases—particularly the marginal ones (that is, the capital goods least likely to pay off). Construction, the other main component of investment spending, also falls as interest rates climb. That's because most people buy houses with credit and businesses rely on credit in order to build factories and offices.

■ Third, many economists believe that investment in capital goods comes in waves or is "lumpy" because of the irregularity of innovation. For example, the development of the auto led to massive investments in related plant and equipment that lasted into the late-1920s, when expansion and innovation slowed. Similarly, computer developments and applications led to mass purchases of equipment in the 1970s and 1980s—which will perhaps fizzle by the late-1990s. If such downturns in capital spending are large enough, other sectors of the economy, such as the suppliers of parts and raw materials, get caught up in it.

The last cause of recession, a decline in government spending, can occur for several reasons: 1) a budget reduction package; 2) election of many conservatives; and 3) the end of a war.

■ First, a move to reduce a budget deficit could mean less government spending. If the United States decides to balance the budget, road projects, the military, and aid to education could all be reduced. This is one reason legislators fought closings of military bases in their districts. Shutting down even a small base can lead to a local "depression" due to "snowballing effects." These fears accompanying a reduced deficit were very evident when Congress, partly spurred by Ross Perot's activities, sought to reduce it in 1993.

■ Second, budgets could decline sharply even without a deficit. One reason could be the election of an overwhelming majority of conservatives, who would reduce government involvement in the economy for philosophical reasons, and, consequently, government spending.

■ The end of a major war would also lead to a sharp decline in government spending. This happened after both world wars. Many people thought the Great Depression, which ended at the start of World War II, would resume after the war. The managers at Montgomery Ward, a leading retailer then, believed that, so they built few new stores. But managers at Sears, a much smaller retailer at the time, thought the opposite. They believed that 10 million ex-servicemen wanted to buy houses—and fill those houses with items that Sears sold. The managers at Sears also believed there was a lot of "stored up" demand for goods because wartime rationing prevented people from buying many items. So Sears greatly expanded its number of stores and leapfrogged its archrival. Thus, the importance of accurate economic forecasting.

End Notes on Recession

Figure 13-8 shows you the four causes of recession: rising savings, rising taxes, falling investment spending, and falling government spending. Any of these can occur alone or in combination with any or all of the others. However, it is possible for one or more of these factors in Figure 13-8 to tend to cause a decline in total spending, while something else might simultaneously tend to *raise* total spending. This would moderate or even completely offset the recessionary effect. For example, while consumers save more (and buy less), the government might cut taxes, giving people even more money to spend. This, as is noted in Chapter 15, is a basis for fighting recession.

★10

Figure 13-8 How Recession Occurs

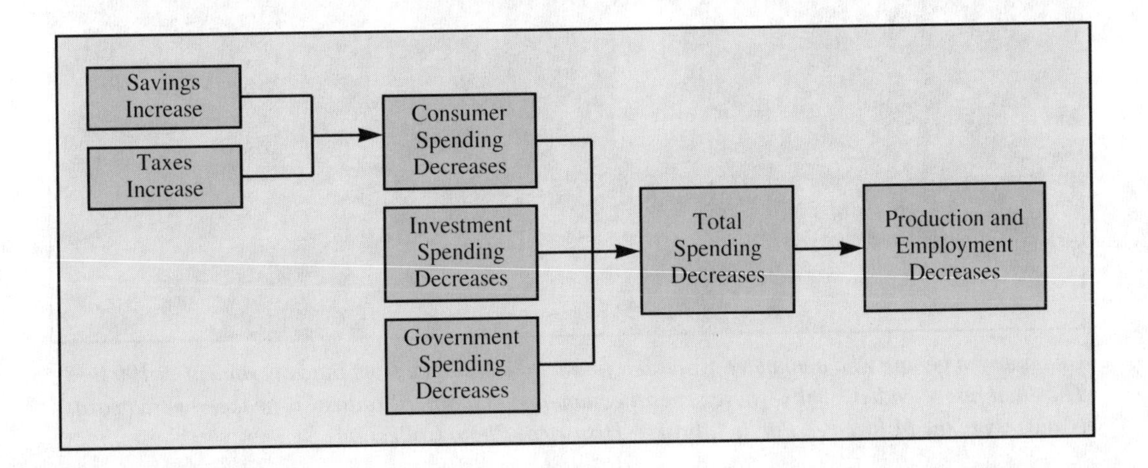

The simple macroeconomic model used in this chapter left out two other causes of recession—rising imports and falling exports. You might want to turn back to Figure 8-2 on page 201 to see the effect a budget deficit can have on exchange rates and imports and exports. The sharp increase in oil prices following Iraq's invasion of Kuwait in August 1990 also led many people to expect recession in Fall 1990. They expected the increases in spending on oil products to "leak out" of the economy. That would mean *less* spending on other goods and services made in the United States, thereby causing a recession. If the assumption of no foreign trade is relaxed, the model will have one more leakage and one more injection.

Some "new-wave" economists reason that the continual shift of the labor force to service jobs and away from the goods sector helps insulate the economy from recession. That's because laborers who produce "big-ticket" durables, such as appliances and cars, experience the worst employment fluctuations during recessions. As such labor shrinks as a factor in the labor force, the economy as a whole will fluctuate less. Also, many economists believe that the increasing diversity the economy is experiencing further protects it from major fluctuation if a few industries suffer decline.

Unemployed people who demanded work and financial assistance from the government in 1993. They had just attended a rally where several communist and other "radical" speakers were heard. (Courtesy of the Milwaukee Public Library - Historical Photo Collection)

Chapter 13 SUMMARY

The macroeconomy in capitalistic economies is subject to business cycles, during which the economy changes from prosperity to recession to recovery and back to prosperity. The macroeconomic model is useful in understanding these cycles because it provides a simplified view of the economy, with only the major macroeconomic variables included.

The macroeconomy is in equilibrium when none of the macroeconomic variables change over a period of time. Equilibrium occurs when the total spending on goods and services equals the total value of goods and services produced at a particular price level. This condition holds when savings and taxes combined equal the combination of investment and government spending. Essentially, all the income that people don't immediately spend will get spent by others, namely, investors and governments.

During a recession, there are decreases in total spending, production, and employment. Also, prices and wages rise less rapidly, businesses cut costs sharply, interest rates fall, and lower tax collections and higher transfer payments lead to budget deficits. Economists try to forecast recessions by building econometric models and by observing certain economic variables.

Recession occurs when total spending falls below the amount needed to bring about full employment and potential GDP. This drop in total spending is caused by increases in savings or taxes and/or decreases in investment spending and government spending. Savings most likely will rise if consumers fear bad economic times are coming. Taxes will rise and/or government spending will fall if the government reduces the budget deficit. Investment spending is most likely to fall if businesses expect profits to fall in the future, generally because of bad times ahead. Any initial fall in spending leads to a drop in spending of a multiple amount.

Chapter 13 RESPONSES TO THE LEARNING OBJECTIVES

1. During prosperity there are high levels of spending, production, and employment, while in recession all of them decline. These variables reach their lowest levels in the trough or depression phase of the business cycle, and the recovery phase begins as soon as they increase.

2. The components of the macroeconomic model include: total spending, level of resource use, level of production, personal income, disposable income, taxes, government spending, savings, investment spending, and consumer spending.

3. Each of the variables in the model ultimately affects all others. However, each variable is directly influenced by only the one(s) preceding it in the model.

4. In macroeconomic equilibrium there are no changes in the levels of total spending, production, resource use, savings, taxes, and so on over a period of time.

5. Macroeconomic equilibrium occurs when total spending equals the total value of goods and services produced. This occurs when the combination of taxes and savings equals the combination of investment plus government spending.

6. During a recession there are declines in total spending, production, and resource use. Also, prices and wages rise less rapidly, businesses cut costs vigorously, interest rates fall, tax collections fall, government budgets increase, and the budget deficit grows.

7. Recession occurs when total spending falls below the level of spending necessary to achieve the potential GDP.

8. Total spending will decline if there is a decrease in consumer, investment, or government spending.

9. Investment spending might fall if: 1) businesses fear lower profits; 2) interest rates rise; or 3) the economy is at the end of an innovative period. Government spending might fall: 1) during a budget reduction program; 2) when the government is conservative; or 3) when a war ends. Consumer spending might fall after an increase in: 1) savings, prompted by an increase in interest rates, patriotism, or fear of bad economic times ahead; or 2) taxes, resulting from a budget-reduction program or from inflation coupled with a progressive income tax

10. If something causes an increase in total spending while something else simultaneously causes a decrease in total spending, these two actions could offset each other and prevent a recession.

Chapter 13 LEARNING ACTIVITIES AND DISCUSSION QUESTIONS

1. On the day you were born, what part of the business cycle was the economy in?
2. Ask someone who remembers the Great Depression what personal problems it caused for them.
3. What stage of the business cycle is the economy in today?
4. If your parents were ever laid off during a recession, what was the ultimate cause(s) of that recession?
5. Do you think there will be a recession next year? Why?

APPENDIX A
EQUILIBRIUM AND CONDITIONS LEADING TO RECESSION

Earlier you learned that macroeconomic equilibrium occurs when the leakages equal the injections—that is, when savings + taxes = investment + government spending. You also learned that recession occurs whenever total spending falls below the value of production.

These elementary propositions must be refined in the case of investment spending (I). The investment considered earlier is actually what is known as intended investment. It includes only the spending people want to do on home construction and what businesses want to invest in plant and equipment. However, recall that investment is defined as also including changes in inventories. During equilibrium there are no changes in business inventories because production exactly matches what buyers want, so warehouse stocks don't rise or fall. Therefore, this refinement causes no difficulty in understanding equilibrium.

Recession is a different matter. Recall that when savings (S) and/or taxes (T) rise, leading to a fall in consumption (C), total spending (C + I + G) falls. In the early stages of a recession, businesses continue to produce at their earlier rates. Thus, they produce more than they sell, placing the excess into warehouses. Of course, the value of such increased inventories is actually part of investment. Economists call the value of these inventories unintended investment because firms don't really intend to produce such an excess. They simply are not yet aware of the recession, or they believe that the slump is temporary and don't want to lay anyone off.

Therefore, as consumption falls because of rising savings or taxes, C + I + G does *not* fall—at least not immediately. The reason is that investment *rises* to match the fall in consumption. However, that investment is the sum of intended investment *plus the unintended investment* in inventories. Because inventories rise in the early part of a recession, investment also rises to match the fall in consumption—leaving C + I + G unchanged.

Eventually, businesses recognize that they are in a recession and cut back on production, which then eliminates the unintended investment in inventories. Therefore, now C + I + G *does* fall.

The necessary condition for recession stated earlier, that leakages exceed injections, also needs refinement. It is when leakages (S + T) exceed *intended* injections (*intended* I + G) that a recession occurs. *Actual* injections (intended *plus unintended*) always equal leakages because of the inventory adjustment accounting procedure.

APPENDIX B CALCULATING THE MULTIPLIER

The multiplier is a concept reflecting the proportional increase in total spending and GDP stemming from an initial increase in one of the components of total spending. For example, suppose investment spending rises $50 billion. This spending becomes the income of capital equipment manufacturers, laborers, business service firms, and so on. In turn, they all spend part of their incomes, adding to the amount of C + I + G, or total spending.

Laborers spend most of their paychecks on consumer goods such as food, autos, and clothes, so consumption rises following an increase in their incomes. In addition, business service firms buy more office supplies, copying machines, and office desks, so investment rises again. In turn, the recipients of all this spending spend part of that money on a wide variety of items.

Suppose that after such "recycling of money" occurs many times over, total spending rises $250 billion. Since the multiplier value can be found by the formula:

$$\text{Multiplier} = \frac{\text{Change in GDP}}{\text{Initial Change in Total Spending}}$$

the multiplier is five in this example, as $250 billion ÷ $50 billion = 5.

The multiplier can be found in an alternative way, but first a new concept needs introduction. The marginal propensity to consume (MPC) is the fraction of an increase in income that people spend on consumption. Suppose everyone combined receives a $40 billion increase in income. If 80 percent of that increase in income is used to buy consumer goods and services, consumption rises by $32 billion, as 0.8 x $40 billion = $32 billion.

The formula for the marginal propensity to consume is:

$$\text{MPC} = \frac{\text{Change in Consumption}}{\text{Change in Income}}$$

In this example, the MPC is 0.8, as $32 billion ÷ $40 billion = 0.8.

A related concept is the marginal propensity to save (MPS), which is the fraction of an increase in income that people save. Its formula is:

$$\text{MPS} = \frac{\text{Change in Saving}}{\text{Change in Income}}$$

In the example, if people save $8 billion of their $40 billion increase in income, MPS = 0.2, as $8 billion ÷ $40 billion = 0.2.

Because people can either spend their income or save it, MPC plus MPS must equal one. This simply means that people will spend and save 100 percent of an increase in income—for there is nothing else they can do with it. As MPC + MPS = 1, then:

$$\text{MPS} = 1 - \text{MPC}$$

Finally, if either the MPC or the MPS is known, the multiplier can be found by using the formula:

$$\text{Multiplier} = \frac{1}{1 - \text{MPC}} = \frac{1}{\text{MPS}}$$

Returning to the example above, where the MPC = 0.8 and the MPS = 0.2, the multiplier is:

$$\text{Multiplier} = \frac{1}{1 - 0.8} = \frac{1}{0.2} = 5$$

CHAPTER 14

INFLATION

★★★★★ LEARNING OBJECTIVES ★★★★★

1. List some consequences of inflation.
2. Explain how the general price level is determined.
3. Explain the ways the general price level increases.
4. Explain how changes in total spending influence changes in output, shortages, and inflation.
5. Explain how demand-pull inflation occurs.
6. Explain how changes in the leakages and injections can increase total spending.
7. Explain the relationship between the money supply and total spending.
8. Explain how cost-push inflation occurs.
9. List the main causes of a decline in production or in the rate of increase of production.
10. Compare and contrast situations in which both wages and productivity can change.

TERMS

inflation
money income
cost-of-living adjustment
interest rate
market interest rate
real interest rate
hyperinflation
demand-pull inflation
velocity of circulation
equation of exchange
cost-push inflation
labor cost

It is easy to understand how recession and unemployment aggravate the economic problem caused by resource scarcity. However, it isn't so obvious how inflation relates to this problem. This chapter begins with a glance at some consequences of inflation and at some of the severe inflations in history. Next is a survey of the factors that determine price levels. Finally, this chapter explains why price levels increase—in other words, why inflation happens. Two such causes of inflation are demand-pull inflation and cost-push inflation.

ECONOMIES WITH INFLATION

Inflation is a condition in which the price level increases, generally over an extended period. The inflation rate refers to the percentage increase in the price level during a year.

Some Consequences of Inflation

★1 Some of the most important consequences of inflation include: 1) a decrease in the purchasing power of the dollar; 2) a redistribution of income and wealth; 3) a reduction in productive work; 4) a reduction in the savings rate; 5) a disruption of business plans; and 6) an increase in market interest rates.

■ First, during inflation the purchasing power of the dollar falls. Suppose that a pencil used to cost a nickel, so that you could buy 20 pencils for a dollar. If pencils now cost a dime, you can buy only 10 for a dollar, or half as many. If prices *in general* double, a given amount of income buys only half as much. Thus, real income, or the amount of goods and services that people can buy with their **money income** (the number of dollars they earn), falls as prices rise.

■ The second consequence of inflation is a redistribution of income and wealth. Income is redistributed primarily because money incomes of different people rise at different rates during inflation. Those whose money incomes rise at a lower rate than prices suffer a drop in real income. Historically, this has included those earning the minimum wage, those receiving pensions, welfare recipients, and many people not represented by unions. However, real income *increases* for those whose money incomes increase faster than prices. This includes many self-employed professionals, other business owners, and laborers in great demand. Occasionally people receiving a **cost-of-living-adjustment** (COLA), including many unionized workers and Social Security recipients, also have a gain in real income, even though COLAs are designed to keep recipients' money incomes rising at the same rate as prices. That occurs when the price index that is used to calculate inflation overstates the extent of inflation.

Inflation can also redistribute wealth. Speculative "investment objects" that often increase in value during inflation include precious metals, art, and rare stamps—bringing windfall gains to their owners. Likewise, real estate values commonly climb sharply during inflations. Thus, people who bought such items before their prices rose earn capital gains income. Another way to gain from inflation is with a long-term loan with a fixed, low-interest rate. Because your income climbs sharply during inflation, the loan payment isn't as large a share of your paycheck assuming that there is no escalator clause (where a lender can increase the rate of interest on a loan). Of course, if there are winners from inflation, there must be losers—the same wealth is merely redistributed.

■ The third consequence of inflation is a reduction in productive work. Entrepreneurs, innovators, and inventors are less productive when they take time from their work to look for tax shelters and other ways to cut their taxable income. The more time they spend seeking to avoid inflationary losses, the less they contribute to the economy.

■ The fourth consequence of inflation is a reduced savings rate. Many people try to beat expected price increases and don't save as much of their incomes. Others spend more than otherwise on houses or other things they believe will increase in value during inflation. A lower savings rate means there are fewer funds to lend to businesses for innovations, capital equipment, and plant expansion. This could lead to a lower rate of economic growth and a slower growth in the standard of living.

■ The fifth consequence of inflation is disruption of business plans for the future. Because capital equipment and factories have long lives, firms want some certainty about future prices of what they buy and sell. Whether investments in capital pay off depends upon such prices. Without knowledge of future prices, firms tend to concentrate on more predictable projects that pay off in the short run, such as a new brand of soap. Revolutionary and innovative projects—such as extreme heat-tolerant ceramics, solar power, and electricity from nuclear fusion—often take expensive, long-term research. Again, long-term economic growth suffers when businesses shy away from such projects.

■ The last noteworthy consequence of inflation is an increase in interest rates. (The interest rate here is the "market interest rate," explained in the paragraph after next.) The **interest rate** is the price of credit for the use of someone else's purchasing power (money) for a certain period. That price must cover the cost of extending credit before a financial institution grants a loan. Part of those costs include bank equipment (typewriters, computers) and labor for the paperwork involved. Another cost is the interest the bank pays depositors (savers). Finally, during inflation, a further cost is the loss in the money's purchasing power during the loan period.

Suppose a bank considers lending you $1,000 for a year on January 1. That money could buy x amount of some good on that day. Also, suppose the bank needs $60 to cover the costs just mentioned (other than the loss of purchasing power)—or six percent of $1,000. You will probably get the loan at six percent—*if* the bank expects that the $1,000 will still have the power to buy x amount of that same good on December 31. But what if the price of that good (and everything else) is expected to rise 10 percent (so that the $1,000 could buy only 0.9x)? Then the bank would have an *extra* cost—it would give up purchasing power when you gave back the $1,000. Therefore, it will charge you interest of $60 *plus* $100 (to cover this extra cost) or 16 percent (= $160 ÷ $1,000). That is why interest rates were so high in the 1970s when inflation rates were very high.

> *Invest in inflation. It's the only thing going up.*
>
> – Will Rogers

During an inflation, people often distinguish between the market interest rate and the real interest rate. The **market interest rate** refers to the actual number of dollars of interest paid in a year for each $100 borrowed, expressed in percentage terms. It is what people usually mean by "the interest rate." The **real interest rate** gives a more accurate view of the true cost of borrowing. It recognizes that during inflation borrowers pay back loans with dollars that have less purchasing power than the ones they borrowed. Thus, borrowers give up less for each dollar repaid than they received. Because this reduces their cost of borrowing, the following formula is used to find the real interest rate:

Real Interest Rate = Market Interest Rate - Inflation Rate

For example, assuming an inflation rate of six percent, suppose a bank charges a market interest rate of nine percent—$90 a year on a $1,000 loan. When the borrower pays back the $1,000 in principal, it *looks* the same as the $1,000 borrowed—but it's worth only $940 of the "old money"(= $1,000 - 0.06 x $1,000)—$60 less. Thus, the loan cost only $30 (= $90 - $60), for a real rate of interest of three percent (= $30 ÷ $1,000 or 9% - 6%).

The Inflation Record in the United States

The United States has faced five periods of significant inflation. The first occurred during the Revolutionary War. Prices rose more than several hundred percent because, rather than raising taxes, the states printed vast amounts of paper currency to pay for the war. Similarly, prices rose several hundred percent during the Civil War. The government had great difficulty raising sufficient taxes and borrowing enough to finance the war. In desperation it printed paper money, called "greenbacks" because of the money's color. The Confederate States printed much more paper money (about $1 billion) and, consequently, suffered ruinous inflation.

During World War I, prices doubled in just two years. Likewise, prices shot up during World War II, though not as much as they would have without price ceilings. However, after removal of these controls, prices zoomed upward in the late 1940s at rates of between 10 and 20 percent each year. The last period of major inflation began in the late 1960s and ended in the early 1980s. It accompanied the large spending increases on the Vietnam War and the social programs of the period. If these increases had been financed by tax increases, much of the inflation would have been avoided. But politicians are usually reluctant to raise taxes.

Figure 14-1 and Table 14-1 show the inflation record of the United States since 1960. In both cases the inflation rate was calculated using the Consumer Price Index.

> *The way to crush the bourgeoisie is to crush them between the millstones of taxation and inflation.*
>
> – Nikolai Lenin

Figure 14-1 Inflation Rates Since 1960

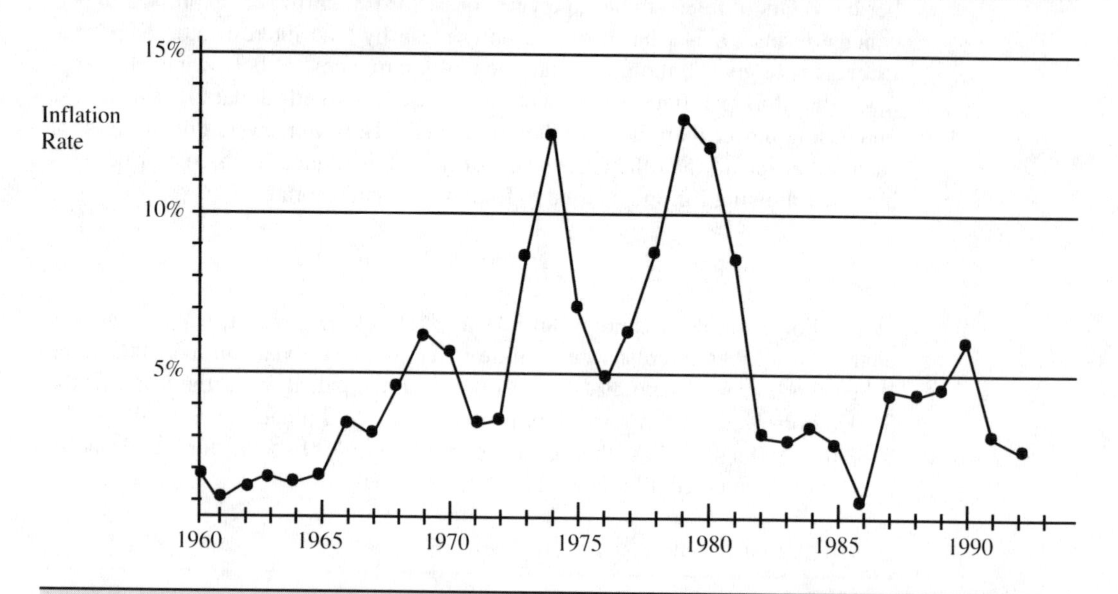

Table 14-1 Inflation Rates Since 1960 (based on December-to-December data)

Year	Inflation Rate	Year	Inflation Rate	Year	Inflation Rate	Year	Inflation Rate
1960	1.5	1970	5.6	1980	12.5	1990	6.1
1961	0.7	1971	3.3	1981	8.9	1991	3.1
1962	1.2	1972	3.4	1982	3.8	1992	2.9
1963	1.6	1973	8.7	1983	3.8	1993	______
1964	1.2	1974	12.3	1984	3.9	1994	______
1965	1.9	1975	6.9	1985	3.8	1995	______
1966	3.4	1976	4.9	1986	1.1		
1967	3.0	1977	6.7	1987	4.4		
1968	4.7	1978	9.0	1988	4.4		
1969	6.2	1979	13.3	1989	4.6		

Some Notable Inflations of the Past

Economists place severe inflations into a special category, called **hyperinflation**. Although there is no strict standard for what constitutes hyperinflation, it generally refers to inflation rates of more than several hundred percent per year.

Hyperinflation is nothing new. The Roman Empire experienced it thousands of years ago. Prices in Europe doubled during the three years of the Black Death around 1350. In the 1500s, European prices more than tripled after the arrival of gold from Spanish plundering of the New World.

So far in the 20th century, there have been several notable hyperinflations. The largest was the Hungarian inflation of 1946. Estimates of price increases range as high as 800 octillion-fold (800 plus 27 zeros). The disruptive effects made it easier for a communist takeover. Similarly, the Chinese inflation of the late 1940s, when prices rose as much as 10 billion-fold over three years, contributed to the economic and political instability that led to the communist takeover in 1949. Prices in Greece rose 4½ billion times from 1943 to 1944.

The most famous inflation occurred in Germany after World War I, from 1919 to 1923. After Germany lost the war, the victors (the United States, Britain, France, Italy, and Russia) imposed heavy money settlements, called reparations, on Germany. For necessary domestic spending and to pay the reparations, Germany printed large amounts of German marks. By 1923, the treasury kept 30 paper mills busy producing paper to make new money. The examples in Table 14-2 give an indication of how fast prices rose in the worst year, 1923. Overall, prices rose as high as six trillion-fold during that period. To put that into perspective, imagine buying a hot dog today for $1—just before you leave for four years in France. Upon your return home, you order a hot dog, which you expect is still $1. Handing you the hot dog, the clerk asks for *six trillion dollars*—or *six million stacks* of *one million* dollars each! Would you be upset? The Germans were. So much so, in fact, that their government, the Weimar Republic, collapsed. That was followed by 10 years of economic and political turmoil until someone led them out of economic depression and political fighting—Adolf Hitler. From 1933 until 1939, the Germans enjoyed rapid economic expansion and high employment, while the rest of the world suffered depression. For many Germans, the loss of political and personal freedom under Hitler was an acceptable price to pay for economic success. But relatively few of them imagined the brutal war—and the deaths of more than 50 million people—that would follow.

Hyperinflations still occur today. Bolivia's inflation rate reached 40,000 percent in 1985, and from 1986 to 1991, prices in Peru rose 2,200,000 percent. Russia may end up having one of the most costly hyperinflations in modern times. In 1992, following the initial sharp price increases in January, prices rose at 25 percent per *month.* This was largely because so much money was printed. In July alone, more Russian rubles were printed (260 billion) than in the previous 30 years *combined.* If the hyperinflation contributes to the collapse of the reforms that are designed to move Russia toward capitalism, civil wars and a possible new cold war could ensue.

Table 14-2 Prices During the German Hyperinflation

	Prices on:		
Product	**August 8, 1923**	**September 29, 1923**	**December 19, 1923**
Liter of Milk	38,000 marks	8 million marks	________
Pound of Butter	900,000 marks	100 million marks	________
Pound of Bread	90,000 marks	27 million marks	________
Pound of Bacon	950,000 marks	130 million marks	________
Newspaper	________	________	200 billion marks
Stamp	________	________	90 million marks

THE PRICE LEVEL OF AN ECONOMY

The price level refers to a collective measure of all prices that exist at some point, and it is reflected by a price index. (You were introduced to the concept of a price index and its use in calculating the inflation rate in Chapter 11. So some of this section will be a review for you.) Figure 14-2 shows you how the price level of the United States changed in recent decades.

Determining the Price Level

The demand for and the supply of a particular product determine its price in an economic tug-of-war. Let's use television sets as an example. The demand for TVs refers to the various numbers of TVs that people are willing to buy (at all possible prices). The supply refers to the various numbers of TVs that firms offer for sale. Buyers compete against one another for the available sets, and sellers are adversaries for the limited customers. Finally, buyers and sellers are adversaries when they haggle over the price.

★2

Likewise, the price level of all goods and services *combined* depends upon demand and supply. However, the critical difference is that now demand refers to the total spending (or aggregate demand) for all products combined—C + I + G, or consumer, investment, and government spending added together. You might think of total spending as the buyers' side of a giant auction where everything imaginable is sold. Imagine millions of consumers, business owners, and government purchasing agents with pockets full of money to spend.

Figure 14-2 The Price Level Since 1946

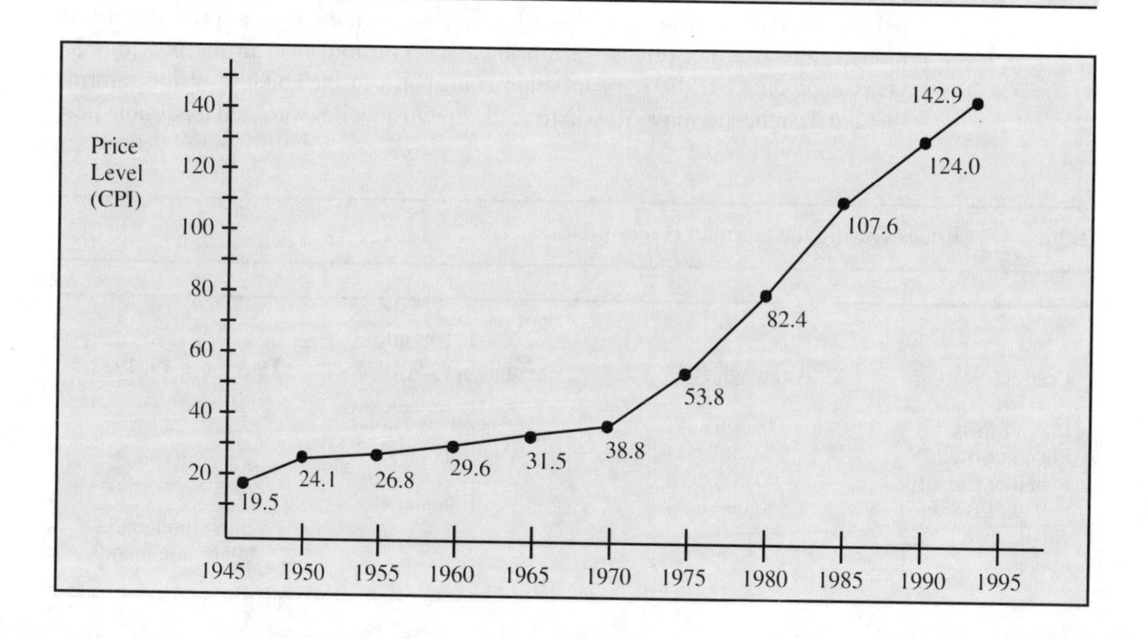

Just as the "strength" of demand for an individual product influences its price, so, too, the "strength of the aggregate demand" influences the price level. This "strength" means *how much* spending that C + I + G entails. A "large amount of total spending" means most buyers bring lots of money to the "giant auction"—which, in reality, refers to all the places where sellers try to sell things. High total spending tends to bring about higher price levels. Conversely, low total spending tends to cause lower price levels.

Consider again the imaginary giant auction. Prices there depend not only upon the amount of money buyers bring to it, but also upon how much the sellers bring to sell. In the real economy, this latter amount refers to how many goods and services of all kinds business firms offer for sale in all the millions of businesses combined. The more goods and services firms offer for sale, the lower the price level tends to be—partly because people buy large amounts only if prices are low. Conversely, lower levels of output tend to lead to higher price levels. The amount firms offer for sale at that auction, measured by GDP, refers to the total output of goods and services.

A 100 million pengo note of Hungary in 1946. The holder of this "small change" of the world's largest inflation didn't even bother to spend it.

A 20 billion mark note, issued at the height of the German hyperinflation. It took 10 of these just to buy a newspaper in December 1923.

The word "tend" in the two preceding paragraphs emphasizes that there are two major factors determining price levels—total spending and the total amount of goods and services available (produced). See the flow chart in Figure 14-3 for an illustration. Note that several concepts you studied earlier in various chapters influence these two primary determinants of the price level. Total production depends upon three factors: 1) the amount of resources used; 2) the output

Figure 14-3 Some Major Determinants of the Price Level

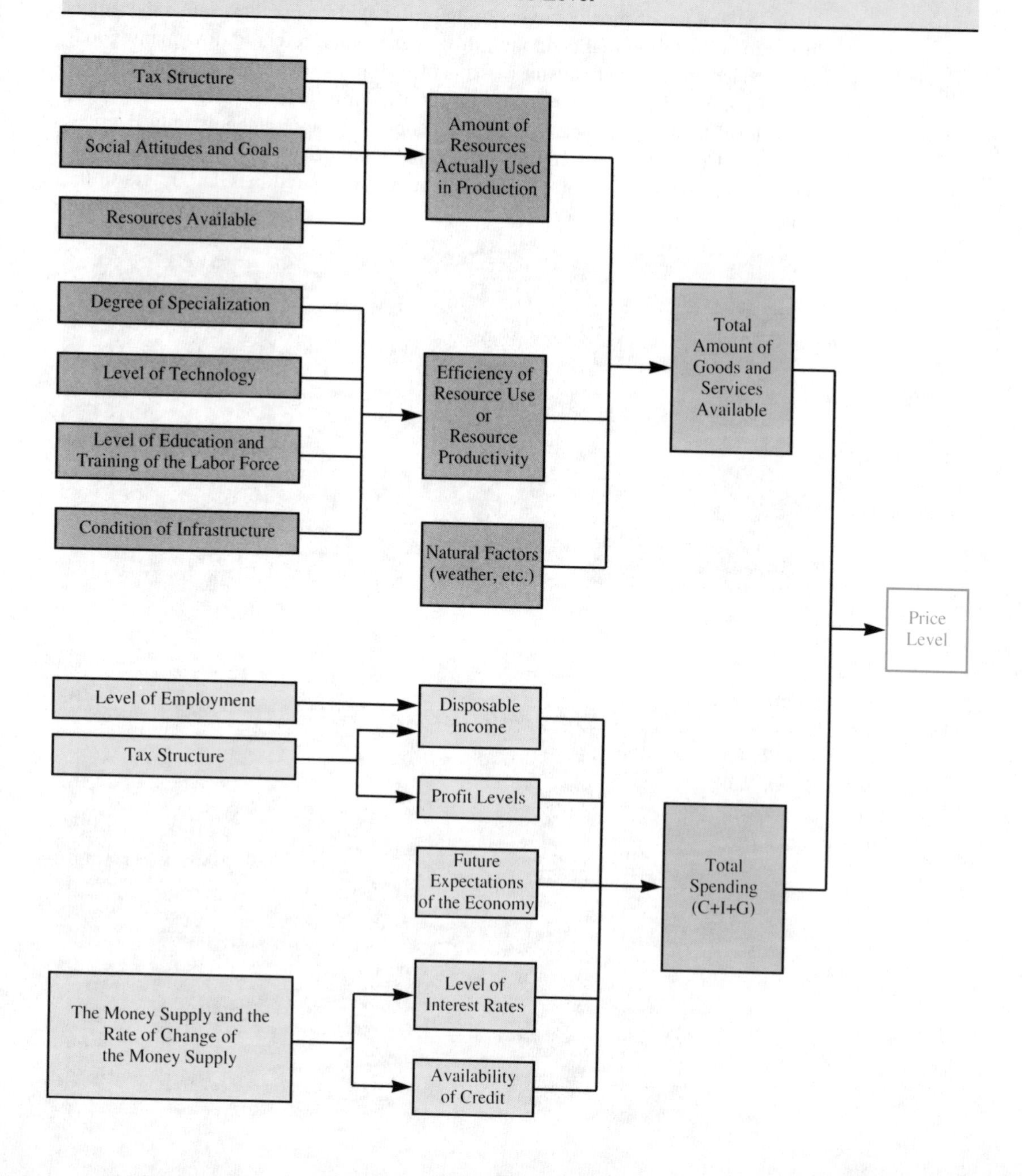

producers get from them (resource efficiency); and 3) natural factors (weather, for example). In turn, these factors depend upon several other factors. The chart doesn't list all factors affecting total spending and total output, only the major ones.

The consumer part of total spending depends largely upon disposable income, which depends primarily upon how many people have jobs. Investment spending depends upon profit levels, the future expectations of the economy, and whether credit is cheap or expensive as well as available. Credit cost and availability depend upon factors studied in Chapter 12.

Changes in the Price Level

To understand inflation (or what causes the price level to rise) it will help to review what causes the price of a particular product, such as shoes, to rise. Remember that whenever there is a shortage of shoes, shoe prices increase for two reasons. First, people who want shoes, but who can't find any to buy at the initial price, offer to pay more for the shoes available—bidding them away from other buyers who *can* get them. Second, shoe store owners realize that they can increase profits by boosting prices. The owners can replace customers they lose with people who want to buy shoes but can't find any to buy. Finally, remember that shortages appear whenever there is an increase in demand or a decrease in supply.

★3 When prices *in general* increase, the situation described for shoes occurs in thousands of markets at the same time. There are widespread shortages brought on by either: 1) a *general* increase in spending (total spending increases); or 2) a *general* decline in production (total output of goods and services decreases).

★4 In reality, production rarely falls—only during recession. Both total spending and production usually increase each year. Generally, widespread shortages and inflation occur whenever total spending rises at a *faster rate* than total production. For example, if consumers, business firms, and governments try to buy eight percent more each year but output increases at merely five percent, shortages appear in thousands of markets. Consequently, prices rise in thousands of markets. There is inflation.

> *Inflation is always and everywhere a monetary phenomenon.*
> – Milton Friedman

> *No civilized country in the world has ever voluntarily adopted the extreme philosophies of either fascism or communism, unless the middle class was first liquidated by inflation.*
> – H. W. Prentiss, Jr.

DEMAND-PULL INFLATION

Until this point it hasn't been necessary to say *why* spending increases faster than output increases. Perhaps spending is increasing too fast. Alternatively, perhaps output is increasing too slowly. In either case, the economy faces shortages and inflation. Now you will learn that both cases are associated with a cause or a type of inflation. The first cause, or the first type of inflation, is called demand-pull inflation. The second, covered later, is called cost-push inflation. Always keep in mind that both work by creating shortages and that, whatever their cause, all shortages look alike. Thus, determining whether an inflation is one type or another often is hard to determine.

Conditions of Demand-Pull Inflation

★5

In its simplest form, **demand-pull inflation** occurs when total spending increases but the total output of goods and services remains constant. Suppose that at some point in the past total spending was $3,600 billion and that all buyers could buy all they wanted. Suppose further that these buyers now want $4,000 billion worth of goods and services—but firms still produce the same $3,600 billion. Buyers do not get the extra $400 billion worth of output they want, and there are widespread shortages to that extent. Consequently, prices rise.

This is most likely to happen at full employment. (Remember that an economy at full employment has also reached its potential GDP.) Virtually all laborers have jobs, factories produce at full capacity, mines produce all the minerals possible, and so on. Firms *would like* to sell more output, but—for the moment—they can't make any more. However, firms that produce goods can temporarily reduce their inventories, thus boosting sales without an increase in output.

Figure 14-4 shows this situation. The column on the far left represents potential GDP. The next two columns reflect the initial, non-inflationary situation: the blue column represents total spending and the grey column total output. Because they are equal, it means the economy starts at macroeconomic equilibrium. The economy is at full employment, as potential GDP equals actual GDP. The last two columns show an inflationary situation: total spending increases but total output does not—because it *can not,* since the economy is still at full employment. The hash-marked area at the top of the total spending column reflects the amount of shortages in the economy. The larger this area, the greater the inflation will be.

The above illustration assumes that only a few months elapse between the two time periods. That's because as time goes on new laborers enter the labor force, new factories are built, firms buy more productive capital equipment, technological advances occur, and countless innovations change the production processes. Suppose that, on average, such changes expand the economy's capacity (potential GDP) by 10 percent each year. (That's more than we can expect, but it makes the graphs easier to follow.) Then there can be an increase in total spending of 10 percent each year *without* creating widespread shortages.

Figure 14-4 Full Employment, Shortages, and Inflation

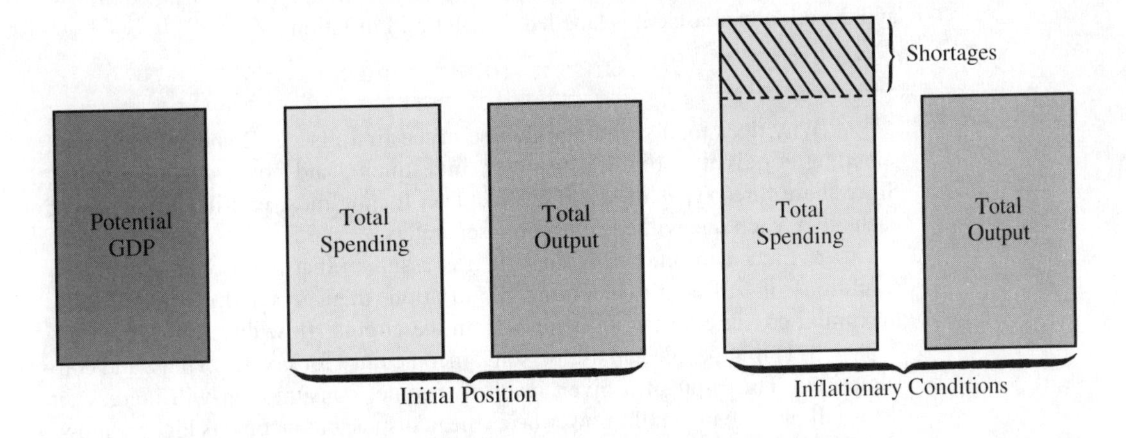

Figure 14-5 A Demand-Pull Inflation Model

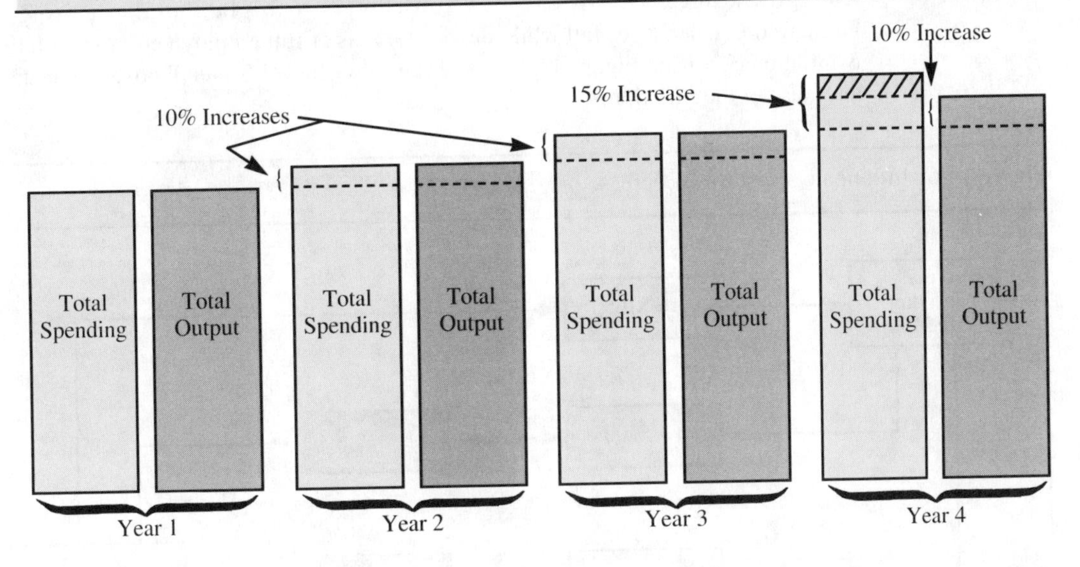

Figure 14-5 shows this situation over a span of several years—from Year 1 through Year 3. Assume that the economy starts at potential GDP in Year 1. Because total spending matches total output, there are no shortages. So there is no inflation. By Year 2 total spending rises 10 percent above Year 1. Since firms *can* produce 10 percent more and *want to*, output also climbs 10 percent above the level in Year 1. Thus, the spending increase does *not* lead to inflation, as it did in the simpler case. Similarly, there is no inflation in Year 3, as again the firms match the spending boost of 10 percent with output boosts of 10 percent.

By Year 4, however, there *is* inflation, because total spending escalates at 15 percent from Year 3 to Year 4. Firms cannot match this abnormal increase, since output can increase at only 10 percent.

In general, the economy will experience demand-pull inflation if total spending increases faster than the total output of goods and services. And because the abnormal increase in spending is seen as the cause of the shortages and the price increases, it is labelled demand-pull inflation.

Why There Are Increases in Total Spending

★6

Why does total spending increase in the first place? Remember that total spending equals the sum of consumer, investment, and government spending. Since these three types of spending fluctuate, for the most part independently of each other, each one will be considered separately.

■ First, consumer spending. If it is assumed that the economy begins at conditions of full employment and no inflation, then personal income is at its maximum possible level. Remember from the circular flow diagram (Figure 13-2, page 311) that people can use personal income only for taxes, savings, and consumption. Thus, out of a given level of income, consumption will increase if taxes fall or if savings fall. Lower taxes mean disposable income is higher, allowing for higher consumption. And, out of a given level of disposable income, lower savings also mean consumption rises. Since taxes and savings are both leakages, a decrease in leakages contributes to higher total spending. Furthermore, if leakages fall while the economy is at full employment, such a fall is inflationary. (See Figure 14-6, where the grey-shaded S and T boxes indicate the cause of the inflation.)

Figure 14-6 Inflation Caused by a Decrease in Leakages

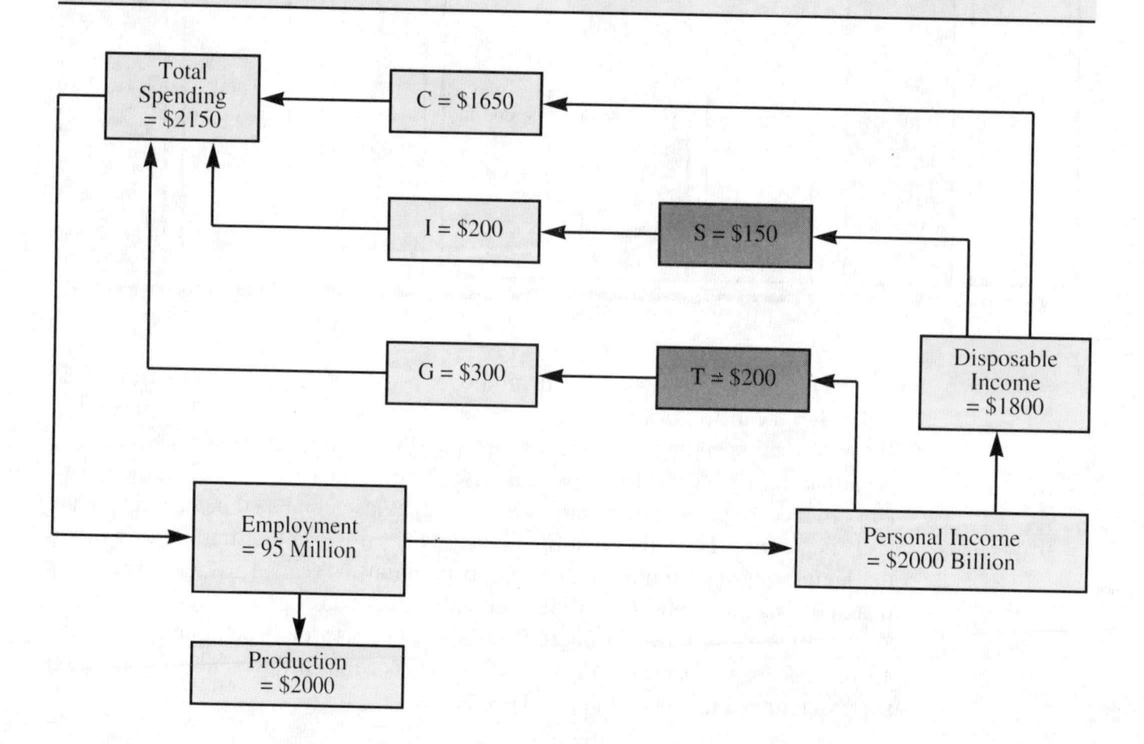

Assume that the economy begins with the same full-employment-equilibrium conditions of Figure 13-3 (page 315). Potential GDP is $2,000 billion, taxes are $300 billion, savings are $200 billion, consumption is $1,500 billion, investment is $200 billion, and government spending is $300 billion. Figure 14-6 shows conditions following a drop in leakages. Since $200 billion, rather than $300 billion, now go for taxes, disposable personal income rises from $1,700 billion to $1,800 billion (allowing consumption to increase by $100 billion). As savings drop to $150 billion (allowing for an additional increase in consumption of $50 billion), consumption jumps $150 billion (= $100 + $50) to $1,650 billion. Adding this to the $300 billion in government spending and the $200 billion in investment spending also pushes total spending up $150 billion to $2,150 billion.

Will employment be the next to climb—perhaps above 95 million? No, for the remaining five million unemployed are the frictionally and structurally unemployed, the type extremely unlikely to find jobs. Consequently, production will not increase, so the extra spending merely creates shortages and inflation.

■ Another way for total spending to increase is for investment spending to increase. Remember, this includes spending for capital equipment, building construction, and increased inventories. Suppose it rises from $200 billion to $250 billion. Then total spending climbs by at least $50 billion.

■ The final source of an increase in total spending is a growth in government expenditures. For example, although government expenditures began with a $300 billion level, suppose these expenditures climb to $400 billion. Again, total spending will rise by at least $100 billion.

Figure 14-7 Inflation Caused by an Increase in Injections

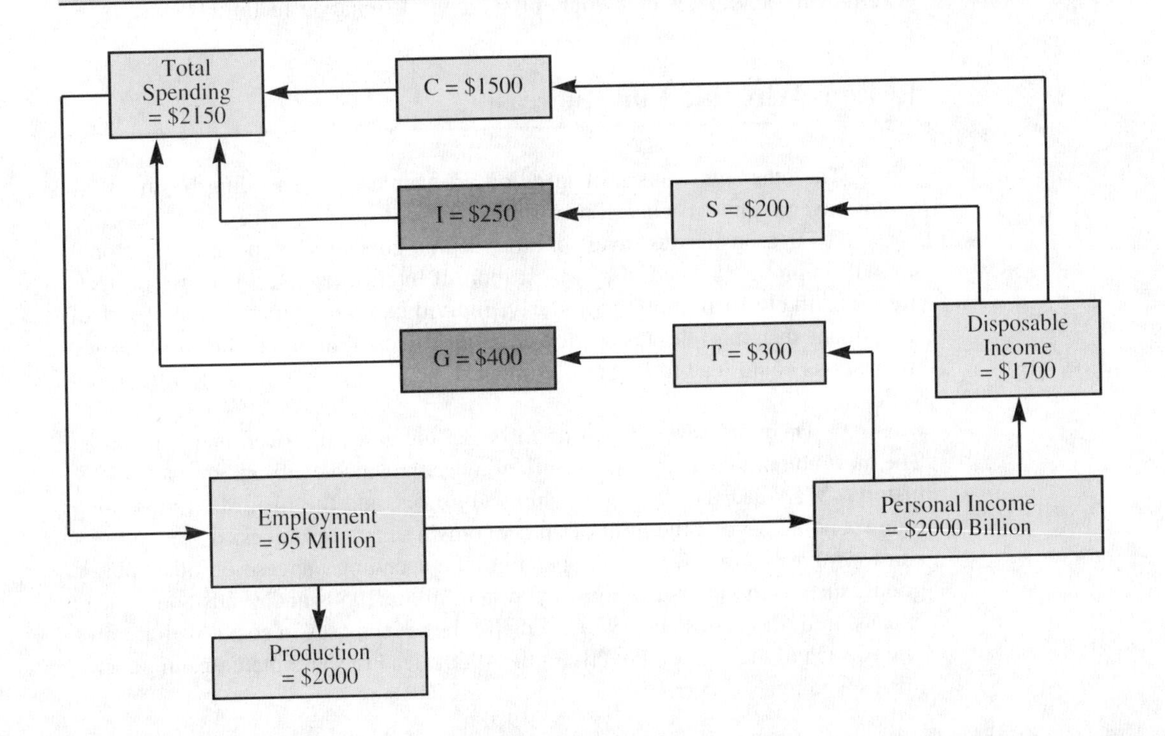

Both of these increases in injections (I and G) combine to boost total spending to $2,150 billion. These changes appear in the circular flow model in Figure 14-7, but now these are shaded grey to note the alternative causes of inflation that you saw in Figure 14-6. This model differs from Figure 14-6 in that leakages and consumption remain the same. However, total spending rises by the same amount. Consequently, the same shortages and inflation appear.

Reasons Why Leakages Decrease

It is now possible to probe deeper into the causes of inflation. The first two causes, lower taxes and lower savings, will be examined in this section.

■ First, consider a drop in the savings rate. A primary factor affecting the savings rate is consumer expectations of the future. If consumers believe that prosperity is on the way, they will probably spend more and save less. They feel especially comfortable about buying durable goods. Many things can promote consumer confidence in the future, such as reports of improved employment, income, or GDP. Consumers also become more confident when they see lots of help-wanted ads or read newspaper stories about a healthy economy. Another reason for lower savings is a drop in interest rates. Finally, the savings rate falls when consumers expect prices to increase sharply in the near future, which, in turn, actually causes prices to increase.

■ Although it isn't likely, a decrease in taxes is the second reason why leakages decline. It is conceivable that a conservative sweep of Congress could lead to sharp tax cuts. On the other hand, conservatives probably would also slash government spending, which would offset the inflationary effect of tax cuts.

Reasons Why Injections Increase

The other two causes of inflation are increases in spending by investors and/or governments. Each will be examined in turn.

■ First, businesses invest in more capital goods if they believe the economy will improve. Second, they invest more if interest rates fall because projects are more likely to pay off. Similarly, individuals build more homes (part of investment spending) because of lower interest rates. Finally, a cluster of related innovations could lead to large investment in new equipment related to the innovations.

■ There are several reasons for steep increases in government spending. The most common reason is war. Inflation accompanied every major war in U.S. history. Wars take guns, aircraft, ships, uniforms, and the like, often increasing total spending beyond the limit of an economy's scarce resources. A second reason for increases in government spending is a spending increase on other public goods, such as the interstate highway system in the 1950s and 1960s and college expansion of the 1960s and 1970s. Finally, large increases in social welfare programs, such as the War on Poverty in the 1960s, lead to sharp increases in government spending.

How Total Spending Can Increase

★7 If total spending increases faster than production, shortages pop up everywhere, and inflation follows. It's clear how production expands, but what makes an increase in total spending possible? Don't people need money in order to buy things? Yes, so if consumers, businesses, and governments spend more money each year, there must be more money around to spend.

Actually, there is an alternative way to increase spending. If people spend money at a faster rate after they receive it, total spending can also rise, even though the money supply does not change. Economists call this rate of spending **velocity of circulation** (also commonly called velocity of money or simply velocity), referring to how often dollars change hands in a year, on average. To illustrate, imagine keeping track of a particular one dollar bill for a year. Eventually it might get used (spent) eight times in the year. Tracing all such dollars would reveal that some dollars change hands only twice a year, some dozens of times.

If the money supply of a particular year is multiplied by velocity, the result equals total spending for that year. Suppose there is $800 billion of M1 (the money supply) this year and that velocity is six. Then total spending is $4,800 billion (= $800 x 6). Total spending could rise to $5,600 billion next year in two ways. First, the money supply could expand to $933.3 billion, for $5,600 = $933.3 x 6. Second, velocity could rise to seven, for $5,600 = $800 x 7.

Why would velocity increase? For one thing, EFT (electronic funds transfer) works faster than a paper check system in moving money around. Thus, widespread adoption of EFT will increase velocity. Various banking and business procedures and equipment also allow velocity to grow. And velocity increases during severe inflations, when people want to unload money before it loses purchasing power. However, there are limits to velocity. First, there is a physical limit to how fast people can spend money. Second, if inflation gets bad enough, people abandon money and resort to barter, at which point velocity falls.

The Equation of Exchange

Total spending is found by multiplying the money supply by velocity, or:

Total Spending = Money Supply x Velocity = MV
or
Total Spending = MV

Recall that total spending, or C + I + G, is one way of thinking about GDP. Thus, MV = Total Spending = GDP. Recall further that you can also think of GDP as the value of goods and services produced. This value could be found by multiplying the price of every item by the number of that item produced, then adding up all these "subtotals." An alternative approach uses the concept of the price level, represented by the letter P, and the *quantity* of goods and services produced in a year, represented by the letter Q. Multiplying the price level (P) by the output level (Q) of the whole economy gives the *dollar value* of that output—namely, GDP. Thus, PQ = Total Value of Output = GDP

As GDP = MV and as GDP = PQ, then MV = PQ, which is known as the **equation of exchange**. Essentially, the equation states the obvious, that total spending in the economy must equal the value of goods and services produced. Yet this obvious statement, usually called an identity rather than an equation, gives insight into the importance of money in causing inflation.

Imagine a greatly simplified economy, with potatoes as the only product and a production of 40,000 pounds of potatoes in some year. Suppose further that 1,000 dollar bills comprise the money supply and that people spend these four times a year. Since total spending on potatoes is $4,000 (= 4 x $1,000), potatoes must be 10¢ per pound (as $4,000 ÷ 40,000 pounds = 10¢/pound). Figure 14-8 shows this situation. The three semicircles labelled "1" reflect the levels of money, spending, and output in the first period.

Figure 14-8 Demand-Pull Inflation in a One-Product Economy

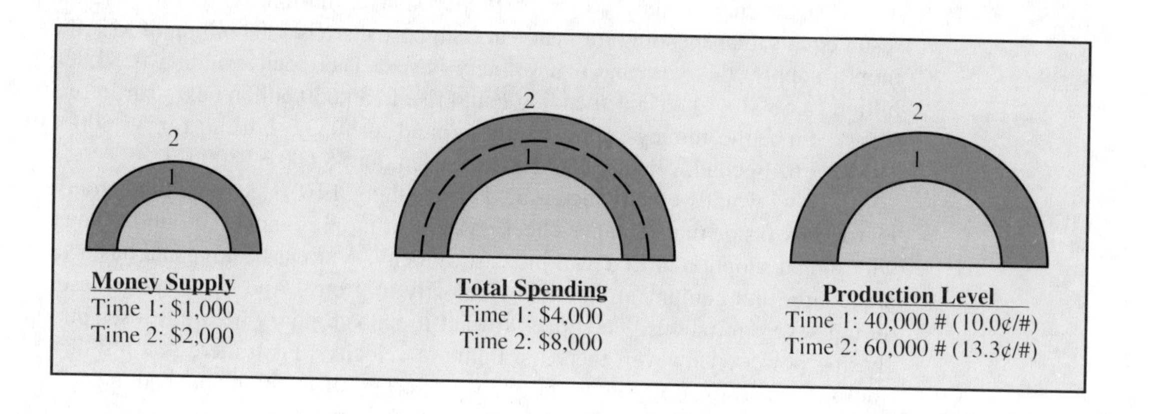

Now consider what happens when these variables increase over some period. Potato output expands four percent a year until it reaches 60,000 pounds per year sometime later in Period 2. The number of dollar bills increases at a six percent yearly rate until there are 2,000 of them by Period 2. This allows people to double their spending as well, to $8,000 per year (assuming no change in velocity).

People now try to buy twice as many potatoes, but they can buy only 50 percent more. Thus, there is a potato shortage, causing prices to climb to 13.3¢ a pound, for $8,000 ÷ 60,000 pounds = 13.3¢ per pound. The larger semicircles in the diagrams labelled "2" reflect these larger levels of money, spending, and output. Note especially the area of the total spending semicircle above the dotted line. That area reflects the shortages caused by the money supply growth in excess of four percent per year.

Of course, economies are more complex than that. Yet the principle is the same: increase the money supply faster than production can increase and there will be inflation. All of history's large inflations have this in common. In all U.S. wars, the money supply increased much faster than in peacetime. The tons of gold of the New World became coins of the Old World in the 1500s—and prices zoomed skyward. In 1923, Germany's 30 paper mills helped the money supply explode by *10 billion-fold* from 1919. Amazingly, those controlling the money supply said the new money had little or nothing to do with the inflation. Instead, they believed that because prices rose so fast, the economy needed *more* money to function! And more money meant that more paper was needed—so they kept cutting down the Black Forest.

Figure 14-9 The Inflation Rate and Changes in M1

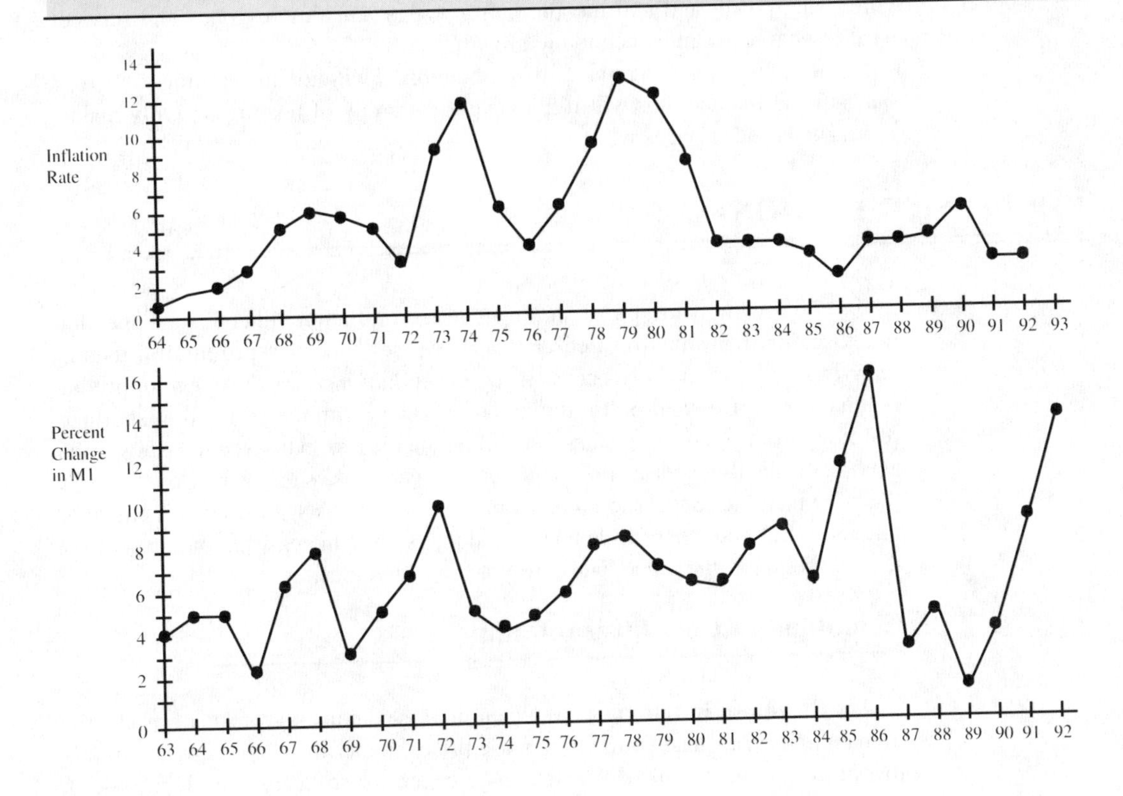

Figure 14-9 shows the recent U.S. data for: 1) changes in M1, the basic money supply; and 2) the inflation rate, as measured by the Consumer Price Index. Note particularly that when the money supply began to climb at a faster rate in the mid-1960s, inflation followed. Inflation generally takes six months to a year to appear after a significant increase in the money supply. This is partly due to the time required for prices to work their way "through the pipeline" from the manufacturer to the retailer. (That is why the inflation chart is shifted one year to the right as compared with the money supply chart.) Also, firms are sometimes reluctant to be the first to raise prices because they don't want to be "over-priced" if competing firms don't raise their prices.

This is a good place to expose a common fallacy about money and income. Money is a medium of exchange. People often say they want more money or that they "make money." What they really want is more *income*, and they earn income at their jobs. Income (actually, *real* income) is the *amount of goods and services* people receive in exchange for what they produce. However, we invariably measure income in dollar value terms. So when you say your income is $20,000, you mean you can exchange that $20,000 for an equal dollar amount of goods and services. Or you can say that you have $20,000 worth of purchasing power.

Earlier you learned that you obtain purchasing power by producing things of value—goods and services. Similarly, as a nation, we *obtain* more collective purchasing power and real income only if we *produce* more goods and services. That is what is meant by economic growth.

If more money is printed in Washington, it will not do anything to increase our national income, nor will it alleviate the scarcity of resources. Only making more goods and services will.

COST-PUSH INFLATION

To review, widespread shortages lead to inflation either if total spending increases or if production decreases. However, because production usually *increases,* inflation usually occurs if total spending increases *faster than* production increases. Demand-pull inflation is associated with the problem of shortages resulting from abnormally large spending increases. This section shows that abnormally small increases in production also can cause shortages. Consequently, the price increases appear to come from increases in costs, so we call it cost-push inflation. But you must still keep in mind that slower increases in output will also lead to shortages, the immediate cause of price increases.

Conditions of Cost-Push Inflation

★8

Cost-push inflation occurs when increases in average costs of production in many industries lead firms to increase prices, rather than to accept abnormally low profit margins. But why will costs escalate for so many firms? In order to answer the question, first review the meaning of average cost. Although average cost is the amount of money needed to make one unit of something, it also reflects *the amount* of resources needed to make something. (Remember, Average Cost = Total Cost ÷ Output.)

Consider the simple potato economy once again. It begins with 1,000 dollar bills in money, total spending of $4,000, and 40,000 pounds of potatoes. The total cost of producing the potatoes for the whole economy is also $4,000. This is because, in order to spend $4,000, people need incomes of $4,000, which they earn by selling resources. So firms have to *pay* $4,000 for these resources—their total costs. Dividing the 40,000 pounds into $4,000 gives 10¢ a pound—but 10¢ of *costs.* This all means that average cost and the price of potatoes are the same—10¢ a pound. (Remember, economists assume that average costs include the implicit or non-cash costs of the business owners. So the owners are just "breaking even," but they are content to stay in business.)

Now what if total spending (and total costs) stays at $4,000 per year in Period 2—but production falls to 30,000 pounds? Firms spend $4,000 to grow 30,000 pounds of potatoes—or 13.3¢ for each pound (= $4,000 ÷ 30,000 pounds). Firms must raise prices to 13.3¢, or they would be better off going out of business. The degree of inflation is exactly the same as in Figure 14-8, when spending increased but production didn't. Figure 14-10 shows this with semicircles representing the money supply, spending (and costs), and production for both periods.

Figure 14-10 Cost-Push Inflation in a One-Product Economy

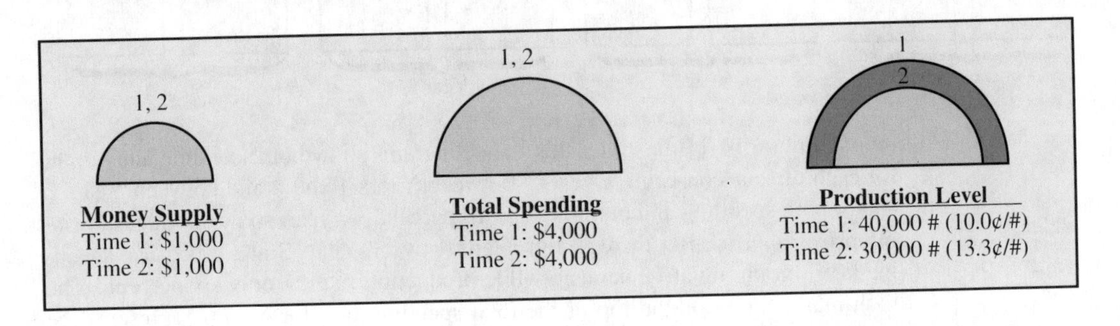

However, in a real economy, would production of all goods and services combined fall over an extended period? It's not likely—but it's possible. That is why prices in Europe rose sharply during the Black Death (the bubonic plague of the mid-1300s). One-third of the population died, so production fell sharply. Thus, the survivors (who inherited the victims' money) spent the same amount of money on fewer goods, creating shortages and inflation.

In modern times, production could fall in wartime if factories, shipping facilities, and cropland were destroyed. This occurred during World War II in Europe, Japan, and China. In the last few years, production also fell in most former communist states while they made the complex transition to market economies. All these economies suffered severe inflations, partly because of lower production.

More commonly, cost-push inflation occurs not when production falls, but when production slows *its rate of expansion*. Suppose that total output usually rises at 10 percent each year. If spending also climbs at 10 percent, there are no shortages or rising prices. But what if output merely grows at six percent during one or more of these years? Then there *will be* shortages—and inflation. People *try* to buy 10 percent more goods and services, but they can buy only six percent more.

Figure 14-11 A Cost-Push Inflation Model

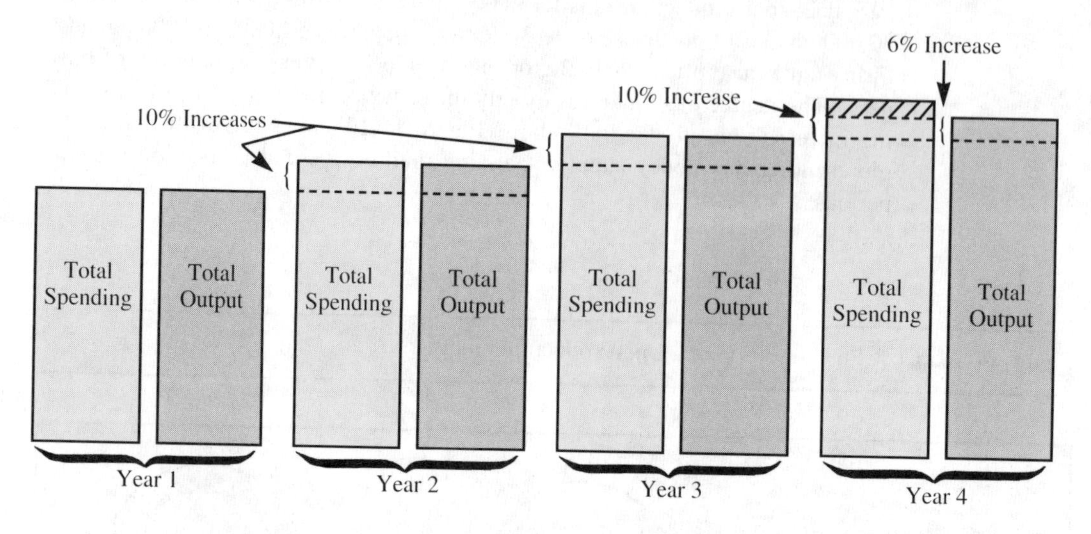

Figure 14-11 illustrates this. The diagrams show both spending and output for each of four consecutive years. Between Years 1 and 2 and between Years 2 and 3, both spending and output rise at 10 percent per year, so no shortages or rising prices appear. But there is a problem between Years 3 and 4 because spending keeps going up at 10 percent, while production rises at only six percent. The hash-marked area on the top of the total spending box for Year 4 represents the amount of shortages caused by these uneven increases. In a sense, that area represents "lost output" that would have been produced if production had increased at the normal rate of 10 percent.

Causes of Production Restrictions

★9

Average costs rise whenever total costs rise faster than output. In a real economy, this can happen for several reasons: 1) restricted expansion of capital; 2) an increase in foreign prices; 3) poor weather; 4) productivity restrictions; and 5) rising labor costs.

■ First, if the increase in capital stock slows and fewer innovations occur, production advances more slowly. This can occur if there is a decline in the savings rate, so that less money is available for purchasing capital equipment. Savings fall during high rates of inflation, during boom periods, and when interest rates are very low. Excess government regulation or unfavorable business tax laws also discourage investment spending.

■ Second, increases in prices that U.S. firms pay for foreign resources are passed along to their customers. This can occur when the dollar depreciates against foreign currencies. It can also happen when foreigners increase their prices, even though exchange rates remain unchanged. Consequently, sales of U.S. firms drop when these increased foreign prices are passed along to U.S. consumers. In turn, production falls in the United States. This occurred in the 1970s when OPEC nations sharply raised the price of oil. Everything made from oil increased in price—from gasoline to plastics to polyester clothing. The same thing happened following Iraq's invasion of Kuwait in August 1990.

■ Third, the primary effect of poor weather is on agricultural output because crop yields plunge and bad weather interferes with harvests. But snow, hurricanes, and extreme cold or hot weather also curtail production in many manufacturing and service industries.

■ Fourth, a decline in labor productivity or even a reduction in the normal rate of advance in productivity restricts output. The slowing of advances in productivity during the last two decades has been attributed to such factors as: 1) new workers with low levels of education; 2) a decline in the work ethic; 3) poorer labor-management relations; 4) an increase in relatively unskilled women and teenagers in the work force; 5) a shift toward labor-intensive service industries; and 6) an increase in drug and alcohol use by workers.

But there are several reasons why the 1990s may see an increase in rates of labor productivity. One reason is that baby boomers will be entering their years of peak productivity. Another is that businesses, forced to become more efficient because of recent recessions as well as increased foreign competition, will continue to strive for higher efficiency.

■ The fifth and last factor that causes cost-push inflation is closely connected to the fourth one. It involves the amount of money a business pays its employees for their labor in order to make one unit of output. This amount is called **labor cost**. It is calculated by the formula:

$$\text{Labor Cost} = \frac{\text{Wages/hour}}{\text{Labor Productivity}}$$

Labor productivity is the amount of a good or service a worker makes in one hour. It includes all workers, from those on the assembly line to the janitors and the secretaries. Labor productivity is calculated by the formula:

$$\text{Labor Productivity} = \frac{\text{Total Output}}{\text{Total Hours Worked}}$$

Thus, combining these two formulas allows us to state that:

$$\text{Labor Cost} = \frac{\text{Wages/hour}}{\text{Output/hour}}$$

Suppose workers in a broom factory produce 6,000 brooms in a day, with 30 people working an eight-hour shift. Total hours worked are then 240 hours (= 8 x 30). Dividing 240 hours into 6,000 brooms gives a labor productivity of 25 brooms per hour (= 6,000 ÷ 240).

Average cost is the amount of money needed to buy the resources used to make one unit of a good or service, including supplies, utilities, machines, labor, and the like. (The part of average cost used to pay employees is called labor cost.) If any one of the parts of average cost for a single item increases, its price will probably go up. However, that is *not* inflation because it is not widespread. But if some part of average cost of a particular resource goes up for *most* firms in the whole economy and, consequently, prices rise for *most* products, that *will* cause cost-push inflation.

When the particular resource that rises in cost is labor, the resulting inflation is sometimes called wage-push inflation. It's merely one form of cost-push inflation. Another was the energy-push inflation of the 1970s.

Figure 14-12 Labor Costs and Prices

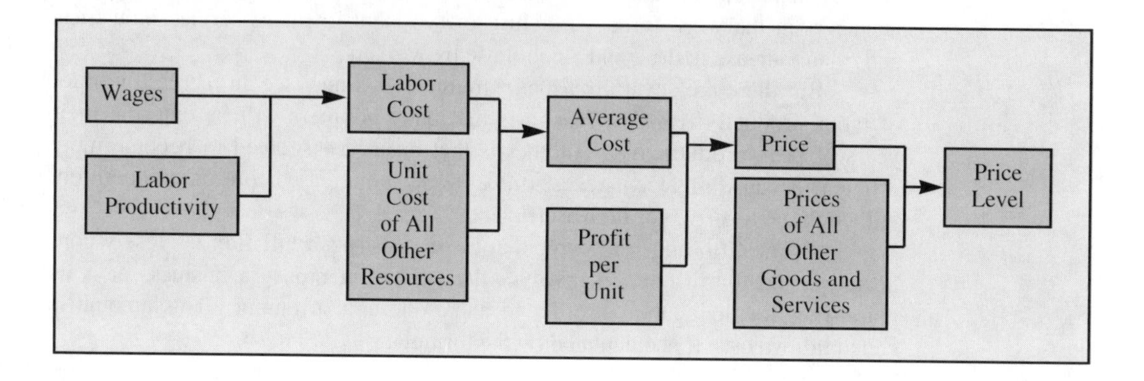

Figure 14-12 shows the major relationships in cost-push inflation. It concentrates on the costs of producing a particular good or service. Beginning at the far right, the price level depends upon the price of some particular item as well as the prices of all other goods and services. Next, that particular price depends upon the average cost and the profit earned on one unit of output (Price = AC + Profit per Unit). Next, average cost equals labor cost plus all the other parts of average cost. Finally, labor cost depends upon labor productivity and wages.

★10

If wages rise over a year in a particular firm or industry, you would expect the price of the good made by that firm or industry to rise as well. But note in Figure 14-12 that labor productivity is equally important in determining labor cost and prices. Like wages, productivity often changes over a year.

Table 14-3 illustrates four situations for a hamburger stand in two time periods—Year 1 and Year 2. Depending upon how much productivity changes between these two years, hamburger prices fall, rise, or remain unchanged. Assume that in both years the shop employs 10 workers who each work 40 hours per week, for a total of 400 hours of labor. They make 8,000 hamburgers a week in Year 1, so labor productivity is 20 hamburgers per hour (= 8,000 hamburgers ÷ 400 hours). Assuming a wage of $4 (400¢) per hour, the labor cost is 20¢/hamburger (= 400¢ ÷ 20 hamburgers per hour). Adding in all the other costs of 50¢ per hamburger (rolls, meat, rent, and so on) plus a nickel profit margin results in a price of 75¢ in Year 1.

Table 14-3 The Effects of Productivity Changes and Wage Changes on Prices

		Production per Week	Total Hours Worked	Labor Productivity	Wage per Hour	Labor Cost	All Other Costs	Profit Margin	Price
Year 1		8,000	400	20	$4	20¢	50¢	5¢	75¢
Year 2	Case A	8,000	400	20	$6	30¢	50¢	5¢	85¢
	Case B	10,000	400	25	$6	24¢	50¢	5¢	79¢
	Case C	12,000	400	30	$6	20¢	50¢	5¢	75¢
	Case D	16,000	400	40	$6	15¢	50¢	5¢	70¢

By Year 2, the wage is $6 per hour, a 50 percent increase, in each of the four possible situations. But output is different in each case. In Case A, production and productivity remain the same as in Year 1. Consequently, the labor cost rises by a dime (or 50 percent) to 30¢. The shop adds this dime to the price, now 85¢.

In Case B, production *does* climb—by 25 percent—as does productivity. This moderates the rise in labor cost, which climbs by only 20 percent (from 20¢ to 24¢). Thus, the shop owner adds only 4¢ to the price, raising it to 79¢.

When extended to many goods and services, Case A and Case B show how cost-push inflation can occur. Case A is extremely rare, but Case B has occurred almost every year since the 1960s in many industries. Generally, cost-push inflation of the wage-push variety occurs when wages rise at a faster rate than labor productivity.

In Case C, production and productivity rise by 50 percent, matching the wage increase. Consequently, labor costs stay at 20¢ per hamburger, and the shop owner can hold the line on prices. The workers gain from higher wages. The owner gains from a 50 percent increase in hamburgers sold (12,000 compared with 8,000), even though the profit per hamburger remains unchanged at 5¢.

In Case D, everybody gains: the workers, the owner (total profit doubles), and the consumers (the price drops to 70¢). This is made possible by the huge 100 percent increase in productivity, which reduces the labor cost to 15¢. This last case explains why the prices of various electronic goods fell so much in the last few decades. Other examples of such price declines include: quartz watches, ball-point pens (the first ones in 1947 cost $12); long-distance telephone calls; automobiles after the moving assembly line was introduced; and hamburgers after Ray Kroc spread the McDonald brothers' methods beyond their single San Bernadino, California, restaurant of the 1950s.

Countless other innovations over our history had an impact on price levels, inflation rates, and living standards. Such innovations reduce the problem caused by resource scarcity—unsatisfied wants. Innovations also tend to hold down the price level and the inflation rate.

Figure 14-13 An Individual Firm Experiencing an Increase in Labor Cost

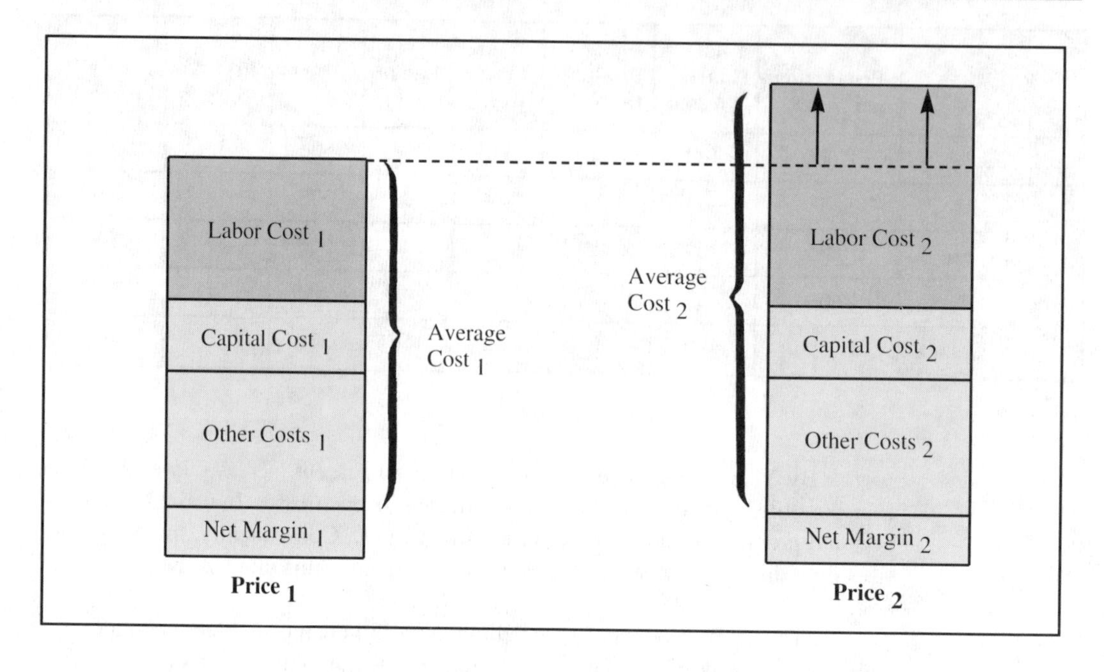

Figure 14-13 presents a graphical illustration of cost-push inflation from the perspective of a business firm. Two periods are shown, with the levels of profit, labor cost, capital cost, other costs, average cost, and price given in each case. Labor cost is the only component of average cost to increase. Thus, it is the cause of an increase in average cost and, in turn, the price. If this happens in thousands of firms nationwide, there is cost-push inflation.

Economists disagree about the importance and even *the existence* of cost-push inflation. Some say cost-push inflation can exist only if there are increases in the money supply that exceed increases in total output. This means demand-pull inflation must occur to make it *appear* that there is cost-push inflation. This is what the Nobel Prize-winning-economist Milton Friedman meant when he said, "Inflation is always and everywhere a monetary phenomenon." Chapter 15 further illustrates such differences of opinion among economists about macroeconomic problems and ways to solve them.

Chapter 14 SUMMARY

Inflation means the price level is rising. It leads to a fall in the purchasing power of money, a redistribution of wealth and income, a reduction in productive work, a lower rate of saving, a disruption in business planning, less investment, and higher interest rates. The United States suffered inflations in every major war.

The price level is primarily determined by: 1) the level of total spending; and 2) the level of output of goods and services. In turn, there are many determinants of each of these factors of the price level. The price level will increase because of: 1) widespread shortages after an increase in total spending; or 2) shortages following a decrease in the output of goods and services. Total spending can increase if there is an increase in consumer, investment, or government spending. Consumer spending will increase if savings or taxes fall.

Before total spending can increase, either there must be more money in the economy or the existing money must be spent faster. Demand-pull inflation occurs if total spending rises faster than the output of goods and services. This generally occurs when the money supply increases faster than the output of goods and services.

Cost-push inflation occurs when production declines or when it doesn't increase as much as usual. This leads to higher production costs, which firms pass on to customers in the form of higher prices. Cost-push inflation can occur if war destroys capital, foreign resource prices increase, or when the weather is poor. The wage-push variant of cost-push inflation is most common if wages increase faster than labor productivity. This leads to higher labor costs, which firms again pass on in higher prices.

Chapter 14 RESPONSES TO THE LEARNING OBJECTIVES

1. Some consequences of inflation include:
   a) the loss of the currency's purchasing power
   b) a redistribution of income and wealth
   c) a reduction in productive work
   d) a reduced rate of savings
   e) a disruption of future business plans
   f) an increase in interest rates

2. The general price level is determined by the amount of total spending and the total amount of goods and services available. In essence, the supplies of and the demands for thousands of items determine all their prices simultaneously to arrive at the general price level.

3. The general price level will increase if there is:
   a) an increase in total spending (with no change in output)
   b) a decrease in the total output of goods and services (with no change in total spending)
   c) an increase in total spending in excess of the increase in production

4. If total spending increases in an economy that is not at full employment, production will increase at about the same rate as spending. Consequently, there will be few or no shortages and no inflation. But if there is full employment, production cannot increase, and the increase in total spending will contribute to shortages. In turn, prices will rise.

5. Demand-pull inflation most commonly occurs when there is an increase in total spending in excess of the increase in the total output of goods and services. The difference in the rates of increase of spending and output most commonly stem from an increase in the rate of spending.

6. If savings and/or taxes decrease and personal income does not change, consumer spending and, in turn, total spending will rise. Also, if the injections (investment and government spending) rise, so will total spending, for it equals C + I + G.

7. Because spending requires money, an increase in the money supply is generally required before there is any significant increase in total spending. The exception is when velocity increases.

8. Cost-push inflation occurs when production costs rise on a widespread basis in many industries. This most commonly occurs when the total output of goods and services increases at a slower rate than normal, causing shortages and price increases.

9. Decreases in production or a reduction in the normal rate of production increases could be caused by:
   a) a slower rise in the capital stock
   b) an increase in prices paid for foreign resources
   c) poor weather
   d) an increase in wages in excess of increases in labor productivity

10. If wages increase by x percent and productivity:
    a) falls, labor costs and prices will rise
    b) rises by less than x percent, labor costs and prices will rise
    c) rises by x percent, labor costs and prices will remain unchanged
    d) rises by more than x percent, labor costs and prices will fall

Chapter 14 LEARNING ACTIVITIES AND DISCUSSION QUESTIONS

1. Calculate the real interest rate on your student loan or a classmate's loan. What will the rate be if the loan is not paid back?
2. How long would it take the purchasing power of money to decrease by half at inflation rates of three, eight, and eighteen percent?
3. Check the price of gold in the last year. If the price changed, did the changes have anything to do with the economy? What are some possible explanations?
4. What things would people buy more of if they expected a sudden increase in the inflation rate? Why would they buy more of some things and not others?
5. List five items that became cheaper in the last 10 years due to rapid increases in productivity. What do you think caused these large productivity increases?

Inflated currency of Uruguay. To deal with the large prices, the government called all paper money (of 1,000 pesos and up) in to be stamped with "new peso" numbers at a 1000:1 ratio. Thus, all prices were to have three zeros dropped off.

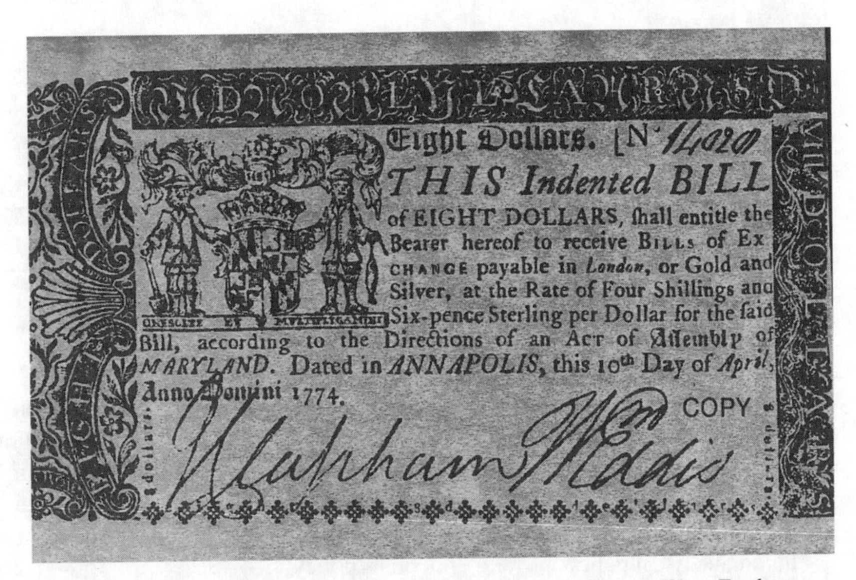

A "continental," or currency used during the Revolutionary War. Each state issued its own currency, none which was "backed" by an equivalent amount of gold or silver. Consequently, the overissued paper currency lead to hyper-inflation.

CHAPTER 15

MACROECONOMIC POLICIES

★★★★★ LEARNING OBJECTIVES ★★★★★

1. Outline the propositions of Classical Theory.
2. Outline the propositions of Keynesian Theory.
3. List the various branches of government involved in controlling the macroeconomy.
4. Describe the three ways that fiscal policy increases total spending.
5. Indicate some problems in using fiscal policy to fight recession.
6. Explain the three methods the Federal Reserve uses to end recession.
7. Explain the two ways fiscal policy is used to reduce total spending and inflation.
8. Explain the three methods the Federal Reserve uses to reduce inflation.
9. Explain the three methods the government can use to end inflation by increasing production.
10. Outline some of the recent issues and developments in macroeconomics.

TERMS

Classical Theory
Say's Law
expansionary policy
fiscal policy
discretionary fiscal policy
automatic fiscal policy
automatic stabilizers
crowding out
monetary policy
contractionary policy
supply-side economics
incomes policy
monetarist
natural rate of unemployment
monetary rule
new classical economics
rational expectations theory

Chapter 11 introduced the goals of macroeconomics—full employment, price stability, and economic growth. Chapters 13 and 14 presented some roadblocks to achieving those goals. This chapter outlines major policy tools the federal government uses to overcome these roadblocks. It introduces two theories of macroeconomics and notes the branches of government involved in the macroeconomy. The chapter also shows how the government tries to stop recession and inflation, and it ends with a summary of major macroeconomic issues.

INTRODUCTION TO MACROECONOMIC THEORIES

Economists use macroeconomic theories to explain changes in such variables as GDP, employment, production, interest rates, and price levels. Such theories also guide the government in making policies that affect the macroeconomy. In the last 200 years, two major macroeconomic theories have evolved: Classical Theory and Keynesian Theory.

Classical Theory

★1 **Classical Theory** was developed in the 1700s and the 1800s by Smith, Ricardo, Malthus, Say, Jevons, and others. It has four major propositions: 1) Say's Law; 2) the normal state of the economy is full employment; 3) recessions and inflations cure themselves; and 4) there is no need for government in the macroeconomy.

■ The major proposition is **Say's Law**, named for Jean Baptiste Say. It essentially states that "supply creates its own demand." Say noted that people sold resources (by working) and thus produced goods and services because they wanted to buy other goods and services. The money earned from creating a *supply* of goods and services created an ability to *demand* other goods and services.

■ Say's Law led to Classical Theory's second proposition that the normal state of the economy is full employment. Because people work in order to earn money to spend on goods and services, then everything people produce will be purchased. In a way, the mass immigration to America from 1880 to 1920 proved this theory. Millions of people immigrated to America to find work—and they found it. Many people believed that these immigrants "stole" jobs from people who were already here. But the more immigrants available to work and to supply goods and services, the more people there were who demanded those goods and services. Actually, the unemployment rate then was generally *lower* than during much of the last 25 years.

■ The third proposition of Classical Theory is that any recession or inflation cures itself because of changes in prices, wages, and interest rates. Consider the problem of recession, caused by "insufficient spending." Remember that recession can begin with an increase in personal savings. But doesn't Say's Law imply that people work to *spend*—and that they don't save? No, merely that people *eventually* spend their earnings before they die. Even though workers may not spend all the money they earn in the year they earn it, they will eventually spend it. In any particular year, there could be "unused" or unspent income. But remember the role played by injections. The Classical economists, who said that all money flowing into leakages reappears as investment spending and government spending, said these injections compensate for leakages.

However, will there be *enough* injections to match leakages? The Classical theorists answered yes because any shortfall that causes a recession also causes some events that compensate for leakages (see Figure 15-1). Three of the main aspects of a recession appear on the left side of Figure 15-1. They are: 1) firms have surpluses of goods and services because sales are down; 2) there are surpluses of laborers (unemployment) because when output is down, firms need fewer workers; and 3) banks have "surplus" money because savers save more than borrowers borrow during a recession. The Classical economists said these three surpluses, like all surpluses, cause price decreases. These decreases are shaded in grey in Figure 15-1.

First, prices of goods and services fall. Consumers, finding bargains, want to (and can) buy more with their paychecks. So firms meet these requests by hiring more workers to produce more. Even if the recession does not end as a result, at least it is not as bad as earlier.

Second, unemployment leads to reduced wages. Either: 1) firms cut wages, knowing they can hire replacements from the pool of the unemployed if some people quit; or 2) the unemployed offer to work at cut-rate wages, just to have a job. Because reduced wages make lower production costs possible, product prices fall, leading to higher sales that moderate the recession. Higher employment also contributes to higher consumer and total spending as the new workers spend their paychecks.

Third, "surplus money" in banks prompts them to have a "sale on money." That is, interest rates tumble. In response, people save less—and spend more. Also, as a result of cheaper credit, investment spending on capital equipment, fac-

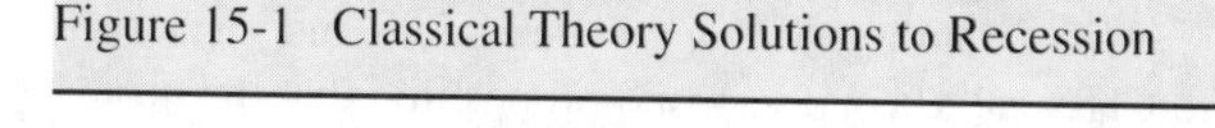
Figure 15-1 Classical Theory Solutions to Recession

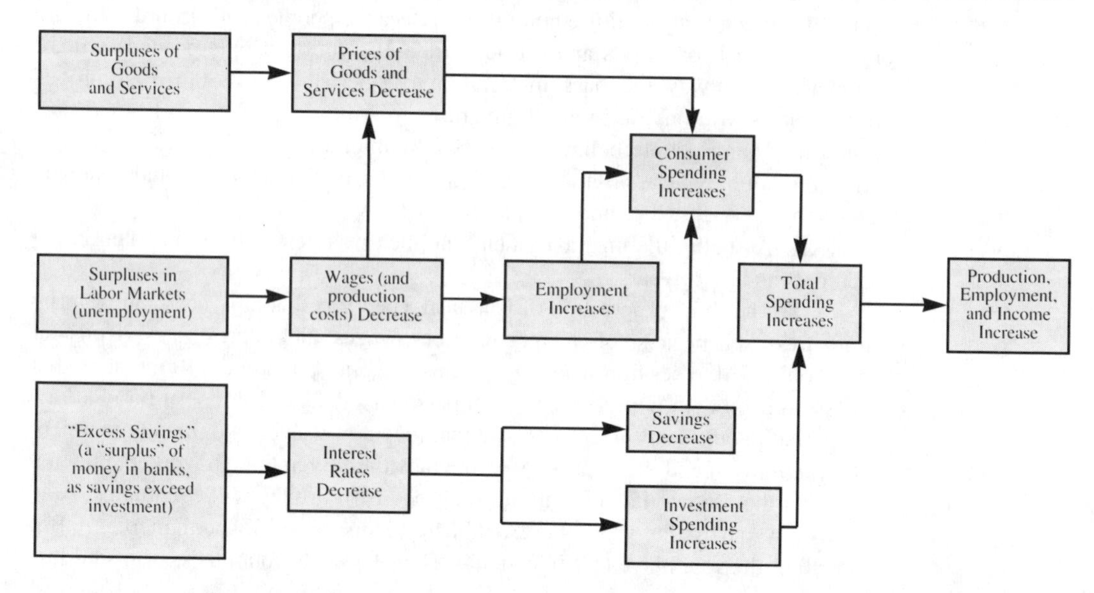

tories, offices, and home construction climbs. Again, the recession moderates because of a flexible price.

Note that the word "government" has not yet appeared. That's because adjustments in prices, wages, and interest rates occur automatically in a market economy.

■ That leads to the final proposition of Classical Theory: the government has no role in ending a recession (or even inflation, since the events will reverse themselves). This complemented the Classical theorists' belief in a *laissez faire* or "hands-off" policy in the microeconomy. That's why, for example, President Cleveland and Congress rejected the demands of Jacob Coxey and his "army" when they came to Washington in 1893 to push for government relief from a severe depression. The next year, however, Cleveland authorized the use of federal troops to crush a strike against the Pullman Palace Car Company, which had been hard hit by the depression. In order to survive and because so many unemployed people were willing to work for almost anything, Pullman cut its workers' wages by one-third.

Keynesian Theory

These Classical Theory solutions to recession prevailed for more than a hundred years, until the 1930s. With some exceptions, recessions and depressions usually lasted only a year or two. However, the Great Depression lasted 12 years, was deeper than any previous one, and was worldwide. A British economist, John Maynard Keynes (pronounced "canes"), set out to determine why Classical Theory failed to explain the Depression. In 1936, he published his major arguments in *The General Theory of Employment, Prices, and Output*. The world was never the same again.

★2 Keynes proposed that: 1) the focus in macroeconomic study should be on total spending; 2) there is no automatic cure for recession; 3) the economy might reach equilibrium at less than full employment; and 4) government action is necessary to ensure full employment.

■ Keynes' first proposition overturned Say's Law by focusing on total spending, rather than total output, as the key to understanding macroeconomic activity. That is why economists today emphasize total spending—by consumers, investors, governments, and foreign traders—as the basis for explaining recession and inflation.

■ Keynes' second proposition was that falling prices, wages, and interest rates no longer provided an automatic escape from recession. First, prices no longer fell as often or as much as in previous depressions. This was due primarily to the growth of oligopolies—industries comprised of big firms that preferred to reduce output, not prices, when recession hit. Second, wages fell less than earlier, partly because of the growing strength of labor unions. Also, cutting people's wages was increasingly considered socially unacceptable. Finally, Keynes believed that even if workers accepted wage cuts (as happened during the 1930s), product demand might fall even faster as poorer workers, who were now even poorer, reduced their spending. Thus, ironically, wage cuts might lead to even more unemployment, not less, as Classical Theory held.

A third attack by Keynes on automatic cures to recession suggested that even though interest rates still fell during a recession, the falling rates failed to end it for two reasons: 1) people didn't save less as rates had fallen, as expected; and 2) investment spending didn't increase much. Keynes said people saved primarily for the future (mainly retirement) and as a precaution against loss of income (during periods of unemployment, for example). The interest rate was only a weak third factor determining savings. Therefore, during the Great Depression, when the thought of losing their jobs terrified workers—for there was no unemployment compensation and little welfare in the early 1930s—people (at least those who had jobs) saved *more,* not less.

Contrary to Classical Theory, Keynes also proposed that investment spending would not increase as predicted when interest rates fell. He noted that both interest rates and investment spending plunged in the 1930s. The explanation, according to Keynes, is that future profit expectations are far more important than interest rates in determining investment. During the Great Depression, expectations of profits from new factories or machines were generally very low to non-existent. Thus, even if interest rates fell to zero, few firms would have borrowed much money.

■ These failures of Classical Theory's automatic solutions to depression led to Keynes' third proposition: the economy might get bogged down in an unacceptably long and deep depression. That is, total spending might not be large enough to allow the economy to reach potential GDP. Thus, it could reach equilibrium at less than full employment. Keynes thought the economy would eventually recover—but over an unacceptably long period.

■ Keynes believed that the government must act to boost spending high enough to allow the economy to achieve full employment. His proposal meant the government should have a budget deficit—thus driving the nation into debt during recessions or depressions. For the United States, this meant the days when the president and Congress sat idly by while the economy floundered were over.

GOVERNMENT SECTORS INVOLVED IN THE MACROECONOMY

Although the Roosevelt administration provided much government assistance to the unemployed in the 1930s and early 1940s, it wasn't until the Employment Act of 1946 that the government committed itself to promoting full employment. Three branches or sectors of the federal government seek to achieve this and other macroeconomic goals: 1) the executive branch; 2) Congress; and 3) the Federal Reserve System.

★3

The Executive Branch

The president is the head of the executive branch. The president's primary control over the economy comes through White House influence on government spending and tax rates (both indirectly influence consumer and investment spending). Another executive branch participant is the budget director, who leads the Office of Management and Budget (OMB) and oversees government spending.

The OMB proposes to the president how much the federal government should spend, and then the president makes the administration's budget proposal to Congress.

The Treasury Department is another vital part of the executive branch. The Secretary of the Treasury influences the president in determining tax rates, user fees, and the size of the budget deficit. The president also consults frequently with the Council of Economic Advisers (CEA). Each January, the Council provides the *Economic Report of the President*, a review of economic conditions and proposals for improving the economy. Finally, the president is also advised by officials from the Commerce Department, the Labor Department, the International Trade Commission, and other agencies.

The Legislative Branch

Congress, the primary institution of the legislative branch, influences total spending in the economy through its power to authorize government spending and to collect taxes. The greatest economic power in Congress is wielded by the House Ways and Means Committee, the Senate Finance Committee, and the Joint Finance Committee. The Congressional Budget Office (CBO) is a counterpart of the OMB in the executive branch. The CBO has a staff of economists who provide members of Congress with information and advice. They also do macroeconomic studies and economic forecasting.

The Federal Reserve System

You studied the Federal Reserve System (the Fed) in Chapter 12. It is headed by the seven-member Board of Governors, and the Federal Open Market Committee engages in open market operations. There are 12 Federal Reserve District Banks, which serve the thousands of commercial banks that are members of the Federal Reserve System. The Fed has several functions, but controlling the availability and the price of credit (the interest rate) is the most important. It exercises this control primarily through: 1) changes in the discount rate; 2) changes in the reserve requirement; and 3) open market operations.

GOVERNMENT POLICIES DEALING WITH RECESSION

How do the various sectors of the government control the macroeconomy? This section explains policies used to end recession. The next section shows how the government tackles inflation.

Recall that recession occurs when a sharp drop in total spending (C + I + G) leads firms to lay off workers, close plants, and cut production. Total spending falls if: 1) savings and/or taxes increase; or 2) investment and/or government spending fall. In essence, recession is caused by "insufficient spending"—insufficient when compared with the (desired) level of spending needed to reach potential GDP. The solution to recession is to boost total spending to that desired level. Any policy to end (or to prevent) recession is called an **expansionary policy**, for the intent is to expand employment and output. Two broad sets of policies for achieving this are fiscal policy and monetary policy.

Expansionary Fiscal Policy

Fiscal policy refers to changes in government spending and/or taxes that are designed to change the level of total spending. If the macroeconomic problem is recession, it is necessary to increase total spending. Business owners will then want to hire more laborers and buy other resources so they can boost output. Implementation of fiscal policy is the responsibility of the president and Congress. Either can propose changes in taxes or government spending. However, generally both must agree on such policies, except when Congress overrides the president's veto. Usually such moves to change taxes and government spending occur during recession or inflation. Economists call such policy changes **discretionary fiscal policy** because such movements in taxing and spending are at the discretion of the president and Congress.

But total spending also changes because of **automatic fiscal policy**. This involves **automatic stabilizers**, which are economic variables that change to moderate recession or inflation without anyone initiating any action. One such automatic stabilizer is unemployment compensation. When unemployment rises during recession, more people collect unemployment benefits. Because the recipients spend most of the money, such spending moderates the recession. Welfare payments, another automatic stabilizer, work similarly, as more people receive such benefits during recession. Farm subsidies represent a third class of stabilizers. Since farm prices and income often fall during recession, the subsequent increase in subsidies somewhat offsets a drop in total spending. The last major automatic stabilizer is the progressive income tax. When their wages or hours are cut, people tend to fall into lower tax brackets. Thus, they get to spend a larger share of their gross paychecks, again offsetting the spending drop that precipitated the recession. (Incidentally, this was much more important before the reduction in the number of brackets from 14 to three in 1986.)

★4

There are two types of discretionary fiscal policy: 1) changes in taxes; and 2) changes in government spending.

■ The first expansionary fiscal policy action is to reduce taxes, either on individuals or businesses, or both. Cutting personal taxes gives people higher disposable incomes. Since this leads to more consumer spending, total spending rises, tending to moderate the recession. Reducing business taxes has a similar effect on businesses because the larger after-tax profits contribute to more investment spending on plant and equipment. Another fiscal policy option for business is an investment tax credit. This is a reduction in taxes for businesses equal to a certain percent of the money spent on capital goods. The United States had an investment tax credit from 1964 until 1986.

■ The second expansionary fiscal policy action is to increase government spending on goods and services. As far as the expansionary effect is concerned, it usually doesn't matter how the money is spent, so long as it *is* spent. The government could buy more street lights or more trucks for the Postal Service—or start a war. Of course, war is an absurd suggestion, but some people believe that war is the only way to ensure full employment. It certainly brought prosperity during

World Wars I and II, the Korean War, and the Vietnam War—but at a horrendous cost. And remember, the Great Depression ended in 1933 in Germany, eight years before it did here, because the Nazis were building up their Wehrmacht (war machine). The consequential creation of jobs was a major reason for Hitler's popularity.

Both expansionary fiscal policies—cutting taxes and raising government spending—result in a budget deficit, but Keynes thought this was an acceptable price to pay for full employment. In the 1930s, however, few politicians accepted his philosophy. President Roosevelt always believed that the government should have a balanced budget each year—even though the huge deficits of World War II brought America out of the Great Depression.

Problems of an Expansionary Fiscal Policy

★5 Besides the deficit problem, an expansionary fiscal policy has other problems, including: 1) timing; 2) politics; 3) inflation from overstimulus; and 4) crowding out.

■ Ideally, a recession should be predicted almost a year in advance. It takes that long to change most tax laws and to initiate major spending projects. Often, however, a recession isn't recognized until well *after* it starts because much government data collection is done quarterly and becomes available well after the economic activity that is measured occurs. Thus, the cure comes later than desired.

■ The second problem is political. Democrats and Republicans often disagree on fiscal policies, a problem that is especially frustrating when one party controls Congress and the other the presidency. But even controlling both branches is often little better, as President Clinton quickly found out when Republicans derailed his economic stimulus package and jobs bill with a filibuster in early 1993.

■ The third problem is overstimulus of the economy, which leads to inflation. Recession occurs when there is not enough total spending to reach potential GDP. Determining the economy's shortfall of this "proper level" of spending might seem easy. Then the government could give the economy the appropriate shot of tax cuts and a government spending boost to close this "spending gap." But it's not that simple, for it's hard to know just how big the gap is. After all, *how big* is potential GDP? The size of potential GDP depends partly on the meaning of full employment. Is it an unemployment rate of three, five, or seven percent, or higher? There is much disagreement on this matter.

Let's say authorities believe total spending should increase by $400 billion to provide full employment, however defined. Suppose Congress then cuts taxes by some amount and also begins some public works projects. But what if these policies unexpectedly create *$600* billion of extra spending? The $200 billion of "excess spending" will merely create shortages and inflation.

A difficulty in applying expansionary policy is that there is no precise level of spending that provides full employment without inflation. If the economy starts from a deep recession and expansionary fiscal policies cause total spending to increase, the unemployment rate steadily drops. At first, prices do not increase much, if at all. This is because most firms have competitors with excess productive capacity, so any price increase pushes buyers to a competitor who does *not* raise prices. Thus, prices stay fairly constant for a while. But eventually, as the economy moves closer to full employment, some industries (the tire industry, for example) will reach their capacities before others. Additional expansionary fiscal policies begin to create shortages in *some* industries, even though the *overall* economy has excess productive capacity. Thus, *some* prices begin to climb (tire prices, in this case) while others stay firm. The closer the economy gets to full employment, the more common such price increases become. Or, the lower the unemployment rate becomes, the higher the inflation rate will be. As commonly stated, there is a tradeoff between these two rates. Unfortunately, there is no point when both rates are at their ideal levels.

■ The last major problem of an expansionary fiscal policy centers on the budget deficit created by that policy. The government finances a deficit by selling government securities (bonds, etc.). But if it wants to sell *many* more securities, it usually must raise the interest rate paid to the buyers of the additional securities sold by the government. This is necessary to draw the buyers' funds away from other forms of saving. In essence, such government borrowing raises the demand for credit, creating a shortage of credit at the original interest rate.

(Technically, what happens when larger deficits lead to higher interest rates is that purchasers of the additional securities sold by the government offer to pay less for them, just like you would be willing to pay less for additional units of any good you buy. For example, instead of paying the \$10,000 face value on a bond, a buyer might offer to pay only \$9,600. Suppose the bond pays \$600 interest per year, or six percent of \$10,000. Because the *number of dollars* of interest paid per year to the bondholder is the same whatever the price, the interest *rate* rises as bond prices fall. The interest rate on a bond, often called the yield, is found by dividing the number of dollars of interest paid per year to the bondholder by the price of the bond. In this case, the yield would be 6.25 percent, or \$600 ÷ \$9,600 x 100.)

To compete against the government for credit, all borrowers, including chargecard users, home buyers, and businesses buying capital equipment and new factories, must pay higher interest rates. But at higher interest rates, *some* spending that consumers and investors plan to do by using credit will not occur because interest rates are too high. Economists call this phenomenon **crowding out**, which means government spending "crowds out" private consumer and investment spending because of increased interest rates. Crowding out can occur in another way. The government could provide goods and services that individuals would otherwise have purchased. Thus, there is no or little net gain in total spending. Examples include: purchases of books by public libraries that lead to fewer books purchased by individuals; spending on government-owned mass transit systems that lead to fewer personal vehicles purchased; and spending on public education that leads to less private education.

Economists disagree about the extent of crowding out. Some say there is very little. Others say it is complete, which means fiscal policy actions can't raise total spending at all because any increase in government spending leads to an equal fall in private spending.

The top section of Figure 15-2 summarizes expansionary fiscal policy. The ultimate goal (on the right) is to increase production and employment. The chart also illustrates two of the problems just examined. The inflation problem appears at top right, where expansion occurs during full employment. The crowding out problem appears in the middle, where it leads to an offsetting effect on total spending.

Expansionary Monetary Policy

The bottom section of Figure 15-2 deals with money or credit expansion, or monetary policy. The Fed always stands ready to help boost total spending if it is a little less than the "desired level." The Fed does not directly control consumer, investment, or government spending. However, it makes it easier for consumers and investors to spend. The Fed does this through **monetary policy**, designed to manipulate both interest rates and the availability of credit. During a recession, the Fed tries to reduce interest rates and to increase excess reserves (see pages 301-303 for review). By reducing the financing cost of purchases made with credit, lower interest rates encourage such spending, whether by consumers

Figure 15-2 Expansionary Fiscal and Monetary Policies

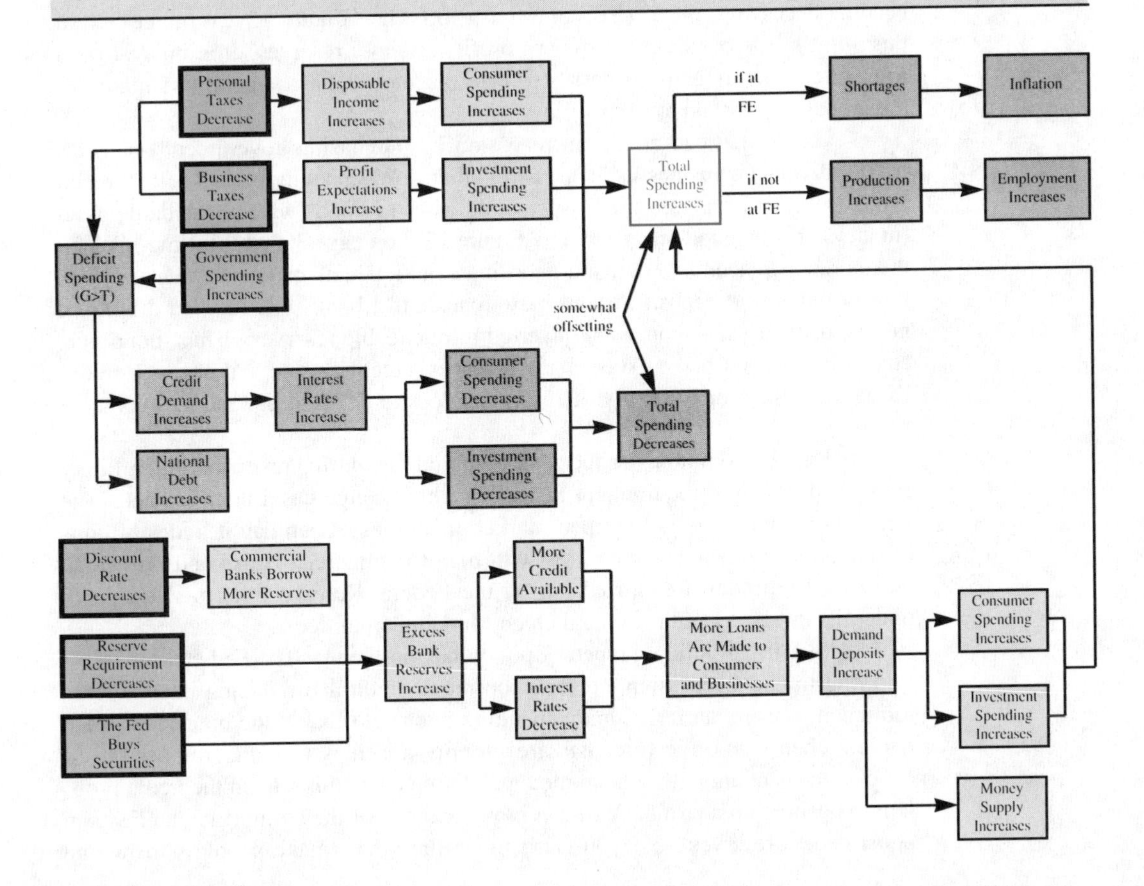

or businesses. By increasing excess reserves, the Fed increases the availability of credit. It also encourages banks to reduce their interest rates on loans. Excess reserves represent a bank's lending capacity that it has not used. Economists refer to expansionary monetary policy as an "easy money" policy—because credit is cheap and plentiful.

★6 The Fed provides "easy money" in three primary ways: 1) it reduces the discount rate; 2) it reduces the reserve requirement; and 3) it buys government securities.

■ A commercial bank bases its decision to borrow reserves from the Fed partly on the cost of those reserves—the discount rate. Thus, if that rate declines, the bank is more likely to borrow more reserves. In turn, the bank passes on these cost savings to its customers by reducing its loan rates. This encourages individuals and businesses to take out more loans to finance consumer and investment spending. Such loans increase the money supply, for the loans usually are deposited in demand deposit accounts. Thus, reducing the discount rate ultimately increases the money supply as well as total spending. To stimulate the economy after the 1990-1991 recession, the Fed cut the discount rate in a series of steps from six percent to three percent.

■ When the Fed reduces the reserve requirement, commercial banks have their excess reserves increased without the banks taking any specific action. It occurs when some of the deposits the banks used to hold as required reserves now become excess reserves. (You may wish to review Figure 12-2 on page 300 at this point.) The banks, eager to earn profits on those reserves, drop interest rates to coax consumers and businesses to take out more loans. Again, this increases the money supply and total spending.

■ The Fed can also fight recession by purchasing government securities from individuals, businesses, banks, and others. When an individual sells the Fed a bond, the Fed replaces a non-spendable asset (a bond) with a spendable asset (money). (It's a good idea to review Figure 12-3 on page 303 at this time.) When the money is placed in a demand deposit account, a bank can generate even more money out of the deposit through new loans. If a bank sells the Fed a bond, a non-lendable asset (a bond) is converted into lendable reserves. Thus, bond purchases by the Fed boost excess bank reserves, creating more and cheaper credit. Eventually, the money supply increases, as does total spending, and the recession moderates.

The Fed commonly reduces the discount rate during recession, but it rarely changes the reserve requirement because such a change has a huge impact. The Fed's most important tool is open market operations. Each day it trades billions of dollars in government securities with major commercial banks and brokerage houses. The trades are carried out by the Federal Reserve Bank of New York under the directives of the Federal Open Market Committee.

Like fiscal policy, monetary policy has problems. The Fed can overreact in trying to end a recession, creating too much credit and reducing interest rates too much, causing an inflationary spending boom. Probably the biggest problem occurs when economic forecasts are gloomy and it is virtually impossible to encourage spending with "cheap money." Often economists liken the Fed's problem to pushing on a string. You can move one end of the string (like the Fed can boost excess reserves), but you can't move the other (make people borrow and spend more). This was partly why the recovery from the 1990-1991 recession was so sluggish and why the weak economy was an issue in the 1992 election. The Fed did seek to ease credit in 1991 and early 1992, and interest rates were very low by recent standards (with the exception of credit card rates). But consumers and, consequently, businesses were reluctant to borrow and spend.

Many business leaders and economists don't agree that a lack of loan demand slowed the recovery. Some blame the Fed for refusing to purchase enough government securities, thereby causing excess reserves to be too low. Others blame the 1991 Federal Deposit Insurance Improvement Act, which requires that more of a bank's capital (net worth) be owned by the bank's managers. This, they say, led to a "credit crunch," as banks refused to make as many loans to otherwise qualified customers in order to comply with the law.

CONTROLLING INFLATION BY RESTRICTING TOTAL SPENDING

The causes of recession and inflation are almost exact opposites. Too little spending causes recession, and too much spending causes shortages and inflation. So you might expect opposite solutions to these problems, and we now turn to such anti-inflation policies. Economists call these actions **contractionary policy**, for the intent is to contract the amount of total spending and, in turn, the amount of shortages and price increases.

Turn back to Figure 14-3 on page 339. Note that the price level depends primarily upon the amount of total spending and the amount of goods and services produced. Contractionary policy seeks to control increases in the price level by restricting total spending. The next section shows how the same thing can be done by boosting production. While reading this section, refer to Figure 15-3, which summarizes contractionary policy.

Contractionary Fiscal Policy

★7

The president and Congress can deal with inflation by: 1) imposing tax increases; and 2) cutting government spending. When they raise taxes on individuals, disposable income falls, as does consumer spending, total spending, shortages, and the inflation rate. (Similarly, if the government raised business taxes, businesses would cut their investment spending on new plant and capital equipment. However, this would lead to less output in the future and lower living standards. Thus, such a fiscal policy is not a good option.) When the government cuts its budget, total spending also drops. For example, the government could put highway projects on hold, reduce public services (such as job-finding services), and close seldom used facilities in some national parks.

The effect of contractionary fiscal policy on the federal budget is the opposite of an expansionary policy's effect. If there was a budget deficit prior to tax increases or budget cuts, the deficit shrinks. If the tax increases and the budget cuts are strong enough, the budget becomes balanced or even ends up in surplus. If the budget was already in balance prior to the tax boosts and the budget cuts, there is a budget surplus.

Figure 15-3 Contractionary Fiscal and Monetary Policies

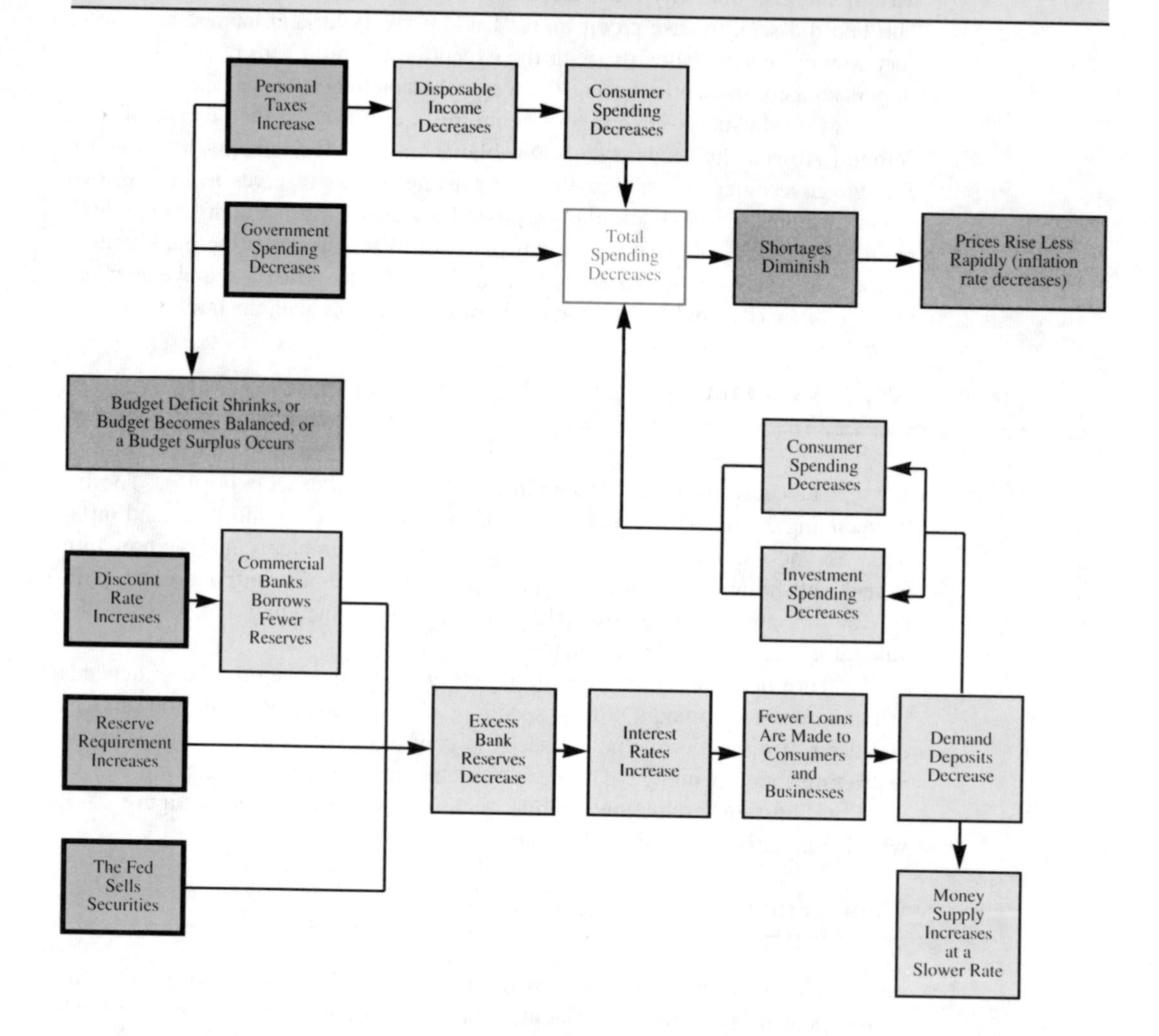

In addition to these discretionary fiscal policy actions, automatic fiscal policy helps to moderate inflation. Unemployment compensation benefits and welfare payments fall as more people work during the prosperity of an inflationary period. Overtime pay, wage increases, and longer hours all push people into higher tax brackets, so they get to spend a smaller share of their income. Farm subsidies fall as farm prices and incomes rise. All these events lead to reduced spending, which then moderates inflation.

Like expansionary policy, contractionary policies have some weaknesses. Again, it's difficult to forecast inflation and the time needed to cure it. Politicians are reluctant to take unpopular actions (tax hikes or budget cuts) that can delay or prevent a necessary cure. An excellent example was the temporary income tax hike in 1968-1970, called a surtax (10 percent was added to each person's taxes). Taxes should have been raised in 1966 or 1967, when inflation began to get out of hand, but President Johnson was reluctant to increase taxes before his re-election campaign. He eventually accepted a tax hike, but it was too late. The severe inflation of the 1970s had been unleashed (though other factors contributed as well). Another problem was that everyone knew the surtax was temporary. So people saved less, and the effect on total spending was minimal.

Another serious problem of a contractionary policy is "overkill." It is possible to moderate the inflation with spending cuts, but excessive cuts create a recession. The last two budget surpluses that were associated with contractionary fiscal policies preceded recessions and occured in 1960 and 1969. Thus, it is possible to overdo contractionary policy just as it is possible to overdo expansionary policy. However, avoiding that overkill is a bit like avoiding an accident on a crowded highway. Pick up speed too fast (expansionary policy) and you hit the car ahead (inflation). Slow down too fast (contractionary policy) and you get rear-ended (recession).

Contractionary Monetary Policy

★8

Suppose the economy experienced inflation in excess of seven percent and that M1 increased at nine percent each year for the last three years. If the Fed suspects that an excessive money supply expansion was the reason for the inflation, it might lower its M1 target to only a four percent increase. This might result in a spending increase equal to the rate of increase in the economy's productive capacity (potential GDP). Consequently, there would be fewer shortages and lower rates of inflation. Thus, contractionary monetary policy, often called a "tight money" policy, occurs when the Fed slows up the money supply's rate of expansion.

The Fed carries out such a move in three ways: 1) it raises the discount rate; 2) it raises the reserve requirement; and 3) it sells government securities. When the discount rate is raised, banks are less likely to borrow reserves from the Fed. Credit becomes a bit less available and more costly (higher interest rates) for consumers and businesses. They take out fewer loans, so the money supply climbs more slowly. Finally, total spending rises at a slower rate. The same effect occurs when the Fed raises the reserve requirement, for banks now must convert some (lendable) excess reserves to (non-lendable) required reserves. Last, when people pay the Fed for the government securities sold by the Fed, their demand deposits fall. In turn, banks have less ability to extend loans.

As with fiscal policy, a major problem with monetary policy is the danger of "overkill." The Fed can easily cut back credit so much that it brings on a recession. This happened in the early 1980s, a time of serious inflation that the Fed, under Chairman Paul Volcker, wanted to end. The Fed successfully reduced inflation to less than three percent by the mid-1980s. But that caused the recessions of 1980 and 1982, the most severe since the Great Depression. Yet many people, including Volcker, believed that such drastic action was necessary to "break the back" of inflation. Another problem of monetary policy is that the timing might be off. If the Fed waits too long to contract credit, inflation can become much worse. By the time credit contraction does occur, the inflationary pressures may have evaporated, and the contraction could actually be harmful, causing an economic slowdown or even recession.

CONTROLLING INFLATION BY INCREASING PRODUCTION

★9

Cutting demand (total spending) is one way to reduce shortages. Increasing supplies (total output) also reduces shortages. This second technique has gained much popularity since the late 1970s, particularly during the early part of the Reagan administration. Such policies to boost production, called **supply-side economics**, became known as Reaganomics. However, the concept is an old one and will never be completely rejected. The ultimate intention of several of President Clinton's major proposals, including infrastructure improvement and workforce education, is to boost total output.

But the better-known supply-side economic policies of the Reagan administration generally fell into three categories: 1) altering the tax system; 2) reforming income redistribution programs; and 3) reducing business regulations. Again, to the extent that they had merit in the 1980s, they will have merit any time in the future.

■ Arthur Laffer, an economics professor, popularized supply-side economics when he theorized that government might increase tax *rates* so much that tax *receipts* (collections) would fall. (For an extreme example, if the government took 95 percent of our incomes, few people would work, at least in jobs where the government could get at their incomes, so the government would collect almost no taxes.) He suggested sharp cuts in tax rates in order to increase tax collections. This is the main policy move favored by supply-siders—to cut taxes in order to spur more work and production. Supply-siders favor three tax reforms. The first is a lower tax rate for everyone. According to supply-side theory, lower taxes encourage people to work longer hours, get second jobs, start businesses, and so on. They do so because the government no longer takes such a big bite out of paychecks. Thus, the 1981-1983 tax cut reduced tax rates over a three-year period so that everyone paid about 25 percent less in federal income taxes. Second, supply-siders support a less progressive income tax, again to encourage working, but also because a less progressive tax provides more after-tax income for upper income people. Because these people save relatively more of their incomes, more money becomes available for capital equipment, new plants, and research and development. This boosts the economy's productive capacity. Third, supply-siders want lower business tax rates, again to encourage investment spending.

■ Another part of the supply-side economics program seeks to reduce or reform various income redistribution programs, so there is more incentive for people to seek employment. Supply-siders believe that welfare and unemployment compensation programs reduce people's willingness to work. They maintain that the budgets for these programs should be cut. Similarly, they believe minimum wage laws reduce the willingness of firms to hire workers and increase production, so these laws should be repealed.

■ Last, supply-side economists want to reduce government regulation of business. They believe less regulation encourages more risk-taking to find more efficient production methods. It also leads to more investment spending, another boost to the nation's productive capacity.

As you have learned, a tax cut leads to a budget deficit. However, according to supply-side theory, the deficit will not last long, since the economic growth created by supply-side policies will yield more tax revenues from the additional people who work and from higher incomes in general.

Throughout the 1980s, economists disagreed about the effectiveness of these programs. The major criticism was that the ballooning deficits of the Reagan years did not shrink as predicted. By the 1990s, few people were championing supply-side economics as our salvation.

CONTROLLING INFLATION WITH INCOMES POLICIES

One final way governments deal with inflation is through **incomes policies**, which are used to control prices and incomes. This is the oldest inflation-fighting technique, dating back to the Roman Empire. But historically (including Roman times) incomes policies have had little success.

Controlling prices directly is the most common incomes policy. During World War II, when heavy government spending was coupled with restrictions on output of consumer goods, huge shortages exerted upward pressure on prices. The federal government established thousands of price ceilings, administered by the Office of Price Administration. To "spread out" the shortages fairly, people received ration coupons needed to buy sugar, gasoline, tires, and other products in short supply.

The Kennedy-Johnson administration instituted "wage-price guidelines." Since productivity gains averaged 3.2 percent, workers were to voluntarily limit their wage demands to that same rate. If they did, labor costs would stay constant, and so would prices. The plan failed, largely because it was voluntary.

In 1971, the Nixon administration imposed price controls, which were gradually lifted during the mid-1970s. Wage controls were part of that same incomes policy. Officials believed that if they could keep wages from rising so sharply, production costs and prices would not rise too much. Most economists deemed the program at least a partial, if not a complete, failure. Some problems included: 1) widespread shortages, especially for oil products; 2) violations of price ceilings; and 3) charges of unfairness by organized labor because they could *not* get away with what many businesses did.

Another incomes policy (which has not yet been implemented) would work indirectly. Firms that kept wage increases below a certain percent would receive a tax break. Firms with sharp wage increases would receive a tax boost.

RECENT MACROECONOMIC ISSUES AND DEVELOPMENTS

In the last few decades, much attention has focused on several macroeconomic issues and theoretical developments. This section introduces you to some of them.

The Budget Deficit Problem

★10

Keynes, who proposed budget deficits during recessions, never suggested that we have them *every* year. However, there have been deficits every year except two since 1960—and every year since 1970. In the 1980s, the United States usually had deficits of between $100 and $200 billion. Many critics blame Reagan's tax cut and the huge military buildup for these deficits. His supporters blame them on the widespread increase in spending initiated by Congress. Whatever the cause, interest on the growing debt eats up about one-sixth of the federal government's current budget.

The problem is that the two main solutions to deficits—raising taxes and cutting government programs—are painful (perhaps suicidal) to politicians. Walter Mondale, the Democratic loser in the 1984 presidential election, didn't get far when he told Americans he would raise their taxes to narrow the deficit. Because so few people wanted to hear that, neither George Bush nor Michael Dukakis said it in the 1988 campaign. In his nomination acceptance speech, Bush even promised, "Read my lips—no new taxes!"

That famous pledge interfered with efforts to reduce the deficit until June 1990, when Bush changed his mind (and ultimately set the stage for his defeat in 1992). Throughout the summer of 1990, a bipartisan committee sought ways to reduce the deficit. Their task was made more difficult by two problems. First, the deepening savings and loan crisis kept adding to the government's budget and, thus, the deficit. Second, the U.S. military buildup in Saudi Arabia and elsewhere in the Middle East added at least $17 billion to the deficit.

A budget-deficit-reduction package was completed in October 1990. The plan was to reduce the budget by an accumulated $500 billion over five years, partly by raising tax revenues by $140 billion. The plan raised the marginal income tax rate for the highest income earners from 28 percent to 31 percent and limited their deductions and exemptions. Taxes were raised on alcoholic beverages, cigarettes, airline tickets, gasoline, and some luxury goods. The Medicare payroll tax was increased, and recipients were required to pay more of their expenses, while doctors and hospitals would be paid lower fees.

In July 1993, Congress passed another budget-reduction bill, largely on President Clinton's proposals. It was a five-year package that was expected to reduce the deficit by $496 billion over that period. Of that, $255 billion would come from spending cuts ($56 billion from Medicare). In addition, $268 billion would come from increased taxes, partly offset by $27 billion in tax breaks. The top income tax rate will be 36 percent (up from 31 percent) for individuals with taxable incomes over $115,000 and couples over $140,000. Also, a 10 percent surtax was added on people earning more than $250,000—in effect, creating a new bracket of 39.6%. The top corporate income tax rate was raised from 34 to 35 percent. The federal gasoline tax was raised 4.3¢ a gallon. Upper-income retirees will be taxed on 85 percent of their Social Security incomes, up from 50 percent. The earned-income credit for the working poor will increase.

It should be noted that many people, including some economists, do not worry much about the deficit and see substantial benefit in it. First, they believe that its size in comparison with GDP is not large. The net public debt is about 54 percent of GDP, so we can easily manage to pay the interest on it. Second, they point to other healthy economies that have even larger deficits (as a percent of total outlays), such as Japan. Third, they believe that the government can do very productive things with the funds that are borrowed (the deficit). Construction and improvement of the infrastructure increases resource efficiency, as you learned earlier. Improved schools can increase labor productivity. And government-sponsored research can lead to cures of diseases and technological breakthroughs that raise productivity.

The Decline of Fiscal Policy

The last time fiscal policy was used to end either recession or inflation was 1975. Jimmy Carter hastened its decline in his 1976 campaign against President Ford when he promised a balanced budget by 1980. The pledge came back to haunt President Carter in 1980 in his race against Ronald Reagan—who made a similar pledge (and was even less successful at keeping it). President Clinton used spending increases in 1993, not to end recession (which ended in 1991), but to get the economy closer to full employment (the unemployment rate was still about seven percent at the time). Many people criticized the move, as the economy was seen to be moving there on its own. But, because Clinton didn't believe that or didn't wish to wait or because of political commitments, he proceeded with the spending increases anyway.

One reason for disenchantment with fiscal policy might be because the nation suffered unacceptable levels of unemployment, inflation, and deficits during the 30 years it was used. Although business cycles have not been as severe as they were prior to World War II, perhaps we expect more today from officials who try to manage the macroeconomy. Perhaps because fiscal policy was oversold as a tool several decades ago, we might expect more to be done than *can* be done.

The Emergence of Monetary Policy

Virtually ignored from the 1930s through the 1960s, monetary policy gained stature again in the 1970s and 1980s. People started to watch the weekly reports of the changes in M1 or M2 as a signal of what the Fed was up to and what the economy would do next.

This was partly due to the failure of fiscal policy. People wanted *some* handle on the macroeconomy. More important, monetary policy's increased stature today is due to a group of economists known as **monetarists**. They believe that, more than anything else, changes in the money supply explain changes in current GDP and prices. Milton Friedman, a long-time professor of economics at the University of Chicago and a Nobel Prize winner, was the leading promoter of this idea. Karl Brunner, who coined the term "monetarist," and Allan Meltzer also were other key advocates of monetarism.

Like the Classical economists, monetarists believe that the economy moves toward a **natural rate of unemployment**. This rate is equal to the frictional unemployment rate plus the structural unemployment rate. It is also the rate of unemployment associated with an economy that has a steady rate of inflation. Monetarists believe that any attempt to reduce unemployment below the natural rate increases the inflation rate as well as interest rates.

They also believe that virtually all business fluctuations are due to erratic and excessive changes in the money supply. That is, a 12 percent increase one year, followed by a four percent increase the next, and so on, lead to periods of recession and inflation. Therefore, because the Fed often *causes* what it attempts to prevent, monetarists say the Fed should not even *attempt* to counteract recession and inflation.

However, monetarists do believe it is possible to have an economy without significant inflation or recession. This could happen if the Fed increased the money supply by the same percentage each year, equal to the rate of increase in the productive capacity of the economy—potential GDP. In that way, all extra output could and would be produced and sold, so there would be no shortages or inflation. Such a policy is called a **monetary rule**, and it would entail selecting some particular monetary aggregate (M1, M2, etc.) to increase at the same percent, year in and year out.

The New Classical Economics

Another body of economic thought, called the **new classical economics**, was developed in the 1970s and 1980s and initially seemed to support the monetarists. Robert Lucas, Thomas Sargent, and Robert Barro are some of the more prominent economists of this group. Their major proposition is called **rational expectations theory**. It maintains that fiscal and monetary policies to end recession or inflation will fail because people have learned what to expect from such policies in the past. For example, they learned that expansionary policy often leads to inflation and, consequently, higher interest rates. Thus, if Congress cuts taxes or the Fed expands the money supply, lenders demand higher interest rates to compensate for the expected inflation. These higher rates then prevent any spending increase the authorities had in mind.

New classical economists also believe that the government (namely, the Fed) cannot control *real* interest rates. They maintain that these rates depend on technological considerations (such as banking technology) and practical considerations (such as present vs. future consumption). Again, this viewpoint coincides with that of the monetarists.

Some say the new classical economists have displaced the monetarists. Others say monetarism is on the decline because it was never capable of accomplishing what it was cracked up to do. Critics of monetarism say it is impossible to control the money supply well enough for a monetary rule to work. Still others, who still believe in monetarism, say the Fed never gave it a chance to work.

No wonder critics say that if you laid all economists end to end, they would never reach a conclusion. This is hardly true, but perhaps their disagreements prove that, contrary to what the dismal Thomas Carlyle said, economics is *not* a dismal science, after all. A bit confusing maybe. But not dismal.

Chapter 15 SUMMARY

Classical Theory was the first body of macroeconomic theory. It was based upon Say's Law, which held that people would always be able to produce and sell as much as they wanted. Thus, there would be no unemployment, at least in the long run. Because recessions and inflations would be automatically cured by flexible prices, wages, and interest rates, there was no need for government to solve these macroeconomic problems.

Keynesian Theory is based upon the role played by total spending. Keynes believed that total spending would not be large enough to provide full employment all the time. Therefore, he proposed that the government make up for this lack of spending with increases in government spending and/or cuts in taxes. Thus, deficit spending was to be used to end recession.

The executive branch of the federal government, Congress, and the Federal Reserve System all attempt to manipulate the economy to promote full employment and stable prices. The president and Congress do this mainly by controlling total spending through tax and budget changes. The Fed controls total spending by influencing the cost and the availability of credit.

Expansionary policy to end recession is carried out by the fiscal policy actions of tax cuts and increases in government spending. It also includes the Fed's monetary policy actions of reducing the discount rate, reducing the reserve requirement, and buying securities. Each of these actions by the Fed increases excess reserves, increases the availability of credit, and reduces interest rates.

Contractionary policy to end inflation uses the fiscal policy actions of raising personal taxes and cutting government spending. Also, the Fed raises the discount rate, raises the reserve requirement, and sells securities. These actions by the Fed decrease excess reserves and the availability of credit, leading to higher interest rates. Inflation can also be reduced through supply-side economics programs that increase the output of goods and services.

In recent years fiscal policy has fallen in popularity, partly because of the growing deficits and the crowding out of private spending by government spending. The role of monetary policy has grown, and more people are paying attention to the role of money in the macroeconomy. The new classical economists point out that people learn from past experiences with government policies and take actions to offset these policies.

Chapter 15 RESPONSES TO THE LEARNING OBJECTIVES

1. Classical Theory states that:
   a) whatever output people want to produce can be sold
   b) the long-run state of the economy is full employment
   c) recession or inflation end because of flexible prices, wages, and interest rates
   d) there is no role for the government in the macroeconomy

2. Keynesian Theory states that:
   a) total spending is the key to understanding the macroeconomy
   b) there are no automatic cures to recession or inflation
   c) the economy might get stuck in a long and deep recession
   d) government is needed to solve macroeconomic problems

3. The branches of the federal government involved in the macroeconomy include: the president, the Office of Management and Budget, the Council of Economic Advisers, the International Trade Commission, Congress, the Congressional Budget Office, the Federal Reserve System, and the Departments of Commerce, Labor, and the Treasury.

4. Total spending increases through the anti-recession fiscal policy actions of:
   a) cutting personal taxes, which raises disposable personal income and, in turn, consumer spending
   b) cutting business taxes, which raises the expectations of profits and, in turn, investment spending
   c) increasing government spending

5. Some problems in using fiscal policy to fight recession include:
   a) timing (not carrying out actions at the right time)
   b) politics (conflicting political and economic goals)
   c) excessive expansionary actions, which lead to inflation
   d) crowding out of private spending by government spending
   e) the reluctance of individuals and businesses to spend money when times are bad

6. The Fed tries to end recession by increasing excess bank reserves and the money supply by:
   a) lowering the discount rate
   b) lowering the reserve requirement
   c) purchasing government securities

7. Total spending decreases after these two anti-inflation fiscal policy actions:
   a) raising personal taxes, which cuts disposable personal income and consumer spending
   b) cutting government spending

8. The Fed tries to end inflation by decreasing excess bank reserves and reducing the rate of increase of the money supply by:
   a) raising the discount rate
   b) raising the reserve requirement
   c) selling government securities

9. The government seeks to increase the output of goods and services to end inflation by:
   a) encouraging people to work more by altering the income redistribution programs
   b) changing the tax system to increase the level of savings, investment, and work effort
   c) reducing the regulation of businesses to encourage investment spending

10. Some recent issues in macroeconomics include:
    a) the budget deficit, which grew substantially from the late 1960s through the 1980s
    b) fiscal policy and its ability to deal with recession and inflation
    c) monetary policy and its effectiveness in dealing with recession and inflation
    d) the effect that expectations of government macro-policies have on the success of those policies

Chapter 15 LEARNING ACTIVITIES AND DISCUSSION QUESTIONS

1. Look up the Democratic and Republican party platforms of 1936 and 1940. What is the evidence of a belief or a disbelief in Keynesian Theory?
2. Would there be any change in the excess reserves of the entire banking system if you found a lot of gold and sold it to a gold merchant? Why or why not?
3. Check the discount rate over the last five years. What explains any changes in the rate?
4. What would you propose for today's fiscal policy? Why?
5. Do the president or the Fed chairman seem to be monetarists? How can you tell?

CHAPTER 16

CONSUMER ECONOMICS

★★★★★ LEARNING OBJECTIVES ★★★★★

1. Explain how consumers use marginal analysis in deciding how much of a good or service to buy.
2. Describe the various financial records and instruments used by consumers to improve their economic welfare.
3. List some publications and other sources of aid for consumers.
4. List the purposes and possible consequences of advertising.
5. Explain the purpose and concept of insurance.
6. List the four primary types of insurance.
7. Outline the pros and cons of consumer credit.
8. Compare and contrast the various types of credit available to consumers.
9. Outline the various laws and other government efforts to aid the consumer.
10. Compare and contrast the various savings forms and investment instruments.

TERMS

consumer equilibrium
marginal utility
law of diminishing marginal utility
conspicuous consumption
consumer sovereignty
savings
dissavings
asset
liability
net worth
equity
bankruptcy
financial plan
beneficiary
liable
mortgage
open account credit
automatic overdraft service
secured loan
collateral
unsecured loan
personal investment

A capitalist or free enterprise economy answers What to Produce? in a system of free markets. Because of the scarcity of resources, people must choose which things they will make and which they will not. They must also decide how much of each good and service to make. The equilibrium quantity in the apple market example in Chapter 5 answered the "how much?" question for apples. Every good or service has a similar equilibrium quantity.

This chapter discusses the source of product demands—that is, the reasons why people buy what they do and in what amounts. In short, this is a closer look at consumer decision making, first explained in Chapter 1. Additionally, this chapter covers the many aids available to consumers, the role of advertising and insurance, the role of consumer credit, and the various forms of personal investing and saving.

CONSUMER DECISION MAKING

Society has scarce resources (labor, capital, entrepreneurship, and natural resources) from which it strives to get as much benefit as possible. Your personal counterparts of these resources are your time and money, since you don't have enough of either to buy and do all you want.

Rational people use scarce time and money so their welfare is maximized. This occurs when the benefit of using any time or money exceeds the opportunity cost. Decision making requires careful thought about the use of your time and money because time and money are not like air—which is *not* scarce. (However, *clean* air may indeed be scarce.) Because you can always find all the air you need, you never have to think about your next breath. However, should you climb a high mountain, careful use of the available air (forced, deep breaths, perhaps) will increase your welfare.

★1

You maximize economic welfare from scarce dollars when the benefits you receive from the last dollar spent on each good and service are equal. This situation is called **consumer equilibrium**. It is a condition when no changes in purchases can increase your economic welfare. Suppose you buy $10 worth of soda in a month and that you spend $9 by the 26th. On the 30th you spend your 10th and "last dollar," and the benefits you get are the "benefits received from the last dollar spent on soda." You can also use the term "last dollar" when you spend several dollars on something *at some point.* Say you buy $12 worth of gasoline at $1 per gallon. The last gallon you put in the tank, the 12th one, takes your "last dollar" spent on gasoline. You maximize economic welfare when the "last dollar" spent on soda provides benefit equal to that of the "last dollar" spent on gasoline, as well as on records, steak, shirts, and so on.

Marginal utility is the amount of satisfaction or benefits received from the last unit of some good or service consumed. In the gasoline example, this "last unit" is the 12th gallon. The marginal utility is the enjoyment (benefit) you receive from going wherever that 12th gallon takes you. Or consider the soda example, where you spend $30 on, let's say, 60 sodas at 50 cents each. The enjoyment from drinking the last soda—the 60th one—is your marginal utility from soda.

The **law of diminishing marginal utility** states that the marginal utility falls as you consume additional units of any good or service. For example, although you might drink several sodas in succession on a hot day, none satisfies you more than the first. For another, a fourth bedroom is less useful than the third, the third less than the second, and so on.

Suppose you want to buy both soda *and* gasoline. How much of each should you buy? You should buy that quantity for which the "last dollar" spent on each gives equal satisfaction. Because gas is $1 per gallon and a soda is 50 cents a can, the gas from your "last dollar" (the 12th gallon) should give satisfaction equal to the "last dollar" spent on soda (the 59th and 60th sodas combined).

Figure 16-1 helps you determine how much soda and gas to buy. The marginal utility, represented by different sized boxes, falls for both soda and gas as you consume more. If you buy only 12 gallons of gas, you get a lot of satisfaction from your 12th and "last dollar." Also, if you buy 60 sodas at 50 cents each, the satisfaction from your 30th and "last dollar" is the combination of the marginal utility from the 59th and 60th cans of soda. Because these two small boxes combined are far smaller than the box for the 12th gallon of gas, it means you get "more bang for the buck" from the last dollar spent on gas than the last dollar spent on soda. This means you incorrectly answered your personal What to Produce (or Buy)? question. You either bought too much soda, too little gas, or

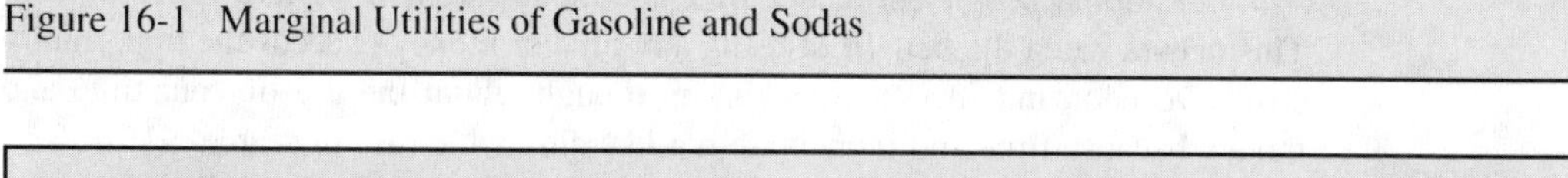
Figure 16-1 Marginal Utilities of Gasoline and Sodas

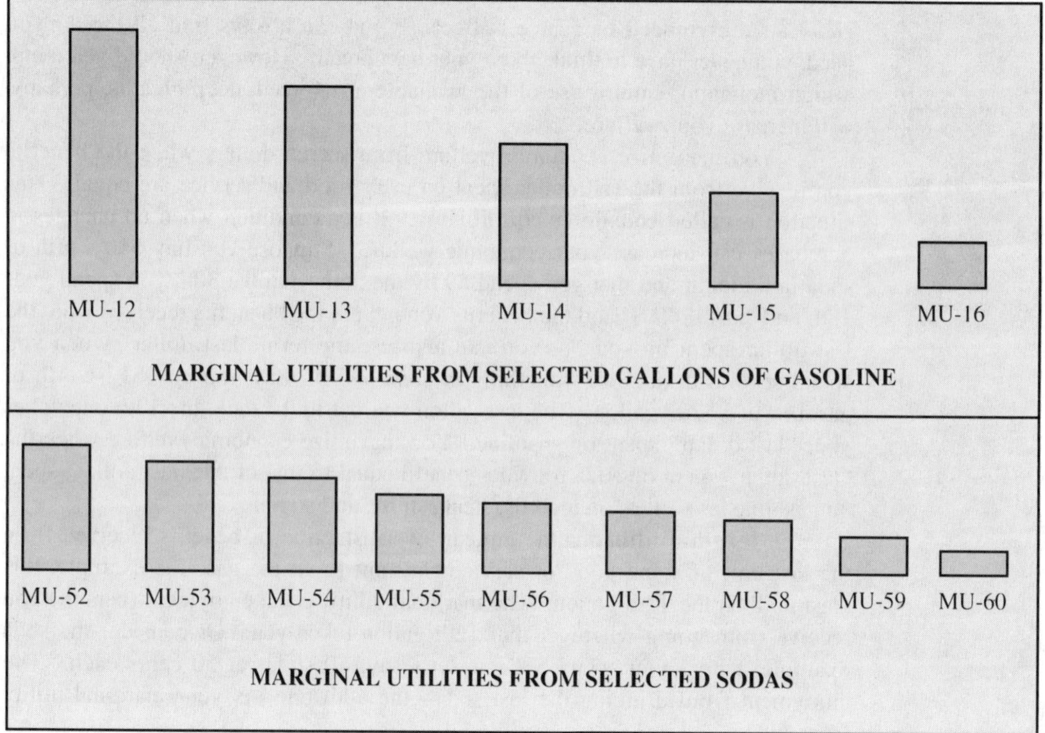

both. The diagrams show that: 1) if you increase gas purchases to, say, 14 gallons, the marginal utility of gas falls; 2) if you decrease soda purchases to, say, 56 cans, the marginal utility of soda rises. Finally, note that the marginal utility of the 14th gallon of gas is exactly double that of the 56th soda. Because the price of gas is double that of soda, you arrived at the point where the "last dollar" (or *half-dollar* in this case) spent on both items gives the same marginal utility.

This analysis can help you in two ways. The first involves what economists call peak demand. Many things come in different sizes or capacities, and you need to decide which size or capacity best suits you. Examples include cars (seating and engine size), houses, VCRs (taping and programming capacity), and luggage. Larger sizes are usually more beneficial because they can accommodate you at your time of greatest need—the point of peak demand. However, larger sizes cost more, so you should buy for your peak demand only if the *extra* benefits you receive from the larger size exceed the *extra* cost. For example, an optional eight-cylinder engine provides more power (and benefit) than a six-cylinder engine. But the larger engine costs more to buy and operate. If you could use the extra money to buy something else that would provide more satisfaction than the extra power, then you should get the six-cylinder engine.

The second way this analysis can help you involves your job. A prospective employer might ask, "Which is more important to you, the salary or the satisfaction from getting a job done?" Your response might be: "It depends upon *which* dollar of my salary you mean. My *first* few thousand dollars in salary, which I will use to keep me alive, will be far more important than any enjoyment I will get from work itself. However, after you pay me $20,000, I will use an *extra* $1,000 to buy luxuries, which will provide less satisfaction than $1,000 worth of necessities. So perhaps a raise of $1,000 to $21,000 will not mean as much as the job itself."

Often people buy things partly to impress others. Examples include: buying a Rolex watch, a BMW, or a two-carat diamond; eating caviar; and vacationing at Club Med. Thorstein Veblen, a plain farm boy who became a famous and controversial economist in the late 1800s, called such purchases **conspicuous consumption**—that is, buying things that make you stand out. Many people say such purchases are irrational and a waste of money. Yet, if someone craves prestige and truly gets happiness from the attention that conspicuous spending attracts—who are we to presume that we know a better way to spend that person's income?

Societies can use different economic systems to answer What to Produce? One purpose of using a market system is to ensure **consumer sovereignty**. This means the consumer is sovereign (has supreme power) in the marketplace and should dictate what products are made, as well as their style and quality. Many people say the reverse is true, that firms control our material lives through their vast economic power. They believe consumers are powerless when confronting business practices that result in less than maximum economic welfare.

> *With money in your pocket, you are wise, and you are handsome, and you sing well, too.*
> – Jewish Proverb

AIDS IN MANAGING YOUR MONEY

Whether your income is $5,000 or $500,000 a year, you can make thousands of *un*wise decisions about how to spend your money. This section provides a general framework on money management and suggests specific aids to help you manage your finances more wisely.

Ways to Use Income

The previous section proposed a framework for the wise spending of money on goods and services. But that section focused on money that is spent *in the present*. However, *all* income need not be spent today. Some can be saved to spend in the future. To find the proper share of income to save, follow the same marginal analysis used earlier. Simply put, you should spend a given amount of dollars in the period when the benefits are the highest. Undoubtedly, some dollars of everyone's income will be spent in the present. But after the basic necessities are bought, usually some of any remaining income is more beneficially spent in the future.

Another way to use income is to swap some of it for an assurance that you will always have a certain amount of income and/or wealth. This is what people do when they buy insurance.

A final way to dispose of income is to give it away. Because money is scarce, giving it away might seem irrational. But the act of giving money, goods, services, or time usually benefits the giver as well as the receiver. People simply feel good (get benefits) when they give to others. People give money to charity or provide estates when they receive more benefits from giving money than from buying goods and services themselves with the money. Of course, this means "unselfish giving" is, from an economic point of view, actually a selfish act.

General Financial Management

★2

After good cost-benefit analysis, record keeping is the next step in converting your income into economic welfare. Specifically, it means: what did you do in the past, what is your present situation, and where do you *want* to be in the future? To help you in this matter, you need at least two financial instruments: 1) a cash flow statement; and 2) a net worth statement.

■ The cash flow statement first lists all sources of income and cash, including that from employment, investments, and businesses, as well as alimony, government assistance, tax refunds, insurance settlements, items you sold, gifts, and gambling winnings. Next, the total of all these cash sources is adjusted by **savings** (cash put into a form that you do not intend to spend on any good or service in the near future). Savings reduces your available cash figure. On the other hand, you might have some **dissavings**, the term used for assets such as savings accounts or a stock portfolio that are turned into cash and used for spending. This dissavings adds to your total cash flow. Next, subtract any money you gave up that did not directly provide you with goods and services in return. This includes taxes, gifts you gave, union dues, charity, and fines. The remainder is what you spent for goods and services.

If you're in financial difficulty, a check of these records can suggest where you can cut spending, especially if you compare yourself to the national average. You might want to set up a budget, a type of cash flow statement for the *next year,* which will help you make ends meet.

■ The second useful financial instrument is the net worth statement. Unlike a cash flow statement, which shows what went on *during some period,* this shows your financial condition *at some point.* You first list all your **assets**—whatever is yours that you can measure in dollar terms. This includes savings and checking accounts, bonds, stocks, real estate holdings, insurance cash value, and auto value. Next, list your **liabilities**—whatever you owe. This includes charge accounts, loans and mortgages, taxes to be paid, and unpaid bills. The difference between your assets and liabilities is your **net worth** or **equity**. It shows what you could spend at that moment if you took everything you owned and paid off everything you owed. If, however, your liabilities exceed your assets, you have a *negative* net worth. A lender probably will not lend you anything, fearing that you will declare **bankruptcy**, a process through which you can be legally absolved of paying your debts.

Table 16-1 shows a hypothetical (but not necessarily typical) balance sheet for an individual. Because all the combined assets ($220,000) exceed the sum of the liabilities ($80,000), this person is "worth" $140,000.

Many professionals can help you when you're in financial difficulty or simply want help. A relatively new financial specialist provides a **financial plan**, designed to ensure that your current and future income, spending, savings, and personal investment patterns will allow you to achieve some specified retirement goals.

Of course, financial specialists also try to make money, so be careful not to be steered into something that earns more money for the specialist than for you. (For example, insurance agents sometimes pass themselves off as financial planners, then try to sell people—guess what?—insurance.)

Table 16-1 A Hypothetical Balance Sheet or Net Worth Statement

Assets		Liabilities	
Checking Account	$300	House Mortgage	$ 64,000
Savings Account	$ 14,000	Unpaid Bills	$200
Bonds	$ 2,600	Taxes Due	$ 1,600
Life Insurance Cash Value	$ 1,100	Auto Loans	$ 6,800
Autos	$ 13,600	Installment Loans	$ 7,400
House Value	$113,000	**Total Liabilities**	**$ 80,000**
Stocks	$ 16,400		
Pension Value	$ 59,000		
Total Assets	**$220,000**	**Net Worth**	**$140,000**

Consumer Publications and Aids

★3

Hundreds of aids are available for consumers. Probably the best known is *Consumer Reports,* a magazine of Consumer's Union, a non-profit organization that compares various brands of products. *Changing Times* is a magazine that covers a wide range of topics, from product evaluation to home ownership to retirement planning. *Consumer Information,* a U.S. Government listing of more than 500 publications for the consumer, is available from your congressional representative. *Consumer News* is a bi-monthly publication of the U.S. Office of Consumer Affairs. The Better Business Bureau publishes a series of booklets to help consumers, and its local offices monitor business practices of local firms. Local and national media provide information to help consumers make better purchases and investment decisions.

Various grades and standards establish a measure of a product's benefits. Private firms or organizations provide some of them. Some examples are: Underwriters Laboratories (UL); Good Housekeeping (Seal of Approval); and the American Association of Nurserymen, which sets grade standards on nursery stock.

Several federal agencies establish grades and regulate product standards. Some examples are: the FDA (Food and Drug Administration), which regulates food and drug safety; the USDA (U.S. Department of Agriculture), which sets grades for meat, milk, and other foods; and the Consumer Product Safety Commission, which tries to reduce product danger (for example, it forced lawn mower manufacturers to add devices that automatically turn off the engine when you leave the mower).

In 1962, President Kennedy declared that consumers should have four "freedoms": 1) to be informed about products; 2) to have safe products; 3) to have product choices; and 4) to have a voice in consumer issues. Consequently, if there was ever a "Decade of the Consumer," it was from the mid-1960s to the mid-1970s. It might be said that the decade began with Ralph Nader and his book *Unsafe at Any Speed,* in which he attacked the Corvair automobile as extremely dangerous. Many other groups arose to represent consumers, and laws were passed to establish consumer rights. It was the beginning of the end of the philosophy of *caveat emptor,* or "Let the buyer beware," which means that it is the consumer's responsibility to guard against faulty or unsafe products. By the 1970s, this responsibility was shifting to the government. The government's role changed, not so much because legislators mistrusted business owners, but because they believed that consumer decisions are so difficult in our complex world that consumers need help.

However, not everyone is happy with this new role of government as well as the anti-business attitude that often accompanied the consumer movement. Regulations and product redesign always add new costs, and these must be passed on to consumers if the firms are to remain profitable. But some firms, especially those that are weaker or are in highly competitive situations, often find it difficult to absorb these costs and/or to raise their prices. Some, therefore, are forced out of business. Such businesses found a sympathetic ear in President Reagan, and many regulations were abandoned or weakened in the 1980s.

ADVERTISING

Advertising has always been a controversial aspect of capitalism. Its primary purpose is to influence the demand for a good or service. A firm uses advertising to: 1) increase demand; and 2) make it more inelastic (or less elastic). When the demand for something increases, more will be purchased at whatever price is charged. That ensures higher sales and, most likely, higher profits. The second goal of advertisers, to increase inelasticity, ensures that if the seller raises the price, buyers will not flock to the competition. Thus, advertising tries to establish brand loyalty.

★4

Advertising is not productive in the normal sense (that is, it doesn't produce an enjoyable or useful item for people so society *as a whole* is better off). Although it *is* useful for the advertiser (for increasing sales receipts), collectively, people are no better off because of advertising. Its primary effect is to shift the way people spend their money. While one firm is better off, its competitors are equally worse off. It appears to be a zero-sum game, where the winnings equal the losses and, collectively, society as a whole is no better off because of advertising. Thus, when viewed from society's perspective, all the labor and other resources used by advertisers are wasted.

Yet, perhaps society as a whole *does* benefit from advertising. After all, it could help consumers make better decisions by providing information about a product, including technical data and a general description of the advertised item. Therefore, the resources used in advertising *are* productive. Moreover, advertising helps firms achieve economies of scale (when they sell more), so resource efficiency increases. Advertising can also increase competition between business firms, which helps keep prices down (although this is somewhat offset by the higher costs of the advertising itself).

However, advertising can have an *unfavorable* consequence if the consumer receives the *wrong* information. You might not receive as much satisfaction from smoking cigarettes, wearing designer jeans, or driving the flashiest car as advertisers promise. So ads may distort the consumer's cost-benefit analysis. This is one reason for the ban on liquor and cigarette advertising on television and radio (another reason is to minimize negative externalities from those products).

Many people believe that a related unfavorable consequence of advertising is "excessive" materialism, which means our values are "distorted." Rather than deriving their primary satisfaction from family, friends, nature, spiritual well-being, and the like, these critics say too many people seek "the almighty dollar" and what it can buy. This leads to sociological problems, including crime, class conflict, and drug abuse, all related to the stress of the "rat race." But economists would argue that it is impossible to determine if materialism is excessive. Again, as when someone buys a showy item, only those who make such "materialistic" decisions know if they are correct.

A final unfavorable consequence of advertising is a preference for spending now rather than in the future. Bombarded with advertising, some people can't stop spending until all their income is gone. If such spending is widespread, total savings in the nation will be too low to finance heavy spending on capital goods and on the research and development needed for innovation. In turn, efficiency of resource use will grow more slowly, as will living standards. People in the United States, on average, save relatively small shares of their income when compared with other industrialized nations.

INSURANCE

In an economy that is largely capitalistic, people have little protection against property losses caused by accidents, thefts, fires, and storms, or against loss of income when they can no longer work. Such losses are financially painful or even catastrophic. Fortunately, they are infrequent. People who consider such potential losses unacceptable join together in a "pool" and agree to share the losses of all those in the pool. The premium is the amount each pool member puts into the "kitty," used to compensate loss-sufferers. Thus, the purpose of insurance is to protect against *unacceptably large* financial losses.

★5

Many years ago, individuals organized and operated the first pools by themselves. Fraternal organizations such as the Elks, the Eagles, and the Moose are remnants of such times. Today, private enterprises create pools that people join when they buy insurance. However, many such enterprises are mutual companies, which technically are owned by the policyholders, so in a way they are similar to the earlier fraternal organizations.

Recent years have brought a rash of extremely large insurance awards, which insurance firms blame for rapidly rising insurance premiums. Higher insurance costs have led to the growth of self-insurance. A self-insured individual, firm, or government unit (such as a city park and recreation department) sets money aside in a budget each year to cover expected *average* losses over several years. If the expectations of losses prove correct, there will be enough money set aside to cover the losses. The "insured" will find this beneficial whenever premiums of a private insurer exceed the self-insured "premiums" or budget set-aside. About two-thirds of business firms are self-insured, but most of them contract with a medical plan administration firm. Because these firms process the claims, they often are mistaken for insurance firms themselves.

★6

Virtually all losses people insure against fall into four categories: 1) property losses; 2) loss of income; 3) liability losses; and 4) medical expenses.

- Most people own property that would be difficult to replace, such as autos, homes, and jewelry. Comprehensive and collision auto insurance and homeowner's insurance guard against losses of property.
- People lose the opportunity to earn income in three main ways. The first is illness and/or injury. "Sick pay" prevents income loss during short-term illness. Of course, firms can pay you for producing things only when you are well. Thus, "sick pay" is a special type of "insurance settlement" provided by the employer.

Disability insurance gives protection against income loss due to long-term injury or illness. Although it replaces only part of the disabled person's income, no income tax is paid on it. Some employers provide such insurance, and individuals can purchase it for themselves. The Social Security Administration also provides payments to the disabled. Workers' compensation provides protection against income loss resulting from job-related injury or illness. State laws require employers to provide such insurance, which they purchase from private companies.

The second main way people lose the ability to earn income is by losing their jobs. State and federal laws require employers to pay a tax to finance a government-operated unemployment compensation program. If you lose your job through no fault of your own, you can collect a certain share of your working income, usually for up to 26 weeks, but occasionally up to 39 weeks or more.

Death is the last major cause of loss of income. Life insurance provides payment to someone—the **beneficiary**—surviving the deceased. Although people generally buy their own life insurance, many employers provide a modest amount as a fringe benefit. The Social Security Administration also provides a small death benefit.

Life insurance comes in three major forms. The first is term insurance, which you buy to provide protection against income loss for a specified term. Whole life insurance, in addition to providing protection against income loss (for your beneficiary, actually) for the length of the policy, provides a method of saving. Part of the premium goes to an account that earns interest over the life of the policy. The amount in this account, called the cash value, is paid to your beneficiary upon your death. But if you do *not* die during the life of the policy, you get this cash value at the end of the policy. You also can borrow against this cash value. Finally, endowment insurance pays the policyholder a sum of money if the holder is alive after a certain period. The beneficiary receives a death benefit if death occurs before that point.

■ People also insure against the loss they would suffer if they caused someone else to lose something of value, such as property, health, or income. Such people are **liable** for these losses, which means that they must repay the person who suffered the loss. Liability insurance for your auto or home provides protection against such losses. Doctors, lawyers, and other professionals buy liability insurance to insure against malpractice suits.

■ Medical expense is the last major loss that people cover with insurance. Everyone knows how expensive modern health care can be. Such costs are high partly because widespread economies of scale are not as feasible in producing medical services as in, say, making pencils and shoes. It is simply impossible to mass produce most medical services, largely because the services provided are unique for each patient. Medical services now comprise 14 percent of GDP, and that percentage is steadily climbing.

To prevent large personal losses from medical bills, people buy accident and medical insurance. However, one person in seven has no such protection. Most people get protection from their employer as a fringe benefit and pay little directly. Medicare, which is part of the Social Security system, is a federal program of medical insurance for the elderly. While many medical insurance policies have limits on payments, the sharp increase in extremely expensive services has led to the popularity of catastrophic insurance, which pays up to several million dollars in bills. In the past few decades, escalating medical costs have spurred a movement supporting federally mandated insurance for everyone. Called national health insurance (or "socialized medicine"), such coverage is common in most other industrialized countries and universal in socialist nations. Because the government is already involved in the payment of medical bills, the United States is more than halfway to such a system.

CREDIT

One way to deal with a financial problem is to use credit. It increases your power to purchase goods and services beyond the limits set by your income. When you use credit, you use part of other people's incomes (their savings).

The Pros of Credit

★7

Credit provides several benefits. First, it allows consumers to buy items when prices are abnormally low, so the price savings exceed the interest charges. Second, when in the form of chargecard credit, it provides convenience. You don't have to carry much cash when traveling to places where no one accepts your checks. Last, credit lets you enjoy the things purchased with credit earlier in life than your scarce income allows. Such things can be enjoyed for a longer period, so you get more satisfaction from them. A home is the best example. Most people would have to save money until they were at least 40 before they could buy a home with cash. People buy homes with credit when they receive loans in exchange for mortgages. A **mortgage**, a borrower's promise to repay a loan, gives the lender the right to foreclose on the property (take it back) if the borrower doesn't repay the loan. (Incidentally, people often mistakenly equate their loan to their mortgage when they say they are "paying off their mortgage.")

Since lenders charge interest for the use of money, is it wise (rational) to buy with credit? If the satisfaction from the extra time you enjoy an item exceeds the satisfaction you would get from the other goods and services you could have bought with the interest money, then it is. Because you have to pay interest when you buy with credit, you can buy *fewer* goods and services *in total* over your lifetime. But most people accept this in order to have some things for a longer time.

The Cons of Credit

Credit has a downside as well. For individuals the major problem is difficulty in repaying the credit, often because of an unexpected decrease in income or an excess use of credit. Many people blame the latter on the ease of obtaining credit cards from firms that are eager to extend credit, regardless of cardholders' ability to repay such loans.

For society as a whole, excess use of credit causes slower economic growth. As with advertising, easy credit might distort the proper balance of spending and saving. A decline in total savings in the nation could lead to less spending on capital goods and research and development, thereby reducing economic growth.

Types of Consumer Credit

★8

Consumer credit usually falls into three categories: 1) open account credit; 2) automatic overdraft service; and 3) loans.

■ The first is revolving or **open account credit**. A credit card account is the best example. The lender extends a pre-arranged amount of credit. As the loan is paid back, the credit again becomes available—it "revolves." Although interest rates are quite high (occasionally more than 20 percent), many people pay off their bills before the next month's statements, avoiding any finance charges. Firms where you use your credit card pay the credit firms a fee in order to be associated with the credit system. In order to reduce such fees, some firms (especially gasoline stations) give discounts for paying in cash.

■ The second form of credit is **automatic overdraft service**, which allows you to write "bad" checks without having to pay for returned ("bounced") checks. Whenever you overdraw your checking account, your bank covers the amount you overdrew with a loan. Although you must pay interest on this credit, it is less than the fee for a bounced check.

■ A loan is the third form of credit. Actually, all credit amounts to a loan, but here a loan means that the borrower asks to borrow a specified amount of money for a specified period. Such loans fall into two broad categories. The first is a **secured loan**. With such a loan, the lender receives security against financial loss should the borrower default (fail to repay the loan). The lender does this by requiring the borrower to provide **collateral**, which is an asset the lender will acquire upon default. In the cases of houses, cars, and large appliances, the item bought with credit is itself the collateral. Usually the lender can't sell such assets at the full purchase price, and there are administrative costs in default that lenders must cover. Consequently, lenders require a down payment, which means that they lend only part of the amount needed for the purchase.

If the lender knows the borrower is an extremely good credit risk, the borrower might be granted an **unsecured loan**, also called a signature loan. Here the lender requires no collateral, only a signature.

Laws Regarding Consumer Credit

★9

Complaints of excessive finance charges, discrimination in obtaining credit, harassment of borrowers who fell behind in payments, and other problems led to several credit laws: 1) the Consumer Credit Protection Act; 2) the Fair Credit Billing Act; 3) the Equal Credit Opportunity Act; and 4) the Fair Debt Collection Practices Act.

■ The first was the Consumer Credit Protection Act of 1969. More commonly known as the Truth in Lending Act, it requires lenders to clearly state all finance charges as simply as possible. It also limits the losses a credit card holder can suffer when some unauthorized person uses the card.

■ The second credit law, the Fair Credit Billing Act of 1969, focuses on applications for credit cards and billing. Related to it is the Fair Credit Billing Act of 1971, which regulates the use of information by credit bureaus. It gives you legal access to your credit files and the right to prohibit specific people from access to your files. It also requires that credit files be monitored for accuracy.

■ The Equal Credit Opportunity Act of 1974 prohibits discrimination in credit application on the basis of color, religion, national origin, race, sex, age, marital status, and whether the applicant receives welfare.

■ The Fair Debt Collection Practices Act of 1979 prohibits lenders from using certain practices to collect from borrowers who are behind on their payments. Such practices include threats of violence, contact at odd hours, and complaints to a borrower's employer.

SAVINGS AND PERSONAL INVESTING

Although people consume (spend) much of their income soon after they earn it, most people save some money, primarily for a "rainy day" or retirement. Saving is after-tax income that is not spent. However, saving differs from **personal investment**, which is the use of savings plus additional borrowed funds for the purpose of earning additional income. Following is a brief introduction to the most common ways of saving and investing.

Ordinary Savings Plans

★10

The passbook account is the most common way to save. Known simply as a savings account, it pays relatively low interest, but it is perfectly safe. If an insured bank fails (goes broke), the Federal Deposit Insurance Corporation (F.D.I.C.), a federal agency, will cover up to $100,000 of each depositor's savings. Similar insured accounts are available at savings and loans and credit unions.

Another common savings form is a certificate of deposit (CD), usually set up for a larger amount for a specified period (six months, two years, and so on). Interest rates are higher than on passbook accounts and increase both with the amount deposited and the period length. CDs also have government protection.

A trust is a savings account at a trust company (often affiliated with a bank) for a minor or one who is not capable of handling funds. Such accounts often are provided by parents or insurance benefits. The trust company invests these funds and dispenses them to the individual according to the wishes of the one who set up the trust.

As you read earlier in this chapter, some people also save when they buy life insurance policies (other than term insurance).

Money market funds, which gained popularity in the 1970s, are set up by (non-bank) firms that collect savings from many people and invest the money in various places (often in large CDs). Although savers have no protection (insurance) for their money because the firms are not banks, the funds often earn higher interest rates. Most banks now have "money market accounts," but they are not true money market plans because they have less risk and are insured.

Retirement Savings Plans

Although they started in the 1960s, Keogh accounts and individual retirement accounts (IRAs) came into their own in the late 1970s. They are strictly for retirement purposes. Keoghs are for self-employed (non-incorporated) people and IRAs for employees. Their great advantage is that the interest earned is not taxable until the money is drawn out after age 59½. Such income is called tax-deferred income. Also, if an employee does not have a pension plan at work, or if the employee has a pension plan but is at a lower-income level ($25,000 for individuals and $40,000 for couples), the IRA contribution itself is "tax deductible." This means the person defers paying income tax on that amount until after retirement (thus, it is not really deductible). There are two major advantages to this. First, you earn interest income on the deferred taxes until you draw the money out. Second, you may be in a lower tax bracket when you retire, so you end up paying less taxes on the amount of income you contributed than if you had paid taxes in the year you earned the money. However, IRA deposits are limited to $2,000 per year for a single person, $2,500 for a married couple when only one person works, and $4,000 if both spouses work.

Another relatively new savings instrument for retirement that allows contributions and interest earned to be tax-deferred is a 401(k) plan, available only through some private enterprise employers. In 1993, you could deposit up to $8,994 in a 401(k) plan, but that figure increases each year. A similar plan, a 403(b) plan, often is available for government employees.

Most larger employers offer their employees a pension, essentially income received after retirement. It shows up neither in gross pay nor take-home pay. Consequently, you pay tax on the pension benefits only when you receive them after retiring. Most pension funds have two parts. One part is financed by the employer, the other by the employee (which should be considered savings rather than income). Sometimes the employer also pays the employee's part as a fringe benefit. To qualify, or be "vested" for a pension, a person generally must be an employee for five years. Usually the benefits become better the longer you work at one job, so frequent job-switching can prove costly when you retire. In 1974, The Pension Benefit Guarantee Corporation was established. It is a federal agency that insures the pensions of over 40 million workers in 85,000 private firms.

Stocks and Bonds

Ownership of a stock by a stockholder means ownership of a share of a corporation. People buy stocks to earn income in two ways: 1) from capital gains, which means they sell stock for more than they paid for it; and 2) from dividends, which is how corporations distribute profits. You can buy stock in many firms, generally through a stockbroker. (See Appendix B for more on the stock market.)

A bond is a promissory note the seller of the bond gives to the buyer. The bond seller promises to pay back the amount stated in the note when it matures (reaches the end of the loan period). Thus, a bond seller borrows money and a bond buyer lends it. The bond states the amount of interest to be paid as well as the maturity date. There are three primary issuers (sellers) of bonds: 1) the federal government, which sells savings bonds, Treasury bills (T-bills), Treasury notes, and Treasury bonds; 2) state and local governments, which issue municipal bonds; and 3) corporations, which sell corporate bonds.

Gentlemen prefer bonds. – Andrew Mellon

Other Methods of Saving and Investing

One of the most common forms of personal investing is in real estate, especially in homes. Paying off a home loan is actually a form of saving for retirement. Because you have paid for your house, you can enjoy it during retirement, while using your retirement income for something else. A home can be an investment if its value escalates faster than prices in general and if the owner sells it and spends those capital gains. Many people also buy income property, which is bought strictly to earn income, whether from the excess of rents over expenses or from capital gains. Such property includes apartments and other dwellings, commercial property (such as stores, factories, and offices), and undeveloped land.

Some people try to strike it rich by investing in commodities, which generally are raw (unprocessed) agricultural goods. Because commodities have wide price swings, caused by changes in weather and yields, people can make a lot of money (or *lose* a lot) in buying and selling them. Commodities are traded in the futures market, so called because a buyer agrees to pay a certain price at a specified future date for a given amount of the commodity. This agreement is called a futures contract. Such buyers, called speculators, bet that the actual market price on that future date will be higher than the price they agreed to pay. The difference in these prices is the speculators' profit (or loss) when they sell the contract to a user of that commodity.

Commodities traded include corn, oats, wheat, pork bellies (for bacon), flaxseed, hogs, cotton, sugar, coffee, cocoa, and orange juice. The primary locations of such trading are the Chicago Board of Trade and the Chicago Mercantile Exchange, where the trading is so hectic and noisy that traders communicate with a complex system of hand signals. Just gaining a "seat" on these exchanges, which you need to make such trades, now costs more than $500,000.

People save or invest in dozens of other ways. They trade in foreign exchange (foreign currency). They also buy gold, silver, platinum, and other precious metals, and they invest in stamps, art, and antiques. Of course, some of these savings methods are safer than others.

Chapter 16 SUMMARY

The overall goal of consumers is to maximize satisfaction from their scarce money. This is accomplished when the last dollar a person spends on any good or service gives the same benefit as the last dollar spent on every other good and service. Under these conditions the person has achieved consumer equilibrium. The benefit from additional units of any good or service consumed is always less than from earlier units. Besides having to decide what to buy, each person must also decide: 1) how much to spend in the present and how much in the future; and 2) how much money to give to others.

Cash flow statements, budgets, net worth statements, and financial plans are designed to ensure that people will maximize their economic welfare from their scarce wealth and income. Many publications are available to help consumers make better choices.

Although advertising is designed to aid the seller, it can serve the consumer by providing information for good decision making. However, advertising could also provide wrong information and might lead to a lower economic growth rate.

Insurance spreads financial risks among many people so that individuals are not financially ruined. People insure themselves against loss of property value, loss of income, loss if liable for another's loss, and loss from medical bills.

Credit allows people to buy more things in the present than they could with their own purchasing power. However, buying on credit means that a person can buy fewer things in total over a lifetime because of the interest paid. Credit usually takes three forms: open account credit, automatic overdraft service, and secured loans. In the last two decades, the federal government passed several laws to protect the consumer in credit matters.

Besides saving money for the future, many people use their savings as well as borrowed money to earn more money in personal investments. These include stocks, bonds, real estate, commodities, and precious metals. Because these investments are somewhat risky, people should also have some assets in regular saving accounts, pensions, and special retirement plans.

Chapter 16 RESPONSES TO THE LEARNING OBJECTIVES

1. A rational consumer will purchase additional amounts of an item until the marginal utility it provides per dollar equals the marginal utility per dollar of all other items purchased.

2. Three useful financial statements or instruments include:
   a) the cash flow statement, which records all sources of income and disbursements of money
   b) the net worth statement, which lists all assets and liabilities
   c) a financial plan, which is designed to ensure that retirement goals will be met

3. Magazines and other sources of consumer information include: *Consumer Reports, Changing Times, Consumer Information, Consumer News,* newspaper columns, trade guides, government standards, testing laboratory results, and the Better Business Bureau.

4. Two purposes of advertising are to change product demand and to provide product information. Among negative consequences of advertising are misleading or incorrect consumer information, excessive reliance on materialistic goals, and a lower economic growth rate.

5. The purpose of insurance is to protect against an unacceptably large financial loss. Risk-avoiders pay premiums that are used to pay the few who actually suffer financial losses.

6. Insurance is purchased primarily to protect against property loss, the loss of income, liability losses, and medical expenses.

7. The benefits of credit include:
   a) the ability to save money when buying at times of low prices
   b) the convenience of not carrying cash or checks
   c) the ability to make earlier purchases (longer possession) of expensive items

   The disadvantages of credit include:
   a) individual financial difficulties from excessive use of credit
   b) a lower economic growth rate

8. Revolving credit is used for smaller purchases, often with credit cards. Automatic overdraft services allow people to overdraw their checking account balances. Secured and non-secured loans are taken out for specific periods, generally for larger amounts.

9. The Consumer Credit Protection (Truth in Lending) Act requires the lender to provide detailed loan cost information. The Fair Credit Billing Act regulates credit card applications and billing practices. The Equal Credit Opportunity Act prevents discrimination in providing credit. The Fair Debt Collection Practices Act prohibits certain debt collection practices.

10. Low-risk savings forms include: passbook accounts, CDs, trusts, life insurance, pensions, and many Keogh, IRA, 401(k), and money market accounts. Somewhat more risky savings/investment forms include: stocks, bonds, real estate, commodity trading, and speculation in an assortment of items such as foreign currencies and art.

Chapter 16 LEARNING ACTIVITIES AND DISCUSSION QUESTIONS

1. Suppose you eat a 50¢ bag of potato chips and do not regret it. How many bags of potato chips would you buy if: 1) your net income is $10,000 per year? 2) your net income is $10 million per year? 3) you have an unlimited income? Also, suppose you do *not* experience diminishing marginal utility with potato chips.
2. Find five examples of people who, you suspect, bought things for the sake of conspicuous consumption. Ask them why they bought the items. Did they lie?
3. Locate a column in your newspaper that offers consumer information for making good consumer decisions.
4. Ask five people who work full time if they have both auto and disability insurance. If they don't have both, ask them why. Do you think they are rational?
5. Under what conditions would it make sense to borrow money at 20 percent interest in order to get into the stock market?

APPENDIX A CONSUMER EQUILIBRIUM

To maximize their economic welfare, consumers need to be aware of the satisfaction received from the last dollar spent on each specific item bought. That amount of satisfaction for a specific item is found by dividing the marginal utility by the price. A consumer is considered to be in equilibrium when this amount is identical for every item bought. Then there is no reason for the consumer to change spending patterns, for the maximum amount of economic welfare has been achieved. Such an equilibrium condition for a consumer who buys n number of items is shown by:

$$MU_1/P_1 = MU_2/P_2 = \ldots\ldots\ldots = MU_n/P_n$$

Thus, for any two goods x and y, the following also holds:

$$MU_x/P_x = MU_y/P_y$$

This condition can be used to show why consumers follow the law of demand. If the price of x rises, then:

MU_x/P_x falls and, consequently, $MU_x/P_x < MU_y/P_y$

The consumer now gets less satisfaction from the last dollar spent on x than from the last dollar spent on y. Now the consumer's welfare is not maximized. One way to correct this is to reduce the quantity of x consumed, which raises MU_x (because of the law of diminishing marginal utility). In turn, this raises:

MU_x/P_x and the consumer buys less of x until $MU_x/P_x = MU_y/P_y$

Therefore, the consumer again is at equilibrium—though facing a higher price at a lower consumption level. This is exactly what you expect when looking at a demand curve.

A second response to an increase in the price of x is an increase in the purchase of a substitute good. If y is a substitute for x, then as more of y is consumed, MU_y declines. In turn, there is a decrease in:

MU_y/P_y and the consumer buys more of y until $MU_x/P_x = MU_y/P_y$

Once again the consumer is at equilibrium, and this consumer response explains shifts in demand caused by price changes of substitutes.

APPENDIX B THE STOCK MARKET

Personal investment in corporate stocks has always been a popular, though risky, form of investment. Stocks are purchased for two primary reasons: 1) to earn dividends; and 2) to reap capital gains, obtained when the stock rises in value.

"The stock market" is actually divided into two sectors. In the first, known as the primary market, corporations issue new stock in order to raise funds for operations and expansion. However, many people will buy stocks only if they can sell them any time they wish. They do so in the secondary market, which is what most people consider "the stock market." In this market, people buy and sell stocks through stockbrokers, who function as middlemen in connecting their clients with other people who want to buy or sell stocks. These are not newly issued stocks, but were bought previously from corporations. Thus, the corporations do not get to use the money that new buyers use to buy the stocks.

The oldest and largest secondary market is the New York Stock Exchange (NYSE), commonly called the Big Board, located on Wall Street in New York City. Around 2,000 stocks of America's major corporations are traded there. Other secondary markets are the American Stock Exchange (AMEX), 14 regional markets, the Over the Counter (OTC) market, and many foreign markets (such as the Japanese Nikkei and the London Exchange).

Most newspapers' financial sections publish the following information on individual stocks: 1) the highest price the stock traded at in the past 52 weeks; 2) the company name; 3) the dividend per share; 4) the percent yield, calculated by dividing the dividend per share by the current stock price; 5) the price-to-earnings (P/E) ratio, found by dividing the stock's price by the (per share) corporate earnings in the previous four quarters; 6) the trading volume for the day, reported in amounts of hundreds of shares; 7) the high and low prices the stock traded at on the previous day; 8) the closing price on the previous day; and 9) the net change in price, or the difference in the closing price for the day and the closing price for the previous day.

People interested in the stock market watch several indicators that measure the price movements of many stocks simultaneously. Dow Jones and Company publishes the best-known indicators, including the Dow Jones Industrial Average (DJIA), the most closely watched one.

The DJIA is an outgrowth of a method used by Charles Henry Dow in 1884 to reflect the level of all stock prices. Dow used the arithmetic average of 11 stocks as a representative of all stocks. Today the DJIA use the stocks of 30 corporations, each a major figure in its industry. Calculation of the DJIA no longer uses a simple average of these 30 representative stocks, as it did in 1884. That is, it doesn't just add the prices of all 30 stocks and divide by 30 (the "divisor"). Partly due to stock splits over the years, the "divisor" was reduced from 30 to less than one today. A stock split means a corporation offers two or more new (and lower-priced) shares of stock for one share of original stock. This often occurs when a stock's price rises too high for it to be an attractive purchase. Thus, the DJIA average is much higher than the price of any particular stock. For example, if the "divisor" was 0.9 and the 30 stocks sold for an average of $96, the DJIA would be 3200, or ($96 x 30) ÷ 0.9.

The Securities and Exchange Commission (SEC) is a federal agency that regulates the stock market. One of its regulations prohibits "inside trading," where someone trades stocks because of information received from an "insider." If someone (such as an accountant or an attorney) has advance knowledge of mergers, stock splits, and so on, that knowledge cannot be passed on to stockbrokers or those wishing to purchase stocks. There were several major indictments for inside trading in the late 1980s.

52 Weeks				Yld	P-E	Sales				Net
High	Low	Stock	Div.	%	Ratio	100s	High	low	Close	Chg.
		— A–A–A —								
17¾	5¾	AAR	.44	2.6	25	50	17¼	16¾	16¾	– ¼
37¾	27½	ACF	1.40	4.1	15	205	34¾	34	34½	+ ½
20	12¼	AMF	.50	3.1	..	380	16⅜	16	16⅛	– ⅜
38¼	13¼	AMR Cp		..	..	2872	34¾	33⅜	33⅝	–1
24½	4	AMR wt		..	..	228	20½	19½	19½	–1⅛
18⅜	13¼	AMR	pf2.18	12.	..	25	18⅛	18	18	.....
39⅜	24⅞	AMR	pf2.13	6.2	..	54	35⅜	34½	34½	–1⅜
10⅝	2½	APL		..	..	58	10¼	10	10	– ⅛
55	26	ARA	2.05	4.1	14	326	49¾	49½	49¾	+ ¼
79⅞	29	ASA	3a	4.6	..	458	67¾	65⅝	65⅞	– ⅜
50	14½	AVX	.32	.8	63	5	39½	39¼	39¼	– ½
48¾	28½	AbtLab	1	2.1	18	1310	47¾	46¼	47¼	+ ¾
30⅛	25¾	AccoW n	.50	1.9	22	93	27⅜	26⅞	26⅞	– ⅜
27½	15⅝	AcmeC	.40	1.6	..	13	24⅝	24¼	24⅜	– ¼
14⅜	5¾	AcmeE	.32b	2.5	42	7	12⅞	12¾	12⅞	.....
19⅞	5½	AdmDg	.04	.2	15	17	17⅞	17⅝	17⅞	.....
17⅞	12½	AdaEx	1.73e	10.	..	35	17⅛	16⅞	17	....
15¼	6⅝	AdmMI	.24	1.6	14	51	15	14½	14¾	– ⅛
28	12⅝	Advest s	.16	.7	13	86	24½	24	24⅜	– ¼
66⅝	13	AMD s		..	63	1043	59¼	57	57¾	–1¼
44⅜	32⅞	AetnLf	2.64	6.9	7	1079	38⅝	38	38⅛	– ¾
65	52⅜	AetL	pf4.94e	8.4	..	7	58¾	58¾	58¾	+ ¾
40½	8¼	Ahmns	.60	1.8	..	1235	33	31⅞	33	+ ⅜
7	2⅜	Aileen		..	..	66	6	5¾	6	+ ¼
50⅞	23⅝	AirPrd	1	2.2	15	215	47¼	46⅛	46⅜	– ⅝
27¼	10	AirbFrt	.60	2.6	24	35	23¼	22⅞	23	+ ⅛
3⅜	2	AlMoa n		..	6	129	2⅞	2¾	2¾	.....
33½	24¾	AlaP	pfA3.92	13.	..	10	29¾	29⅜	29¾	+ ⅜
7⅝	5¾	AlaP	dpf.87	12.	..	26	7⅛	7	7⅛	– ⅛
74½	56	AlaP	pf 9	13.	..	z650	69	68	68	–1
99	74	AlaP	pf 11	11.	..	z70	98½	98½	98½	+1
81½	58	AlaP	pf 9.44	13.	..	z350	71½	71	71	–1¾
70	51	AlaP	pf 8.28	13.	..	z100	64½	64½	64½	+1¼
20¼	13	Alagsco	1.76	9.0	7	6	19¾	19⅝	19⅝	.....
18⅝	4⅞	AlskAir	.12	.7	14	452	18⅛	17½	17½	.....
39⅝	23¾	Albany	1.40	3.5	20	116	39⅝	39⅝	39⅝	.....
24⅛	10¾	Alberto	.54	3.2	14	6	16¾	16¾	16¾	– ¼
29	16	Albtsn s	.60	2.2	14	70	27⅞	26¾	26¾	–1⅛
35¼	17⅞	Alcan	.90	2.8	..	785	32½	31⅞	32	– ½
36⅛	18	AlcoStd	1.12	3.2	13	88	35⅜	34⅞	34⅞	– ⅜
27⅝	18⅝	AlexAlx	1	3.9	259	8278	26¾	24¼	25⅞	+1¾
17	7½	Alexdr		..	15	25	16⅞	16⅝	16¾	+ ⅛
95	35⅝	AllgCp	1.08	1.3	18	299	84⅞	81¾	81¾	–2½
27¼	20	AlgCp	pf2.86	11.	..	33	26⅞	26⅞	26⅞	....
36¼	16⅜	AlgInt	1.40	4.7	..	1646	30⅝	29⅞	29⅞	– ⅞
22⅛	14	AlgIn	pf2.19	11.	..	11	19¾	19⅝	19¾	.....
98	68½	AlgI	pfC11.25	12.	..	3	91¾	91½	91½	– ¼
25⅜	18½	AllgPw	2.40	10.	7	213	23½	23¼	23½	+ ⅛
20	12⅜	AllenG	.40b	2.1	..	221	18⅞	18⅝	18¾	.....
53	29¼	AlldCp	2.40	4.8	7	1409	50⅜	49⅞	50⅜	– ⅛
65½	48⅛	AldCp	pf6.74	11.	..	9	60¾	60½	60¾	+ ⅜
114¾	84⅝	AldCp	pf 12	11.	..	3	110¾	110¾	110¾	– ½
110¼	97¾	AldCp	pf4.45e	4.3	..	50	102⅞	102⅞	102⅞	+ ⅜
56⅛	22⅝	AlldStr	1.80	3.5	13	95	52¾	51⅝	51⅞	–1
31½	14⅝	AlldTel	1	4.3	9	153	23½	23	23⅜	+ ⅛
18⅜	6¼	AllisCh		..	..	291	16⅜	16	16⅜	– ⅛
37¼	20	AlisCh pf		..	..	22	34	33¾	34	.....
24⅛	12⅜	AlphPr		..	6	38	24	24	24	+ ¼
41⅛	22¾	Alcoa	1.20	3.3	.	2179	37⅛	36⅝	36⅝	– ⅝
32¾	17½	Amax	.20	.8	..	756	26⅝	25¾	26⅛	– ⅜
45	33	Amax	pf 3	7.1	..	3	42	41¼	42	+ ¾
29¼	14⅛	Amrce	.40	1.5	..	2	27¼	27¼	27¼	– ⅛
33½	15⅞	AmHes	1.10	3.8	13	993	29⅛	28⅝	28¾	– ½
3¾	1¼	AmAgr		..	..	356	2⅞	2¾	2⅞	+ ⅛
20⅝	8	ABakr		..	..	22	16⅞	16¾	16¾	– ⅛
55⅜	37⅛	ABrand	3.50	6.9	8	233	51	50⅝	50⅝	.....
69¾	35⅝	ABdcst	1.60	2.7	12	217	60¾	59¾	60⅜	– ¼
24⅝	19⅞	ACan	pf2.80	12.	..	1	23½	23½	23½	.....
19½	7½	ACntC n		..	29	82	u19⅞	19⅜	19⅞	+ ½
50¼	27	ACyan	1.75	3.7	19	876	47⅝	46½	47½	+ ⅝
32⅝	28½	ADT s	.92	3.2	13	73	29	28⅝	28⅞	+ ⅛
20	15⅞	AEIPw	2.26	12.	10	4154	18⅝	18¼	18½	+ ⅛
74⅜	26⅜	AExp s	1.92	2.9	14	3920	68	65⅞	66½	– ¾
49⅝	17⅝	AExp wi		..	..	78	46	44⅝	45	–1
24⅛	9⅜	AFamil	.60	2.8	13	55	21¼	21⅛	21¼	.....
24⅛	10½	AGnCp s	.80	3.5	9	188	23	22⅝	22⅞	– ⅛
58¾	49⅜	AGnl	pfA3.67e	6.8	..	103	53⅞	53⅝	53⅝	– ¼
67	50⅝	AGnl	pfB3.43e	5.5	..	26	63	62¾	62¾	+ ⅜
52¾	31	AGn	ipf3.25	6.6	..	3	49½	49½	49½	.....
20⅞	15⅝	AGIBd	2.16	12.	..	56	18⅜	17⅞	18⅛	+ ⅜
35½	21¼	AGnCv	5.07e	16.	..	10	32⅛	31¼	31¼	– ½
23⅞	17¼	AHerit	.96	4.4	10	4	22⅛	22	22	– ¼
16⅛	8¾	AHoist		..	..	68	15¼	14½	14⅞	– ¼
52¼	35⅝	AHome	2.40	5.3	12	2592	45⅝	44⅞	45⅛	– ½
49	28	AHosp s	1	2.2	15	1277	45⅜	44⅞	45	.....
37¼	14½	AMI s	.48	1.5	17	618	33½	32⅝	32⅞	– ⅝
11¼	3	AmMot		..	..	1008	9⅜	9⅛	9¼	.....
40	25¼	ANatRs	3.16	8.6	6	143	38⅛	36¼	36¾	–1⅝
26⅜	3½	ASLFI s		..	..	387	20¼	19¼	20	– ¼
13¾	8⅜	AShip	.80	6.4	14	35	12½	12¼	12½	+ ¼
38⅛	17	AmStd	1.60	5.0	21	223	32⅛	31¾	31¾	– ⅜
24¼	11¼	ASteril	.40	2.0	13	309	19⅝	18⅞	19⅝	+ ¼
105½	42¾	AmStr	1.44	1.4	12	35	100¾	98⅝	99¾	– ⅞
35½	14¼	AmStr wi		..	..	1	34	34	34	–1
52⅝	39⅛	AStr	pf 5.51	11.	..	3	50⅞	50⅞	50⅞	– ⅛
70¼	50	ATT	5.40a	8.6	8	7211	63⅛	62¾	62¾	– ¼
73¼	52½	ATT	pf 4	6.1	..	71	66	65¾	65¾	– ⅛
38½	30¼	ATT	pf 3.64	9.8	..	115	37¼	36¾	37	+ ¼
39¾	31⅝	ATT	pf 3.74	9.8	..	627	38	37¾	38	+ ⅜
29¼	14	AWatr	1.40	5.2	6	45	27⅛	26⅞	27⅛	+ ¼
11¾	8⅝	AWat	pf1.25	11.	..	z50	11	11	11	+ ¼
26⅝	19⅞	AHotl n	.59e	2.5	..	204	23⅜	23	23¼	– ⅛
36¼	19⅜	Ameron	1.60	4.8	9	15	33¾	33¼	33½	– ½
65¼	21½	AmesD	.40	.6	20	152	62⅛	61½	61⅝	+ ¾
50	25⅛	Ametk	1.20	2.7	17	88	44¼	44	44¼	.....
24¾	12½	Ametk wi		..	..	5	22½	22½	22½	.....
30¼	17⅛	Amfac	1.44	5.5	14	115	27	26⅜	26⅜	– ⅜
26⅝	15¾	Amfes	n2.12t	11.	7	413	19½	18½	19⅛	– ½
106¼	45½	AMPIn	1.60	1.7	29	527	97¾	95⅞	96	–2¼
15¾	11⅞	Ampco	.30	2.1	..	3	14⅝	14⅝	14⅝	+ ⅛
19¾	7⅜	Amrep		..	15	355	18⅞	18½	18⅞	+ ⅜
33¼	17¼	AmSth	1.76	5.8	7	47	30¾	30⅛	30¼	– ½
33⅝	18¾	Amstar	1.90	6.2	22	35	31⅛	30⅝	30⅝	– ½
6½	4⅞	Amst	pf .68	12.	..	11	5¾	5¾	5¾	.....
30⅜	18⅝	Amsted	.80	2.9	52	18	27⅞	27½	27⅝	+ ⅛
23¼	9⅜	Anacmp	.12	.8	20	782	15⅜	15⅛	15⅛	– ⅛
39	11¾	Analog s		..	56	79	38¼	37	37	–1¼
34½	13½	Anchor	1.36	4.3	21	69	31¾	31½	31¾	.....
33⅜	19⅞	AnClay	1.32	4.4	20	47	30⅜	30	30	– ½
18	9½	AndrGr	.18b	1.2	12	12	15	14⅞	15	– ⅛
35	12¾	Angelc s	.48	1.5	21	36	32½	32¼	32⅜	– ⅝
77	45	Anheus	1.48	2.3	11	1033	64⅛	62⅞	63¼	– ⅞
57¾	48	Anheu	pf3.60	7.2	..	17	50	49¾	49⅞	– ⅛
29	9⅜	Anixtr	.24	1.0	28	152	23¾	23½	23⅝	.....
18⅜	9⅞	Anta	.56	3.2	12	24	17½	17¼	17⅜	– ⅜
18½	6⅛	Anthny	.44b	3.2	14	70	14½	13¼	13⅝	–1
16⅛	7¾	Apache	.28	1.9	13	553	14¾	14¼	14½	– ⅛
23⅜	18	ApchP	un2e	9.7	..	222	21	20⅝	20⅝	– ¼
68	51	ApPw	pf8.12	13.	..	z50	62½	62¼	62¼	– ¾
35½	26	ApPw	pf4.18	13.	..	12	31⅜	31¼	31¼	+ ¼
36½	12½	ApplMg	1.14t	3.8	21	97	31⅛	29½	29⅝	–1⅜
26½	12½	ArchDn	.14b	.6	18	1345	25⅛	25	25⅛	+ ⅛
26⅛	19⅛	ArizPS	2.52	10.	8	1350	25⅛	24⅞	25⅛	+ ⅛
31⅞	24⅛	AriP	pf 3.58	12.	..	13	30⅛	30	30⅛	+ ⅜
103½	87½	AriPpf	10.70	11.	..	z980	101⅞	100⅝	101⅞	+1¼

A listing of selected stocks on the New York Stock Exchange, along with data that appear in many newspapers.

EPILOGUE

It is time to survey what you learned about the economy—and what you need to consider in your future.

WHAT YOU LEARNED

Economics concerns our efforts to achieve more of the unlimited amounts of goods and services we want than our scarce resources will provide. We do this—that is, we achieve economic growth and raise our living standards—by obtaining more resources or by using resources more efficiently. The primary ways to increase the efficiency of resource use include specializing, innovating, and eliminating resource waste.

Societies can choose from several economic systems available to them to accomplish this. Two such systems, capitalism and socialism , dominated the 20th century. Capitalism is founded upon the private ownership of resources as well as a system of free markets. In these markets individuals seek to maximize their self-interest. Competition assures that almost everyone ultimately gains through these self-seeking actions of individuals.

Prices in these markets largely determine what actions these individuals will take. The supply of and the demand for the items in these markets determine such prices. No government intervention is required. Business firms consider the prices in both resource and product markets to decide how to maximize their economic welfare (profit). Individuals need to follow similar principles in selling resources and buying consumer goods and services if they are to maximize their economic welfare.

The world is composed of individual buyers and sellers seeking to exchange their specialized goods, services, or resources. People occasionally establish arbitrary restrictions and barriers that interfere with that trade and the quest to raise economic welfare.

An unrestrained capitalist economy doesn't automatically lead to the maximum level of economic welfare. Externalities, the lack of social goods, imperfect competition, and an unequal income distribution are problems of capitalism addressed by governments, for which taxes must be raised.

Similarly, the economic goals of society—economic growth, full employment, and price stability—often require government intervention before they are achieved. Fiscal policies of tax and government spending changes and monetary policies of changes in credit and interest rates are designed to accomplish these goals. Not everyone believes that such policies are necessary.

OTHER CONSIDERATIONS

References were made in the text to issues and concepts just out of the mainstream of economic principles. They include: 1) the limits imposed by scarcity; and 2) the need to place materialistic goals in proper perspective to non-materialistic goals.

Realizing the Limits Imposed by Scarcity

Although scarcity is a fact of life, people often create problems for themselves by acting as if there is no scarcity. If you are fully aware of your personal scarcity, you will be extremely cautious when spending time, spending money, and using credit. You will consider each year of the future as important as the present year. You will not saddle yourself with massive debt and will not face destitution in your retirement years.

You will not squander time and merely live for the moment—for you realize that the future holds vastly more moments than the present. Thus, you show concern for those *future* moments by being diligent today.

In addition, people who realize that they're materially comfortable are often much happier than those who seek ever more goods and services. People with such awareness count their blessings.

Members of societies get into similar *collective* problems when they demand that governments solve an impossibly large number of economic problems. It's not that governments couldn't or shouldn't solve them. But governments face a scarcity of tax revenues from citizens. Nevertheless, many people refuse to accept the limits of government spending imposed by the limits of funds available to any government. The result is a budget deficit and problems such as the United States has faced in the last 20 years.

To avoid such problems, people must be fully aware of the tradeoffs forced upon them by resource scarcity. Having a luxurious home might mean doing without vacations, college, or adequate food or clothing. Beyond economics, "excessive" eating and drinking means trading away health and possibly some years of life. Economists say "excessive" with quotation marks, for they are not judgmental about individual lifestyles. Yet, they realize that people can't have it all—perfect health *and* all the food and drink imaginable. So, whatever balance between these goals that a person chooses *is* the right balance for that person and not excessive—so long as the person is rational (one who weighs all the costs and benefits of all the options and decides accordingly). Thus, being rational implies constant awareness of scarcity and the consequential tradeoffs.

Placing Materialistic Goals in Perspective

It's often observed that people in poorer countries don't seem less happy than those in the rich West. If it's true that material richness does not make people happier, why strive for more?

A high income is not enough for happiness. We must all fulfill some non-materialistic goals. It's as if some "law-of-the-minimum" is at work—dooming us to the level of happiness provided by the goal we least achieve. Suppose we need to respect the rights of others in order to be a happy people. If we all ignore that goal and achieve financial (materialistic) success by cheating, lying, and stealing, we will be a (materialistically) rich but miserable lot.

There are many such non-materialistic goals to consider besides the respect for others. A major one is the maintenance of a clean, healthy, viable earth that will be habitable for all humans, animals, and plants for thousands of years—or forever. The Industrial Revolution brought about vast increases in materialistic wealth. Yet, we were often blind to the havoc it caused. Pollution, over-crowded cities, stress, the loss of thousands of plant and animal species, and dozens of related problems must lead a thinking people to reconsider their society. Awareness of our plight grew substantially in the 1960s, 1970s, and 1980s. Unfortunately, vast and ominous dangers still face the dwellers of the 21st century. Perhaps there is still time to stave off these problems. Or perhaps Chief Seattle, speaking in the 1800s, was right when he said:

> How can one buy or sell the air, the warmth of the land? That is difficult for us (Indians) to imagine. We do not own the sweet air or the sparkle of the water. How, then, can you buy them from us?
>
> We are part of the Earth and the Earth is part of us. The fragrant flowers are our sisters. The reindeer, the horse, the great eagle are our brothers. The rocky heights, the foamy crests of waves in the river, the sap of meadow flowers, the body heat of the pony—and of human beings—all along to the same family.
>
> So when the Great Chief in Washington sends word that he wants to buy our land, he asks a great deal of us. He treats his Mother the Earth and his Brother the Sky like merchandise. His hunger will eat the Earth bare and leave only a desert.
>
> I have seen a thousand buffalo left behind by the White Man—shot from a passing train. I am a savage and I cannot understand why the puffing iron horse should be more important than the buffalo, which we kill only in order to stay alive. What are human beings without animals? Whatever happens to the animals will happen soon also to human beings. Continue to soil your bed and one night you will suffocate in your own waste.
>
> Whatever befalls the Earth befalls also the Children of the Earth.

GLOSSARY

Words in **bold print** are listed as terms in the beginning of each chapter. They are printed as bold the first time they appear in a chapter. Words in *italics* also are part of the jargon of economists and people in business. Many of them are part of your everyday life, whether the news, the job, or as a consumer. The numbers following both sets of words indicate the page it first appears.

ability-to-pay principle - the taxing philosophy stating that the more a person is able to pay taxes, as evidenced by income or wealth, the more taxes that person should pay 258

absolute advantage - occurs when a particular resource of a class of resources is the most efficient or productive at a task than any other resource of that class 34

absolute price - the amount of money that is paid for one unit of an item 69

accounting loss - the excess of a firm's explicit costs over its total revenue 146

accounting profit - the excess of a firm's total revenue over its explicit costs 146

actual GDP - the value of final goods and services actually produced, as opposed to the amount that could potentially be produced 273

aggregate demand - refers to total spending (C+I+G) 279

allocative efficiency - refers to the situation where firms produce the goods and services most preferred by consumers, and in a broader sense, how much economic welfare results from using all our resources 31

allotment program - also called a quota program, in which farmers need a permit to grow and market a product 190

amended capitalism - a system in which the market's answers to economic questions are changed somewhat by government actions 92

antitrust legislation - laws restricting acts of firms that might lead to imperfect competition 232

apprenticeship - the period of training some laborers go through to learn a skilled trade 178

arbitration - a process of settling differences between labor and management, where the terms of a third party must be accepted 182

asset - anything of value that can be expressed in money terms 386

authoritarian capitalism - an economic system where most resources are privately owned and where heavy use is made of the command economic system 91

authoritarian socialism - an economic system where most resources are publicly owned and where government authorities answer most economic questions 93

automatic fiscal policy - changes in total spending that occur during recession or inflation to offset these problems, where such changes do not require specific actions by the government 365

automatic overdraft service - a form of credit received when a financial institution covers an overdrawn demand deposit account with a loan 392

automatic stabilizers - instruments that are used to carry out automatic fiscal policy, including transfer payments, farm subsidies, and the progressive income tax 365

automation - the automatic control of one machine by another machine 38

average cost - the amount of expenses in producing one unit of a good or service, on average 142

average fixed cost - the amount of fixed expenses in producing one unit of a good or service, on average 142

average variable cost - the amount of variable expenses in producing one unit of a good or service, on average 142

balance of payments - the difference between the combined credits and debits of a nation in its international transactions 221

balance of trade - the difference between a nation's exports and imports of goods and services 220 *balance on current account* - the difference between 1) the combined value of a nation's exports and money which its government or individuals receive from abroad and 2) the combined value of its imports and money gifts its government or individuals send abroad 220

balance sheet - a financial statement listing a firm's assets, liabilities, and equity 141

balanced budget - occurs when total outlays of a government equal total receipts 250

ban - a prohibition of the import of a specific product 211

bankruptcy - occurs when an individual or a business is legally absolved of its debts 386

barrier to entry - anything which prevents a new firm from entering an industry, including patents, copyrights, licenses, permits, franchising requirements, and high capital costs 153

barter - a system of exchange or trade where some item is exchanged for some other good, service, or resource without any use of money 288

base year - a reference point for a price index, to which its price level of every year is compared 275

Basic Economic Questions - the questions to be considered in allocating resources, including What to Produce? How to Produce? and For Whom to Produce? 13

Basic Economic Systems - the systems upon which the structure of all economies are based, including the traditional, the command, and the market systems 86

basic industries - industries that produce relatively simple-to-make, common products, including steel, autos, and textiles 216

batch process - a production process where a relatively small number of identical products is made 63

beneficiary - the person receiving the payment in the event of the death of someone having life insurance 390

benefit - any satisfaction received from an economic activity 6

benefits-received principle - the taxing philosophy stating that as people receive more benefits from government services, they should pay more in taxes 258

bilateral consensus agreement - a pact between nations to restrict nations from subsidizing their firms' exports 214

black market - an illegal market, either where an item is produced or sold that is prohibited or where an item is sold at a price other than the prices that are allowed 87

block grant - money given to local governments by the federal government for a specific purpose 247

bond - a note given by a borrower promising to pay back a loan 139

boom - a period of very strong prosperity 309

break-even point - the level of a firm's output at which its total revenue equals its total costs 149

budget deficit - occurs when total outlays of a government exceed the total receipts 250

budget surplus - occurs when total receipts of a government exceed the total outlays 250

bureaucratic control - a method of reducing imports by establishing government "red tape" that importers must deal with 212

business cycle - irregular changes in macroeconomic conditions, ranging from prosperity to recession and back to prosperity 308

bust - a term used mainly in the past to describe a recession 310

capital - any good used to produce another good or service 3

capital consumption allowances - the name for depreciation in the national income accounts 285

capital formation - the increase in the capital stock of a firm or in the nation 185

capital gains - the increase in value of an asset over the period in which it was owned 394

capital-intensive - a production process where the largest share of the costs involve capital resources 68

capital productivity - the amount of output produced in one hour by a given amount of capital 32

capital stock - the amount of capital resources of a firm or an economy 31

capitalism - an economic system whose main characteristics include individuals making decisions about their privately owned resources in a system of competitive, free markets 90

cartel - an organization of sellers that seeks to control a market, which usually involves raising the price in that market above equilibrium, accompanied by a restriction in output 126

cash flow statement - a personal financial instrument that lists all sources and amounts of income and all categories and amounts of expenditures over a period of time 385

cash grant - a transfer payment involving the payment of money 245

cash value - the value of savings that builds up in a whole life insurance policy 390

caveat emptor - a Latin phrase which means, "Let the buyer beware," or that the consumer, not the seller, is responsible for making a good purchasing decision 387

central bank - a government "bankers' bank," which provides financial services for banks as well as controlling the availability and the cost of credit 294

centrally directed - refers to an economic system where economic decisions are largely made by government authorities 94

certificate of deposit (CD) - a form of savings in a bank or a savings and loan where a larger amount of money is deposited for a specified period 393

ceteris paribus - refers to the assumption that all other influences on desires to purchases (or offers to sell) do not change as price changes 110

change in demand - a change in the amount buyers are willing to purchase at each price, even though there is no change in price 113

change in supply - a change in the amount sellers wish to sell at each price, even though there is no change in price 117

Classical Theory - a body of economic thought developed in the late 1700s and 1800s, centering on the establishment of a free-market economy 360

closed shop - a workplace in which a person must be a member of the labor union before beginning to work 182

closely held corporation - a synonym for private corporation 139

coefficient of elasticity - a measure of the change in consumer purchases following a change in price 135

collateral - some asset a borrower agrees to give to a lender if a loan is not repaid 392

collective bargaining - refers to the actions of a group of laborers operating in unison to determine their wages, fringe benefits, and working conditions 180

collusion - an agreement between sellers to raise prices, usually accompanied by restricting output 126

command economic system - a Basic Economic System in which the economic decisions are made by government authorities 87

commercial bank - a financial intermediary that provides checking accounts and makes commercial loans 298

commercial paper - all the various debt instruments sold by a corporation 185

commodity - often used as a synonym for good, but generally agricultural goods 395

commodity money - a good that serves as a medium of exchange 291

common stock - corporate stock that gives stockholders the right to vote at stockholders' meetings 139

commune - a community of individuals in which resources are publicly or collectively owned and where most economic decisions are made by the entire community 100

communism - a form of authoritarian socialism popularized by Marx and Engels, where eventually the state would disappear and all production and consumption would be carried out in the best interest of the community 93

comparative advantage - occurs when a particular resource has the lowest opportunity cost in producing something of all resources of that type 34

compensatory justice - refers to the achievement of "fair prices" for goods and services 16

competition - refers to the struggles of market participants for the purpose of maximizing their economic welfare 90

complementary good - a good commonly used in tandem or together with another good 109

Composite Index of Leading Economic Indicators - an index of 11 macroeconomic variables used to predict the future 318

conglomerate merger - a combination of two or more firms that produce unrelated items 140

conservative - one who favors an economy that is somewhat more capitalistic than the current one 103

conspicuous consumption - the purchase of luxury goods and services primarily to show off to others 384

constant dollar GDP - a synonym for real GDP 276

constant returns to scale - describes a production process in which an increase in inputs of x percent results in output increasing by x percent 57

consumer equilibrium - a condition where a consumer receives the same amount of satisfaction from the last dollar spent on each item and where it is impossible to improve economic welfare by changing buying patterns 382

Consumer Price Index - a reflection of the price level, found by calculating the cost of 400 items commonly bought by consumers 275

consumer sovereignty - refers to a condition in which the consumer ultimately directs which goods and services get produced 384

consumption - the part of total spending that reflects the purchase of consumer goods and services 279

consumption process - the using of goods and services by individuals for the purpose of gaining benefits or satisfaction 2

continuous production process - refers to a situation where a product's manufacture is broken down into a series of steps, where specialized machines do a large share of the production, and where raw materials continually enter the production process and finished products continually exit the process 65

contraction - the part of the business cycle extending from the beginning of the recession to the beginning of the recovery 310

contractionary policy - government policy designed to end inflation by reducing total spending and, in turn, shortages 370

cooperative - a form of business where those who are served by the business are the owners and where control of the business is shared by all equally 139

corporate bond - a promissory note issued by a corporation 185

corporate raider - someone or some firm seeking to gain a controlling share of a corporation 140

corporation - a form of business owned by stockholders, each having limited liability, and where the business is considered to be a person in legal matters 138

cost-benefit analysis - a method of comparing costs and benefits to determine whether resources should be used in a certain way 6

cost of living - the amount of money needed to buy the necessities of life, or things in general 275

cost-of-living-adjustment - a clause in a labor contract which raises wages in accordance with changes in the price index, also known as a COLA 332

cost-push inflation - an increase in prices caused by an increase in the cost of producing most goods and services 349

craft union - a labor union composed of workers working in the same craft or job description 180

credit - in international economics, anything having monetary value that enters a nation 219

credit union - a thrift institution associated with a place of employment or a union, operated as a cooperative 298 *creditor nation* - a nation whose citizens collectively have more assets abroad than liabilities 222

crowding out - occurs when an increase in the budget deficit due to an expansionary policy leads to higher interest rates and reduced consumer and investment spending 367

currency devaluation - a government-sponsored reduction in the amount of a nation's currency that will exchange for other nations' currencies, occasionally done in order to increase exports and decrease imports 212

current GDP - the value of final goods and services when using the prices existing at the time of production 276

cyclical unemployment - unemployment due to a downturn or recession in the economy 282

debit - in international economics, anything having monetary value that leaves a nation 219

debit card - a plastic card, that when placed in a special cash register, transfers money out of one's checking account to someone else's account in a process known as electronic funds transfer 293

debt financing - refers to a corporation obtaining money by selling debt instruments, such as bonds 185

debtor nation - a nation whose citizens collectively have more liabilities abroad than assets 222

decrease in demand - a decrease in the amount buyers are willing to purchase at each price 115

decrease in supply - a decrease in the amount sellers offer for sale at each price 117

decreasing returns to scale - describes a production process in which an increase in inputs of x percent results in output increasing by less than x percent 57

deduction - an amount of income on which you do not have to pay federal income tax, often tied to a specific reason 264

default - non-payment of a loan 141

demand - the relationship between the various amounts that buyers are willing to purchase of some item and all possible prices of th at item 110

demand deposit - a checking account in a commercial bank 292

demand-pull inflation - an increase in the price level caused by an increase in total spending that exceeds the increase in available goods and services 341

deposit multiplier - the number of times the money supply can expand if all excess reserves are lent 301

depreciation - a year's share of the purchase price of a capital good that lasts more than one year 142

depression - traditionally, the worst part of the business cycle, but today usually referring to a prolonged period of unemployment greater than 10 percent 310

derived demand - the demand for a resource which stems from the demand for the good or service which that resource produces 168

direct capital - capital that directly produces goods and services and which is usually mobile and privately owned 184

directors - people hired by stockholders to oversee the managers of a corporation and who appoint the officers 140

dirty float - a synonym for a managed-float exchange rate system 214

discount rate - the rate of interest the Fed charges member banks that borrow reserves from it 301

discouraged unemployed - those who wish to work but have given up looking for work 281

discretionary fiscal policy - changes in taxes and/or government spending designed to change total spending in order to achieve a full-employment, non-inflationary economy 365

diseconomies of scale - a synonym for decreasing return to scale 59

disposable income - income that is available for consumption and personal saving 286

disposable income - the income people have available to them for spending on consumer goods and services as well as for saving 312

dissavings - the excess of spending on consumer goods and services over disposable income 385

distributive efficiency - refers to how well a nation's total output of goods and services is distributed 31

distributive justice - refers to the achievement of an equitable distribution of the goods and services produced 16

diversified company - a corporation that produces many unrelated goods and services, often the result of a conglomerate merger 140

divestiture - the selling of one or more divisions or subsidiaries of a diversified company 140

dividend - the share of corporate profits given to stockholders for each share of stock held 139

division of labor - where laborers produce only one product or carry out only one task in the production process of a single product 33

division of labor by process - when a resource participates in only one part of a production process 33

division of labor by product - when a resource produces only one or a few goods or services 33

domestic content and mixing requirement - an obstacle to trade, where a nation requires that a minimum percentage of a product's parts be made in that country 212

double coincidence of wants - a necessary condition in barter exchanges, where each trader has what the other trader wants and who wants what the other trader has 288

dumping - selling a product abroad for less money than it sells for domestically 210

durable goods - more expensive, larger goods lasting at least several years, such as appliances and cars 318

duty - a synonym for tariff 211

dynamic equilibrium - a state of macroeconomic equilibrium in which economic growth occurs 313

easy money policy - an expansionary monetary policy, where credit is relatively cheap and easy to obtain 369

econometric model - a mathematical model of the macroeconomy used for forecasting 318

economic growth - an increase in the output of goods and services 28

economic growth rate - the percent increase in a year's time of the amount of goods and services produced in the economy 278

economic loss - the shortfall of a firm's total revenue compared with the sum of its explicit plus implicit costs 146

economic model - a simplified view of an economy or part of an economy, where only the major elements and relationships are shown 2

economic profit - the excess of a firm's total revenue over its explicit plus implicit costs 146

economic system - the institutions, concepts, and procedures a society uses to deal with the problem created by a scarcity of resources 86

economic welfare - the satisfaction derived from consuming materialistic goals 3

economics - the study of how members of society choose to use scarce resources in order to maximize economic welfare 5

economies of scale - a synonym for increasing returns to scale 59

efficiency - refers to the ratio of inputs to outputs, or how well resources are used, either in a specific production process or in an entire nation 5

elastic - refers to a demand relationship where a given price change results in a proportionately greater change in purchases 112

elastic currency - a money whose volume the central bank is able to expand or contract with the needs of the economy 294

elasticity of demand - refers to the responsiveness of buyers to changes in price with respect to the amount purchased 112

electronic funds transfer - the transfer of funds into and out of a checking account electronically 293

empowerment - where decision-making authority is given to the lowest-level workers as possible 78

employed - someone who works at least one hour per week 281

Employee Stock Ownership Plan (ESOP) - a mechanism through which employees own shares of stock in the firm where they work 140

energy-push inflation - a type of cost-push inflation where rising energy costs lead to inflation 353

entrepreneurship - refers to the characteristics of an enterprising person, one who provides financial backing and management for a business and who often has an innovative idea 4

equation of exchange - MV=PQ, which shows how the money supply (M), the velocity of money (V), the price level (P), and the level of output (Q) are all related 347

equilibrium GDP - the level of GDP, where once reached, at which the economy remains 313

equilibrium price - the price where the amount buyers are willing to purchase equals the amount sellers offer for sale 122

equilibrium quantity - the amount of an item that is purchased at the equilibrium price 122

equilibrium wage - the wage where the number of workers employers wish to hire equals the number of people looking for work 173

equity - the difference between total assets and total liabilities, also known as net worth 386

equity financing - refers to a corporation obtaining money by selling new corporate stock 185

equity in taxation - refers to the fairness in how taxes are assessed 259

escalator clause - part of a loan agreement that gives the lender the right to raise the interest during the period of the loan 299

excess reserves - the difference between what a bank is allowed to lend and how much it has lent out 301

exchange rate - the rate of exchange between the currencies of two nations, or the price of one currency in terms of another currency 198

excise tax - a tax placed on a specific good or service 247

exemption - a certain amount of income for each dependent on which federal income taxes are not paid 265

expansion - the part of the business cycle extending from the beginning of the recovery to the beginning of the next recession 310

expansionary policy - government policy designed to end recession or to increase the rate of economic growth, which is carried out through an increase in total spending 364

explicit cost - a business cost that involves payment of money to a seller of resources 145

exploitation - where workers are denied part of the value of the product they produced that is believed to be rightly theirs 93

export subsidy - payment by a government to an exporter to encourage exports by reducing the price of the item to be exported 212

external benefit - any satisfaction received by a second party when a first party carries out some activity 228

external cost - any negative effect or cost a second party suffers when a first party carries out some activity 224

external debt - part of the national debt of a nation that is owed to people who are not citizens of that nation 251

externality - any effect that some party experiences when a second party makes an economic decision and carries out a subsequent economic activity 224

fact-finding - the study of the issues in a labor-management dispute by an appointed board 182

factor market - a market in which a resource is traded or exchanged 166

factor of production - a synonym for resource, or anything necessary to produce a good or service 3

favorable balance of trade - the condition where a nation's exports exceed its imports 202

featherbedding - work rules that are extremely restrictive of management concerning the production process and which result in union members being insulated from normal competitive conditions 177

federal funds rate - the rate of interest paid by a commercial bank for borrowing excess reserves of another commercial bank 304

Federal Reserve System - the central bank of the United States, whose functions include regulating banks, providing financial services, and controlling the money supply 294

final good - a good ready for use, which needs no more production on it 271

financial capital - money or other assets readily convertible into money to be used in a business 4

financial intermediary - any institution that serves as a "middleman" between savers and borrowers when it accepts deposits and extends credit, including commercial banks and thrifts 297

financial plan - a financial instrument designed to ensure that one's retirement goals will be met by considering the earnings, spending, and savings of the working years 386

fiscal policy - changes in taxes and/or government spending designed to influence the level of total spending 365

fiscal year - the 12-month period a government or business uses for its records 256

fixed exchange rate - an exchange rate between the currencies of two nations that is established by government authorities 199

flat tax - a proportional tax, where everyone pays the same percentage of their income into the tax 260

flexible manufacturing system - where small amounts of different products are made in batch processes 77

floating exchange rate - an exchange rate between the currencies of two nations that is established in foreign exchange markets by the supply of and the demand for currencies 199

foreign exchange markets - places where currencies of many nations are traded 199

franchisee - a person or firm that owns a franchise 141

franchiser - a firm that gives a franchisee the right to do business in a specified way and area 141

free trade - trade occurring between parties across international borders without any interference from governments 205

free-rider effect - when individuals don't buy social goods because other people will get to use them 230

French Utopians - a group of early socialists of the 1700s who were concentrated in France 18

frictional unemployment - unemployment caused by people between jobs, seasonal unemployment, and ignorance of job openings 282

fringe benefits - benefits workers receive other than wages and salaries 182

full employment - a condition of zero cyclical unemployment, corresponding to approximately five to six percent of the labor force 282

futures contract - an agreement to buy/sell a given amount of something for a specific price at a specified date in the future 395

futures market - a place where futures contracts are traded 395

GDP per capita - a monetary measure of the amount of final goods and services produced in a year for each person, on average 273

general equilibrium analysis - refers to the study of the inter-relationships between all markets 17

gold standard - a system where international accounts are settled by shipments of gold and where a nation's money supply and macroeconomic policy is dependent upon the gold supply 214

good - anything that has physical substance that is produced by humans with resources 2

government spending - part of total spending, including only spending for which governments receive goods and services in return 279

greenmail - money paid to a corporate raider for his stock, amounting to a bribe, in return to giving up plans to purchase the firm sought 140

gross domestic product - the dollar value of all final goods and services produced in a nation in a year with resources located in that nation 271 *gross national product* - the dollar value of all final goods and services produced in a year by the resources of a nation, regardless of where those resources were used 272

growth recession - a state of economic growth so slight that the unemployment rate rises 317

guild - a group of medieval craftsmen who established rules covering skill levels of the craftsmen, trading practices, and the like 180

hard-core unemployed - those unable to find jobs because they have very few skills 282

horizontal equity - occurs when people in the same economic situation pay about the same amount in taxes 259

horizontal merger - a combination of two or more firms that produce identical or closely related items 140

hostile takeover - the act of buying out a corporation that is strongly resisted by the management of the firm being sought 140

human capital - the education and training received by human resources 4

hyperinflation - a very severe rate of inflation, usually exceeding 100 percent annually 335

imperfect competition - refers to the market structures of monopolistic competition, oligopoly, and monopoly 231

implicit cost - a business cost that does not involve any payment of money to a seller of a resource 146

implicit price deflator - the price index used to calculate the real GDP 275

in-kind income - goods and services received by someone from the government as a transfer payment as part of an income redistribution program 245

income - goods and services produced for one's use, or the money earned or otherwise received which can be exchanged for such goods and services 233

income distribution - refers to how the money income or the goods and services are allocated among the various members of society 233

income effect - the increase in purchases made possible by an item's price decrease, as one's income can go further, and vice versa 110

income redistribution program - a government program to make the income distribution somewhat closer to equality by taking more taxes from those with higher incomes and giving transfer payments to those with lower incomes 236

income statement - a business statement showing the condition of the business over a period of time, containing information on revenues, costs, and profits or losses 141

income tax bracket - a range of one's income that is subject to the same percentage of income tax 265

incomes policy - direct intervention by government into markets to reduce inflation, including wage and price controls 374

increase in demand - an increase in the amount buyers are willing to purchase at each price 115

increase in supply - an increase in the amount sellers offer for sale at each price 117

increasing returns to scale - describes a production process in which an increase in inputs of x percent results in output increasing by more than x percent 57

independent union - a national union that is not affiliated with other national unions in a federation 181

indirect business taxes - sales, property, and excise taxes 285

individual retirement account (IRA) - a tax-deferred savings account set up by an employee for retirement purposes 393

industrial policy - a government policy in a capitalist economy that targets certain industries for expansion and development and where government assistance is provided 92

industrial union - a labor union composed of workers who all work in the same industry at many different crafts 181

industry - refers to all the firms that produce a particular good or service 152

inelastic - refers to a demand relationship where a given price change results in a proportionately smaller change in purchases 112 *infant industry* - an industry so new to a nation that its firms have not yet had time to become as efficient as possible 210

inferior good - a good of which consumers wish to purchase less if their incomes increase 109

inflation - a condition in which the price level increases, generally over an extended period 332

inflation rate - the percentage increase in the price level in a year, calculated by the percent increase in the price index 275

infrastructure - a synonym for social overhead capital 185

injection - an addition to total spending in the macroeconomic circular flow, in the form of either investment or government spending 314

injunction - a court order to cease and desist a certain activity 181

innovation - a change in the way resources are used 38

inside trading - trading of corporate stock done on the basis of obtaining information about that stock illegally 400

insolvent - refers to a condition where a firm's liabilities exceed its assets and which often leads to bankruptcy 299

institutionalists - a group of economists of the early 1900s who believed that institutions, customs, and values explained economic behavior better than the traditional principles 19

intended investment - the value of private capital goods purchased plus private construction 328

interchangeable parts - refers to a situation where each of the parts of one unit of a product is identical to the respective parts of all other units 64

interest rate - the percentage of a loan that is paid for the use of that money by the borrower over the period of the loan 333

intermediate good - a good which needs to have more production done on it before it is ready for use 271

internal debt - that part of the national debt of a nation that is owed to citizens of that nation 251

internalizing external cost - when decision makers are forced to pay some or all of the external costs resulting from their decisions 227

investment - that part of total spending that involves spending on capital goods, construction, and a change in business inventories 279

investment tax credit - a reduction in the taxes a business pays when it purchases capital equipment 365

iron law of wages - the philosophy that wages would gravitate towards subsistence levels 17

junk bond - a bond with a high risk of default by the issuer, often issued in leveraged buyouts of firms 141

just-in-time manufacturing - where a manufacturer receives parts from suppliers just prior to assembly, called *kanban* in Japanese 77

kaizen - a Japanese word that refers to the continuous improvement sought in the production process 39

kanban - a Japanese word for just-in-time manufacturing 77

Keogh account - a tax-deferred savings account set up by the owner of a business for retirement purposes 393

labor - non-organizational human effort needed to produce a good or service 3

labor cost - the part of average cost that goes to pay laborers 352

labor demand - the relationship between wages and the number of people employers are willing to hire 168

labor force - all the people who are employed plus those that are unemployed 280

labor-intensive - a production process where the largest share of the costs involve labor resources 68

labor productivity - the output produced by a laborer working one hour 32

labor shortage - a condition in a labor market where employers want to hire more workers at a specific wage than there are people willing to work 173

labor supply - the relationship between the wages and the number of people willing and qualified to work 171

labor surplus - a condition in a labor market where there are more people willing to work at a specific wage than employers are willing to hire 173

labor union - an organization of laborers who intend to raise their economic welfare and improve their working conditions by eliminating competition between themselves 180

laissez faire - a government policy of minimum interference into the economic affairs of businesses and into all markets 91

land grant college - colleges established in each state in the 1800s with money earned by the states from selling land given to them by the federal government 190

land productivity - the output from one acre of land 32

law of comparative advantage - a resource will specialize in producing a product in which it has the lowest opportunity cost of all other resources 195

law of demand - at higher prices for an item, buyers want to purchase less of it, and at lower prices, they want to purchase more of it 110

law of diminishing marginal returns - as additional amounts of a single resource are added to a production process, eventually the marginal product declines 54

law of diminishing marginal utility - each additional unit of a good or service that is consumed by an individual will provide less satisfaction than the previous unit 383

law of diminishing marginal utility of income - a given amount of additional income received provides less satisfaction than a similar amount of income already earned 259

law of increasing cost - higher levels of output of a good or service are increasingly costly 26

law of supply - at higher prices for an item, sellers will offer more of it for sale, and at lower prices, they will offer less for sale 116

leakage - a part of peoples' income that they do not immediately spend on goods and services, including taxes and savings 314

lease - a contract giving a firm the right to use someone's capital for a specified period 185

left - includes individuals who want to move their economy closer to a system of public ownership of resources and heavy use of the command economic system 101

legal reserves - what a bank can use to meet its reserve requirement, including its deposits at the Fed and its vault cash 301

leveraged buyout (LBO) - refers to the purchase of a corporation with a large amount of credit (leverage) 140

levy - refers either to the assessment of a tax or the establishment of a tariff 221, 258

liability - anything of monetary value that is owed 386

liable - being responsible for a loss suffered by another person 390

liberal - someone who wants the government to become more involved in making economic decisions and in providing goods and services 103

libertarian - someone who wants an economic system that is very close to pure capitalism, with almost no government involvement in the economy 103

limited liability - where stockholders in corporations are only liable for the firm's debts to the extent of their investment in the firm 139

living standard - the amount of goods and services produced in a nation in a year for each person, on average 29

long run - a period of time long enough for a firm to increase or decrease its capital stock 156

machine tool - a machine that cuts or shapes metal 64

macroeconomic equilibrium - a condition where there is no change in the major macroeconomic variables, occurring when total spending equals the value of total output 312

macroeconomics - the branch of economics that studies the behavior of large sectors of the economy and their related variables and r elationships, including the rates of inflation and unemployment, total output, and interest 15

managed float - a system where exchange rates are influenced by supply and demand but are kept within certain bounds by government interference in foreign exchange markets 214

maquiladora - an American-owned Mexican factory along the U.S. border 43

marginal - extra or additional 8

marginal analysis - decision making that involves the comparison of the extra benefits and extra costs of a decision beyond those already encountered 7

marginal cost - the additional cost in producing an additional unit of output of a good or service 142

marginal product - the additional output of a good or service that results from the addition of one more unit of a particular resource to a production process 54

marginal propensity to consume (MPC) - the fraction of an increase in income that people spend on consumer goods 329

marginal propensity to save (MPS) - the fraction of an increase in income that people save 329

marginal revenue - the additional sales or total revenue for a seller as a consequence of producing and selling one more unit of output of a good or service 143

marginal revenue product - the value of the output of a good or service produced by adding one additional unit of a resource, such as a laborer 168

marginal tax rate - the percent of taxes paid on an extra dollar of earned income 265

marginal utility - the additional satisfaction received from consuming one more unit of a good or service 382

market - a place where people meet to exchange things of value 87

market basket - a sample of goods and services used to calculate a price index 275

market failures - refers to the four main problems in the microeconomy in a capitalist economy, including externalities, social goods, imperfect competition, and an unequal distribution of income 224

market interest rate - the rate of interest as stated on the loan agreement, which is unadjusted for inflation 334

market share - a particular firm's percentage of the total sales of all the firms combined in an industry 154

market socialism - an economic system that combines the public ownership of resources with a system of markets that largely directs resource use 94

market structure - refers to characteristics of an industry, including the number and size of firms, the degree of competition, the similarity of the firms' products, and the ease of entering the industry 152

marketing order - a government program that restricts the output of an agricultural commodity by controlling the quality of the product that is marketed 190

Marxist - one who follows the teachings of Karl Marx, but also referring to one who supports revolution to overthrow capitalism in order to establish authoritarian socialism 94

mass markets - markets for goods and services where there are very many buyers, made possible by a large population and efficient transportation and communication systems 66

materialistic goal - refers to anything produced with economic resources, including all goods and services 2

mechanization - the replacement of labor with capital 3

mediation - a process of settling differences between labor and management, where a third party's opinion is requested by both sides but does not have to be accepted 182

medium of exchange - something that represents purchasing power and is used to obtain goods and services in market exchanges 290

mercantilism - a system where governmental policies were established to promote exports and discourage imports for the purpose of accumulating gold and silver 16

merchandise trade deficit - the excess of the value of a nation's imports of goods over its exports of goods 202

merchandise trade surplus - the excess of the value of a nation's exports of goods over its imports of goods 202

merger - a combination of two or more corporations into one 140

microeconomics - the branch of economics that studies the economic behavior of individuals, including consumers, firms, and resource sellers, and the variables and relationships relating to them 15

micromachines - extremely small machines 77

minimum wage law - legislation establishing a price floor for wages in labor markets 180

mixed economy - an economic system where there is: 1) neither dominance of private nor public ownership of resources; and 2) where there is neither dominance of the market system nor the command system 101

moderate - one who does not wish to make significant changes in the economic system, also known as a middle-of-the-roader 103

monetarist - someone who believes the amount of the money supply is a primary factor explaining macroeconomic activity and that recession and inflation can be avoided with a steady increase in the money supply equal to the rate of increase in total output 376

monetary aggregate - refers to one of four classifications of the money supply, M1 being the most commonly used one 291

monetary policy - the manipulation of interest rates and the availability of excess reserves and credit by the Federal Reserve System in order to influence total spending 368

monetary rule - a monetary policy in which the Fed would increase the money supply at a constant rate that is determined by the rate of increase in the capacity of the economy 377

money income - the amount of money someone receives, usually from the sale of resources, such as labor 332

money market mutual funds - refers to accounts in which you can save money other than commercial banks and thrifts and which are not insured 299

monopolistic competition - a market structure where there are very many firms, each having a slightly different product that is sold at slightly different prices, and where there usually is ease of entry into and exit from the industry 152

monopoly - a market structure where there is only one firm and where there is a barrier to entering the industry 152

monopsony - the single buyer in an industry 153

mortgage - a document given to a lender by a borrower, stating that the lender can take possession of the property in the event of default 391

most-favored-nation - a nation that is given the lowest possible tariff rates by the United States 211

multinational - a firm with major operations and/or subsidiaries in several nations 215

multiplier - the factor change in total spending and the GDP following an initial change in consumer, investment, or government spending 329

municipal bond - a bond issued by a state or local government 247

national health insurance - a health insurance program operated by the national government 390

national income - the total of factor payments paid to resource owners 285

national income accounts - refers to the system of various measures of the macroeconomy 285

national socialism - a political-economic system in which most resources are privately owned, but which has heavy government involvement in economic decisions 91

national union - an organization of all the local unions of one type in the nation 180

nationalization - the takeover of privately owned resources by the national government 89

natural exchange rate - the exchange rate that reflects identical purchasing power of given quantities of two currencies 198

natural law - the set of rules that 18th century philosophers believed people should follow in economic affairs 16 *natural monopoly* - a firm, usually a public utility, whose production process is most efficiently carried out if only one firm produces the good or service 153

natural rate of unemployment - the rate of unemployment the economy will gravitate towards in the long run in the absence of government intervention and which equals the combined rates of frictional and structural unemployment 376

natural resource - anything necessary in a production process that appears in nature 4

near money - certain assets which serve as a store of value but not as a medium of exchange, such as individual savings accounts 291

negative externality - any negative effect or cost a second party suffers when a first party carries out some activity 224

negotiated order of withdrawal (NOW account) - a checking account at a savings and loan 292

net domestic product - GDP minus depreciation 285

net exports - the difference in the value of exports minus imports 280

net income per share - profit expressed as the amount of earnings for each share of corporate stock 143

net margin - a way to measure after-taxes profit, referring either to the profit as a percent of sales or as the dollar amount of profit per unit of sales 143

net worth - the difference between total assets and total liabilities, also known as equity 386

net worth statement - a statement listing all assets, all liabilities, and the difference between them, known as net worth or equity 386

new classical economics - a school of economic thought centering on rational expectations theory, which discounts the government's ability to be successful in macroeconomic policy due to people making adjustments in their behavior of allowing such policy 377

non-exclusionary - refers to the inability to stop anyone from using a good or service 230

non-materialistic goal - anything providing satisfaction that does not require economic resources to achieve 2

non-rival - the characteristic of a good or service where increasing the amount of its consumption does not mean there is less for anyone else to enjoy 230

normal good - a good of which consumers wish to purchase more if their incomes increase 109

normal profit - the total of a typical firm's implicit costs in an industry 146

officers - people who are the top managers of a corporation 140

oligopoly - a market structure characterized by a few large firms with significant price-setting power and unique products and where there are significant barriers to entry 153

open account credit - also known as revolving credit, where one receives a certain amount of credit to be used and which can be used again after the loan is repaid 392

open market operations - sales and purchases of securities by the Fed in order to carry out monetary policy by influencing the level of excess reserves in the commercial banking system 302

operating costs - a synonym for total variable costs 142

opportunity cost - the satisfaction given up from the best of the remaining alternative ways of using resources when they are used in a specific way 6

optimum scale of plant - the size of a firm's capital stock associated with the lowest average cost 155

overhead - a synonym for total fixed costs 142

overnight repurchase agreement - refers to the sale of a security by a commercial bank which agrees to purchase it back at a certain time and price 293

owner's equity - the difference between a firm's assets and liabilities 141

panic - a term used in the past to describe a very sharp recession 310

partnership - a type of business structure with more than one owner, each sharing responsibilities and being liable for the debts of the firm 138 *passbook account* - the most common form of saving money in a bank, usually called a savings account 393

peak demand - the point where the greatest use is made of a good 384

perestroika - a Russian term meaning restructuring, referring to the introduction in the Soviet Union of market incentives as well as private enterprises into the economy, designed to raise economic growth 96

personal income - as shown in the model of the macroeconomy, the total income earned by the sale of resources, but which, in reality, includes transfer payments as well 311

personal investment - the use of savings and/or borrowed funds for the purpose of earning more money 393

personal saving - equal to disposable income minus consumption 286

physical capital - a synonym for capital goods 4

Physiocrats - the first true economists, who believed in natural law and that all wealth came from the land or working it 16

point of diminishing returns - the level of inputs used where the marginal product begins to fall 57

poison pill - a financially disastrous action faced by a corporate raider following the purchase of a firm 141

political economy - issues and concepts in which politics and economics cannot be separated 100

positive externality - any satisfaction received by a second party when a first party carries out some activity 224

potential GDP - the value of final goods and services produced at full employment 273

poverty level - an official measure of the amount of income needed to stay out of poverty 234

preferred stock - corporate stock that does not give stockholders voting rights 139

premium - an amount of money paid by those who are insured to cover their share of the losses of the group 389

present value - the value at the present of an asset that will be received at some point in the future 233

price - the rate of exchange of money for one unit of what is sold 108

price ceiling - the maximum price allowed by law in some market 127

price controls - government laws restricting how high or how low prices can be 126

price floor - the minimum price allowed by law in some market 127

price index - a representation of all prices 275

price level - refers to the collection of all prices of all final goods and services 275

price support - a price floor, generally in reference to certain agricultural commodities 190

price taker - a firm, usually one in a purely competitive industry, that must accept the market price for its product 152

price-to-earnings ratio - a measure of corporate stock's performance, found by dividing the stock's price by the earning per share of the firm 399

primary market - that part of the stock market where firms obtain money by selling new corporate stock 399

private benefit - the benefits received by the person who carries out an economic activity 224

private corporation - also known as a closely held corporation, where only a few people are allowed to own stock 139

private cost - the cost experienced by the person who carries out an economic activity 224

private enterprise - an organization that produces a good or service and is owned by one or more individuals 88

private good - a good whose use can be denied to specific people and whose consumption results in a smaller amount available for others to consume 230

private property - resources owned by one or several individuals 88 *privatization* - either refers to the sale of publicly owned resources to private individuals or the contracting out to private firms services that were previously provided by the government 89

Producers' Price Index - a price index that reflects wholesale prices 275

product market - a market in which a good or service is exchanged 166

production possibilities curve - a graph showing all possible combinations of two goods that it is possible to produce with a set of resources 7

production process - the conversion of resources into a good or service 3

profit and loss statement - a synonym for income statement 141

progressive tax - a tax that takes a higher percentage of the incomes of higher income taxpayers than from those with lower incomes 261

proletariat - a Marxist term for the working class 93

proportional tax - a tax in which every taxpayer pays the same percentage of income into the tax 261

prosperity - the part of the business cycle where output, employment, and spending are at high levels, also called the peak 309

protectionism - government policies designed to protect firms and their employees from foreign competition 211

public corporation - a corporation whose stock anyone can purchase 139

public debt - the money owed by citizens of the national government to those who purchase the government's securities 250

public enterprise - a government enterprise that produces a good or service 89

public goods - a synonym for social goods 230

public property - resources owned by all the citizens of a government 89

public service commission - a government agency that controls the natural monopolies in its jurisdiction, usually public utilities 153

purchasing power - the ability to demand and receive goods and services in markets 290

purchasing power parity - a synonym for natural exchange rate 198

pure capitalism - an economic system in which all resources are privately owned and the market system is used in all economic decisions 90

pure competition - a market structure characterized by many small firms having identical products, where no firm can influence the price, and where there is easy entry into and exit from the industry 152

quit rate - the percentage of the labor force that has quit jobs to start new ones 316

quota - in international economics, it refers to a physical limit on imports, and in domestic economics it refers to a limit on acreage of a certain crop that can be marketed 211

rank and file - members of a labor union 182

rate of exchange - how much one thing of value trades for another thing of value 88

rate of return on equity - profit expressed as the percentage of owner's equity 143

ratification - passage of a collective bargaining agreement by the union membership 182

rational - the attribute of having behavior that is expected to result in an increase in one's welfare following a decision and subsequent activity 2

rational expectations theory - the belief that any macroeconomic policy will be offset by actions of the private sector due to anticipated problems following those policies 377

real GDP - the current or nominal GDP after adjusting for inflation, which gives a more accurate measure of production 276

real income - the amount of goods and services that can be purchased with a given money income 41

real interest rate - the rate of interest after adjusting for inflation, equal to the nominal rate of interest minus the inflation rate 334 *reallocation of resources* - when resources previously used to make some good or service are switched to making some other good or service 149

recession - the part of the business cycle when spending, output, and employment are falling, usually for a period of two or more quarters 310

recovery - the part of the business cycle when macroeconomic conditions have begun to improve, but before prosperity has been reached 310

regressive tax - a tax that takes a smaller percentage of the incomes of higher income taxpayers than from those with lower incomes 261

reindustrialization - refers to large investment in new facilities and production processes in certain industries to make them more efficient, especially in basic industries 216

relative price - the amount of some other good or service that will exchange for one unit of some particular good 69

required reserves - the amount of deposits upon which a commercial bank is not allowed to make loans and must keep on reserve, which it usually does with the Fed 300

reserve ratio - the percentage of a bank's deposits which it cannot lend 300

reserve requirement - the percentage of a commercial bank's deposit it must keep as required reserves 300

resource - anything necessary to produce a good or service 3

resource allocation - refers to how resources are directed to specific uses 5

resource misallocation - occurs when resources are used unwisely 5

restraint of trade - any act to control any market to gain monopoly power 232

restricted capitalism - a synonym for authoritarian capitalism 91

retained earnings - that part of after-tax profits that a corporation does not distribute in dividends 185

right - includes individuals who want to move their economy closer to a system of private ownership of resources and heavy use of the market economic system 101

right-to-work law - a state law, authorized by the Taft-Hartley Act, outlawing union shops in that state 182

savings - income that is not spent on consumer goods and services 385

savings and loan - a thrift institution that concentrates its loans in real estate 298

savings bank - a thrift institution that usually accepts small deposits and is owned by the depositors 298

Say's Law - the proposition that there will be an equivalent demand for goods and services for all the output people wish to produce 360

scarce - something available in limited amounts and which provides utility or benefit 4

secondary boycott - where striking workers pressure a third party not to deal with their employer 182

secondary market - that part of the stock market where previously owned corporate stocks are traded 399

secured loan - a loan which requires the borrower to provide collateral of which the lender takes possession if the loan is not repaid 392

self-insurance - refers to when a firm or government sets money aside to cover its expected losses that are usually covered by insurance 389

service - anything that has no physical substance that is produced by humans with resources 2

share draft - a checking account at a credit union 292

short run - a period of time when a business is not able to change the amount of its capital stock 156

shortage - the excess of what buyers wish to purchase over what sellers offer for sale at some given price 122

signature loan - a loan where the borrower is not required to put up any collateral, also called an unsecured loan 392 *sin taxes* - taxes on alcoholic beverages and tobacco products 227

single proprietorship - a type of business firm where there is only one owner, who faces unlimited liability and earns all the profits 138

small business set-aside program - a government program that gives small firms a break in bidding against large firms for federal projects 232

smallholder agriculture - a system of small farms established by a series of laws and policies early in the history of the United States 17

social benefit - the combination of private benefits and external benefits of an economic activity 229

social cost - the combination of private costs and external costs of an economic activity 225

social good - a good which is non-rival and non-exclusionary, or one whose use can be shared by all and whose consumption does not leave less for others 230

social overhead capital - capital goods which provide the foundation for all production by providing such services as electricity, transportation, communication, education, and public safety 184

social science - a study of how humans think, act, and relate to one another 2

Special Drawing Right (SDR) - a financial instrument that is set to be equal in value to a given amount of gold 221

specialization - the use of a resource to produce only one (or several) item, or perhaps to produce only part of an item 33

standard of value - something that allows comparisons of value between goods and services, often called a unit of account 290

standardization - refers to the identical size, shape, and pattern of parts of products of different firms 64

static equilibrium - a state of macroeconomic equilibrium in which no economic growth occurs 313

stock split - refers to when a corporation exchanges each share of its stock for two or more new shares, often done when the stock price rises very high 399

stockholder - someone who owns part of a corporation by virtue of owning stock in the corporation 140

store of value - something in which purchasing power is stored until the holder is ready to use it 290

strategic industry - an industry whose firms make products vital to a country's national security 210

strike - a refusal by unionized laborers to sell labor resources 180

structural unemployment - unemployment which results from the structure of the economy being such that the needs of employers are not met by everyone in the labor force 282

subsidiary - a company that is owned by another company 141

subsidy - a payment by the government without expecting anything in return, usually given to business firms, in order to achieve a particular social goal 229

substitute good - a good which provides approximately the same amount of satisfaction as another good 109

substitution effect - the act of buyers purchasing less of an item whose price rises because a substitute good becomes a better purchase, and vice versa 110

supply - the relationship between the amount that sellers offer for sale of some item and all possible prices of that item 117

supply restriction program - any of various government programs to restrict the output of certain agricultural products in order to keep their prices higher 190

supply-side economics - government policies designed to increase total output for the purposes of increasing economic growth and moderating inflation 373

surplus - the excess of how much sellers offer for sale over what buyers are willing to purchase 123

target corporation - a company that a corporate raider is seeking to obtain control of 140 *target price* - a price guaranteed to farmers for certain crops, often in the form of loans that do not have to be repaid and where the crop itself is the collateral 190

tariff - a tax on an import, designed to reduce the level of imports 211

tatonement process - the process of how prices are established by adjustments in markets 17

tax shifting - refers to the passing on to consumers of a tax placed on a business 240

tax-deferred income - the income that is put into Keogh accounts and IRAs on which taxes are paid after it is drawn out after retiring 394

taxable income - the part of one's income that is subject to the federal income tax 264

technological unemployment - occurs when people lose their jobs because of an improvement in technology, often in the form of mechanization 282

technology - the level of sophistication, complexity, and scientific knowledge used in capital goods 4

the economic problem - the difficulty caused by the combination of an unlimited desire for goods and services and limited resources 5

thrifts - financial intermediaries that include savings and loans, savings banks, and credit unions 298

tight money policy - a contractionary monetary policy, when credit is relatively expensive and difficult to obtain 372

time deposit - a bank deposit which is made for a specified period of time 293

total cost - includes all the costs of producing a specific amount of output of a good or service 142

total fixed cost - includes all the overhead or fixed costs of producing a specific amount of output of a good or service 142

total funding - the total amount of money a government has available to spend, including borrowed funds 247

total outlays - the total amount of money spent by government, including spending for goods and services as well as transfer payments 246

total receipts - includes all the money received by a government other than borrowed funds 247

total revenue - the total sales received by a firm from producing and selling a specific amount of output a good or service 112

total variable cost - includes all the operating or variable costs of producing a specific amount of output a good or service 142

traditional conservative - an individual who generally favors a capitalist system but who wishes to expand the government's role in issues relating to personal morals and behavior 103

traditional economic system - a Basic Economic System where all economic decisions are made the way they were made in the past 86

transaction costs - the costs involved in making an exchange, including money costs as well as the costs of time and aggravation 288

transfer payment - money given by a government for which it receives nothing in return 245

trough - the worst part of the business cycle, which occurs just prior to the recovery phase 310

trust - an account usually set up for a person who is not capable of handling funds 393

underemployment - occurs when workers are employed in positions that do not make full use of their skills 281

underground economy - refers to market exchanges that are not recorded by the government in its measure of the GDP 272

unemployed - a person who is not working and who is actively seeking work 281

unemployment rate - the percentage of the labor force that is unemployed 281

unfair competition - occurs when certain individuals are able to restrict market activity to their benefit 92

unfair labor practice - employer interference into certain labor union activity and discrimination against union laborers 181

unfavorable balance of trade - the condition where a nation's imports exceed its exports 202 *unintended investment* - the value of an increase in business inventories 328

union shop - a workplace in which a person is required to join a union following a brief period 182

unit of account - the unit of a nation's currency, such as a dollar or mark 290

unlimited liability - the condition where an individual is responsible for all the debts incurred by a business 138

unsecured loan - a loan which requires no collateral from the borrower 392

user fee - a charge assessed by the government for the use of its goods or services 247

user fee - also called a user charge, amounting to the price charged by a government for the use of its facilities 185

uskoreniye - a Russian word meaning accelerated production 96

usury - lending for the purpose of earning interest 15

vault cash - currency located in banks 292

velocity of circulation - refers to how many times money is used in a year, on average 346

venture capital - money provided to a new firm to start up its operations 141

vertical equity - occurs when people who earn higher incomes and/or who have greater wealth pay a larger share of the taxes 259

vertical merger - a combination of two or more firms involved in different stages of the production process 140

voluntary restraint agreement - when a foreign nation agrees to limit how much it exports to another, even though it is not forced to do so 212

wage bill - the total amount of wages earned by all laborers combined, usually in one firm or industry 182

wage-push inflation - a type of cost-push inflation where rising labor costs lead to inflation, usually the result of wage increases that exceed increases in labor productivity 353

wealth - how much power a person has to purchase goods and services at any given moment 223

wealth distribution - refers to how much wealth the different members of society have in relation to one another 223

welfare states - nations that are basically capitalistic but which have income distribution heavily influenced by the government in order to reduce income inequality 93

white knight - a firm sought by a company under attack by a corporate raider that is a more favorable purchaser 140

wildcat bank - a state-chartered bank of the 1800s, many of which printed more currency than was authorized and which were located in remote areas 294

work rule - worker-influenced guidelines on how to perform a certain job 177

yellow-dog contract - an agreement by a worker not to join a union 181

zero-sum game - a game or situation in which the combined winnings of all participants equal the combined losses of all participants, so if someone wins more, someone else must lose more 213

zone of impossibility - all points located outside a production possibilities curve, which refer to combinations of two items that it is not possible to produce with a set of resources 7

zone of inefficiency - all points located within a production possibilities curve 7